General Editors

Garrett A. Sullivan, Jr is Professor of English at Penn State University. He is the author of *The drama of landscape: land, property, and social relations on the early modern stage* (1998) and *Memory and forgetting in English Renaissance drama: Shakespeare, Marlowe, Webster* (2005).

Alan Stewart is Professor of English and Comparative Literature at Columbia University, and International Director of the Centre for Editing Lives and Letters, University of London. He is the author most recently of *Shakespeare's Letters* (2008), and editor of volume I of the Oxford Francis Bacon, *Early writings, 1584–1596* (forthcoming).

Associate Editors

Rebecca Lemon is Associate Professor of English at the University of Southern California. She is author *of Treason by words: literature, law, and rebellion in Shakespeare's England* (2006) and one of the editors for *The Blackwell companion to literature and the Bible* (2009).

Nicholas McDowell is Associate Professor of English at the University of Exeter. His publications include *Poetry and allegiance in the English Civil Wars: Marvell and the cause of wit* (2008), and he is co-editor of *The Oxford handbook of Milton* (2009).

Jennifer Richards is Professor of Early Modern Literature and Culture at Newcastle University UK. Her publications include *Rhetoric and courtliness in early modern literature* (2003) and *Rhetoric* (2007) in the New Critical Idiom series.

The Wiley-Blackwell Encyclopedia of Literature
www.literatureencyclopedia.com

The Wiley-Blackwell Encyclopedia of Literature is a comprehensive, scholarly, authoritative, and critical overview of literature and theory comprising individual titles covering key literary genres, periods, and sub-disciplines. Available both in print and online, this groundbreaking resource provides students, teachers, and researchers with cutting-edge scholarship in literature and literary studies.

Published:

The Encyclopedia of Literary and Cultural Theory, General Editor: Michael Ryan

The Encyclopedia of the Novel, General Editor: Peter Melville Logan

The Encyclopedia of Twentieth-Century Fiction, General Editor: Brian W. Shaffer

The Encyclopedia of English Renaissance Literature, General Editors: Garrett A. Sullivan, Jr and Alan Stewart

The Encyclopedia of Romantic Literature, General Editor: Frederick Burwick

Forthcoming:

The Encyclopedia of the Gothic, General Editors: William Hughes, David Punter, and Andrew Smith

The Encyclopedia of Postcolonial Studies, General Editors: Sangeeta Ray and Henry Schwarz

The Encyclopedia of English Renaissance Literature

General Editors:
Garrett A. Sullivan, Jr and Alan Stewart

Associate editors:
Rebecca Lemon, Nicholas McDowell, and Jennifer Richards

Volume I
A–F

WILEY-BLACKWELL

A John Wiley & Sons, Ltd., Publication

This edition first published 2012
© 2012 Blackwell Publishing Ltd

Blackwell Publishing was acquired by John Wiley & Sons in February 2007. Blackwell's publishing program has been merged with Wiley's global Scientific, Technical, and Medical business to form Wiley-Blackwell.

Registered Office
John Wiley & Sons Ltd, The Atrium, Southern Gate, Chichester, West Sussex, PO19 8SQ, United Kingdom

Editorial Offices
350 Main Street, Malden, MA 02148-5020, USA
9600 Garsington Road, Oxford, OX4 2DQ, UK
The Atrium, Southern Gate, Chichester, West Sussex, PO19 8SQ, UK

For details of our global editorial offices, for customer services, and for information about how to apply for permission to reuse the copyright material in this book please see our website at www.wiley.com/wiley-blackwell.

The right of Garrett A. Sullivan, Jr and Alan Stewart to be identified as the authors of the editorial material in this work has been asserted in accordance with the UK Copyright, Designs and Patents Act 1988.

Library of Congress Cataloging-in-Publication Data
ISBN 9781405194495

The encyclopedia of English renaissance literature / edited by Garrett A. Sullivan, Jr and Alan Stewart.
   p. cm.
  Includes bibliographical references and index.
   ISBN 978-1-4051-9449-5 (hardcover : alk. paper) 1. English literature–Early modern, 1500-1700–Encyclopedias. 2. Renaissance–England–Encyclopedias. I. Sullivan, Garrett A. II. Stewart, Alan, 1967-
  PR411.E53 2012
  820.9'003–dc22

                                                                                2011015326

A catalogue record for this book is available from the British Library.

Set in 10/12 Minion by Thomson Digital, Noida, India
Printed and bound in Singapore by Markono Print Media Pte Ltd

01 2012

The *Encyclopedia of English Renaissance literature* is dedicated to two eminent colleagues, Patrick Cheney and Anne Lake Prescott, in gratitude not only for their major contributions to literary scholarship, but also for their friendship and support.

Contents

Volume I

List of entries   ix
Notes on contributors   xv
Introduction   xlv
Acknowledgements   liii

English Renaissance Literature A–F   1

Volume II

List of entries   ix
Notes on contributors   xv

English Renaissance Literature G–O   375

Volume III

List of entries   ix
Notes on contributors   xv

English Renaissance Literature P–Z   757

Index   1089

Contents

List of Entries

VOLUME I

Alabaster, William   1
Allen, William   3
Andrewes, Lancelot   5
Anger, Jane   7
anonymity   8
Ascham, Roger   12
Askew, Anne   17
Aubrey, John   21
Audland/Audley, Anne   22
Avery, Elizabeth   24
Aylmer, John   26
Bacon, Anne (Cooke)   29
Bacon, Francis   30
Baldwin, William   38
Bale, John   40
Barclay, Alexander   44
Barnes, Barnabe   46
Barnfield, Richard   47
Barry, Lording   49
Basset, Mary Roper Clarke   51
Baxter, Richard   52
Bayly, Lewis   57
Beaufort, Margaret   59
Beaumont, Francis   60
Beaumont, John   65
Benlowes, Edward   66
Berkenhead, John   68
Bible, the   70
Biddle, Hester   76
Birch, William   77
Blundeville, Thomas   79
Bodley, Thomas   80
Boece, Hector   82

Bolton, Edmund   84
Book of Common Prayer, the   85
Boorde, Andrew   89
Boyle, Robert   91
Brackley, Elizabeth   92
Bradstreet, Anne   94
Brandon, Samuel   99
Breton, Nicholas   101
Brewer, Anthony   103
broadside ballads   104
Brome, Alexander   108
Brome, Richard   110
Brooke, Christopher   114
Browne, Thomas   115
Browne, William   120
Bryan, Francis   122
Bryskett, Lodowick   123
Buchanan, George   125
Bullein, William   127
Bunyan, John   129
Burton, Robert   134
Camden, William   140
Campion, Thomas   145
Carew, Thomas   147
Cartwright, William   148
Cary, Elizabeth   150
Cary, Lucius, Lord Falkland   154
Cary, Mary   156
Cavendish, George   158
Cavendish, Jane   159
Cavendish, Margaret   161
Cavendish, William   169
Caxton, William   171
Chaloner, Thomas   175
Chapman, George   177

Cheke, John   182
Chettle, Henry   184
Chidley, Katherine   185
Chillingworth, William   187
Churchyard, Thomas   189
Chute, Anthony   190
Clarkson, Lawrence   192
Cleveland, John   194
Clifford, Anne   196
Clinton, Elizabeth   201
Colet, John   202
Collins, An   204
commonplace books   206
Constable, Henry   209
Copland, Robert   210
Coppe, Abiezer   212
Corbett, Richard   214
Coryate, Thomas   216
Cotton, Charles, the younger   221
Cowley, Abraham   223
Cox, Leonard   227
Cranmer, Thomas   229
Crashaw, Richard   231
Crooke, Helkiah   236
Crowley, Robert   238
Cudworth, Ralph   243
Daniel, Samuel   245
Davenant, William   249
Davies, Eleanor   254
Davies, John   255
Day, John   257
de Vere, Edward, earl of Oxford   259
Dekker, Thomas   260
Delaval, Elizabeth   265
Deloney, Thomas   267
Denham, John   271
Devereux, Robert, earl of Essex   273
Digby, Kenelm   275
Donne, John   277
Douglas, Gawin   285
Dowland, John   287
Dowriche, Anne   289
Drant, Thomas   290
Drayton, Michael   292
Drummond, William   297
Dryden, John   299

Dunbar, William   304
Dury, John   306
Dyer, Edward   307
Edwards, Richard   310
Edwards, Thomas   312
Elizabeth I   313
Elyot, Thomas   317
emblem books   322
Evelyn, John   326
Fage, Mary   328
Fairfax, Edward   329
Fanshawe, Ann   331
Fanshawe, Richard   332
Farnaby, Thomas   334
Fell, Margaret   336
Fenner, Dudley   337
Fenton, Geoffrey   339
Ferrers, George   341
Fisher, Payne   342
Fitzgeffrey, Henry   344
Fleming, Abraham   346
Fletcher, John   347
Fletcher, Phineas   352
Florio, John   354
Ford, John   356
Fox, George   360
Foxe, John   364
Fraunce, Abraham   369
Fulwell, Ulpian   371

VOLUME II

Gardiner, Stephen   375
Gascoigne, George   376
Gilbert, Humphrey   381
Godolphin, Sidney   383
Godwin, Francis   385
Golding, Arthur   386
Goodman, Christopher   388
Googe, Barnabe   390
Gorges, Arthur   392
Gosson, Stephen   393
Gouge, William   395
Grafton, Richard   396
Greene, Robert   398
Greville, Fulke   403

Griffin, Bartholomew 408
Grimald, Nicholas 410
Grymeston, Elizabeth 412
Guilpin, Everard 414
Habington, William 416
Hake, Edward 417
Hakluyt, Richard 419
Hales, John 423
Halkett, Anne 425
Hall, Edward 426
Hall, John, of Durham 428
Hall, Joseph 430
Harington, John, the elder 431
Harington, John, the younger 433
Harley, Brilliana 434
Harrington, James 437
Harriot, Thomas 441
Harrison, William 444
Hartlib, Samuel 446
Harvey, Gabriel 451
Harvey, Richard 455
Harvey, William 457
Haughton, William 458
Hawes, Stephen 460
Hayward, John 461
Herbert, Edward,
   Lord Herbert of Cherbury 463
Herbert, George 465
Herbert, Mary (Sidney), countess
   of Pembroke 473
Herrick, Robert 477
Heywood, John 482
Heywood, Thomas 486
Higgins, John 489
Hobbes, Thomas 491
Hoby, Margaret 496
Hoby, Thomas 497
Holinshed, Raphael 499
Holland, Philemon 504
Hooker, Richard 505
Horman, William 507
Hoskyns, John 508
Howard, Anne, countess of Arundel 510
Howard, Henry, earl of Surrey 511
Howell, James 516
Howell, Thomas 518

Hughes, Thomas 520
Hume, Alexander 521
Hume, Anna 523
Humphrey, Laurence 524
Hutchinson, Lucy 526
Hyde, Edward, earl of Clarendon 531
James VI and I 536
Jekyll, Elizabeth 540
Jewel, John 542
Jinner, Sarah 544
Jocelin, Elizabeth 545
Johnson, Cicely and Thurgood, Rose 547
Johnson, Richard 548
Jones, Inigo 550
Jonson, Ben 551
Jordan, Thomas 559
Kempe, William 562
Kendall, Timothy 564
King, Henry 565
Knolles, Richard 567
Knox, John 569
Kyd, Thomas 572
Lanyer, Aemilia 577
Latimer, Hugh 582
Leigh, Dorothy 584
Leland, John 585
Leslie, John 590
letters in print 592
Lilburne, John 596
Lilly, William 601
Lindsay, David 602
Lisle, William 604
Lithgow, William 606
Llwyd, Humphrey 608
Llwyd, Morgan 609
Lodge, Thomas 611
Lodwick, Francis 614
Lok, Anne 616
Love, Mary 618
Lovelace, Richard 620
Lumley, Jane 624
Lupton, Thomas 626
Lyly, John 627
Mair, John 633
Major, Elizabeth 634
marginalia 636

Markham, Gervase   639
Marlowe, Christopher   641
Marprelate, Martin   649
Marshall, William   651
Marston, John   653
Martin, Dorcas   658
Marvell, Andrew   660
Massinger, Philip   668
May, Thomas   672
Medwall, Henry   674
Melville, Elizabeth   676
Mennes, John, and Smith, James   677
Meres, Francis   679
Middleton, Elizabeth   680
Middleton, Thomas   682
Mildmay, Grace   690
Milton, John   691
Moffett, Thomas   700
Montagu, Walter   702
More, Henry   703
More, Thomas   705
Morison, Richard   714
Moryson, Fynes   715
Moulsworth, Martha   717
Moulton, Thomas   718
Munday, Anthony   720
Nashe, Thomas   723
Nedham, Marchamont   727
Neville, Frances   733
Neville, Henry   734
newsletters   736
Niccols, Richard   739
Norden, John   741
Northbrooke, John   743
Norton, Thomas   745
Ogilby, John   747
Osborne, Dorothy   748
Overton, Richard   750
Owen, Jane   752
Oxlie, Mary   753

VOLUME III

Pace, Richard   757
Painter, William   759
Palsgrave, John   761

Parker, Henry   762
Parker, Martin   764
Parr, Katherine   766
Paynell, Thomas   767
Peacham, Henry   769
Peele, George   770
Peend, Thomas   775
Percy, William   777
Pettie, George   779
Petty, William   780
Philips, Katherine   782
Phillips, John   786
Platt, Hugh   788
Ponet, John   790
Poole, Elizabeth   791
Porter, Henry   793
Preston, Thomas   794
Primrose, Diana   796
Prynne, William   798
psalms and psalters, metrical   800
Pulter, Hester   803
Purchas, Samuel   805
Puttenham, George   807
Quarles, Francis   809
Rainolds, John   812
Ralegh, Walter   815
Randolph, Thomas   820
Rastell, John   821
Ravenscroft, Thomas   826
recipe books   827
Rich, Barnabe   830
Rich, Mary   832
Richardson, Elizabeth   834
Rogers, John   836
Roper, Margaret   838
Roper, William   839
Rowlands, Samuel   841
Rowley, William   843
Russell, Lucy, countess of Bedford   847
Sackville, Thomas, earl of Dorset   849
Sander, Nicholas   851
Sandys, George   852
Saxton, Christopher   854
Scot, Reginald   855
Scott, Alexander   857
Selden, John   859

sermons 860
Sexby, Edward 864
Seymour sisters 865
Shakespeare, William 867
Shelton, Mary 875
Shepherd, Luke 876
Shirley, James 878
Sidney, Philip 883
Sidney, Robert, earl of Leicester 890
Skelton, John 892
Smith, Thomas 897
Southwell, Anne 898
Southwell, Robert 900
Sowernam, Ester 905
Speed, John 906
Speght, Rachel 908
Spenser, Edmund 910
St German, Christopher 917
Stafford, Dorothy 920
Stanbridge, John 921
Stanley, Thomas 923
Stanyhurst, Richard 925
Starkey, Thomas 927
Sterry, Peter 928
Stow, John 930
Streater, John 935
Strode, William 937
Stubbes, Philip 938
Suckling, John 940
Sutcliffe, Alice 942
Swetnam, Joseph 943
Sylvester, Joshua 945
Taylor, Jeremy 947
Taylor, John 949
Thimelby, Gertrude 950
Thomas, William 952
Thornton, Alice 954
Tichborne, Chidiock 955
Tofte, Robert 957
Totney, Thomas 959
Tourneur, Cyril 960
Townshend, Aurelian 962
Traherne, Thomas 964
Trapnel, Anna 968

Turbervile, George 972
Tusser, Thomas 975
Tyler, Margaret 976
Tyndale, William 978
Tyrwhit, Elizabeth 985
Udall, Nicholas 988
Underdowne, Thomas 993
Urquhart, Thomas 994
Vaughan, Henry 997
Vaughan, Thomas 1001
verse miscellanies, manuscript 1002
verse miscellanies, printed 1006
Verstegan, Richard 1010
Waller, Edmund 1013
Walton, Izaak 1017
Walwyn, William 1019
Warner, William 1021
Watson, Thomas 1022
Weamys, Anna 1024
Webbe, William 1026
Webster, John 1027
Weever, John 1032
Weston, Elizabeth Jane 1034
Wheare, Degory 1036
Wheathill, Anne 1037
Whetstone, George 1039
Whichcote, Benjamin 1040
White, Robert 1042
Whitney, Geoffrey 1044
Whitney, Isabella 1046
Whittinton, Robert 1050
Whythorne, Thomas 1052
Wight, Sarah 1054
Wild, Robert 1055
Wilkins, John 1057
Wilson, Robert 1059
Wilson, Thomas 1060
Winstanley, Gerrard 1062
Wither, George 1067
Wolley, Hannah 1071
Wotton, Henry 1073
Wright, Thomas 1075
Wroth, Mary 1076
Wyatt, Thomas 1081

Notes on Contributors

Matthew Adams is a freelance writer who has contributed to *Review of English Studies, Essays in Criticism*, and *Standpoint* magazine as well as the *Times Literary Supplement, New Humanist*, the *Spectator*, the *Guardian, Literary Review*, and the *Los Angeles Review of Books*. He is currently writing a book about Richard Overton.

Ruth Ahnert is a lecturer in Renaissance English Literature at Queen Mary, University of London, and is editor of Bulletin of the Society for Renaissance Studies. Her research interests lie at the intersection of religious history, literary form, and book history. She has written a number of articles and chapters on early modern prison literature, including a forthcoming article on the representation of Henry VIII in Robert Bolt's A man for all seasons. She is currently preparing a monograph entitled The rise of prison literature in the sixteenth century, which charts innovations in English prison writing following the Reformation.

Bernadette Andrea is a professor of English at the University of Texas at San Antonio, where she chaired the Department of English, Classics, and Philosophy. Her most recent books include *Women and Islam in early modern English literature* (2007) and *Delarivier Manley and Mary Pix: English women staging Islam, 1696–1707* (forthcoming). She has published widely on English women writers of the sixteenth and seventeenth centuries, early Quaker women writers, the first women playwrights for the public stage, and the first feminists.

Jayne Elisabeth Archer is a lecturer in Medieval and Renaissance Literature at Aberystwyth University. She has co-edited essay collections on Elizabethan progresses entertainments, and the early modern Inns of Court, and is general editor of a five-volume edition of John Nichols's *The progresses of Queen Elizabeth I* (forthcoming).

M. G. Aune is Assistant Professor in the English Department at California University of Pennsylvania. His research interests include travel writing, Shakespeare and film, and Shakespeare and performance. His articles and reviews have appeared in *Shakespeare Bulletin, Renaissance Quarterly*, and *Borrowers and Lenders*.

Gillian Austen is a Visiting Fellow in the Department of English, University of Bristol. She did her PhD research at Lincoln College, Oxford. Her book *George Gascoigne* is the first on Gascoigne to discuss all of his work, including his illustrations. She is currently preparing a fully annotated *Gascoigne bibliography* and editing the collection *New essays on George Gascoigne*.

Laura Aydelotte is a PhD candidate at the University of Chicago where she is completing a dissertation on literature and architecture in late medieval and early modern England.

Rebecca A. Bailey is Senior Lecturer in English Literature at the University of Gloucestershire. She has published *Staging the Old Faith: Queen Henrietta Maria and the theatre of Caroline England, 1625–1642* (2009) and is currently editing *The young admiral* for a forthcoming edition of the complete works of James Shirley.

Naomi Baker is Lecturer in English Literature at the University of Manchester. She has published articles on seventeenth-century autobiographical and radical religious writing, and edited the conversion narratives of two early modern women in *Scripture Women* (2005). Her most recent book, *Plain ugly: the unattractive body in early modern culture* (2010), discusses representations of the body in relation to early modern forms of identity.

Crystal Bartolovich is an associate professor of English at Syracuse University. She has published over thirty essays on early modern literature and culture, as well as theoretical topics in publications such as *Journal of Medieval and Renaissance Studies*, *Renaissance Drama* and *Cultural Critique*. She also edits the e-journal *Early Modern Culture*.

Thomas Betteridge is Professor of English Literature and Drama at Oxford Brookes University. He is author of *Literature and politics in the English Reformation* (2004).

Dennis Austin Britton is an assistant professor of English at the University of New Hampshire. He is the author of 'Re-'turning' Othello: transformative and restorative romance' (2011) and 'Allegory and difference in Ralegh and de Bry: reading and seeing "the Discoverie"' (2011). He is completing a book on race, Protestant theology, and 'infidels' converting to Christianity in early modern English romance.

Meaghan Brown is a doctoral candidate in History of Text Technologies at Florida State University. She is currently researching communities of printers in Elizabethan England and the transnational book trade's interactions with the Anglo-Spanish war.

John R. Burton is a graduate student at the University of Wales, Trinity St David's, where he is completing his PhD thesis on the early modern English sonnet sequence tradition. He has authored several review articles for *Year's Work in English Studies*.

Brooke A. Carlson is an assistant professor of English at Hanluk University of Foreign Studies in Seoul, South Korea 2010. His interests include early modern drama, gender, economic and poetic theory. He is currently creating a monograph from his dissertation, 'Printing pleasing profit: the crafting of capital selves and sales in the English early modern period'.

Peter Carlson is Professor of Church History at Bloy House/Episcopal School of Theology, Claremont, California. His work focuses on the intersection of text and religion in the late medieval and early modern periods. He is currently investigating the role of the 'erased biography' in medieval and early modern LGBT and gender studies, using as a primary example the founder of the monastic college at Ashridge.

Dermot Cavanagh is Senior Lecturer in English at the University of Edinburgh. He is the author of *Language and politics in the sixteenth-century history play* (2003) and co-editor with Stuart Hampton-Reeves and Stephen Longstaffe of *Shakespeare's histories and counter-histories* (2006). He has published essays on Shakespeare and early modern drama.

Paul Cefalu is Associate Professor of English at Lafayette College, Easton, PA. He is the author of *Moral identity in early modern literature* (2004), *Revisionist Shakespeare: transitional ideologies in texts and contexts* (2004), and *English Renaissance literature and contemporary theory: sublime objects of theology* (2007), and co-editor of *The return of theory in early modern cultural studies* (2011).

Elizabeth Clarke is Reader in English at Warwick University, where she leads the Perdita Project investigating women's manuscript writing in the early modern period. She also leads the Warwick John Nichols Project, whose four-volume *Progresses of queen Elizabeth I* appeared in 2010. Her latest monograph is *Politics, religion and the* Song of songs *in seventeenth-century England* (2011).

Jason E. Cohen is an assistant professor of English at Berea College, Kentucky. His publications have appeared in the *Shakespeare Bulletin* and *Upstart Crow*. He has held fellowships at the National Humanities Center, Folger Shakespeare Library, and the Institute for Research in the Humanities at the University of Wisconsin-Madison. He is preparing a monograph on Francis Bacon's political and natural philosophies.

Kimberly Ann Coles is Associate Professor of English at the University of Maryland. She is the author of *Religion, reform, and women's writing in early modern England* (2008), as well as a number of articles on the topics of women's writing, gender, and religious ideology. She is currently writing a book on the constitution of belief in early modern England.

Annaliese Connolly is Senior Lecturer in English at Sheffield Hallam University. Her publications include 'Peele's *David and Bethsabe*: reconsidering the drama of the long 1590s') and 'Evaluating virginity: *A midsummer night's dream* and the iconography of marriage' (both 2007). She is also managing editor of *Early Modern Literary Studies.*

Ruth Connolly is a lecturer in seventeenth-century literature at Newcastle University (UK). She has published articles and chapters on early modern women's manuscript writings and has recently co-edited the collection *Community and conviviality in the work of Robert Herrick* (2011) with Tom Cain. She is also co-editor of *Robert Herrick: the complete poetry* (forthcoming).

Marie-Louise Coolahan is Lecturer in English at the National University of Ireland Galway. Her research interests lie in early modern women's writing, devotional prose, and Renaissance manuscript culture. She is the author of *Women, writing, and* *language in early modern Ireland* (2010) and articles on early modern women's writing, devotional prose, and Renaissance manuscript culture.

Tim Cooper is Senior Lecturer in the History of Christianity in the Department of Theology and Religion at the University of Otago, New Zealand. He is the author of *Fear and polemic in seventeenth-century England* (2001) and scholarly articles on Richard Baxter, John Owen, and radical religion in seventeenth-century England.

Katharine A. Craik is Senior Lecturer in Early Modern Literature at Oxford Brookes University. She has particular interests in the history of the body and the history of reading. She is the author of *Reading sensations in early modern England* (2007) and has also published widely on the works of Shakespeare and his contemporaries. Her edition of Jane Collier's *An essay on the art of ingeniously tormenting* appeared in 2006.

Julie Crawford is Associate Professor of English and Comparative Literature at Columbia University. She is the author of *Marvelous Protestantism* (2005), editor of *The Merchant of Venice* (2008), and is currently completing a book about women and the politics of literary production in early modern England.

Christopher Crosbie is an assistant professor of English at North Carolina State University, and specializes in Renaissance drama with a particular interest in intellectual history. The recipient of the Shakespeare Association of America's J. Leeds Barroll Dissertation Prize for 2008, he has published articles on Shakespeare and his contemporaries in *Shakespeare Quarterly*, *English Literary Renaissance*, *Renaissance Papers*, and *Arthuriana*.

Timothy D. Crowley is Assistant Professor of English and Comparative Literature at Texas Tech University. His research interests include Anglo-Spanish relations and early modern English reception of classical and continental literature.

Robert Darcy is Associate Professor of English at the University of Nebraska-Omaha. His work on early modern drama and poetics has appeared in *Renaissance Drama* and the *Journal for Early Modern Cultural Studies*, as well as in edited collections on Marlowe and Shakespeare. He is currently at work on an edition of early modern verse satire, as well as on a monograph on 'misanthropoetics', or the poetics of misanthropy in the early modern period.

Michael Davies is Senior Lecturer in English at the University of Liverpool. He is the author of *Graceful reading: theology and narrative in the works of John Bunyan* (2002) and has published a number of essays on Bunyan, including a chapter on Bunyan's *Grace abounding* in *The Cambridge companion to John Bunyan* (2010). He is currently preparing an edition of *The Bunyan church book 1656–1702*.

S. F. Davies is currently researching witchcraft writing and the book trade in England, 1563–1660, for a DPhil at the University of Sussex. He has edited George Gifford's *Dialogue concerning witches and witchcrafts* (2007), Matthew Hopkins's

Discovery of witches, and John Stearne's *A confirmation and discovery of witchcraft*, both published as *The discovery of witches and witchcraft* (2007).

Alex Davis is a lecturer in English at the University of St Andrews. He is the author of *Chivalry and romance in the English Renaissance* (2003), and *Renaissance historical fiction: Sidney, Delaney, Nashe* (2011).

Matthew Day is Head of English at Newman University College. He is working on a reception history of *The principal navigations* and has published articles on censorship and early modern travel writing, and the relationship between Hakluyt, Gabriel Harvey, and Thomas Nashe. His forthcoming work concerns the influence of Hakluyt's collection on eighteenth-century travel-narrative compilations.

James Daybell is Professor of Early Modern British History at the University of Plymouth and Fellow of the Royal Historical Society. He is author of *Women letter-writers in Tudor England* (2006), and *The material letter: manuscript letters and the culture and practices of letter-writing in early modern England, 1580–1635* (forthcoming). He edited *Early modern women's letter-writing, 1450–1700* (2001), *Women and politics in early modern England, 1450–1700* (2004), and, with Peter Hinds, *Material readings of early modern culture, 1580–1720* (2010).

Mario DiGangi is Professor of English at Lehman College and the Graduate Center, CUNY. He is the author of *The homoerotics of early modern drama* (1997), *Sexual types: embodiment, agency, and dramatic character from Shakespeare to Shirley* (2011), and he has published editions of *Romeo and Juliet*, *A midsummer night's dream*, and *The winter's tale*.

Jeff Dolven is an associate professor of English at Princeton University, and author of *Scenes of instruction in Renaissance romance* (2007).

Michelle M. Dowd is Associate Professor of English at the University of North Carolina, Greensboro. She is the author of *Women's work in early modern English literature and culture* (2009), which won the Sara A. Whaley Book Award from the National Women's Studies Association. She is also the co-editor of *Genre and women's life writing in early modern England* (2007), *Working subjects in early modern English drama* (2011), and *Early modern women on the Fall: an anthology* (forthcoming). Her essays have appeared in the journals *English Literary Renaissance*, *Modern Philology*, and *Medieval and Renaissance Drama in England*.

Alice Eardley is Research Fellow in Early Modern Poetry at the University of Reading. Her publications include articles on editing, women's manuscript writing, Hester Pulter and Elizabeth Isham, and an edition of Lady Hester Pulter's Complete works (2011). She is currently completing a monograph on Pulter's poetry and prose.

Daniel Ebalo is a cultural historian and literary scholar of the early modern period. He has published his work in the *New Yorker*.

Joshua Eckhardt is an associate professor of English at Virginia Commonwealth University, where he teaches the literature of early modern England and, occasionally, Virginia. His research has focused on manuscript verse miscellanies. His recent book on the subject is *Manuscript verse collectors and the politics of anti-courtly love poetry* (2009).

Jess Edwards is Principal Lecturer in English at Manchester Metropolitan University. He has published a number of articles and essays on various aspects of early modern geometry, geography, travel, and literature, and is the author of *Writing, geometry and space in seventeenth-century England and America* (2006). He is now working on a book-length study of Daniel Defoe's contribution to eighteenth-century geographic culture.

Martine van Elk is an associate professor of English at California State University, Long Beach. She is co-editor of *Tudor drama before Shakespeare, 1485–1590* (2004) and has published numerous articles on Shakespeare, vagrancy, and early modern women.

Elizabeth Elliott is a Leverhulme early career fellow at the Centre for the History of the Book, University of Edinburgh. She has published articles on medieval and Renaissance Scottish literature, and she is currently completing a book on the reception of Boethius in the vernacular literature of the Middle Ages.

William E. Engel is Professor of English at Sewanee: The University of the South (USA). He is the author of *Mapping mortality: the persistence of memory and melancholy in early modern England* (1995), *Death and drama in Renaissance England* (2002), and *Chiastic designs in English Literature from Sidney to Shakespeare* (2009). His current research concerns 'Slips of thought from Chaucer to Milton'.

Lukas Erne is Professor of English Literature at the University of Geneva. He is the author of *Shakespeare's modern collaborators* (2008), *Shakespeare as literary dramatist* (2003), and *Beyond 'The Spanish tragedy': A study of the works of Thomas Kyd* (2001), and the editor of *The first quarto of Romeo and Juliet* (2007) and *Textual performances: The modern reproduction of Shakespeare's drama* (2004).

Susan M. Felch is Professor of English at Calvin College. She has published numerous essays on sixteenth-century British literature, as well as books, including *The collected works of Anne Vaughan Lock* (1999); *Elizabeth Tyrwhit's morning and evening prayers* (2008), which won the Josephine A. Roberts award from the Society for the Study of Early Modern Women; and *Elizabeth I and her age*, co-edited with Donald Stump (2009).

Andrew Fleck is an associate professor of English at San José State University. He has published articles on Renaissance poetry, prose, and drama. His research focuses on the place of the Dutch in the English imagination.

Jennifer Forsyth is an associate professor of English at Kutztown University of Pennsylvania where she specializes in Shakespeare, Fletcher, and other early modern British dramatists, textual theory, collaboration, attribution studies, and conditions of early modern dramatic authorship and textual production.

Rachel Foxley is a lecturer in early modern history at the University of Reading. Her articles on the political thought of the Levellers have appeared in *Historical Journal*, *History of Political Thought*, and *The Seventeenth Century*. She is presently completing a monograph on the Levellers.

Penelope Geng is a graduate student in the English Department at the University of Southern California. She studies law and literature in Renaissance drama and has forthcoming articles in the *Ben Jonson Journal* and *Sixteenth Century Journal*.

Jonathan Gibson works at the English Subject Centre at Royal Holloway, University of London. He has published articles on a wide range of early modern topics, including letters, manuscript construction, Elizabethan prose fiction, Elizabeth I, Ralegh, Sidney, and Shakespeare, and has co-edited books on the *Gawain*-poet and on early modern women's manuscript writings.

Daniel Juan Gil is Associate Professor of English Literature at Texas Christian University. He is the author of *Before intimacy: asocial sexuality in early modern England* (2006), and numerous articles on early modern literature and culture.

Jacqueline Glomski is Visiting Research Fellow in the History Department at King's College London. She is the author of *Patronage and humanist literature in the age of the Jagiellons: court and career in the writings of Rudolf Agricola Junior, Valentin Eck, and Leonard Cox* (2007).

David B. Goldstein is Assistant Professor of English at York University, Toronto, where he teaches courses on Renaissance literature, food and writing, and poetry. He has published articles on Shakespeare, Martha Stewart, and the poet Robert Duncan, and is currently writing a book about eating and ethics in early modern England.

Jaime Goodrich is Assistant Professor of English at Wayne State University. She has written articles on early modern women's learning and religious translations in the journals *Sixteenth Century Journal and English Literary Renaissance*, and she has also contributed to several collections of essays.

Andrew Gordon is Lecturer in Sixteenth and Seventeenth Century Literature, and co-director of the Centre for Early Modern Studies, at the University of Aberdeen. He has written on various aspects of the culture of early modern London, from urban mapping to civic community and has also published widely on correspondence and manuscript culture in the early modern period. He is currently completing a book entitled 'Writing the city: memory, text and community in early modern London'.

Kenneth J. E. Graham is Associate Professor of English at the University of Waterloo. He is the author of *The performance of conviction: plainness and rhetoric in the early English Renaissance* (1994), and co-editor of *Shakespeare and religious change* (2009). He is completing a monograph on the relationship between post-Reformation English poetry and Protestant church discipline.

Tobias B. Gregory is Associate Professor of English at the Catholic University of America, Washington, DC. He is the author of *From many gods to one: divine action in*

Renaissance epic (2006) and of articles on Milton, Tasso, Spenser, and William Empson.

Crawford Gribben is Long Room Hub Senior Lecturer in Early Modern Print Culture in the School of English, Trinity College Dublin, and the author of a number of books on the literary cultures of puritanism and evangelicalism, including *The Puritan millennium: literature and theology, 1550–1682* (2000) and *God's Irishmen: theological debates in Cromwellian Ireland* (2007).

Jane Griffiths is a lecturer in English at the University of Bristol. Her publications include *John Skelton and poetic authority: defining the liberty to speak* (2006) and she is working on a study of marginal glosses in the early decades of print in England.

Jerome de Groot is Lecturer in Renaissance Literature and Culture at the University of Manchester. He has written *Royalist identities* (2004) and numerous articles on Royalism, manuscript culture, gender, and pedagogy in the early modern period.

Stephen Guy-Bray is Professor of English at the University of British Columbia. He specializes in Renaissance poetry and queer theory. Most recently, he has co-edited *Queer renaissance historiography: backward gaze* (2009) and published his third monograph, *Against reproduction: where Renaissance poems come from* (2009).

Helen Hackett is Professor of English at University College London, and co-director of the UCL Centre for Early Modern Exchanges. She has written extensively on Elizabeth I, including *Virgin mother, maiden Queen: Elizabeth I and the cult of the Virgin Mary* (1995) and *Shakespeare and Elizabeth: the meeting of two myths* (2009). Other publications include the introduction to the Penguin edition of *A midsummer night's dream* (2005), and *Women and romance fiction in the English Renaissance* (2000).

Andrew Hadfield is Professor of English at the University of Sussex. His publications include *Shakespeare, Spenser and the matter of Britain* (2003), *Shakespeare and Republicanism* (2005, 2008), and *The history of the Irish book, vol III: the Irish book in English 1550 – 1800* (2006). He is currently working on a biography of Edmund Spenser, editing *The Oxford handbook of English prose, 1500–1640*, and co-editing the Norton Spenser.

Hannibal Hamlin is Associate Professor of English at Ohio State University. He is the author of *Psalm culture and early modern English literature* (2004), and co-editor of *The Sidney Psalter: the psalms of Philip and Mary Sidney* (2009) and *The King James Bible after four hundred years: literary, linguistic, and cultural influences* (2010). He is editor of the journal *Reformation* and is currently completing a book on the Bible in Shakespeare.

Stephen Hamrick is Associate Professor of English at Minnesota State University, Moorhead. He has published *The Catholic imaginary and the cults of Elizabeth* (2009), as well as articles on *Tottel's miscellany* and the English reformation (2002) and on George Gascoigne (2005, 2008).

Peter Happé is a Visiting Fellow in the Department of English, Southampton University. His research interests range from medieval drama to the work of Ben Jonson and James Shirley. In addition he has edited texts and written on the work of John Bale and John Heywood, on the English interludes and on cyclic drama in England and Europe. He is co-editor of the Ludus series (Rodopi).

Johanna Harris is Lecturer in Renaissance Literature at the University of Exeter. She is writing a monography on Puritan epistolary communities in early modern England, and is co-editor of *The intellectual culture of Puritan women, 1558–1680* (2011), She has also published articles in *The Seventeenth Century* and *Literature Compass* and is editing the manuscript writings of Lady Brilliana Harley.

Theo van Heijnsbergen is a lecturer in the Department of Scottish Literature at the University of Glasgow. He specializes in late medieval and early modern Scottish literature and its relationship with its English and Continental equivalents. He is co-editor with Nicola Royan of *Literature, letters and the canonical in early modern Scotland* (2002) and is currently preparing an edition of the poems of Alexander Scott.

Jennifer Wynne Hellwarth is an associate professor of English at Allegheny College where she teaches and writes about gender, sexuality, medical practices, and medieval and early modern English literature. She has published articles in *Critical Survey*, a book, *The reproductive unconscious in medieval and early modern England* (2002), and the Afterword for Douglas Brooks' *Printing and parenting* (2005). She is currently working on a book titled 'Sexual healing: charms, potions, and the female healer managing the sexual body in medieval and early modern romance'.

Erin Henriksen recently taught in the Department of English and American Studies at Tel Aviv University, Israel. She is the author of *Milton and the Reformation aesthetics of the Passion* (2010), and co-editor of *Fiction of unknown or questionable attribution*, in the series *The early modern Englishwoman: a facsimile library* (2006). She has also written on the women writers of the Renaissance.

Roze Hentschell is Associate Professor of English at Colorado State University in Fort Collins, Colorado. She is the author of *The culture of cloth in early modern England: textual constructions of a national identity* (2008) and co-editor of *Masculinity and the metropolis of vice: 1550-1650* (2010). She is currently at work on a new book, 'The cultural geography of St Paul's precinct'.

Thomas Herron is Assistant Professor of English at East Carolina University. He has published widely on topics related to Spenser and Ireland, as well as to Ireland in the Renaissance, including the monograph *Spenser's Irish work: poetry, plantation and colonial reformation* (2007). He has recently been appointed editor of the journal *Explorations in Renaissance Culture*.

Ariel Hessayon is Lecturer in the Department of History at Goldsmiths, University of London. He is the author of *'Gold tried in the fire': the prophet TheaurauJohn Tany and the English Revolution* (2007), as well as co-editor of *Scripture and* *scholarship in early modern England* (2006) and *Varieties of seventeenth- and early eighteenth-century English Radicalism in context* (2011). His current research is primarily focused on the reception of the writings of the German mystic Jacob Boehme, Gerrard Winstanley and the Diggers, and Jews and crypto-Jews in early modern England.

Hilary Hinds is Senior Lecturer in English at Lancaster University. Her research has focused on early modern sectarian writing; publications include *God's English-women: seventeenth-century sectarian writing and feminist criticism* (1996), *George Fox and early Quaker culture* (2011), and an edition of Anna Trapnel's *The cry of a stone* (2000).

Elizabeth Hodgson is an associate professor in English at the University of British Columbia. She is the author of *Gender and the sacred self in John Donne* (1999) and is currently completing a book project entitled 'The weapon of grief for women writers of the English Renaissance'.

Adam G. Hooks is an assistant professor of English at the University of Iowa. His research projects focus on Shakespeare and the book trade, the history of authorship, and the forms and practices of textual circulation. He has published articles in *Shakespeare Survey*, PBSA, and the *Oxford handbook of Shakespeare*, and is finishing a book called 'Vendible Shakespeare'.

Lisa Hopkins is Professor of English at Sheffield Hallam University. She has published many notes and articles on Ford and edited the volume on *'Tis pity* in the Continuum Renaissance Drama series. She has also edited *The lady's trial* for the Revels series and *The broken heart* and *The fancies, chaste and noble* for the Oxford Complete Ford.

Brenda M. Hosington is Professeur associé at the Université de Montréal and research associate in the Centre for the Study of the Renaissance at the University of Warwick. She has published widely on medieval and early modern translation and has written on and edited women's Neo-Latin writings. She has just completed an online annotated catalogue of translations in early modern Britain.

Chloë Houston is a lecturer at the University of Reading. She is the editor of *New worlds reflected: travel and utopia in the early modern period* (2010), and a number of articles on utopias, travel writing, and early modern Persia. She is currently working on a monograph on the Renaissance utopia, and a study of representations of Safavid Persia and Islam in early modern Europe.

Judith Hudson is currently completing doctoral studies at Birkbeck College, University of London. She works primarily in the field of law and literature, with a particular interest in pamphlet texts and popular controversies. Forthcoming publications include a chapter on sixteenth-century perjury.

Ann Hughes is Professor of Early Modern History at Keele University. She is the author of many books and articles on the religion and politics of mid-seventeenth century England including *The causes of the English Civil War* (1998), *Gangraena and the struggle for the English revolution* (2004), and *Gender and the English Revolution* (2011), and co-editor of the *Writings of Gerrard Winstanley* (2009).

Elizabeth Human completed her PhD in English while teaching at Saint Louis University, Missouri. Her research interests include medieval and early modern historiography and the literature of religious controversy.

Sarah Hutton is Professor of English at Aberystwyth University. Her main area of research is seventeenth-century intellectual history, with a special interest in the Cambridge Platonists. Her publications include an edition of Ralph Cudworth's *Treatise concerning eternal and immutable morality* (1996), *Anne Conway: a woman philosopher* (2004), and *Platonism at the origins of modernity* (co-editor, 2008). She is the director of the series *International archives of the history of ideas*.

Bradley J. Irish is a doctoral candidate in English at the University of Texas at Austin; his dissertation project examines Tudor aristocratic culture via contemporary, cross-disciplinary research on affect and emotion. His previous work has appeared in *Renaissance Quarterly, Renaissance Drama,* and *Early Theatre.*

Nicole A. Jacobs is a lecturer at California Polytechnic State University in San Luis Obispo. She has written an article on Charles I and John Milton in *Criticism* (forthcoming) and is working on a book-length study on romance and political theory.

Grace Jones is Junior Teaching Fellow at Sino-British College, Shanghai. Her thesis was entitled 'The Romans in Britain: reading Renaissance views of imperialism'. She has contributed an essay to the collection *Writing Wales from the Reformation to Romanticism* (forthcoming).

Mike Rodman Jones is Leverhulme Early Career Fellow at the English Faculty, Cambridge University. He is author of *Radical pastoral, 1381–1594: appropriation and the writing of religious controversy* (2011) and articles on medieval and early modern literature in *Sixteenth Century Journal, New Medieval Literatures,* and *Leeds Studies in English.*

Claire Jowitt is Professor of Renaissance Literature at Nottingham Trent University. She is the author of *Voyage drama and gender politics 1589–1642* (2003) and *The culture of piracy 1580–1630: English literature and seaborne crime* (2010). She is currently editing volume 14, *The south seas,* in a new edition of Richard Hakluyt's *The principal navigations* (1598–1600).

David Kathman is an independent scholar in Chicago, Illinois. He has published numerous scholarly articles on Elizabethan theatre history, and was a contributor to the *Oxford Dictionary of National Biography* and the *Shakespeare Encyclopedia.* His archival research has focused on theatrical apprenticeship, boy actors, and the inns, taverns, and halls where plays were performed in sixteenth-century London.

Lloyd Edward Kermode is Professor of English at California State University at Long Beach. He works on early modern drama, sixteenth-century ethnicity in England, and British Renaissance cultural studies. His books include *Aliens and Englishness in Elizabethan drama* (2009), *Three Renaissance usury plays* (2009), and *Tudor drama before Shakespeare* (ed.) (2004).

Margaret Jane Kidnie is Professor of English at the University of Western Ontario. She has published widely in early modern textual studies, performance, and adaptation. Her edition of Philip Stubbes, *The Anatomie of Abuses* (2002) was awarded 'Honorable Mention' by the Modern Language Association Committee on Scholarly Editions in 2003.

Adam H. Kitzes is Associate Professor of English literature at the University of North Dakota. He has published *The politics of melancholy from Spenser to Milton* (2006) and articles on John Donne and Thomas Browne.

Bernhard Klein is Professor of English at the University of Kent where he coordinates the Erasmus Mundus Joint Doctoral Programme *TEEME – Text and Event in Early Modern Europe*. His publications in early modern studies include the monograph *Maps and the Writing of Space in Early Modern England and Ireland* (2001) and the essay collections *Literature, Mapping and the Politics of Space in Early Modern Britain* (2001) and *Sea Changes: Historicizing the Ocean* (2004). He is currently working on a monograph on the early modern ocean as a historical space and cultural contact zone, as well as co-editing Volume 7 for the forthcoming 14-volume critical edition of Richard Hakluyt's *Principal Navigations*.

Gregory Kneidel is Associate Professor of English at the University of Connecticut. He is author of *Rethinking the turn to religion in early modern English literature* (2008) and several articles on John Donne and the law.

Jeffrey Todd Knight is Assistant Professor of English at the University of Washington. His essays have appeared in Shakespeare Quarterly, Textual Cultures, Criticism, and Book History, and he is currently working on a book-length study of compiling practices in early modern England.

Sarah Knight is Senior Lecturer in Shakespeare and Renaissance Literature in the School of English at the University of Leicester. She works on sixteenth- and seventeenth-century literature in English and Latin. Her editions and translations include Leon Battista Alberti's *Momus*, John Milton's *Prolusions*, the accounts of Elizabeth I's visits to Oxford in 1566 and 1592, and Fulke Greville's plays.

Gary Kuchar is Associate Professor of English at the University of Victoria. He is the author of *Divine subjection: the rhetoric of sacramental devotion in early modern England* (2005), *The poetry of religious sorrow in early modern England* (2008), and articles on, among other figures, Henry Constable, John Donne, Ben Jonson, Aemilia Lanyer, Andrew Marvell, Shakespeare, and Thomas Traherne.

John Kuhn is a doctoral student in the Department of English and Comparative Literature at Columbia University.

Chris R. Kyle is an associate professor of History at Syracuse University. He has published extensively on seventeenth-century parliaments and the news culture of England. At present he is working on the Oxford Francis Bacon (Vol. VII) and on a monograph on proclamations.

Edel Lamb is an Australian Research Council Fellow at the University of Sydney. She is the author of *Performing childhood in the early modern theatre: the children's playing companies (1599–1613)* (2008) and of various essays on early modern drama. She is currently writing a monograph on early modern books for children, *Reading children in early modern culture.*

Jesse M. Lander is Associate Professor of English at the University of Notre Dame. He is the author of *Inventing polemic: religion, print, and literary culture in early modern England* (2006), and is currently writing a book on the staging of the supernatural in Tudor–Stuart drama.

Rebecca Lemon is Associate Professor of English at the University of Southern California. She is author *of Treason by words: literature, law, and rebellion in Shakespeare's England* (2006) and co-editor of *The Blackwell companion to literature and the Bible* (2009).

Carole Levin is Willa Cather Professor of History and Director of the Medieval and Renaissance Studies Program at the University of Nebraska, Lincoln, specializing in early modern cultural history and women's history. Her publications include: *The heart and stomach of a king: Elizabeth I and the politics of sex and power* (1994), *The reign of Elizabeth I* (2002), *Dreaming the English Renaissance: politics and desire in court and culture* (2008), and most recently, with John Watkins, *Shakespeare's foreign worlds* (2009).

Rhodri Lewis is Fellow and University Lecturer in English at St Hugh's College, Oxford. He has written widely on early modern literary and intellectual history, and is the author of: *Language, mind and nature* (2007) and *William Petty on the order of nature* (2011). He is currently editing John Aubrey's correspondence and Francis Bacon's early philosophical writings.

Daniel T. Lochman is a Professor of English at Texas State University-San Marcos. He has published chapters and articles on John Colet, is completing a critical edition and translation of Colet's commentary on Dionysius's *Ecclesiastical hierarchy*, and is co-editing a collection of scholarly essays on early modern friendship. He teaches early modern literature and culture with interests in romance and pastoral literature as well as friendship studies.

Sandra Logan is Associate Professor of Early Modern English Literature and Culture at Michigan State University. She is the author of *Text/events in early modern England: poetics of history* (2007), as well as articles on Elizabeth I, Shakespeare's *Othello*, Catherine de Valois, and Michael Drayton's *Poly-olbion.* She is currently researching and writing monographs on early modern sovereignty and disenfranchisement and on silent Shakespeare films and nineteenth-century Shakespeare culture.

Jeremy Lopez is Associate Professor of English at the University of Toronto. He is the author of *Theatrical convention and audience response in early modern drama* (2003) as well as numerous articles on Shakespeare and his contemporaries. He is also the theatre review editor of *Shakespeare Bulletin.*

Joyce Lorimer is Professor Emeritus of History at Wilfrid Laurier University, Waterloo, Ontario, Canada. Her research and publications focus on the history of English and Irish exploration, trade, and settlement in the Guianas during the reign of Queen Elizabeth I and the early Stuarts, and on the travel literature which arose from it. She has published *English and Irish settlement on the river Amazon 1550–1646* (1989), *Settlement patterns in early modern colonization* (1998), and *Sir Walter Ralegh's Discoverie of Guiana* (2006).

Genevieve Love is Associate Professor of English at Colorado College. She has published on non-Shakespearean early modern drama in the journals *Renaissance Drama* and *Shakespeare Bulletin,* and in the essay collections *Thunder at a playhouse* and *New directions in Renaissance drama and performance studies.* She has written about the field of Shakespeare performance studies for *Literature Compass,* and serves as book review editor for *Shakespeare Bulletin.*

Scott Lucas is Professor of English at The Citadel, the Military College of South Carolina. He is the author of *'A mirror for magistrates' and the politics of the English Reformation* (2009) as well as several articles on the literature and historiography of the Tudor period.

Christina Luckyj is Professor of English at Dalhousie University in Halifax, Nova Scotia, Canada. Author of *A winter's snake: dramatic form in the tragedies of John Webster* (1989) and *A moving rhetoricke: gender and silence in early modern England* (2002), and editor of *The Duchess of Malfi: a critical guide* (2011), she has also published two essays on Rachel Speght in *English Literary Renaissance.*

Rory Lukins received his PhD in English from the University of Southern California. His areas of specialty include Shakespeare, Renaissance literature, genre theory, poetics and literary history.

Philip Major Lecturer in Early Modern English Literature at the University of Ghent. He has published widely on seventeenth-century English literature, including the edited collection *Literatures of exile in the English Revolution and its aftermath, 1640–1690.*

Willy Maley is Professor of Renaissance Studies at the University of Glasgow. He is the author of *A Spenser chronology* (1994), *Salvaging Spenser: colonialism, culture and identity* (1997), and *Nation, state and empire in English Renaissance literature: Shakespeare to Milton* (2003).

Elizabeth Malson-Huddle teaches at the University of Wisconsin-Madison. She recently published an article on Anne Askew in *Studies in English Literature, 1550–1900* (2010). Her present book project addresses religious controversy in early modern English utopian literature.

James Mardock is Associate Professor of English at the University of Nevada. He has published articles on Shakespeare and Dickens, Jonson and transvestism, John Taylor and religion, and King James I and plague. His book *Our scene is London* (2008) examines Jonson's representation of urban space as an element in his strategy of self-definition. Dr Mardock is at work on an edition of *Henry V* and a book-length study of Calvin's influence on early modern drama. He also serves as the dramaturge for the Lake Tahoe Shakespeare Festival.

James J. Marino is Associate Professor of English at Cleveland State University. He is the author of *Owning William Shakespeare: the King's Men and their intellectual property* (2011).

Christopher Martin is Associate Professor of English at Boston University. He specializes in English and continental literature of the early modern period. He has published *Policy in love: lyric and public in Ovid, Petrarch and Shakespeare* (1994) and *Ovid in English* (1998). He is presently completing a book on old age in Elizabethan literature.

R. W. Maslen is Senior Lecturer at the University of Glasgow. He has published two monographs, *Elizabethan fictions* (1997) and *Shakespeare and comedy* (2005), two editions of early modern texts, and many articles on English Renaissance poetry, prose and drama. He also writes on modern fantasy and science fiction.

Kris McAbee is Assistant Professor of English at the University of Arkansas, Little Rock. She works on the circulation of popular poetry in the English Renaissance and is Technical Consultant of the English Broadside Ballad Archive.

John F. McDiarmid is Professor Emeritus of British and American Literature at New College of Florida. He has published on various topics in the history of early modern English literature, English humanism, and the English Reformation, and edited *The monarchical republic of early modern England: essays in response to Patrick Collinson* (2007). He is currently writing a biography of Sir John Cheke.

Nicholas McDowell is Associate Professor of English at the University of Exeter. His publications include *Poetry and allegiance in the English Civil Wars: Marvell and the cause of wit* (2008), and he is co-editor of *The Oxford handbook of Milton* (2009).

Sean H. McDowell is an associate professor at Seattle University, where he teaches courses on Renaissance literature, Irish literature, creative writing, and film studies. He is the Executive Director of the John Donne Society, and has published numerous articles in *John Donne Journal, George Herbert Journal, ANQ, Discoveries, Literature Compass*, and chapters in various edited collections. In 2009 he edited a special issue of *Explorations in Renaissance Culture* entitled 'The social character of Andrew Marvell's imagination'.

Angela McShane is Tutor in Graduate Studies (1600–1800) in History of Design for the joint Royal College of Art/V&A postgraduate programme. She is the author of *Political broadside ballads of seventeenth century England: a critical bibliography* (2011) and co-editor with Garthine Walker, of *The extraordinary and the everyday in early modern England (2010)*.

M. Barbara Mello is a PhD candidate at the University of Southern California. Her dissertation is entitled 'From the hellmouth to the witch's cauldron: feeding evil on the early modern stage'.

Kirk Melnikoff is an associate professor of English at the University of North Carolina at Charlotte. He has edited two collections of essays on Robert Greene and is finishing a book on Elizabethan publishing practices and the literary sphere.

Steve Mentz is Associate Professor of English at St John's University, New York City. He is the author of *Romance for sale in early modern England* (2004) and *At the bottom of Shakespeare's ocean* (2009), and co-editor of *Rogues and early modern English culture* (2004). He has also published numerous articles and book chapters on Shakespeare, Nashe, early modern prose fiction, ecocriticism, and maritime literature. His current work on early modern maritime culture included an exhibition in 2010 at the Folger Shakespeare Library, entitled 'Lost at sea: the ocean in the English imagination, 1550–1750'.

Eleanor Merchant teaches Latin at the Centre for Editing Lives and Letters, University of London. Publications include her translation of *Erasmus: a handbook on good manners for children* (2008). She is currently completing a doctoral thesis on biography and translation in sixteenth-century Europe.

Gretchen E. Minton is Associate Professor of English at Montana State University. She is the co-editor of the Arden 3 edition of *Timon of Athens* (2008) and has published articles on the English Reformation, Augustine, Shakespeare, and modern drama. Currently she is working on a critical edition of John Bale's *The image of both churches.*

Susannah Brietz Monta is John Cardinal O'Hara, C.S.C. and Glynn Family Honors Associate Professor of English at the University of Notre Dame and the editor of *Religion and Literature.* She has published *Martyrdom and literature in early modern England* (2005), and articles on Edmund Spenser, William Shakespeare, Robert Southwell, Henry Vaughan, history plays, early modern women writers, and early modern Catholicism.

Helen Moore is Fellow and Tutor in English at Corpus Christi College, Oxford and Lecturer in the Faculty of English, University of Oxford. She has edited *Amadis de Gaule* (2004) and *Guy of Warwick* (2007), and co-edited *Classical literary careers and their reception* (2010). She has also published essays on early modern drama and fiction, and the reception and translation of classical and continental texts in England.

Sarah Mortimer is Lecturer in History at Christ Church, Oxford. Her monograph, *Reason and religion in the English Revolution* (2010), discusses the religious and political influence of Socinian ideas during the civil wars. She is currently working on a broader study of the development and impact of heterodox religious and political ideas within the Protestant world.

Stewart Mottram is Lecturer in English at the University of Hull. He is author of *Empire and nation in early English Renaissance literature* (2008) and has articles published or forthcoming on a range of Renaissance authors, from Spenser to Shakespeare, Wyatt to William Browne. He is currently co-editing the volume *Writing Wales: from the Reformation to Romanticism*, and is preparing a second monograph, a study of ruins in Renaissance literature.

Ian Frederick Moulton is Head of Interdisciplinary Humanities and Communication in Arizona State University's School of Letters and Sciences. He has published widely on the representation of gender and sexuality in early modern literature, including *Before pornography: erotic writing in early modern England* (2000). He is also editor and translator of Antonio Vignali's *La cazzaria*, an erotic and political dialogue from Renaissance Italy (2003). He is currently writing a book on the cultural dissemination of notions of romantic love in sixteenth century Europe.

Andy Mousley is Reader in Critical Theory and Renaissance Literature at De Montfort University, Leicester. His publications include: *Re-humanising Shakespeare* (2007) and, as editor, *Towards a new literary humanism* (2011).

Ayesha Mukherjee is a lecturer in the English Department at the University of Exeter, Cornwall Campus. Her research specialism lies in early modern literature and culture, and she is currently completing a book on the Elizabethan scientific practitioner and poet Sir Hugh Platt.

Lucy Munro is a senior lecturer in English at Keele University. Her publications include *Children of the Queen's Revels: a Jacobean theatre repertory* (2005), various essays on early modern drama, and editions of Shakespeare and of Wilkins' *Pericles*, Sharpham's *The fleer*, Brome's *The queen and concubine* and *The demoiselle*, and Fletcher's *The tamer tamed*.

Kathryn Murphy is Fellow and Tutor in English at Oriel College, Oxford. She has published widely on early modern literature and intellectual history, and edited, with Richard Todd, the essay collection *A man very well studied: new contexts for Thomas Browne* (2008). With Claire Preston, she is editing *Urne-buriall* and *The garden of Cyrus* for the Oxford edition of Thomas Browne.

Molly Murray is Associate Professor of English at Columbia University. She is the author of *The poetics of conversion in early modern English literature* (2009), as well as a number of articles on early modern literature and culture. She is currently at work on a study of literature in the early modern English prison.

Vin Nardizzi is Assistant Professor of English at the University of British Columbia. He is co-editor of *Queer Renaissance historiography: backward gaze* (2009) and *The indistinct human in Renaissance literature* (forthcoming). He has completed a book manuscript entitled 'Evergreen fantasies: Shakespeare's theatre in the age of wood'.

Joseph Navitsky is an assistant professor of English at West Chester University Pennsylvania, where he teaches Shakespeare, sixteenth-century literature, and early modern print culture. His book manuscript, *The Marprelate effect: religious conflict, satire, and the late Tudor state*, examines the relationship between religious controversy and the rise of satiric discourse in early modern literary culture. He has also written articles on the religious satirist Martin Marprelate and on verbal violence on the early modern stage.

Marcus Nevitt is Senior Lecturer in Renaissance Literature at the University of Sheffield. He is the author of *Women and the pamphlet culture of revolutionary England* (2006). He is currently working on two book-length projects: 'Poetry and the art of English newswriting, 1640–1660' and 'William Davenant and the making of Restoration culture'.

David Nicol is Assistant Professor of Theatre at Dalhousie University. He has published articles on the plays of William Rowley in *Comparative Drama*, *Early Theatre*, *Medieval and Renaissance Drama in England*, *Cahiers Élisabéthains*, and *Studies in English Literature*. A book entitled *Middleton and Rowley: forms of collaboration in the Jacobean playhouse* is forthcoming.

Marcy L. North is Associate Professor of English at Pennsylvania State University. She is the author of *The anonymous Renaissance* (2003) and several articles on early modern authorship, print, and manuscript culture. She is currently completing a book on the way the material production of early modern verse manuscripts reflects and influences the fashions and taste for poetry in the period.

Liz Oakley-Brown is a lecturer in Renaissance writing at Lancaster University. Her publications include *Ovid and the cultural politics of translation in early modern England* (2006) and the edited collection *Shakespeare and the translation of identity in early modern England* (2011).

Michelle O'Callaghan is Reader in Early Modern English Literature in the Department of English and American Studies at the University of Reading, and the author of *The 'shepheards nation': Jacobean Spenserians and early Stuart political culture* (2000), *The English wits: literature and sociability in early modern England* (2007), and *Thomas Middleton, Renaissance dramatist* (2008).

Niamh J. O'Leary is an assistant professor of English at Xavier University in Cincinnati, Ohio. She has published on Shakespeare and film and is working on a book-length project about communities of women in Renaissance drama.

Melanie Ord is Senior Lecturer in Renaissance Literature at the University of the West of England, Bristol. She is the author of *Travel and experience in early modern English literature* (2008) and has written articles on Roger Ascham, Thomas Coryat, Anthony Munday, and Sir Henry Wotton.

Clare Painting-Stubbs teaches History at a grammar school in Kent. She wrote her PhD on Abraham Fleming at Royal Holloway, University of London, and has published articles on Fleming in *The Indexer* and *Fortean Times*. She is now working on a biography of folklorist Theodora Brown.

Edward Paleit is a lecturer in English at the University of Exeter. He has published a number of articles including 'The 'Caesarist' Reader and Lucan's *Bellum Ciuile, CA.* 1590 to 1610' (2010). His book on the reception of Lucan in early modern England is forthcoming.

Michael P. Parker is a professor of English at the United States Naval Academy. He has published on Carew, Suckling, Davenant, and other Caroline poets. He is currently collaborating with Timothy Raylor on an edition of Edmund Waller's poems.

Jason Peacey is Senior Lecturer in History at University College London. He is the author of *Politicians and pamphleteers: propaganda in the Civil Wars and Interregnum* (2004), the editor of *The regicides and the execution of Charles I* (2001) and *The print culture of parliament, 1600-1800* (2007), and the co-editor of *Parliament at work* (2002). He is currently writing a book about popular political participation during the mid-seventeenth century.

Patricia Pender is a postdoctoral Research Fellow in the School of Humanities and Social Science at the University of Newcastle, Australia. She has published two articles on Anne Askew, in the *Huntington Library Quarterly* and in the edited collection *Expanding the canon of early modern women's writing* (both 2010). She has previously published essays on the early modern women writers Anne Bradstreet, Aphra Behn, and Mary Sidney Herbert.

Elizabeth Pentland is Assistant Professor of English at York University in Toronto. She has published work on Jacobean representations of Elizabeth I, and her essay on Shakespeare's Illyria recently appeared in the edited collection *Twelfth night: new critical essays* (2010). She is currently at work on a book-length study of Elizabethan and Jacobean writing about France.

Mike Pincombe is Professor of Tudor and Elizabethan literature at Newcastle University, UK, He has published books on *The plays of John Lyly* (1996) and *Elizabethan humanism* (2001), and co-edited (with Cathy Shrank) *The Oxford handbook of Tudor literature* (2009).

Tanya Pollard is Associate Professor of English at the Graduate Center and Brooklyn College, City University of New York. Her publications include *Drugs and theater in early modern England* (2005), *Shakespeare's theater: a sourcebook* (2003), and essays on early modern theatre and medicine in a number of journals and edited volumes. She is currently writing on the development of popular dramatic genres in early modern England, and their debts to classical Greek plays and genre theory.

William Poole is John Galsworthy Fellow of New College, Oxford. Publications include *Milton and the idea of the Fall* (2005), *John Aubrey and the advancement of learning* (2010), and *The world makers* (2010). He also edited (2009) Francis Godwin's *The man in the moone*, and co-edited (2011) the complete writings of Francis Lodwick.

Jason Powell is an assistant professor of English at St Joseph's University, Philadelphia. He is working on a two-volume edition of *Thomas Wyatt's complete works*. Tudor literature and diplomacy, manuscripts, and the transmission of Henrician literature are among his primary research interests.

Henry Power is Lecturer in English at the University of Exeter. His publications include 'Virgil's Georgics and the Landscape of the English Civil War' and 'The Aeneid in the Age of Milton' (both 2010). He is currently writing a book on Henry Fielding and the Scriblerians.

Sarah Poynting is an independent scholar with a particular interest in interdisciplinary research on the Caroline court. She has taught English literature at the universities of Oxford, Keele, Roehampton, and Warwick. Recent contributed chapters include '"I doe desire to be rightly vnderstood": rhetorical strategies in the letters of Charles I' (2007) and '"The rare and excellent partes of Mr. Walter Montague": Henrietta Maria and her playwright' (2008). She is currently working on a three-volume scholarly edition of the writings of Charles I.

Aaron T. Pratt is a PhD student at Yale University. His recent work concerning the materiality and history of the English Bible appears in a co-authored chapter in *The King James Bible after four hundred years: literary, linguistic, and cultural influences* (2011).

Beth Quitslund is Associate Professor of English at Ohio University. She is the author of *The Reformation in rhyme: Sternhold, Hopkins and the English metrical psalter, 1547–1603* (2008) and the co-editor of a critical edition of *The whole booke of Psalmes* (forthcoming).

Noël Clare Radley is a doctoral candidate at the University of Texas at Austin. Her dissertation focuses on embodied poetics during the transition from medieval to Renaissance verse, with emphasis on the reform poetry of Sir Thomas Wyatt and Anne Vaughan Locke.

Mark Rankin is Assistant Professor of English at James Madison University. He is the co-editor of *Henry VIII and his afterlives: literature, politics, and art* (2009). In addition to his and chapters on English Renaissance literature and culture, he is completing a monograph entitled *Representing Henry VIII in early modern England: literature, history, and polemic*.

Jamie Reid-Baxter is a Research Fellow in Scottish History, University of Glasgow. He has published widely on Scottish Jacobean writing, music and history, including most recently *Poems of Elizabeth Melville, Lady Culross* (2010), and is currently editing *The poems of John Burel.*

Jennifer Richards is Professor of Early Modern Literature at Newcastle University, UK. Her publications include *Rhetoric and courtliness in early modern literature* (2003) and *Rhetoric* (2007) in the New Critical Idiom series.

Jane Rickard is Lecturer in Seventeenth-Century English Literature at the University of Leeds. Her publications include *Authorship and authority: the writings of James VI and I* (2007). She is currently completing a book entitled 'Writing the monarch in Jacobean England'.

Timothy Rosendale is an associate professor of English at Southern Methodist University, Texas. He is the author of *Liturgy and literature in the making of Protestant England* (2007), and is currently pursuing projects on early modern historiography and doctrinal problems of agency in Renaissance literature.

Sarah C. E. Ross is Senior Lecturer in English at Massey University, New Zealand. She is the editor of *Katherine Austen's Book M* (2010) and several articles on early modern women writers. She is currently working on a book entitled 'Women, poetry, and politics in seventeenth-century Britain'.

Nicola Royan is a lecturer in late medieval and early modern literature in the School of English Studies, University of Nottingham. She has published several articles and essays on Hector Boece and Scottish historiography, and continues to work on Scottish literary representations of national identity. She is the Editorial Secretary of the Scottish Text Society.

Eleanor Rycroft is Lecturer in Early Modern Literature at Lancaster University. She has published essays and articles in contributed volumes and journals including Locating the Queen's Men, The Oxford handbook to Tudor Drama, Henry VIII and the Tudor court, and Medieval English Theatre. She is currently working on a book provisionally entitled 'Hair, beards and the performance of gender on the early modern English stage'.

Melissa E. Sanchez is Stephen M. Gorn Family Assistant of English at the University of Pennsylvania. She has been an Andrew W. Mellon Fellow at the Huntington Library, California, and her articles have appeared in *PMLA, Eighteenth-Century Studies, The Sidney Journal, The Huntington Library Quarterly, English Literary History, English Literary Renaissance, Studies in Philology*, and several edited collections. She is the author of *Erotic subjects: the sexuality of politics in early modern English literature* (2011).

Julie Sanders is Professor of Englih Literature and Drama at the University of Nottingham. She has published widely on Ben Jonson and Caroline drama as well as editing plays by James Shirley and Richard Brome, including the edited collection

Ben Jonson in context (2010) and the monograph *The cultural geography of early modern drama, 1620–1650* (2011).

Rhonda Lemke Sanford is Professor of English at Fairmont State University. She is the author of *Maps and memory in early modern England: a sense of place* (2002); her current project centres upon different forms of legitimacy.

Gary Schneider is Associate Professor at the University of Texas – Pan American. He is the author of *The culture of epistolarity: vernacular letters and letter writing in early modern England, 1500–1700* (2005) and is completing a monograph on print letters in sixteenth- and seventeenth-century England.

Lisa J. Schnell is an associate professor of English and Associate Dean of the Honors College at the University of Vermont. She is the co-author of *Literate experience: the work of knowing in seventeenth-century English writing* (2002), and has published articles on Aemilia Lanyer, Rachel Speght and Aphra Behn, as well as on medicine and narrative theory. She is one of the editors of *Women's worlds: the McGraw-Hill anthology of women's writing* (2008).

Fred Schurink is Lecturer in Early Modern English Literature at Northumbria University. He is the editor of *Tudor translation* (forthcoming) and co-editor of a Special Issue of *Huntington Library Quarterly* on early modern reading (2010) and has published articles and chapters in *Review of English Studies*, *Yearbook of English Studies*, and *The Oxford handbook of Tudor literature*. He is currently completing a monograph on Tudor translations of the classics and a scholarly edition for the MHRA Tudor & Stuart Translations series, *Plutarch: 'Essays' and 'Lives'*.

Philip Schwyzer is Associate Professor of Renaissance Literature at the University of Exeter. He is the author of *Literature, nationalism and memory in early modern England and Wales* (2004) and *Archaeologies of English Renaissance literature* (2007), and is currently completing a study of Shakespeare and the historical Richard III.

Elizabeth Scott-Baumann is a Research fellow at Wolfson College, Oxford and Lecturer in Early Modern Literature at Wadham College, Oxford. As well as publishing articles on Lucy Hutchinson and Margaret Cavendish, she co-edited an essay collection on *The intellectual culture of Puritan women 1558–1680* (2010). She is currently completing a book entitled 'Forms of engagement: women, poetry and culture, 1640–1680' and working on a project on early modern women critics as well as co-editing an anthology of *Women Poets of the English Civil War*.

R. W. Serjeantson teaches early modern history at Trinity College, Cambridge. He is the editor of *Meric Casaubon, 'Generall learning: A seventeenth-century treatise on the formation of the general scholar'* (1999) and co-editor of Volume III of the Oxford Francis Bacon (forthcoming).

Manish Sharma is an associate professor at Concordia University in Montréal, Québec, Canada. He specializes in Old and Middle English literature. He has published articles on a variety of topics pertaining to medieval English poetry in several journals including *Journal of English and Germanic Philology*, *English Studies*, *Studies in Philology*, and *Papers on Language and Literature*.

Lauren Shohet is Professor of English at Villanova University. She is the author of *Reading masques: the English masque and public culture in the seventeenth century* (2010) and is working on a study of adaptation and genre theory.

Cathy Shrank is Professor of Tudor and Renaissance Literature at the University of Sheffield. She is author of *Writing the nation in Reformation England, 1530–1580* (2004) and the co-editor of *The Oxford handbook of Tudor literature, 1485–1603* (2009). She is currently editing Shakespeare's poems for Longman Annotated English Poets and researching a monograph on sixteenth-century dialogue.

Emma Smith is Fellow and Tutor in English at Hertford College, University of Oxford. She has published on Shakespeare in performance, on critical reception of his works, and on editing, including *The Cambridge Introduction to Shakespeare* (2007).

Matthew J. Smith is a PhD candidate at the University of Southern California where he studies Renaissance English literature in religious and philosophical contexts. His dissertation is entitled 'The phenomena of literary belief in Renaissance England'.

Adam Smyth is a senior lecturer in Renaissance Literature at Birkbeck College, London. His publications include *Profit and delight: printed miscellanies in England, 1640–82* (2004); an edited collection, *A pleasing sinne: drink and conviviality in seventeenth-century England* (also 2004); and *Autobiography in early modern England* (2010).

Edith Snook is an associate professor of English at the University of New Brunswick in Fredericton, Canada. She has published articles on beauty practices, reading, and politics in early modern women's writing in print and manuscript, and is the author of *Women, reading, and the cultural politics of early modern England* (2005) and *Women, beauty and power in early modern England: a feminist literary history* (2011).

George Southcombe is a British Academy Postdoctoral Fellow at Somerville College, Oxford. He is the co-author of *Restoration politics, religion, and culture: Britain and Ireland, 1660–1714* (2010) and is currently editing a collection of late seventeenth-century Nonconformist poetry.

Michael R. G. Spiller is Honorary Senior Lecturer in English and Cultural History at the University of Aberdeen and the author of *The development of the sonnet* (1992), *The sonnet sequence: a study of its strategies* (1997), and *Early modern sonneteers: from Wyatt to Milton* (2001); his articles on poetry, literary theory, and the Scottish court can be found in numerous edited collections and scholarly journals.

Matthew Steggle is Reader in English at Sheffield Hallam University. His publications include *Richard Brome: place and politics on the Caroline stage* (2004), *Laughing and weeping in early modern theatres* (2007), and an edition of *The English moor* for *The Richard Brome Project* (gen. ed. Richard A. Cave, 2010).

Paul D. Stegner is an assistant professor of English at California Polytechnic, San Luis Obispo. His articles have appeared or are scheduled to appear in *Shakespeare Studies*, *Studies in Philology*, and the *Journal of English and Germanic Philology*, and he has contributed to edited collections on Shakespeare and Spenser. His current book project focuses on representations of auricular confession in early modern English literature.

Alan Stewart is Professor of English and Comparative Literature at Columbia University, and International Director of the Centre for Editing Lives and Letters in London. He is the author, most recently, of *Shakespeare's letters* (2008), and editor of volume I of the Oxford Francis Bacon, *Early writings, 1584–1596* (forthcoming).

Robin S. Stewart is an English doctoral candidate at the University of California, Irvine, specializing in Tudor and Stuart drama. He is currently examining the shifting conceptions of temporality in the development of the English history play from the reign of Henry VIII to that of James I.

Emily E. Stockard is Associate Professor of English at Florida Atlantic University, Davie campus. Her publications include: 'Patterns of consolation in Shakespeare's sonnets 1–126' (1997) and 'The power of fantasy in Middleton's *Chaste Maid*: A cost/benefit analysis' (2006).

Robert Stretter is Assistant Professor of English at Providence College (Rhode Island), where he teaches Medieval and Renaissance English Literature. He has published articles on Chaucer, Lydgate, and early English Renaissance drama, and is currently at work on a book entitled *Other selves: theorizing friendship from Chaucer to Shakespeare*.

Ceri Sullivan is Professor in the School of English, Bangor University. Her principal books include *Dismembered Rhetoric. English Recusant Writing, 1580–1603* (1995) and *The rhetoric of the conscience in Donne, Herbert and Vaughan* (2008). She is currently working on a monograph on the relation between institutional ethics and creativity in public servants from John Milton to David Hare.

Erin Sullivan is a lecturer at the Shakespeare Institute, University of Birmingham. Her research focuses on the intersection between medicine, religion, and morality in sixteenth- and seventeenth-century England, with particular emphasis on the management of emotions. Her publications include 'Physical and spiritual illness: narrative appropriations of the bills of mortality' (2010), as well as short pieces contributed to *The Lancet* on early modern health. She is currently working on a monograph on sadness in medicine and religion in the early modern period.

Garrett A. Sullivan, Jr is Professor of English at Penn State University. He is the author of *The drama of landscape: land, property, and social relations on the early modern stage* (1998), *Memory and forgetting in English Renaissance drama: Shakespeare, Marlowe, Webster* (2005), and *Sleep, romance and human embodiment: vitality from Spenser to Milton* (forthcoming).

David Swain is Associate Professor of English at Southern New Hampshire University. He writes on early modern medicine and social history, and is co-editor of *The Routledge encyclopedia of Tudor England* (2001; 2011) and editor of *Twelfth night* for *The Broadview anthology of British literature*.

Mark S. Sweetnam is a research fellow in the School of History at Trinity College Dublin, where he works particularly in the area of Digital Humanities. He has wide-ranging research interests in the area of literature and theology, with a particular focus on the literature of the early-modern period. He has published chapters on the sermons of John Donne, Alexander Montgomerie, and a number of articles on evangelical millennialism. He has recently completed an edition of the manuscript minutes of the Antrim Ministers' Meeting, 1654–58, and is working on a monograph study of the theology of John Donne.

Ramie Targoff is Professor of English, and director of the Mandel Humanities Center, at Brandeis University. She is the author of *Common prayer: the language of public devotion in early modern England* (2001), *John Donne, body and soul* (2008); and articles in journals such as *PMLA, Representations, Word and Image,* and *English Literary Renaissance*. She is currently completing a book entitled 'Posthumous love: Romeo and Juliet's tomb'.

Joseph Tate is an independent scholar in Seattle, Washington. He taught Renaissance literature for more than seven years at the University of Washington, Lewis and Clark College, and Oregon State University. He has lectured in the US, Canada, UK, and France, on Renaissance literature, with a focus on Renaissance prose and verse practices. He has also published essays on Karl Marx for Open Court's Popular Culture and Philosophy series.

Alison Taufer is Professor of English, teaching medieval and Renaissance Literature, at California State University, Los Angeles. Her publications include *Holinshed's Chronicles*, a volume in the Twayne English Author series, as well as articles and book reviews on medieval and Renaissance English and Spanish literature.

Joseph R. Teller is an Edward Sorin Postdoctoral Fellow in the English Department at the University of Notre Dame. He is currently developing a project on the poetics of Christ's Passion in early modern England. His recent publications include '"Bodying truth": mediation, prophecy, and sacrament in Milton's early prose', and 'The (dis)possession of Lear's two bodies: madness, demystification, and domestic space in Peter Brook's *King Lear*'.

Edward M. Test is an assistant professor of English at Boise State University. He is author of several articles on the transatlantic Renaissance, most recently 'Seeds of sacrifice: Amaranth, the Gardens of Tenochtitlan and Spenser's *Faerie Queene*' (2010).

Amy L. Tigner is an assistant professor of Renaissance Studies in the English Department at University of Texas, Arlington. Tigner has published articles in

Milton Quarterly, Modern Drama, English Literary Renaissance, Drama Criticism, and *Global traffic: discourses and practices of trade in English literature and culture from 1550 to 1700.* She is the author of *Literature and the Renaissance garden, from Elizabeth I to Charles II: England's Paradise* (forthcoming).

Rebecca Totaro is a Professor of English at Florida Gulf University and Editor of the book series Medieval & Renaissance Literary Studies. She is author of *Suffering in paradise: the bubonic plague in English literature from More to Milton* (2005); recipient of the 2010 SEL Monroe Kirk Spears Award for 'Securing sleep in *Hamlet*'; editor of *The plague in print: essential Elizabethan sources, 1558–1603* (2009), and co-editor of *Representing the plague in early modern England* (2010).

Shaina Trapedo is a graduate student in English at University of California, Irvine. Her research interests include early modern studies, religious studies (especially Hebrew and Christian Biblical literature), and rhetoric. Her dissertation examines how Judeo-Christian texts and exegesis migrated into secular literary works of the Renaissance.

Deborah Uman is Associate Professor of English at St John Fisher College. Among her publications are articles on the works of Aphra Behn, Jane Lumley, and Margaret Tyler. She is currently completing a book on female translators in early modern England and co-editing a collection on dramatizing the blazon.

David Vaisey is Bodley's Librarian Emeritus, a Fellow of Exeter College, Oxford, an Honorary Fellow of Kellogg College, and a Fellow of the Society of Antiquaries of London and the Royal Historical Society. He was Keeper of Western Manuscripts of the Bodleian Library, Oxford, from 1975 to 1986 and Bodley's Librarian from 1986 to 1996. He also held the post of Keeper of the University Archives at Oxford from 1995 to 2000.

Angus Vine is Lecturer in Early Modern Literature at the University of Sussex. He is the author of *In defiance of time: antiquarian writing in early modern England* (2010), and is also one of the editors working on the Oxford Francis Bacon project.

Daniel Vitkus is associate professor of English at Florida State University. He is the author of *Turning Turk: English theater and the multicultural Mediterranean* (2003) and the editor of *Three Turk plays* (2000) and *Piracy, slavery and redemption: Barbary captivity narratives from early modern England* (2001). He serves as co-editor of the *Journal for Early Modern Cultural Studies* and has published numerous articles and book chapters on early modern culture and literature.

Daniel Wakelin is the Jeremy Griffiths Professor of Medieval English Palaeography at the University of Oxford and a fellow of St Hilda's College. He has published *Humanism, reading & English literature, 1430–1530* (2007) and is currently research-ing scribal corrections in Middle English and editing William Worcester's *The boke of noblesse* (1475).

Melissa Walter teaches Renaissance literature at the University of the Fraser Valley in Abbotsford, British Columbia, Canada. She writes on early modern prose, drama, transnational exchange, and especially the Italian novella in England.

Allyna E. Ward is Assistant Professor of Early Modern Literature at Booth University College, Winnipeg. She edited Richard Robinson's *The reward of wickedensse* for publication (2009). Her published articles include 'Lucanic Irony in Marlowe's *Tamburlaine*' (2008), and 'The rare triumphs of love and fortune' for the *Oxford handbook of Tudor drama* (2010).

Christopher N. Warren is Assistant Professor of English and Literary and Cultural Studies at Carnegie Mellon University in Pittsburgh. His published essays include 'When self-preservation bids: approaching Milton, Hobbes, and Dissent' (2007) and 'Hobbes's Thucydides and the colonial law of nations' (2009).

Tiffany Jo Werth is Assistant Professor of English at Simon Fraser University in British Columbia. She has published 'The Reformation of Romance in Sir Philip Sidney's *The New Arcadia*' (2010) and has completed a monograph *The fabulous dark cloister: romance in England after the Reformation* (forthcoming). Currently, she is researching the status of the godless in early modern England.

Philip West is Tutorial Fellow in English at Somerville College, Oxford, and a lecturer in the Oxford English Faculty. He is the author of *Henry Vaughan's Silex scintillans: scripture uses* (2001), editor of *Sermons preached for the nobility and gentry*, Volume VI of *The Oxford edition of the sermons of John Donne*, and has published several articles on early modern devotional poetry and religion. His current project is an edition of the poems of James Shirley.

Martin White is Foundation Chair of Drama and Professor of Theatre at the University of Bristol. He has published extensively as a critic, editor, and theatre historian, including *Renaissance drama in action* (1998), an edition of Massinger's *The Roman actor* (2007), a study of *A midsummer night's dream* (2009) and an interactive DVD, *The chamber of demonstrations: reconstructing the Jacobean indoor playhouse* (2009). At Bristol he has directed a large number of early modern plays, and also acts as an adviser to the Royal Shakespeare Company and Shakespeare's Globe.

Micheline White is an associate professor in the College of the Humanities at Carleton University in Canada. She has edited *Ashgate critical essays on women writers in England, 1550–1700: Anne Lock, Isabella Whitney, and Aemilia Lanyer* (2009) and *English women, religion, and textual production, 1500–1625* (2011).

Robert Wilcher is an Honorary Fellow of the Shakespeare Institute in Stratford-upon-Avon. He was formerly Reader in Early Modern Studies in the English Department at the University of Birmingham. His publications include *The writing of royalism 1628–1660* (2001); *The discontented cavalier: the work of Sir John Suckling in its social, religious, political, and literary contexts* (2007), as well as books, articles and chapters on Shakespeare, Milton, Marvell, Henry Vaughan, Quarles, and *Eikon Basilike*.

Deanne Williams is an associate professor of English at York University. She is the author of *The French fetish from Chaucer to Shakespeare* (2004), which won the Roland Bainton prize from the Sixteenth Century Society and Conference, and co-editor, with Ananya Kabir, of *Postcolonial approaches to the European middle ages* (2005).

Grant Williams is Associate Professor in the Department of English at Carleton University. His research focuses on the rhetoric of memory, forgetting, and fantasy in early modern English Literature and culture. His publications include *Forgetting in early modern English literature and culture: Lethe's legacies*, co-edited with Christopher (2004) and *Ars reminiscendi: memory and culture in the Renaissance*, co-edited with Donald Beecher (2009).

Emma Annette Wilson is a Postdoctoral Fellow at the University of Pittsburgh, working on early modern logic and its use on stage from the 1580s to the 1630s. She completed her Ph.D. on 'John Milton's use of logic in *Paradise Lost*' in 2009 at the University of St Andrews, after which she was a Canadian DFAIT Commonwealth Post-Doctoral Research Fellow at the University of Western Ontario until her appointment at Pittsburgh. She is the co-editor of two essay collections on the logician and pedagogue Petrus Ramus, and has published essays on John Milton. She is currently working on a monograph history of early modern logic, and a co-authored work on early modern jestbooks.

Luke Wilson is an associate professor of English at the Ohio State University. He is author of *Theaters of intention: Drama and the law in early modern England* (2000) and of a number of articles on Renaissance law and literature.

Edward Wilson-Lee is a fellow of Sidney Sussex College, Cambridge and an affiliated lecturer in the English Faculty at the University of Cambridge. His work focuses on early and mid-Tudor poetry and romance, and he is currently completing a monograph on readers of Sidney's *Arcadia* in its first century.

Phil Withington is an early modern social and cultural historian at the University of Cambridge. He is the author of *The politics of commonwealth: citizens and freemen in early modern England* (2005) and *Society in early modern England: the vernacular origins of some powerful ideas* (2010), and co-editor of *Communities in early modern England* (2000).

Matthew Woodcock is Senior Lecturer in Medieval and Renaissance Literature at the University of East Anglia, Norwich. He is the author of *Fairy in The Faerie Queene* (2004), *Henry V: a reader's guide to essential criticism* (2008), and *Sir Philip Sidney and the Sidney circle* (2010).

Jonathan Woolfson is Director of Semester and Summer Programmes, Sotheby's Institute of Art, London. He has written widely on Anglo-Italian cultural and intellectual relations during the sixteenth century, including *Padua and the Tudors: English students in Italy, 1485–1603* (1998). He is also the editor of *Reassessing Tudor humanism* (2002) and *Palgrave advances in Renaissance historiography* (2004).

Matthew Zarnowiecki is an assistant professor of English at Auburn University, Alabama. He has published on English poetry in manuscript and print, including articles about Sir Philip Sidney and George Gascoigne. He is currently at work on a project focused on reproductive strategies in early modern English poetry.

Introduction to *The encyclopedia of English Renaissance literature*

GARRETT A. SULLIVAN, JR AND ALAN STEWART

The encyclopedia of English Renaissance literature presents the most comprehensive picture of sixteenth- and seventeenth-century English literature available today. It covers the period from the reign of Henry VII to that of Charles II (roughly 1485 to 1670), two momentous centuries in the history of England that saw the end of the Wars of the Roses, the rise of the Tudor and then Stuart dynasties, the Civil Wars and the overthrow of royal government, and the Restoration of the monarchy. Historians have located in these two centuries the transitions from feudalism to capitalism and from Catholicism to Protestantism, the crisis of the aristocracy and the rise of the middling classes, the emergence of the nation-state, the dawn of empire, and the birth of modern science. For literary historians, too, this is an exciting, fruitful, and contested time – when the printing press came into its own, the English language expanded exponentially, while its literature adapted forms from the classical past and the Continental present and forged ahead in new, unprecedented ways. As a result this period produced some of the giants of world literature, among them William Shakespeare and John Milton, and a fascinatingly rich and diverse array of lesser-known writers. Over its three volumes, *The encyclopedia of English Renaissance literature* celebrates and analyses this legacy, providing readers with a clear sense of the vibrancy and variety of early modern writing, in over 430 specially commissioned entries by a distinguished team of international scholars, overseen by us and our associate editors, Rebecca Lemon, Nicholas McDowell, and Jennifer Richards. And while the appearance of an encyclopedia in print might seem to signal the endpoint of an amassing of knowledge, we hope instead that the *Encyclopedia* will excite new debate and provoke new discoveries about English Renaissance literature that will allow the work to continue to develop in its online incarnation.

As straightforward as this encyclopedia's title appears, each of its three keywords – English, Renaissance, literature – raises important questions. What precisely constitutes an 'English' work? Is such a work necessarily written within the boundaries of the country of England? Or only by a writer born in England? Or is it best defined as a work written in the English language? Or published in England? We should state at the outset that we have deliberately chosen to buck the current trend that simply replaces the word 'English' with the word 'British' without materially altering the content of what is being discussed. We are not aiming here to provide a picture of literature emanating from the entire British–Irish archipelago, but specifically to describe the literature of England, and literature in English. Even with this aim in mind, however, the sixteenth and seventeenth centuries pose particularly acute problems of definition. Latin remained the international *lingua franca* of intellectual and political exchange for much of this period, and so it could be argued that much 'English Renaissance literature' was not written in English. And the English vernacular itself was the subject of ongoing controversy – first, about its suitability as a vehicle for Scripture, and more lastingly, about its qualities as a language for poetry. As late as the 1580s, writers such as Philip Sidney and George Puttenham were agonizing over the merits of English metrical forms, often deemed far inferior to those of Latin literature. Yet by early in the seventeenth century, English had come into its own as a poetic language, and a stigma no longer attached to writing verse in the vernacular. Part of what we aim to tell in the *Encyclopedia* is the very specific story of *English*.

A different, geographical challenge to our 'English' definition is posed by English-born writers who fled their homeland in the face of religious persecution – for example, Protestants who flocked to the Continent while Mary Tudor was on the throne, recusant Catholics who sought refuge in Europe during her half-sister Elizabeth's reign, or Puritans who migrated to the New World in the first half of the seventeenth century. The case of the Puritan poet Anne Bradstreet, author of the volume *The tenth muse lately sprung up in America* (1650), is instructive. As her book-title suggests, Bradstreet is commonly thought of as one of the first American writers; she wrote her poetry in Massachusetts and her work is a major part of the colonial American canon. And yet, she was also English-born (in Northampton) and educated; her volume of poems was published in London, and circulated in her native land. Just how English was she? More complexly, if we (very plausibly) understand Bradstreet as contributing to, or even helping to inaugurate, a fundamentally transatlantic form of cultural exchange, how much sense does it make to label her as either English or colonial American?

While the Englishness (or lack thereof) of a given work poses specific editorial difficulties, the term 'Renaissance' offers conceptual ones. No English writer of the period thought herself part of the 'Renaissance': indeed, the word 'Renaissance' is of nineteenth-century vintage, more the product of John Ruskin or Walter Pater than of Shakespeare or Milton. The concept was first applied to the political, cultural, and artistic developments of *trecento* and *quattrocento* Italy, some of which gradually migrated northward until making their belated arrival in England. The concept of the Renaissance period is ideologically charged, describing a 'rebirth' of classical learning – a revival conducted in England on several fronts, perhaps most influentially through the *studia humanitatis*, a curriculum of works, and a philological and pedagogical methodology derived from Italian universities and central to what has come to be termed 'Renaissance humanism'. In its emphasis on rebirth, the term *Renaissance* effaces important continuities between medieval and 'Renaissance' literatures, while often belittling the former: in the most influential nineteenth-century account of the Italian Renaissance, the Swiss historian Jacob Burckhardt describes that period as lifting the veil that the Middle Ages had placed over human consciousness. Additionally, the term 'Renaissance' is better suited to high cultural artistic productions than, say, to almanacs or broadsheet ballads. In short, to construe this period as 'the Renaissance' is to run the risk of emphasizing certain cultural developments and artistic products over others.

Finally there is the question of what precisely constitutes 'literature'. Today, the word has a range of meanings, all of them centered upon the written word. The *Oxford English dictionary* shows us definitions that include, first, 'Literary work or production; the activity or profession of a man of letters'; second, 'Literary productions as a whole; the body of writings produced in a particular country or period, or in the world in general'; or, third, 'Printed matter of any kind', although this final meaning is identified as colloquial. In other words, literature can mean anything from a specialized form of writing that we would now term 'literary' to all forms of writing. If the shifting scope of these meanings poses one problem, their anachronism poses another: all of these definitions postdate the seventeenth century. Indeed, the only meaning of the word current in the Renaissance is one the *OED* identifies as 'Now *rare* and *obs[olete]*': 'Acquaintance with "letters" or books; polite or humane learning'. Here, literature describes not a body of texts, but a sensibility and a capacity achieved through reading. Moreover, literature in this sense is an elitist endeavour; it tacitly differentiates learned texts from popular texts, and explicitly separates learned people from popular consumers.

In planning this encyclopedia, we as editors attempted to respond to these categorical challenges. Our answers are both simple and somewhat unsatisfying, precisely because the *Encyclopedia* includes some exceptions to our rules. In the main, the writers contained in this encyclopedia were born and wrote in England (exceptions include not only Bradstreet, featured because of the Anglocentric nature of her publication history, but a small handful of Scottish-born writers, such as Hector Boece and George Buchanan, who had a major impact on English literature and culture). We have opted to feature primarily writers who wrote in the English vernacular, rather than in Latin: but once again, this is by no means a hard and fast rule, since many writers (from Thomas More to Francis Bacon to Thomas Hobbes) wrote in both.

The only viable option to 'Renaissance' as a period designator is the oft-used term 'early modern', which introduces distortions of its own: instead of looking back to a classical past, it looks forward to a future not yet realized. We have opted in our title for 'Renaissance' – which captures something of the classical humanist and republican cultural engagements that played a major role in the period – but both 'Renaissance' and 'early modern' will be used by contributors throughout the *Encyclopedia* (and, indeed, in this introduction).

Finally, we have opted for as catholic a definition of 'literature' as is feasible. Readers of these volumes will encounter a rich variety of texts: from medical treatises to cookbooks, sonnets to sermons, broadside ballads to epic poems, prose romances to plays, chronicle histories to conduct manuals, anatomies to emblem books. They will also encounter writers from diverse socio-cultural and educational backgrounds: from the self-educated waterman-poet, John Taylor, to the highly educated female monarch, Elizabeth I. (Because of their literary endeavours, Elizabeth and James VI and I both have entries devoted to them.) This eclectic approach helps us to avoid the pitfalls of anachronism, whereby 'literary' texts – products of men and women of letters – are artificially cordoned off from other kinds of writing, and offers a rich and varied account of Renaissance textual production. At the same time, and in contradistinction to other encyclopedias focused on the period, *The encyclopedia of English Renaissance literature* restricts itself to the written word, introducing cultural or historical topics only in so far as they illuminate some aspect of a 'literary' one.

As mentioned above, our primary organizational mode is the author-based entry. Each entry is carefully cross-referenced, so that the reader interested in, say, women who wrote books of advice to their children is prompted to turn from the entry on Elizabeth Jocelin to one on Dorothy Leigh. In the case of genres or forms not suited to an approach based on single authors, such as commonplace books or printed verse miscellanies, we include an entry on the genre itself. In a few exceptional instances, we have entries on individual works of tremendous historical and cultural significance that do not have authors in the traditional sense: the Bible and the Book of Common Prayer are notable examples.

While the *Encyclopedia* strives to accommodate writings of various kinds, it does not neglect the major writers of the period: it contains cutting-edge scholarship on both canonical authors and lesser-known writers. Literary history can too easily abstract major writers from their literary and cultural milieus – or even assume for these writers a dominance they did not achieve in their lifetimes. *The encyclopedia of English Renaissance literature* invites the reader to consider these writers in a broader context. That reader browsing these volumes might be surprised to discover the popularity of now marginal writers like Nicholas Breton, whose many and various works went through almost 120 editions by the beginning of the Civil War; and conversely, the comparative contemporary marginality of writers who now routinely feature in modern anthologies of Renaissance literature – such as Isabella Whitney, whose two published works each survive in a single copy.

The *Encyclopedia* will offer readers fresh insights into sixteenth- and seventeenth-century writing in additional ways. Rather than focusing primarily on the most well-trodden terrain of English literature between 1579 and 1640, it gives significant space to earlier Tudor authors, and the new types of writers who found their voices during the Civil Wars and Interregnum of the 1640s and 1650s. It includes entries on over 80 women writers, not just those who have been integrated into the literary canon over the last twenty years. It throws new light on writers whose output was primarily legal, or educational, or religious; or whose chosen generic forms were private and devotional.

The *Encyclopedia* also gives space to the manuscript culture that coexisted alongside the printing press. Whereas earlier critics focused largely on the manuscript writings of already canonical poets such as Thomas Wyatt and John Donne, more recent work has uncovered authors whose writings never circulated in print – such as Cicely Johnson and Rose Thurgood, whose handwritten conversion narratives are bound together in the same volume; and Lady Hester Pulter, whose writings survive in a single manuscript volume that was only brought to light as recently as 1996. The *Encyclopedia* also attends to the very popular manuscript forms of miscellany and commonplace book in which texts and extracts were copied and organized, most often without any authorial attribution.

While the author-based entries in the *Encyclopedia* have a biographical component, they are not centrally about writers' lives. (For such information, we recommend the reader consult *The Oxford dictionary of national biography*.) Instead, their emphasis is on the literary productions of the author. As a result, the content of individual entries is necessarily various. Some figures who achieved major importance in other aspects of their lives – such as archbishop of Canterbury Thomas Cranmer, bishop of Salisbury John Jewel, and Robert Devereux, second earl of Essex – have shorter entries here, because the focus is on their literary output. Some of the writers in this encyclopedia are known for only a single work (such as Chidiock Tichborne with his 'Lamentation', and Mary Oxlie with her commendatory verse, 'To William Drummond of Hawthornden'), while others produced dozens; they neither could nor should be provided the same treatment. What the essays do share is a commitment to describing clearly the nature and significance (both literary and historical) of the works under examination. They are informed by current scholarship without being dominated by recent critical debates. Taken together, these entries offer a lucid and engaging introduction to English Renaissance literature in all its myriad forms.

The *Encyclopedia*'s index makes apparent the power of certain political or celebrity figures to inspire a wealth of literary making – from charismatic royals like Richard III, Henry VIII, and the two executed monarchs Mary Queen of Scots and Charles I, to those from less exalted background, such as Edward IV's mistress Jane Shore, and the Protector Oliver Cromwell – as well as the importance of key historical events, such as the Babington Plot of 1586, the discovery of the 1605 Gunpowder Plot, or the 1612 death of Prince Henry, to inspire waves of writing.

As inclusive as *The encyclopedia of English Renaissance literature* is, there will inevitably be omissions, some the result of editorial choice and others of oversight. This is one of the reasons we are excited about the electronic version of the *Encyclopedia* that forms part of the Wiley-Blackwell Encyclopedia of Literature. The existence of an electronic version opens up an entirely new way of thinking about this or any *Encyclopedia*. At the most basic level, it will allow us to update lists of suggested readings, or correct or expand entries in line with new discoveries and new critical approaches. But perhaps more exciting is the possibility to add to the *Encyclopedia* – to fill the gaps, and exploit the connections, that have become visible as we worked on this large-scale project. Although we have devoted space to several forms of religious writing – notably sermons and psalters – this barely scratches the surface of this most popular of genres. We have already mentioned the important place of neo-Latin writing in Renaissance literature; we might also point to the role of translators of classical and Continental works – and indeed, consider the centrality of those classical and Continental authors, among the most published in England during the period. The writers of incunabula (printed books before 1500), Catholic exiles, and early writers in America are under-represented. While we have chosen to use the traditional 'author' category to organize much of the material, some writing falls through the cracks – anonymous plays such as the 1592 *Arden of Feversham* are still actively seeking an author, while, increasingly, plays are being ascribed to multiple authors working in collaboration.

The existing author entries have, moreover, highlighted other possible modes of organization that might dictate future commissions for this project. As recent scholarship shows, both the role and importance of printers and publishers have been routinely underestimated. While a few printers (including William Caxton and John Streater) appear in these volumes because of their other literary endeavours, it is clear that other figures deserve recognition. Thomas Berthelet, the King's Printer in the 1530s, was responsible for many of the works we now recognize as the founding texts of English humanism, by the likes of Thomas Elyot, Richard Morison, and Thomas Paynell. Richard Tottel, a printer known for his legal textbooks, not only introduced the verse of Thomas Wyatt and Henry Howard, earl of Surrey, to a wide print audience, but actively intervened as an editor to mould the reception of these poems in the collection of *Songes and sonettes* now known as 'Tottel's Miscellany'. Reginald (Reyner) Wolfe was the driving force behind the project that came down to posterity under another's name, as 'Holinshed's *Chronicles*' – and so on.

Another structuring framework would be the phenomenon of patronage. The identification of individuals who patronized writers helps us to identify networks of social, political, and artistic alliance, and to see anew the importance of figures such as Essex, Robert Dudley, earl of Leicester, William Cecil, Lord Burghley, Queen Anna, consort to James VI and I, and her son Prince Henry. One sees anew the significance of certain places or communities for literary writing – not only the major locations of Oxford and Cambridge, London's Inns of Court, and the European cities where the Marian exiles settled, but also rural venues like Nicholas Ferrar's Anglican community at Little Gidding, which attracted Richard Crashaw, and where a manuscript of George Herbert's poetry was copied. Kin relationships prove equally illuminating – for example, the family (and doctrinal) ties that link Thomas More, Margaret More, William Roper, and John Donne. Some figures prove central to entire networks of patronage and kinship: Mary Herbert, countess of Pembroke, for example, was sister to Philip and Robert Sidney, and aunt to Robert's daughter Mary Wroth; a co-author with her brother Philip, and editor (with Fulke Greville) of his works; her country marital home at Wilton saw the composition of Philip's *Arcadia*, and provided a shelter for many writers, among them Nicholas Breton, Samuel Daniel, and Abraham Fraunce.

All these connections will reward further study. It is our sincere hope that the publication of this print version of *The encyclopedia of English Renaissance literature* will provoke its readers to challenge our decisions, augment our picture, and help us to continue to develop this resource online. These volumes represent only the first phase of an ongoing project, one that will keep this reference work fresh and relevant for years to come.

Garrett A. Sullivan, Jr
Alan Stewart

Acknowledgements

On more than one occasion along the way, we wondered what we were thinking when we took on a project of this scale. In the end, however, the *Encyclopedia of English Renaissance literature* came together surprisingly smoothly, and there are numerous people to thank for this: our contributors, who produced wonderful work in a timely fashion, and who remained gracious as we peppered them with queries; our associate editors, Rebecca Lemon, Nicholas McDowell, and Jennifer Richards, who were crucial to every facet of this project and without whom it never would have gotten off the ground; our editor, Emma Bennett, who proposed the project, supported it throughout, and helped ensure that we kept to schedule; and our able production team whose professionalism and good humour were exemplary: Barbara Duke and Tom Bates (production editors at Wiley-Blackwell), and the freelancers Jennifer Cassidento (project manager), Janey Fisher (project manager and copyeditor), Jacqueline Harvey (copyeditor), Helen Kemp, Caroline Richards, and Alta Bridges (proofreaders) and Zeb Korycinska (indexer).

Garrett A. Sullivan, Jr. and Alan Stewart

NOTES ON TITLES

Titles to primary texts are given in original spelling, except in the case of works whose modernized titles are so familiar as to generate confusion by altering them (e.g. Shakespeare).

Alabaster, William

MOLLY MURRAY

Clergyman and writer of Latin and English poetry, prose, and polemic, William Alabaster (1568–1640), through his eventful life and varied writings, vividly illustrates the heterodoxy of post-Reformation English Christianity. Spending a significant portion of his life in prison or in voluntary exile for his religious beliefs, he is the author of a Senecan tragedy, a projected epic poem on Elizabeth's reign, a long prose spiritual autobiography on his conversion to Catholicism, as well as works of theology and hermeneutics, and a significant body of lyric poetry, including a well-known collection of sonnets.

Born into a staunchly Protestant family in Hadleigh, Suffolk, in 1567, Alabaster was educated at Westminster School and Trinity College, Cambridge, from which he graduated BA in 1587/88, and seemed destined for a successful career in the English clergy. After serving as a Protestant chaplain to Robert Devereux, earl of Essex, on the 1596 voyage to Cadiz, however, Alabaster announced his conversion to Roman Catholicism, and was promptly imprisoned by the English authorities in Cambridge, and then in London. He managed to escape from prison and return to the Continent, entering the English Catholic College at Rome in 1598. Returning to England the following year, Alabaster was once more imprisoned, then pardoned by King James

in 1603, only to be imprisoned for recusancy yet again in 1604. Alabaster spent the next several years on the Continent, where he may have served as a spy for England; in 1610 he was imprisoned again, this time by the Inquisition, for the unlicensed publishing of a book of occult theology, *Apparatus in revelationem Christi* (Antwerp, 1607). Although he publicly declared his intention 'to live and die a Catholic' after his arrest, Alabaster soon returned to England, and to the English church. In 1614 he was made doctor of divinity at Cambridge, served as royal chaplain to James I, and received the livings of Thetford, Hertfordshire, and then Little Shelford in Cambridgeshire, where he lived with his wife, Katherine Fludd (mother of the occult philosopher Dr Robert Fludd), until his death in 1640.

Many of Alabaster's contemporaries expressed bewilderment over his serial conversions; John Chamberlain dismissed him as 'the double or treble turncoat', while Oliver Cromwell's maiden speech in the Commons in 1629 indicted the 'flat popery' of one of Alabaster's sermons before the king. Although Alabaster seems not to have returned to the Roman Church after 1614, his religious interests remained highly idiosyncratic. He spent the last years of his life writing works of biblical hermeneutics deeply influenced by Kabbalistic theology, including *Tractata de bestia apocaliptica* (1621), *Ecce sponsus venit* (1633), and *Spiraculum tubarum* (1633). It is probably this last text to which Robert Herrick refers

The Encyclopedia of English Renaissance Literature, First Edition. Edited by Garrett A. Sullivan, Jr and Alan Stewart.
© 2012 Blackwell Publishing Ltd. Published 2012 by Blackwell Publishing Ltd.

in *Hesperides* (1648) when he praises 'Dr. Alablaster' [*sic*] for 'the Trumpet which thou late hast found'. Alabaster's last published work was an abridgement of Valentin Schindler's *Lexicon pentaglotton* (1637).

These works of theology and hermeneutics, however, represent only the final phase of Alabaster's extraordinarily wide-ranging writerly career. While still at Cambridge, the young Alabaster earned a reputation as a skilled Latin poet for his *Roxana*: a Senecan tragedy in dactylic hexameters adapted from Luigi Groto's *La dalida* (Alabaster eventually published the play in 1623, after the appearance of a number of unauthorized editions). By 1591, he had completed the first book of another Latin work, the *Elisaeis*: a projected epic poem celebrating Queen Elizabeth's victory over the forces of Roman Catholicism. Edmund Spenser celebrated the *Elisaeis* in *Colin Clouts come home againe* as 'that heroick song, / Which he hath of that mighty Princesse made', predicting that 'when he finisht hath as it should be, / No braver Poeme can be under Sun'. In his modern edition, Michael McConnell (1979) suggests that Alabaster's epic project influenced Spenser's own *Faerie Queene,* as well as John Milton's Latin epyllion on the Gunpowder Plot, *In quintum Novembris* (1626).

After converting to the same church he had so recently maligned, however, Alabaster left the *Elisaeis* decidedly un-'finisht', turning to other genres in order to reflect upon his experience of religious change. First, perhaps inspired by the autobiographical questionnaire administered to all entrants at the English College in Rome, Alabaster composed a long prose spiritual autobiography in English, possibly at the urging of the college's director, the Jesuit Robert Parsons. In this text, which remained unpublished until the late twentieth century, Alabaster details his early life and education, and his eventual estrangement from his family, friends, and former patrons and teachers in England. He also narrates the climactic moment of conversion in a scene clearly modelled on book 8 of St Augustine's

Confessions. Here, Alabaster describes taking up a book of Catholic theology loaned to him by Thomas Wright (the Jesuit priest rumoured to have converted Ben Jonson), and reading a few pages. Suddenly, he recalls, 'I lept up from the place where I satt, and saide to myself, now I ame a Catholique, and then fell down upon my knees and thanked God.' Shortly after his first return to England as a Catholic, Alabaster also circulated a work of prose polemic, the *Seven motives,* in which he explained the particular theological tenets behind his conversion; this text is no longer extant, but extensive portions are reprinted in two Protestant texts of refutation, John Racster's *Booke of the seven planets, or seven wandring motives of William Alabaster* (1598) and Roger Fenton's *Answere to William Alablaster* [*sic*] *his motives* (1599).

During this time, Alabaster also wrote a number of short English and Latin lyric poems on religious subjects, including his own experience of conversion. These poems were not published until the twentieth century, although they also seem to have circulated widely in manuscript during Alabaster's lifetime. The surviving Latin poetry has been published by Sutton (1997), who also reprints Abraham Cowley's 1636 English translation of a series of Latin verses on the Virgin Mary, now no longer extant. Alabaster is perhaps best known to modern critics for his English sonnets, thanks to the scholarly edition produced by G. M. Story and Helen Gardner (1959). Louis Martz (1967) classifies the poems as 'meditative verse', seeing in them the specific influence of the Jesuit spiritual exercises developed by Ignatius of Loyola. For Martz, as for Story and Gardner, Alabaster's sonnets should be understood as important early instances of 'metaphysical' poetry, anticipating the later work of John Donne and Richard Crashaw in the elaborate complexity of their conceits and the paradoxical and dialectical quality of their style.

SEE ALSO: Crashaw, Richard; Donne, John; Herrick, Robert; Jonson, Ben; Milton, John; Spenser, Edmund

REFERENCES AND SUGGESTED READINGS

Caro, Robert (1988) William Alabaster: rhetor, meditator, devotional poet. *Recusant History* 19, 62–79; 155–170.

Marotti, Arthur (2005) *Religious ideology and cultural fantasy: Catholic and anti-Catholic discourses in early modern England.* University of Notre Dame Press, Notre Dame.

Martz, Louis (1967) *The meditative poem.* New York University Press, New York.

McConnell, Michael (ed. and trans.) (1979) The *Elisaeis* of William Alabaster. *Studies in Philology* 76(5).

Murray, Molly (2009) *The poetics of conversion in early modern English literature: verse and change from Donne to Dryden.* Cambridge University Press, Cambridge.

Shell, Alison (1996) *Catholicism, controversy and the English literary imagination 1558–1660.* Cambridge University Press, Cambridge.

Story, G. M. & Gardner, Helen (eds) (1959) *Sonnets of William Alabaster.* Oxford University Press, Oxford.

Sutton, Dana (ed.) (1997) *Unpublished works of William Alabaster.* University of Salzburg, Salzburg and Oxford.

Allen, William

JOSEPH NAVITSKY

William Allen (1532–94) was Tudor England's last Roman Catholic cardinal and principal leader of the English Catholic community for most of Elizabeth I's reign. His impressive record of missionary, academic, and diplomatic attainments was achieved in the service of a single lifelong goal: the restoration of Catholicism in his native land. After he began to organize and train Catholic expatriates in the colleges he founded in Douai (in northern France) and Rome, this tireless – and highly controversial – crusade secured Allen access to courts and dignitaries across Europe. During the attempted Spanish invasion in 1588, which he did much to encourage, Allen stood ready to preside over England's reunion with Rome in the double capacity of archbishop of Canterbury and lord chancellor. Although the Armada's ruin suspended the dreams of the Catholic resistance, Allen continued until his death to press European leaders on the fate of his homeland.

The story of Allen's rise from modest Lancashire gentry to international power-broker began during the disruptive power shifts following Henry VIII's death. Little is known of Allen's life before his Oxford career, during which he held a succession of academic positions under three monarchs. Allen graduated BA (1550) and MA (1554) from Oriel College before becoming university proctor in 1556. When the Elizabethan regime reconsolidated the university's Protestant leadership, Allen emigrated to the Low Countries in 1561. He visited England once more in 1564/65 when he witnessed at first hand the accommodations made by fearful Catholics in his native Lancashire. Upon returning to the Continent, Allen made his way to Louvain and Malines (now Mechelen in Belgium) and began teaching theology after his 1565 ordination.

Allen laboured to preserve the faith on a number of fronts. His brief visit to England launched a career as a controversialist that would eventually see him write nearly 20 books, many of them in English, on topics as diverse as purgatory and military affairs. Versatile and economical, Allen's style is perfectly suited to the thrust and parry of pamphlet warfare and rarely descends into the tedium that marks theological controversy of the era. In this regard, Allen was no common polemicist, excelling at such increasingly relevant genres as the news bulletin and political essay. An appreciation for the efficacy of vernacular speech led him to fund an English translation of the Bible known as the Douay–Rheims version. He also helped to coordinate the academic and seminary training of a growing number of exiles and, in the fragile early years of Douai College, to secure funding from Philip II of Spain and the Papal See. Ostensibly, the mission of the college was to educate and ordain a capable body of clergy to return to England upon the country's reconversion (Bossy 1976). Its members were mostly scholars who, like

Allen, had departed Oxford. As college head, Allen enforced discipline while confronting fiscal collapse, town–gown animosity, and (after 1578 when the college temporarily relocated to Rheims) the outbreak of hostilities in the Low Countries. Soon Rome, too, sponsored an English college, which Allen placed under Jesuit direction in 1579. Missionary fervour, meanwhile, intensified at Douai: by 1580 nearly 100 priests had joined the underground operations in England (Knox 1965). It fell to Allen not only to train the young priests but also to prepare them for the travails they would face in England, including privation, imprisonment, and – in the cases of Edmund Campion, Cuthbert Mayne, and others – martyrdom. On several occasions, Allen defended the mission's objectives through eulogies for his fallen students. *A briefe historie of the glorious martyrdom of xii reverend priests* (1582) honours the sacrifice of Campion by revealing how the Elizabethan magistrates, incited by religious hatred, trod on individual consciences and ignored legal precedent. Allen's early writings do not implicate Elizabeth or her leading ministers in the torture and execution of Catholic priests but instead reserve their strongest censure for spies, informants, and Protestant hardliners.

The success of the college and the expansion of the Elizabethan mission resulted in Allen's de facto appointment as leader of the English Catholic community. Under his leadership, the spiritual and material preparation of the missionaries prospered from beneficial collaboration with the Society of Jesus. Allen thought highly of the Jesuit emphasis on scholarly and spiritual attainment, borrowing freely from the Jesuit academic model when crafting the course of study at Douai. A capable administrator, he proved a sensitive pastoral guide as well – a fact often overshadowed by his subsequent political activism.

English interference in the Low Countries hardened Allen's resolve for military intervention against his homeland. For him, the surest way to re-establish Catholicism in England was to secure the accession of a Catholic monarch who would forcibly remove the heretical Elizabeth. While Allen proclaimed an apolitical agenda in his writings, his rigid beliefs necessarily placed him within the sphere of Spain, the dominant Catholic power of the day (Duffy 1995). He helped plan invasions of Ireland and England in the late 1570s and early 1580s that sought to place on the throne Mary, Queen of Scots, with whom he maintained a lengthy correspondence (Knox 1965). Before Mary's execution in 1587, Allen stepped up his efforts to obtain support for military action, balancing Spanish exertions at hegemony (which he doubtless saw himself as advancing) against the scepticism of Pope Sixtus V. Under pressure from the Spanish diplomatic corps and the Jesuit Robert Parsons, Sixtus elevated Allen to the office of cardinal in 1587 (Haile 1914).

For the Armada invasion, Allen wrote his most virulent piece of propaganda, *An admonition to the nobility and people of England* (1588). Along with *A copy of a letter written by M. Doctor Allen* (1587), the brief *Admonition* exhibits a polemical intensity and partisan outlook that eclipses his earlier, historically grounded defences of English Catholicism. Condemning Elizabeth as an apostate, usurper, and sexual deviant, Allen urges English Catholics to rise in revolt against their queen. Disappointment over the Armada's defeat did not render Allen ineffective, yet he was increasingly burdened by political setbacks, such as the assassination of Henri, duc de Guise in 1588, and Elizabeth's alliance with France's king Henri IV (Haile 1914). Allen turned down an opportunity to return to the Netherlands as archbishop of Malines, opting to remain in Rome to attend to his curia duties and to an appointment as apostolic librarian.

Following his death in 1594, internecine conflict greatly weakened the English Catholic community. The office of English cardinal fell vacant, and the clergy that Allen had done so much to equip and inspire resisted the influence of their newly ascendant Jesuit masters.

SEE ALSO: Bible, the

REFERENCES AND SUGGESTED READINGS

Bossy, John (1976) *The English Catholic community, 1570–1850.* Oxford University Press, New York.

Duffy, Eamon (1995) William Allen, 1532–1594. *Recusant History* 22(3), 265–290.

Haile, Martin (1914) *An Elizabethan cardinal, William Allen.* Sir Isaac Pitman & Sons, London.

Knox, Thomas Francis (ed.) (1878) *The first and second diaries of the English College, Douay.* David Nutt, London.

Knox, Thomas Francis (ed.) (1965) *The letters and memorials of William, Cardinal Allen (1532–1594).* Gregg Press, Ridgewood.

Law, Thomas Graves (1889) *A historical sketch of the conflicts between Jesuits and seculars in the reign of queen Elizabeth.* David Nutt, London.

Andrewes, Lancelot

ADAM SMYTH

Born in Barking, and one of 12 children, Lancelot Andrewes (1555–1626) might well have followed an apprenticeship in trade – but (according to some accounts) his great academic potential was glimpsed by a master of the local charity school who persuaded Andrewes's parents to keep the boy behind a desk. After an academic career marked equally by success and a remarkable diligence (he mastered 15 languages, ancient and modern, and his only recreation was said to be walking), Andrewes rose to become bishop of Winchester in 1618. He was a crucial figure in the seventeenth-century articulation of Anglicanism's theology and culture, most centrally through his sermons and his role in the production of the Authorized (or King James) Version of the Bible (1611). Posthumously, Andrewes's importance was perhaps even greater – his *Preces privatae* (*Private prayers*) has been popular from its first publication in 1648 – and many have turned to his life, writings, and career as exemplary expressions of high Anglicanism.

From about 1565, Andrewes was educated, first at Merchant Taylors' School, where headmaster Richard Mulcaster did much to encourage a sense of English (and not only Latin) as a potentially capacious and literary language; and then at Puritan-leaning Pembroke College, Cambridge, where he would have met Gabriel Harvey, a junior fellow, and Edmund Spenser, an undergraduate. In 1578 Andrewes became a fellow of Pembroke and, appointed to the office of catechist, delivered crowd-drawing sermons in the college chapel on the Ten Commandments.

Many hagiographical assessments stress Andrewes's almost unworldly selflessness, but the facts of his career show his capacity to attract the backing of political heavyweights at key moments: among them, Francis Walsingham, Elizabeth's secretary of state and head of her intelligence network, who helped secure Andrewes's early appointments outside university (including as prebendary of St Pancras in St Paul's, in 1589); Fulke Greville and Robert Cecil (who both, in 1601, helped Andrewes in his appointment as dean of Westminster, a post which involved Andrewes in teaching and administration at Westminster School); John Whitgift, archbishop of Canterbury (1583–1604), to whom Andrewes was appointed chaplain in 1590; Richard Bancroft, archbishop of Canterbury (1604–10); and King James I.

Andrewes's career as a churchman coincided with a period of upheaval and conflict in the English church. Perceptions of him as consistently anti-Calvinist, and a proponent of 1630s Laudianism *avant la lettre*, are in part the product of Archbishop William Laud's selective editing of Andrewes's works in 1629 (*XCVI Sermons*, in English; and *Opuscula . . . posthuma*, in Latin). In fact, there is evidence to suggest that the youthful Andrewes assumed a more strongly Protestant position on issues such as the Sabbath and predestination. Nonetheless, his preaching and writing have as refrains a dedication to the Church of England and its position as part of the Catholic Church, purged of errors; a defence of episcopacy; and a deep respect for the monarchy.

Andrewes worked as a loyal servant to the crown. As court preacher, he delivered sermons on the anniversaries of the Gunpowder Plot (1605) and the Gowrie Conspiracy (1600) that were, among other things, powerful assertions of the divine right of kings. Andrewes was also involved in a printed dispute with Cardinal Bellarmine, in which Andrewes defended the king's supremacy over the English church in response to Bellarmine's criticisms of James's attempts to distinguish between loyal and subversive Roman Catholics in his Oath of Allegiance, issued after the Gunpowder Plot. The exchange was in many ways characteristic of theological controversy at this historical moment: rapid answers and counter-answers constructed through point-by-point refutation, circulating across Europe in public, printed Latin texts. Andrewes's appointment as bishop of Winchester owed much to James's desire to appoint anti-Calvinists to central positions; and Andrewes embraced the king's less anti-Spanish foreign policy, culminating in his support for the hugely unpopular Spanish match of 1623, in which the future Charles I came close to a Spanish marriage. Andrewes's loyalty to the crown sometimes tipped over into an apparently less principled meekness: his assent to Frances Howard's infamous divorce of Robert Devereux – on the grounds of impotence – has been interpreted as Andrewes ceding to James's desires despite his convictions.

At the Hampton Court Conference of 1604, Andrewes was part of a group that resisted many Puritan demands made to James I in the Millenary Petition (1603), but the Conference did bow to the request for a new translation of the Bible into English. Andrewes was chairman of one 'company', responsible for the Pentateuch (Genesis, Exodus, Leviticus, Numbers, Deuteronomy), and the books of Judges, Ruth, 1 and 2 Samuel, and 1 and 2 Kings. There had been several sixteenth-century English translations, including William Tyndale's New Testament (1525); Miles Coverdale's Bible (1537); the Great Bible (1538), the first official Bible supplied to all parish churches; the Shakespeare-favoured Geneva Bible (1557); and the Bishops' Bible (1568). The collectively authored Authorized Version, or King James Bible (1611), in fact drew heavily on these precedents: hence its already (but compellingly)

anachronistic prose at its moment of publication. The publication of the Authorized Version also represents a crucial moment in the broader cultural assertion of the potential and legitimacy of the English language – a shift that was also being enacted in the writings of literary figures such as Andrewes's former undergraduate contemporary, Edmund Spenser.

Andrewes's health began to fail in about 1621, three years after he became bishop of Winchester: his final sermon at court was preached on Christmas day 1624. His frailty meant that he was unable to respond to King James's request that he be present at his deathbed, and that he could not preach the king's funeral sermon. When his brothers, Thomas and Nicholas, died in the 1625/26 plague, Andrewes saw this as a preface to his own death, which came on 25 September 1626.

Andrewes was widely admired for his preaching, and drew praise from Queen Elizabeth and King James. The sudden, almost broken, style of his sermons fell out of favour after the Restoration, but most modern readers have been persuaded by T. S. Eliot's encomia and attempts to connect Andrewes with metaphysical writing, especially in terms of irony and paradox, a condensed brevity, the combination of high and low registers, and the ability to move quickly from the particular to the expansive. Eliot (1928) noted that 'Andrewes takes a word and derives the world from it', and certainly his sermons are based around creative, frequently brilliant anatomizations of short biblical passages. These writings have an abrupt, often jolting, quality that creates the effect of thought in process: a sometimes thrilling sense of meaning being continually refined.

SEE ALSO: Bible, the; Greville, Fulke; Harvey, Gabriel; James VI and I; Spenser, Edmund; Tyndale, William

REFERENCES AND SUGGESTED READINGS

Chapman, Raymond (2008) *Before the king's majesty: Lancelot Andrewes and his writings.* Canterbury Press, Norwich.

Eliot, T.S. (1928) *For Lancelot Andrewes: essays in style and order.* Faber & Gwyer, London.

Lake, Peter (1991) Lancelot Andrewes, John Buckeridge, and avant-garde conformity at the court of James I. In: Peck, Linda Levy (ed.) *The mental world of the Jacobean court.* Cambridge University Press, Cambridge, pp. 113–133.

McCullough, Peter (2004) Andrewes, Lancelot. In: *Oxford dictionary of national biography.* Oxford University Press, Oxford.

McCullough, Peter (ed.) (2005) *Lancelot Andrewes: selected sermons and lectures.* Oxford University Press, Oxford.

McCullough, Peter (2008) Lancelot Andrewes's transforming passions. *Huntington Library Quarterly* 71(4), 573–589.

Tyacke, Nicholas (1987) *Anti-Calvinists: the rise of English Arminianism, c.1590–1640.* Oxford University Press, Oxford.

Anger, Jane

JUDITH HUDSON

The pamphlet writer and 'gentlewoman' Jane Anger (*fl.* 1588/89) was the author of *Jane Anger, her protection for women, to defend them against the scandalous reportes of a late surfeiting lover, and all otherlike venerians that complaine so to bee overcloyed with womens kindnesse*, written in 1588 and published in 1589 by the London printer Thomas Orwin. The first 'defence of women' written by a female author in English, and explicitly dedicated to a female readership, Anger's text has precedents in European works, including those of Christine de Pisan and Hélisenne de Crenne; it is also an important forerunner of such seventeenth-century defences as Rachel Speght's *A mouzell for Melastomus* (1617), Ester Sowernam's *Ester hath hang'd Haman* (1617), and Constantia Munda's *The worming of a mad dogge* (1617). As such, Anger's work represents a particular milestone in the English Renaissance experience of the literary debate on women known as the *querelle des femmes*.

Beyond her gentle status, there is almost nothing known about Anger herself. Her name may have been a pseudonym, although Anger was a well-known surname in southern England in the sixteenth century. While its 'chollericke vaine' is peculiarly apt, facilitating a series of puns throughout the text, as a pseudonym it is oddly plain, with little of the biblical or classical allusive weight one might expect. Anger's gender has also been debated, although there seems little reason for a male writer to have posed as a woman to deliver this particular text. There was certainly a tradition of men writing defences of, as well as attacks upon, women in the period – see, for example, Thomas Elyot's *Defence of good women* (1540), and Nicholas Breton's *Praise of vertuous ladies* (1597), which has echoes of Anger's own work. Whatever her true gender, Anger's textual persona is avowedly female, and she is notably conscious of her role as a woman writing, craving 'pardon' of her reader both for her authorship and for the emotion that impels it: 'it was Anger that did write it.'

The *Protection* is offered as a response to an earlier work, the 'Surfeit of an old lover'. This is usually identified as a now lost pamphlet, *Boke his surfeit in love*, entered into the Stationers' Register in 1588, and thought to have been heavily influenced by sections of John Lyly's *Euphues his censure to Philautus* (1578). Lyly's work is a textbook 'attack'. It creates sweeping categorizations of 'good' and 'bad' women, offering biblical and classical exemplars as illustrations. Reading Anger's response to the *Boke* it is clear that the lost pamphlet had a similar schema.

Anger's primary intent is to challenge the *Boke*'s central argument, that women are to blame both for inspiring men's desire and for fulfilling it. Her strategy is twofold: she mounts a counter-attack on the male sex in general, but also seeks to expose a double standard inherent in literary assaults upon women. For Anger, such slanderous depictions are merely expressions of men's own weaknesses: 'they have been so daintily fed with our good natures that ... they surfeit of our kindness.' This is linked explicitly to the act of writing: 'their wits must be shown in telling the manner how.' She has little sympathy with male appetite: 'the lion rageth when he is hungry,' she notes, 'but man raileth when he is glutted.' 'Diet their greedy paunches', she advises readers, her tongue firmly in her cheek.

Anger repeatedly decries male rhetorical self-indulgence. Yet, her own work is by no means rhetorically unsophisticated. She asserts that 'like a scholar' she will 'prove our wisdom more excellent than theirs', and to this end she draws on a wide range of sources, quoting from Plato and deploying Latin maxims with confidence. She avoids any overt engagement with Christian doctrine, however, and, unlike her successors Speght, Sowernam, and Munda, spends little time dealing with images of Eve, merely noting that unlike man, who was formed from 'dust', woman was created from man's flesh 'that she might be purer than he'.

Anger's style is at times euphuistic; she uses alliteration, balance, and antithesis and she clearly relishes the dramatic possibilities of verbal play. Whilst its tone ranges from frank irritation to vitriol, her displeasure primarily manifests itself via a rich vein of wit – including, for example, a highly original explanation of the origin of cuckold's horns, allegedly a safety measure introduced by the gods to prevent men from breaking 'their pates' when running after 'the smocke'. Interestingly, however, she also employs a number of classic anti-feminist tropes in her descriptions of men 'whose minds goe oft a madding, and whose tongues cannot so soone be wagging', and her text is scattered with sexual puns.

It is perhaps suggestive to note that the printer of *Boke his surfeit in love* was also Thomas Orwin, and some scholars have proposed that Orwin actively commissioned Anger's response in order to provoke controversy. In fact, the debate around women was immensely popular fare in the period and it is likely that Orwin had an eye on market trends in issuing the *Protection*. Nonetheless, there seems to have been little contemporary response to Anger's work, this particular skirmish within the *querelle des femmes* apparently concluding with her text.

SEE ALSO: Breton, Nicholas; Elyot, Thomas; Lyly, John; Sowernam, Ester; Speght, Rachel

REFERENCES AND SUGGESTED READINGS

Gushee O'Malley, Susan (ed.) (1996) *The early modern Englishwoman: a facsimile library of essential works, part 1: Printed writings, 1500–1640*. Scolar Press, Aldershot.

Henderson, Katherine Usher & McManus, Barbara F. (1985) *Half humankind: contexts and texts of the controversy about women in England, 1540–1640*. University of Illinois Press, Urbana.

Kelly, Joan (1982) Early feminist theory and the 'querelle des femmes', 1400–1789. *Signs* 8, 4–28.

Shepherd, Simon (ed.) (1985) *The women's sharp revenge: five women's pamphlets from the Renaissance*. Fourth Estate, London.

anonymity

MARCY L. NORTH

Although English Renaissance print culture granted celebrity status to authors such as William Shakespeare and Ben Jonson, many writers still chose the privacy and discretion of anonymity when they published or circulated their literature. In the sixteenth and seventeenth centuries, anonymity was a well-known authorial practice, a useful printer's convention, and sometimes simply the condition of a text that had lost its author over time or through manuscript transmission. It was less a bibliographical category and more a set of devices, traditions, expectations, and circumstances that framed and introduced a text. Pseudonyms and ambiguous initials as well as missing names functioned to make a text anonymous. Early readers encountered anonymity every day. Anonymity commonly accompanied ephemeral and cheaply printed literature, but it also introduced readers to some of the more influential and innovative writing of the period, including Bishop John Jewel's *Apologie of the Church of England* (whose 1564 edition was translated by 'A.B.' – Lady Anne Bacon), the incendiary Catholic publication *A true reporte of the death and martyrdome of*

M. Campion (1582), the important revenge prototype *The Spanish tragedie* (1592), and Joseph Swetnam's provocative *Araignment of lewd, idle, froward, and unconstant women* (1615), which reinvigorated an ongoing debate about the worth of women. Among the types of authors likely to publish anonymously, one finds new literary authors awaiting favourable public reception, writers of popular plays, news pamphlets, and other genres composed for profit, and certain elite authors who were reluctant to subject their names to the censure of an increasingly 'common' readership. Authors of illegal literature and satire adopted disguises, often for reasons of self-protection, and parodists found anonymity useful, too, in affecting the voice of another writer. Authors of religious texts might publish anonymously as an act of humility, political self-protection, or both.

Anonymity marks several important moments in literary history. Edmund Spenser began his career with the anonymous *Shepheardes calender* (1579) and announced his authorship officially when he published his Protestant epic *The Faerie Queene* (1590). His early experiment with genre, prosody, and literary personae became a touchstone for other writers. The Puritan satirists lurking behind the name of Martin Marprelate challenged church government in the late 1580s and, with their caustic *ad hominem* attacks, influenced the tone and vocabulary of much late Elizabethan and Stuart satire and libel. Fashionable sixteenth-century lyric miscellanies such as the *Phoenix nest* (1593) and a second wave of miscellanies in the 1640s (*Wits recreation* 1640, for example), introduced anonymous court, coterie, and university verse to a broader audience. Similarly, the explosion of the popular press in the late sixteenth and early seventeenth centuries saw the publication of hundreds of anonymous ballads, pamphlets, and short fictions. Anonymity's influence in the popular press is especially noticeable during periods of lax print regulation, such as the early 1640s. Throughout the first two centuries of print, anonymity was an exceptionally influential convention; the rise of the author

seems only to have encouraged writers and printers to experiment with new types of name suppression and authorial disguise.

An author's or printer's choice to publish a text anonymously was often determined by the genre of the work, the author's status, political pressures, or traditional conventions of authorship currently in play. Conventions of naming and anonymity spread quickly in early print culture and were often shared by like groups of authors. After the Marprelate scandal in the late 1580s, satirists popularized the use of satirical pseudonyms. Many women authors, including Isabella Whitney (*Copy of a letter*, 1567) and Elizabeth Cary (*Tragedie of Mariam*, 1613), preferred to publish using initials and some description of their status. Published play-texts were likely to name the acting company and first audience rather than the playwright. These attribution patterns meant that the same author could publish one work anonymously and set his name proudly to another. Very early in his career, John Milton was discreet in his publication of a masque (commonly known as *Comus*, 1637) and his anti-episcopal pamphlets defending the pseudonymous SMECTYMNUUS authors (*Of reformation*, 1641, for example). He commonly used his initials to announce other mid-career political works from his *Doctrine and discipline of divorce* (1643) to *The readie and easie way to establish a free commonwealth* (1660), and he used his full name with *Areopagitica* (1644), his *Poems* (1645), and *Paradise lost* (1567).

Modern bibliographers have long assumed that early modern authors preferred attribution and that only unscrupulous or careless printers rendered them anonymous. In fact, it was often authors who set anonymity in motion. In an age without authorial copyright, however, authors could not necessarily control the fate of their attribution choices once the texts left their hands, and printers did indeed reveal some authorial names and suppress others for reasons of their own. Printers notoriously left individual poems unascribed, perhaps because their source manuscripts did the same. In response to market pressures, they might foreground the most prominent name in a collected volume at the expense of other authors, as William Jaggard did when he credited *The passionate pilgrime* (1599) to Shakespeare. When political pressures intensified, they might suppress a controversial author's name. Richard Tottel is thought to have relegated Sir Thomas Wyatt's name to the preface of *Songes and sonettes* (*Tottel's miscellany*) (1557) because Wyatt's son and namesake fought in a rebellion to keep Mary Tudor off the throne. Printers and authors could also work together to preserve the secrecy of a dangerous text. The anonymity of Jesuit Robert Southwell's *Epistle of comfort* (1587) helped protect the secret English press where it had been printed and Southwell himself as he ministered secretly to English Catholics.

Anonymity's many visible forms in early print and manuscript are too various to document outside of a bibliography, but authors and book producers frequently utilized designators such as 'Anonymus' and 'Ignoto', serious and satirical pseudonyms, ambiguous initials, and the simple absence of a name where a reader might expect one. Standards for author attribution were still inchoate, and the variety of forms anonymity took mirrored the diversity of naming conventions in use. Today the name of an author serves as a marketing tool and legal claim to intellectual property, but in Renaissance England the name of the author functioned more often as a claim to authority – the authority of social class, professional status, institutional affiliation, religious vocation, or classical precedent. Anonymity conventions built upon these naming functions. Some offered readers the status of an author but no other identifying information. The Catholic Philip Howard, thirteenth earl of Arundel, translator of Johann Justus Lansperger's *An epistle in the person of Christ* (1595), is identified on the title page as 'one of no small fame'. Some anonymous works manipulated naming conventions more playfully, mocking status, occupation, and authority, as in *A wonderfull*

... astrologicall prognostication for 1591 attributed to 'Adam Fouleweather, student in assetronomy'. Playful pseudonyms provided an opportunity for authors to assume satirical personae. The pseudonym Misacmos allowed Sir John Harington to discourse about privies under a shallow disguise in *An anatomie of the metamorphosed Ajax* (1596). Martin Marprelate, Pasquil (Thomas Nashe), and even Misacmos provoked other authors to join the fray with their own pseudonyms in what became a competition of pseudonyms in the late sixteenth-century satire wars.

Many manifestations of anonymity are subtle rather than conspicuous. They can appear to be correct attributions or cases of lost names even though their actual purpose is disguise. It is no surprise that one of the most dangerous genres of literature produced domestically in England, the manuscript libel, called very little attention to its own authorship or anonymity, even though it relished naming its subjects. That an anonymous author could hide behind a satirical disguise, a seemingly correct attribution, or a nameless voice gave early critics a reason to label anonymity an immoral deception. Anonymity was too ubiquitous and useful, however, to fall out of favour because of this criticism, and its association with the religious virtue of humility helped in its moral defence. The government and the church never found a successful way to regulate anonymity in print or manuscript, and the variety and creativity of its visible forms continued into the Restoration and eighteenth century.

As often as it was employed satirically or surreptitiously, anonymity was also used to aid an author in creating a seemingly authentic voice different from his or her own. Male authors regularly used anonymity to ventriloquize the opposite sex, and they particularly enjoyed the challenge of composing female-voiced laments, erotic verse, and even defences of women. For many anonymous female-voiced works, it is impossible to determine the author's biological sex. Victorian women authors would later conventionalize the use of male pen-names, but this practice was rare in Renaissance England, and most documented cases of cross-gendered ventriloquism involve men imitating women. For some scholars, this enduring male tradition is a good reason to exclude anonymous female-voiced work from the canon of women's literature. For others, these anonymous works are an opportunity to see how anonymity helped craft a gendered voice and character. Among the questionable publications are the oft-studied prose defences of women by Jane Anger (*Protection for women*, 1589), Ester Sowernam (*Ester hath hang'd Haman*, 1617), and Constantia Munda (*The worming of a mad dogge*, 1617).

Several other critical debates about early modern authorship are informed and complicated by the study of anonymity. For instance, there is no consensus as to when the figure of the author became the artistic and professional celebrity that he or she can be today. The prevalence of anonymity in the Renaissance, even among literary authors, suggests that celebrity and professional authorship were less important than market contingencies, decorum, class, and protection from censorship. A related debate explores whether Renaissance literature was governed by an 'author-function', a concept proposed by Michel Foucault (1977) to describe the cultural control that a known author's name exerts over a body of literature. Some genres of early literature, one could argue, did not have authors in any modern sense; the reading public interpreted and categorized these works through some other cultural lenses such as common knowledge, folk traditions, or shared histories. These genres included several that today might merit iconic authors, such as prose romance and drama. While romance and drama were less authored in the Renaissance, Foucault's author-function seems especially applicable to sets of texts attributed to a single pseudonym.

A third debate asks if authorial collaboration in the Renaissance renders modern attribution standards anachronistic. In other words, was Renaissance authorship less individualized than it is today, making the singular author's name less relevant? The most familiar models of collaboration involve two playwrights working together or one playwright adapting a previous author's work for a new audience. But collaboration could also include acts of translation and compilation or the accretion of a popular title, such as the *Mirrour for magistrates*, as new authors and editors added material to subsequent editions. Publications that included multiple authors' works were extremely marketable in early print culture, and it was relatively common for at least some of the included authors to remain unnamed. Modern bibliographical efforts to determine exactly who wrote what in collaborative publications can obscure the complex and dynamic modes of authorship that define this period in literary history.

Bibliographers and editors have replaced missing authors' names whenever possible in their reference works and editions, so it is not easy for scholars of early modern literature to reimagine the full extent of anonymous publication in early modern England. The association of the Renaissance with the birth of the modern author and the modern book has done little to motivate the recovery of early anonymity, though digital access to archival materials and critical attention to the material characteristics of early publications have helped make some examples of anonymity visible again. For readers in Renaissance England, however, anonymity would have been a common condition for much of the literature they encountered, and they came to associate it with particular genres, publication formats, political stances, and literary styles. This does not mean that early readers were not curious about the authors behind the text – they often did their best to guess. But their expectations about attribution were tempered by the usefulness and meaningfulness of anonymity.

SEE ALSO: Anger, Jane; Cary, Elizabeth; Harington, John, the younger; Marprelate,

Martin; Milton, John; Southwell, Robert;
Sowernam, Ester; Spenser, Edmund; Swetnam,
Joseph; verse miscellanies, printed; Whitney,
Isabella; Wyatt, Thomas

REFERENCES AND SUGGESTED READINGS

Clarke, Danielle & Clarke, Elizabeth (eds) (2000)
'This double voice': gendered writing in early modern England. Macmillan Press, Basingstoke.
Coiro, Ann Baynes (2004) Anonymous Milton, or, 'A maske' masked. ELH 71, 609–629.
Farmer, Alan B. & Lesser, Zachary (2000) Vile arts: the marketing of English printed drama, 1512–1660. Research Opportunities in Renaissance Drama 39, 77–165.
Foucault, Michel (1977) What is an author? Trans. Donald F. Bouchard & Sherry Simon. In: Bouchard, Donald F. (ed.) Language, counter-memory, practice. Cornell University Press, Ithaca, pp. 124–127.
Fox, Adam (2000) Oral and literate culture in England: 1500–1700. Clarendon Press, Oxford.
Griffin, Robert (ed.) (2003) Faces of anonymity: anonymous and pseudonymous publication from the sixteenth to the twentieth century. Palgrave Macmillan, Basingstoke.
Halkett, Samuel, Laing, John, & Horden, John (eds) (1980) Dictionary of anonymous and pseudonymous publications in the English language, 3rd edn. Longman, Harlow.
Hirschfeld, Heather (2004) Joint enterprises: collaborative drama and the institutionalization of the English Renaissance theater. University of Massachusetts Press, Amherst.
Knapp, Jeffrey (2005) What is a co-author? Representations 89, 1–29.
McRae, Andrew (2004) Literature, satire and the early Stuart state. Cambridge University Press, Cambridge.
North, Marcy L. (2003) The anonymous Renaissance: cultures of discretion in Tudor–Stuart England. University of Chicago Press, Chicago.
Raymond, Joad (2003) Pamphlets and pamphleteering in early modern Britain. Cambridge University Press, Cambridge.
Robson, Mark (2008) The ethics of anonymity. Modern Language Review 103, 350–363.
Wayne, Valerie (1999) The dearth of the author: anonymity's allies and Swetnam the woman-hater. In: Frye, Susan & Robertson, Karen (eds) Maids and mistresses, cousins and queens. Oxford University Press, Oxford, pp. 221–240.

Ascham, Roger

MELANIE ORD

Roger Ascham (1514/15–1568), Tudor humanist and courtier, was the author of three main literary works in English: *Toxophilus* (1545), a dialogue promoting the sport of archery; *A report and discourse written by Roger Ascham, of the affaires and state of Germany and the Emperour Charles his court, duryng certaine yeares while the sayd Roger was there* (written in 1552 and published posthumously in 1570), a commentary on the current state of European politics; and his most popular text, *The scholemaster* (also published posthumously in 1570), which sets out Ascham's plans for a reformed grammar school practice and which is best known today for its vociferous objection to travel to Italy and its extended opposition to the process of Italianization.

Ascham was born at Kirby Wiske, near Northallerton, to a family of Yorkshire yeomen; his younger brother Anthony (c.1517–59) became a noted astronomical writer and almanac-maker. Ascham progressed from the local school to the household of the lawyer Humphrey Wingfield in Suffolk. In 1530 he went on to matriculate at St John's College, Cambridge, gaining his BA in 1534 and his MA in 1537, and serving as a college fellow and tutor. Various university and court appointments followed, including public orator and Greek reader at Cambridge University, and tutor to Princess Elizabeth (the future Elizabeth I); during this period his *Toxophilus* (1545) was published. From September 1550 to August 1553 he accompanied Sir Richard Morison, English ambassador to the court of the emperor Charles V, on his travels to Germany, an experience that gave rise to *A report and discourse of the affaires and state of Germany* (1552). In Strasbourg, he met the humanist educator Johann Sturm, with whom he maintained a correspondence; two of their letters were published under the title 'Epistolae duae de nobilitate Anglicana' ('Two letters on the English nobility') in Conrad Heresbach's *De laudibus Graecorum literarum oratio* (*Oration in praise of Greek letters*, 1551). Returning to England, Ascham married Margaret Howe in June 1554: they were to have at least seven children. The marriage came a month after Ascham's appointment as Latin secretary to Queen Mary, a post he retained under Elizabeth I. Ascham died on 30 September 1568; his widow arranged for the publication of his *Report and discourse* and *The scholemaster* by John Day in 1570, and of his Latin letters, edited by Edward Grant, in 1576.

An early instance of Ascham's pursuit of royal favour – the dedication of *Toxophilus* to Henry VIII – led to the granting of a royal pension. Subtitled *The schole of shootynge contained in two books. To all gentlemen and yomen [sic] of Englande, pleasaunte for theyr pastyme to rede, and profitable for theyr use to follow, both in war and peace*, this project provided Ascham with the opportunity to write in defence of archery, a sport he had enjoyed since his days in Wingfield's household. An important early contribution to the development of prose writing in the vernacular, *Toxophilus* takes the form of a dialogue between the characters Philologus (lover of study) and the eponymous Toxophilus (lover of the bow). Book I covers such topics as the history of archery and its suitability as an exercise for scholars as well as for members of the nobility. Here, Toxophilus successfully counters Philologus's view that 'we Scholers have more earnest & weightie matters in hand [than such sports as archery], nor we be not borne to pastime and pley' by arguing that, on the contrary, manual exercise – provided it is, as is archery, 'honest' – offers a necessary respite from study, enabling one to return refreshed to one's books and therefore to be a better (more efficient, committed, and enthusiastic) scholar. Book II offers practical advice on how best to 'hit the marke', explaining how to handle and care for one's bow and what posture to adopt in drawing the shaft.

The best known of Ascham's writings is *The scholemaster*, a text in which one finds numerous biographical details, many of which centre on Ascham's early college life, including the favour he received at the hands of the master of St John's College, Nicholas Metcalfe; his support for the reformed pronunciation of Greek; and his indebtedness to Sir John Cheke for 'all the poor learning I have' (as well as, more generally, for the flourishing state of humanist learning at St John's). One also finds in *The scholemaster* an anecdotal account of Ascham's visit to Lady Jane Grey before he left England for Germany in September 1550 (which led to experiences that were to find their way into his *Report and discourse of the affaires and state of Germany*). The 'Preface to the reader' in *The scholemaster* roots the text in a historically specific incident: a debate at Windsor Castle on 10 December 1563 about the efficacy of physical punishment in the instruction of youth. This debate places Ascham in distinguished company dominated by members of Elizabeth's Privy Council who have gathered in the rooms of Sir William Cecil, Elizabeth's principal secretary, and the man to whom *The scholemaster* was posthumously dedicated by Ascham's widow, Margaret.

The full published title of Ascham's work is: *The scholemaster, or plaine and perfite way of teachyng children, to vnderstand, write, and speake, the Latin tong but specially purposed for the priuate bryngyng vp of youth in ientlemen and noble mens houses, and commodious also for all such, as haue forgot the Latin tonge*. Like *Toxophilus*, *The scholemaster* comprises two books. Book II, which has often been overlooked by scholars, provides a detailed discussion of Ascham's pedagogical programme, including his account of how to practise literary *imitatio*. Book I is divided into three main sections: on education, on the court, and on travel to Italy. Ascham connects the sections on education and on the court by means of an extended contrast between 'quick' and 'hard' wits, which he allies to a further distinction between speech and writing. These students are of opposed natures and serve to illustrate and to represent competing educational trajectories. Whilst the hard wit achieves his social and educational aims through the effort he expends in reading and writing, the precocity of the quick wit leads him to eschew further study and to succumb, instead, to vain courtly pursuits and a pleasure-led experience of Continental travel. Ascham's paired distinctions of quick and hard wits, and speech and writing, not only encapsulate his pedagogical preferences but also accompany and animate a series of related contrasts in the text between the university and the court, England and Italy, and learning and experience.

Ascham's suspicion of verbal fluency is not a narrowly pedagogical issue. It is also a rejection of courtly show, given that those accounted graceful at court are said to be 'able to raise taulke, and make discourse of everie rishe [trifle]' and 'to have a verie good will, to heare him selfe speake'. This distinction between speech and writing is one means used in *The scholemaster* to conceptualize relations between the court and the university, to object further to the range of behavioural misdemeanours thought to be found at court, and to articulate his humanist recommendations to the court. It also provides Ascham with a means of offering perspectives on courtliness both directly and indirectly. Directly since eloquent quick wits are seen as those most likely to be seduced by the vanity, hypocrisy, and one-upmanship that characterizes the negative image of the court. The quick wit even doubles as a type of courtier in that he appears learned without having undergone a sufficiently rigorous and sustained programme of study. (The gap between appearing and being was a standard charge levelled against courtliness in the period.) The danger detected by Ascham is that this flashy brilliance puts in the shade those who *have* acquired their learning in a proper, painstaking fashion, and it leads onlookers to mis-evaluate the respective worth of quick and hard wits. This poses a threat to social stability and cohesion, as well as to the place of humanist pedagogy at court.

The opposition between speech and writing provides an indirect commentary on the court in that quick wits are seen as most vulnerable to the destabilizing effects of travel to Italy, a country that was virtually synonymous with courtliness in this period. Whilst Ascham imagines a pedagogical programme in which good examples are 'the best kinde of teaching', the court and contemporary Italy are imagined as sites where imitative examples, in the form of 'ill companie', are powerful inciters to corruption. Ascham's anti-courtly prejudices are linked to his nervousness about travel to Italy. Not only are extemporary speakers, or quick wits, seen as particularly prone to moral deterioration at court and in Italy, but travel gives rise in the unwary to courtier-like characteristics, denoted in part through a facility for speech. According to Ascham, travellers to Italy learn to become 'faire readie speakers' because travelling is a tickling of the senses, and involves surrendering the self to the vagaries of experience. As such, travel acts as a threat to a humanist project based on stable foundations and clearly delineated paths through learning as instituted in writing. Whereas the hard-witted scholar achieves his educational goals through steady textual application, the quick wit's pursuit of 'unlearned experience' equates to a kind of wandering or errancy in which he acquires knowledge only by chance. Travel in youth is implicitly 'quick', for it requires acts of discernment and discrimination from those not yet equipped to make them. In order to profit from an experience of overseas travel, one needs the kind of maturity that Ascham sees as acquirable only through a serious commitment to the practice of writing, as well as the reading of approved texts: these are the only means for knowledge properly to take root. The fact that quick wits are exposed to certain dangers overseas lends support to Ascham's concern to privilege textual over experiential forms of education: he argues that books facilitate a greater, swifter, and safer transmission of knowledge than that available through travel. Untrammelled experience, glibness, and a lack of learning are, for Ascham, inextricably related.

Ascham famously centres his anxieties about travel on Italy. He worries that unsupervised travel leads to a decline in learning on the part of the young traveller, and specifically to his inability to 'speake learnedlie' given his acquisition there of a 'discoursing tong'. Like other English Protestant writers at this time, Ascham draws a sharp distinction between the glories of Italy's classical past and its present perceived degradation as the home of Roman Catholicism and the purported scene of sexual immorality and political expediency. At times in *The scholemaster* Ascham is able to dissociate his disapprobation of Catholic doctrine from his approbation of those educational works produced by Catholic controversialists, in the knowledge that Protestant hostility to Italy as the home of the papacy runs the risk of impeding the educational projects of Europe. Yet as a Protestant committed to the reading of the vernacular Bible by individuals, Ascham reveals a suspicion of fluently spoken Latin as a sign of Catholic practices. These include the centrality of speech to the act of confession; the renowned linguistic skills of Jesuit missionaries, for whom language was a tool of persuasion and a means of self-protection; and the performance of the Roman Mass, which was frequently held to enact a divorce between the tongue and the heart, a perception that recalls Ascham's objection to both the superficial practices of (courtly) Italianate Englishmen and to abuses in learning.

Ascham notes that on arriving in Italy the young Englishman will be assailed by '*Siren* songes' which signify the corrupting effects of pleasure. Given that '*Siren* songes' recall the temptations that beset Ulysses on his travels whilst also referring to Catholicism and to the seductive nature of Italian court culture (especially music), their inclusion in the closing section of book I of *The scholemaster* provides a means of further connecting Ascham's anti-travel and anti-courtly prejudices. (Ascham had earlier accompanied a gift to his friend John Astley of Cicero's *De officiis* with a letter referring to Cicero as inoculating his readers against the 'pernicious charms of the court,

which catch the inexperienced sooner than any songs of the Sirens'). Ascham's *Toxophilus* explains how the court is the natural home for such 'softe' instruments as the lute, and claims that playing or hearing such music saps the practitioner or auditor of the intellectual and moral discipline needed for a proper engagement with the classics. In *The scholemaster*, Ascham objects not only to courtly music but also to poetry, a form intimately associated with the court. Unlike quantified metre, rhyme seems to have been perceived by some in the period as a natural gift, requiring little or no educational effort. 'The Poet' writes Henry Peacham in *The compleat gentleman* (1634), 'is made by miracle from his mothers wombe, and like the Diamond onely polished and pointed of himselfe, disdaining the file and midwifery of forraine helpe', a comment that recalls Ascham's objection to self-determination in study. Ascham advocates a pruning away of 'superfluous' reading material in order to produce a fruitful body of learning, and productive members of society, and might therefore be said to object to rhyme because it is associated with the perceived profuseness and self-indulgence of courtly love.

Ascham expresses the desire that students should cultivate a supremely polished writing style, carefully matching thought and expression (or *res* and *verba*), on the basis that this can act as an antidote to the false show of the court and of contemporary Italy. It is ironic, then, that Ascham should himself come to be accused by Francis Bacon and others of an over-concern for stylistic show; that the kind of assiduous imitation of Cicero that Ascham recommends in *The scholemaster* should be identified as a stylistic affectation (i.e., 'Ciceronianism') and branded an Italianism; and that attempts to cure what Erasmus calls (in his *Ciceronianus*, 1528) this 'style-addiction' by privileging 'the ripe fruitage of reason and thought' over 'the flowering verdure of style' (Gabriel Harvey, in his *Ciceronianus*, 1576), should see an implicit turning of the language used by Ascham against quick wits, persuasive speakers,

courtiers, and Italianates, against his own pedagogical recommendations.

These objections aside, *The scholemaster* was
an influential text in the late sixteenth century,
going into five editions between 1570 and
1589. It is, perhaps, best known today for its
heated attacks on undirected travel to contemporary, Catholic Italy (imagined as a
debased version of its glorious classical past)
and its memorable identification of a contemporary cultural stereotype: the Italianate
Englishman as a 'devil incarnate': aspects of
the text where Ascham is at his most polemical. Alongside such texts as Richard
Mulcaster's *Positions* (1581) and *Elementarie*
(1582), *The scholemaster* is regarded as a key
work of Tudor pedagogy, providing valuable
commentary on the educational fashioning of
youth and the relationship between schoolmaster and pupil, and outlining Ascham's
recommendations for the scope and nature
of a reformed educational programme; it is
also the text in which Ascham theorizes his
practice of 'double translation' (or translation
from Latin to English, then back again into
Latin). *The scholemaster* also made an important contribution to the now arcane sixteenth-
century debate over whether English poetry
should adopt rhyme or be modelled on classical, quantified metre, and gave impetus to
experiments in quantitative verse that continued throughout the sixteenth century.
Ascham's text exerted the most visible literary
influence in helping to fuel the prodigal-son
fictions of the next two decades (most notably,
John Lyly's *Euphues: the anatomy of wyt*, 1578)
which depict the ill fortune and ultimate
repentance of various recalcitrant youths
who rebel against the kind of pedagogical and
behavioural recommendations contained in
Ascham's text. Ascham expresses his own literary preferences in *The scholemaster*, providing trenchant views on suitable reading
material and sources of literary imitation, and
objecting to the 'bold bawdry' of chivalric
romance which he uses to point a cultural
contrast between classical and medieval

culture, and to exhort Englishmen to follow
the example of the ancients in shaping
England's national identity (for example, by
improving the vernacular) rather than resting
content with native traditions and customs.
Ascham's *Scholemaster* is, then, not only of
pedagogical interest but also of wider cultural
significance in giving forceful expression to the
contrast between classical and medieval that
Richard Helgerson (1992) argues structures the
English mind-set from the sixteenth to the
nineteenth century.

SEE ALSO: Bacon, Francis; Cheke, John; Harvey,
Gabriel; Jonson, Ben; Lyly, John; Peacham,
Henry; Puttenham, George

REFERENCES AND SUGGESTED READINGS

Aldis Wright, W. (ed.) (1904) *English works of Roger Ascham: Toxophilus; Report of the affaires and state of Germany; The scholemaster*. Cambridge University Press, Cambridge.
Bushnell, Rebecca W. (1996) *A culture of teaching: early modern humanism in theory and practice*. Cornell University Press, Ithaca.
Grafton, Anthony & Jardine, Lisa (1986) *From humanism to the humanities: education and the liberal arts in fifteenth- and sixteenth-century Europe*. Gerald Duckworth, London.
Hatch, Maurice & Vos, Alvin (eds) (1989) *Letters of Roger Ascham*, trans. Alvin Vos. Peter Lang, New York.
Helgerson, Richard (1992) *Forms of nationhood: the Elizabethan writing of England*. University of Chicago Press, Chicago.
Hunter, G. K. (1962) *John Lyly: the humanist as courtier*. Routledge & Kegan Paul, London.
Ord, Melanie (2002) Classical and contemporary Italy in Roger Ascham's *The scholemaster* (1570). *Renaissance Studies* 16(2), 202–216.
Ord, Melanie (2008) *Travel and experience in early modern English literature*. Palgrave Macmillan, New York.
Pincombe, Mike (2001) *Elizabethan humanism: literature and learning in the later sixteenth century*. Longman, Harlow.
Richards, Jennifer (2003) *Rhetoric and courtliness in early modern literature*. Cambridge University Press, Cambridge.

Askew, Anne

PATRICIA PENDER

Protestant martyr Anne Askew (c.1521–46) was burnt at the stake as a heretic, leaving behind the unusual first-person record of her trials at the hands of Henry VIII's officials. *The examinations of Anne Askew*, first published by John Bale in 1546/47, bear eloquent testimony to her unlawful torture, her defence of the right of women to read and interpret the Bible, and her concerted defiance of Catholic doctrine. She was born c.1521 to Sir William Askew or Ayscough (1498–1541) and Elizabeth Wrottesley in Stallingborough, Lincolnshire, a family with Protestant sympathies. After her elder sister Martha died, Anne was married, apparently against her will, to Martha's fiancé, Thomas Kyme. Askew bore him two children, but her open conversion to Protestantism led Kyme to drive her 'vyolently' away, possibly at the urging of the priests at Lincoln. In framing Askew's *Examinations* for publication Bale cites 1 Corinthians 7 ('If a faytfull woman have an unbelevynge husbande, which wyll not tarrye with her, she may leave hym') as the scriptural authority for Askew's separation from her husband, and relates that she sought to divorce him. It is possible that Askew went first to the bishop's court at Lincoln, and failing to win support there, to the Court of Chancery in London to secure her divorce, although no extant evidence appears to exist (Beilin 1996). Askew herself recounts, however, her provocative reading of the Bible in Lincoln Cathedral, a performance that publicly defied the Act for the Advancement of True Religion which prohibited women and men of lesser rank from reading the Bible in English. Askew relates that the Lincoln priests had expressly warned her against her actions, which she maintained, in the face of their disapproval, for six days.

It is upon Askew's arrival in London that the events recounted in the *Examinations* begin to unfold. Divided into two books, *The first examinacyon* records her detention in March 1545 on suspicion of heresy and her release without indictment by the London commission. *The lattre examinacyon* describes her subsequent arrest in June 1546 when she was brought before the king's Privy Council, and records her examination and eventual torture by Lord Chancellor Richard Wriothesley and Richard Rich. While she is initially questioned about her position on several of the Six Articles, it is her position on the first of these – mandating the belief in Christ's physical presence in the eucharist – that ensures Askew's subsequent arrest on suspicion of heresy and her eventual execution. The Six Articles, originally known as the 'Acte Abolishing Diversity in Opynions', offered the legal definition of orthodox religious belief in England and forbade that any English citizens 'hold any opinion contrary to His Magesty's government'. According to the first of the Act's articles, those who denied the dogma of real presence would be 'demed and adjudged hereticke' and would suffer the 'paynes of death by way of burning'. Arrested on suspicion of heresy, Askew maintained the reformist position on the Eucharist, affirming that, rather than Christ being physically present in the host, the bread 'is onlye a sygne or sacrament' and 'but a remembraunce of hys death'. In maintaining this position in the face of extended interrogations, in submitting to torture and eventual immolation rather than offering the recantation that was demanded of her, and in recording her own spirited testimony of her trials, Askew herself became a powerful sign of the religious battles being waged between English Catholics and Protestant reformers in the last years of Henry VIII's reign.

While no manuscript survives of Askew's original testimony, one can surmise that she wrote the record of her trials either in separate instalments, or at one time in the intervening days between her condemnation and her execution (Coles 2002). After Askew's execution for heresy in July 1546, her manuscript was smuggled out of England, ostensibly by Dutch merchants, and came into the hands of the Protestant bibliographer John Bale, then living in exile on the Continent. Bale published *The first examinacyon* in November 1546 and *The lattyre examinacyon* in January 1547, probably in Wesel in the Protestant duchy of Cleves. Bale's editions surround Askew's text with what he terms 'my simple elucydacyon', a volmunious paratextual apparatus which he uses to frame, position, annotate, and interpret Askew's own representation of her trials. He repeatedly intersperses Askew's narrative with an emphatic and didactic exegesis designed to demonstrate that Askew's words, actions, and beliefs are far closer to the Scriptures than those of her Roman Catholic interrogators. Peter Happé (1996) has suggested that in editing Askew so systematically, Bale developed a new technique of textual production, both within his own editorial practice and within the history of the book more generally. While the current state of scholarship does not allow us to determine the precise place Askew's text occupies in this chronology, it is clear that Bale's editions of Askew represent some of the first early modern English versions of the 'scholarly edition' (Pender 2010).

The *Examinations* subsequently appeared in editions throughout the Renaissance with and without Bale's commentary. Bale's friend and protégé, the historian and martyrologist John Foxe, published them alone as *The two examinations of the worthy servant of God, Maistris An Askew* in his history of the Reformation, *Actes and monuments of these latter and perilous dayes* (1563). He also included them in his Latin edition, *Rerum in Ecclesia Gestarum commentarii* (1559). Like Bale, Foxe gathered documents and eyewitness accounts to support his narrative of the religious and political struggle to establish the English Protestant church. Foxe added the 'true copy' of Askew's confession from the bishop's register, arguing that her enemies had altered the original document in order to incriminate her. He also concluded Askew's text with a dramatic woodcut of her execution at Smithfield. A brief excerpt from the *Examinations* appears in Thomas Bentley's *Monument of matrones* (1582) alongside 'The praier of Anne Askue

the martyr, before hir death'. By 1596, when Thomas Nashe mentions it, a 'Ballad of Anne Askew' was circulating in England; it was first printed after 1642 as 'A ballad of Anne Askew, intitled I am a Woman poore and Blinde'. While it is possible that Askew herself wrote the ballad, it may also have been written by a later writer in an exercise of imitation or *prosopopoeia*. The ballad is not mentioned by Bale, who includes two songs written by Askew in his own edition: 'The voice of Anne Askewe out of the 54. Psalme of David' and 'The Balade whych Anne Askewe made and sange whan she was in Newgate'.

While these paratexts are fascinating and historically rich documents, it is the extended record of her trials and testimony in the *Examinations* that ensures Askew's unique place in English Renaissance literary culture. Part spiritual autobiography, part dramatic dialogue, the work is a generically challenging text, one which provides an extraordinary history of political and religious life in Reformation London. Written by a woman who presents herself as the worthy opponent of civil, ecclesiastical, and state officials, the work also offers an unusually female perspective on contemporary religious controversies. Throughout the *Examinations*, Askew's style is elliptical and elusive yet implicitly combative; she mobilizes a remarkable rhetorical repertoire – initially to avoid articulating her specific beliefs, and eventually to defend her reformist position. Asked in the *First examinacyon* whether she believes that the sacrament over the altar is the 'verye bodye of Christ reallye', for example, Askew poses a counter question ('wherfore S[aint] Steven was stoned to deathe?'). Her interrogator being unable to answer this challenge, Askew replies 'that no more wolde I assoyle hys vayne questyon'. Asked later whether she believes that 'God was not in the temples made with handes', Askew directs her interrogator to chapters 7 and 17 of the apostles' Acts. When pressed to interpret these sentences herself, Askew replies that she 'wolde not throwe pearles amonge swine, for acornes were good ynough'. At other times Askew is more direct.

Called upon to confirm whether she would rather 'read five lynes in the Bible, than to heare five masses in the temple', Askew agrees: 'I confessed, that I sayd no lesse', because the first did 'greatlye edyfye' and the second 'nothinge at all'.

The *Lattyre examinacyon* is more direct than the first and records the position Askew ultimately articulates to defend her faith. Comprising a series of documents that mark the stages of her journey to Smithfield, the *Lattyre examinacyon* begins with Askew's brief exposition on the Lord's Supper and continues with her account of her examination before the king's council at Greenwich where she is again questioned about her husband and her beliefs about the sacrament. When she refuses to sign a document recanting her position, she is sent to Newgate prison. Bale includes Askew's 'confessyon' of faith, various prayers and meditations, and a summary of her condemnation for heresy at Guildhall on 28 June. Also included are Askew's letters to Lord Chancellor Wriothesley and the king and a chilling account of her transfer from Newgate to the Tower where, contrary to existing law, Wriothesley and Rich tortured her on the rack. The last items included are Askew's 'confessyon of faith' and the ballad she ostensibly wrote and sang in Newgate.

One of the key differences between Askew's testimony and the accounts of contemporary Protestant dissenters is her explicit reference to gender. In reconstructing her trials, Askew repeatedly shapes her encounters with powerful male officials by revealing their discomfiture by an ostensibly 'weak' woman (Beilin 1996). Henry's officials challenge Askew with the Pauline proscription that 'forbode women to speake or talke of the word of God'. In response, Askew adamantly defends her right to discuss Scripture so long as she obeys Paul's injunction not to 'speake in the congregacyon by the waye of teachynge'. In a fiercely contested battle of wills, in which the stakes are unaccountably high, Askew marshals her own questions (both rhetorical and pointed), her sarcasm, her

silence, and perhaps most powerfully, her smile. When asked to explain St Paul's passage, she cannily manipulates the humility and ignorance expected of early modern women as weapons in her own defence: 'I answered, that it was against saynt Paules lernynge, that I beynge a woman, shuld interprete the scriptures, specyallye where so manye wyse lerned men were.' In response to a question that recurs throughout her interrogations ('whether a mouse eatynge of the hoste, received God or no?'), she relates: 'I made them no answere, but smyled.' Askew uses a woman's silence, figured as strict obedience to the Scriptures, in order to deflect, or at least defer, the accusations of heresy that are made against her.

Askew's rhetorical dexterity, her trenchant defence of her beliefs, and her unflinching commitment to her faith have made her a compelling subject for feminist scholarship. Critics suggest that her defence of her own interpretation of the sacrament against the directives of church officials has 'deeply subversive implications' (Coles 2002). Others applaud the way that she defends 'her right to read and interpret Scripture, to examine religious doctrine, and to debate religious practice' (Beilin 1996). Her sacramentarian beliefs, it is suggested, render the priest unnecessary as mediator between the faithful and God, 'effectively contesting royal and state power as well' (Kemp 1999), and her sophisticated negotiation of incongruities between contemporary common law and ecclesiastical law challenge 'our standing notions of the relationship between gender and jurisprudence in this period' (McQuade 1994). Askew's *Examinations* thus shed light on many of the textual, historical, and historiographical issues of concern to the study of early modern women's literary history as it has developed over the past 40 years. Her articulation and defence of her position on the sacrament illuminates how women's writing contributed to the reformulation of devotional norms during the English Reformation. Her confrontation with Henrician civil and ecclesiastical authority sheds new light on the ways in which we understand women's participation in English debates about theology and gender in the period, suggesting that some women may have had more experience and agency in their encounters with patriarchal institutions than we have hitherto suspected.

While Askew's willingness to defend and die for her beliefs has made her an important figure for feminist literary history, she also poses intriguing problems for textual scholarship because her original manuscript has never been recovered. Askew's 'own' text has always been framed by the work of male editors, most notably Bale and Foxe. Viewing Askew's text as problematically compromised by its process of transmission, some scholars see her text as overwhelmed, undermined, and even occluded by her male editors. Kimberly Ann Coles (2002) views Bale's commentary as 'invasive annotations' that are 'intended to direct our reading' of Askew's text; Theresa D. Kemp (1999) calls Bale's an 'overwhelming intertextual commentary' through which he is able to 'tame her voice' and transform Askew into 'a mere conduit for a battle between male figures'; and Elaine V. Beilin (2005) suggests that Bale appears to have construed Askew's text 'as the guided writing of a medium more than the work of a writer . . . she becomes a vessel and an exemplum rather than an agent or author'. Other scholars have explored Askew's relationships with her male editors in the context of the material history of the early modern book or the legacy of poststructural editorial theory (Betteridge 1997; Freeman & Wall 2001; Pender 2010). The *Examinations* have also been of interest to scholars tracing broader cultural and historical shifts in the English Renaissance. Edith Snook (2005) situates Askew in the context of a history of early modern reading practices, Coles (2008) in the context of women's contributions to religious discourse in the early modern period, and Megan Matchinske (2004) in the context of early modern discourses of nationhood.

Anne Askew occupies a unique place in feminist literary scholarship on the early modern period and in research devoted to tracing the religious and intellectual conflicts of the English Reformation. The rhetorical richness of the *Examinations*, the challenges posed by their complex publication history, puzzling paratexts, and process of transmission, and the ways in which they engage with emerging critical interests in early modern legal theory, editorial theory, and gender theory, to name but a few, suggest that these texts have only begun to attract a fraction of the scholarly attention they are capable of sustaining.

SEE ALSO: Bale, John; Foxe, John; Nashe, Thomas

REFERENCES AND SUGGESTED READINGS

Beilin, Elaine V. (1985) Anne Askew's self-portrait in the *Examinations*. In: Hannay, Margaret P. (ed.) *Silent but for the word: Tudor women as patrons, translators, and writers of religious works*. Kent State University Press, Kent, pp. 77–91.

Beilin, Elaine V. (1991) Anne Askew's dialogue with authority. In: Logan, Marie-Rose & Rudnytsky, Peter L. (eds) *Contending kingdoms: historical, psychological and feminist approaches to the literature of sixteenth-century England and France*. Wayne State University Press, Detroit, pp. 313–322.

Beilin, Elaine V. (ed.) (1996) *The examinations of Anne Askew*. Oxford University Press, Oxford.

Beilin, Elaine V. (2005) A woman for all seasons: the reinvention of Anne Askew. In: Benson, Pamela Joseph & Kirkham, Victoria (eds) *Strong voices, weak history: early modern women writers and canons in England, France, and Italy*. University of Michigan Press, Ann Arbor, pp. 341–364.

Betteridge, Thomas (1997) Anne Askewe, John Bale, and Protestant history. *Journal of Medieval and Renaissance Studies* 27, 265–284.

Coles, Kimberly Anne (2002) The death of the author (and the appropriation of the text): the case of Anne Askew's *Examinations*. *Modern Philology* 99, 515–539.

Coles, Kimberly Anne (2008) *Religion, reform, and women's writing in early modern England*. Cambridge University Press, Cambridge.

Freeman, Thomas S. & Wall, Sarah Elizabeth (2001) Racking the body, shaping the text: the account of

Anne Askew in Foxe's 'Book of martyrs'. *Renaissance Quarterly* 54, 1165–1196.

Happé, Peter (1996) *John Bale*. Twayne, New York.

Kemp, Theresa D. (1999) Translating (Anne) Askew: the textual remains of the sixteenth-century heretic and saint. *Renaissance Quarterly* 52, 1021–1045.

Linton, Joan Pong (2001) The plural voices of Anne Askew. In: Smith, Barbara & Appelt, Ursula (eds) *Write or be written: early modern women and cultural constraints*. Ashgate, Aldershot, pp. 137–153.

Matchinske, Megan (2004) *Writing, gender, and state in early modern England*. Cambridge University Press, Cambridge.

Mazzola, Elizabeth (1995) Expert witnesses and secret subjects: Anne Askew's *Examinations* and Renaissance self-incrimination. In: Levin, Carole & Sullivan, Patricia A. (eds) *Political rhetoric, power, and Renaissance women*. State University of New York Press, Albany, pp. 151–171.

McQuade, Paula (1994) 'Except that they had offended the lawe': gender and jurisprudence in the *Examinations* of Anne Askew. *Literature and History* 3(2), 1–14.

Pender, Patricia (2010) Reading Bale and reading Askew: contested collaboration in *The examinations*. *Huntington Library Quarterly* 73, 507–522.

Snook, Edith (2005) *Women, reading, and the cultural politics of early modern England*. Ashgate, Aldershot.

Aubrey, John

ANGUS VINE

John Aubrey (1626–97) was an antiquary, biographer, and miscellanist. His works range from mathematics and natural philosophy to archaeology and antiquarianism, and from folklore and fieldwork to the biographical sketches for which he is most famous today.

Aubrey was born on 12 March 1626 at Easton Pierce, near Kington St Michael in Wiltshire. He received his early education from John Brome and then, from the age of eight, he attended the school of the Reverend Robert Latimer in Leigh Delamere. In 1638 he was sent as a boarder to the grammar school at Blandford St Mary in Dorset. Despite excelling academically, his time there was not happy, as he fell victim to both the 'envy and treachery' of other schoolboys and the 'tyrannie' and thwacking of his masters. He seems to have drawn on these unhappy experiences later in life, when he argues in *An idea of the education of a young gentleman* (1684) for a less disciplined pedagogy and complains of 'the tedious effects of grammar' and the 'tyrannical beating and dispiriting of children'. In 1642 he went up to Oxford, entering Trinity College as a gentleman commoner. But his studies were disrupted, first by the Civil War, and then by his decision to enrol at the Middle Temple. By the end of the decade his studies were further disrupted by his father's ill health and his return to Wiltshire to take control of the family estates.

In January 1649, while back in Wiltshire, Aubrey visited for the first time a site that would become a formative influence on his literary career: the now famous megaliths at Avebury. Remembering the encounter, Aubrey remarked that he 'was wonderfully surprised at the sight of those vast stones, of which [he] had never heard before'. Matters antiquarian and megalithic would then exercise him for the rest of his life. In 1663 he was commissioned by Charles II to survey Avebury, and in 1665 he completed two papers on stone circles: 'Templa druidum' and 'Review of Stonehenge'. Despite the best efforts of friends such as Thomas Browne and John Locke, neither paper was published. But together they did form the basis of his best-known antiquarian book, *Monumenta Britannica, or a miscellanie of British antiquities* (1691). Important arguments in this work include his suggestion in the first part that Avebury and Stonehenge might have been built by the druids, a considerable advance on the Roman and Danish theories of Inigo Jones and Walter Charleton; also significant is his comparative history of architectural styles in the fourth part.

Aubrey was also the author of a number of studies of natural history and topography. These, too, speak of his curiosity and his capacity for miscellanea. The longest and most important was *The naturall historie of Wiltshire* (1691), whose contents range from flora and fauna to stones, minerals, and medicinal springs. Related works include 'An essay towards the description of the north division of Wiltshire', modelled on William Dugdale's survey of Warwickshire; 'The interpretation of villare Anglicanum', a study of English place names; 'Remains of gentilisme and judaisme', a collection of customs and folk traditions; and the unfinished 'A Perambulation of Surrey'.

Aubrey's greatest contribution to the literary culture of the seventeenth century, however, was undoubtedly the *Brief lives*. The origins for this work may be found in biographical research that he carried out for his one-time friend, the Oxford antiquary Anthony a Wood. His subjects include authors, mathematicians, statesmen, and soldiers, and by the time he finished he had written the lives of more than 400 famous (and not so famous) men and women. His method of composition was as follows. First, he took a folio paperbook and wrote at the top of a page the name of a person. Then, he wrote down his recollections of that person; where he could not remember, he left a gap or mark of omission (an ellipsis or dash). If those recollections exceeded a page, he copied the material in whatever space he could find: in the margins, between paragraphs, on the opposite page, and so on. He also revised his recollections, adding and deleting material, substituting words, and transposing whole passages. The *Lives* are, therefore, disordered, and they also vary wildly in length: from the 50 or so leaves devoted to his great friend Thomas Hobbes, to the two words given to Abraham Wheelock ('simple man'), to the lives of Richard Blackbourne, John Flamsted, Peter Ramus, and the duke of Monmouth, which do not go further than their names.

Aubrey died at the beginning of June 1697, and a week later he was buried in the church of St Mary Magdalene, Oxford. Only one of his works was printed in his lifetime: the *Miscellanies*, 'a collection of hermetick philosophy' that emerged from the press of Edward Castle in 1696. Posthumously, though, editions did begin to appear. In 1718, for example,

A perambulation of Surrey was published by Richard Rawlinson, and by the nineteenth century editions of *Brief lives* were being printed. Selections were published in 1797 and 1813, and in 1898 Andrew Clark's monumental two-volume edition appeared. Although bowdlerized, and lacking the salacious details so characteristic of the work, this remains the most complete edition available to scholars today. Aubrey also left behind three large mathematical volumes, now deposited in the library of Worcester College, Oxford, and a scientific commonplace book, the 'Adversaria physica'. This manuscript is lost, but its contents can be ascertained from a transcript made by Henry Oldenburg, now preserved in the papers of the Royal Society, to which Aubrey himself had been elected in 1663.

SEE ALSO: Browne, Thomas; commonplace books; Hobbes, Thomas; Jones, Inigo

REFERENCES AND SUGGESTED READINGS

Bennett, Kate (2001) John Aubrey's collections and the early modern museum. *Bodleian Library Record* 17, 213–245.

Hunter, Michael (1975) *John Aubrey and the realm of learning.* Gerald Duckworth, London.

Poole, William (2010) *John Aubrey and the advancement of learning.* Oxford University Press, Oxford.

Powell, Anthony (1948) *John Aubrey and his friends.* Heinemann, London.

Audland/Audley, Anne

ELIZABETH MALSON-HUDDLE

Anne Audland/Audley, née Newby, later Camm (1627–1705), Quaker preacher, missionary, and writer, was baptized on 28 October 1627 in Kendal, Westmorland; her father, Richard Newby, gave his daughter a religious education. When she was 13, she went to live with her aunt to continue her education in London, where she remained for seven years (Evans & Evans 1837). Upon returning home, she joined a small Independent church in which she met her first husband, John Audland, a dissenting preacher and linen draper. They were married in 1650 and were converted to Quakerism in 1652 by George Fox (Leachman 2004). Together they worked as missionaries and preachers in the Society of Friends.

On her first missionary trip through Durham, Audland preached on market day in Auckland and was arrested and gaoled; she continued to preach from the window of her cell, moved a number of witnesses, and was taken in by sympathetic locals upon her release later that day (Evans & Evans 1837). She pursued her missionary travels with Mabel Camm, her future mother-in-law, and preached throughout Yorkshire, Derbyshire, Leicestershire, and Oxfordshire. On 14 November 1653 Audland and Camm 'were moved to go to the Steeple-house, to speake the word of the Lord to Priest and People' in Banbury. The congregation drove them away and accused Audland of blasphemy before William Allen, the justice of the peace. Although she was imprisoned briefly, she continued her missionary work and helped to establish a large meeting of Friends in Banbury; later she was tried again and incarcerated for some months under harsh conditions until her release in 1656 (Evans & Evans 1837).

In 1655 Audland related her account of the Banbury incident with grim prophetic warnings in *A true declaration of the suffering of the innocent.* Giles Calvert, a London printer well known for producing the pamphlets of religious radicals, especially Quakers, published the text. Writing from prison, Audland denies the charges of blasphemy and argues that she is not guilty of 'causing a tumult in a Church' because the practices of the congregation are not supported by the Scriptures. A true church, she asserts, 'is built of living stones, elect and precious, and there is order kept in the Church'. She contends, 'And I did not cause a tumult, neither did I assault the Minister (as ye call him) and that which is part of his Function, is an invention; and there is neither command nor example in all the Scripture, that ever any of the Ministers of Christ did sprinkle

Infants, and call it a Function.' Unlike some Quaker writers who stress the importance of the spirit within the individual, Audland argues that the Scriptures hold the ultimate religious authority. Her repetition of the phrase 'as you call it' throughout the text emphasizes her belief that the institution, leaders, and practices of the Church of England are human 'inventions' not sanctioned by the Gospels.

In the midst of debates about religious toleration in the 1640s and 1650s, Audland argues that true Christians do not persecute the godly: 'you know that the blood of the innocent hath been shed in your streets; one that came amongst you and offered violence to none, was beat and abused, and lost much blood amongst you: and yet you are not ashamed to professe your selves Christians.' Like her co-religionist Hester Biddle, Audland prophesies that God will punish sinners for persecuting the godly and the poor: 'he will judge all you that respects persons, for the Lord regards the rich no more than the poor; but this is hee that that Lord regardeth, who is humble and contrite spirit, and trembleth at his word.' Here Audland shares the egalitarian beliefs of the Quakers and contemporary radical religious groups such as the Diggers; Gerrard Winstanley, leader of the Diggers, repeatedly argues that God 'is no respecter of persons'.

In later texts, Audland articulates the difficulty of simultaneously grieving the loss of her loved ones and submitting herself to God's will. Just before the birth of her second child in 1664, her husband, John Audland, died at the age of 34. In 'The testimony of Ann Camm concerning her late husband deceased' (published in 1689), she recounts their happy marriage, 'our hearts being knit together in the unspeakable love of Truth, which was our Life, Joy and Delight, and made our days together exceeding comfortable'. The Audlands' shared desire to serve as Quaker missionaries, however, often separated them. In 'Testimony', Anne reconciles herself to the loss of her spouse in the terms of her faith: 'yet nevertheless in submission to the Will of God (whose chosen vessel he was) and also in respect to the honourable

Service of Truth, and the publication thereof which he was called unto; I could freely give him up as to be separated from in the outward a great part of our time after we were convinced of Gods blessed Truth.'

In 1666 Anne married Thomas Camm, with whom she continued to serve as a leader among the Friends; however, she travelled less so as to maintain their home and business during her husband's frequent missionary journeys and incarcerations (Evans & Evans 1837). Together, they wrote a moving account of their daughter's death from smallpox at the age of nine in *The admirable and glorious appearance of the eternal God in and through a child* (1684). Praising Sarah's faith and emphasizing her pious submission to God's will, her parents relate that she 'kissed most about her one by one, saying, *Do not cry, but be content in the will of God, for I am so.*' Anne continued to participate actively in Quaker meetings until 1705, when she died at the age of 78.

Throughout her long and productive life, Anne strove to strengthen the Quaker movement, establish new meetings, and increase toleration for the Friends in England.

SEE ALSO: Biddle, Hester; Fell, Margaret; Fox, George; Winstanley, Gerrard

REFERENCES AND SUGGESTED READINGS

Evans, William & Evans, Thomas (eds) (1837) *The Friends' library.* Joseph Rakestraw, Philadelphia.

Leachman, Caroline L. (2004) Camm, Anne. In: *Oxford dictionary of national biography.* Oxford University Press, Oxford.

Mack, Phyllis (1992) *Visionary women: ecstatic prophecy in seventeenth-century England.* University of California Press, Berkeley.

Avery, Elizabeth

MARIE-LOUISE COOLAHAN

Elizabeth Avery (*fl.* 1614–53), prophet and author, was a radical religious voice and a significant figure in women's prophecy of the mid-seventeenth century. She believed herself to be an instrument through which God spoke, and her experiential understanding of the 'last things' led her to express a realized eschatology that anticipated Quakerism. Feminist critics have addressed her as a woman writer and recent scholarship has focused on her visionary theology and its contemporary contexts.

Avery's family background was immersed in the politics of Presbyterianism and millennial thinking. Her father, Robert Parker, was a Puritan with Congregational sympathies whose first published work resulted in suspension from his ministry in Wiltshire, whence he fled to the Netherlands in 1607 or 1610. His wife and children joined him in Amsterdam in 1612 but returned on his death in 1614. Avery's brother, Thomas Parker, was educated at Oxford, Dublin, Leiden, and Franeker. He emigrated to America in 1634, where he co-founded Newbury, Massachussetts. As pastor there, he promoted Presbyterian church discipline and published an exegesis of the book of Daniel in 1646. Elizabeth married Timothy Avery, who is described in 1653 as having been a 'commissionary' in Ireland by the Independent and later Fifth Monarchist John Rogers. In 1647 Avery published *Scripture-prophecies opened*, in which she sets forth for the first time in print her millenarian vision. Her move to Dublin in the early 1650s and membership of John Rogers's Independent congregation led to the publication of her conversion narrative in his *Ohel, or Beth-shemesh* (1653). The discovery of the christening of Avery's child on 14 June 1653 places her in Ireland at that time, although nothing is known of her subsequent life (Gribben 2007).

In *Scripture-prophecies opened*, Avery speaks as a prophet. Although her preface initially attends to the conventional topos of female modesty, this is quickly abandoned in favour of her mystical experience and the imperative to communicate her revelations. Avery subscribed to the doctrine of progressive revelation, the belief that God would impart further discoveries to his people as the second coming grew closer, and she placed herself at the centre of this drama, laying claim to secrets that had been hidden even from the apostles.

Presented as three letters, originally addressed to Christian friends, the text offers her vision of the fall of Babylon, the dissolution of heaven and earth in the last days, and the final resurrection. She rejects interpretation of Scripture 'in the letter', positing instead her own spiritual, or metaphorical, understanding. Avery's is a realized eschatology – a vision of the 'last things' which is accomplished in the present. She asserts that the last days have already begun; Great Britain is the tenth city of Revelation whose fall signals the fall of Babylon. She critiques arbitrary government, manifest in monarchy and parliament, and draws particular attention to the events of spring 1647, a moment when the Presbyterians (then dominant in parliament) urged the suppression of the Independents and the disbanding of the army. The end is calculated as occurring in three and a half years' time. Avery rejected church ordinances entirely, believing that even the reformed church was tainted with corruption. Her theory of the final resurrection distinguishes between the natural and the mystical body. The godly who have died prior to the second coming will be saved. The demise of ordinances means that the wicked will then be left to perdition, and she maintains that the physical universe will continue after the day of judgement.

Her prophecies provoked a hostile reception on both sides of the Atlantic. Avery was the only woman to be named among the false teachers cited in *A glasse for the times* (1648), attributed to 'T.C.'. In his *Copy of a letter . . . to his sister, Mrs Elizabeth Avery* (1650), her brother accused her of heresy. Parker – who had not read her pamphlet – denounced his sister in strongly patriarchal terms. The episode emphasizes the potential subversiveness of the female prophet's claim to experiential authority.

Avery's testimony of her assurance of salvation was edited and published by Rogers, whose belief in women's church participation was supported by the quantity of female conversion narratives collected in *Ohel*. Avery's narrative locates her composition of *Scripture-prophecies opened* in a biographical context, postdating the moment of assurance. Her life was punctuated by agonized periods in search of sufficiently godly ministers. The deaths of three children constituted a low point of despair. Invited to Oxford by the then governor, the Parliamentarian colonel John Lambert, she dismissed the debates held there by the Particular Baptist William Kiffin. The period of the Civil Wars was one of great contentment for Avery, as godly ministers were plentiful. But the close of the wars brought renewed anguish. Her husband is only fleetingly mentioned in this account.

Avery's teleological understanding of grace is conceived in terms of the seven seals of Revelation. When in despair in Oxford, she is told by a voice that she is under the fifth seal, referring to the preparation of the saints for salvation, and near unto the sixth, the day of wrath. Avery saw herself as excluded from the elect, but rejoiced at their salvation. For a period of nine months, she expected her imminent destruction. Ultimately, she experienced assurance, figuring herself as the woman who bears the man-child of Revelation 12 and is saved in the wilderness.

Scholarly interest in Avery has located her in the contexts of radical religion (Smith 1988; Gribben 2000; 2007; Hindmarsh 2005), female prophecy (Mack 1992), and women's writing in Ireland (Coolahan 2010). Susan Wiseman (2006) has focused on the American dimension of her brother's reaction, comparing Avery's reception with that of Anne Bradstreet (her niece by marriage) to illuminate the parameters of acceptability for women's eschatological writing. Crawford Gribben (2007) argues that Avery gradually moderated her radical vision; his discovery of the record of her child's christening in 1653 suggests a spiritual trajectory from radicalism to the mainstream church. He suggests that her changing voices have underpinned scholars' uncertainty as to how to label her theological position, but notes her consistency in rejecting patriarchal authority.

SEE ALSO: Bradstreet, Anne; Rogers, John

REFERENCES AND SUGGESTED READINGS

Coolahan, Marie-Louise (2010) *Women, writing, and language in early modern Ireland*. Oxford University Press, Oxford.

Gribben, Crawford (2000) *The Puritan millennium: literature and theology, 1550–1682*. Four Courts Press, Dublin.

Gribben, Crawford (2007) *God's Irishmen: theological debates in Cromwellian Ireland*. Oxford University Press, Oxford.

Hindmarsh, Bruce (2005) *The evangelical conversion narrative: spiritual autobiography in early modern England*. Oxford University Press, Oxford.

Kreitzer, Larry J. (2010) Elizabeth Avery's encounter with William Kiffen in 1647: Mis-recollection, or mis-attribution? In: Larry J. Kreitzer *William Kiffen and his world*. Regent's Park College Publications, Oxford, pp. 351–62.

Mack, Phyllis (1992) *Visionary women: ecstatic prophecy in seventeenth-century England*. University of California Press, Berkeley.

Smith, Nigel (1988) *Perfection proclaimed: language and literature in English radical religion 1640–1660*. Clarendon Press, Oxford.

Wiseman, Susan (2006) *Conspiracy and virtue: women, writing, and politics in seventeenth-century England*. Oxford University Press, Oxford.

Aylmer, John

ALLYNA E. WARD

John Aylmer (1520/21–94) was bishop of London from 1577 until his death. During Elizabeth's reign, this position was one of the most political in the Church of England and one that most historians, with the exception of John Strype (1821), believe that Aylmer was ill suited to. John Aylmer was born at Aylmer Hall in Tilney, Norfolk, younger brother to Sir Robert Aylmer, to whom their family estate was left. Henry Grey, third marquess of Dorset, and father to Lady Jane Grey, recognized a high level of intellectualism in John and helped him

through his studies at Cambridge. Aylmer later attended Oxford University where he took a degree in divinity. In his early twenties he was made chaplain to Grey and appointed as tutor to Lady Jane Grey, also holding positions as the rector of Rodney Stoke and Stoke Gilford (1541) and as the vicar of Wellington (1543).

In 1553 Aylmer was made the archdeacon of Stow in the diocese of Lincoln but when he opposed Marian officials on the doctrine of transubstantiation his position was revoked and he fled into exile. He first resided in Strasbourg but later moved to Zurich, supporting himself by undertaking private tutoring. Strype (1821) tells us that while he was in Switzerland Aylmer helped John Foxe, first on the martyrology that became *Actes and monuments* (1563) and then on *A vindication of the most reverend Thomas Cranmer*, a defence of Cranmer against Stephen Gardiner which Foxe translated into Latin (this was never printed). During his time in exile Aylmer travelled to Europe and visited the universities of Italy and Germany.

When Mary I died in 1558, and Elizabeth acceded to the English throne, Aylmer published a book in response to John Knox's *First blast of the trumpet* entitled *An harborowe for faithfull and trewe subjectes, against the late blowne blaste, concerning the government of women*, printed anonymously in Strasbourg in 1559, and in April of that year by John Day in London. This text contributed to the discussions of the reformers in Continental Europe, in Scotland, and in England, and would shape and inform Elizabethan polemic on both religion and the debates concerning female regency. Aylmer attacks Knox's use of divine and natural law to castigate women rulers and instead advocates absolute obedience to the divinely sanctioned monarch. However, obedience to an ordained female monarch – that is Elizabeth – necessitates wider participation in government. In the *Harborowe* Aylmer writes that, because women are by nature the weaker sex, a woman ruler requires good counsellors. The blame for political wrongdoing will lie with the (male) counsellors, not the queen, or God.

In the case of Mary Tudor, Aylmer points out, the counsellors chosen were from the Catholic ascendancy and this contributed to the depraved nature of her reign. Elizabeth, he assumes, would choose better counsellors: that is, godly (male) advisors. Aylmer does not argue that women are as capable as men of ruling but instead proposes the theory that the monarch has two bodies: one political and one physical. Though Elizabeth's physical body may be female and weak, her political body, ordained by God, takes precedence; it is parliament, Aylmer finally argues, that has the final authority in England. This concept of a mixed monarchy (with the queen, her counsellors, and parliament sharing the duties of ruling) would later shape English political thought, especially in the period before the seventeenth-century English Civil Wars.

Aylmer's career was clouded by various disputes over conformity to the regulations of the new English church. A serious disagreement arose between Aylmer and the newly appointed bishop of London Thomas Cooper in 1571, after a grave incident concerning parish allocation left Aylmer without a jurisdiction (Usher 2004). Aylmer would eventually accuse Cooper of lying in response to Edmund Grindal, archbishop of York (later archbishop of Canterbury), when he requested information on the practice of 'prophesyings' in his diocese.

Despite the efforts of the archbishop of Canterbury, Matthew Parker, to advance Aylmer's career in the 1570s, it was the courtier and politician Sir Christopher Hatton who would in the end patronize and promote Aylmer following his attempted sabotage of Cooper's reputation. In December 1576 Grindal refused to suppress the prophesyings as Elizabeth had requested, Aylmer's advancement (with Hatton's assistance) was assured; Aylmer was initiated as bishop of London in the spring of 1577 and printed *Articles to be enquired of within the dioces of London in the visitation of the reverend father in God, Jhon bishop of London* the same year. In the 1580s Aylmer attempted to purge his diocese of any obstinate clergy.

Approximately 30 well-established nonconformists were accused in total but Aylmer's attempts were futile and most of the accused remained in their positions until their deaths.

As a result of his condemnation of Thomas Cooper, Edmund Spenser characterized Aylmer in *The shepheardes calendar* (1579) as Morrell, a goatherd rather than a true pastor. In the July eclogue Aylmer is characterized as ambitious; his motto is *In summo foelicitas* ('happiness is found in the highest'). Following his 1586 injunction in which he forbade the publication of books, pamphlets, or tracts not authorized by the archbishop of Canterbury John Whitgift or by the bishop of London (i.e., Aylmer himself), he was severely criticized in the Martin Marprelate tracts which characterize him as 'Dumb John of London', and chastise his use of puns and jokes in ecclesiastical matters (see especially *The epistle*). The Marprelate tracts refer to him as 'John Elmer' and quote from his *Harborowe*. Further, the tracts represent him as 'Mar-elm' with a tin-can tied to his tail because of his rumoured profiteering in the timber industry, from which he made a small fortune of £6,000 (Usher 2004). After the abuses of 1586 regarding preaching licences Aylmer's career was more closely examined and he appears to have withdrawn considerably from public scrutiny.

His successor as bishop of London, Richard Fletcher, commented on Aylmer's achievement in monitoring England's clergy as a university-trained ministry, something that had been lacking in the English church until his time. Aylmer died at Fulham Palace on 3 June 1594 and was buried in St Paul's Cathedral.

SEE ALSO: Cranmer, Thomas; Foxe, John; Gardiner, Stephen; Spenser, Edmund

REFERENCES AND SUGGESTED READINGS

Black, Joseph L. (ed.) (2008) *The Martin Marprelate tracts: a modernized and annotated edition.* Cambridge University Press, Cambridge.

Jordan, Constance (1987) Women's rule in six-teenth-century British political thought. *Renaissance Quarterly* 40, 421–451.

McLaren, A. N. (1996) Delineating the Elizabethan body politic: Knox, Aylmer and the definition of counsel 1558–88. *History of Political Thought* 17, 224–252.

Strype, John (1821) *Historical collections of the life and acts of the right Reverend Father in God, John Aylmer, lord bishop of London in the reign of Queen Elizabeth . . . A new edition.* Clarendon Press, Oxford.

Usher, Brett (2004) Aylmer, John. In: *Oxford dictionary of national biography.* Oxford University Press, Oxford.

B

Bacon, Anne (Cooke)

JONATHAN GIBSON

Anne Cooke Bacon (c.1528–1610), famous in her own day for her scholarship, was the translator of evangelical texts by Bernardino Ochino and John Jewel and a lively letter-writer. She makes a fleeting appearance in many recent works on early modern women's writing, but has yet to be studied in detail by modern scholars. Anne was one of the five famously learned daughters of Anthony Cooke and his wife, Anne, sisters frequently praised by contemporaries for their expertise in Latin and Greek and their interest in reformed theology and the church fathers. Their father, a tutor to Edward VI, educated his children himself at the family home in Essex, Gidea Hall (McIntosh 1975).

During Edward's reign, the Cookes were part of a pious court circle keen to establish the fledgling Edwardian church on a strongly Protestant footing. Among the reformers invited to England at this time was Bernardino Ochino, the charismatic preacher from Siena. An anonymous translation of five of his *Sermons* that appeared in July 1547, seven months after his arrival, is sometimes attributed to Anne. These sermons repeatedly state the doctrine of justification by faith alone. Nothing material can be done to assure salvation, Ochino stresses: one must simply have faith in Christ. This position is taken further in a second English selection from Ochino, *Fouretene sermons* (c.1551),

more certainly Anne's work. Here Ochino focuses on predestination – the idea that God has decided in advance who will be saved. He anatomizes one after another the dizzying challenges that such a belief presents to the individual Christian. The book's prefatory material is intriguing: a publisher's note claims that the female translator ('A.C.') was reluctant to appear in print; meanwhile, dedicating the book to her mother, 'A.C.' defends daughterly disobedience, arguing that her rebellious decision to study Italian can now be justified. Both these sets of Ochino sermons reappeared in a 1551 volume, along with six more translated by Richard Argentine and first published in 1548. A similar collection came out in about 1570, this time attributed *in toto* to 'A.C.'.

By February 1553 Anne had married Nicholas Bacon, a recently widowed government lawyer with six young children. Surprisingly, given the Cookes' commitment to reformed religion, the Bacons prospered during the return of Catholicism in the reign of Mary I. Lady Bacon belonged, in fact, to Mary's inner circle, at one point helping her brother-in-law, the statesman William Cecil (later Lord Burghley) into Mary's favour. A touching poem written by Nicholas at this period testifies to the couple's shared devotion to Latin literature.

On Elizabeth's accession, the newly knighted Sir Nicholas became lord keeper of the great seal, one of the most senior of government offices. In the same year, 1558, Anne's first son, Anthony, was born; her only other child

The Encyclopedia of English Renaissance Literature, First Edition. Edited by Garrett A. Sullivan, Jr and Alan Stewart.
© 2012 Blackwell Publishing Ltd. Published 2012 by Blackwell Publishing Ltd.

to survive babyhood, the future philosopher and statesman Francis, followed in 1561. Three years later, Lady Bacon's most important publication appeared. *An apologie or answere in defence of the Churche of Englande* is a translation (attributed to 'the Ladie A.B.') of John Jewel's official rebuttal to scurrilous accusations against the church from abroad, superseding an earlier authorized English version. According to its preface by Matthew Parker, archbishop of Canterbury – not necessarily to be taken at face value (Stewart 2000) – she had presented her work unbidden and it had passed the scrutiny of both Parker and Jewel. Jewel's text, stuffed with attacks on Catholic abuses and detailed precedents for Anglican practice, is very different from Ochino's inward-looking sermons. Lady Bacon's lively turns of phrase adhere closely to the detail of Jewel's Latin, a remarkable feat fulsomely praised by C. S. Lewis (1954).

Lady Bacon's most vivid texts are her letters. Most of those that survive were written to her grown-up sons in the years following her husband's death in 1579, when she was looking after the family estate, Gorhambury in Hertfordshire (Jardine & Stewart 1998). These letters are shot through with anxiety about Anthony and Francis: social, religious, political, medical. She frets constantly about their involvement with deceitful people (particularly papists); she sends gifts, relays estate news, and offers stern advice about court politics, cloaking sensitive topics in Latin and Greek.

Gorhambury at this time was a notorious stronghold for Puritan clergy, sheltered from the authorities by the mistress of the house, who also perhaps helped in the collection of nonconformist texts for publication. Little is known of the 10 years leading up to her death in 1610, though several contemporaries expressed horror at her eccentricities. It has been suggested that widowhood prevented her intellectualism from being taken seriously: with no father or husband behind her, she ceased literary production and her strength of character was interpreted as madness (Stewart 2000). In 1572 commendatory Latin verse by Lady Bacon

had appeared in a manuscript treatise presented to Robert Dudley, earl of Leicester (Schleiner 1994): probably other original work, religious and secular, in poetry and prose, is lost.

SEE ALSO: Bacon, Francis; Jewel, John

REFERENCES AND SUGGESTED READINGS

Jardine, Lisa & Stewart, Alan (1998) *Hostage to fortune: the troubled life of Francis Bacon.* Gollancz, London.

Lamb, Mary Ellen (1985) The Cooke sisters: attitudes toward learned women in the Renaissance. In: Hannay, Margaret P. (ed.) *Silent but for the word: Tudor women as patrons, translators, and writers of religious works.* Kent State University Press, Kent, pp. 107–125.

Lewis, C. S. (1954) *English literature in the sixteenth century, excluding drama.* Clarendon Press, Oxford.

Magnusson, Lynne (2001) Widowhood and linguistic capital: the rhetoric and reception of Anne Bacon's epistolary advice. *English Literary Renaissance* 31, 3–33.

McIntosh, Marjorie Keniston (1975) Sir Anthony Cooke: Tudor humanist, educator, and religious reformer. *Proceedings of the American Philosophical Society* 119, 233–250.

Schleiner, Louise (1994) *Tudor and Stuart women writers.* Indiana University Press, Bloomington.

Stewart, Alan (2000) The voices of Anne Cooke, Lady Anne and Lady Bacon. In: Clarke, Danielle & Clarke, Elizabeth (eds) *This double voice: gendered writing in early modern England.* Palgrave Macmillan, Basingstoke, pp. 88–102.

Bacon, Francis

R. W. SERJEANTSON

Francis Bacon (1561–1626) was acknowledged in his lifetime, and has been known ever since, as one of the foremost authors of his age. His publications encompassed the fields of the moral essay and political thought; the fable; history; and especially philosophy, above all natural philosophy. He also had a prominent career in law and politics, culminating in his appointment to the highest legal office in England, that of lord chancellor, in 1618. Although fascinated by practical ways of prolonging human life, Bacon was also determined that future ages should remember him for his books. The good number of these books printed in his lifetime are matched at least in quantity by writings that he never published, or indeed never finished. The unusually large amount of seventeenth-century manuscript material relating to Bacon testifies to an unusual level of interest in his writings both during his lifetime and in the years following his death.

Bacon was born in London in 1561 into a prominent family with an established tradition of service to the Tudor monarchy. He was the second son of his mother, Anne Cooke, the daughter of Sir Anthony Cooke, who had been a tutor to Edward VI. Francis remained close to his elder brother Anthony Bacon until the latter's death in 1601. Their father was Sir Nicholas Bacon (1510–79) who from the accession of Elizabeth I in 1558 until his death held the office of lord keeper of the great seal, with all the powers of lord chancellor except a title of nobility. Bacon recalled his father's office with pride when he in turn was appointed to the same position. When Anthony went up to Trinity College, Cambridge, in 1573 Francis, then only 12, also went up with him; the brothers were tutored by the master of Trinity, and future archbishop of Canterbury, John Whitgift. Although Bacon was critical of university learning in general in his later writings, he remained loyal to Cambridge, dedicating *De sapientia veterum* (*On the wisdom of the ancients*) (1609), a collection of idiosyncratic interpretations of classical fables, to the university and also presenting copies of his other books to its library. Leaving Cambridge after two years without taking a degree, Bacon joined the household of the English ambassador to France, Sir Amias Paulet, in 1576. In Paris his tuition continued; in particular, it was at this point in his life that he first studied civil (or Roman) law, which he later drew on in

various abortive efforts to reform English common-law jurisprudence. This legal inclination continued when he returned to England in 1579 on the death of his father. Left, unexpectedly, without an estate, Bacon had to seek a means of earning a living, and – although he later developed serious interests in both medicine and divinity – his father's profession of the law was the obvious choice. He entered Gray's Inn and became in due course an utter barrister, a bencher, and a reader there. He also sat in every parliament from 1581 to 1621.

These experiences can be seen as shaping the course of Bacon's later intellectual and authorial life. In his numerous proposals for the reform of philosophy he developed to an unusual degree an interest first provoked at Cambridge. In his professional life as a lawyer he produced numerous arguments and, later, judgements, some of which shaped the development of the common-law tradition in the seventeenth and eighteenth centuries. Throughout his life, he regarded his pen as something to be put at the service (in composing letters of advice, proclamations, and speeches) of his patrons and political superiors: Elizabeth I; Robert Devereux, earl of Essex; James VI and I; and George Villiers, duke of Buckingham. Intimately involved in national politics both as a parliamentarian and as a counsellor to monarchs, Bacon wrote a number of 'advertisements' and 'considerations' giving counsel in specific political circumstances. From these arose, in part, his more general, and more public, *Essays* – or, to give them the title of their final 1625 edition, *Essays or counsels, civill and morall*.

It was with these *Essays* that first Bacon emerged into print, albeit unwillingly, as an author. In 1597 an enterprising stationer set about printing, without his permission, a circulating manuscript of the *Essays*. Bacon got wind of this, suppressed the unauthorized edition, and arranged for his own version to appear – dedicated, not to a great and useful patron, but to his brother Anthony. These essays inaugurated a new genre of literature, and were widely imitated. Quite different from the *Essais* (1580, 1588, 1595) of the French author Michel de Montaigne, whose title he nonetheless adopted, Bacon's essays were abrupt forays into subjects of pressing interest to his readership in the late Renaissance court: studies, friendship, suits (appeals to someone in authority), honour. Collections of terse and sometimes only loosely articulated maxims, these early essays reflect and offer guidance to success in a culture of favour, faction, and connection: 'If you would worke any man, you must either know his nature, and fashions and so leade him, or his ends, and so winne him, or his weaknesses or disaduantages, and so awe him, or those that haue interest in him and so gouerne him' ('Of negociating', 1597).

Bacon worked on his *Essays* throughout his life: adding both new ones and fresh material to existing ones. From a slender octavo volume in 1597 they evolved into a substantial quarto in 1625, with an intermediate edition of 1612 intended for dedication to James I's heir, Prince Henry, before his untimely death that year. The growing volumes of essays reflect Bacon's mature political experiences, and several of them have a kernel in specific events or in particular intellectual preoccupations. His essay 'Of seditions and troubles' (written by 1612) may have its origin in the Midland Rising of 1607: Bacon's rigorous analysis of 'the *Materials*, the *Motives* and the *Remedies* of sedition' reflects the origins of that popular revolt in dearth, enclosure, and libelling. Similarly, his meditation 'Of plantations' (1625) reflects not only the experience of English settlers in Virginia and Newfoundland, but also the Scottish and English planting of Tyrone in Ireland in the wake of the Flight of the Earls, about which Bacon had written *Certaine considerations touching the plantations in Ireland* in late 1608. More generally, as suggested in particular by the essays 'Of simulation and dissimulation' (1625), on the one hand, and 'Of the greatnesse of kingdomes' (1612), on the other, the *Essays* arise from the prevalent intellectual culture of 'Tacitean' humanism, with its concern to analyse both the hidden motives of the powerful and the well-springs of popular opinion, and its Machiavellian preoccupation with successful military expansion.

The 1597 volume of *Essays* holds a key to understanding how Bacon understood himself, and how others saw him. It contains a piece entitled 'Places of perswasion and disswasion', the subject of which is the art of rhetoric. The systematic analysis of rhetoric preoccupied Bacon throughout his life, although unlike many other spheres of late-Renaissance learning he regarded it as 'A Science excellent, and excellently well laboured' (*The advancement of learning*). But it was not only the theory of rhetoric that was important for Bacon; all his public writings are framed and expressed with a consciousness of their nature as rhetorical performance. Book I of *The advancement of learning* (1605), for instance, must be understood as a printed oration delivered to the person of King James, to whom it is directly addressed. In other works Bacon used the dialogue form, with different characters giving different, often opposed, speeches on points of deliberation. The early *Gesta Grayorum* (1594) (commonly and probably securely attributed to Bacon) offers a virtuoso instance of this: written for performance at the Christmas-time revels of Gray's Inn, it is a feigned debate between six different counsellors to a prince on how best to attain the happiness of a state – whether by war, philosophy, riches, or virtue. Bacon's late, unfinished, *Advertisement touching a holy war* (written in 1623, published in 1629) is also a dialogue, on the merits and demerits of launching a new crusade against the Turks. Speeches on opposed sides in political debate were something which Bacon had constant experience of as a parliamentarian. He was also celebrated for his own eloquence as an orator. The art apparent in all of Bacon's writings for publication reflects that verbal eloquence.

One final extra item was printed in the 1597 *Essays*: a slim collection, in Latin, of *Religious meditations*. Bacon's relationship in his writings to Christianity and to the Christian churches has divided interpreters. A number of his writings were placed on the Index of Prohibited Books maintained by the Inquisition in

Rome. While this did not stop his works from being widely read both in Italy and elsewhere throughout the seventeenth and eighteenth centuries, it may have contributed to his reputation, in Italian scholarship in particular, as a libertine and Machiavellian critic of religion. This image does not quite do justice to the nature of Bacon's engagement with religious matters. We possess, for instance, an apparently personal document entitled 'A confession of faith by Mr Bacon' which evinces a reasonably orthodox Calvinist theology. Nonetheless, besides this unusual piece Bacon's engagement with religion was largely concerned with the external aspects of religious belief, with, to use the contemporary distinction, questions of church discipline rather than of theological doctrine. In 1589 or 1590 Bacon wrote and circulated a trenchant intervention into the controversy over the illegal 'Martin Marprelate' pamphlets which was critical of the official response to them of the bishops, and particularly of another future archbishop of Canterbury, Richard Bancroft. Bacon reprised this role as a layman commenting judiciously on church affairs in 1603 in his *Certaine considerations touching the better pacification and edification of the Church of England*, in which he showed himself to be guardedly sympathetic to the demands of Puritan reformers of the Elizabethan church settlement. The printing of this pamphlet in 1604, however, was suppressed by authority, and thereafter Bacon, no doubt encouraged by James's expressed distaste for such things, refrained from commenting directly on the church's affairs. Subsequently, his most elaborate consideration of religion came at the end of his *The advancement of learning*, in which he pronounced that he could find 'no space or ground that lieth vacant and vnsowne in the matter of Diunitie'.

Nonetheless certain religious preoccupations emerge: consistent with his approbation of the exercise of 'prophesying' in the earlier *Certaine considerations*, Bacon praised sermons over systematic theology and biblical commentary. In particular, he attacked 'The consumption of all that euer can be said in controuersies

of Religion, which haue so much diuerted men from other Sciences'. He always found place in his writings for biblical quotations, often in the Latin of the Vulgate, and this is consistent too with his insistence in the *Religious meditations* that the soul of the church was the testimony of the Bible. These *Meditations* also contain one last telling thought: that only persons of corrupt understanding suppose that goodness arises from 'ignorance and simplicity of manners'. Bacon, by contrast, insisted forcefully that if goodness is to be fruitful in the world, men need to experience all things, even 'Satan's depths'.

Though Bacon wrote a great deal during the reign of Elizabeth I, not always in his own name, it was after the accession of James VI of Scotland to the throne of England in 1603 that both his political and his authorial career began to flourish – the former, at first, more than the latter. Successfully attracting the attention, both by his designs and by his talents, of the king, of James's lord chancellor, Thomas Egerton, and latterly also of James's favourite, George Villiers (later duke of Buckingham), Bacon became solicitor general in 1607, attorney general in 1613, a privy councillor in 1616, lord keeper in 1617, and lord chancellor in 1618. In tandem with these offices he also received civil honours: a knighthood in 1603; elevation to the peerage in 1618 as Baron Verulam (after the Roman name for his home town of St Albans – hence his sometimes being known in Latin as 'Verulamius'); and further elevation within the peerage in 1621 to the viscountcy of St Albans.

While this impressive ascent to the pinnacle of Jacobean government was very largely owing to Bacon's legal ability, and also to his defence of the crown's interest in the House of Commons, it also owed something to his abilities with a pen. He wrote a number of papers of advice for James and his Privy Council. He also took it upon himself, and was also increasingly called upon explicitly, to draft royal proclamations for distribution throughout James's realm on a large number of subjects. But of all the works Bacon wrote to and for the king in this period one stands out: *The advancement of learning* (1605).

Of the proficience and advancement of learning (to give it its full title) is a book about knowledge: its acquisition, its advantages, its institutions, but above all its scope for improvement. Bacon speaks in the *Advancement* of his extreme love of learning, and 'learning', for him as for his contemporaries, comprehended the entire range of human intellectual endeavour: in language, logic, rhetoric, poetry (in its broadest sense of imaginative literature), history, and philosophy. It also included that sphere of knowledge with which Bacon has been associated ever since the seventeenth century: experimental science. Bacon's map of learning – he calls it a 'Globe of the Intellectuall world' at the end of the book – is therefore encyclopedic and universal. It is concerned with 'general' learning, rather than the specifics of 'action'. But it is not an encyclopedia in any formal sense: rather it is a selective survey of the world of learning as Bacon saw it in 1605, with numerous suggestions for how its different provinces might be 'advanced'.

The *Advancement* consists of two books, of which the first is (as Bacon puts it) 'a page' – that is, a young servant who precedes his master – to the other. This first book is a forensic oration, weighing the true value of learning in the balance by means of evidence and arguments, and refuting those detractors who undervalued it. The second book is a less rhetorical affair, written without digression or dilation. After an assessment of the ways in which learning is advanced through places, books, and people, Bacon turns to his principal purpose, which is to take a survey of learning, noting omissions and deficiencies in all the different disciplines. This often gives the discussion of individual aspects of learning a rather abrupt character: Bacon does not in general linger long on any single art or science. He effectively offers numerous suggestions for further endowment of the world with sound and fruitful knowledge, rather than a summary of existing information. This in itself is a

striking phenomenon: for future generations, Bacon would exemplify the thought that knowledge could be, and ought to be, advanced. Out of such a conviction ultimately emerges, in due course, the assumption that the goal of a university, for instance, is 'research' and the acquisition of new knowledge. For Bacon this conviction expressed itself above all in an antipathy to the standing of certain ancient authors as authorities in their particular spheres – above all, Aristotle in philosophy, and Galen in medicine: 'For why should a fewe receiued Authors stand vp like *Hercules Columnes*, beyond which, there should be no sayling, or discouering'? It is for this reason, perhaps, that Bacon is reticent in mentioning the names of particular authorities in the different sciences he discusses.

In a celebrated letter of 1592/93 written to Queen Elizabeth's lord treasurer and his own uncle, William Cecil, Lord Burghley, Bacon had confessed, in terms that might then have appeared grandiose, that he had 'taken all knowledge to be my province'; and he went on to speak of his desire to 'purge' knowledge of its different enemies, including 'frivolous disputations' and 'auricular traditions'. *The advancement of learning* was a manifest expression of the universality of his ambitions for the world of learning. But even this book was only a precursor to Bacon's grandest intellectual design: a project that he spent much effort working out over the last 25 years of his life, but one that bore public fruit only when he was at the height of his political power as lord chancellor.

In 1620 an elaborate and imposing Latin folio appeared from the presses of the king's printing house. The engraved title page depicts a ship passing through the pillars of Hercules (the entrance to the Mediterranean, and hence the gates of the Old World of knowledge) of which he had earlier spoken in the *Advancement*. The title identifies proudly that 'Francis of Verulam, High Chancellor of England', has composed an *Instauratio magna*: a 'Great Instauration' of knowledge. In the dedication to King James and the several prefaces that follow it becomes clear that this 1620 volume constitutes just one part of this great instauration. Specifically, it is the second part: the *Novum organum* (*New organon*), a 'New Instrument' of 'Directions concerning the interpretation of nature'. Of all his writings, Bacon later wrote, it was this one that he most esteemed.

By its very title this *New organon* announces that it is intended as a replacement for the old organon, that is, for the logical writings of Aristotle. Aristotelian logic served in the early modern period, and especially in the universities, as the basis of all the sciences, whether natural, human, or divine. Bacon has little to say about the role of logic in the knowledge of human and divine things. But he was very sure that in the investigation of nature, the old logic fell far short of grasping 'the subtlety of nature'. Productive of controversies, bloated with questions, it nonetheless lacked the capacity to generate 'works' from a true understanding of the operations of nature. The first book of the two-book *Novum organum* develops this critique by identifying the different 'idols' (of the tribe, of the cave, of the market-place, and of the theatre), falsely followed by the human mind, that lead it into error and misunderstanding. The second book offers a series of procedures, called by Bacon 'Instances of Special Powers', which – again unlike the old logic – will 'slice into nature'. The natural knowledge thereby gained, however, is but a 'first vintage'; better and more rarefied wine was to follow in the later parts of the *Instauration*. In fact, even the *Novum organum* itself was unfinished. Book II contains information about only one of the eight different procedures that were planned to help the understanding to the interpretation of nature by means of what he called 'true and perfect Induction'. But no doubt Bacon had thought that it was better to publish something than nothing.

In 1621 an event occurred that had fatal consequences for Bacon's political career, but that also gave rise to a dramatic period of literary fertility that lasted until his death five years later in 1626: he was impeached, and removed from the office of lord chancellor.

The ostensible cause of this catastrophe was bribery: Bacon was charged with, and in due course admitted to, improperly accepting gifts from those to whom he was dispensing justice. Behind this charge, which was levelled at him by enemies in the House of Commons, lay a popular and political hostility to the practice of granting patents to protect trade monopolies. The chief culprit here, and also a principal gainer by it, was Bacon's patron, the duke of Buckingham. Bacon was 'guilty of corruption', as he acknowledged; but he was also the instrument by which the parliament hoped to bring down James's favourite. Buckingham, however, retained James's protection and survived, whereas Bacon was convicted, fined, imprisoned, barred from sitting in the Lords or holding any state office, and banished from coming within 12 miles of the court, and hence from visiting London.

The leisure that Bacon's exile in St Albans provided gave him time to devote to concluding the *Great Instauration*, time that he had previously complained his professional duties did not allow him. Part I of the *Instauration* was to be a partition or organization of all the sciences. Abandoning his hope that he might produce such a thing from scratch – though an incomplete draft exists, entitled *Descriptio globi intellectualis* (*A description of the intellectual globe*) – Bacon expanded *The advancement of learning* into a work of nine books, and arranged for it to be translated into Latin as the *De augmentis scientiarum*. It appeared in 1623, and Bacon subsequently wrote that it would serve in lieu of the first part of the *Instauration*.

Of parts III to VI of the *Great Instauration* Bacon wrote even less. In 1622 and 1623 he published two specimen volumes of natural histories as a contribution to Part III. The first of these volumes was a *Historia ventorum* (*History of the winds*) (1622), in which he explored, among other aspects of their nature, the names, qualities, origins, generation, motions, and 'simulations' of winds. The second published natural history, *Historia vitae et mortis* (*The history of life and death*) (1623), had as a prominent theme one that had long been close to his heart: the prolongation of life. Here Bacon may be regarded as continuing a common preoccupation of earlier Italian authors such as Marsilio Ficino and Alvise Cornaro in his interest in the roles of place, family, alimentation, birth date, and profession, as well as medicine, in lengthening or shortening life.

More generally, natural history played a crucial role in Bacon's mature conception of how to go about attaining useful natural knowledge. It was through the knowledge systematically gathered in natural histories that the 'Empirical Faculty' of the human mind could be fruitfully married with the 'Rational Faculty'. An indication of the seriousness with which Bacon pursued this thought is offered by perhaps his most popular work among later seventeenth-century readers: his *Sylva sylvarum, or a naturali historie*, published posthumously in late 1626 or 1627 by his former chaplain, William Rawley. Though not formally a part of the *Great Instauration*, not least because it was in English rather than Latin, this collection of exactly 1,000 experiments was intended to draw Bacon's philosophy 'downe to the sense'. Along with his own observations, the *Sylva* drew upon a number of authors who had evidently long inspired his interest in natural philosophy: in particular, from antiquity, the elder Pliny and Aristotle; and from his own time, Julius Caesar Scaliger and Girolamo Cardano.

Together with the *Sylva* there was also published a short work unlike anything else Bacon ever wrote. *New Atlantis*, like so many of his other writings, was 'a work unfinished', as its editor Rawley explained on its title page. Nonetheless, Bacon wrote enough of his 'Fable' to join Thomas More and Tommaso Campanella as one of the most inventive and thought-provoking of all early modern utopian authors. Unusually for a utopia written before the eighteenth century, Bacon's imaginary island of Bensalem is located not in an 'unknown southern land' of the Atlantic, but in the Pacific, and the European sailors who find it speak Spanish. What they find when they arrive is an ancient

and advanced society, converted to Christianity by a special revelation, but notable above all for their achievements in natural knowledge. On Bensalem this knowledge was pursued by the Fellows of an institution calls 'Salomon's House' – the kind of foundation Bacon always hoped, in vain, that James might endow. As one of these Fellows explains to the narrator: 'The End of our Foundation is the knowledge of Causes, and secret motions of things; and the enlarging of the bounds of Human Empire, to the effecting of all things possible.' Here, vividly represented in imaginative form, is a vision of Bacon's ambitions for what putting his *Instauration* into effect might one day achieve.

Bacon nonetheless feared that the philosophy of the *Novum organum* 'flies too high over Mens Heads', and indeed James I is recorded as joking that the book, like the peace of God, 'passeth all understanding'. The physician William Harvey, who had studied natural philosophy and medicine extensively at the leading place for these subjects in the period, the University of Padua, observed that Bacon wrote philosophy 'like a Lord Chancellor'. This hostile witticism catches both Bacon's characteristically magisterial tone and his status as an amateur by contrast with the largely medically trained natural philosophers of this period. Harvey may not have intended it in any more exact sense, but a number of modern scholars have been attracted to the thought that there is a connection of some kind between Bacon's legal and political learning and his natural philosophy. In favour of this thought is a certain emphasis he places on investigating 'matters of fact', his scorn for 'contemplative' conceptions of natural philosophy in favour of 'active' ones, and also, one might add, his insistence that even more than searching for its causes philosophy should be concerned with the characteristically legal procedure of 'interpreting' nature. A very few of his writings also encourage this connection between law and science explicitly, in particular his early *A briefe discourse, touching the happie union of the kingdomes of England, and Scotland* (1603), in which he pursued a systematic parallel between the rules of nature and politics. The question remains open, yet it is difficult to avoid the thought that there is something, at least, to encourage it.

If Bacon never completed the *Great Instauration* this was no doubt mostly owing to the enormous scope of his planned project – the *Novum organum* is, after all, a sixth part of a sixth part of the projected *Instauration*. But it is also owing to the other literary projects with which Bacon also busied himself in the last years of his life. Practically his first action upon his impeachment was to write, at impressive speed, but also drawing upon manuscript evidence supplied to him by Sir Robert Cotton, a work of civil history: *The historie of the reigne of King Henry the seventh* (1622). To write the history of the Tudor dynasty that Bacon had served under Elizabeth and to which James traced the legitimacy of his claim as king of England (he was Henry VII's great-great-grandson) was a long-standing ambition for Bacon, dating back to at least 1605; he also wrote fragments of histories of Henry VIII, of the Tudor dynasty as a whole, and of a *History of Great Britain*. The ancient Roman historians, above all Tacitus and Livy, offered important models for his own history. But Bacon was also familiar with the modern historical writings of Niccolò Machiavelli and Francesco Guicciardini, and indeed in 1608 or so had sent the foremost contemporary historian, the French statesman Jacques-August de Thou, a eulogy of Queen Elizabeth for incorporation into de Thou's ongoing *Historia sui temporis* (*History of his own time*). Like all Renaissance historians, Bacon wrote with one eye on the application of his story to contemporary circumstances, and (for instance) his comment that Henry knew the way to peace was not to seem to be desirous to avoid wars may be a covert reproach to what was, in Bacon's eyes, James I's undue pacifism.

For Bacon's political vision, expressed in several of his essays, in his *Advertisement touching an holy war* (1623), and in his *Considerations touching a war with Spain* (1624), was a bellicose one that emphasized the 'greatness' as the supreme achievement of kingdoms and republics, and which sought the consolidation of the new British state followed by its expansion into Ireland, into North America, and ultimately also back onto the continent of Europe: in a private memorandum from 1608 Bacon advocates 'annexing the Low Countries', an ambition closely connected to his consistent hostility to Catholic Spain. Behind this desire for greatness there always lay for Bacon the example of the Roman republic. Ancient Rome was the polity most admired by Bacon, as it had been for Machiavelli, whom he admired for writing about what men do, and not what they ought to do.

In intellectual matters Bacon was similarly expansive in his ambitions, if more tolerant and less imperial. Latin was the 'Generall Language' into which he caused all his most important writings to be translated, and through textual alterations he made systematic efforts to render them acceptable to Roman Catholic audiences. He sent copies of his books abroad, and even prepared a copy of his *De augmentis*, in characteristically extravagant purple velvet, for presentation to Pope Urban VIII (it seems never to have been sent). In his lifetime there were also Italian and French translations of his *Essays*, *De sapientia veterum* (by Arthur Gorges), and *The advancement of learning*.

When Bacon died in 1626 the debts that he had incurred in maintaining a position he regarded as appropriate to his condition meant that his executors were unable to endow his planned Oxford and Cambridge lectureships in natural philosophy. But if he did not have a direct legacy in this way his indirect legacy in the natural sciences of the seventeenth-century was profound. Though scholars debate the extent to which the inductive procedures of the *Novum organum* were employed in practice by later natural philosophers, it is certainly the case that his example was often invoked in the early Royal Society after its founding in 1660. Before then he had influenced a range of social and scientific reformers in England, and his philosophical writings were reprinted in France, the Netherlands, and Germany throughout the seventeenth century. In the eighteenth century his partition of knowledge, and his advocacy of practical learning, inspired the contributors to the *Encyclopédie* (1751–72). In the nineteenth century there was a renewed interest in the philosophy of the inductive sciences and hence of the *Novum organum*, while an edition of the *The advancement of learning* (1876) was reprinted with a complete course of examination questions at the back for hopeful members of the civil and colonial services. And in the twentieth century Bacon became canonized as one of the great figures of what was then regarded as the greatest age of new field of 'English Literature'; so much so, in fact, that the idea even arose that in addition to all his other writings Bacon must have written the plays of William Shakespeare as well. Absurdly mistaken though it is, this thought is indicative of the qualities that could be attributed to one of the most powerful and original intellects of the English Renaissance.

SEE ALSO: Bacon, Anne (Cooke); Devereux, Robert, earl of Essex; Elizabeth I; Gorges, Arthur; Harvey, William; James VI and I; Marprelate, Martin; More, Thomas

REFERENCES AND SUGGESTED READINGS

Coquillette, Daniel R. (1992) *Francis Bacon*. Stanford University Press, Stanford.

Findlen, Paula (1997) Francis Bacon and the reform of natural history in the seventeenth century. In: Kelley, Donald R. (ed.) *History and the disciplines: the reclassification of knowledge in early modern Europe*. University of Rochester Press, Rochester, pp. 239–260.

Gaukroger, Stephen (2001) *Francis Bacon and the transformation of early modern philosophy*. Cambridge University Press, Cambridge.

Jardine, Lisa & Stewart, Alan (1998) *Hostage to fortune: the troubled life of Francis Bacon 1561–1726*. Gollancz, London.

Leary, John E., Jr (1994) *Francis Bacon and the politics of science*. Iowa State University Press, Ames.

Martin, Julian (1992) *Francis Bacon, the state and the reform of natural philosophy*. Cambridge University Press, Cambridge.

Peltonen, Markku (ed.) (1996) *The Cambridge companion to Bacon*. Cambridge University Press, Cambridge.

Pérez-Ramos, Antonio (1988) *Francis Bacon's idea of science and the maker's knowledge tradition*. Clarendon Press, Oxford.

Price, Bronwen (ed.) (2002) *Francis Bacon's 'The new Atlantis': new interdisciplinary essays*. Manchester University Press, Manchester.

Rossi, Paolo (1968) *Francis Bacon: from magic to science*, trans. Sacha Rabinovitch. Routledge & Kegan Paul, London.

Serjeantson, R. W. (2002) Natural knowledge in the *New Atlantis*. In: Price, Bronwen (ed.) *Francis Bacon's 'New Atlantis'*. Manchester University Press, Manchester, pp. 82–105.

Serjeantson, R. W. & Woolford, Thomas (2009) The scribal publication of a printed book: Francis Bacon's *Certaine considerations touching ... the Church of England* (1604). *The Library* 10(2), 119–156.

Sessions, William A. (ed.) (1990) *Francis Bacon's legacy of texts: 'The art of discovery grows with discovery'*. AMS Press, New York.

Solomon, Julie Robin & Martin, Catherine Gimelli (eds) (2005) *Francis Bacon and the refiguring of early modern thought*. Ashgate, Aldershot.

Tuck, Richard (1993) *Philosophy and government 1572–1651*. Cambridge University Press, Cambridge.

Zagorin, Perez (1998) *Francis Bacon*. Princeton University Press, Princeton.

Baldwin, William

SCOTT LUCAS

William Baldwin (d.1563) was a leading light of mid-Tudor literature. Nearly everything to which Baldwin turned his hand during the period 1547–63, including poetry, prose fiction, translation, and edited collections, won success in its own time and, in many cases, for long after.

The details of Baldwin's early life are unknown. He first appears at the opening of Edward VI's reign (1547–53), where he is found in the employ of the zealously Protestant printer Edward Whitchurch. Baldwin composed his first known work in 1547, a commendatory sonnet that became the first English sonnet ever to appear in print. In the year following, Baldwin released *A treatise of morall phylosophie*, a collection of classical aphorisms translated into his native tongue. Baldwin's *Treatise* became one of Renaissance England's greatest print success stories: the work appeared in a remarkable 24 editions over the next century, and numerous later authors drew upon its many pithy sayings to embellish their own creations.

With his next two projects, Baldwin sought to further the ends of the English Reformation. In 1549 he published a metrical translation of the Song of Songs, titled *The canticles or balades of Salomon*. He followed this with an English rendering of the anonymous Latin anti-papal satire *Wonderfull newes of the death of Paul the Third* (c.1552), a lively and often shockingly scurrilous piece of invective purporting to describe the reception of Pope Paul's soul in Hell by Satan and his minions.

In 1553 Baldwin composed his comic masterpiece *Beware the cat*, a wildly inventive, multilayered work of prose fiction that William A. Ringler, Jr, and Michael Flachmann (1995) hold to be the first English novel. In its narrative, one Gregory Streamer recounts to Baldwin how he came to understand the speech of cats. What follows is a dizzying array of imaginative vignettes, including an account of Streamer's farcical alchemical experiments, an erotic fabliau, and even the proceedings of a court trial conducted entirely by felines. Along the way, Baldwin indulges in anti-Catholic satire and the humorous exposure of the foibles of English citizens, whose guilty practices are revealed by the talking cats who witness them. Since Baldwin finished *Beware the cat* at the time the Catholic Queen Mary came to the throne, the text's anti-Catholic content necessarily prevented its publication until after Mary's death in 1558. A similar fate befell Baldwin's poem *The funeralles of King Edward the Sixt* (1553; published 1560), which blamed the loss of England's Protestant monarch on divine anger at the unwillingness of so many

English men and women to accept the Reformation fully.

After King Edward's death, Baldwin's strongly Protestant employer Whitchurch left the print trade and sublet his shop to a new man, John Wayland. As one of his first works, Wayland sought to print John Lydgate's medieval classic *The fall of princes* (c.1431–39), an enormous verse compendium recounting tales of historical figures who came to tragic ends. Wayland decided to add to this tome a continuation describing the falls of specifically English leaders. Wayland assigned the task of creating this continuation to Baldwin, who gathered seven other men to assist him in composing tragic verse monologues cast in the voices of ghostly political leaders from the reigns of Richard II through to Edward IV. This compilation, titled *A memorial of suche princes* (1554), was the first version of the work published five years later as *A mirrour for magistrates*.

Initially, Baldwin sought to fulfil his employer's demand for an uncontroversial literary exercise in Lydgate's style. However, in the wake of the rebellion of Sir Thomas Wyatt the younger in early 1554 and the perceived governmental attacks on the rights of citizens that followed, Baldwin and other contributors began to compose poetic exempla that were topically allusive in form and politically contentious in purpose. Some of these sought to address supporters of the previous reign's high officers, allusively urging them to contest the dominant Marian accounts that blamed the failings of the Edwardian period on the faults of its leaders and on God's judgement against the Reformation. Other poems sought to admonish the chief members of the current queen's government, moving them to believe that many of the policies they were currently pursuing were the very same as those that, according to the *Memorial* tragedies, led to some of the worst disasters of the late Plantagenet era. For both sorts of poems, the authors extensively altered the accounts found in their historical sources in order to 'mirror' the events of their own time better.

The authors' attempts to communicate with Marian readers were unsuccessful, as Mary's government prohibited the *Memorial* before it could be released. The work appeared only after Elizabeth's accession under the title *A mirrour for magistrates* (1559). In 1563 Baldwin began compiling an expanded edition of the *Mirrour*, which augmented the original gathering of tragedies with a combination of Marian poems created after the suppression of the *Memorial* and newly penned Elizabethan historical narratives. This edition of the *Mirrour* contained the most celebrated work of the collection, Thomas Sackville's 'Induction'. Baldwin's two *Mirrour* editions exerted a profound influence on subsequent English literature. Numerous Elizabethan and Jacobean poets penned verse tragedies in emulation of Baldwin's collection, while playwrights, including Shakespeare, drew upon its contents to enrich their own historical dramas. The *Mirrour* itself appeared in seven ever expanding editions between 1559 and 1610, each enlarged by later authors who eagerly contributed their own compositions to new printings of Baldwin's text. Unfortunately, Baldwin himself did not live to witness his works' enduring fame. He died of the plague in London in September 1563.

SEE ALSO: Churchyard, Thomas; Ferrers, George; Higgins, John; Sackville, Thomas, earl of Dorset; Shakespeare, William

REFERENCES AND SUGGESTED READINGS

Lucas, Scott C. (2009) '*A mirror for magistrates*' and *the politics of the English Reformation.* University of Massachusetts Press, Amherst.

Maslen, R. W. (2009) William Baldwin and the Tudor imagination. In: Pincombe, M. & Shrank, Cathy (eds) *The Oxford handbook of Tudor literature.* Oxford University Press, Oxford, pp. 291–305.

Ringler, William A., Jr, & Flachmann, Michael (1995) Introduction. In: Ringler, William & Flachmann, Michael (eds) *Beware the cat: The first English novel,* by William Baldwin. Huntington Library Press, San Marino, pp. xiii–xxx.

Bale, John

STEWART MOTTRAM

A writer of Protestant plays and prose attacks on the Roman Catholic Church, John Bale (1495–1563) also won esteem in his lifetime as a serious scholar: a bibliographer, antiquarian, and author of the first full-length Protestant commentary on the book of Revelation. His coarse humour and acerbic prose appealed little to later Renaissance tastes; by the 1660s Thomas Fuller had dubbed him 'bilious Bale'. Recent criticism has done much to redeem his reputation. Today he is recognized for his influence on John Foxe and Edmund Spenser, and for his key contribution to the development of a Protestant English national identity in the early modern period.

Born November 1495 at Covehithe near Lowestoft, Suffolk, Bale was sent to the Carmelite priory at Norwich at the age of 12, thence to Jesus College, Cambridge. In the early 1530s he was prior of Carmelite houses at Maldon, Ipswich, and Doncaster, but by 1536 he had left the White Friars, married, and taken up post as a priest in his native Suffolk. His career as a dramatist dates from around this time, and in 1538/39 Bale was being paid by Thomas Cromwell, earl of Essex, to stage Protestant plays in Canterbury and perhaps elsewhere. The Act of Six Articles (1539) reversed much of the work of the English Reformation, reinstating in England a Roman Catholic Church in all but name. Bale fled to Germany, returning to England only after the accession of Edward VI. In this, his first exile, Bale turned his hand to prose, publishing anti-papal polemics, Protestant martyr histories, a catalogue of British writers, and a commentary on Revelation, *The image of bothe churches* (1545). In an extraordinarily prolific period, Bale also saw four of his five extant plays through the press. After the accession of Edward VI, he found favour with the Protestant regime in England. In 1552 Bale was sent to Ireland as bishop of Ossory, where for eight months he tried to enforce Protestant church services on the largely Catholic local population. Bale fled his bishopric after Mary Tudor was proclaimed queen in Ireland in August 1553. His parting shot was to stage three of his Protestant plays at the market cross at Kilkenny. From Ireland Bale escaped to the Continent, living in Basel with fellow exile John Foxe. His second exile saw him publish the *Vocacyon of Johan Bale* (1553), an account of his time in Ireland, and the *Catalogus* (1557), an expanded second edition of his bibliography of British writers. He returned to England upon Elizabeth's accession, and died soon after in 1563.

Even before his break with the Carmelites, Bale was attracting attention as a Protestant preacher. He faced heresy charges for preaching in 1534 and imprisonment in 1537. His release, Bale would later recall, was at the request of Thomas Cromwell and 'on account of my comedies'. That Bale was already active as a dramatist at this time is clear from a list of 14 plays to appear in his *Anglorum Heliades*, his history of the English Carmelites, datable to 1536. Of these plays at least two – the now lost *Treasons of Thomas Beckett* and the extant *King Johan* – were revised for performance at Canterbury in September 1538 and January 1539. Cromwell paid for both performances and in the late 1530s may have acted more formally as patron of Bale's company of players, perhaps even sending them on tours of the provinces, as Paul Whitfield White (1993) suggests.

By 1548 Bale had written or translated a total of 24 plays, of which only five survive today. Of these, the most well known is *King Johan*. The oldest extant English history play, it develops a patriotic Protestant English identity that anticipates the tone of Shakespeare's histories. The play survives in a single manuscript (Huntington Library, San Marino, HM 3) written around 1538 and revised some 20 years later, perhaps for performance before Elizabeth I on her visit to Ipswich in August 1561 (Blatt 1968). Bale's four other extant plays were printed between 1547 and 1548. All are biblical in theme, staging the prophecies of the Old Testament and their fulfilment in the New Testament. Three of these plays – *The chefe promyses of God*, *Johan Baptystes preachynge*, and *The*

temptacyon of our Lorde – may have been written as a trilogy. We know they were performed together in a single sitting at the market cross at Kilkenny on 20 August 1553.

No performance context survives for Bale's other extant play, *The thre lawes*, written in 1538 and revised for publication a decade later. In this play Bale exposes the corrupt practices of the Roman Catholic clergy, accusing nuns and clergymen of a host of crimes both sexual and spiritual. The three laws of this play's title are the laws of Nature, Moses, and Christ, the first of which dominates human history between Adam and Moses, the second between Moses and Christ, and the third between Christ's Advent and his return on the Day of Judgement. The play dramatizes the successive perversions of the three laws by a series of Vice figures dressed as bishops, monks, and friars – Sodomy and Idolatry (Nature), Ambition and Avarice (Moses), and Pseudo-doctrine and Hypocrisy (Christ) – who work alongside the play's chief Vice, Infidelity, to undermine God's plans for humanity's salvation. Only in the apocalyptic fifth act is Infidelity finally banished to Hell, and the play ends optimistically with a vision of England as the New Jerusalem, its three laws restored, through the triple blessings of England's Reformation, break with Rome, and English Bible. The Bible is key to Bale's identity as a Protestant writer. His plays, pamphlets, histories, and book catalogues all take their theme and inspiration directly from Scripture. Bale's identification with the Bible is reflected in the several woodcut illustrations of the writer to survive, in which he always appears with a Bible in hand. It is reflected also in his conscious alignment in the Irish *Vocacyon* and *The image of both churches* with the evangelical apostles St Paul and St John. Bale likens their experiences of hardship and persecution to his own, to his sufferings in Ireland and his forced exile abroad.

Originality was not a quality Bale valued in writers, least of all in himself. On the title pages of plays and other works he refers to himself not as an author but as a 'compiler' of scriptural material. For Bale, God alone was the one true author, his apostles the secretaries of his word. To this extent, Bale speaks of apostleship as the highest category of authorship, since it is through apostles that God speaks to his church. That Bale identifies himself with the apostles Paul and John speaks volumes, of course, for his own authorial self-image as an apostle, or secretary of the word of God. That word is never far beneath the surface of Bale's work. In his edition of the *Examinations* of Anne Askew (1547), for example, each character takes on a sacred role in his imagination, their 'real life' personalities subsumed into the types of the saint or the sinner. Bale likens Henry VIII to King David, and Anne Askew to the early Christian martyr Blandina. Conversely, at Askew's heresy trial the conservative bishop Stephen Gardiner is recast in the villain's role as Caiaphas, the Jewish judge at Christ's trial.

The Bible also plays its role in Bale's dramatic writing, exercising a direct influence on his three plays on biblical themes, and a more diffuse impact on the structure and stagecraft of all five extant plays. Bale's indebtedness to medieval civic drama has long been recognized, but from this drama his biblical plays also represent a significant departure. Civic plays at York and elsewhere dramatized sacred history but took the opportunity also to embellish on Scripture, introducing local colour and costumes, and at times even subsuming entirely fictional characters into the Bible narrative. By contrast, Bale's biblical plays stick closely to the text of the Bible. Where medieval biblical plays were collaborative affairs embedded in a given locale, Bale's plays were designed for touring and written for a national rather than a local community, their aim being to promote the interests of the developing Tudor nation-state. The expense of touring dictated that Bale's plays were sparse on scenery and special effects. However, the decision to avoid elaborate stagecraft was also an ideological one. In all his plays, Bale's focus is on dialogue, a counterpart to his focus on the word. It is telling that his most colourful characters are his vices and villains. With their songs, costume changes, and knockabout humour, the Vices in *King Johan* and *Thre lawes* are quite self-consciously theatrical. Yet for Bale this very staginess carries a polemical charge, marking the Vices out as suspect in the eyes of his plain-speaking Protestant characters, like England and King John. Theatricality stands for hypocrisy in Bale's plays, and more often than not, Bale's Vices, dressed as monks and priests, embody the staginess of the Roman Catholic Church. Its rites and ceremonies Bale sees as an elaborate pageant, designed to conceal Bible truths beneath a smoke-and-mirrors facade.

Yet it is not just the Bible message that Bale accuses the Roman Catholic Church of corrupting. As products of this church, Bale argues, the chronicles also serve Roman interests, their business to distort history so that it shows off monks and priests in the best possible light. In *King Johan* Bale speaks of the need to rehabilitate John's tarnished reputation in the English chronicles as a tyrant king. But how was Bale to go about this task? How was he to sift fact from fiction? With so much of history buried in monastic libraries, Bale turned characteristically to the Bible as the touchstone against which to try the truth of chronicle history.

Throughout his works, Bale reads the chronicles of history through a sacred lens, seeing history's heroes and villains prefigured in Scripture, and in particular in the prophecies of the book of Revelation. Bale's first period of exile gave rise to three influential Protestant martyrologies – the *Examinations* of Sir John Oldcastle, William Thorpe, and Anne Askew – and his catalogue of British authors, the *Summarium* (1548), later enlarged to form the two-volume *Catalogus* of 1557–59. Both these bio-bibliographies arrange manuscripts chronologically by author, grouping authors into 'centuries' in a schema that divides British history into the seven ages foretold in the book of Revelation. Bale sees the whole of Christian history as a battle across these seven ages between Christ and Antichrist, Protestant and papist. Protestantism for Bale is no newfangled belief invented by Martin Luther. Instead, the Protestant church – like Augustine's City of God – has for centuries remained largely invisible, forced underground by the ascendancy of Antichrist at Rome in the fifth century AD. The re-emergence of Protestantism in the sixteenth century Bale reads as a sign that his generation stands on the threshold of the final, seventh age of history.

For Bale, British history is patterned and preordained; it plays out in mirror image the battle between the two churches of good and evil, light and dark, that he reads in the book of Revelation. This idea runs throughout his writings and receives its fullest expression in his commentary on Revelation, *The image of both churches* (1545), easily his most influential work. Bale's is the first Protestant commentary on Revelation printed in English, but Bale was also the first writer to 'English' the Revelation in another important sense. In his *Actes of Englysh votaryes* (1546) and his preface to the *Lattre examinacyon of Anne Askewe* (1547) he sets out to rewrite British history as a centuries-long struggle between good and evil, effectively recasting the chronicles of England and Wales in an apocalyptic light.

Bale argues that the true church took up roots in Britain in the first century, surviving into the sixteenth century in the faith of the reformed English church. He contrasts this true church with the false Roman Catholic faith, a comparative newcomer to these isles, brought to Britain, he alleges, by Augustine and the Saxons only in the sixth century. It is a foreign church on British soil, Bale writes, and yet, he fears, it is a faith that still thrives in England, despite recent efforts to reform the English church along Protestant lines.

Bale's approach to the book of Revelation had a major impact on the English Renaissance, his account of the two churches in history a direct influence on the commentaries of the Geneva Bible (1560), on Foxe's *Actes and monuments* (1563), and on the battle between Una and Duessa in book I of Spenser's *Faerie*

Queene (1590). Particularly influential was Bale's reading of Britain's two churches along nationalist lines. For Bale, the Roman Church is not just false, it is foreign; like the Saxons, it arrived from abroad. Not so Bale's Protestant church. Rooted in pre-Saxon soil, this faith is claimed by Bale as the more British because the more ancient. Protestantism is as much about national belonging as religious belief, its battle with Rome a patriotic defence both of church and of nation.

Recent years have seen an outpouring of scholarship on Bale and national identity, with studies exploring the national significance of Bale's apocalyptic approach to history (Hadfield 1994), his nostalgia for the past (Schwyzer 2004), and his enthusiasm for the English Bible (Mottram 2008). Recent critics have noted the ironies of the fact that Bale builds his 'English' Protestant identity upon the foundations of a pre-Saxon – and therefore a pre-English – Celtic British church. This has been explored within the context of England's wider tendency in Tudor times to lay claim to the history, and through history to the geography, of Britain's Celtic fringe (Schwyzer 2004). Bale's near-interchangeable use in his writing of the terms 'English' and 'British' can also be seen to reflect on England's British colonial ambitions in this period, as can his ill-fated attempts as bishop in Ireland to impose an English Protestant identity on the native Irish population (Hadfield 1993).

Bale built his identity as an author and an Englishman on his reading of Scripture alongside the chronicle histories of England and Wales. The Bible is the source of his identity as an author, an inspiration for his fiction, and also a mirror reflecting the 'facts' of history. Yet with so much invested in Scripture, how could Bale be sure he was reading it aright? Like William Tyndale and other reformers of his generation, Bale put his trust in the transparency of the newly licensed English Bible. For him, this Bible was written in plain and simple English, its meaning self-evident to all. To understand Scripture, then, one needed only to have the text of the Bible to hand. In

King Johan and elsewhere Bale castigates the Roman Catholic Church for obscuring Scripture beneath layers of interpretation and commentary. In stark contrast Bale presents himself as a bluff Englishman, a plain-speaking exponent of scriptural truths. The image of Scripture written or printed on the heart is a recurrent one in Bale's prose.

But the Bible was never as plain-speaking as Bale claimed it to be. In Bale's lifetime the 'plain and simple' text of the English Bible was always accompanied in print by prefaces, tables, and marginal glosses. When the Act for the Advancement of True Religion (1543) commanded that such material be expunged from English Bibles, Bale wrote to defend their usefulness in guiding the reader in their interpretation of Scripture. He was eager to promote the English Bible as a glass of truth: simple, clear, transparent. Yet he was more pragmatic than he cared to admit about the need to regulate and control the interpretation of Scripture.

Several recent studies have explored the ironies and contradictions inherent in Bale's approach to the English Bible, together with their impact on his vision for the English nation (Hadfield 1994; Kastan 1994; Mottram 2008). Bale's nation inhabited shifting ground, anchored in a Protestant interpretation of the Bible more contestable and contingent than he would have us believe. In the absence of a plain-speaking Bible, Bale's nation stood or fell wholly on the ability of his plays and prose to persuade us that his reading of the Bible was the right one. Critics are beginning to recognize the modernity of this national vision. For all his rootedness in a medieval literary tradition, Bale's nation has a very contemporary feel to it. Partial and partisan, more rhetorical than real, Bale's nation looks forward to a modern age, anticipating the fictions of community and origin that define our experience of national identity today.

SEE ALSO: Askew, Anne; Bible, the; Foxe, John; Gardiner, Stephen; Spenser, Edmund; Tyndale, William

REFERENCES AND SUGGESTED READINGS

Blatt, Thora B. (1968) *The plays of John Bale: a study of ideas, technique and style*. Gad, Copenhagen.

Hadfield, Andrew (1993) Translating the Reformation: John Bale's Irish vocacyon. In: Bradshaw, Brendan, Hadfield, Andrew, & Maley, Willy (eds) *Representing Ireland: literature and the origins of conflict, 1534–1660*. Cambridge University Press, Cambridge, pp. 43–59.

Hadfield, Andrew (1994) *Literature, politics and national identity: Reformation to Renaissance*. Cambridge University Press, Cambridge.

Kastan, David S. (1994) 'Holy wurdes' and 'slipper wit': John Bale's *King Johan* and the poetics of propaganda. In: Herman, Peter C. (ed.) *Rethinking the Henrician era: essays on early Tudor texts and contexts*. University of Illinois Press, Urbana, pp. 267–282.

King, John N. (1982) *English Reformation literature: the Tudor origins of the Protestant tradition*. Princeton University Press, Princeton.

Mottram, Stewart (2008) *Empire and nation in early English Renaissance literature*. D. S. Brewer, Cambridge.

Schwyzer, Philip (2004) *Literature, nationalism, and memory in early modern England and Wales*. Cambridge University Press, Cambridge.

Shrank, Cathy (2007) John Bale and reconfiguring the 'medieval' in Reformation England. In: McMullan, Gordon & Matthews, David (eds) *Rethinking the medieval in early modern England*. Cambridge University Press, Cambridge, pp. 179–192.

Simpson, James (1997) Ageism: Leland, Bale, and the laborious start of English literary history. In: Copeland, Rita, Lawton, David, & Scase, Wendy (eds) *New medieval literatures*, vol. 1 Clarendon Press, Oxford, pp. 213–236.

White, Paul W. (1993) *Theatre and Reformation: Protestantism, patronage, and playing in Tudor England*. Cambridge University Press, Cambridge.

Barclay, Alexander

MIKE PINCOMBE

Alexander Barclay (c.1484–1552) was one of the most important early Tudor authors, yet he has still to receive the recognition bestowed by a serious scholarly monograph. He was essentially a modern writer, who made translations and adaptations of contemporary neo-Latin classics by Continental authors: Sebastian Brant's *Shyppe of fooles* (1509), five *Eglogs* (c.1518–30) based principally on Aeneas Sylvius Piccolomini (Pope Pius II) and 'Mantuan' (Baptista Spagnuoli), Mantuan's *Life of Saint George* (c.1515), and Domenico Mancini's *The myrrour of good maners* (c.1518). All this indicates that we should place him squarely in the camp of the 'moderns', as does his attention to more traditionally recognizable 'humanist' works such as his translation of Sallust's *Jugurthine wars* (c.1520), his revision of John Stanbridge's school-room text *Vocabula* (*Words*, 1519 and several reprints), and his *Introductory to wryte, and to pronounce French* (1521). For all this, he has attracted relatively little attention from the critics, unlike his rival and sparring partner, John Skelton. Why? Sadly, one suspects it is because he was a monk and then a friar, and that the Anglo-Protestant literary-historical tradition – which has its roots in the Reformation as much as the Renaissance – has tended to write him off as hopelessly 'medieval' (Carlson 1995). In this, his fate resembles his great predecessor, John Lydgate, 'the monk of Bury'. But just as modern scholars are beginning to appreciate the true value of Lydgate's works, so, too, it may be hoped, Barclay's star may soon rise again.

The date and place of Barclay's birth are a matter of debate. Until recently, and on quite good evidence, it was thought that Barclay was a Scot born around 1475; but new research suggests that he was actually a Lincolnshire man (Lyall 1969) who came into the world in the mid-1480s (Orme 2004). In either case, Barclay had certainly received a good education – probably not only at home but also in France and Germany – by the time he started to publish in 1509. The previous year, he had been ordained priest in Exeter Cathedral, so that he could take up a position at the collegiate church in Ottery St Mary in Devon. Here he was a chaplain with special responsibility for the choristers and 'secondaries', a group of young clerics whose mischievous behaviour he

notes, with relative good humour, in his translation of *The shyppe of fooles*. These personal allusions, of which there are many more, help to set off the otherwise general nature of Brant's satirical attacks on the folly and vanity of worldly occupations.

They also indicate Barclay's insertion of himself into a tradition of self-advertisingly public 'laureate' poetry initiated by John Lydgate and pursued by several writers in the later fifteenth century and in early Tudor England, such as Stephen Hawes and Barclay's rival Skelton (Meyer-Lee 2007). Barclay's choice of a monastic career in the Benedictine house at Ely did not signal an intention to leave the world behind him; rather, it gave him time and space for his literary work, and it was whilst he was a Benedictine monk that he produced most of his copious and various *oeuvre*. In addition to the works cited above, Barclay is supposed to have written an attack on the French king Louis XII and hagiographies of St Katherine and St Margaret. And as in the case of Lydgate, monastic life did not prevent Barclay from participating in the life at court, where he seems to have special links with the Chapel Royal and its members. Barclay was a client of the great Howard family, and dedicated several works to Thomas Howard, second duke of Norfolk (grandfather to the poet earl of Surrey, Henry Howard).

It was at Ely that Barclay wrote the work for which he is most famous: his five *Eglogs*. These are the only poems which may be said to have had any influence on later Tudor writers, and they may still be read for pleasure (Cooper 1977). Barclay does not merely translate his sources, but uses them as the basis for his own imaginative reworking of their thematic material (Lyall 1972). The well-known description of the English winter at the start of his final eclogue owes less to Mantuan, for example, than to Barclay's own creative genius. The anti-courtly sentiments of the first three eclogues (all from Aeneas Sylvius) are also well observed.

Barclay ceased to write in the mid-1520s, and thereafter his life becomes a matter for the religious rather than the literary historian.

He left the Benedictines for the Franciscans about this time, and after the dissolution of the order in England, he moved from one part of the country to another rather restlessly. He seems to have led a double life: on the one hand, he accumulated a number of church livings, which means he must have conformed to some extent to the Reformation; but on the other hand, he was clearly also resistant to the changes and was still saying Mass for Princess Mary in the reign of Edward VI (Lyall 1969). He died in 1552.

SEE ALSO: Hawes, Stephen; Howard, Henry, earl of Surrey; Skelton, John; Stanbridge, John

REFERENCES AND SUGGESTED READINGS

Carlson, David R. (1995) Skelton and Barclay, medieval and modern. *Early Modern Literary Studies* 1. http://extra.shu.ac.uk/emls/01-1/carlskel.html

Cooper, Helen (1977) *Pastoral: Mediaeval into Renaissance.* D. S. Brewer, Ipswich; Rowman & Littlefield, Totowa.

Lyall, R. J. (1969) Alexander Barclay and the Edwardian Reformation, 1548–52. *Review of English Studies* 20, 455–461.

Lyall, R. J. (1972) Tradition and innovation in Alexander Barclay's 'Towre of vertue and honoure'. *Review of English Studies* 23, 1–18.

Meyer-Lee, Robert J. (2007) *Poets and power from Chaucer to Wyatt.* Cambridge University Press, Cambridge.

Orme, Nicholas (2004) Barclay, Alexander. In: *Oxford dictionary of national biography.* Oxford University Press, Oxford.

White, Beatrice (ed.) (1928) *The eclogues of Alexander Barclay.* Early English Text Society, Oxford.

Barnes, Barnabe

TANYA POLLARD

Barnabe Barnes (1571–1609) was a poet and playwright best known for Petrarchan poems, an Italianate revenge play, and personal scandals. He associated with the controversial Robert Devereux, earl of Essex, became involved in a number of literary quarrels, and burst into notoriety in 1598 when he was prosecuted and imprisoned for attempted murder through poisoning. Barnes is primarily remembered as a sonneteer, but his life and writings alike are notable for embodying the sixteenth-century English fascination with Italian ideas and fashions, as well as the lively competition between young literary wits in early modern London.

Barnes was born in York to Dr Richard Barnes, bishop of Durham, and Fridismunda Gifford. He began studies at Brasenose College, Oxford, in 1586, but did not receive a degree. After travelling with Essex to Normandy in 1591, he began his literary career with *Parthenophil and Parthenophe* (1593), a collection of Petrarchan sonnets and other verse forms. Although Barnes's story of an unrequited lover pursuing a beautiful virgin closely follows the conventions of the Italian sonnet sequence, it veers sharply away from these conventions in the closing poem, in which Parthenophil turns to black magic in order to conjure up, and make love to, a naked Parthenophe riding on a goat. Scholars have identified Parthenophil's forceful taking of a virgin with political schemes surrounding Elizabeth I, especially in the light of Barnes's association with Essex. Even aside from possible political implications, however, the poem is striking for its implicit critique of the literary traditions linked with courtly love.

When *Parthenophil* was published, Barnes appended a sonnet praising Henry Wriothesley, earl of Southampton, apparently putting himself in competition for Southampton's patronage with William Shakespeare, who dedicated his *Venus and Adonis* to the earl in the same year. Based on this and other details, some scholars have identified Barnes as the rival poet to whom Shakespeare refers in his sonnets. He has also been seen as the model for a number of Shakespeare's braggart soldiers, including Parolles in *All's well that ends well*, Don Armado in *Love's labour's lost*, and Pistol in *Henry IV, part one* and *Henry V*, as well as for Basilisco in Thomas Kyd's *Tragedie of Solimon and Perseda*. If so, these would not be the only instances in which Barnes was caricatured in print. In his *Poemata* (1595), Thomas Campion mocked his lack of military prowess in a Latin epigram, 'In Barnum', and made fun of a cuckolded 'Barnzy' in his 'Eight Epigram'. After attacking Thomas Nashe as a liar and buffoon in commendatory verses to Gabriel Harvey's *Pierces supererogation* (1593), Barnes was excoriated by Nashe as a coward, a bad poet, and badly dressed, in *Have with you to Saffron-walden* (1596). His peers seem to have found his writing as forceful as his personality: Thomas Bastard wrote in 'De Barnei poesi' that 'Barneus verse, (vnlesse I doe him wrong,) / Is like a cupp of sacke, heady and strong' (*Chrestoleros*, 1598).

Barnes's notoriety increased dramatically in 1598, when he was accused of attempting to murder John Browne through poisoning lemonade and a flagon of wine with mercury sublimate. Scholars have suggested that Barnes undertook the murder on behalf of Lord Ever, a noted enemy of Browne; in any case, Barnes had powerful allies, and after managing to escape from prison he was not recaptured. There is a curious parallel between this incident and the numerous poisonings in Barnes's elaborately Machiavellian revenge drama, *The divils charter*. The play, which depicted Caesar Borgia's machinations to become Pope Alexander VI, echoed Marlowe's *Doctor Faustus* in its protagonist selling his soul to the devil, and Shakespeare's *Macbeth* in its fascination with dark magic. It was performed at court before James I by the King's Men in February 1607, and published in October of the same year.

Although Barnes claimed not to have travelled to Italy, his works demonstrate the impact of its literary and cultural influences. Just as *Parthenophil and Parthenophe* imitate the forms and themes of Petrarch's poems, *The divils charter* not only exploits an Italian setting but explicitly echoes Machiavelli. In *Foure bookes of offices* (1606), a prose work on virtue and government dedicated to King James, Barnes quotes Machiavelli in Italian. Nashe's criticism of his fashion sense, furthermore, suggests at least popular ideas about Italian

influences, as does his imaginative poisoning scheme. Barnes also produced a collection of religious poetry, *A divine centurie of spirituall sonnets* (1595), and wrote another play, *The battle of Hexham*, which is no longer extant. He was buried at Durham in 1609.

SEE ALSO: Harvey, Gabriel; Kyd, Thomas; Marlowe, Christopher; Nashe, Thomas; Shakespeare, William

REFERENCES AND SUGGESTED READINGS

Cox, John D. (1998) Stage devilry in two King's Men plays of 1606. *Modern Language Review* 93, 934–947.

Creighton, Charles (1904) Shakespeare's literary 'devil': Barnabe Barnes. In: *Shakespeare's story of his life*. Grant Richards, London, pp. 144–181.

Dodds, Madeleine (1946) Barnabe Barnes. *Archaeologia Aeliana* ser. 4, 24, 1–59.

Eccles, Mark (1933) Barnabe Barnes. In: Sisson, Charles J. (ed.) *Thomas Lodge and other Elizabethans*. Harvard University Press, Cambridge, MA, pp. 166–241.

Lee, Sidney (1898) *A life of William Shakespeare*. Macmillan, London.

Nelson, Jeffrey (1994) Lust and black magic in Barnabe Barnes's *Parthenophil and Parthenophe*. *Sixteenth Century Journal* 25, 595–608.

Barnfield, Richard

LAURA AYDELOTTE

Richard Barnfield (1574–1620/26) wrote lyric and pastoral verse. His best-known works are *The affectionate shepheard* and the poems 'If musique and sweet poetry agree' and 'As it fell upon a day', which were long misattributed to William Shakespeare. Barnfield is often regarded as one of the better of the minor Elizabethan poets, the most notable and controversial aspect of his poetry being his frank expression of homoerotic themes. In response to this candid homoeroticism, critics once either suppressed or qualified his claims to a substantial literary reputation; but his verse has excited the interest of many recent critics who find in him both an accomplished poetic talent and a fascinating figure for studies of homosexual literature and early modern sexuality.

Barnfield was born on 13 June 1574, the eldest son of Richard Barnfield, a gentleman and landowner from Shropshire, and Mary Skrymsher. He was probably raised by his aunt, Elizabeth Skrymsher, following his mother's probable suicide when he was seven. He attended Brasenose College, Oxford, where he matriculated in 1589, attained his BA in 1592, and spent an additional year working towards an MA without taking the degree. It was during his four years at Oxford that he began writing poetry and made literary acquaintances such as the poet and playwright John Marston.

Following his Oxford years, Barnfield lived in London, possibly spending some time in one of the Inns of Court where he might have known any number of Elizabethan literary lights. He may have been in the literary circle of Abraham Fraunce and Mary Herbert, countess of Pembroke (Morris 1963; Klawitter 1990), and the writer Francis Meres refers to Barnfield as a friend. Several critics have suggested that Barnfield was the author of *Greenes funerals*, a collection of sonnets written on the death of author Robert Greene (Klawitter 1990) and published under the initials 'R.B.', which would suggest a friendship with Greene. In terms of poetic inspiration, Barnfield himself mentions Edmund Spenser as a significant influence on his verse as well as Drayton, Daniel, and Shakespeare, but there is no way of knowing if he ever crossed paths with any of these poets.

Barnfield's first book of poems was *The affectionate shepheard* (1594). The title poem describes a love triangle between the poet/ shepherd Daphnis, the beautiful youth Ganymede, and the married Queen Guendolena with some possible clear parallels to the poet himself, the Lady Penelope Devereux Rich, and her lover Charles Blount, whom Barnfield possibly knew at Brasenose. The poem includes extended passages of praise and enticement directed at Ganymede, often in imitation of

Christopher Marlowe's 'The passionate shepherd to his love'. However, the misogynistic condemnation directed at the woman in the poem is as unflattering as the praise of Ganymede is charming, and if the insult was indeed directed at Lady Rich – to whom the poem is also dedicated – then this is perhaps the offence for which Barnfield later apologized in the introduction to *Cynthia* (1595). He made no such apology for *The affectionate shepheard*'s homoerotic themes, which he defended as in imitation of Virgil's eclogues.

Within the space of a few years Barnfield published his final two works. *Cynthia* includes the titular poem, 'The legend of Cassandra', and a fine collection of 20 sonnets, again addressed to 'Ganymede'. *The encomion of Lady Pecunia* (1598; reprinted 1605) showcases a humorous work loosely based on Erasmus's *Praise of Folly*, and includes 'As it fell upon a day' and 'If musique and sweet poetry agree', which became well known due to their publication in the printed verse miscellany *The passionate pilgrime* (1599) and their subsequent misattribution to Shakespeare. Both 'As it fell' and sonnet 15 from *Cynthia* appeared in the miscellany *Englands Helicon* (1600).

The poems attributed to Shakespeare demonstrate two aspects of Barnfield's poetic style. 'As it fell', entitled 'An ode' in its original publication, belongs with some of his other lighter verses, which tend to either charm or annoy critics. Written in heavily rhymed, mostly seven-syllable couplets, it was set to music more than once in the eighteenth and nineteenth centuries. The sonnet 'If musique', dedicated 'To HIS FRIEND Maister R.L.', is an enjoyable example of a sixteenth-century sonnet built around the conceit that 'If Musique and sweet Poetrie agree / ... Then must the Love be great, twixt thee and me', since the friend 'R.L.' is a lover of music and the poet of poetry. The sonnet exemplifies Barnfield's smooth control over the form and the engaging, intimate warmth towards a male friend characteristic of many of his sonnets and other poems. However, 'If musique' stops just short of the passionate intensity of *Cynthia*'s

Ganymede sonnets, apparent in the opening of sonnet 8: 'Sometimes I wish that I his pillow were, / So might I steale a kisse, and yet not seene.' Owing to a will dated 1627, it was long believed that Barnfield married and lived his final years in comfortable prosperity. As Andrew Worrall (2001) has proven, this will was that of the poet's father, also named Richard Barnfield. The poet himself was disowned by his family and deprived of his birthright. He died in either 1620 or 1626, probably in financial distress.

The critical reception of Barnfield's verse has been varied. The first collection of his poems, edited by Alexander Grosart, appeared in 1876, and critics throughout the Victorian age and the first part of the twentieth century praised his pastoral verses and his lyric style. Yet even those who admitted the quality of Barnfield's poetry felt the need to apologize for his homoerotic themes as imitations of classical poetry, or to conclude that they negated any real claim to poetic worth. Many critics betray conflicting views. C. S. Lewis flatly condemns Barnfield for his 'pederasty', but cannot seem to help admiring that he could 'steal from Shakespeare and add something worth adding' (Lewis 1954). For some time, the only twentieth-century critical book devoted to Barnfield (Morris 1963) was one that celebrated his poetry but still referred to the homoerotic aspects as 'unnatural'. The last few decades have seen a marked shift with the publication of a new edition of Barnfield's works (Klawitter 1990), a useful collection of critical essays (Borris & Klawitter 2001), and various articles. These have contributed valuable new readings of his poems and offered a reassessment of Barnfield's life and work in light of an acceptance of and interest in homoeroticism as a theme in literature. This renewed take on Barnfield's poetry opens up potentially fertile ground for future thought and research on a poet who merits the attention.

SEE ALSO: Fraunce, Abraham; Greene, Robert; Herbert, Mary (Sidney), countess of Pembroke; Marston, John; Meres, Francis; Shakespeare, William; Spenser, Edmund; verse miscellanies, printed

REFERENCES AND SUGGESTED READINGS

Borris, Kenneth & Klawitter, George (eds) (2001) *The affectionate shepherd: celebrating Richard Barnfield.* Associated University Presses, Cranbury.

Bredbeck, Gregory W. (1992) Tradition and the individual sodomite: Barnfield, Shakespeare and subjective desire. In: Summers, Claude J. (ed.) *Homosexuality in Renaissance and Enlightenment England: literary representations in historical context.* Haworth-Harrington Park, New York, pp. 41–68.

Klawitter, George (ed.) (1990) *Richard Barnfield: the complete poems.* Associated University Presses, Cranbury.

Lewis, C. S. (1954) *English literature in the sixteenth century, excluding drama.* Clarendon Press, Oxford.

Morris, Harry (1963) *Richard Barnfield: Colin's child.* Florida State University Press, Tallahassee.

See, Sam (2007) Richard Barnfield and the limits of homoerotic literary history. *GLQ: A Journal of Lesbian and Gay Studies* 13(1), 63–91.

Worrall, Andrew (2001) Biographical introduction: Barnfield's feast of 'all varietie'. In: Borris, Kenneth & Klawitter, George (eds) (2001) *The affectionate shepherd: celebrating Richard Barnfield.* Associated University Presses, Cranbury, pp. 25–40.

Barry, Lording

JEREMY LOPEZ

Lording Barry (1580–1629) left only one play, *Ram-alley* (printed 1611), to posterity, and a wealth of tantalizing biographical traces which hint at a life of adventure, occasional desperation, and remarkable luck.

From 1607 to 1608 the Children of the King's Revels performed in a theatre in the seedy Whitefriars neighbourhood, just beyond the City of London's western wall. Barry, whose father died in 1607 and left him £10, seems to have been a driving force behind getting this playing company up and running: he probably invested his inheritance, and, between August and November 1607, borrowed a great deal of money to put towards the theatrical enterprise. His theatrical expenditures seem to have left Barry with little money for himself: in March 1608, Nicholas Haley, baker, brought a lawsuit against Barry, for non-payment of 40 shillings for 'dozens of bread'.

The playing company in Whitefriars was a complicated venture, with a large number of shareholders, separately and jointly bound for large sums of money. The venture was speculative (the London theatrical market was always very tight) and, as a number of internecine lawsuits indicate, somewhat contentious. Still, there is no reason to assume the company might not have succeeded if a long plague had not closed the theatres in mid-1608. While Mary Bly (2000) and other critics have generally found the eight known plays of the King's Revels to be 'tawdry and imitative', there is also a vital consistency across the repertory – a sense of close collaboration among the playwrights and of an intimate, familiar engagement between the playwrights and their imagined audiences. The plays are bawdy, funny, and wildly theatrical: it is easy to see how they might have appealed to students from the nearby Inns of Court (or even other playwrights – Ben Jonson's *Epicene* borrows a great deal from *Ram-alley*), or to theatre-goers from elsewhere in London, seeking an evening of rowdy entertainment in a bad part of town. But for the untimely plague, Barry might today be a more immediately recognizable figure in the pantheon of early modern dramatists.

Ram-alley takes its name from an alley in Whitefriars (probably very near to the theatre itself) which was known as a haunt for disreputable types – 'cookes, alemen, and laundresses' as Barry puts it in his play. The overlap between dramatic location and the theatre's location suggests that Barry was interested in the theatrical possibilities of local culture – a playwright immersed in his milieu. But the play's protagonist, Will Smallshanks, is a young man who, having squandered all the

money his father has given him, resorts to Whitefriars where, with the help of a prostitute, he schemes his way back into city life. The fantasy of success represented in Smallshanks (he bests his father in pursuit of a rich widow), together with Barry's optimistic investment in the theatre company and his behaviour subsequent to its collapse, all suggest that Barry was also interested in success that would take him out of the seedy part of town.

After the collapse of the King's Revels, Barry's inability to pay his debts landed him in the Marshalsea prison. He was bailed out and immediately left town. On 13 August 1608, Barry and some companions hijacked a Flemish fishing boat on the Thames, and by early 1609 Barry was in Ireland, working as a pirate on a ship called the *Fly*. In 1609, the *Fly* was taken by a king's ship and most of its crew were tried and executed in London. Those executed included two men, Roger Notting and Richard Baker, whom Barry actually seems to have shanghaied aboard. Notting had sold Barry a horse on credit in London and, by a remarkable coincidence, bumped into Barry in Ireland while visiting his brother-in-law Baker. Perhaps improvising his way out of a jam, Barry invited the men aboard the *Fly* and got them drunk and sleepy; when they awoke, they were at sea.

Astonishingly, Barry himself was not punished for piracy. It is just possible that, when the ship was taken, he fabricated a connection to nobility, taking advantage of the fact that his father's coat of arms was that of the cadets of the Lords Barry of Ireland, and that one of those Lords Barry was an Admiralty commissioner in piracy in 1609. Not insignificantly, literary historians through the early twentieth century were uncertain whether Barry's first name (abbreviated 'Lo.' on *Ram-alley*'s title page) was 'Lodowick' or 'Lording', and whether or not he was a lord himself ('Lodowick, Lord Barry') or nicknamed ('Lording') because the son of a lord.

Barry's father was not a lord; he was a fishmonger, and in 1611 Barry became free of the Company of Fishmongers as well. In

1617 he had another nearly disastrous priva-teering adventure, as part of Sir Walter Ralegh's gold-mining expedition to Guyana. Back in London, Barry became part-owner of a trading vessel called the *Edward of London,* whose principal owner was Edward Bennett, a com-missioner of Virginia at the court of England. This ship was, in 1627, granted a letter of marque to take pirates and enemy ships. Barry's career at sea seems to have come full circle.

Barry wrote no other plays and seems not to have married or had children. His niece Hannah Scarburgh, however, emigrated to Virginia, and had children and grandchildren there. Some small genetic remnant of Barry was, perhaps, at last enjoying the riches and freedom of a new world which the playwright had so vigorously pursued.

SEE ALSO: Jonson, Ben; Ralegh, Walter

REFERENCES AND SUGGESTED READINGS

Adams, J. Q. (1912) Lordinge (alias 'Lodowick') Barry. *Modern Philology* 9(4), 567–570.

Bly, Mary (2000) *Queer virgins and virgin queans on the early modern stage.* Oxford University Press, Oxford.

Cathcart, Charles (2005) Authorship, indebtedness, and the Children of the King's Revels. *Studies in English Literature, 1500–1900* 45(2), 357–374.

Ewen, C. L. (1938) *Lording Barry, poet and pirate.* Privately printed, London.

Hillebrand, Harold (1926) *The child actors.* University of Illinois Press, Urbana.

Ingram, William (1985) The playhouse as an invest-ment, 1607–14: Thomas Woodford and White-friars. *Medieval and Renaissance Drama in England* 2, 209–230.

Basset, Mary Roper Clarke

BRENDA M. HOSINGTON

Among the learned women of the mid-Tudor period, Mary Roper Clarke Basset (1526/30–1572) stands out for the excellence of her two works, both models of accurate, eloquent,

and fluent translation, one from Greek, the other from Latin. The first is a Latin rendering of book I of Eusebius's fourth-century *Ecclesi-astical history,* followed by an English rendering of the first five books. This was a particularly ambitious undertaking and her Latin version was abandoned, Mary says in her dedicatory epistle to Mary Tudor (now British Library, Harley MS 1860), only because 'a greate learned man' (John Christopherson, one of her former tutors) had just finished his version. Eusebius's Greek was particularly challenging; his text was a web of cultural, historical and theological references; and the only printed copy, dated 1544, contained many errors. Mary's second translation is an English rendering of her grandfather Thomas More's *De tristitia, tedio, pauore et oratione Christi ante captionem eius,* his last work, written in difficult circumstances in the Tower. Mary not only translates this text, entitling it *Of the sorowe, werinesse, feare, and prayer of Christ before hys taking,* but also edits it, supplying missing references and emending More's original when necessary.

Born probably between 1526 and 1530, Mary was the second daughter of the equally learned Margaret Roper, née More, herself a translator and renowned for her knowledge of Greek and Latin, and William Roper, trained at Lincoln's Inn, a member of parliament, and the author of the first biography of More. From one letter written by John Morwen to William and another by Roger Ascham to Mary, we know that Margaret sought the best tutors possible for her daughter and that the young woman was a talented linguist. We also know, from certain features of Mary's translations, that she followed closely in the footsteps of both her mother, who had translated Erasmus's *Precatio domenica* a quarter of a century before, and her grandfather, respecting their translating prin-ciples and sharing their love of the classical languages. Both mother and daughter also played a crucial role in defending More's rep-utation and perpetuating his memory through his writings.

A few biographical details can be gleaned from Mary's two translations. Her Eusebius was composed between 1547 and 1553, since in her dedicatory epistle she mentions King Edward VI and calls her dedicatee 'the Lady Mary'. She describes herself as the widow of Stephen Clarke. He was the son of a well-to-do Suffolk clothier and ardent Catholic, and a relative by marriage to William Roper (Guy 2009). Mary also mentions 'learned men' who have seen and approved her translation and friends who have encouraged her to present it to a 'noble personage'. This suggests she was part of a circle of well-educated and well-connected Catholics, one that would soon include the Princess Mary herself. Indeed, in September 1553, Mary was invited to ride in the royal procession in London on the eve of the queen's coronation, along with eight other young women, including one Anne Basset. Both Mary and Anne were subsequently made gentlewomen of the privy chamber and by 1556, Mary had married Anne's brother, James Basset, private secretary to Stephen Gardiner, then to Mary Tudor, and future chief gentleman to Mary's husband King Philip. Basset died in 1558, leaving Mary with one son and pregnant with a second.

In 1557, when her cousin William Rastell needed financial aid for his publication of *The workes of Sir Thomas More, knyght . . . written by him in the Englysh tonge*, Mary was able to come to the rescue. His inclusion of her translation of the *De tristitia Christi* (*Of the sorowe of Christ*) was a gesture of gratitude, although not entirely altruistic, since Mary was very well connected at court. Rastell also certainly had another motive. Since More's original work was written in Latin, not English, it should not normally have been included; however, its subject, the capture and martyrdom of Christ, was particularly valuable in reminding readers of More's own analogous fate and contributing to his rehabilitation; an English translation would make the text available to a far wider audience.

Mary lived for another 15 years after Rastell's publication but nothing is known of her during this time. More's early biographers, although not Roper, tell us she translated the whole of Eusebius, as well as his successors, but none of

these translations is extant. In 1566 she drew up her will, bequeathing lands to one son and jewels and a gold cross to the other, on condition they never become heretics. Mary died on 20 March 1572 and although neither son continued their mother's and grandmother's scholarly pursuits, they did remain in the faith. Both were later involved with Edmund Campion's Catholic Association in England and with recusant establishments on the Continent.

SEE ALSO: Ascham, Roger; More, Thomas; Roper, Margaret; Roper, William

REFERENCES AND SUGGESTED READINGS

Goodrich, Jaime (2010) The dedicatory preface to Mary Roper Clarke Basset's translation of Eusebius' *Ecclesiastical history*. *English Literary Renaissance* 40, 301–328.

Guy, John (2009) *A daughter's love: Thomas More and his dearest Meg*. HarperCollins, London.

Hosington, Brenda (2010) Translation in the service of politics and religion: a family tradition for Thomas More, Margaret Roper and Mary Clarke Basset. In: De Landtsheer, Jeanine & Nellen, Henk (eds) *Between Scylla and Charybdis: learned letter writers navigating the reefs of religious and political controversy in early modern Europe*. Brill, Leiden, pp. 93–108.

Baxter, Richard

TIM COOPER

Richard Baxter (1615–91) was a significant Puritan pastor and author. He was the only child of freehold, Puritan parents. His track into ministry was unusual in that he did not go to university. He remained a voracious reader, sharp thinker, and accomplished autodidact all his life. He is best known for his ministry at Kidderminster where he served for a cumulative total of 14 years, interrupted early on by the Civil War and two years of service as a chaplain in the New Model Army. The town experienced something of a reformation under his ministry, and he looked back on the 1650s as the most rewarding season of his life. During that time he developed a pastoral model he hoped other ministers might follow in order to bring about a comparable, national reformation. He turned to print to advance his various agendas, to engage in controversy, and to minister to his many readers; he wrote 141 books in the course of his life, 37 of them before 1660. His labours at Kidderminster ended with the Restoration. Baxter then became a leading nonconformist figure, and he continued to write and teach whenever possible until his death in 1691. In 1662 he married Margaret Charlton, a woman 21 years his junior who had been among his parishioners at Kidderminster. They had no children; Margaret predeceased him in 1683.

Baxter's experience of the First Civil War (1642–46) provides the most immediate and important context for his career as both pastor and author. His proximity to many of the main battles is striking: he witnessed the first skirmish at Powicke Bridge, was on hand to view the carnage at Edgehill, visited the army at Naseby, and acted as chaplain in Colonel Edward Whalley's regiment as it toiled through the final battles and sieges of the war. Even then, he stayed on to battle the outbreak of bad doctrine he saw among the soldiers. His service ended only with the collapse of his health early in 1647. Sensing death at hand, Baxter began to write his funeral sermon. It was, in fact, the beginning of a very long writing career.

Baxter rarely showed any great interest in brevity; this funeral sermon quickly blossomed into the four-part, 856-page *Saints everlasting rest*, first published in 1650. It became a devotional classic, running through eight editions in the 1650s and is still in print today. In it Baxter encourages his readers to cultivate the disciplined habit of meditating on heaven. Not surprisingly, the work is coloured by his experience of the trauma that he and England have both just endured. The injunction to think on heaven acknowledges the very dismal reality of life on earth, especially during a time of civil war 'when nothing appears to our sight, but ruine . . . scarce a month, scarce a week, without

the sight or noise of blood. Surely there is none of this in Heaven.' While the work was not received without controversy, it helped to shape his reputation as a warm-hearted, spiritually minded pastor.

A second book emerged from that crisis of ill health, *The aphorismes of justification*, published in 1649. Still writing his funeral sermon, Baxter had come to Matthew 25, where Christ judges the sheep and the goats. At that moment a 'great light that I could not resist' came upon him; in an experience not unlike a religious conversion his soteriological system was entirely recast, 'and I suddenly wrote down the bare propositions'. He presented those propositions in *The aphorismes of justification*. This new system remained Calvinist. Indeed, the first 10 pages of the book are strikingly so. But the remaining 300 pages warded off any potential abuse of Calvinist doctrine. And the most flagrant abusers were, in Baxter's mind, the Antinomians, whom he had encountered in the army. Leading Antinomian authors such as the army chaplains John Saltmarsh and William Dell, along with the lately published Tobias Crisp, adhered very literally to the Protestant nostrum that the believer is justified by faith alone through grace without works. Baxter's new system was the mirror image of Antinomian theology as he understood it, an elaborate network of qualifications that preserved a place for obedience in the scheme of salvation. He distinguished between God's will of purpose, by which the elect shall infallibly be saved, and his will of precept, by which each believer must provide his or her own 'evangelical righteousness' in order to be saved. That required faith, which comprised repentance, obedience, and lifelong perseverance. *Pace* the Antinomians, Christ did not supply the believer's righteousness in the place of the believer; he supplied the 'legal righteousness' the law demanded, but other conditions had still to be met.

The book's reception was mixed, at best. Several people wrote privately to Baxter expressing their appreciation, but the public response was unmistakably hostile. What was, to him, merely a preventative against the Antinomian disease seemed to many others a betrayal of the Calvinist cause. By arguing for some sort of human contribution, even if only a 'pepper corn', as a condition of salvation, Baxter seemed to have moved beyond the hypothetical universalism that marked out moderate Calvinism into something like Arminianism or even, with his cautious talk of merit, Catholicism. Faced with such accusations and criticisms, he was thrown irreparably on the defensive. In private manuscripts, he responded at length to a series of animadversions of the *Aphorismes*. In public, he issued his *Apology* in 1654. This massive work was a compilation of five discrete books against the main authors who had taken him to task. In all of these defensive manoeuvres, Baxter gave little ground. His concessions amounted only to matters of style; his one regret was to have rushed the book into print without a more careful consideration of some of his choice of words. For that reason, 'I do repent that ever I published it.' *Rich: Baxter's confession of his faith* (1655) was a more positive statement of his theology designed to rectify some of the damage the *Aphorismes* had done without abandoning the system it expounded, mainly by presenting Baxter's soteriology as a middle way between Arminianism and Antinomianism.

The *Confession* marks something of an end point to the trail of wreckage left behind by the *Aphorismes*, in the year in which Baxter's restless concern with the Antinomians began noticeably to abate. In its place, a much more positive agenda emerged: national unity and godly reformation. Much of the energy of the Interregnum was spent in search of a religious settlement that would remedy the imperfections of the former system along Puritan lines and put an end to the present confusion in which the fragmented state of the English church left it largely bereft of central direction and countrywide consistency. But it was much easier for the Puritans to agree on what they did not like than it was to agree on what they wanted to put in its place. This was especially fraught, given that complex political forces were at work. The Congregationalist architects of the Interregnum church – men like Philip Nye, Thomas Goodwin, and John Owen – supported a national church but with room for more than one congregation in each parish, allowing the godly to gather together with a degree of purity of worship and membership impossible in the parish church. They also favoured a policy of toleration that involved freedom of worship for those who were of orthodox belief; that is, for those whose theology was consistent with the 'fundamentals' of the faith.

Increasingly, Baxter inserted himself into all these debates, and, again, his war experience helped to shape his concerns. It left him with an understandable aversion to social disorder and national disunity. Returning to Kidderminster, he had to restore a sense of order from the ground up, and he did this extremely successfully. The innovation he introduced was to catechize not just children, but adults as well. Once a year each family in the parish was invited to meet with him or his assistant to receive instruction and to assess the state of their souls. In this way, Baxter was able to transform the effectiveness of parish discipline, thereby negating the main argument of the Congregationalists that the parish system was too much a mixed bag of impure members and worship. His system was, then, a vocal affirmation of the parish system. Baxter believed it was sheer laziness, and the death of evangelism, to abandon the hard work of discipline for the easy road of gathering only the visibly godly. Though costly and time-consuming, Baxter's system of annual visitations helped to bring about an effective reformation in the parish. He also added another layer: the Worcestershire Association. This voluntary group of ministers from differing ecclesiological parties within the county met monthly for teaching (often provided by Baxter), mutual encouragement, and to handle the most difficult cases of discipline in their respective congregations. It 'set the benchmark for pastoral ministry during the remainder of the

Interregnum' (Lim 2004). In 1653 Baxter wrote *Christian concord* on behalf of the association. It laid out the agreement the ministers had reached for the administration of discipline; it included the profession of faith that would serve as a test of orthodoxy and as the basis of their theological unity; and it concluded with a long explication of the propositions written in Baxter's own name. The book made its mark. By 1654 Baxter had gained enough national credibility to be invited to join a group of divines assembled to advise parliament in its search for the elusive list of fundamentals of the faith.

Baxter's ecclesiological writings during the remainder of the 1650s were designed to do two things. First, he wanted to promote to other ministers the Kidderminster model of systematic adult catechizing. He wrote *The reformed pastor*, first published in 1656 and also still in print today, to that end. Secondly, he wanted to bring together the main parties who broadly agreed on a national church with some form of discipline. Beginning in the first edition of *The saints everlasting rest* and advocated in many other contexts, both public and private, he urged that a small number of representatives from each party be brought together to thrash out a basis for unity that would recognize all the points they had in common while allowing each its own distinctive positions in matters that were not of fundamental importance. Thus he supported the search for a list of fundamentals, as long as it did not go beyond the words of Scripture in defining those essential beliefs, since Scripture was the only thing on which all parties could be guaranteed to agree. And he was broadly comfortable tolerating those who adhered to the fundamentals, but he never countenanced splitting off into effectively rival congregations in the one parish. Despite numerous setbacks and discouragements, Baxter never stopped advocating a consistent scheme for national unity. The only change he made was to allow a place for the Baptists among the parties he wanted to bring together in the late 1650s. He had begun the decade attacking them in *Plain Scripture proof of infants church-membership* (1651) but by

early 1659 he had some hopes of finding unity with the moderates among them.

Cultivating and maintaining disunity in the English church was, in Baxter's mind, the special project of the Roman Catholics, and his opposition to them is another important strand in his publications in the later 1650s. While he showed uncommon sympathy for Catholic soteriology and was famously reluctant to call the pope the Antichrist, Baxter retained a consistent fear of papist political subversion in England. In *The Grotian religion discovered* (1658) he alerted the nation to a plot to reunite the English church with the Catholic Church along moderate French Catholic lines. Ongoing division in the English church simply played into the hands of the plotters. Baxter regarded the Quakers as advancing papist objectives and he attacked them as well, beginning with *The Quakers catechism* in 1655.

In the midst of these controversial writings Baxter kept up an impressive stream of devotional works that further enhanced the reputation he had gained with *The saints everlasting rest*. In this vein, his most notable works were *The right method for a settled peace of conscience* (1653), *A treatise of conversion* (1657), *A call to the unconverted* (1658), and *Directions and perswasions to a sound conversion* (1658). These works often comprised the content of sermons he delivered from the pulpit at Kidderminster. They offer evidence of his evangelistic and pastoral concern. These books sold well and enjoyed a generally positive reception. Part of that can be attributed to Baxter's engaging and autobiographical writing style. In the words of the historian Geoffrey Nuttall, 'there is something about Baxter's writing which I find peculiarly affecting: the style, the self-expression, is so direct, penetrating, sure, yet so sincerely modest, almost ingenuous, and produces a strange feeling that that the man is personally present, at least that he wrote this only yesterday and wrote it to *you*' (Nuttall 1967). Baxter consistently showed a remarkable (and sometimes exhausting) comprehensiveness and a particularly shrewd understanding of human nature. His devotional works reveal him at his most appealing. Even he distinguished between his devotional and his controversial works, but there is a danger of misrepresenting Baxter by focusing only on the devotional works, especially as only those works were republished in the eighteenth century (and are still available today). Baxter's manner could also be rude, arrogant, tactless, sharp, and offensive. There was no shortage of people he offended in the course of his life, and even he conceded that his determination to speak the truth could come across as overly personal and critical. Despite his genuine desire for peace, his methods invariably extended controversy and provoked further division and argument, from the very beginning until the very end. As William Lamont (1979) puts it, 'The pathos in his career is the gap between magnanimous aim and divisive means.' Baxter simply could not keep himself out of his writing. That is what makes him so engaging, then and now, but it means that in his published works we see him at his best and at his worst. Both sides of the man must be comprehended.

By the late 1650s, Baxter looked for all the world like an author at the height of his powers. He published nine books in 1657 and eight more in 1658; *The saints everlasting rest* appeared in its seventh edition and sales showed no signs of slowing. Baxter had discovered that the English climate under Oliver Cromwell was surprisingly conducive to the kind of fruit he was trying to grow, and that seemed only more apparent with the advent of his more benign son, Richard, in 1658. But in 1659 things went horribly wrong. Senior figures in the army, and their Congregationalists allies, effectively brought down Richard's government. Baxter's hopes for national unity and reformation, then at their height, came crashing down with it. This is the decisive event of his career, not least in the way Baxter himself conceived it. Worse still, just as Richard fell, Baxter published his only work in political theory, *A holy commonwealth* (1659), which set out his views on civil government and explained why he supported Parliament in the war. The book offers good evidence of Baxter's

poor political timing; it was among those burned at Oxford University in 1683.

During the late 1650s, then, Baxter came as close as he would ever get to the kind of reformation he desired. With characteristic political ineptitude he played a part in discussions that led to the Restoration settlement in religion; he became one of the foremost leaders among those excluded by the terms of that settlement. As opportunity allowed, he continued to publish a prodigious amount. As he aged, he also sustained a warm pastoral heart shaped by extensive experience of human nature and affairs. He wrote his autobiography in stages during the Restoration period, published as *Reliquiae Baxterianae* in 1696. It is a lucrative source for seventeenth-century English history, but it must also be read cautiously as a project in self-justification. Baxter's post-1660 career is remarkably accomplished, especially given the conditions within which he worked, but it is difficult to avoid the impression that the period of the Interregnum saw the best of Baxter, the years in which his reputation as a skilled writer and pastor was well earned.

SEE ALSO: sermons

REFERENCES AND SUGGESTED READINGS

Black, J. William (2004) *Reformation pastors: Richard Baxter and the ideal of the reformed pastor.* Paternoster Press, Carlisle.

Boersma, Hans (1993) *A hot pepper corn: Richard Baxter's doctrine of justification in its seventeenth-century context of controversy.* Boekencentrum, Zoetermeer.

Cooper, Tim (2001) *Fear and polemic in seventeenth-century England: Richard Baxter and Antinomianism.* Ashgate, Aldershot.

Keeble, N. H. (1982) *Richard Baxter, Puritan man of letters.* Clarendon Press, Oxford.

Keeble, N. H. & Nuttall, Geoffrey F. (eds) (1991) *Calendar of the correspondence of Richard Baxter.* 2 vols. Clarendon Press, Oxford.

Lamont, William M. (1979) *Richard Baxter and the millennium: Protestant imperialism and the English Revolution.* Croom Helm, London.

Lamont, William M. (1996) *Puritanism and historical controversy*. UCL Press, London.

Lim, Paul Chang-Ha (2004) *In pursuit of purity, unity and liberty: Richard Baxter's Puritan ecclesiology in its seventeenth-century context*. Brill, Leiden.

Nuttall, Geoffrey F. (1965) *Richard Baxter*. Nelson, London.

Nuttall, Geoffrey F. (1967) The personality of Richard Baxter. In: Nuttall, Geoffrey F. (ed.) *The holy spirit: essays and addresses*. Epworth Press, London, pp. 104–117.

Packer, J. I. (2003) *The redemption and restoration of man in the thought of Richard Baxter*. Paternoster Press, Carlisle.

Powicke, Frederick J. (1924) *A life of the Reverend Richard Baxter 1615–1691*. Jonathan Cape, London.

Powicke, Frederick J. (1927) *The Reverend Richard Baxter under the cross (1662–1691)*. Jonathan Cape, London.

Bayly, Lewis

TIFFANY JO WERTH

Lewis Bayly (c.1575–1631), bishop of Bangor and author of one of the most popular and enduring manuals of Christian piety, enters literary history as an in-joke. The 'shee-puritan' or 'Shee-precise Hypocrite' caricatured in John Earle's 1627 *Micro-cosmographie* wields as her weapon to cudgel her maids *The practise of pietie*, Bayly's phenomenally successful guide to living the good life. Often expanded and reissued, the text's initial date of publication is unknown.

Bayly was probably born in Carmarthen, but little of his early life and education is known. He was, by some accounts, quarrelsome and grasping, an intolerant vigilante and an embezzler suspected of illicit passions, impiously nicknamed 'my Lord Bang-whore'. A courtier within the clerical hierarchy, Bayly wrangled, and some say bought, his way into notoriety. Although scant evidence exists for his early formal education, he acquired significant learning in biblical and classical subjects and became a renowned preacher. Despite his

criticism of the monarchy (he was imprisoned briefly for denouncing Prince Charles's proposed Spanish marriage and had a 'hot encounter' with James I over his opposition to the royal *Book of sports*), he curried royal favour. Chaplain first to Prince Henry, who died in 1612, Bayly quickly dedicated his 1613 edition of *Practise* to the new Prince of Wales, Charles, perhaps to garner royal attention for the diocese of Bangor. He found himself in 'extraordinary favour' with James I's favourite, George Villiers, first duke of Buckingham in 1626, which probably aggravated his case before the House of Commons where he was accused of simony and 'incontinency the most palpably proved that ever I heard' (Hill 1988). Bayly justified himself against such malicious accusations and proved vigilant against perceived Catholic recusants. He died leaving substantial property and was buried in Bangor Cathedral.

The irony of an 'incontinent' prelate who counselled discretion and a 'plaine description' for how every 'every Christian should competently endeavour' to live a modest life seems not to have troubled his contemporaries, and newly amplified editions of Bayly's devotional guide sold briskly to godly readers. Within its compact, but thick, duodecimo format, *The practise of pietie* offers practical guidance on: prayer in the mornings, in the evenings, and on special occasions; reading the Bible through once a year; meditations on important doctrinal issues such as Sabbath-keeping; observing fasts and communion; persevering through sickness; practising the *ars moriendi*; and identifying 'Christs Martyrs' (denied inclusion are those who die for 'popery'). Its iconic frontispiece depicts a gentleman at prayer, dressed in an elaborate fur-trimmed coat. Behind him rests an open Bible; before him, prayers ascend to a chorus of angels, who hover above a flaming heart on an altar. The eye-catching imagery suggests how the busy layman might use pious tools in order to join a spiritual – and social – elite. It promises a well-dressed humbleness.

Despite Bayly's popular success at home and abroad (his work was translated into

French, Welsh, German, Polish, Romanian, Hungarian, and a Native American language), when recalled by scholars of literature, he is frequently the butt of comparison to later, and most literary critics agree, better authors. His meditations are 'stones in a wall' to the 'great chords of music' made by men such as Thomas Traherne and Henry Vaughan (Stranks 1961; Day 1988). Bayly's sober reflections on the soul's miseries are remembered as the dull antidote to the licentious romances and ribald jestbooks that Arthur Dent's 'caviler' adored. His book is a literary footnote, credited for the spiritual quickening of John Bunyan, prompting him to put down the tales of King Arthur and Bevis of Hampton to take up the trials of Pilgrim. Yet this unassuming Puritan devotional discipline was an instant classic, with some 60 editions in print during the seventeenth century alone. One might speculate that it both had a role in the development of early Stuart prose and reached across the Atlantic to shape the emerging literature of New England and America.

Bayly's devotional guide indeed exceeds its caricature. In the process of providing a Puritan catechism, he demonstrates a virtuosic prose range. When writing on the explanation for God, or the doctrine of the Trinity, his sentences take on an almost Baconian cadence, with characteristic aphoristic, balanced clauses that produce a dispassionate proto-scientific language. 'The *third person* is named the *holy ghost*,' he intones as if cataloguing flora and fauna from a New World colony, 'first, because hee is *spirituall* without a body: secondly, because he is *spired*, and as it were breathed from both the *Father* and the *Sonne*, that is, proceedeth from them both.' In other sections, when for instance he meditates on the 'the Soules Soliloquy, ravished in contemplating the Passions of her Lord', his prose becomes confrontational, densely metaphysical in its conceit and rich with hortatory oratory. 'But, O my Lord, though knowest, that since that losse of thine image . . . I cannot love thee with all my might, and my minde, as I should,' Bayly cries in prose that approaches

the agonized voice of Donne's Holy Sonnets, 'therefore as thou didst first cast they love upon mee, when I was a *childe of wrath*, and a lumpe of the lost and condemned world; so now, I beseech thee, shead abroad thy love by thy spirits through all my faculties and affections.' Such a stylistic and formal diversity well suits the Anglican need at once to scorn the obsessive devotions of papists and yet, in the end, to seek exactly this depth of religiosity. It is a text whose proclaimed 'plainness' and habituation to basic routines reveals a paradoxical love for ritual and flourish. It registers the contradictions and unique triumphs of the Church of England's middle way as a cultural and historical phenomenon.

His legacy continues albeit predominantly among Christian readers. Bayly's 'plain' guide remains available in multiple languages and media: the Kindle edition came out in 2010. After over 800 pages, Bayly concludes the 1616 *Practise of pietie*: 'if thou wilt not bestoy on mee the loaves, yet, Lord, deny mee not the crums of they mercy; and those shall suffice they hungrie handmaid.' His plea presciently realizes its crumb-like place within the English canon, yet, like the proverbial loaves and fishes, from it multitudes have been fed.

SEE ALSO: Bunyan, John; Donne, John; Traherne, Thomas; Vaughan, Henry

REFERENCES AND SUGGESTED READINGS

Day, Hilary (1988) Bayly's *The practice of piety*: a new source for Henry Vaughan's *The mount of olives*. *Notes and Queries* 35(2), 163–165.

Fincham, Kenneth (1990) *Prelate as pastor: the episcopate of James I*. Clarendon Press, Oxford.

Green, Ian (2000) *Print and Protestantism in early modern England*. Oxford University Press, Oxford.

Hambrick-Stowe, Charles (1982) *The practice of piety: Puritan devotional disciplines in seventeenth-century New England*. University of North Carolina Press, Chapel Hill.

Heal, Felicity & Holmes, Clive (1994) *The gentry in England and Wales, 1500–1700*. Stanford University Press, Stanford.

Hill, Christopher (1988) *A tinker and a poor man: John Bunyan and his church, 1628–1688.* Alfred Knopf, New York.

Sasek, Lawrence A. (1961) *The literary temper of the English Puritans.* Louisiana State University Press, Baton Rouge.

Stranks, Charles James (1961) *Anglican devotion: studies in the spiritual life of the Church of England between the Reformation and the Oxford movement.* SCM Press, London.

Wright, Louis B. (1935) *Middle-class culture in Elizabethan England.* University of North Carolina Press, Chapel Hill.

Beaufort, Margaret

BRENDA M. HOSINGTON

Lady Margaret Beaufort, countess of Richmond and Derby (1443–1509), exercised considerable power in the political arena of her day, especially after her son, Henry Tudor, became king of England in 1485. However, she was also an active patron of learning, using her remarkable intellectual ability and energy to encourage scholars, support university education, finance the publication of both religious and secular works, and study and translate spiritual writings for her own and others' edification.

Born in 1443 to John Beaufort, grandson of John of Gaunt and Katherine Swynford, in the very year he suffered military disgrace and banishment from court, Margaret became acquainted at an early age with the intrigues and uncertainties of the courtier's life. She was betrothed at six, released from the contract at 10, married at 12 to Edmund Tudor, and widowed, six months pregnant, one year later. In 1457 she married Henry Stafford, second son of Humphrey Stafford, duke of Buckingham, and like herself a Lancastrian supporter. Five years later, the Yorkist Edward IV made her son Henry a ward of William, Lord Herbert, but Margaret maintained contact with him, energetically consolidating his finances and preparing his future. In September 1471, believing he could be perceived as a Lancastrian pretender to the throne, Margaret had him flee to France. One month later Stafford died and within eight months Margaret remarried, this time to a wealthier and more powerful courtier, Thomas Stanley, second Baron Stanley. She spent the next decade dividing her time between their estates and court but also unsuccessfully negotiating her son's rehabilitation. In 1483 she became embroiled in the rebellion by Buckingham against Richard III, for which she was severely punished. Success was finally hers with Henry Tudor's military victory at the battle of Bosworth in 1485, and his subsequent marriage to Elizabeth Woodville, a bride chosen by Margaret.

Her relationship with Henry would never weaken and Margaret, now *femme sole* and thus independent of her husband in legal matters, became a wealthy landowner in her own right and enjoyed a special status at court, wielding privilege and influence. She reached the pinnacle of her power in the two decades leading up to her death in 1509 and it is at this time that she turned to the intellectual and spiritual pursuits that would mark her final years. These too were characterized by the practical streak that had governed her political and social activities and similarly enabled her to establish networks of power.

Margaret's interest in education extended to all levels of schooling. She financed the primary instruction and apprenticeships of children living in her household, supported choral scholars from her chapel at Eton, and sent students to Oxford and Cambridge. Her patronage of both universities was extremely generous, with endowed lectureships in theology, a preachership at Cambridge, and other gifts made to Jesus College and Queens' College, where her former chaplain, John Fisher, was president. Her grandest gestures, however, were reserved for refounding God's House as Christ's College and establishing a new college, St John's, which she did not live to see.

Margaret's interest in learning also manifested itself in a practical way, with her support of the nascent book trade through patronage of the first printers and the purchase and dissemination of religious works, particularly with regard to the Syon Bridgettine monastery. Her first commissioned book was a French romance from William Caxton in 1489 but this was followed by a devotional work, one of his final publications. His successor, Wynkyn de Worde, also enjoyed Margaret's patronage, printing commissioned religious works like Walter Hilton's *Scala perfectionis* and John Fisher's sermons, but also, as he claims, Sebastian Brant's *Shyppe of fooles*.

Richard Pynson, too, was entrusted with various works, among which were Margaret's own translations. These are quite remarkable for two reasons. First, neither of the two devotional texts Margaret translated had ever been turned into English. Book IV of the most significant work of the *devotio moderna*, *De imitatione Christi*, was not included in the manuscripts available in England and thus found no place in William Atkinson's English translation, itself commissioned by Margaret in 1503. However, when she encountered a complete French translation, she translated book IV and added it to Atkinson's version. Entitled *A ful deuout gostely treatyse of the imytacion and folowynge the blessed lyfe of our sauyour cryste*, the volume was published in 1503, going through six editions and reprintings by 1528 and remaining unrivalled for 28 years, when its new translator nevertheless asserted he had retained its 'substaunce' and 'effect'. The second text, Jacobus de Gruytroede's *Speculum aureum animae peccatricis*, a 'mirror' representing the *contemptu mundi* theme in lay terms, was also made available for the first time in English through Margaret's translation of a French version. Her *The mirroure of golde for the synfull soule* was printed in 1506 and went through two new editions in 1522 and 1526.

The other remarkable feature of Margaret's translations is that they were made in the context of a field dominated by male religious elites, namely the translation of monastic Latin devotional texts into vernacular versions suitable for a wider, less educated, lay audience. This dominance certainly characterized English translations. The medieval translator and scribes of the *De imitatione* were all Carthusians, Atkinson was a cleric, the 1531 anonymous translator was a Bridgettine, and the 1584 translator an Anglican clergyman. The 1567 male translator, although not a cleric, was a lawyer. As for the *Speculum*, its only translator was Margaret. She was in fact not only the first to translate these texts into English, but remained the *only* woman to do so until the twentieth century, commanding a place among monks, priests, and university men.

SEE ALSO: Caxton, William

REFERENCES AND SUGGESTED READINGS

Hosington, Brenda M. (2011) Margaret Beaufort's translations as mirrors of piety. In: White, Micheline (ed.) *English women, religion, and textual production, 1500–1625*. Ashgate, Aldershot, pp. 185–203.

Jones, Michael K. & Underwood, Malcolm G. (1992) *The king's mother: Lady Margaret Beaufort, countess of Richmond and Derby*. Cambridge University Press, Cambridge.

Powell, Susan (1998) Lady Margaret Beaufort and her books. *The Library* 30, 197–240.

Beaumont, Francis

EDEL LAMB

Francis Beaumont (1584/85–1616), playwright and poet, is most often remembered alongside his theatrical collaborator, John Fletcher. This pair continues to be known for their distinctive dramaturgy, which contributed significantly to the development of tragicomedy and courtly drama in the playhouses of Jacobean and Caroline London.

A member of a Nottinghamshire recusant family, Beaumont was educated at Broadgates Hall (later Pembroke College), Oxford, from 1597 to 1598. From 1600 until 1606 he was a student at the Inns of Court, and during his residence in the Inner Temple he wrote his earliest poetical works. His Ovidian narrative poem *Salmacis and Hermaphroditus* was published anonymously in 1602, and in the same year he wrote a prefatory verse for *The metamorphosis of tobacco* (1602), a poem by his brother, Sir John Beaumont. Francis Beaumont wrote a number of commendatory verses during his career, including one for John Fletcher's *The faithful shepherdess* (c.1609) and a number on the plays of Ben Jonson, as well as various elegies. Some of this poetry is collected in *Poems, by Francis Beaumont, gent* (1640), alongside elegies to the poet himself, including one by the character writer John Earle. Beaumont's position within a community of poets and wits in Renaissance England is further demonstrated by his tribute to the artists who gathered at the Mermaid tavern in 'Master Francis Beaumont's letter to Ben Jonson' (written c.1605).

However, Beaumont was, and continues to be, more widely recognized for his plays and for his position in the theatrical community of early modern London. His first attempt at dramatic writing took place during his residency at the Inns of Court and comprised a mock grammar lecture, probably delivered as part of the Inner Temple's Christmas revels between 1601 and 1606. This piece is often overlooked, yet as a burlesque text it establishes his interest in a form of writing that he would continue to explore as a professional playwright.

Beaumont's subsequent dramatic works were, for the most part, written for the professional London theatres. They are contained in two often examined folio editions of the *Comedies and tragedies, written by Francis Beaumont and John Fletcher, gentlemen* printed in 1647 and 1679. The first folio collection, probably modelled on the collected works of Shakespeare and Jonson, was a shrewd economic venture by the King's Men, the playing company with which both Beaumont and Fletcher finished their careers. The troupe sold the playwrights' scripts in their possession for publication at this time of playhouse closure. However, the collected edition may also have capitalized on nostalgia for earlier times during this period of civil war (Finkelpearl 1990).

Whatever the motive, the seventeenth-century folios firmly established the connection between these two dramatists, who, according to John Aubrey, lived as well as worked together.

Beaumont's plays are, therefore, the products of a collaborative venture. Collaboration was integral to the professional theatres of early seventeenth-century London. Playwrights worked together to produce scripts; they added to and revised earlier plays; and censors, managers, and players altered the play during the processes of production – an aspect recognized by the stationer of the 1647 folio collection, Humphrey Moseley, who claims to provide readers with 'both All that was *Acted*, and all that was not'. These collaborative processes and the particular practices of the relevant playing company are crucial to an evaluation of the plays of any early modern dramatist. They have been allocated heightened significance in critical scholarship on Beaumont's works as bibliographic and textual scholars in the nineteenth and twentieth centuries have attempted to determine his precise contributions to this collection of plays (Oliphant 1927; Hoy 1956–62). Such scholarship has revealed that the 1647 folio collection, in fact, contained a limited amount of Beaumont's theatrical work. It does include his sole-authored masque, *The maskue of the gentlemen of Grayes-Inne and the Inner Temple*, written as part of the 1613 marriage celebrations of Princess Elizabeth to Frederick V, elector palatine, rather than for the professional playhouses, and some plays that he co-authored with Fletcher (*The coxcomb*, *The captain*, and *The noble gentleman*, and possibly also *Loves pilgrimage*, *Loves cure*, and *The beggars bush*). However, his other works (the sole-authored *The Knight of the Burning Pestle*, and the co-authored *The woman hater*, *The scorneful ladie*, *Philaster*, *The maids tragedie*, *A king and no king*, and possibly also *Thierry and Theodoret*) are absent from this edition and later appeared in the second folio as part of the Beaumont and Fletcher canon. The remaining 29 plays in the 1647 edition were not only by Fletcher, but have been shown to incorporate the hands of Shakespeare, Philip Massinger, and Nathan Field. As a result, many late twentieth-century and early twenty-first-century critics have followed Jeffrey Masten's (1992) line of argument that authorship is indeterminable in this collaborative theatre, and consequently refer to all the plays from these folios as the drama of 'Beaumont and Fletcher'.

Beaumont and Fletcher's partnership began at an early stage in both their careers as professional dramatists for the children's playing companies. They wrote for two of these troupes (the Children of Paul's and the Children of the Queen's Revels), which were composed mostly of young children who performed in the indoor theatres at St Paul's, the Blackfriars and the Whitefriars under the mastership of theatre managers. The working relationship between the two writers may have commenced as early as 1606 when the boy players of Paul's performed *The woman hater*. This play was suited to the repertoires of the children's companies, which were characterized by their self-reflexive commentaries on theatre practices and were well known for their satirical elements. *The woman hater* offers a satirical representation of the court, and also provides comic observations on out-of-date inductions and verse prologues in its mocking prose prologue. This opening technique sets the tone for the innovative drama produced throughout Beaumont's career in questioning conventions of genre as well as of staging when it states 'I dare not call it Comedie, or Tragedie'.

Beaumont and Fletcher, working separately on their next plays, continued to disrupt generic expectations within the context of the children's companies. While Fletcher famously defended the generic form of tragicomedy in the publication of his Children of the Queen's Revels' play, *The faithful shepherdess*, around 1609, Beaumont wrote his most experimental piece, *The Knight of the Burning Pestle*, for performance by this children's company around 1607. This play presents a city comedy, *The London merchant*, interrupted by fictional audience members who insist on having their apprentice, Rafe, perform a new plot which runs alongside and at times intersects with the original plot. The narrative is derived from chivalric romance, and through its comic presentation Beaumont mocks many contemporary plays. It also, as Lucy Munro (2006) points out, combines elements from a range of sources (dramatic and non-dramatic romance, comedy, tragedy, ballads and songs) to change the genre itself into 'something that is capable of both literary and social satire'. Unfortunately, this experimentation (one of the most admired aspects of Beaumont's work in the twenty-first century) proved too radical for the play's original audience, and when Walter Burre published the play in 1613, he admitted that they had 'utterly rejected it'.

In spite of this, Beaumont continued to engage interestingly with a range of genres in subsequent plays for the Children of the Queen's Revels co-written with Fletcher. *Cupids revenge*, a tragedy that adapted material from Philip Sidney's *Arcadia* and, according to Philip Finkelpearl (1990), created the character type of the antihero appropriate to the Jacobean and Caroline age, was performed around 1607–8; *The coxcomb*, a comedy partially based on part one of *Don Quixote*, around 1608; and *The scorneful ladie*, a city comedy showing the young heir how to act in order to achieve money and women, around 1609–10. This last play is exemplary of the playwrights' tendencies to direct much of their drama towards the young gentry, and goes some way towards explaining the humorous suggestion of James Shirley that the plays of Beaumont and Fletcher 'were usually of more advantage to the hopefull young Heire, then a costly, dangerous, forraigne Travell' to the 'young spirits of the Time'. It was one of their most popular plays, appearing in quarto format 10 times in the seventeenth century and performed steadily until the mid-eighteenth century. One of these performances in particular emphasizes early modern regard for the play: in 1641/42, it was the only play performed at court during the Christmas season.

Around 1608, the playwrights also began writing for the King's Men. Beaumont co-wrote *Philaster, The captain, The maids tragedy, A king and no king*, and possibly also *The noble gentleman, Loves cure, Loves pilgrimage, Thierry and Theodoret*, and *The beggars bush* for performance by this company. As Suzanne Gossett (2007) has suggested, the move of the two dramatists to the adult company may have been prompted in part by the unstable position of the Children of the Queen's Revels, who had been temporarily dissolved in 1608 and 1609, but it provided an opportunity for them to find a new framework for their plays, perhaps influenced by, but also influencing, this company's most well-known playwright, Shakespeare. Beaumont and Fletcher's first play for this troupe, *Philaster* (performed between 1608 and 1610), was their first successful tragedy and was also the play that, according to John Dryden's later praise, first brought them 'Esteem'. Although *Philaster* signals a fresh direction in the playwrights' work, its treatment of the motif of cross-dressing also demonstrates the ongoing influence of their early careers in the children's companies. The female disguised as a page is a common theme in prose romance, one which Beaumont draws on a number of occasions in his dramatic work, and also on the Renaissance stage, used famously in Shakespearean comedies such as *Twelfth night* and *As you like it. Philaster* uses this trope in the character of Euphrasia, who is disguised as the page, Bellario. Yet by withholding knowledge of this disguise from the audience until the final scene, the play disrupts the audience's expectations of narrative conventions (a recurrent feature of Beaumont's drama) and utilizes a technique of audience surprise that was more common in the children's theatres.

Cross-dressing, gender, and sexuality are recurrent themes in Beaumont and Fletcher's plays for the King's Men, and recent scholarship on both playwrights has analysed the political undercurrents of their depictions of these themes. Sandra Clark (1994), for example, has suggested that the theatrical strategies deployed in the representation of these topics provide a medium for exploring, and even critiquing, power, and particularly royal authority. Therefore, although Samuel Taylor Coleridge emphasized the royalist dimension of Beaumont and Fletcher's plays – a dimension that has been invoked as an explanation for their popularity in the Restoration – to dismiss them as 'the most servile *jure divino* royalists' (Clark 1994), Beaumont's King's Men plays have also been interpreted as politicized interrogations of the authority of the king. An examination of royal lineage in *A king and no king*, performed by the King's Men around 1610–11, is undertaken via the play's depiction of incest. *The maids tragedie*, performed by the King's Men around 1610–11, also explores the misuse of royal authority through a story of sexual deviance (that of a king who insists that his courtier, Amintor, marry his lover, Evadne, so that he can continue his relationship with her). It is through an innovative manipulation of narrative and genre that the play provides its potentially most condemning critique of king and court. The play's intricate plot is unpredictable and involves constant reversals of the audience's expectations. This is combined with the use of the revenge tragedy genre to depict a court filled with competing, and ultimately destructive, ideologies of kingship. Moreover, the play appropriates the performance traditions of the court in order to do this. It opens with a wedding masque, a form associated with the contemporary Jacobean court and frequently incorporated into plays for the professional theatres in Jacobean London (though not normally at this length). This masque, Suzanne Gossett (1972) argues, provides an anticipatory and ironic commentary on the action of the play, but it also disrupts generic conventions to the extent that it distances the audience so that they are unable to tell if the play will be a tragedy or a comedy.

The inclusion of a masque in *The maids tragedie* highlights the concurrent influences on Beaumont's drama of the multiple theatrical traditions in which he worked: the Inns of Court, the children's stages, the adult theatres, and the royal courts. A number of his plays were subsequently commissioned for performance at court, including *The maids tragedie*, despite its courtly critique. As already noted, Beaumont's last dramatic work, *The maskue of the gentlemen of Grayes-Inne and the Inner Temple*, was written specifically for the court and was performed in February 1613 as part of the marriage celebrations for Princess Elizabeth. Beaumont's dramatic writing, from his burlesque revels to the comic children's company play, *The Knight of the Burning Pestle*, to this late tragic King's Men piece, combines various theatrical traditions and appropriates a range of genres and narratives in experimental ways. It is perhaps this distinctive theatricality that most characterizes Beaumont's literary career.

This literary career, however, was brief. Following his marriage to the heiress Ursula Isley in 1613, Beaumont stopped writing, possibly as a result of his changed economic status or because of a stroke (Finkelpearl 1990). Yet in spite of the original audience rejection of his early *The Knight of the Burning Pestle*, Beaumont received critical acclaim from his contemporaries. He was praised by Ben Jonson during his lifetime and was the subject of various accolades from writers following his death in 1616, when he was buried in what is now known as Poets' Corner in Westminster Abbey. By 1638, he was recognized by Owen Feltham in a eulogy 'To the memory of immortal Ben', alongside Jonson and Shakespeare, as one of the three main playwrights of 'our halcyon days'. Following Fletcher's death in 1625, the plays of Beaumont and his writing partner were regularly performed in the London theatres. Attending to courts and aristocrats and dynamically adapting chivalric and romance narratives, these plays remained at the centre of courtly drama through the Restoration and continued to figure as some of the most frequently performed pieces at theatres throughout Britain in the seventeenth century. Between 1615/16 and 1642, 41 of the King's Men's plays performed at court came from the Beaumont

and Fletcher canon (Wallis 1947); in 1647, a clandestine performance of *A king and no king* was interrupted by the authorities (Appleton 1956); and 14 of 27 Interregnum drolls gathered in Francis Kirkman's *The wits* (1662) came from Beaumont and Fletcher's plays, including *The scorneful ladie*, *Philaster*, *Cupids revenge*, *A king and no king*, and *The maids tragedie*. During the Restoration, their drama, according to Dryden, continued to outperform Shakespeare's and Jonson's by two plays to one. Plays from the Beaumont and Fletcher canon were also prominent in the repertoires of theatres in Edinburgh and Dublin, indicating the ongoing and wide-ranging popularity of the plays written in part by Beaumont. Yet this popularity soon declined. During the eighteenth and nineteenth centuries Beaumont and Fletcher's work was overlooked first as indecent, and then as immoral – a critical tradition that has impacted on their standing today. Although recent attention to Beaumont's work has not restored him to his previous critical standing on a par with Shakespeare and Jonson, this early modern playwright continues to be recognized for his role as a professional dramatist, his novel engagement with theatre and dramatic form, and his influence, alongside Fletcher, on the development of drama in Renaissance England.

SEE ALSO: Aubrey, John; Beaumont, John; Dryden, John; Fletcher, John; Jonson, Ben; Shakespeare, William; Shirley, James

REFERENCES AND SUGGESTED READINGS

Appleton, William W. (1956) *Beaumont and Fletcher: a critical study*. Allen & Unwin, London.

Berek, Peter (2004) Cross-dressing, gender, and absolutism in the Beaumont and Fletcher plays. *Studies in English Literature, 1500–1900* 44(2), 359–377.

Bliss, Lee (1987) *Francis Beaumont*. Twayne, Boston.

Clark, Sandra (1994) *The plays of Beaumont and Fletcher: sexual themes and dramatic representation*. Harvester Wheatsheaf, London.

Eccles, Mark (1940) Francis Beaumont's grammar lecture. *Review of English Studies* 16(64), 402–414.

Finkelpearl, Philip (1990) *Court and country politics in the plays of Beaumont and Fletcher.* Princeton University Press, Princeton.

Gayley, Charles Mills (1914) *Francis Beaumont: dramatist.* Gerald Duckworth, London.

Gossett, Suzanne (1972) Masque influence on the dramaturgy of Beaumont and Fletcher. *Modern Philology* 69(3), 199–208.

Gossett, Suzanne (2007) Taking *Pericles* seriously. In: Mukherji, Subha & Lyne, Raphael (eds) *Early modern tragicomedy.* D. S. Brewer, Cambridge, pp. 101–114.

Hoy, Cyrus (1956–62) The shares of Fletcher and his collaborators in the Beaumont and Fletcher canon [in 7 parts]. *Studies in Bibliography* 8, 124–146; 9, 143–162; 11, 85–99; 12, 91–116; 13, 77–108; 14, 45–67; 15, 71–90.

Masten, Jeffrey (1992) Beaumont and / or Fletcher: collaboration and the interpretation of Renaissance drama. *ELH* 59, 337–356.

McLuskie, Kathleen (1992) 'A maidenhead, *Amintor,* at my yeares': chastity and tragicomedy in the Fletcher plays. In: McMullan, Gordon & Hope, Jonathan (eds) *The politics of tragicomedy: Shakespeare and after.* Routledge, London, pp. 92–121.

Munro, Lucy (2006) *The Knight of the Burning Pestle* and generic experimentation. In: Sullivan, Garrett A., Cheney, Patrick, & Hadfield, Andrew (eds) *Early modern English drama: a critical companion.* Oxford University Press, Oxford, pp. 189–199.

Oliphant, E. H. C. (1927) *The plays of Beaumont and Fletcher.* Yale University Press, New Haven.

Wallis, Lawrence B. (1947) *Fletcher, Beaumont & company: entertainers to the Jacobean gentry.* King's Crown, New York.

Beaumont, John

JOSEPH R. TELLER

Sir John Beaumont (c.1584–1627), baronet and brother of the dramatist Francis Beaumont, was a Catholic devotional and court poet whose output includes an Ovidian satire, *The metamorphosis of tabacco* (1602), and a collection of poems titled *Bosworth-field* (1629), containing verse on English political history, courtly lyrics to King James, King Charles, and royal favourites, Latin verse translations, and devotional poems on the Christian mysteries. Beaumont also composed the longest English poem on Christ's Passion, a 12-book epic titled *The crowne of thornes,* preserved in only one extant manuscript (British Library, Additional MS 33392). Though Beaumont's modest popularity waned after the seventeenth century, in his own time he was revered by Ben Jonson and Michael Drayton as a poet encouraging Christian devotion and stoic virtue. Beaumont's use of the heroic couplet and his preference for 'noble subject[s] which the mind may lift' ('To his late Majesty, concerning the true forme of English Poetry') suggests his stylistic affinity with Jonson as well as his anticipation of John Dryden and Alexander Pope. Though there is relatively little scholarship on Beaumont, his biography and literary output embody a rich synthesis of recusant Catholicism and courtly verse during the politically charged early seventeenth century.

The second of four children, John Beaumont was born in 1583 or 1584 to Francis Beaumont and Anne Pierrepoint. Though John's father conformed to the Established Church, the Beaumont and Pierrepoint families had deep Catholic recusant sympathies; his uncle, Gervase Pierrepoint, was imprisoned for aiding Edmund Campion in 1581. In 1597 Beaumont and his brothers matriculated at Broadgates Hall, Oxford, and proceeded to the Inner Temple. In London, he became acquainted with Jonson and Drayton. During this time Beaumont wrote *The metamorphosis of tabacco,* a satirical defence of Virginian tobacco written as an Ovidian epyllion, a form popular at the turn of the century. In 1607 Beaumont married Elizabeth Fortescue, daughter of a prominent London Catholic family, with whom he would have seven sons and four daughters. The same year two-thirds of Beaumont's estates were confiscated for his refusal to attend Protestant services. From 1607 until 1620, he was confined to Grace Dieu, the family home in Belton parish, and its immediate environs. During his confinement, Beaumont composed many of his translations of Latin poets, including Virgil, Horace, Persius, and Ausonius, as well as much of his devotional poetry. Beaumont also probably began the 800-line *Bosworth-field* (on the 1485 battle ending the Wars of the Roses) and the 11,000-line *The crowne of thornes* during this period.

Beaumont became a court poet in 1620 through the influence of his cousin, Maria, countess of Buckingham, whose son George Villiers later became the duke of Buckingham, a royal favourite. From 1620 to 1627, Beaumont wrote epithalamia, panegyrics, and various occasional lyrics celebrating events in the lives of King James, King Charles, and the duke of Buckingham. He also wrote a masque, *The theatre of Apollo*, casting James as the title character. On 31 January 1627 John was made a baronet by King Charles, but he died four months later, and was buried on 19 April in Westminster Abbey. His eldest son, John, supervised the publication of Beaumont's poetry in 1629, under the title *Bosworth-field: with a taste of the variety of other poems, left by Sir John Beaumont*. This volume, *The metamorphosis of tabacco*, *The theatre of Apollo*, the unpublished *The crowne of thornes*, and a few manuscript poems on overtly Catholic topics (e.g., 'Of the Assumption of our Blessed Lady'), represent Beaumont's extant *oeuvre*.

Beaumont's poetry is characterized by his Christian humanism, his Catholic devotion, and his preoccupation with the connection between poetry, politics, and virtue. In addition to his poetry's stylistic similarities to Jonson's, Beaumont's religious verse is also indebted to John Donne: one of Beaumont's best lyrics, 'Upon the two great feasts of the Annunciation and Resurrection falling on the same day, March 25. 1627', imitates Donne's earlier poem 'Upon the Annunciation and Passion falling on one day. 1608'.

More expansively than any other of his works, *The crowne of thornes* synthesizes Beaumont's interests in devotional poetry, contemporary English politics, and Christianized stoic virtue. Celebrating Christ's Passion as the source of all meaning, the epic offers comfort to persecuted English Catholics and encourages all readers to imitate Christ's patient self-abnegation. The epic also

advocates a unified Christendom under Kings James and Charles, revealing the poem's turbulent relationship to the politics of the 1620s. Like much of Beaumont's verse, *The crowne of thornes* exemplifies the aesthetic possibilities and potential appeal of Catholic-influenced religious poetry in seventeenth-century England.

SEE ALSO: Beaumont, Francis; Donne, John; Drayton, Michael; Dryden, John; Jonson, Ben

REFERENCES AND SUGGESTED READINGS

Cousins, A. D. (1991) *The Catholic religious poets from Southwell to Crashaw*. Sheed & Ward, London.

Eccles, Mark (1942) A biographical dictionary of Elizabethan authors. *Huntington Library Quarterly* 5, 293–300.

Huttar, Charles A. (1992) Sir John Beaumont. In: Hester, M. Thomas (ed.) *Seventeenth-century British nondramatic poets*, 1st series. Gale, Detroit, pp. 25–35.

Newdigate, B. H. (1942) Sir John Beaumont's 'The crowne of thornes'. *Review of English Studies* 18 (71), 284- 290.

Sell, Roger D. (2010) Sir John Beaumont and his three audiences. In: Sell, Roger D. & Johnson, Anthony W. (eds) *Writing and religion in England, 1558–1689: studies in community-making and cultural memory*. Ashgate, Farnham, pp. 195–221.

Wadsworth, Randolph Lincoln (1967) 'The bound, and frontier of our poetry': a study of Sir John Beaumont (1583–1627). PhD dissertation, Stanford University.

Wallerstein, Ruth (1954) Sir John Beaumont's 'Crowne of thornes': a report. *Journal of English and Germanic Philology* 53, 410–434.

Benlowes, Edward

ROBERT WILCHER

The literary culture to which Edward Benlowes (1602–76) contributed as patron and poet was already in decline when he set about composing *Theophila, or loves sacrifice* (1652), the long poem for which he is chiefly remembered, and his reputation has never recovered from the ridicule directed at him by the Restoration satirist Samuel Butler in 'Character of a small poet'. Nevertheless, he is of interest to both social and literary historians as an articulate representative of his class (Hill 1953) and as one of the first poets to borrow phrases and images from John Milton's 1645 *Poems*.

Born into a wealthy Catholic family on 12 July 1602, Benlowes inherited extensive property near Great Bardfield in Essex. Both his parents were recusants who sent two of his younger brothers abroad to be educated by Jesuits, but Edward was admitted to St John's College, Cambridge, in 1620, and two years later to Lincoln's Inn. Acquaintance with polemical Protestant literature and travel in Europe between 1627 and 1630 led to his apostasy from the Roman Catholic Church.

During the 1630s, Benlowes settled into a quiet life at Brent Hall, the family seat in Finchingfield. Leaving the management of his estates to John Schoren, a Dutch printer who had entered his service in Brussels, he earned the name of Benevolus (an anagram of Benlowes) for his generous patronage of the arts. In 1633 he encouraged Phineas Fletcher to publish *The purple island*, some copies of which were embellished with engravings printed by Schoren on a private rolling-press at Brent Hall. He also instigated and financed the publication of Francis Quarles's *Emblemes* (1635), another project that reflected his taste for allegorical poetry and the art of the engraver. He wrote complimentary verses for both these volumes and in 1636 published *Sphinx theologica*, a devotional work of his own in Latin prose and verse.

Benlowes kept a low profile during the First Civil War, but was lucky to escape sequestration when he refused to subscribe to Parliament's Solemn League and Covenant in 1644. From the seclusion of Brent Hall, he sponsored Alexander Ross's *Medicus medicatus* (1645), which attacked the toleration of Catholics advocated in Sir Thomas Browne's *Religio medici* (1643). His own bitter antagonism towards his former religion was vented in a Latin echo-poem, *Papa perstrictus*, published

in 1645. Most of his energies, however, were devoted to *Theophila*, which was more or less completed by the time he emerged briefly to take command of a troop of cavalry in the abortive Royalist rising of 1648. As a consequence of this action, he was declared a delinquent and had to pay a considerable sum to retain possession of his estates.

He had already begun to mortgage land to meet parliamentary war taxes; and, since he himself never married, he felt obliged to raise a dowry for his niece and only heir, Philippa, by mortgaging the rest of his property. Undeterred by growing financial difficulties, he published *A Poetick descant upon a private musick-meeting* (1649), his longest English poem to date; he subsidized the printing of Payne Fisher's *Marston-moor* (1650), a Latin poem for which Benlowes supplied some commendatory verses in Latin; and he brought to fruition the most ambitious artistic undertaking of his life with an elegant folio volume of *Theophila*. When Brent Hall was destroyed by fire in 1653, he took lodgings in London, where mounting debts forced him to negotiate the outright sale of his ancestral estates in 1657. Swindled out of the proceeds and pursued by writs and duns, he sought refuge with Philippa at Mapledurham in Oxfordshire. After his niece's death in 1667, he spent the rest of his life in Oxford, subsisting on a small annuity from her husband and the charity of friends at the university. He passed his days in the Bodleian Library and in 1673 issued three sets of Latin verses, one of which reworked material from the more substantial *Oxonii encomium* (1672). He died on 18 December 1676 and was buried in St Mary's church three days later.

All the published works of Benlowes, in Latin and English, bear witness to his liking for enigmatic and decorative detail in the form of epigrams, allegories, mottoes, paradoxes, anagrams, emblems, impresas; and the extravagant conceits in which his poetry abounds led George Williamson (1930) to describe him as the most fantastic of the late metaphysical poets, whose flights of fancy plunge into absurdity more often than they soar to the heights of devotional intensity. According to a prose preface, *Theophila* was conceived as 'a Heroic Poem' in eight cantos, which charts the personified soul's combat 'with the world, hell, and her own corruptions' on a journey from 'the life of Nature' by way of 'the life of Grace' to an ecstatic foretaste of 'the life of Glory'. Benlowes occasionally succeeds in condensing spiritual concepts and mystical experiences into vividly concrete images, but the poem lacks narrative coherence and the original plan was obscured by the accretion of supplementary items, including a ninth canto that recapitulated the entire poem in parallel Latin and English texts, Latin translations of cantos I and III inserted after canto IX, and two discrete poems, a satire on 'the Vanity of the World' and a celebration of 'the Sweetness and Pleasure of Retirement', which are misleadingly labelled cantos X–XIII as if they were integral to the foregoing argument. Harold Jenkins (1952) notes the debt to Milton in the second of the retirement cantos and considers that the poet is at his best in its description of a summer day in the countryside. The habit of appropriating poetic material from such writers as Milton, John Donne, Guillaume de Salluste Du Bartas, William Shakespeare, Thomas Randolph, and Richard Crashaw prompted H. J. L. Robbie (1928) to dismiss Benlowes as a plagiarist, but Maren-Sofie Røstvig (1962) sees the extensive borrowings from the odes of the Polish Jesuit Casimire Sarbiewski, which reach a peak in canto XIII, as evidence of a fervent assent to the literary convention of spiritual ecstasy in a rural environment.

Quite apart from its literary qualities, *Theophila* is of interest to bibliographers and students of fine art for the care with which Benlowes oversaw its production. Illustrations were provided by some of the best engravers of the age, including a portrait of the poet by Francis Barlow; the title page was handsomely printed in red and black ink; initial letters were decorated as in medieval manuscripts; and different fonts and letter sizes were used consistently to distinguish significant words. The bare text of *Theophila* edited by G. Saintsbury (1905) makes available to the modern reader only one dimension of the fastidious craftsmanship that Benlowes bestowed upon the surviving presentation copies listed by Jenkins (1952), some of them meticulously corrected and inscribed in his own exquisite handwriting.

SEE ALSO: Browne, Thomas; Fisher, Payne; Fletcher, Phineas; Milton, John; Quarles, Francis

REFERENCES AND SUGGESTED READINGS

Hill, Christopher (1953) Benlowes and his times. *Essays in Criticism* 3, 143–151.

Jenkins, Hugh (1948) Benlowes and Milton. *Modern Language Review* 43, 186–195.

Jenkins, Harold (1952) *Edward Benlowes (1602–1676): biography of a minor poet.* Harvard University Press, Cambridge, MA.

Robbie, H. J. L. (1928) Benlowes: a seventeenth-century plagiarist. *Modern Language Review* 23, 342–344.

Roditi, Edouard (1950) The wisdom and folly of Edward Benlowes. *Comparative Literature* 2, 343–353.

Røstvig, Maren-Sofie (1962) *The happy man: studies in the metamorphoses of a classical ideal*, vol. 1, 2nd edn. Norwegian Universities Press, Oslo; Humanities Press, New York.

Saintsbury, George (ed.) (1905) *Minor poets of the Caroline period*, vol. 1 Clarendon Press, Oxford.

Williamson, George (1930) *The Donne tradition.* Harvard University Press, Cambridge, MA.

Berkenhead, John

PHILIP MAJOR

John Berkenhead (1617–79) was a pre-eminent Royalist propagandist who gained a considerable contemporary reputation – on both sides of the main factional divide of the English Revolution – for the withering acerbity of his polemical writings. The foremost vehicle for his arch satirical wit was the first official Royalist newsbook to be based in Oxford – indeed, the first newsbook to be published anywhere in England, *Mercurius aulicus* (1643–45), of which Berkenhead was both editor (in succession to Peter Heylin) and chief writer. Recent scholarship has emphasized the significant influence on *Aulicus* of the court faction centring on William Laud, archbishop of Canterbury, at the expense of more moderate Royalist figures such as Edward Hyde. Berkenhead had been patronized by Laud during the 1630s, gaining a fellowship at All Souls College, Oxford, on the latter's recommendation. It is a testament to Berkenhead's industry and talent that *Aulicus* is held to have been among the most influential – and feared – of the nascent newspapers of its day, so much so that various manifestations of the Parliamentarian opposition, official and unofficial, felt compelled to counter it with nearly two dozen new such publications of their own during its run.

Born in Northwich, Cheshire, into a family of modest means, Berkenhead was educated at the free Witton grammar school and, from 1632, at Oriel College, Oxford, where by all accounts he was an outstanding student; by 1639 he had been awarded BA and MA degrees by All Souls. Berkenhead's posthumous reputation rests not solely on the political potency of his unyieldingly mordant pen, exhibited also in numerous, often anonymously published pamphlets, but also on his raising of journalistic standards: he is widely regarded as one of the first professional journalists in England; and, notwithstanding its overt partisanship, *Aulicus*'s attention to detail, in providing in-depth descriptions of major events and meticulously referencing source material, brought a new sense of literary authority to an era when the 'war of the pen' as it was waged in other genres and idioms often paid lip service to notions of historical accuracy. Its supporting infrastructure of first-hand intelligence, improved print quality, and efficient distribution combined to make *Aulicus* a formidably effective agent of court opinion.

Nonetheless, it is its vivid and hard-hitting satirical wit for which *Aulicus* – and by extension Berkenhead – is best remembered. Beneath its overarching goal of ruthlessly undermining the unity of and basis for popular Parliamentarian support lay a series of interlocking literary strategies. This included asserting the self-seeking and parvenu nature of Parliament, twinned with a pervasive stress on the unsustainable fragmentation in its ranks. Parliament's alleged incessant law-making was another recurrent motif, dovetailed with its penchant for punitive taxation of the ordinary citizen. As with other prominent Royalist polemicists, such as Marchamont Nedham, Samuel Sheppard, and John Cleveland, Berkenhead's caustic anti-Parliamentarianism was also characterized by a relentless assault on the perceived cultural ignorance of Puritanism. It was at the level of direct personal attack, however, where Berkenhead's most memorably sly invective is found: the parliamentarian leader John Pym was mercilessly lampooned as a self-interested dissembler and womanizer; the speaker of the House of Commons, William Lenthall, cruelly mocked for his speech impediment.

The undoubted intransigency of *Aulicus*'s political credo has helped to fuel the notion of a monochrome and homogeneous Royalist opposition during the Interregnum. Yet it is one measure of what is now more commonly viewed as Royalism's fluidity and contingency that Berkenhead himself modified his position appreciably in his writings of the late 1640s and 1650s by engaging in more consistently reasoned argument for the restoration of the king, though he remained more than capable of producing savagely sardonic pamphlets, such as *The assembly-man* (1647), which targeted the Assembly of Divines, and *The earle of Pembrokes last speech* (1650), designed to create opposition in London to the republican parliament.

If the acuity of his prose work has justifiably received critical attention, the merits of Berkenhead's poetry have been comparatively neglected. Yet he was a competent enough versifier to have several pieces set to music by Henry Lawes, the illustrious mid-seventeenth-century musician and song-writer. One of these was 'Staying in London after the Act for Banishment, and going to meet a friend who fail'd the hour appointed', published in Lawes's *Ayres and dialogues for one, two, and three voyces* (1653). It is a poem which breathes an atmosphere of both enabling subversion (Berkenhead is believed to have been a royalist spy in London at the time of its composition) and enervating submission, opening windows into the complexities of royalist 'internal exile' and the literary responses to it. 'Loyalties tears', published anonymously in June 1649 and again on the first anniversary of the regicide, in January 1650, is a lengthy elegy on the execution of Charles I which communicates a sense of bewilderment at political and religious disenfranchisement adopted also, if in markedly different registers, by more widely acknowledged royalist poets such as Robert Herrick and Henry Vaughan.

The Restoration brought new challenges and achievements, notably editorship of the official newsbook, *Mercurius publicus*, and founding membership (with responsibility for promoting better use of the English vernacular) of the Royal Society. It is his earlier corpus, however, that has inevitably shaped Berkenhead's literary standing. He died unmarried, and without issue, in Whitehall, soon after failing to retain his seat as member of parliament for Wilton, Wiltshire, which he had held since 1661. He was buried in the grounds of St Martin-in-the-Fields, Westminster.

SEE ALSO: Cleveland, John; Herrick, Robert; Hyde, Edward, earl of Clarendon; Nedham, Marchamont; Vaughan, Henry

REFERENCES AND SUGGESTED READINGS

Blackwell, Mark R. (1999) Bestial metaphors: John Berkenhead and satiric royalist propaganda of the 1640s and 50s. *Modern Language Studies* 29(1), 103–130.

de Groot, Jerome (2004) *Royalist identities.* Palgrave Macmillan, Basingstoke.

Major, Philip (2008) ''Twixt hope and fear': John Berkenhead, Henry Lawes, and banishment from London during the English Revolution. *Review of English Studies* 59, 270–280.

McDowell, Nicholas (2008) *Poetry and allegiance in the English civil wars: Marvell and the cause of wit.* Oxford University Press, Oxford.

McElligott, Jason (2007) *Royalism, print and censorship in revolutionary England.* Boydell Press, Woodbridge.

Peacey, Jason (2004) *Politicians and pamphleteers: propaganda during the English Civil Wars and Interregnum.* Ashgate, Aldershot.

Raymond, Joad (1999) *The invention of the newspaper: English newsbooks, 1641–1649.* Clarendon Press, Oxford.

Thomas, Peter (1969) *Sir John Berkenhead (1617–1679): a royalist career in politics and polemics.* Clarendon Press, Oxford.

Wilcher, Robert (2001) *The writing of royalism, 1628–1660.* Cambridge University Press, Cambridge.

Bible, the

HANNIBAL HAMLIN

The influence of the Bible on English Renaissance literature can hardly be exaggerated. With the proliferation of vernacular Bible translations following the Protestant Reformation, the Bible itself became the best-known work of literature in England. It is estimated that the total number of Bibles, New Testaments, and selections from the Bible printed in England between 1526 and 1640 was over two million copies. The principal English Bible translations were the Coverdale Bible (1535), Matthew's Bible (1537), the Great Bible (1539), the Geneva Bible (1560), the Bishops' Bible (1568), and the King James Bible or Authorized Version (1611).

The most influential English Bible translator was also the earliest (barring the translators of the Wycliffite versions, which circulated widely from the late fifteenth century on): William Tyndale did not live to complete his Bible translation, but his translations of select books from the original languages were printed in Antwerp in the 1520s and 1530s. Arrested as a heretic, Tyndale was publicly strangled in the Netherlands in 1536, but his translations were incorporated into all subsequent Renaissance English Bibles. Even the influential King James Bible is based largely on Tyndale's work. The Coverdale Bible was the first complete Bible in English, but was translated second-hand, from Latin and German sources. Matthew's Bible, actually the work of John Rogers, was a revised compilation of Tyndale's extant translations with the rest of the Bible from Coverdale. The Great Bible, commissioned by Henry VIII and the only Bible ever officially 'authorized', was a further revision by Coverdale of the Matthew's text. The Geneva Bible, translated by Protestant exiles in Calvin's city in the reign of Catholic Queen Mary, was the first complete English Bible translated from the original languages, Hebrew and Greek. It also featured an extensive scholarly and editorial apparatus, including maps, tables, illustrations, introductions, and extensive marginal notes offering alternative readings, cross-references, and interpretive glosses. It was the most widely available and popular Bible for the next century. The Bishops' Bible, supervised by archbishop of Canterbury Matthew Parker, was an attempt to supplant the Geneva by a more conservatively edited translation. It was the Bible read aloud in churches from 1568 to 1602, but was never popular. An English translation of the New Testament was produced by Catholic exiles at Rheims in 1582 (the Old Testament at Douai in 1610). It remained the Bible of English Catholics for many years, but had little wider influence. The King James Bible was also an attempt to replace Geneva, some of whose marginal notes James I found offensive. A thorough revision of the Bishops' Bible, which took into account all other previous translations and the latest scholarship, the King James was the work of six teams of the best English scholars of the Bible and ancient languages. Though it eventually became *the* English Bible, shaping English language, literature, and culture for four centuries, it was initially greeted with disinterest, even criticism. The Geneva Bible remained dominant until after the Restoration.

Bibles (especially the Geneva) were widely available to readers of even modest means, and, since everyone was required by law to attend church, they heard most of the Bible read aloud on Sundays and holidays over the course of their lives. Some biblical books and stories were exceptionally well known by everyone. The Psalms were sung around the country, in church and outside of it, in sophisticated musical settings as well as with the simpler tunes of the Sternhold and Hopkins psalter (printed in hundreds of editions from 1562 to 1696 and beyond). Parts of the story of Jesus told in the Gospels were lodged in the collective memory from the annual celebrations of the Nativity and the Crucifixion at Christmas and Easter. But many Old Testament and Apocryphal stories were almost as well known: Adam and Eve and the serpent, Cain and Abel, Noah and the Flood, Abraham and Isaac, Jacob and Esau, Joseph and his brothers, Samson and Delilah, David and Goliath (or Bathsheba, or Absalom), Susanna and the Elders. These stories were part of popular culture as well as of church worship, sung in broadside ballads, staged in religious dramas and puppet plays, and represented on painted cloths, embroidered fabrics, carved furniture, and engraved tableware. Countless writers translated, paraphrased, adapted, and alluded to the Bible in almost every conceivable literary form. Renaissance England was a biblical culture to an extent that is difficult to imagine today, which makes the familiar modern distinction between the sacred and the secular an irrelevant anachronism.

The range of biblical literature is wide. The Bible itself began to be recognized as a literary work in the Renaissance, based partly on comments by Jerome and other church fathers that not only was biblical poetry written in hexameters, pentameters, Sapphics, and other familiar classical forms, but that the Hebrew writers were actually the originators of the later Greek poetics. Literary scholars like Gabriel Harvey, Sir Philip Sidney, George Puttenham, Thomas Lodge, and others popularized this view, as did influential Continental scholars writing in Latin, including Immanuel Tremellius,

Franciscus Gomarus, J. J. Scaliger, and G. J. Vossius. Countless poets, professional and amateur, brilliant and incompetent, responded by trying to cast the prose of the Bible – especially the Psalms and other Old Testament songs like those of Moses and Deborah, but also Ecclesiastes, the Song of Solomon, and Job – into English poetry that captured the notional sense of the poetic excellence of the Hebrew originals. That no one understood the formal principles of Hebrew 'poetry' only encouraged these literary experiments. Some literary translations (including free paraphrases) were written with the godly intention to provide a spiritually edifying alternative to secular poetry. One example was the metrical psalms published by John Hall in his *Courte of virtue* (1565), which were designed to counter the love poems in the anonymous *Courte of Venus*, printed in the 1530s and 1540s. William Hunnis wrote an extended paraphrase of the seven penitential psalms, *Seven sobs of a sorrowfull soule for sinne* (1583), in the common metre used by Sternhold and Hopkins, and provided tunes for singing them. Coverdale's *Goostly psalmes and spirituall songes* (?1535) were perhaps the earliest paraphrases for godly pastimes. Strongly Lutheran in influence, the book was prohibited in 1530 and most copies were publicly burned. Other psalm translations were designed for practical use in public worship or domestic devotion. Sternhold himself wrote for the godly entertainment of Edward VI, but the Sternhold and Hopkins psalms as a whole were intended for church singing, as were the metrical psalters of George Joye, Robert Crowley, Matthew Parker, George Wither, James I (written with William Alexander), and Henry King, among others. Some metrical psalters are difficult to categorize, especially those that were never printed. The manuscript psalters, for instance, by Francis Davison (incomplete), Sir John Denham, and Thomas Fairfax may have been intended as alternatives to Sternhold and Hopkins, though they may also have been written for literary or for private devotional purposes. John Milton's common metre translations of Psalms 80–88,

printed in his 1671 *Poems*, also seem to have been written for congregational singing.

Another group of psalm translations seems to have been motivated primarily, though not necessarily exclusively, by literary concerns. Pre-eminent in this category is the Sidney psalter, by Sir Philip Sidney and Mary Sidney Herbert, countess of Pembroke. Mary Sidney's psalms, two-thirds of the whole, are particularly brilliant. Though bound by the biblical content, which as Scripture could not be significantly altered, or at least not by translators aiming at fidelity to the original, the Sidneys nevertheless exercised remarkable formal ingenuity, using metres, rhyme schemes, stanza forms, and other schematic devices so variously that their psalter has been called a school of English versification. Not printed until the nineteenth century, the Sidney psalter circulated widely in manuscript and was greatly admired. (For other deliberately literary versions of the Psalms, see the entry on 'psalms and psalters, metrical'.)

The Psalms were not the only biblical book translated separately. George Joye produced early prose versions of Isaiah, Jeremiah, and Lamentations. In addition to his psalms, Surrey also translated Ecclesiastes 1–5 into poulter's measure (alternating hexameters and fourteeners). Critics have argued that Surrey's Ecclesiastes, some of his psalms, and the penitential psalms of Wyatt were written partly as coded political statements which criticized the abuses of Henry VIII and his court. Biblical paraphrases provided a relatively safe mode for political commentary, since the authority of Scripture was unassailable and the level of plausible deniability for the translator was comfortably high. Another perhaps less political translation of Ecclesiastes was written by Henry Lok, son of Anne Vaughan Lok, and dedicated to Queen Elizabeth (1597). The Song of Solomon was an especially popular choice for paraphrase, not surprisingly, given its rich metaphorical language and evidently erotic content (despite the tradition of spiritual allegorizing). William Baldwin, author of *Beware the cat* (1552) and *A mirrour for magistrates* (c.1554), published his *Canticles or ballads of Solomon* in 1549 (in the Great Bible the Song of Solomon was entitled 'The Ballad of Ballads'). Further metrical versions of the Song were published by Jud Smith (1575), Dudley Fenner (1587), and Gervase Markham (1596, translated into 'eight Eclogues'). Robert Aylett's *Song of Songs, which was Salomon's, metaphrased in English heroiks, by way of dialogue*, was published in 1621. Aylett continued his biblical writing with paraphrases of Susanna and the Elders (1622), the Joseph story (1623), and *Davids troubles remembered* (1638). These were all republished in a collected edition, *Divine and moral speculations in metrical numbers* (1654). Other paraphrases of the Song of Solomon were published by Bishop Joseph Hall (1609), the separatist Henry Ainsworth (1623), George Sandys (1643, dedicated to King Charles I; Sandys also versified the Psalms and other books), and John Mason (in the extremely popular *Spiritual songs, or songs of praise*, 1683). One of the oddest biblical paraphrases was *The actes of the apostles* by the composer Christopher Tye (1553), in a common metre translation he seems to have written himself, designed 'to synge and also to play upon the Lute'. As well as the penitential psalms, Hunnis wrote a metrical paraphrase of Genesis (*A hive full of honey*, 1578). John Donne wrote *The lamentations of Jeremy* based, as his title admits, *for the most part according to Tremellius*, though he also relied on an earlier English version of Lamentations by Christopher Fetherstone. Fetherstone's *Lamentations* (1587) actually included two versions, one by himself in prose and one by an anonymous friend in verse. Perhaps the most ambitious, if not the most accomplished, biblical paraphrast was Henoch Clapham, who in just over 200 pages managed *A briefe of the Bibles history, drawne first into English poësy, and then illustrated by apt annotations: whereto is now added a synopsis of the Bibles doctrine* (1603).

Many English writers retold biblical stories in free adaptations. In her long poem *Salve Deus rex Judaeorum* (1611), for instance, Aemelia Lanyer gives an account of Christ's Passion, in which she also includes the boldly revisionist 'Eve's apology in defence of women'. Giles Fletcher, the younger, cast the Gospel story of Christ as a Christian biblical epic, *Christs victorie, and triumph in heaven, and earth, over, and after death* (1610). After the Passion, the David story was among the most popular, as evidenced by the unfinished epic poem, *Davideis* by Abraham Cowley (1656). In the previous century, the composer John Merbecke had published a retelling of the David story, 'drawn into English meter for the youth to read' (1579). George Peele wrote a dramatic version of the story, *The love of King David and fair Bethsabe with the tragedy of Absalon*, published in 1599. Early modern English biblical drama had its roots in the medieval mystery plays, which were performed in some places (Coventry was the last) until well into Elizabeth's reign. In 1538, the fiercely evangelical John Bale wrote the plays *Johan the baptists preaching*, and *The temptation of Jesus Christ*, as well as *The chief promises of God*, consisting of dialogues between God and Adam, Noah, Abraham, Moses, David, Isaiah, and John the Baptist. Bale's acting company was patronized by Sir Thomas Cromwell. Biblical drama was common fare not only at schools and universities but elsewhere too. *Jacob and Esau* (printed 1568), *Godly queen Hester* (printed 1561), and Thomas Garter's *Susanna* (printed 1578) were performed for private audiences. Surviving public theatre plays are few: Robert Greene's *David and Bethsabe* and Thomas Lodge and Greene's *A looking glass for London* (printed 1594), about Jonah and the fall of Nineveh. Biblical plays that have not survived included Greene's *The history or tragedy of Job*, and the anonymous *Abraham and Lot* (performed 1593), *Esther and Ahasuerus* (performed 1594), *Nebuchadnezzar* (performed 1596–97), and *Samson*. Philip Henslowe's diary also references payments to Thomas Dekker for work on *Pontius Pilate*, Dekker and Anthony Munday for *Tobias*, William Haughton and Samuel Rowley for *Judas*, and Rowley for *Joshua*. The Admiral's Men at the Rose were clearly specialists in biblical drama. Beyond the public theatres, biblical dramas were also told in puppet plays, including *Jephtha's rash vow*, performed at London's Bartholomew Fair, and *The fall of Jerusalem*, performed in Coventry in 1584, 1605, and 1614. A 1628 puppet play in Oxford featured Adam and Eve in Eden, the expulsion from Paradise, Cain and Abel, Abraham and Isaac, Nebuchadnezzar and the fiery furnace, the nativity and the adoration of the three kings, the flight into Egypt and the slaughter of the innocents, and the parable of Dives and Lazarus.

English Renaissance literature's most famous biblical adaptations are the poems of John Milton, especially *Paradise lost*, *Paradise regained*, and *Samson agonistes*. Each of these major works developed out of a distinct tradition of biblical literature. First, in his preface to *Samson agonistes*, Milton notes that Paul cited Euripides in 1 Corinthians 15.33, that the church father Gregory Nazianzen wrote a tragedy on Christ's Passion, and that Calvinist theologian David Paraeus read Revelation as a tragedy. There were precedents for biblical closet drama closer to home, however. *A tragedie of Abrahams sacrifice*, for example, though written originally in French by Calvin's successor Theodore Beza, was translated into English by Arthur Golding. (Beza's play was performed in Lausanne, but Golding's translation seems not to have been intended for performance.) Similar plays include George Sandys's translation of Hugo Grotius's Latin *Christus patiens* (1608), *Christ's passion: a tragedy* (1640), as well as the Latin biblical plays of George Buchanan. Buchanan, who also wrote widely admired Latin metrical psalms, wrote his *Jephthes sive votum* (on Jephtha and his daughter) and *Baptistes sive calumnia* (on John the Baptist) in the 1540s for his students at the Collège de Guyenne in Bordeaux. They were published many times, including in London and Edinburgh in 1577 and 1578. While at Cambridge, John Christopherson, later chaplain to Mary I, also wrote a school play on Jephtha, but in Greek (c.1554–55).

Secondly, Milton's *Paradise regained* has been described as a brief epic, like that of Giles Fletcher, ultimately deriving from the book of Job, as it was understood by Renaissance scholars in terms of classical genre. Many believed Jerome's assertion that Job was somehow composed in epic hexameters, and the term 'brief epic' is Milton's own, applied to Job in *The reason of church government*. Job, *Christs victorie, and triumph*, and *Paradise regained* also redefine heroism as patient suffering. Thirdly, *Paradise lost* derives in part from the tradition of hexameral epic, based on the six-day Creation account in Genesis. Though it has ancient roots, the most influential hexameral poem in the Renaissance was *La sepmaine, ou, creation du monde*, by the French Huguenot poet Guillaume de Salluste Du Bartas, translated into English as *The deuine weekes and works* by Joshua Sylvester (1605). Partial translations of Du Bartas had appeared earlier: Thomas Hudson's *Historie of Judith* (1584), commissioned by James VI of Scotland (later James I of England), Sylvester's *The sacrifice of Isaac* and *The ship-wreck of Jonah* (1592), and William L'Isle's *Babylon* (1595). Sir Philip Sidney and Thomas Churchyard also translated portions of Du Bartas, but they are now lost. It was Sylvester's complete translation that had the greatest influence of any English version, however, culminating in *Paradise lost*, which, like the *Divine weeks*, invokes Urania, the muse of astronomy reconceived as the heavenly muse of Christian poetry. *Paradise lost* is also, of course, primarily concerned with explicating Genesis 1–3, and along the way it recounts the Creation, as well as much else in biblical and extra-biblical history. Sylvester's Du Bartas was nearly universally praised, and its influence may be seen in biblical poems including Michael Drayton's *Noah's flood* (1630), Aylett's *Susanna*, John Davies of Hereford's Passion poem, *The holy roode* (1609), and Francis Quarles's poems on Jonah, Esther, Job, and Samson (1638), as well as Fletcher's *Christ's victory*, Cowley's *Davideis*, and Milton's *Paradise lost*.

Even the huge number of biblical translations, paraphrases, and adaptations does not adequately convey the extent of the Bible's influence on Renaissance literature. Another effective measure of literary influence is allusion, and there is no work more frequently alluded to in the period than the Bible. Shakespeare's plays are studded with biblical allusions, some of them, like those in *The merchant of Venice*, *Richard II*, and *King Lear*, so densely constellated that they fundamentally shape their meaning. Shylock cites the story of Jacob and Laban (Genesis 31), for instance; Richard II attempts to describe his deposition as another Crucifixion by means of allusions to Judas and Pilate; and *King Lear* is Shakespeare's extended response to the problem of suffering in the book of Job. *Measure for measure* takes its title from Matthew 7.2. Other ostensibly non-biblical plays use biblical allusion in the same way: Thomas Kyd's *The Spanish tragedie* and Christopher Marlowe's *The Jew of Malta*, for example. Spenser's *Amoretti* allude to the Bible, especially the Song of Solomon, as does *The Faerie Queene*, most thickly in book I, where St George rescues King Adam and Queen Eve from a great dragon. Renaissance lyric poetry is also rich with biblical allusion, even in love poems like Wyatt's 'Whoso list to hunt', Sir Walter Ralegh's 'Nature, that washed her hands in milk', and Thomas Campion's 'There is a garden in her face', to give only a sample, and more overtly religious poems by John Donne, George Herbert, Henry Vaughan, Andrew Marvell, Thomas Traherne, and countless others. In England, religious verse was an especially Protestant concern, since it was Protestants who were keen to translate the Bible. Yet Catholic poets also wrote poetry that derived from or responded to the Bible: Robert Southwell's 'St Peter's complaint', William Alabaster's 'Over the brook Cedron Christ is gone', and Richard Crashaw's 'The weeper', a meditation on Mary Magdalene. Catholics even wrote metrical psalm paraphrases, like Richard Verstegan's 'Odes in imitation of the seven penitential psalms' (1601), Crashaw's Psalms 23 and 137, and the common metre psalms of William Forrest, chaplain to Mary I.

The English Bible also profoundly influenced the development of prose style, especially in works aiming at a grand, oracular, or prophetic tone. The translators, especially of the King James Bible, aimed at a high, antiquated style, and tried to render the Hebrew and Greek as literally as possible. This influence is most obvious in English sermons and religious writing, but also in political oratory (and treatises like those of Thomas Hobbes and John Locke), the many influential tracts printed during the Commonwealth, and in the fiction and non-fiction of John Bunyan and Daniel Defoe. Finally, the Bible also altered the English language, introducing many Hebraic usages and idioms, including biblical 'knowledge' (meaning 'sex', based on Genesis 4.1), and phrases like 'the apple of his eye' (Deut. 32.10), 'by the skin of my teeth' (Job 19.20), 'an eye for an eye' (Exod. 21.24), and 'the salt of the earth' (Matt. 5.13). When anyone refers to the writing on the wall, the mighty who have fallen, turning the other cheek, or biting the dust, they are using biblical idioms (Dan. 5.5; 2 Sam. 1.19; Matt. 5.39; Ps. 72.9). Among Bible translators, Coverdale seems to have been a particularly creative wordsmith. His Bibles are cited by the *Oxford English Dictionary* for the first use of the words 'belly-full', 'birthright', bloodthirsty', 'daytime', 'forecast', 'killer', 'kind-hearted', 'spider-web', 'swaddling-clothes', and 'unpleasant'. To Tyndale we owe the words 'scapegoat', 'brokenhearted', 'busybody', and 'castaway'. Many Renaissance writers invented new words and idioms, but those in the English Bibles were repeatedly read and heard by English speakers throughout their lives, and hence became everyday language.

SEE ALSO: Crowley, Robert; Donne, John; Golding, Arthur; Herbert, George; Herbert, Mary (Sidney), countess of Pembroke; Howard, Henry, earl of Surrey; Milton, John; psalms and psalters, metrical; Sandys, George; Shakespeare, William; Sidney, Philip; Sylvester, Joshua; Tyndale, William

REFERENCES AND SUGGESTED READINGS

Campbell, Lily B. (1959) *Divine poetry and drama in sixteenth-century England.* Cambridge University Press, Cambridge.

Daniell, David (2003) *The Bible in English.* Yale University Press, New Haven.

Lewalski, Barbara Keefer (1979) *Protestant poetics and the seventeenth-century religious lyric.* Princeton University Press, Princeton.

Norton, David (2000) *A history of the English Bible as literature.* Cambridge University Press, Cambridge.

Shaheen, Naseeb (1999) *Biblical references in Shakespeare's plays.* University of Delaware Press, Newark.

Biddle, Hester

ELIZABETH MALSON-HUDDLE

Hester Biddle (1629/30–97), Quaker writer and itinerant preacher, addressed pugnacious pamphlets to those who persecuted religious dissenters, worshipped in the Anglican Church, or refused to help the poor. Raised in Oxford, she grew up in the Anglican Church; no record of her early life survives but the brief account in her writing. She moved to London, where she mourned the burning of the prayer books and the beheading of Charles I so greatly 'that I was even weary of life . . . then did the Lord take away my hearing that I was deaf as to all Teachings of Men for a year' (*The trumpet of the Lord sounded forth unto these three nations*, 1662). After attending Quaker meetings and being inspired by the preaching of Edward Burrough and Francis Howgill, she converted to Quakerism in 1654. With her husband, Thomas Biddle (d.1682), a cobbler, she had four sons; after his death, charitable funds from a local Quaker meeting helped to support her. Irrepressible in spite of frequent arrests, imprisonments, even beatings, during the fiercest periods of Quaker persecution, she continued publishing provocative pamphlets and composed *The trumpet of the Lord sounded forth unto these three nations* from Newgate prison in 1662. Like her

Quaker sisters Katherine Evans, Sarah Cheevers, and Mary Fisher, Biddle travelled as a missionary not only across England, Ireland, and Scotland but also to the Netherlands, Barbados, Egypt, and finally, in her last years, to France. In her last years, she delivered her message of peace to Louis XIV of France. She died of natural causes in London at the age of 67.

Biddle shared the millenarian excitement of many radical sectarians of the 1650s, who anticipated the justification of the oppressed godly saints and the bloody punishment of those who persecuted them when Christ returned to rule the earth. While Fifth Monarchist prophet Mary Cary describes at length the spiritual benefits for the saints during the millennial rule of Christ, Biddle focuses on God's wrath and the punishment of the sinful. She evokes the upheaval of apocalyptic judgement with the language of natural disaster. She combines the symbolic imagery of scriptural prophecies with her own vision of nature overturned by God's wrath: 'I will roar and thunder forth my voice out of my Holy Mountain, and the Beasts shall tremble, the Earth shall be as a smoke, the tall Cedars shall fall, and the stirdy Oakes shall be plucked up by the Roots, and all things of this World shall be afraid' (*Trumpet*). As Elaine Hobby (1991) observes, she often conflates her own prophetic voice with the voice of God spoken through Old Testament prophets to lend authority to her message. When Christ's millennial kingdom begins, Biddle asserts that creatures may hide but God's enemies cannot escape punishment: 'the Bats shall go into their Holes, and the Lyons into their Dens, when the Lord appeareth in his Beauty, to make Inquisition for blood, then shall your hearts fail you for fear of those things that are coming to you' (*Trumpet*).

In her polemical tracts, Biddle issued scathing critiques of the Anglican Church. In twin pamphlets from 1655, *Wo to thee city of Oxford* and *Wo to thee town of Cambridge*, Biddle condemns the cities, their universities, and especially their priests, 'your hearts are full of dirt, and filth, thy pride shall become as filthy rags upon the dunghill' (*City of Oxford*). Reflecting upon her Anglican experience, she writes in *A warning from the Lord God of life and power* (1660), 'whilest I was one with you in your Religion and Worship, my soul was hungry, and was even black with thirst, I had almost fallen in your streets for want of the Bread of Life'. She also warns the Anglican clergy against ceremonial worship and prophesies, 'your Surplices and Tippets, and all your loathsome Robes, which you dress your selves withall, which are like unto a menstrous Cloth before the Eye of the pure Jehovah, he will rent them all off'.

Like the Digger leader Gerrard Winstanley, Biddle contends that rich landowners, clergy, judges, and lawyers uphold interdependent systems of oppression to enrich themselves. She stresses the hypocrisy of Christians who ignore the poor: 'He that saith he loves God, and doth not feed the hungry, and cloath the naked, and judge the cause of the poor and needy, he is a lyar, and doth not the truth' (*Warning*). Biddle often denounces religious persecution, Anglican government, and sinful amusements in a single sentence to show that the church, local magistrates, and popular entertainers have created a new Sodom; for example, she berates London, 'Oh! the blood of the innocent is found in thee, which cryeth aloud for Vengeance unto my Throne, Drunkenness, Whoredom, and Gluttony, and all manner of Ungodliness, Tyranny and Oppression, is found in thee; Thy Priests Preach for hire, and thy People love to have it so; Rioting and ungodly meetings, Stage-Plays, Ballad Singing, Cards, and Dice, and all manner of Folly (not in corners only, but in the high places of thy streets) wicked works & actions are not punished by thee' (*Trumpet*). Biddle's highly poetical tracts are important for scholars of early Quakers, millennialism, early modern women writers, and the pamphlet literature of seventeenth-century religious controversy.

SEE ALSO: Cary, Mary; Fell, Margaret; Winstanley, Gerrard

REFERENCES AND SUGGESTED READINGS

Hobby, Elaine (1991) 'Oh Oxford thou art full of filth': the prophetical writing of Hester Biddle, 1629[?]–1696. In: Sellers, Susan (ed.) *Feminist criticism: theory and practice*. Harvester Wheatsheaf, New York, pp. 157–169.

Hobby, Elaine (1995) Handmaids of the Lord and mothers in Israel: early vindications of Quaker women's prophecy. In: Loewenstein, David & Corns, Thomas N. (eds) *The emergence of Quaker writing: dissenting literature in seventeenth-century England*. Frank Cass, London, pp. 88–98.

Hobby, Elaine & Gill, Catie (2004) Biddle, Hester. In: *Oxford dictionary of national biography*. Oxford University Press, Oxford.

Loewenstein, David & Morrill, Janel (2002) Literature and religion. In: Loewenstein, David & Mueller, Janel (eds) *The Cambridge history of early modern English literature*. Cambridge University Press, Cambridge, pp. 703–706.

Birch, William

EDWARD WILSON-LEE

William Birch (*fl.* 1562–71) is the author of five extant broadside ballads treating a variety of political and religious topics, ranging in date from 1562 to 1571. His writings notably include an early poetic representation of Elizabeth I as England's lover and a version of a ballad which was quoted by Shakespeare. No biographical details have been established: the scriptural learning and evangelical tone of many of his writings makes it possible that he is the same William Birch, MA, who was preferred to the wardenship of the college and parish church of Manchester on 30 July 1560 (*Calendar of patent rolls*), although his concern with the moral fibre of London in a number of his ballads might undermine any suggestion of residence outside of the capital.

Birch's first surviving publication is *A new balade of the worthy seruice of late doen by Maister Strangwige in Fraunce, and of his death* (?1562) which celebrates the transformation of Henry Strangeways from pirate to soldier and his heroic death from wounds sustained during the Newhaven campaign in October 1562. Probably published shortly after Strangeways's death, Birch's ballad is an early example of heavily nationalistic maritime literature which first flourished with late Elizabethan texts such as Gervase Markham's *The most honorable tragedie of Sir Richard Grinuile, knight* (1595). In 1563 Birch published *The complaint of a sinner, vexed with paine, desyring the ioye, that euer shall remayne*, which advertises itself as a 'moralized' version of a popular ballad by the pre-eminent early Elizabethan balladeer William Elderton. Elderton's poem is lost, although a snatch of it is sung by Benedick in *Much ado about nothing*. After beginning with a line from Elderton about 'The god of love, that sits above', Birch's new lyrics transfer the focus from Cupid to Christ and issue a call for penance; it is unclear how closely Birch's words would have continued to follow and play upon Elderton's. This tactic of hijacking already popular ballads by composing new words was to become increasingly widespread, and Birch's third extant ballad, *A songe betwene the quenes maiestie and Englande* (?1558–64) uses a traditional Tudor ballad ('Come over the burn, Bessy') as the basis for a lovers' duet between Elizabeth and her realm of England, which 'this long space ... loved [her] grace' but could not speak it for fear of reprisal: 'But no man durst speak, / but they wuld him threat / and quickly make him repent'. After recounting Elizabeth's difficulties during the reign of Queen Mary and excusing the general populace, who were not among those who 'would have decayed her wealth' because she was 'not of their religion', the ballad ends by putting a note of reconciliation into Elizabeth's mouth – all the more noble as it goes against the country's fury at her treatment – and she vows to 'forgive, / al such as do live, / if they do hereafter amend'. The surviving copy of the ballad in the library of the Society of Antiquaries has been dated to 1564, but the ballad was registered by William Copland as early as 1558/59, and the text may have been intended to sound a conciliatory note in the first months of Elizabeth's reign.

The next ballad signed by Birch, *A warnyng to England, let London begin: to repent their iniquitie, & flie from their sin* (1565), gathers evidence of God's displeasure with England in the form of plague, threatened invasion, and the burning of St Paul's spire after a lightning strike in 1561. It castigates Londoners for their gluttony and lust, comparing the city to Sodom and Gomorrah, Nineveh, and Jerusalem, and providing relevant scriptural passages to spur them to penance. Birch's final ballad appeared in 1571, after a gap of some years, and forms part of a group of ballads written in the aftermath of the Northern Rising of 1569–70 which warn recusants of the dire consequences of supporting rebels against their rightful queen. *A free admonition without any fees, to warne the papistes to beware of three trees* cites biblical antecedents of chastised rebels and reminds readers of the failure of the Prayer Book Rebellion and Kett's Rebellion of 1549. The ballad strikes a tone of defiance, but is also evidence of the widespread anxiety that there were more disturbances to follow.

The printing by Alexander Lacy of three of Birch's ballads from the early 1560s strongly suggests an increasing awareness of marketplace demand; Birch seems to have had a keen sense of how to exploit popular media for polemical purposes, and his writings certainly aimed to be among those 'texts [which move] freely between printed and non-printed media, from the pamphlet or printed ballad, into petitions, oral traditions, or crowd behaviour, and back again' (Lake & Pincus 2007).

SEE ALSO: Markham, Gervase; Shakespeare, William

REFERENCES AND SUGGESTED READINGS

Fox, Adam (2000) *Oral and literate culture in England 1500–1700*. Oxford University Press, Oxford.
Lake, Peter & Pincus, Steven (2007) Rethinking the public sphere. In: Lake, Peter & Pincus, Steven (eds) *The politics of the public sphere in early modern England*. Manchester University Press, Manchester, pp. 1–30.

Livingstone, Carol Rose (ed.) (1991) *British broad-side ballads of the sixteenth century: a catalogue of the extant sheets and an essay*. Garland, New York.

Watt, Tessa (1991) *Cheap print and popular piety, 1550–1640*. Cambridge University Press, Cambridge.

Blundeville, Thomas

MATTHEW WOODCOCK

The works of Thomas Blundeville (?1522–1606) represent two of the most popular and frequently reprinted kinds of books to be published during the Elizabethan period: vernacular translations of classical and contemporary European authorities, and practical manuals of instruction (themselves translations from Continental sources). These are also the kinds of works most commonly overlooked by modern critics of English Renaissance literature.

Blundeville was descended from a gentry family based in Newton Flotman, five miles south of Norwich, Norfolk. His educational background is not known. Although there is little evidence of his being at Cambridge University, as is sometimes suggested, he was clearly skilled in logic and mathematics and a proficient linguist who had perfected his knowledge of Italian through travel overseas. Blundeville lived in London for some time though he returned to Norfolk upon his father's death in 1568 and inherited the family estate. He died in 1606 and is buried in Newton Flotman church in the family monument that bears an effigy of him dressed in armour and accompanied by a book. Since the bulk of his works are translations, it is Blundeville's prefaces that provide the most personal information and represent the best illustration of his narrative voice and style. Blundeville's explicit aim throughout his writings is to elucidate, though this is accompanied by reflection on the national and public utility of the expertise he sets forth, be it horsemanship, historiography, or navigation.

Blundeville's early works signal his connections to courtly circles, which were facilitated by his friend in the royal household, John Astley, and, perhaps indirectly, the pedagogue Roger Ascham. Blundeville's *Three morall treatises* (1561), a translation of Plutarch's *Moralia* prefaced by dedicatory verses to Queen Elizabeth and a commendatory poem by Ascham, is clearly a bid for royal patronage, positioning the translator and his friends as counsellors to Elizabeth (Schurink 2008). Blundeville translated two further works on counsel in 1570, the latter of which was based on a Latin work by Ascham's friend Johannes Sturm: *A very briefe and profitable treatise declaring howe many counsells, and what maner of counselers a prince that will governe well ought to have* and *A ritch storehouse or treasurie for nobilitye and gentlemen, which in Latine is called nobilitas literata*. The courtly associations of equestrian accomplishment may have informed Blundeville's decision to publish several treatises on horsemanship. *The arte of ryding, and breakinge greate horses* (1561), adapted from Federico Grisone's 1550 *Gli ordini di cavalcare*, was the first such manual produced in English. This was followed in 1566 by the longer, illustrated *Fower chiefyst offices belongyng to horsemanshippe*.

The most commonly cited work in recent scholarship on Blundeville is *The true order and methode of wryting and reading hystories* (1574), a syncretic translation of the work of sixteenth-century Italian historians Jacopo Aconcio and Francesco Patrizzi. It was the first published treatise on historiography in English. Its prefatory dedication argues that historians do not simply supply diversionary entertainment; they also provide an instructive resource for counsellors to employ when advising in public office. The treatise is a good example of the emerging humanist historiography, emphasizing the historian's duty to present more than a simple linear record of events (as found in medieval chronicles) by combining attention to detail with logical organization and analysis of causation, that is, the exploration of *why* things happened. The treatise also champions historical veracity and criticizes ancient historians, like Livy and

Plutarch, who regularly invented speeches to put into the mouths of people they wrote about.

Blundeville possessed a wide-ranging interest in mathematics and its practical applications. He was tutor in the household of the keeper of the great seal, Sir Nicholas Bacon, and his most frequently reprinted work, *M. Blundevile his exercises* (1594) started life as an arithmetic textbook for Bacon's daughter. Blundeville expanded this to direct the reader towards different areas of applied mathematics, particularly astronomy, cartography, and geography. When first printed as *Exercises*, it comprised six separate treatises, eight in later editions. It was clearly conceived as a luxury volume intended more for a wealthy, erudite gentleman reader than for a penurious sailor seeking navigational instruction (Ash 2004). By the time *Exercises* first appeared Blundeville was already well connected to the Elizabethan 'scientific' community, which included Edward Wright, John Dee, and Henry Briggs, and had published a guide to reading contemporary maps in which he argued that geographical knowledge was essential for reading histories (*A briefe description of vniuersal mappes and cardes, and of their vse*, 1589). Blundeville's *Theoriques of the seven planets* (1602) presented detailed descriptions of the movements of heavenly bodies and contained diagrams of navigational instruments for mariners, although its preface is also addressed to land-based gentlemen of the city and court. Blundeville's mathematical texts are largely collections of existing sources and theories, rather than statements of original or empirical research, though this was by no means an unusual method of composition in technical and instructional works of the Renaissance period (Ash 2004). Indeed, Blundeville's overall strength as a writer was founded upon skills of scholarly repackaging and transmission as evinced by his expertise in translation, compilation, and exposition for courtly and learned audiences.

SEE ALSO: Ascham, Roger

REFERENCES AND SUGGESTED READINGS

Ash, Eric H. (2004) *Power, knowledge, and expertise in Elizabethan England*. Johns Hopkins University Press, Baltimore.

Campling, Arthur (1921–23) Thomas Blundeville of Newton Flotman. *Norfolk Archaeology* 21, 336–360.

Kintgen, Eugene R. (1996) *Reading in Tudor England*. University of Pittsburgh Press, Pittsburgh.

Schurink, Fred (2008) Print, patronage, and occasion: translations of Plutarch's *Moralia* in Tudor England. *Yearbook of English Studies* 38, 86–101.

Bodley, Thomas

DAVID VAISEY

Thomas Bodley (1545–1613) was the founder and benefactor of the library in Oxford University that bears his name. Opening on 8 November 1602 the Bodleian (as it came to be called) replaced an earlier library in the university that had developed from the collection of manuscripts given by Humfrey, duke of Gloucester, between 1439 and 1444. That library had lacked endowment and was slow to respond to the changes in teaching at Oxford brought about by the advent of printing. Its final disintegration came with the Protestant reformers in the 1550s, and the room which once contained the library was empty when Thomas Bodley went to the university as a 15-year-old undergraduate in 1560.

Thomas Bodley was born in Exeter on 2 March 1545, the eldest son of John Bodley, a prominent Protestant merchant, and his wife Joan. On the accession of Queen Mary I, the family left England, eventually joining other Protestant exiles in Geneva where the young Thomas studied under Antoine Chevalier, François Bérault, Theodore Beza, Jean Calvin, and others. The family returned to England when Elizabeth I came to the throne and Thomas went to Magdalen College, Oxford, in 1560, subsequently moving to a fellowship at Merton College in 1564. He remained there for 12 years, gaining a reputation as a gifted linguist and Hebrew scholar before being recruited into the service of the government, travelling abroad on various state missions. In 1583 he became gentleman usher to the queen, and served two terms as a member of parliament – for Portsmouth in 1584 and subsequently for St German's. In 1586 he resigned his Oxford fellowship on his marriage to Ann Ball, the widow of a wealthy fish merchant from Totnes, Devon. It was this marriage that provided the wealth which was subsequently devoted to the foundation of the library. Two years later in 1588 he was appointed Queen Elizabeth's resident in the United Provinces, a post with which he became increasingly disillusioned but nevertheless held until 1597. There is evidence that he had ambitions to become secretary of state but, caught between the feuding factions of the Cecils and Robert Devereux, earl of Essex, he was frustrated and left the service of the state to devote the remaining 15 years of his life to the project for which he is now chiefly remembered. His letter to the vice chancellor of Oxford University announcing his intention of refurbishing and restocking the old library room is dated 28 February 1598.

Two years after the library opened in 1602 Bodley was knighted by James I, who had also in that year issued letters patent styling the institution as the Public Library of Oxford on the foundation of Sir Thomas Bodley. Until his death on 28 January 1613, Bodley controlled in minute detail the way the library was administered and augmented, financing two further extensions of its building and negotiating the agreement with the Stationers' Company in 1610 which made it the first library of legal deposit in Great Britain. He was buried in the chapel of Merton College where a fine monument to his memory by Nicholas Stone depicts him surrounded by books and by allegorical figures representing branches of learning.

In 1608 Bodley wrote a short account of his own life which remained unpublished until 1647. It is in the eyes of some the first real autobiography in English. It is, however, notable for what it omits as much as for what it includes and others have seen it as a self-glorifying apologia for a journey through a life fulfilled only in the foundation of his library. Though Bodley's letter to the vice chancellor of Oxford University makes it clear that he wished to benefit posterity by devoting the means at his disposal to the support of learning, his motives for founding a library are far from clear. He was much influenced by his friend Sir Henry Savile who had restored and enlarged the library at Merton College and, having seen while in the Netherlands in 1587 the newly opened library at the University of Leiden, it is likely that he saw at Oxford the opportunity to establish an equivalent arsenal for Protestant scholarship in England. He chose as his first librarian the Protestant scholar Thomas James, but prevailed on friends and acquaintances of all religious persuasions to donate money or books and manuscripts in all branches of learning. Ecclesiastical bodies such as the dean and chapter of Exeter and the dean and canons of Windsor saw the new foundation as a safe and permanent home for collections of manuscripts which might be threatened during times of religious upheaval. As early as 1604 works in, for instance, Chinese were acquired even though no one in Oxford at the time could read the language and consequently the books stood upside down on the shelf. The new library rapidly attracted scholars from throughout Europe, and its catalogue of 1605 was the earliest general catalogue of any European public library.

Bodley himself remained opposed to the acquisition of books in the vernacular since English was not the language for the communication of scholarship; the 1605 catalogue, which covered some 5,000 titles, contained only around 170 books in English of which only three were literary works. After the agreement with the Stationers' Company, and after Bodley's death, the situation changed, though not all such works once received were retained. The most notorious example was the First Folio of Shakespeare, received on publication in 1623 but eliminated as a duplicate when the Third Folio was received in 1664 and not bought back until 1906. Throughout the seventeenth century, however, under Thomas James's successors, the Bodleian developed as the principal home of a great variety of collections generated by others. Those of, for example, archbishop of Canterbury William Laud in the 1630s, Robert Burton in 1640, John Selden in 1659, Francis Junius in 1677, and many more meant the Bodleian was regarded until the foundation of the British Museum in 1753 as the national library, and in the centuries since as an institution which has, as was Bodley's intention, acquired and stored the raw materials for scholarship to the benefit of the republic of the learned.

SEE ALSO: Burton, Robert; Selden, John; Shakespeare, William

REFERENCES AND SUGGESTED READINGS

Clennell, William (2002) Bodley before the Bodleian: a lecture to the Friends of the Bodleian, 21 February 2002. *Bodleian Library Record* (400th anniversary commemorative issue) 17(6), 371–384.

Clennell, William (ed.) (2006) *The autobiography of Sir Thomas Bodley*. Bodleian Library, Oxford.

Macray, William D. (1890) *Annals of the Bodleian Library Oxford*, 2nd edn. Clarendon Press, Oxford.

Philip, Ian (1983) *The Bodleian Library in the seventeenth and eighteenth centuries*. Clarendon Press, Oxford.

Trecentale Bodleianum: a memorial volume for the three hundredth anniversary of the public funeral of Sir Thomas Bodley March 29, 1613 (1913). Clarendon Press, Oxford.

Vaisey, David (2002) The legacy of Sir Thomas Bodley. *Bodleian Library Record* (400th anniversary commemorative issue) 17(6), 419–430.

Wheeler, G. W. (ed.) (1926) *Letters of Sir Thomas Bodley to Thomas James first keeper of the Bodleian Library*. Oxford University Press, Oxford.

Wheeler, G. W. (ed.) (1927) *Letters of Sir Thomas Bodley to the University of Oxford 1598–1611*. Oxford University Press, Oxford.

Boece, Hector

NICOLA ROYAN

Hector Boece (c.1465–1536) was the author of *Scotorum historia a prima gentis origine* (Paris, 1527; reprinted with two additional books, 1574 and 1575), a work that became hugely influential on the presentation and understanding of the Scottish past throughout the sixteenth century and into the seventeenth. Its style, its deployment of moral exemplars and its sure view of Scottish nationhood ensured its initial circulation in Scotland and beyond (a copy owned by William Cecil, Lord Burghley, is still extant). It underlies the polemical histories of the later sixteenth century, John Leslie's *De origine, moribus et rebus gestis Scotorum* (Rome, 1578) and George Buchanan's *Historia rerum Scoticarum* (Edinburgh, 1582). Its success was reinforced by John Bellenden's English translation, printed around 1540, a major source of Scottish history in Raphael Holinshed's *Chronicle*, and thus a key text for Shakespeare's *Macbeth*.

Boece was born in Dundee, around 1465. He Latinized his name to 'Boethius'; the common use of 'Boece' represents a re-anglicization. He was educated at Montaigu College, Paris, and he happily describes his time there, drawing attention to his friendship with Desiderius Erasmus of Rotterdam. Boece's training was largely in scholastic philosophy: he published a work on logic (*Explicatio quorundam vocabulorum*, c.1519). He was also clearly enthralled by humanism, demonstrated by his signature (a handsome italic), through his knowledge of recently rediscovered works of Tacitus, and through his Latin style, evoking the classical historian Livy.

In 1492, Boece was invited back to Scotland by William Elphinstone, bishop of Aberdeen, first to teach at, and then in 1497, to serve as first principal of King's College, Aberdeen, a post he held until his death in 1536. Boece wrote all his books while at Aberdeen: in addition to *Explicatio* and *Scotorum historia*, he also wrote *Murthlacensium et Aberdonensium episcoporum vitae* (*Lives of the bishops of Aberdeen*, Paris, 1522), essentially a commemoration of Elphinstone.

The *Scotorum historia* records the history of the Scots – the people rather than the country – from their origins in Greece and Egypt (contained in the introduction), and their first settlement of mainland Scotland in 330 BC (book 1). The work is divided into 17 books, and reaches the assassination of James I. The king is central to Boece's narrative. Boece traces an unbroken line of kings from the first settlement by Fergus mac Ferquhard to James I: this line symbolizes Scottish sovereignty independent of any authority apart from the pope. As in many other histories, the reign forms an important narrative arc, and kingly deeds are central to the action. What makes this contentious for many readers of Boece's history, both in the sixteenth century and subsequently, is that many of the kings he names do not appear in any other narrative chronicle. Boece claims a no longer extant source, 'Veremundus' (which translates as 'true world'): as a result, he has been accused both of duplicity in forging his source, and of being deceived as to the nature of a text put in front of him. Recent research, however, has made a cogent case for 'Veremundus' being genuine; at worst, therefore, Boece stands accused of embellishment, a crime common to his contemporary historiographers.

Nevertheless, Boece's account is contentious for other, ideological, reasons. First, his early kings are chosen by the elders; the imposition of primogeniture, by one Kenneth, just before Macbeth, is problematic, because of Kenneth's motives and methods. Many of these elected kings are virtuous on accession but degenerate into viciousness. Then the correlative of election, deposition by the Scots elders, occurs (although not consistently, as some evil kings die without additional intervention). Thus Boece's account can be interpreted to suggest a model of kingship which demanded certain standards of the sovereign, and which allowed the subjects to judge the efficacy of their king. While commentators are divided as to how radical Boece actually was, this interpretation was available to and developed most strongly by George Buchanan, and resisted, naturally enough, by his pupil James VI of Scotland.

Boece dramatizes his narratives: between the summaries of events, there are set-pieces allowing key figures speeches for argument, reflection, instruction. Thematically, the speeches allow Boece to investigate one of the key themes of Scotorum historia: the tension between private and public behaviour. Such scenes include parents having to choose between the lives of their children and the success of a siege, or a queen admitting to murdering her husband and reflecting on its public significance. Sometimes the tension spans a larger narrative: the scene of King Kenneth's imposition of primogeniture contrasts with the initial conciliar choice of election.

Boece's narrative appeals, therefore, for a number of reasons. It is rich in human success and failure; its narrative is fast-paced and dramatic; its style was of the moment, and translated well into Scots. For all these reasons, Boece's view of the Scots and their past came to dominate the imagining of Scotland for centuries to come.

SEE ALSO: Buchanan, George; Holinshed, Raphael; James VI and I; Leslie, John; Mair, John; Shakespeare, William

REFERENCES AND SUGGESTED READINGS

Broun, Dauvit (2007) Scottish independence and the idea of Britain from the Picts to Alexander III. Edinburgh University Press, Edinburgh.

Mapstone, Sally (1998) Shakespeare and Scottish kingship: a case history. In: Mapstone, Sally & Wood, Juliette (eds) The rose and the thistle: essays on the culture of late medieval and Renaissance Scotland. Tuckwell Press, East Linton, pp. 158–193.

Mason, Roger (1998) Kingship and the commonweal: political thought in Renaissance and Reformation Scotland. Tuckwell Press, East Linton.

Moir, James (ed. and trans.) (1894) Murthacensium et Aberdonensium episcoporum vitae, by Hector Boece. New Spalding Club (NS 12), Aberdeen.

Royan, Nicola (1998) The relationship between the Scotorum historia of Hector Boece and John Bellenden's Chronicles of Scotland. In: Mapstone, Sally & Wood, Juliette (eds) The rose and the thistle: essays on the culture of late medieval and *renaissance Scotland.* Tuckwell Press, East Linton, pp. 136–157.

Royan, Nicola (2000) The uses of speech in Hector Boece's Scotorum historia. In: Houwen, L. A. J. R., MacDonald, A. A., & Mapstone, S. L. (eds) *A palace in the wild: essays on the vernacular culture and humanism in late-medieval and renaissance Scotland.* Peeters, Leuven, pp. 75–93.

Royan, Nicola (2001) Hector Boece and the question of Veremund. *Innes Review* 52(1), 42–62.

Bolton, Edmund

ROBIN S. STEWART

Edmund Mary Bolton (1574/75–1634 or after) was a historian, antiquarian, and minor poet best known to contemporary scholars as the author of *Hypercritica*, a critical essay discussing the work of many contemporary writers and historians, and as an advocate for an English 'academ roial', an unrealized royal institution that would have been similar to the Académie française.

Bolton matriculated to Cambridge in 1589, entering Trinity Hall as a pensioner. Not officially recorded in any of the Inns of Court, Bolton himself reports that he lived in the Inner Temple until 1606 when he married Margaret Porter. Margaret's brother, Endymion Porter, later entered the service of the Villiers family and became a notable figure at court through the aid of James VI and I's favourite Sir George Villiers, the duke of Buckingham. Despite these family connections, which initially provided him with a small position in James's court, Bolton never enjoyed a successful public career, due in part to his staunch Catholicism. He was officially indicted for recusancy first in 1605 – along with Ben Jonson and Thomas Lodge (Eccles 1982) – and again in 1628 when, unable to pay the accompanying fine, he was imprisoned, where he remained probably until his death in 1634 (Woolf 2004).

Bolton's earliest works are pastoral poems included in *Englands Helicon* (1600), and his commendatory verses to William Camden's *Britannia* (1600), Thomas Andrew's *Unmasking of a female Machiauell* (1605), and Ben Jonson's *Volpone* (1605). His first antiquarian work, *The elements of armories* (1610), consists of a dialogue between two fictitious knights as they discuss the nature, history, and meaning of heraldry. It was one of many works that contributed to the rapid systemization of heraldry in the period (Day 1990). Bolton's first extended historical work, 'The life of Henry II' (1610), was written for inclusion in the *History of Great Britaine* (1611) compiled by John Speed, but was ultimately rejected for its overly sympathetic portrayal of Thomas à Becket, the archbishop of Canterbury.

Bolton then produced works dealing with Roman history, the first of which was a translation of *The Roman histories of Lucius Iulius Florus* (1618), an epitome of Livy's history. Bolton's only full-length, original Roman history, *Nero Caesar, or monarchie depraued* (1624), endeavours to demonstrate that 'No Prince is so bad as not to make monarckie seem the best forme of gouernment'. Beyond its didactic monarchism, however, Bolton's *Nero* represents a watershed moment in Renaissance historiography, as it is the first work to incorporate numismatics (the study of coins and currency) and epigraphy (the study of inscriptions) in order to verify the versions of events reported by ancient authors (Woolf 1990). Bolton's papers also indicate that he composed a history dealing with the reign of Tiberius, which has not survived.

Throughout his life, Bolton was a passionate champion of two great projects – both of which remained unrealized. The first was the composition of a worthy *Corpus rerum anglicarum* (a new and definitive history of England), for which his most well-known work, *Hypercritica* (1618), was written as a kind of historiographic manifesto. In *Hypercritica*, Bolton expresses his opinion that an improved history should go beyond the chronicle style of simply listing events, asserting that 'he who relates Events without their Premisses and Circumstances deserves not the name of an Historian, as being like to him who . . . presenteth unto us the Bare Skeleton, without declaring the Nature of the

Fabrick or teaching the Use of Parts'. In the work he also offers a rather ambivalent evaluation of Geoffrey of Monmouth as a historical source, outlines a scheme for the division of English history, and provides a critical evaluation of the best examples of English prose and poetry to aid the historian in elegant composition. The work concludes with Bolton enumerating the four most important roles the writer of this great history should fulfil: (1) as a 'Christian Cosmopolite', he must show the workings of God in the world to blast the atheist; (2) as a 'Christian Patriot', he must disclose the causes and authors of his country's good or evil for the liberty of nations; (3) as a 'Christian Subject', he must show the damage of rebellion and the benefit of obedience; and (4) as a 'Christian Paterfamilias', he must tend to his own family and everyday affairs. Though Bolton never materialized this ambition for a definitive English history, he did work laboriously in his final years on a history of London, the *Vindiciae britannicae*, which was never published and has not survived in manuscript (Woolf 2004).

The second great project was the establishment of an English 'academ roial', which he unsuccessfully advocated to both James I and Charles I in a series of pamphlets. Initially, James was receptive to the idea, and a plan for the academy was considered by the House of Peers in 1624 at Buckingham's request. According to the plan, the academy would have included 'tutelaries' consisting of knights of the garter as well as the lord chancellor, 'auxiliaries' consisting of other prominent noblemen, and 'essentials' drawn from prominent English writers, scholars, and intellectuals. Most importantly, the academy would have had the power of reviewing and censoring all English translations of secular learning. With James's death, however, the project failed to capture the favour of Charles I, despite Bolton's continued promotion of the idea in later works, such as *The cabanet royal* (1627).

SEE ALSO: Camden, William; Jonson, Ben; Lodge, Thomas; Speed, John

REFERENCES AND SUGGESTED READINGS

Blackburn, Thomas H. (1967) Edmund Bolton's *The cabanet royal*: a belated reply to Sidney's *Apology for poetry*. Studies in the Renaissance 14, 159–171.

Day, J. F. R. (1990) Primers of honor: heraldry, heraldry books, and English Renaissance literature. Sixteenth Century Journal 21(1), 93–103.

Eccles, Mark (1982) Brief lives: Tudor and Stuart authors. Studies in Philology 79(4), 1–135.

Woolf, D. R. (1990) *The idea of history in early Stuart England*. University of Toronto Press, Toronto.

Woolf, D. R. (2004) Bolton, Edmund Mary. In: *Oxford dictionary of national biography*. Oxford University Press, Oxford.

Book of Common Prayer, the

TIMOTHY ROSENDALE

The Book of Common Prayer, first published in 1549, was and technically still is the official liturgy of the Church of England, and is arguably one of the most important texts in English history. It is primarily the work of archbishop of Canterbury Thomas Cranmer, assisted by a range of scholars, bishops, and theologians, and its purpose was to provide nationally standardized forms of worship, in English, and with generally (if sometimes ambiguously) Protestant commitments.

The contents of the 1549 Book of Common Prayer are as follows:

1 A preface, written by Cranmer, substantially a translation of the introduction to Cardinal Francesco de Quinones's 1535 Breviary
2 Table and Kalendar for determining daily scriptural readings
3 Liturgical forms for Mattins and Evensong (morning and evening prayer)
4 Proper readings for each Sunday and feast day throughout the year
5 Holy Communion
6 The Litany
7 Baptism

8 Confirmation
9 Matrimony
10 Visitation of the Sick
11 Burial
12 Purification of Women
13 Ash Wednesday
14 An original concluding essay titled 'Of Ceremonies, why some be abolished and some retained', in which Cranmer explains the logic of liturgical reform embodied in the Prayer Book
15 Concluding rubrics.

Subsequent editions (1552, 1559, 1604, 1662) revised, rearranged, and supplemented these, but this structure formed the basic skeleton for all of them.

But the history of the Book of Common Prayer is quite complex. While it is largely a modified translation of the Latin liturgy of the Roman Catholic Church (specifically the Sarum Use prevalent in England), it was also considerably influenced by Continental Protestant liturgies, Lutheran and other, and also owes some debts to the liturgies of the Eastern Church. While the impulse for an English liturgy grew directly out of the Reformation, it was preceded by a corresponding movement for liturgical reform within Catholicism (hence the influence of Quinones). And while a liturgy is of course a primarily religious form, the development of the Book of Common Prayer, like everything else about the English Reformation, was complicated by political factors and counter-currents.

Evidence from Cranmer's letters and drafts suggests that purposeful movement towards an English liturgy began in the 1530s, after the break with Rome, and especially late in the decade, at the same time as the successful and legal publication of the first English Bibles. The Protestant objection to Latin scripture and service made liturgical translation and reform the obvious (and, some have argued, equally important) corollary to the vernacular Bible. But Henry VIII's religious conservatism prevented the implementation of thorough reform, and the only piece officially remade

during his lifetime was the English Litany in 1544. Upon his death and Edward VI's accession in 1547, however, the process quickened, with an English eucharistic liturgy distributed for insertion into the Mass in 1548, and all the while Cranmer and his advisers were drafting and finalizing the entire liturgy for immediate publication.

There is much of interest surrounding the official publication of the first Prayer Book in 1549. To begin with, it was issued by parliamentary authority, not that of Convocation, indicating that political as well as theological and ecclesiastical interests were at stake. That authorization took the form of the first Act of Uniformity, which decreed the uniform and exclusive use of the new liturgy throughout the king's dominions, outlawed the use of any other, and prescribed significant penalties – ranging up to life imprisonment and forfeiture of all property – for clergy who violated these provisions. The other major event attending the Book of Common Prayer's introduction was a serious uprising in Devon and Cornwall, known as the Western or Prayer Book Rebellion, which was triggered by the new liturgy, demanded the restoration of the old religion, grew quite large and dangerous, and was in the end rather brutally suppressed by the Somerset regime. (The written grievances and demands of the rebels, and the government's responses to them, are interesting reading.)

The text itself appears to be a calculated compromise that took Catholic forms, adapted them in Protestant directions, and aimed for a studied ambiguity that avoided giving direct offence at crucial moments. The 1549 words of consecration, for example, ask God to 'blesse and sanctifie these thy gyftes, and creatures of bread and wyne, that they maie *be unto us* the bodye and bloude of thy moste derely beloued sonne Jesus Christe' – thereby dodging any clear (and thus divisive) theological declaration of belief in either transubstantiation or the symbolic function of the eucharist by resorting to ambiguity and metaphor. Of course, ideologues and true believers at the far ends of the religious spectrum were appalled at this waffling, in which Protestants smelled residual popery, while Catholics caught more than a whiff of heresy and falsehood. But for most people, ambiguity seems to have worked, as it could be interpreted by individuals in a wide variety of ways, and thus formed a basis for more or less harmonious collective practice.

This modus operandi was largely abandoned when the Book of Common Prayer was revised and re-released in 1552. This second Edwardian Book of Common Prayer was doctrinally clearer and ceremonially leaner than the first, and was in many respects the most stripped down and decisively Protestant liturgy in the history of the Church of England, before or since. Its words of invocation, for example, articulate a strongly memorial and symbolic view of the sacrament: 'graunt that wee, receiving these thy creatures of bread and wyne, according to thy sonne our Savioure Jesus Christ's holy institucion, in remembraunce of his death and passion, maye be partakers of his most blessed body and bloud'. The elements are not transformed, but emphatically remain mere 'creatures' which inspire and signify spiritual participation in Christ without literalizing it.

The 1552 Prayer Book was successfully introduced, but doomed by the death of Edward VI the following year. His half-sister Mary I quickly banned it and restored England to Rome; Cranmer was burned at the stake; and the Prayer Book was preserved in exile, particularly in the English congregation at Frankfurt, where there was a battle between liturgical and anti-liturgical Protestants (including John Knox, John Foxe, and Jean Calvin himself) that foreshadowed the future of the Book of Common Prayer.

When Elizabeth I succeeded Mary in 1558, the Prayer Book was quickly restored, in a form which significantly re-ambiguized what 1552 had striven to clarify, thus signalling one fundamental principle of the Elizabethan settlement: its recourse to latitude, ambiguity, and adiaphora ('things indifferent', that is, the position that some religious issues are matters of individual discretion, and thus do not require coercive institutional declaration) for the purpose of neutralizing religious conflict. The other main principle – an insistence on royal prerogative and supremacy – was embodied in the Act of Uniformity that authorized it, which greatly increased the penalties for violation, and specifically mandated weekly church attendance for all the queen's subjects. This did not entirely prevent early Puritan critiques of the Book of Common Prayer during her reign, but these were swiftly dealt with and resoundingly rebutted by Richard Hooker.

Nevertheless, the reformists sensed further opportunity at the 1603 accession of James I, who called the Hampton Court Conference (January 1604) in response to the Millennary Petition. This resulted in only minor alterations to the liturgy, but complaints about the inadequacies of the Bible translation used in the Prayer Book resulted in the commissioning of the Authorized Version, or King James Bible. The remainder of the early Stuart era saw a general polarization of reformists and a reactionary high-church party associated with William Laud, archbishop of Canterbury from 1633, and this division was an important dimension in the fissures that developed into the Civil War in the 1640s. Parliament banned the Book of Common Prayer in 1645; conversely, it was the textual centrepiece of Charles II's restoration in 1660.

The resulting 1662 text survived more or less intact to the present day. It remained the sole authorized liturgy of the Church of England until 1965, when parliament allowed its supplementation with more recent forms. In 1974 parliament stepped out of matters liturgical, but only with the provision that the 1662 Book of Common Prayer be permanently protected. And in 1980, the Alternative Service Book took its place as the first ever full-scale liturgical alternative to exist alongside the Prayer Book legally. This event prompted organized defence of the Book of Common Prayer by a surprising number and variety of public figures, including C. H. Sisson, John Gielgud, Laurence Olivier, Philip Larkin, Iris Murdoch, Henry Moore, and Andrew Lloyd Webber.

As the preceding account suggests, there are many reasons why this critically underappreciated text is of enormous importance in understanding the religious, political, and literary history of England in the early modern period and beyond. First, it is a foundational text of the English Reformation, and its significance approaches, and at times arguably exceeds, that of the English Bible, with which it is inextricably, if sometimes tensely, linked. Secondly, even more than the English Bible, it is a text that we can say with considerable confidence was familiar to virtually everyone. Thirdly, it is a core text of English identity generally, as it was from the start deeply connected to both vernacular English and nationally uniform practice as well as autonomous Protestantism. Fourthly, it was the primary vehicle by which the vast majority of the populace experienced theology. Fifthly, by virtue of the necessarily collective commitments of liturgy, and especially a legally mandatory liturgy, it implicitly and explicitly articulated fundamental principles regarding the political and social order, and the individual's relation to them. Sixthly, these principles helped to counterbalance and moderate the chaotic potentialities of unrestricted individual Bible-reading, and thus create an importantly qualified understanding of the nature of Protestant England. Seventhly, for all these reasons, the Book of Common Prayer is a text quietly central to England's sense of itself over four centuries, and noisily epicentral to the religious and political conflicts that so deeply affected England in the early modern period.

This all has deep interest and broad implications for literary studies. The Prayer Book's language demonstrably saturates the works of Shakespeare; this was shown long ago by Richmond Noble, who further argued that most of Shakespeare's allusions to the Psalms are recognizably derived from the Book of Common Prayer's Coverdale version and not more contemporary translations (Noble 1935). Hundreds of terms and phrases from the liturgy echo throughout the Shakespeare canon:

Hamlet's 'pickers and stealers', Wolsey's 'vain pomp and glory of this world', Prince Hal's 'good amendment of life'. But Shakespeare's engagement with liturgy runs deeper than mere echoes. *Richard III*, for example, makes use of prayer-books as true and false signs of piety, and when Richard II, at his deposition, cries out 'God save the king! Will no man say amen? / Am I both priest and clerk? Well then, amen', he heartbreakingly figures his political and social isolation in terms of the breakdown of an explicitly liturgical order.

Many other major early modern British writers took explicit positions for (e.g., Hooker, John Donne, George Herbert, Thomas Browne, Thomas Hobbes) and against (John Milton, pre-eminently) the Book of Common Prayer and what it stood for. Many others wrestled more indirectly with its implications in terms of theology, devotional expression, and the tensions between individual and communal identity. Much of Herbert's *Temple*, from its overall structure to the refrains and responsories of individual poems, is clearly derived from the liturgy, and even the violently anti-liturgical Milton seemingly could not resist the beauty of morning and evening prayer spoken in unison by Adam and Eve.

Similar demonstrations of the Book of Common Prayer's influence could be made in any period up to, and including, our own. From Ernest Hemingway's (and Neville Chamberlain's) '[peace] in our time' to Neil Young's 'ashes to ashes, dust to dust' to much of the typical modern wedding service (starting with 'Dearly beloved'), English-speaking culture has repeated and echoed Cranmer's language for four and a half centuries, often without being aware of doing so. And in this, we can see further evidence of the depth of its embeddedness in our thinking and speaking, and of our unconscious indebtedness to its legacy.

SEE ALSO: Bible, the; Browne, Thomas; Cranmer, Thomas; Donne, John; Herbert, George; Hobbes, Thomas; Hooker, Richard; Milton, John; Shakespeare, William

REFERENCES AND SUGGESTED READINGS

Booty, John (ed.) (1981) *The godly kingdom of Tudor England*. Morehouse-Barlow, Wilton.

Booty, John (ed.) (2005) *The Book of Common Prayer 1559*. University of Virginia Press, for Folger Shakespeare Library, Charlottesville.

Brightman, F. E. (1915) *The English rite*. 2 vols. Rivingtons, London.

Brook, Stella (1965) *The language of the Book of Common Prayer*. Oxford University Press, New York.

Cuming, G. J. (1982) *A history of Anglican liturgy*. Macmillan, London.

Cuming, G. J. (1983) *The godly order: texts and studies relating to the Book of Common Prayer*. Macmillan, London.

Green, Ian (2000) *Print and Protestantism in early modern England*. Oxford University Press, New York.

MacCulloch, Diarmaid (1996) *Thomas Cranmer: a life*. Yale University Press, New Haven.

Maltby, Judith (1998) *Prayer book and people in Elizabethan and early Stuart England*. Cambridge University Press, Cambridge.

Noble, Richmond (1935) *Shakespeare's biblical knowledge and use of the Book of Common Prayer*. SPCK, London.

Ratcliff, E. C. (ed.) (1949) *The first and second prayer books of Edward VI*. J. M. Dent, London.

Rosendale, Timothy (2007) *Liturgy and literature in the making of Protestant England*. Cambridge University Press, Cambridge.

Targoff, Ramie (2001) *Common prayer: the language of public devotion in early modern England*. University of Chicago Press, Chicago.

Wall, John N. (1988) *Transformations of the word: Spenser, Herbert, Vaughan*. University of Georgia Press, Athens.

Boorde, Andrew

ERIN SULLIVAN

Best known for his vernacular medical treatises and travel writings, Andrew Boorde (c.1490–1549) cuts a picaresque figure in English Tudor history. He began his professional life in 1515 as a Carthusian monk at the London Charterhouse, receiving permission in 1529 to travel to the Continent to study medicine. Upon his return he began practising medicine in England, caring for Thomas Howard, third duke of Norfolk, and possibly for Henry VIII. Having already distanced himself from the strict vegetarianism and austere lifestyle of the Carthusian order, he obtained a full release from his monastic vows after Henry VIII's split from Rome. In contrast to many Carthusians, who were well known for their enduring allegiance to the pope, Boorde took the oath of conformity as required under the Act of Succession of 1534. The following year Thomas Cromwell, Henry's chief reforming minister, employed him as a government informant in Continental Europe and later Scotland, where he reported on public feeling concerning the king and his divorce. During this time Boorde continued to pursue his medical studies, and in the late 1530s, with Cromwell's fall from favour, he began writing and publishing handbooks on the maintenance of health. Although in his writings he presented himself as a committed loyalist, he never fully escaped persecution for his Catholic past (Shrank 2000; 2004; Maslen 2003). In 1547 he was imprisoned, allegedly for engaging the services of prostitutes, and he died in prison in 1549.

Boorde wrote his medical treatises for a popular audience, composing them in English and tailoring his advice to the needs and means of lay readers. His most successful publications, *A dyetary of helth* (1542) and *The breviary of helth* (1547), went through eight and seven editions respectively by the end of the century (Slack 1979; Shrank 2004). Both books emphasize the importance of diet, exercise, and environment to the preservation of good health, as was typical of medicine at the time. Readers are encouraged to know their humoral temperament and to tailor their daily regimen accordingly; those with a hot, choleric constitution, for instance, are encouraged to avoid spicy foods, while those with an earthy, melancholic nature should eat boiled rather than roasted meats. In his *Dyetary* Boorde stresses the importance of eating properly; he describes the health-giving qualities of many kinds of food and drink and notes that 'a good coke is halfe a phisicion' since so many medical treatments 'come from the kytchyn'. His *Breviary*, an encyclopedia of illnesses and their remedies, bears out this statement, as most prescriptions focus on the patient's eating habits and recommend particular foods as treatments. In all cases temperance is advocated as essential for health and longevity, a principle central to contemporary orthodox medicine, which relied principally on the theories of Hippocrates and Galen of Pergamum (Siraisi 1990; Wear 2000).

Boorde's other major publication is *The fyrst boke of the introduction of knowledge* (written 1542, published c.1549), an early travel guide intended to 'teache a man to speake parte of all maner of languages, and to know the usage and fashion of all maner of countreys'. The first in a series of three books (the other two have been lost), the *Introduction* begins in England and takes its readers on a tour through Europe and its neighbouring countries, wittily and satirically detailing information about local customs, dialects, foods, currencies, and weather. Each chapter begins with a woodcut illustration of a stereotypical countryman, followed by a humorous poem written from his point of view. While Boorde's depiction of England is largely flattering, his representations of foreign countries generally poke fun at commonly held cultural stereotypes. His Hollander, for instance, is shown at a table eating and drinking, and the accompanying poem focuses on his fondness for drink: 'I am a Holander, good cloth I do make / To much of englyshe bere dyvers tymes I do take.' Such commentary has been of particular interest to scholars researching both the construction of national identity and the representation of foreignness in Renaissance England (Sousa 1999; Floyd-Wilson 2003; Shrank 2004).

Recent scholarly work on Boorde has focused on his efforts to adapt to the dramatically changing religious and political landscape in Tudor England (Shrank 2000; 2004), as well as the nature of his reputation in the years after his death (Maslen 2003). Several posthumous jestbooks were attributed to Boorde in the early seventeenth century, and while nineteenth-century historians largely denied his authorship (Furnivall 1870), recent work has argued for their reattribution (Maslen 2003). Boorde's medical works emphasize the health benefits of mirth and laughter, encouraging readers to enjoy the company of friends and avoid sorrow and worry. He gained a reputation as a jolly man, and he may have even provided inspiration for the character of Gregory Streamer in William Baldwin's *Beware the cat* (1553), a humorous work of prose fiction that imagines the stories cats might tell if they could speak (Maslen 2003). In his full and diverse life he worked as a monk, doctor, spy, travel writer, and jester, adjusting his interests to suit the needs of the time and producing a variety of written works interested in the idiosyncrasies of human nature.

SEE ALSO: Baldwin, William

REFERENCES AND SUGGESTED READINGS

Floyd-Wilson, Mary (2003) *English ethnicity and race in early modern drama.* Cambridge University Press, Cambridge.

Furnivall, F. J. (ed.) (1870) *The fyrst boke of the introduction of knowledge made by Andrew Borde.* Early English Text Society, London.

Maslen, R. W. (2003) The afterlife of Andrew Borde. *Studies in Philology* 100(4), 463–492.

Shrank, Cathy (2000) Andrew Borde and the politics of identity in Reformation England. *Reformation* 5, 1–26.

Shrank, Cathy (2004) *Writing the nation in Reformation England, 1530–1580.* Oxford University Press, Oxford.

Siraisi, Nancy G. (1990) *Medieval and early Renaissance medicine.* Chicago University Press, Chicago.

Slack, Paul (1979) Mirrors of health and treasures of poor men: the uses of the vernacular medical literature of Tudor England. In: Webster, Charles (ed.) *Health, medicine and mortality in the sixteenth century.* Cambridge University Press, Cambridge, pp. 237–273.

Sousa, Geraldo U. de (1999) *Shakespeare's cross-cultural encounters.* Macmillan Press, Basingstoke.

Wear, Andrew (2000) *Knowledge and practice in English medicine, 1550–1680.* Cambridge University Press, Cambridge.

Boyle, Robert

KATHRYN MURPHY

Robert Boyle (1627–91), natural historian and philosopher, and writer on religious and ethical topics, was a key figure in the development of science, particularly important for contributions to chemistry and experimental methodology. He wrote prolifically in various genres, and is especially notable in the development of the essay.

Boyle was born on 25 January 1627 in Lismore, Ireland, the fourteenth child of Richard Boyle, the wealthy first earl of Cork. He was educated at Eton College from 1635 to 1638, and went on a Continental tour from 1639 to 1644. On his return he began to write, mostly on ethics and religion, experimenting with genres including the essay, meditation, and romance. Important early writings include the 'Account of Philaretus during his minority' (1648 or 1649), a spiritual autobiography, and *The martyrdom of Theodora and of Didymus*, a romance allegorizing love and piety, first published, anonymously and much revised, in 1687. He studied biblical languages and history, and produced essays and letters later incorporated into *Some motives and incentives to the love of God* (1659), also known as *Seraphick love*, his most reprinted work in the seventeenth century.

In the late 1640s he started a correspondence with the intelligencer Samuel Hartlib. In three letters and a manuscript dating from 1646 and 1647 he referred to an 'Invisible College', dedicated to the improvement of natural philosophy and husbandry, but there is no indication of the other members or of their activities. In 1649 Boyle established a laboratory at his house in Stalbridge, Dorset, inaugurating an interest in experimentation that dominated his later life and writings. His first publication was the 'Invitation to a free and generous communication of secrets and receits in physick', couched as a letter between imaginary correspondents, which was probably composed in 1649 and appeared anonymously in *Chymical, medicinal, and chyrurgical addresses: made to Samuel Hartlib* (1655).

The developing interest in natural philosophy coincided with a change in style: elaborate rhetorical self-consciousness and literary imitation gave way to plainness and lack of ambiguity, though his difficult subjects often demanded convolution. The shift was also influenced by a medical crisis: in the early 1650s, a serious illness permanently damaged Boyle's eyesight. He relied thereafter on amanuenses to record his works, resulting in a digressive and oral style.

In the winter of 1655/56 Boyle moved to Oxford and became part of a group around John Wilkins of Wadham College who met to conduct experiments and discuss natural philosophy. Boyle was much influenced by reading Francis Bacon, while his fraught engagement with the writings of Thomas Hobbes and René Descartes convinced him to counter the threat of materialistic atheism through a combination of Christian apologetics and natural philosophy. From 1660, he began to publish extensively. Several volumes narrated experiments investigating specific topics, including *New experiments physico-mechanical, touching the spring of air and its effects* (1660), which contained experiments done with an air-pump designed by his assistant Robert Hooke, and prompted a controversial exchange with Thomas Hobbes. The year 1661 saw the publication of both the dialogue *The sceptical chymist*, and *Certain physiological essays*, which included a 'Proemial Essay . . . with some considerations touching experimental *essays* in General', on the literary methodology of natural philosophy, preferring rather a 'Philosophical than a Rhetorical strain'. The exclamatory style and homely subjects of his pious *Occasional reflections* (1665) prompted parodies by Jonathan Swift and Samuel Butler. *Physiological essays* and *The origine of formes and qualities* (1666) argued for the superiority of corpuscularian accounts of matter over scholastic philosophy.

Boyle was an inaugural member of the Royal Society in 1660, and an active participant throughout the 1660s, despite his continued residence in Oxford. He published frequently and copiously in their journal, the *Philosophical Transactions*. From 1668 Boyle lived in London with his sister, Katherine, Viscountess Ranelagh, who shared his intellectual interests and facilitated his natural enquiries. In 1670 he suffered a stroke which hindered his participation in the Royal Society. He nonetheless continued his experimental work and published on natural philosophical, alchemical, and religious topics, including several works in an apologetic vein, including *The excellency of theology, compar'd with natural philosophy* (1674), *A disquisition about the final causes of natural things* (1688), and *The Christian virtuoso* (1690). His influence on natural theology continued after his death on 31 December 1691: his will provided for annual lectures against atheism.

Boyle wrote prolifically, and in addition to his voluminous publications, he left much in manuscript, preserved as the Boyle Papers at the Royal Society. He was preoccupied with the reception of his works, and strived to ensure their persuasive impact, whether through genre, style, or strategic dissemination in print. He was involved in proselytizing schemes to translate the Bible into Turkish and Irish Gaelic. His consciousness of rhetoric is evident in *Some considerations touching the style of the holy Scriptures* (1661). His concern to secure trust in his experimental observations, and assent to conclusions based on them, led to the development of what Steven Shapin and Simon Schaffer (1985) called 'literary technology' and 'virtual witnessing', in which narratives of experiments, endorsed by trustworthy witnesses, substituted for readers' direct experience of the phenomena described. An important component was an emphasis on doubts and probability, and an ethos of gentlemanly civility and moral scrupulosity. He was solicitous about his works' reception, arranging for their publication in Latin, supplying book-lists and adverts for forthcoming titles, and adding lengthy prefaces, explaining how illness, the theft or loss of manuscripts, and his chaotic system of composition had hindered the optimal presentation of his work.

SEE ALSO: Bacon, Francis; Bible, the; Hartlib, Samuel; Hobbes, Thomas

REFERENCES AND SUGGESTED READINGS

Black, Scott (2007) Boyle's essay: genre and the making of early modern knowledge. In: Smith, Pamela H. & Schmidt, Benjamin (eds) *Making knowledge in early modern Europe: practices, objects, and texts 1400–1800*. University of Chicago Press, Chicago, pp. 178–195.

Hunter, Michael (ed.) (1994a) *Robert Boyle by himself and his friends*. William Pickering, London.

Hunter, Michael (ed.) (1994b) *Robert Boyle reconsidered*. Cambridge University Press, Cambridge.

Hunter, Michael (2000) *Robert Boyle (1627–91): scrupulosity and science*. Boydell Press, Woodbridge.

Hunter, Michael (2009) *Boyle: between God and science*. Yale University Press, New Haven.

Sargent, Rose-Mary (1995) *The diffident naturalist: Robert Boyle and the philosophy of experiment*. University of Chicago Press, Chicago.

Shapin, Steven (1984) Pump and circumstance: Robert Boyle's literary technology. *Social Studies of Science* 14(4), 481–520.

Shapin, Steven & Schaffer, Simon (1985) *Leviathan and the air-pump: Hobbes, Boyle, and the experimental life*. Princeton University Press, Princeton.

Wojcik, Jan W. (1997) *Robert Boyle and the limits of reason*. Cambridge University Press, Cambridge.

Brackley, Elizabeth

DEANNE WILLIAMS

Elizabeth Brackley (1626–63), born Elizabeth Cavendish, was an author and dramatist. The daughter of William Cavendish, duke of

Newcastle (1593–1676), stepdaughter of Margaret Cavendish (1623–73), and great-granddaughter of Bess of Hardwick (Elizabeth Talbot, countess of Shrewsbury, ?1527–1608), Elizabeth grew up in a literary family that supported her literary and dramatic efforts. She is best known for her play *The concealed fancyes* (c.1644–45), which she co-authored with her sister, Lady Jane Cavendish (1621–69), and which survives, along with a pastoral masque and their poems, in manuscripts at the Bodleian and Beineke Libraries (Beinecke Library, Osborn MS b. 223; Bodleian Library, MS Rawl. Poet. 16). She is also the author of a substantial number of writings on the Bible, prayers, and other meditations held at the British Library and the Huntington Library (British Library, MS Egerton 607; Huntington Library, MS EL 8374, 8376, 8377).

Brackley married John Egerton (1622–86), then Viscount Brackley, in 1641. Egerton, later the second earl of Bridgewater, had played the role of the elder brother in Milton's *Comus*. Elizabeth was just 15, and, in the opinion of her family, 'too young to be bedded', and so she remained at home for some years. When the Civil War broke out, Elizabeth's father and brothers fought with the Royalist forces while she remained at the family estate at Welbeck Abbey with her sisters Jane and Frances, and their mother, Elizabeth Basset, who died in 1643. As Welbeck was captured and held by Parliamentary troops, the sisters passed the time writing *The concealed fancyes*.

The concealed fancyes is a kind of dramatic *roman à clef*, concerning the marriage of Luceny and Tattiney (Jane and Elizabeth). Through the characters of Lord Calsindow and Lady Tranquillity, the sisters express their disapproval of their father's courtship of Margaret Lucas (later Margaret Cavendish), 30 years his junior, during his exile in France. The sisters also cast their brothers, the two Stellows, as heroes who liberate them from imprisonment. In this sense, the play also serves as a form of wish fulfilment. The unusual context in which

The concealed fancyes was written anchors the play's reflections on companionate marriage and women's autonomy with accurate depictions of warfare and bloodshed, yet it also conveys nostalgia for witty and sophisticated court culture.

Elizabeth and Jane had served as ladies-in-waiting to Henrietta Maria, and the elaborate masques performed at court and during Charles and Henrietta Maria's visits to Welbeck, in which they may have participated, inspired their own masque, *A pastorall* (1645). Three shepherdesses (Jane, Elizabeth, and Frances) are so upset by the absence of their father and brothers that they are unwilling to entertain the amorous advances of three shepherds. Anti-masques presented by witches and country wives reflect the political climate of warfare and espionage, just as the pastoral narrative allegorizes the sisters' condition. An allusion to Elizabeth's position as married but not yet a wife illustrates the authors' particular state of suspended animation.

Elizabeth and Jane elaborately dedicated *The concealed fancyes* and *A pastorall* to their father, in his absence. Their poems and songs are also dedicated to the king, queen, prince of Wales, and various family members. Although Elizabeth and Jane often signal their independent authorship by initialling the verses they composed, their collaboration reinforces the emotional, political, and symbolic power of family ties. It possesses, as well, an elegiac quality, memorializing a way of life that was no more.

Elizabeth eventually joined John Egerton at Ashridge, the family home, and their marriage produced four children. Elizabeth's writings as wife and mother are almost exclusively devoted to the genres of prayer and meditation, revealing a wholeheartedly pious character whose devotion infuses her family life with religious meaning. Elizabeth's 'Meditations on generall chapters of the Holy Bible' present a substantial collection of extended meditations on biblical chapters. 'True copies of certain loose papers left by the right honourable Elizabeth, countess of Bridgewater', which John had gathered up after her death and made into multiple copies, contain prayers and meditations, along with the odd verse, that explore her experiences as wife and mother. They include numerous prayers and meditations concerning her husband and marriage, sick children and children who died, pregnancy, labour, and the recovery after childbirth. In a verse dialogue written when she was a girl, Elizabeth's father had asked her, teasingly, to learn to 'dissemble' as a writer. Yet this comprehensive and substantial body of work, which totals hundreds of pages, contains honest examinations of her status as a mother and wife and heartfelt considerations of her spiritual condition.

Elizabeth died in 1663. After joining her husband in prison following a duelling charge, she went into premature labour. Jane's poem, 'On the death of my dear sister', records the deaths of Elizabeth and her baby. Illustrating the centrality of family to the sisters' literary productivity, the work of Elizabeth Brackley conveys not only the royalist ideas of aristocratic lineage, but also the personal and affective bonds of the household, focusing on everything from the vacuum created by an absent father and brothers to the powerful presence of a wife and mother as spiritual nurturer and guide. In Elizabeth's independent writing, she creates a genre and vocabulary for expressing the longings and anxieties of motherhood and conveys a sharp and humanizing awareness of the fragility of life.

SEE ALSO: Cavendish, Jane; Cavendish, Margaret; Milton, John

REFERENCES AND SUGGESTED READINGS

Bennett, Alexandra G. (2005) Now let my language speake: the authorship, rewriting, and audience(s) of Jane Cavendish and Elizabeth Brackley. *Early Modern Literary Studies* 11(2), 1–13.

Ezell, Margaret (1988) To be your daughter in your pen: the social functions of literature in the writings of Lady Elizabeth Brackley and Lady Jane Cavendish. *Huntington Library Quarterly* 51, 281–296.

Findlay, Alison (2006) *Playing spaces in early women's drama.* Cambridge University Press, Cambridge.

Travitsky, Betty (1999) *Subordination and authorship in early modern England: the case of Elizabeth Cavendish Egerton and her 'Loose papers'.* Arizona Center for Medieval and Renaissance Studies, Tempe.

Bradstreet, Anne

JOHANNA HARRIS

Interest in Anne Bradstreet (1612/13–1672) has traditionally focused upon her status as a woman writer and early American Puritan poet, yet her literary legacy extends beyond both these categories. Her major poetry publications were *The tenth muse* (1650) and the posthumous *Several poems* (1678), but she also wrote in prose, leaving a collection of further writings known as the Andover manuscripts ('Andover MSS', Stevens Memorial Library, North Andover, Massachusetts; now deposited in the Houghton Library, Harvard University). As well as additional poems, these writings include aphorisms for her son, prose meditations on her daily and spiritual life, and an autobiographical legacy in epistolary form to her children. Interest in Bradstreet stretches across several discursive terrains, including her contributions to early modern English political thought and early American philosophy; her views on ecology, natural science, transatlantic travel and expansion, and education; and her discourses on suffering, mourning, and survival. Her writings are deeply influenced by her Calvinist providentialism and the intellectual outlook and literary expression of a transatlantic Puritan culture. In turn, Bradstreet's influence upon modern feminist literary criticism and upon the discourses of English and American Puritanism is well established. Her Prologue to *The tenth muse* is well known and self-effacing, yet her apology for her poems on the grounds of modest skill and gender are at odds with the outspoken and agile defence of the woman's right to write in the poem's fifth verse:

> I am obnoxious to each carping tongue
> Who says my hand a needle better fits,
> A Poets pen all scorn I should thus wrong,
> For such despite they cast on Female wits:
> If what I do prove well, it won't advance,
> They'l say it's stoln, or else it was by chance.

Anne Bradstreet (née Dudley) was born in 1612/13, probably in Northampton, the second of five children to Thomas Dudley (1576–1653) and his first wife, Dorothy Yorke (1581/82–1643). According to the New England Puritan minister Cotton Mather, her father was of great 'Natural and Acquired Abilities' and 'excellent Moral Qualities', and her mother 'a gentlewoman both of good estate and good extraction'. In 1619 the family moved to Sempringham, Lincolnshire, where Dudley became chief steward to the estates of Theophilus Clinton, fourth earl of Lincoln, the son of the third earl Thomas and his wife the countess, Elizabeth Clinton (née Knyvett). *The countesse of Lincolnes nurserie* (1622) was published while the Dudley family were in the Clinton household. Thomas Dudley was recommended to his position by the leading Puritan aristocrat of Broughton, Oxfordshire, William Fiennes, first Viscount Saye and Sele, whose daughter, Bridget, married the fourth earl in 1620; she was the countess of Lincoln with whom Thomas Dudley corresponded from New England. The Dudleys' close association with some of the leading families of early Stuart Puritanism in England provides an insight into Anne Bradstreet's early intellectual formation. Along with her father's example and encouragement of reading across a wide range of subjects, including classical as well as English and French literature, history, philosophy, astronomy, medicine, and natural science, and his encouragement of her writing (he too was a poet), Bradstreet had access to the earl of Lincoln's books as well as a wider literary and intellectual coterie. It was during this period that she met Simon Bradstreet, the son of the

Puritan minister (also Simon Bradstreet) of Horbling, Lincolnshire, who had arrived at the earl of Lincoln's household in 1621. Thomas Dudley moved his family to Boston, Lincolnshire, in 1623, to join the congregation of St Botolph's, then under the strongly Puritan preacher, John Cotton, who migrated to Boston, New England, in 1633. Anne Hutchinson travelled 24 miles to attend this same congregation, and was also a future migrant to America, though she was later tried and banished during the colony's Antinomian Controversy.

Anne Dudley and the younger Simon Bradstreet married in 1628, when he was steward to Frances Rich, dowager countess of Warwick and mother of Robert Rich, second earl of Warwick, the most consistent supporter of the Puritan cause and its ministers. At the Warwick seat of Leighs Priory in Felstead, Essex, Anne Bradstreet probably knew and participated in the godly activities of the Rich household with the little-known Puritan woman writer, Lucy Robartes (née Rich, c.1615–1645/46), daughter of the second earl and her near contemporary in age.

The Bradstreets sailed for New England in March 1630 on board the flagship *Arbella* to New England, arriving in Salem, Massachusetts, on 12 June 1630. Thomas Dudley sailed with his family on the same ship as one of the founding members and shareholders of the Massachusetts Bay Company, and as deputy to John Winthrop's governorship of the new colony. Mather suggests that it was Bradstreet who encouraged her husband to agree to emigrate, although according to her account to her children she felt an initial reluctance: 'I found a new world and new manners, at which my heart rose. But after I was convinced it was the way of God, I submitted to it and joined to the church at Boston.' The Bradstreets lived for short periods in Charlestown, Boston, and Newtown (now Cambridge), before settling in Ipswich from 1635 until 1640 when they moved to Merrimack (now Andover). There is little evidence of Bradstreet's activities beyond her home and family during this time, but her literary output was already making an artistic and intellectual contribution to English and American cultural posterity as early as 1642 when a manuscript collection of her poetry, dedicated to her father, was in circulation.

Bradstreet's printed works consist of two volumes of poetry. *The tenth muse lately sprung up in America*, a small sextodecimo volume, was published in London in 1650 by her brother-in-law, John Woodbridge, though only with the attribution, 'By a Gentlewoman in those parts'. *Several poems* (1678) posthumously published Bradstreet's additions to and corrections of *The tenth muse* and, as the title page states, 'several other Poems found amongst her Papers after her Death'. The volume, also in sextodecimo size but greater in page length and with a larger typeface, was printed by John Foster in Boston. The volume also printed further poetic epitaphs written in Bradstreet's honour, including 'Upon Mrs. Anne Bradstreet her poems, & c.', by the president of Harvard College, John Rogers, and the Puritan minister John Norton's funeral elegy on Bradstreet.

As the first Anglo-American to publish poetry, and arriving in New England at the age of 17, Bradstreet exhibits in her poems an ongoing dual allegiance. *The tenth muse* gives notice of her new location in its full title and in the appended poem 'In praise of the Author ... At present residing in the Occidentall parts of the World, in *America*, alias *NOV-ANGLIA*'. The allegiance, however, is rooted in Bradstreet's firm commitment to an international radical Protestantism. 'A dialogue between Old *England* and New; concerning their present troubles, *Anno*, 1642' is styled as a poetic exchange between mother and daughter. It is the younger 'New England' who frames the dialogue, and mother England responds to her questions with passionate laments on the origins of the religio-political crisis at the root of the English Civil War. Bradstreet clearly indicates the colony's ongoing concern for home: 'And for my self let miseries abound, / If mindless of thy State I e're be found.' Extensive evidence of transatlantic correspondence between the English and American Puritan communities contemporary

with Bradstreet's poem testify that this mindfulness was sustained. England's turmoil is described from the characteristic Puritan Parliamentarian perspective upon her 'breach of sacred Laws', 'Idolatry', 'foolish Superstitious Adoration', the threat of papal insurgency, 'Sabbath-breaking' and drunkenness, 'The Gospel trodden down' and 'Church Offices ... bought for gain'. The voice of the daughter points to the future, proposing an outlook of eschatological hope by reminding her in covenantal terms:

> Oh *Abraham*'s seed lift up your heads on high,
> For sure the day of your Redemption's nigh ...
> Then follows dayes of happiness and rest;
> Whose lot doth fall to live therein is blest:
> No Canaanite shall then be found i'th' Land,
> And holiness on horses bells shall stand.

Among Bradstreet's early poems are elegiac homages to her literary and other influences. In these 'Elegies and epitaphs' she registers both appropriate praise and a degree of regard for herself as a poet in her own right. For instance, 'An elegie upon that honourable and renowned knight *Sir Philip Sidney*' positions the poet as inadequate to celebrate her subject: 'The more I say, the more thy worth I stain, / Thy fame and praise is far beyond my strain.' In the same form of heroic couplets, she wrote the elegy 'In honour of that high and mighty princess Queen Elizabeth', defending the legitimacy of female monarchical rule and women's sufficiency of reason: 'She hath wip'd off th' aspersion of her Sex, / That women wisdome lack to play the Rex', and downplaying her own claim to literary credit: 'my pride doth but aspire / To read what others write, and so admire.' However, Bradstreet's feminist argument is unequivocal and is here conveyed with witty rhetorical questions:

> Now say, have women worth? Or have they none?
> Or had they some, but with our Queen is't gone?
> Nay Masculines, you have thus taxt us long,
> But she, though dead, will vindicate our wrong.
> Let such as say our Sex is void of Reason,
> Know tis a Slander now, but once was Treason.

Bradstreet also recorded a deep literary and intellectual debt to the French Huguenot poet Guillaume de Salluste, sieur du Bartas, of whom she claimed 'A thousand thousand times my senseless senses / Moveless stand charm'd by thy sweet influences' ('On Du Bartas, 1641'). The Puritan clergyman Nathaniel Ward noted that Bradstreet was 'a right *Du Bartas* Girle', and the influence of Du Bartas was pre-emptively noted in her dedication of *Several poems* to her father, warning that she 'fear'd you'ld judge *Du Bartas* was my friend / I honour him, but dare not wear his wealth' ('The epistle dedicatory'). Bradstreet finds both stylistic and substantive sources in Du Bartas, and her quaternions – *The four elements* (composed 1641–43), *The four constitutions* (1641–43), *The four ages of man* (1643), and *The four seasons of the year* (1643) – are both an imitation of his *Devine weekes and workes* (1605; translated into English by Joshua Sylvester in 1621), and of Thomas Dudley's own quaternions: 'I bring my four times four, now meanly clad / To do homage, unto yours, full glad' ('The epistle dedicatory'). They also draw on Helkiah Crooke's anatomical treatise, *Mikrokosmographia* (1615), among many other sources of natural philosophy and biblical commentary.

The quaternions (four long poems of four parts each) are perhaps the most technically and intellectually ambitious of Bradstreet's poetic works, although they are often placed amongst her earlier and less-well-regarded poems: they are judged as 'wooden' and 'forced' (Rich 1967), 'bald / Didactic rime' (Berryman 1989), and typical of Bradstreet's juvenilia. They are also generally neglected in anthologies of seventeenth-century poetry. In a format of four related debates – the first two of which have solely female speakers (sisters) – she describes and classifies the world according to categories of the four elements, humours, ages, and seasons, at the same time exhibiting extensive classical, geographical, theological, and scientific knowledge and reasoning. Their composition also coincided with the Massachusetts Bay Colony's mandate that all children be taught literacy, and thus were possibly also designed to be didactic texts, systematizing knowledge for a pedagogical context, possibly a 'dame school' in which Bradstreet taught her own children and others. A similar tone of questioning and debate between sisters recurs in the later poem 'The flesh and the spirit', on the struggle to quench the 'unregenerate part' and pursue a 'setled heart'.

Following the four long, four-part poems is an incomplete poem, 'The four monarchies', a biblical history in heroic couplets of iambic pentameter, influenced by Sir Walter Ralegh's *History of the world* (1614) and based on the four kingdoms represented in the book of Daniel: Assyria, Persia, Greece, and Rome. This work was abandoned after her papers were destroyed by fire, an event Simon Bradstreet also noted in his diary when he lost his books and papers, and his father a library of 800 volumes. Bradstreet later revisited this event in manuscript, in 'Some verses upon the burning of our house, July 10th, 1666', and she turned the loss of her books and papers into a broader moral reflection on the undulating fortunes of civilizations throughout history. In the 'Apology' printed at the end of the fourth, (incomplete) part, 'Roman monarchy', she speculates on the poem's incompletion in the light of these fortunes:

> No more I'le do sith I have suffer'd wrack,
> Although my Monarchies their legs do lack:
> Nor matter is't this last, the world now sees,
> Hath many Ages been upon his knees.

During the years in which she composed the quaternions, Bradstreet wrote four epistolary poems to her husband. The first, 'To my dear and loving husband', opens with the well-known lines, 'If ever two were one, then surely we. / If ever man were lov'd by wife, then thee.' The second, 'To her husband, absent upon publick employment', develops the same theme: 'If two be one, as surely thou and I, / How stayest thou there, whilst I at *Ipswich* lye?'

One of Bradstreet's most admired works is 'Contemplations', the 33-stanza emblem poem written at Andover and published in the 1678 volume. Appreciation for the poem's artistry and complexity has developed since her nineteenth-century editor J. H. Ellis (1867) declared that it 'proves she had true poetic feeling, and ... could rise when she was willing to throw aside her musty folios and read the fresh book of nature'. Bradstreet's accomplishment has been critically situated in terms of her intellectual and literary influences, including conventional emblem forms, classical and biblical allusions, the Neoplatonism of Sidney and Edmund Spenser, Protestant devotional exercises and Puritan sermons. The poem is set by the river Merrimack, with the poet's eyes looking first at 'the autumnal tide', then lifting to gaze at 'a stately oak', and finally rising to the 'glistering Sun'. Her magnification of God's majesty is inspired by the earth's intricate natural harmony: the revelation of God is discerned in Creation, and reflections on Creation consistently prompt a scriptural association. The poem reviews biblical history and the New Testament redemption narrative and concludes with her literary Calvinist devotion to enduring faith in the context of election.

'The Author to her book' is among the most celebrated poems within the authorized 1678 collection. Bradstreet here demonstrates her capacity for self-reflection as an author, modelling the modesty of unexpected publication – her works were 'snatcht' and 'expos'd' 'by friends'. However, the poem opens with the metaphoric casting of her book as 'ill-form'd offspring', suggesting that her maternal attitude towards her literary production was not an apology to a patriarchal literary culture for her inclination to write, but rather an expression of pride in her capacity for an improved literary aesthetic. She denies the role of a 'Father' figure in the poem's creation, and possibly even admits to a degree of complicity in the publication: 'And for thy Mother, she alas is poor, / Which caus'd her thus to send thee out of door.'

The 'Andover' manuscript writings were first printed in 1867 from the leather-bound notebook in Bradstreet's hand, part of which she titled 'Meditations diuine and morall'. Over 20 pages of this book feature her son Simon's copying of another of her manuscript books. The first section is a short epistolary autobiography addressed 'To my dear children', a legacy designed for posterity and for them to 'Make vse of'. She relates her 'experiences of God's gratious Dealings' since her 'young years, about 6 or 7' when she 'began to make conscience of [her] wayes and what ... was sinfull'. The account records her consumptive illness not long after her arrival in America, which she interpreted as sent by God 'to humble and try me and doe mee Good'. It was, she notes, 'not altogether ineffectuall', and is marked in one of her earliest poems, 'Upon a fit of sickness, *Anno.* 1632'. It was a 'great greif' to her to be kept from conceiving a child 'a long time', although after her first, Samuel, in 1633, Bradstreet went on to have seven more children: Dorothy, Sarah, Simon, Hannah, Mercy, Dudley, and John. The legacy also describes how God dealt with her during times of affliction and doubt and her experiences of answered prayer; it is peppered with biblical paraphrases, particularly from the Psalms and the Pauline epistles. Several meditations follow in both prose and lyric, mostly dated between 1656 and 1661, with direct addresses made to her children as well as poems on various personal themes, including her bouts of illness and the safe travels of her son Samuel, with several on her husband's travels and absence, on letters received from her husband, on her daughter Hannah's recovery from a fever, and on further spiritual themes. Bradstreet's psalms also appear in the manuscripts, technically and thematically imitating the Geneva Bible's rendering of the Psalms and the *Bay psalm book*, the metrical translation designed for use in worship and used in the Colony.

The last of Bradstreet's extant poems was dated 31 August 1669, three years before her death. 'As weary pilgrim' represents a waning interest in the present world, and concludes in the same tone as the final words of Revelation: 'Lord make me ready for that day / then Come deare bridgrome Come away.' Bradstreet died from consumption on 16 September 1672. Though absent from her, her son Simon recorded 'her pious & memorable Expressions uttered in her sicknesse'. Edward Phillips, John Milton's nephew, memorialized her in *Theatrum poetarum* (1675) as 'a *New-England* poetess, no less in title', and Cotton Mather lavished the following praise on her poems in his *Magnalia* (1702), as having 'afforded a grateful Entertainment unto the Ingenious, and a Monument for her Memory beyond the Stateliest *Marbles*'.

SEE ALSO: Cavendish, Margaret; Clinton, Elizabeth; Crooke, Helkiah; psalms and psalters, metrical; Ralegh, Walter; Rich, Mary; Sidney, Philip; Spenser, Edmund

REFERENCES AND SUGGESTED READINGS

Berryman, John (1989) Homage to Mistress Bradstreet. In: *Collected Poems, 1937–71*. Farrar, Straus & Giroux, New York.

Doriani, Beth M. (1989) 'Then have I . . . said with David': Anne Bradstreet's Andover manuscript poems and the influences of the psalm tradition. *Early American Literature* 24(1), 52–69.

Eaton, Sara (1997) Anne Bradstreet's 'personal' Protestant poetics. *Women's Writing* 4(1), 57–71.

Eberwein, Jane Donahue (1974) The 'unrefined ore' of Anne Bradstreet's quaternions. *Early American Literature* 9(1), 19–26.

Ellis, J. H. (ed.) (1867) *The works of Anne Bradstreet in prose and verse*. Abram E. Cutter, Charlestown.

Harvey, Tamara (2000) 'Now sisters . . . impart your usefulness and force': Anne Bradstreet's feminist functionalism in the *Tenth muse* (1650). *Early American Literature* 35(1), 5–28.

Rich, Adrienne (1967) Anne Bradstreet and her poetry. In: Hensley, Jeannine (ed.) *The works of Anne Bradstreet*. Harvard University Press, Cambridge, MA, pp. ix–xxii.

Wiseman, Susan J. (2006) *Conspiracy and virtue: women, writing, and politics in seventeenth-century England*. Oxford University Press, Oxford.

Wright, Nancy E. (1996) Epitaphic conventions and the reception of Anne Bradstreet's public voice. *Early American Literature* 31(3), 243–263.

Brandon, Samuel

DAVID KATHMAN

Samuel Brandon, whose birth and death dates are unknown, was the author of a late Elizabethan closet drama, *The vertuous Octavia*. It depicts the story of Octavia, wife of Marc Antony and sister of Octavius (the future Roman emperor Augustus), who patiently suffered while Antony had his notorious affair with Cleopatra. The play was entered in the Stationers' Register on 5 October 1598 by William Ponsonby and printed by Edward Allde. Following the title page, which identifies the play as a 'tragicomoedi' (presumably because the heroine does not die), there is a dedicatory sonnet to Lucy Touchet, Lady Audley; a sonnet 'All' autore' signed 'Mia'; a poem 'Prosopopeia al libro' signed 'S.B.'; a prose argument; and a list of the play's characters. Following the text of the play are two long verse epistles between Octavia and Antony, dedicated to Lady Audley's daughter Maria Thynne and modelled on Michael Drayton's *Englands heroicall epistles* (1597).

Essentially nothing is known of Brandon other than what can be inferred from the sole printed edition of his play. The dedicatee, Lady Audley, was married to Mervyn Touchet, Lord Audley, who was active in Ireland in the 1590s and governor of Kells in 1599. Brandon's dedications indicate some personal familiarity with the family, suggesting that he may have served Lord Audley in Ireland. This, in turn, might help explain his close familiarity with the works of Edmund Spenser, who was also in Ireland at the time, and whose publisher, William Ponsonby, also published *The vertuous Octavia*. Critics since Frederick Ives Carpenter (1923) have noted that Brandon's play alludes to Spenser's *The Faerie Queene*, and Andrew Hadfield (2009) has recently demonstrated convincingly that Brandon was also familiar with Spenser's Mutability Cantos in manuscript.

Brandon also appears to have been part of the literary circle of Mary Sidney Herbert, countess of Pembroke, whose father, Sir Henry Sidney, had been lord deputy of Ireland (Lamb 1981). Although the main source for the plot of *The vertuous Octavia* is the life of Antony in Thomas North's translation of Plutarch's *Lives*, Brandon was also familiar with two other closet dramas on the same subject matter: the countess of Pembroke's translation of Robert Garnier's *Marc Antonie* (printed 1592) and Samuel Daniel's *Cleopatra* (1594), which was dedicated to the countess and commissioned by her as a companion piece. *The vertuous Octavia*, though not dedicated to the countess, may have been meant as another play in the series, focusing on the third member of the love triangle. Eve Rachele Sanders (1999) has argued that *The vertuous Octavia* was a direct response to the countess' play, which Brandon certainly knew in its printed version, since his prose argument directly quotes the countess' prose argument. Daniel and Brandon were clearly familiar with each other's plays. Daniel's *Poetical essays*, published in 1599, the year after *The vertuous Octavia*, included 'A letter from Octavia to Marcus Antonius' with close similarities to the first epistle appended to Brandon's play, though it is not absolutely clear in which direction the influence ran.

While critics in the early twentieth century tended to dismiss *The vertuous Octavia* as a mere knock-off of Daniel's *Cleopatra* featuring a duller main character, more recent scholars have looked at the play in context and found a more complex and subtle work. The Octavia figure had long been the standard classical representation of the virtuous, long-suffering wife of a straying husband, an epitome of feminine Stoic constancy and resolve. She was used in this way by several late Elizabethan writers besides Brandon, notably Daniel in the above-mentioned 'A letter from Octavia to Marcus Antonius' and Fulke Greville in 'Letter to an honourable lady', both of which, like Brandon's play, were dedicated or addressed to an aristocratic woman meant to identify with Octavia. All of these authors used the Octavia character to criticize the Christianized version of classical Stoicism promoted by such contemporaries as Guillaume du Vair and Justus Lipsius, in which the Stoic ideal of constancy is made difficult or impossible by the presence of the soul in the human body. In *The vertuous Octavia*, the title character is explicitly contrasted with the licentious woman Sylvia, who attacks Octavia's constancy in the face of Antony's infidelity, shocking the other Roman women but ultimately helping to undermine the assumed connection between constancy and virtue (Bruce 2009). As Hadfield (2009) notes, Sylvia's rhetoric is a clever inversion of the arguments in Spenser's Mutability Cantos, in which Nature rejects Mutability's arguments and defends the universe as fixed and stable.

John Bodenham's *Bel-vedere, or the garden of the muses* (1600), edited by Anthony Munday, includes nearly 50 excerpts from *The virtuous Octavia* (Crawford 1911). The title page of *The vertuous Octavia* includes a Latin motto from Claudian's *De consulatu Stilichonis*, 'Carmen amat, quisquis carmine digna gerit' ('He loves song whose deeds are worthy of song'), which Samuel Daniel also used in 1603 on the title page of his *Panegyrike congratulatorie* for King James; this is probably not a coincidence, given the mutual influence between Brandon and Daniel noted above. John Dryden quoted the same motto 75 years later in the epistle dedicatory for his version of the Antony and Cleopatra story, *All for love* (1678), suggesting the possibility that he had read Brandon's play.

SEE ALSO: Daniel, Samuel; Dryden, John; Greville, Fulke; Herbert, Mary (Sidney), countess of Pembroke; Munday, Anthony; Spenser, Edmund

REFERENCES AND SUGGESTED READINGS

Bruce, Yvonne (2009) 'That which marreth all': constancy and gender in *The virtuous Octavia*.

Medieval and Renaissance Drama in England 22, 42–59.

Carpenter, Frederick Ives (1923) *A reference guide to Edmund Spenser.* University of Chicago Press, Chicago.

Crawford, Charles (1911) Bodenham's *Belvedere*, quotations from *The virtuous Octavia* and *A knack to know an honest man.* In: Greg, W. W. (ed.) *Collections*, parts 4 and 5. Malone Society, Oxford.

Farmer, John S. (1912) *The virtuous Octavia by Samuel Brandon 1598.* Tudor Facsimile Texts, London.

Hadfield, Andrew (2009) Edmund Spenser and Samuel Brandon. *Notes and Queries* 254, 536–538.

Lamb, Mary Ellen (1981) The myth of the countess of Pembroke: the dramatic circle. *Yearbook of English Studies* 11, 194–202.

McKerrow, Ronald B. (ed.) (1909) *The virtuous Octavia 1598.* Malone Society, Oxford.

Sanders, Eve Rachele (1999) *Gender and literacy on stage in early modern England.* Cambridge University Press, Cambridge.

Breton, Nicholas

ALAN STEWART

Nicholas Breton (1554/55–after 1626?) was one of the most prolific writers of Elizabethan and Jacobean England, with almost 120 editions of his multifarious works published by the beginning of the Civil Wars, and more surviving in manuscript form (Robertson 1952; Brennan 2004). Breton's father, William, a wealthy London trader, died in 1559; his mother, Elizabeth, quickly remarried one Edward Boyes, and then in November 1561, though still wed to Boyes, married the poet George Gascoigne. This led in September 1562 (according to diarist Henry Machyn) to 'a great fray in Redcrosse Street' between Boyes and Gascoigne and their men, in which 'divers were hurt'. Elizabeth divorced Boyes, remarried Gascoigne (probably in 1566), and she and her two sons sued to recover the Breton lands from Boyes. Nicholas's whereabouts during this period are uncertain, although he has been placed at Oriel College, Oxford in the late 1560s and early 1570s, which would explain why his *The pilgrimage to paradise* (1592) was addressed 'To the Gentlemen students and scholars of Oxforde', and printed there.

By 1577 Breton was living in a 'Chamber in Holborne' in London, from where he published *A floorish upon fancie*; he may have spent much of the 1580s (when his publications cease) abroad, perhaps in Italy. He may be the 'Brittan a schoolmaster' mentioned in a 1590 letter by Henry Herbert, second earl of Pembroke (Brennan 2004). In January 1593 he married Anne Sutton, and they had at least five children. He was actively publishing until 1622, and appears to have been alive for his daughter's marriage in 1626 (Brennan 2004). Any other information about his life is speculative, gleaned from his publications, which are dedicated to a bewildering array of people from King James downwards who may or may not have known Breton.

Breton's earliest publications were the collections of verse *A smale handful of fragrant flowers* (1575), *A floorish vpon fancie* (also known as *The toyes of an idle head*) (1577, 1582), and *The workes of a young wyt, trust vp with a fardell of pretie fancies* (1577); five prose pieces entitled *The wil of wit* (entered 1580, first surviving edition 1597); and the self-explanatory *A discourse in commendation of the valiant gentleman, Maister Frauncis Drake* (1581). His writings had some impact: in his 1589 *Arte of English poesie*, George Puttenham put Breton last on his list of 'Courtly makers Noble men and Gentlemen of her Maiesties owne seruantes, who haue written excellently well as it would appeare if their doings could be found out and made publicke with the rest'. In 1591 a collection appeared entitled *Brittons bowre of delights. Contayning many, rare epitaphs, pleasant poems, pastorals and sonets*, but the following year, Breton complained that the miscellany featured 'many thinges of other mens mingled with a few of mine' (he was happy to claim one piece, an elegy on Philip Sidney entitled 'Amoris lachrimae'). A printed marginal list of poets in William Covell's *Polimanteia* (1595) places 'Britton' at the head of what appears to be an Oxford contingent:

'Britton. Percie. Willobie. Fraunce'. In Francis Meres's *Palladis tamia* (1598), he is the most recent on a list of 'the most passionate among vs to bewaile & bemoane the perplexities of Loue'. His verses appeared in the leading verse miscellanies of the decade, *The phoenix nest* (1593), *The arbor of amorous devices* (1597), and *Englands Helicon* (1600).

In the 1590s Breton moved into the circle of Mary Herbert, countess of Pembroke (Brennan 1987; 2004; Trill 1997). His 1592 *The pilgrimage to paradise, joyned with the countess of Pembrokes love* tells the countess that 'the hand of your honour' had favoured him, and one of Breton's works *The passions of the spirit* (entered 1594) was for some time believed to be by Herbert (Brennan 2004). It has been suggested that this Mary was the presiding inspiration behind *Marie Magdalens love: a solemne passion of the soules love* (1595) and *Auspicante Jehova, Maries exercise* (1597), while a passage in *Wits Trenchmour* (1597) recounts how Breton temporarily lost the countess's favour. Whatever the case, by 1601 he could once again dedicate *A divine poeme, divided into two partes: the ravisht soule and the blessed weeper* to the countess (Robertson 1952; Brennan 1987; 2004).

Breton continued to expand his generic range. He authored (or perhaps adapted) prose romances *The historie of ... Don Federigo di Terra Nuova* (1590) and *The strange fortunes of two excellent princes* (1600). Early in the new century, he capitalized with great success on the vogue for verse satire, producing a series of 'Pasquil' Pamphlets including *Pasquils madcappe* (in two parts), *Pasquils passe, and passeth not*, *Pasquils mistresse*, and *Melancholike humours* (also known as *Pasquilles swullen humours*), all in 1600. In 1601 he joined John Weever and Everard Guilpin in producing the so-called 'Whipper pamphlets' with his *No whipping, nor tripping, but a kinde friendly snippinge*. He also became known for compilations of versified moral aphorisms such as *The mothers blessing* (1602), *A true description of unthankfulnesse* (1602), *Honest counsaile* (1605), and *A murmurer* (1607). Spiritual

concerns were addressed in his longer poems, *The soules heavenly exercise* (1601), *An excellent poeme, upon the longing of a blessed heart* (1601), *The passion of a discontented minde* (1601), and *The soules immortall crowne* (1605). His most popular devotional work, going through 11 editions by 1676, was a manual of verse entitled *The soules harmony* (1602). There were to be other poetic works, including the collections *The passionate shepheard* (credited to 'Bonerto', 1604) and *The honour of valour* (1605); two poems peddling standard anti-Machiavellian sentiments, *The uncasing of Machivils instructions to his sonne* (1613) and *Machivells dogge* (1617); and *The hate of treason, with a touch of the late treason* (1616), on the Gunpowder Plot. But Breton increasingly explored prose.

The impetus for this move was his 1602 work *A poste with a packet of madde letters*, the conceit of which had the author chancing upon a packet of letters dropped by a careless 'poste' or mail-carrier. The reader is thus allowed to catch sight of 'A Letter of comfortable aduise to a friend, and his answere', 'A Letter of aduise to a yong Courtier, and his answere', and so on. Although it is never explained how the answers to these letters came to be in the same dropped packet, Breton's publication of intercepted correspondence proved another best-seller, with at least 16 editions by 1685.

Characteristically, Breton tried out other prose genres. The essay collection, pioneered by Francis Bacon and John Florio's translation of Montaigne, inspired *Fantasticks: serving for a perpetuall prognostication* (entered 1604), *Characters upon essaies morall, and divine* (1615, dedicated to Bacon), and *The good and the badde* (1616). There was a brief flirtation with the dialogue: *A dialogue ... between three phylosophers* (1603), *A merrie dialogue betwixt the taker and mistaker* (1603, reprinted as *A mad world my masters* in 1635), *Grimellos fortunes* (1604), *I pray you be not angrie: a pleasant and merry dialogue, between two travellers* (1605), and *An olde mans lesson, and a young man's love* (1605). The miscellany form foregrounded his skill for pulling together all kinds of aphoristic and proverbial wisdom in titles like *The figure of foure* (entered 1597); *Wits private wealth, stored with choice commodities to content the minde* (1607), another best-seller with 12 editions; *The figure of foure: the second part* (entered 1614); *Crossing of proverbs* (in two parts, 1616); and *Soothing of proverbs* (1626). In 1608 he produced a devotional piece entitled *Divine considerations of the soule.* His final surviving printed work, *Strange newes out of divers countries* (1622), saw Breton doing what he did best: capitalizing on a trend, in this case the newsletter emerging from the battlefields of the Thirty Years War.

SEE ALSO: Bacon, Francis; Florio, John; Gascoigne, George; Guilpin, Everard; Herbert, Mary (Sidney), countess of Pembroke; Meres, Francis; Puttenham, George; verse miscellanies, printed; Weever, John

REFERENCES AND SUGGESTED READINGS

Brennan, Michael G. (1987) Nicholas Breton's *The passions of the spirit* and the countess of Pembroke. *Review of English Studies* 38, 221–225.

Brennan, Michael G. (2004) Breton, Nicholas. In: *Oxford dictionary of national biography.* Oxford University Press, Oxford.

Grosart, A. B. (ed.) (1879) The works in verse and prose of Nicholas Breton. Printed for private circulation, Edinburgh.

Robertson, Jean (ed.) (1952) *Poems by Nicholas Breton.* Liverpool University Press, Liverpool.

Trill, Suzanne (1997) Engendering penitence: Nicholas Breton and 'the Countesse of Penbrooke'. In: Chedgzoy, Kate, Hansen, Melanie, & Trill, Suzanne (eds) *Voicing women: gender and sexuality in early modern writing.* Duquesne University Press, Pittsburgh, pp. 25–44.

Brewer, Anthony

DAVID KATHMAN

Anthony Brewer was the author of a Jacobean pseudo-history play, *The love-sick king.* The play was printed in 1655 with a title page attribution to 'Anth. Brewer, Gent.', but internal evidence indicates that it was written more than 30 years earlier, during the reign of James I. In fact, the play was probably performed before James in Newcastle in 1617 during a progress to Scotland, as argued most thoroughly by Randall Martin (1991), and may have been written for that occasion. Gerard Langbaine wrote in 1691 that it was revived in 1680 under the name *The perjured nun,* and the first modern edition was by A. E. H. Swaen in 1907.

The identity of the Anthony Brewer who wrote the play is uncertain, but perhaps the most likely candidate is the minor actor 'Anth: Brew:', who appears in a stage direction playing a Lord of Babylon in the manuscript play *Two noble ladies* (British Library, Egerton MS 1994). Among the other plays in the same manuscript is *Edmond Ironside,* a play set in the same historical period as *The love-sick king* and apparently known to Brewer, as both G.E. Bentley (1956) and Martin (1991) argue. Actors' names in other plays in the manuscript led Martin to conclude that it was probably compiled in the early 1620s, most likely for either Lady Elizabeth's Men or the Revels company at the Red Bull. Some early critics speculated that Anthony Brewer was the T.B. (for 'Tony Brewer') who wrote the play *The countrie girle* or the prose pamphlet *The merry of Edmonton,* but such identifications lack evidence and are not accepted by modern scholars.

The action of *The love-sick king,* much of which is closely based on John Speed's *The history devill Great Britaine* (1611), nominally takes place during the Danish conquest of England in the eleventh century. However, Brewer mixes in people and events from other eras of English history for dramatic and thematic purposes, in keeping with the loose way seventeenth-century writers often used medieval history. The play opens with the Danish king Canute conquering England and killing its king, Ethelred, after which he is opposed by the new English king, Ethelred's brother Alured, who eventually defeats Canute and allows him to return to Denmark. Alured is aided in this reconquest by the Scots, an ahistorical plot element presumably meant to flatter King James. Canute is based on the historical Danish king of that name who ruled England from 1016 to 1035, but Alured is based on King Alfred the Great, who opposed a different Danish invasion more than a century earlier, from 871 to 899. The Ethelred of the play conflates Ethelred I, Alfred the Great's brother and predecessor, and Ethelred II ('the Unready'), whose reign was ended by the Danish invasion that eventually brought Canute to the throne.

Both opposing kings fall in love with doomed women during the course of the play. Alured falls for Canute's sister Elgina, who was raised in England as a Danish princess. After her accidental death midway through the play, Alured expresses a desire for the two nations to be friends. Canute falls in love with a nun named Cartesmunda, and the distraction of this love affair eventually allows Alured to triumph; Canute cannot bring himself to kill Cartesmunda, as his advisers want, but he accidentally kills her anyway shortly before the climactic battle with the English and the Scots. As Robert Dent (1961) first noted, the Canute–Cartesmunda plot is based not on anything in English history, but on the story of Turkish sultan Mahomet's love affair with the Greek maiden Irene during the sack of Constantinople, as romanticized in William Barksted's 1611 poem *Hiren, or the faire Greeke* and elsewhere. This connection identifies the invading Danes with Turks, the stereotypical other in early modern England, though the two stories differ in that Mahomet recovers from his infatuation and goes on to victory, while Canute is defeated.

There is also a comic subplot set in Newcastle (where the play was probably performed) and centred around a character named Thornton, based loosely on a real fifteenth-century Newcastle merchant named Roger Thornton. The Thornton of the play is a rags-to-riches success story who becomes mayor, and bears many similarities to the semi-legendary London merchant and lord mayor Dick Whittington. After becoming rich, Thornton considers marrying a rich widow but instead starts giving his money

away, providing a contrast to the tyrannical Canute and his doting on Cartesmunda. Plot and subplot become intertwined when Alured arrives in Newcastle and meets Thornton, who fortifies the city and helps defeat Canute. The Thornton subplot has evident similarities to London city comedies from around the turn of the seventeenth century, such as Thomas Dekker's *The shomaker's holiday* (1600), as well as other plays from the same period, such as William Haughton's *Grim the collier of Croydon* (?1600). A song sung by Thornton is an adaptation of one that appears in Francis Beaumont's *The Knight of the Burning Pestle* (1607) and Thomas Heywood's *The rape of Lucrece* (1608).

SEE ALSO: Beaumont, Francis; Dekker, Thomas; Haughton, William; Heywood, Thomas; Speed, John

REFERENCES AND SUGGESTED READINGS

Bentley, G. E. (1956) Anthony Brewer. In: *The Jacobean and Caroline stage*, vol. 3. Oxford University Press, Oxford, pp. 42–45.

Dent, Robert W. (1961) *The love-sick king*: Turk turned Dane. *Modern Language Review* 56, 555–557.

Martin, Randall (ed.) (1991) *Edmond Ironside and Anthony Brewer's 'The love-sick king'*. Garland, New York.

McMullan, Gordon (2007) The colonisation of early Britain on the Jacobean stage. In: McMullan, Gordon & Matthews, David (eds) *Reading the medieval in early modern England*. Cambridge University Press, Cambridge, pp. 119–140.

Perry, Curtis (2009) 'For they are Englishmen': national identities and the early modern drama of medieval conquest. In Perry, Curtis & Watkins, John (eds) *Shakespeare and the Middle Ages*. Oxford University Press, Oxford, pp. 172–195.

broadside ballads

KRIS McABEE

The broadside ballad was one of the most popular Renaissance genres of cheap print. In a general sense, a ballad is a story set to song. However, the term 'ballad' resists singular definition. Ballads intersect with many literary and artistic genres in the Renaissance, lending the term multiple meanings. In fourteenth- and fifteenth-century references to ballads, it can be difficult to distinguish between the notion of a light, simple song and the more formal *ballade*, a verse form consisting of two or three stanzas composed of seven or eight metrically consistent lines. The ballade form entails an envoy, or refrain, from stanza to stanza, yet many light songs that may be recognized as ballads also employ refrains, further blurring the lines between the two ostensibly distinct terms. Similarly, ballads of the Renaissance were frequently songs that accompanied dances, as in the *Oxford English dictionary*'s example from John Olde's 1594 translation of Erasmus: 'That can stirre vs, not to wanton dauncynges or folyshe ballettes'. Because of this practice of joining song and dance, by the seventeenth century ballads can be easily conflated with the choreographed dramatic entertainments known as 'ballets'. What tends to distinguish ballads from the myriad of musical, theatrical, and verse forms with which they intersect, is the perception of the genre as popular (as opposed to purely elite), if not downright frivolous. However, to think of ballads as merely 'low' culture would be to misread their tremendous reach across not only generic boundaries but social ones as well.

Much of the popular reputation of ballads stems from their means of dissemination, which was primarily twofold. On the one hand, ballads have origins in oral traditions, as popular lore of ill-fated love, noble heroes, or the likes of Robin Hood. On the other, the printed broadside provided a ready vehicle for short tales and widened ballads' topics to include more current events, especially of such topical or salacious interest as politics, religion, or wondrous happenings. Broadside ballads frequently identify a popular tune to which they can be sung, typifying their reliance on popular oral culture. Thus traditional ballads (or folk ballads of the type Francis Child was to collect

much later in the nineteenth century) and broadside ballads are interdependent phenomena. For example, popular English folk-songs could be picked up and printed as broadside ballads, while the circulation of a broadside ballad in print aids in its oral transmission, especially through the voices of the ballad-hawkers who, in the practice of the other criers in the town square, sell their wares by singing the ballads aloud.

As cheap print, costing on average a mere penny for a single sheet, ballads did not participate in the complex system of patronage associated with more elite verse forms of the Renaissance. Much to the contrary, authors of ballads were often mocked or reviled in those rare cases where they were identified. Some ballad-writers, like Martin Parker (*fl.* 1624–47), played recognizable roles in ballad production and trade; many of Parker's ballads bear his name or his initials. Parker, however, offers a notable exception to the general rule. In contrast, other prolific ballad writers, such as Thomas Deloney (d. in or before 1600), are not identified by name on the ballads attributed to them. Likewise, broadside ballads that offer the cheap print version of poetry already made famous in more privileged circulation do not identify the authors of their contents. For example, Richard Barnfield's ode known as 'Address to a nightingale', published in his 1598 *Poems in divers humours*, appears again as 'A louers newest curranto, or the lamentation of a young mans folly' in a broadside ballad usually dated to 1625. Christopher Marlowe's 'The passionate shepherd to his love' and 'The nymph's reply to the shepherd', then attributed to Walter Ralegh, are printed together as a two-part ballad on a single broadside from the 1620s, entitled 'A most excellent ditty of the louers promises to his beloued' and 'The ladies prudent answer to her loue', respectively. These broadsides indicate the degree to which identifiable authorship in and of itself played a limited role in the marketing of ballads.

While the majority of broadside ballads do not identify an author, they frequently feature the names of the printers or publishers. A preponderance of extant ballads include at the bottom of the sheet, below the text proper, an imprint naming the location of the publishing house alongside the name of the printer and / or publisher. As participants in the book trade, all ballad publishers were required by the royal charter of 1557 to purchase and record the right to publish every ballad in the Stationers' Register. As with other publications of the day, some ballads were likely to have been registered but never printed. This phenomenon is especially likely in the case of ballads because their topical nature might tempt a potential publisher to pre-empt his competition by registering titles about upcoming events, such as impending executions, for example, where the ballads would be sold as part of the event. Conversely, many ballads were printed, but never registered. In a further attempt to regulate the printing of ballads, in 1624 members of the Stationers' Company formed a group called the Ballad Partners, originally comprising Cuthbert Wright, John Wright, Edward Wright, John Grismond, Thomas Pavier, and Henry Gosson. However, some publishers resisted the monopoly posed by this syndicate, and smaller associations like the Philip Brooksby group (consisting of Brooksby, Jonah Deacon, Josiah Blare, and John Back), known for printing more topical material, managed to offer prolific competition. When ballads were written, they were sold to such figures as Wright, Gosson, or Brooksby and the authors would not see any further remuneration for the circulation of their work; it was the printers and publishers who stood to gain profit and hence it is their names that appear in ballad imprints.

Imprints played an important role as identifiers for the marketing of ballads. Though consumers may or may not have been attracted to the offerings of a particular print-house, the imprint informed the chapmen where they could buy their wares in bulk. An individual consumer might buy ballads from a bookseller's shop, but it was these chapmen, travelling in the city and out into the countryside, who sold the preponderance of ballads. Requiring no special permission to push these wares, ballad-mongers trafficked alongside other itinerant workers and carried the reputation of being engaged in a seedy line of work. They relied heavily on showmanship to achieve success in peddling them, using the ability to perform the ballads to attract customers.

And, indeed, they attracted all kinds. The ballad easily circulated among all classes and found its way into the collections of some of the most prominent members of society. The largest collection of ballads from the sixteenth and seventeenth centuries, consisting of approximately 1,800 broadsides, belonged to the famous diarist, naval administrator, and member of parliament Samuel Pepys. The first volume of the five-volume Pepys ballads set contains the collection's oldest ballads, almost entirely originally collected by the seventeenth-century scholar of English history and law John Selden, and purchased by Pepys at some point in the 1680s. The eighteenth century saw other prominent collectors of Renaissance ballads in Sir Robert Harley, first earl of Oxford, for whom John Bagford assembled much of what would become the Roxburghe collection, now at the British Library. Bagford also gathered his own significant collection of ballads from the seventeenth century. Without the careful efforts of these collectors, we would have few remaining ballads extant despite their having been printed, as scholars estimate, in the millions by the late sixteenth century.

The organizing systems inherent in these collections also reveal a great deal about broad categories of themes and subjects seen most frequently in ballads. For example, Samuel Pepys's collection is divided into 10 topics and one catch-all, miscellaneous category. These groupings, loosely discernible in other collections, are formally identified in the Pepys collection as: devotion and morality; state and times; history; tragedy; love pleasant; love unfortunate; marriage; sea; drinking and good fellowship; and humour and frolics. That three of these categories concern love and marriage, combined with the fact that over one-third of the ballads of the Pepys collection are categorized as 'love pleasant', suggests that the preponderance of ballads (or at least of those that invited collecting) deal with matters of the heart. While these categories are permeable, they provide a useful rubric through which to understand the breadth of topics on which ballads touched: from the religious to the frivolous and from the historical to the whimsical, ballads run the gamut of possible subjects, no doubt contributing to their widespread appeal.

The wide reach of the ballad genre can be seen throughout other literary genres of the Renaissance. Among the many verse miscellanies that emerged in the second half of the sixteenth century, Richard Jones's *A handefull of pleasant delites* (1566) offers a collection of previously printed broadside ballads. Later, the plays of William Shakespeare and Ben Jonson draw heavily from ballad culture. Many of Shakespeare's plays, including *Taming of the shrew*, *Titus Andronicus*, and *The merchant of Venice*, have ballads among their sources. Ballads enter the action of the drama in plays like *The winter's tale*, in which the rogue Autolycus carries a sack full of ballads, describes several, and leads other characters in their performance. It is in these plays that we find much evidence of the social function of the ballad at the time. For example, the notion that the broadside ballad served as an aesthetic object that would be purchased and placed on the walls of taverns or homes finds support in Jonson's *Bartholomew Fayre*, in which the country simpleton Cokes recollects the ballads he had once pasted on the walls of his home.

Even as broadside ballads functioned as aural and textual artefacts, they presented distinctive aesthetic qualities that probably broadened their consumption to the illiterate and semi-literate. The ballads of the seventeenth-century heyday generally followed a several-column layout, frequently exhibiting cast fleurons and other ornamentation as well as multiple woodcut illustrations. Many of the woodcut illustrations have a 'stock image' quality appropriate to almost any ballad content. One might show simply an aristocratic-looking woman holding a fan, while another might depict a dapper man with a hat and cane. Other illustrations portray more elaborate scenarios, suited to only particular texts. For example, one popular woodcut illustration of a woman being burned at the stake appears on a number of broadsides of the goodnight ballad sub-genre. Goodnight ballads take on the voice of a criminal lamenting a crime in the moments leading up to his or her execution; among these ballads are several from the perspective of husband-murderers, of which both 'Anne Wallens lamentation for the murthering of her husband' and 'A warning for all desperate women by the example of Alice Dauis' share the same execution illustration. Still other ballads employ woodcuts that appear also on the title pages of related texts, as with 'The complaint and lamentation of Mistresse Arden of Feversham', which pictures the same woodcut illustration as the 1633 edition of the anonymous play *Arden of Feversham*.

In the same way as one woodcut illustration may appear on multiple ballads, multiple ballads can be sung to the same tune, which, like many of the stories the ballads tell, would be well known to British audiences. Some popular ballad tunes, like 'Greensleeves', continue to have wide recognition today. However, many ballads either do not identify their tunes or identify tunes for which the melody has now been lost. Though it is not uncommon for ballads of the late seventeenth century to include musical notation (as the formal features of broadside ballads begin to morph to resemble slip-songs), some of the notation appears purely ornamental, either not matching the ballad text or not capable of being rendered musically. Complicating matters of tune identification further, the names of ballad tunes themselves frequently changed over time. For example, 'A lamentable ballad of the ladies fall' identifies its tune as 'In peascod time' but the ballad became so popular that later ballads sung to this melody, such as 'The brides burial', identify their tune as 'The ladies fall'. Following this pattern, some even later ballads identify this same melody as the tune named 'The brides burial'. These complicated transformations in titles epitomize how ballad culture depended upon the overlapping of folkloric and print transmission, and are indicative of the wide cultural reach of ballads.

SEE ALSO: Barnfield, Richard; Deloney, Thomas; Marlowe, Christopher; Parker, Martin; Ralegh, Walter; Selden, John; Shakespeare, William; verse miscellanies, printed

REFERENCES AND SUGGESTED READINGS

Fumerton, Patricia & Anita Guerrini (eds) (2010) *Ballads and broadsides in Britain, 1500–1800.* Ashgate, Aldershot.

Smith, Bruce (2006) Shakespeare's residuals: the circulation of ballads in cultural memory. In: Rhodes, Neil & Gillespie, Stuart (eds) *Shakespeare and Elizabethan popular culture.* Thompson, London, pp. 193–217.

Watt, Tessa (1991) *Cheap print and popular piety, 1550–1650.* Cambridge University Press, Cambridge.

Wurzbach, Natascha (1990) *The rise of the English street ballad, 1550–1650,* trans. Gayna Walls. Cambridge University Press, Cambridge.

Brome, Alexander

EDWARD PALEIT

Alexander Brome (1620–66) was a Royalist poet active mainly during the 1640s and 1650s. The majority of his verse circulated in manuscript or appeared in front of other Royalist publications until *Songs and other poems* (1661) collected most of it. He wrote one comedy, *The cunning lovers* (1654), and also saw *Five new playes* (1653) by Richard Brome (no relation) through the press in 1653. After the Restoration he supervised a multi-authored translation, *The poems of Horace* (1666), to which he also contributed. He was the brother of Henry Brome, the printer-publisher. Brome's poetry associates him with several Royalist literary coteries of the period, including Thomas Stanley's circle. It concentrates on the conventional themes of Royalist poetry, especially in defeat – wine, love, friendship, the happy life – alongside some frank, vigorous satires, and distinctively couples verbal and imaginative plainness with metrical diversity.

Brome was born around 1620 in Evershot in Dorset, and educated nearby, probably by the as yet unidentified 'W.H.' whom he celebrates in two poems. No further information on his parentage or education is known. His one play, *The cunning lovers,* a derivative aristocratic romance set in Italy, belonged to William Beeston's company at the Cockpit Theatre in August 1639, placing him in London. In around 1640 he began a moderately successful legal career, probably as a clerk of the King's Bench; he was admitted to Gray's Inn in 1648 and Lincoln's Inn in 1659. In 1650 he married Martha Whitaker, the widow of the bookseller Thomas Whitaker, and fathered five daughters. Brome died on 30 June 1666, having been based in London all his adult life.

Brome never took up arms to aid his king. Nonetheless, an unflinching royalism emerges in his political verse, in the values underpinning his poems on love, drink, and retirement and in his use of dedicatory poems and epistles to assert a Royalist sociability in the face of defeat. Poems by Brome appeared in front of programmatically pro-Royalist publications such as Beaumont and Fletcher's first folio collection (1647), the volume of elegies *Lachrymae musarum* (1649) and the plays and poems of William Cartwright (1651). Poems for other publications suggest intimacy with Stanley's circle, based at the Middle Temple from the late 1640s onwards. A poem for Richard Lovelace's *Lucasta* (1649) was printed only in 1661. Brome was friendly with Charles Cotton, with whom he exchanged poetic epistles, and Izaak Walton, contributing a poem to the second edition of *The compleat angler* (1655). In addition to his sociable poems, Brome composed several political satires, the earliest datable to 1643. While possessed of various voices and tones, collectively they represent Charles I as an innocent Christian martyr and his followers as loyal patriots, undone by the hypocrisy, greed, and social envy of lower-class upstarts. The 1650s satires are increasingly bitter; a poem on the Restoration shows that Brome thought it too conciliatory.

Brome's other poetry also has a strongly political inflection, discussing themes familiar to the 'Cavalier' mode outlined by Earl Miner (1971). As with Robert Herrick, Cotton, Lovelace, and others, Brome celebrates drink and conviviality, drawing on Horace and the *Anacreontea* (translated by his friend Stanley in 1651); he is termed the 'English Anacreon' in Edward Phillips's *Theatrum poetarum* (1674). Political defeat alters Brome's emphasis from wine as inspirational lubricant to welcome inducer of oblivion. His love poetry, somewhat like Sir John Suckling's, explores various amatory situations and, raffishly but charmlessly, expresses intermittent scorn for 'such Toyes as Ladies are'. Another group of poems suggests the appeal of an 'Epicurean' life of leisured rural retirement. Sir Aston Cokain's *A chain of golden poems* (1658) suggests Brome considered translating Lucretius, but the chief model for the 'happy life' poems is Horace.

Horace also stands behind Brome's *Songs and other poems*, his volume of collected verse. The volume's structure, placing 'Poems' or lyrics (in two parts) before 'ballads' and 'epistles', is Horatian-inspired; the epistles are clearly modelled on Horace. A final section consists mostly of epigrams translated from various Latin and neo-Latin authors, before ending with Brome's celebrations of the Restoration. The 1661 edition of *Songs and other poems* came with dedicatory poems by Brome's lawyer friends of the Middle Temple as well as Izaak Walton; later editions of 1664 and 1668 added poems by Cotton and Valentine Oldis and a prose epistle by Ralph Bathurst. Some of Brome's satires had already appeared in *The Rump* (1st edn 1660), an exuberant collection of Royalist songs and ballads. *The poems of Horace*, which Brome edited, is arguably a companion volume to *Songs and other poems*. It draws on the published Horaces of Sir Thomas Hawkins (1625),

Sir Richard Fanshawe (1652), and Barten Holyday (1652), but also on other printed renditions, such as Abraham Cowley's, and many contributors whose work Brome knew of or solicited in manuscript; Harold Brooks (1938) conjectures that Charles Cotton, Thomas Flatman, Sir William Petty, and Thomas Sprat were amongst them. Brome himself contributed 23 satires and epistles. His edition presents Horace as, like himself, a survivor into better times from a period of upheaval. A frontispiece engraving places the Roman poet in front of a rural English church. His dedication compliments John Denham and Edmund Waller as the 'Standard-bearers' of poetic excellence.

Songs and other poems was not reissued after the posthumous 1668 edition; *The poems of Horace* was republished in 1671 (with changes to some contributions) and 1680, but then faced competition from Thomas Creech's translation. Positive biographical notices appeared in Phillips's *Theatrum poetarum* and Gerard Langbaine's *An account of the English dramatick poets* (1691), suggesting that Brome was still popular; Phillips records that many of his 'songs', which are now read as poems, were actually sung to music. Thereafter oblivion began to gather. The edition of Roman Dubinski (1982) has restored him to view.

SEE ALSO: Beaumont, Francis; Brome, Richard; Cartwright, William; Cotton, Charles, the younger; Denham, John; Fanshawe, Richard; Fletcher, John; Herrick, Robert; Lovelace, Richard; Stanley, Thomas; Waller, Edmund; Walton, Izaak

REFERENCES AND SUGGESTED READINGS

Brooks, Harold (1938) Contributors to Brome's Horace. *Notes and Queries* 174, 200–201.
Dubinski, Roman (ed.) (1982) *Alexander Brome: poems.* 2 vols. Toronto University Press, Toronto.
McDowell, Nicholas (2008) *Poetry and allegiance in the English Civil Wars: Marvell and the cause of wit.* Oxford University Press, Oxford.
Miner, Earl (1971) *The Cavalier mode from Jonson to Cotton.* Princeton University Press, Princeton.

Brome, Richard

MATTHEW STEGGLE

Richard Brome (c.1590–1652) was one of London's leading playwrights in the reign of Charles I. Brome wrote or co-wrote 16 surviving plays, all comedies, of which perhaps the best known are *The Antipodes* (1636) and *A joviall crew* (1642). Brome is an early inheritor of Shakespeare, one of the most important and distinctive voices of the 1630s, and one of the most successful of all Renaissance playwrights on the post-Restoration stage.

The date of Brome's birth is unknown, and nothing is known of his family background beyond the fact that it was poor and unprivileged. He is first heard of working as a manservant to Ben Jonson, and is named as Jonson's servant in the Induction to *Bartholomew fayre* (1614). This reference is generally taken to indicate that Brome was working for Jonson by 1614, the date of *Bartholomew fayre*'s first performance (although it has also been suggested that the reference might be an interpolation from as late as 1631, the date of that play's first publication). Brome was certainly working for Jonson by 1625, the date of John Fletcher's death: in his commendatory verses on the Beaumont and Fletcher folio (1647) he refers to having known Fletcher personally, and to how Jonson, then his master, praised Fletcher's work.

By 1628, Brome himself was involved in theatre. In that year he was named among the members of a new theatrical venture, Lady Elizabeth's Men. The company seems to have been a strange mix of veterans and new, untried, talent, and did not enjoy a particularly good reputation in the years that followed, but by 1629 Brome was with the King's Men, Shakespeare's former company and also the one for which Jonson himself was then writing. Jonson had written a new play for them, *The new inn*, which was badly received on its first performance. Shortly afterwards, Brome's play *The love-sick maid, or the honour of young ladies* was performed by the same company to extraordinary applause. Regrettably,

The love-sick maid was never printed and is now lost.

Brome followed it, in 1629, with *The northern lass*, another very successful play performed by the King's Men. *The northern lass* revolves around Sir Philip Luckless, who wishes to marry Mistress Fitchow, a rich but domineering city widow. Luckless's friend, Tridewell, believes Luckless is making a mistake, and tries to dissuade Fitchow from going ahead with the marriage, only to fall in love himself with her independent spirit and resolve. Further confusion is added by the arrival of the northern lass herself, an innocent young girl from the north who has met Luckless briefly and fallen hopelessly in love with him; and of Constance Holdup, a London prostitute. Disguises, lies, and problems of mistaken identity multiply, until at last the knot is untied in a happy ending. As this summary suggests, *The northern lass* is a racy, well-plotted city comedy in what could broadly be called the Jonsonian humours tradition. But what gives it its particular appeal is something typical of much of Brome: the combination of theatrical energy with a more considered and 'sentimental' streak, represented in this play in the love-melancholy of the naive northern lass.

Jonson's anger at the failure of *The new inne* had bubbled over into a sarcastic reference, in his poem 'Ode to himself', to 'Brome's sweepings': but he seems quickly to have repented of this, and when *The northern lass* was printed in 1632, it bore commendatory verses by Jonson praising Brome's craftsmanship. But Brome inherits not merely the legacy of Jonson, but also that of many of the other leading Elizabethan and Jacobean playwrights. Thomas Dekker called Brome his 'son'; and Brome also has an interesting relation with Shakespeare, seen, for instance, in *The queenes exchange* (c.1634). *The queenes exchange* is not a city comedy but a historical tragicomedy, set in Anglo-Saxon England, centred upon a proposed marriage between the king of Northumbria and the queen of Wessex. It is full of echoes and semi-quotations of Shakespeare, especially of *King Lear* and *Macbeth*, as it explores, in effect, the prehistory of Britain. One such moment is when one of the characters has a miraculous vision confirming that the Wessexians will *not* permanently be shackled to the Northumbrians: 'Enter six Saxon Kings ghosts crowned, with sceptres in their hands, etc. They come one after another to Anthynus; then fall into a dance; loud music; after the dance, the first leads away the second, he the third, so all: the last takes up Anthynus, and leaves him standing upright.' This is both a knowing imitation of the vision-scene in *Macbeth* and also a remaking of it for an audience in Caroline England who were increasingly aware of the tensions involved in their ongoing relationship with the Scots.

Other Brome plays thought to date from the first phase of his career include *The city wit* (?1629), a lively comedy about a merchant ruined by his honesty who must turn trickster to regain his fortune; *The novella* (1632), a comedy set in Venice about a woman who appears to be a very expensive prostitute; and *The witches of Lancashire* (1634), also known as *The late Lancashire witches*. Co-written with Thomas Heywood, this dramatizes current events in the form of a series of alleged episodes of witchcraft that took place in Lancashire in 1633–34. In the hands of Brome and Heywood, the whole play is a balancing act: the witchcraft is both a sinister, demonic force, and also something playful, anarchic, and entertaining. According to one eyewitness of the early performances at the Globe in summer 1634, 'it consisteth from the beginning to the end of odd passages and fopperies to provoke laughter, and is mixed with diverse songs and dances . . . it passeth for a merry and excellent new play' (Berry 1984).

In summer 1635, Brome signed a contract binding him exclusively to one theatrical company: the King's Revels, under the leadership of the theatrical impresario Richard Heton. While the contract itself does not survive, a good account of it can be reconstructed from later legal action surrounding it. The contract required Brome to produce three plays a year for the company, and to refrain from doing any work for any other company. In return, he received a retainer of 15 shillings a week, and a day's takings for each new play he produced. Brome's contract is unique of its kind in early modern theatre history, and it serves as the basis from which one extrapolates about the usual terms and conditions of professional dramatists of the period – although recent work has suggested that one cannot assume that it was entirely typical of other contracts of the period, since the very fact that it resulted in legal action, and therefore survives, at least in summary, makes it unlike all the others.

For the King's Revels, Brome wrote *The Sparagus Garden* (1635), a comedy of intrigue, mistaken identity, and marriage set in a London pleasure-garden where a cross-section of London society – plus an interloper from Somerset – meet and mingle. The insistently specific detail of the setting means that the play can be described as 'place-realism' comedy, a genre that flourished in the 1630s. Brome, in particular, is fascinated by the possibilities of place-realism, representing specific London locations, streets, and taverns throughout his career, and using it as the organizing principle of other plays including *The weeding of Covent-Garden* (c.1632) and *The new academy, or new exchange* (1636). But in *The Sparagus Garden* in particular, this journalistic reportage coincides with a surrealist streak, as the phallic asparagus becomes a symbol of social climbing and sexual desire, and is said to possess near-miraculous medicinal powers. The Sparagus Garden itself, a site both of Edenic plenty and potentially of Edenic sin, becomes symbolic of the whole garden of England. Brome later claimed that the play had earned the King's Revels company £1,000 in takings. Also from this part of his career is *The queen and concubine* (1635), Brome's most sustained experiment in 'serious' tragicomedy, describing the saint-like patience of Eulalia, a queen of Sicily falsely accused of adultery and sent into internal exile.

In May 1636, plague broke out in London, and the city authorities closed the theatres, as was usual in such cases. Early on in the closure, the King's Revels company ceased to pay Brome the weekly retainer to which he was entitled under his contract. Short of money, Brome ended up breaching the terms of his contract by writing a play for another company entirely, Christopher and William Beeston's company at the Cockpit theatre. Although professional theatre was still banned because of the plague, the Beestons were staging performances of plays, or rather (as they claimed) rehearsals at which an audience happened to be present. In these unpropitious and illicit circumstances, Brome wrote for the Beestons what is often thought to be his masterpiece: *The Antipodes.*

The Antipodes concerns a young man, Peregrine, who has been driven mad by reading the works of the medieval traveller Sir John Mandeville, to the point where he is so distracted by thoughts of travel that he has not even consummated his marriage. In desperation, his father brings him to the London house of an eccentric nobleman, Letoy, who keeps a company of players. There, the psychiatrist Dr Hughball resolves to drug Peregrine and create an immersive illusion around him with the help of the players, making him think he has actually travelled to the other side of the world so that he can act out and neutralize his fantasies of travel. Thus, most of *The Antipodes* is a play-within-a-play, as Peregrine travels to a world where everything is the opposite of normal: the mice chase the cats, the young are prim and pious while the old behave disgracefully, and the lawyers are honest. Peregrine is delighted and throws himself into the illusory world while the players scramble and improvise to keep up. Soon he has killed the local monsters and crowned himself king of the Antipodes, while the onstage audience, watching his delusions and conducting intrigues with one another as they do so, struggle with their own demons of jealousy and desire. *The Antipodes* is a play which taps a particularly rich vein of the Caroline subconscious, a travel play with a colonialist slant which is also a satire on the state of Britain and yet also a meditation on metadrama. In its imagination, energy, and

originality, it is often reckoned to be Brome's best play.

The plague closure continued for almost 18 months, and Brome continued to be in dispute with his employers. During the closure Brome wrote *The English moor,* a comedy in which a jealous London usurer makes his wife disguise herself as a black maidservant. Although relatively little is known about it compared to *The Antipodes, The English moor,* too, explores the nexus of sexual desire, the geographically and racially exotic, and theatrical illusion. The two plays could be considered companion pieces.

The theatres reopened in October 1637. The King's Revels, now renamed Queen Henrietta's Men, started performing again, and Brome resumed his writing career with them. As well as *The English moor,* to this period belong Brome plays including *The demoiselle* (1637–39), a city comedy critiquing law and lawyers; *The love-sick court* (1638), a satire on Neoplatonic tragicomedy; a lost play, *The Florentine friend* (1638); and *The madd couple well matcht* (1639), a city comedy featuring a debauched rake-hero who utterly refuses to reform himself as required by the usual conventions of plays about prodigals. *The Antipodes* was also performed by Queen Henrietta's Men during this period, as well as a revival of Thomas Goffe's pastoral *The careles shepherdess.* This last item was accompanied by a 'Praeludium', an extended comic sketch in which different character types argue over what sort of drama they prefer, and it is generally thought that Brome, as the company's retained professional dramatist, was the author of this lively reflection on the current state of theatre.

By Easter 1639, Brome's relationship with Heton's company, long strained, had become unworkable. Brome left Salisbury Court and started working, instead, for William Beeston. His erstwhile employers made a bill of complaint against him for breach of contract, to which Brome's lawyer wrote a rebuttal, arguing that he owed them nothing. These documents still exist in the National Archives, Kew, and are the source from which our knowledge of Brome's contract derives.

Writing for Beeston, Brome again found his career disrupted by events outside his control. Caroline courtiers were becoming increasingly interested in the power of public drama, and a number of them had written plays for the professional theatre, giving them over for free or even paying for their performance. Throughout the prologues and epilogues of Brome's plays, such courtier playwrights are a frequent target. Even worse, Sir John Suckling – a particular *bête noire* of Brome's – and his friend William Davenant were looking to gain control of an entire theatre. In summer 1640, they succeeded by gaining a royal warrant giving them control of William Beeston's, and Beeston was briefly imprisoned: it is not clear how long it was before Beeston got his theatre back, possibly as late as May 1641 when both Suckling and Davenant were involved in the treasonous Army Plot and utterly disgraced. *The court begger* (1640–41), a cheerfully satirical attack on monopolies and monopolists, was written at some point in this sequence of events. The play is given extra edge by its references to the war against Scotland, and by its rather savage personal satire of Sir John Suckling, put on stage as Ferdinando, a mad and lustful courtier.

Brome's next and last play is *A joviall crew*. This play concerns the relationship between Oldrents, a traditional English landlord, and the groups of wandering beggars to whom he gives charity. In the course of the play, his daughters disappear, electing to adopt the life of the beggars for a while, only to discover the hardships and difficulties it brings; the beggars turn out to be an entire society in themselves, made up of displaced actors, musicians, and even former courtiers; and Oldrents's steward, Springlove, is revealed to be king of the beggars and the great-grandson of the man whose ruin enabled the Oldrents family to become rich. The play seems astonishingly prescient of the Civil War, forecasting the grim outlook for players and poets in the event of serious civil disruption. In the assessment of Martin Butler, one of the most influential critics of Caroline drama, 'While in political life the question of the good of the country was being bandied back and forth, Brome asks insistently what the "country" *is* . . . *A jovial crew* is a truly national play written at a turning point in the history of the English stage and the English nation' (Butler 1984).

The closure of the theatres seems to have ended Brome's theatrical career, with the exception of one strange text possibly by him, the allegorical entertainment *Times distractions* (c.1643). Brome wrote commendatory verses for the 1647 Beaumont and Fletcher folio; acted as the editor of *Lachrymae musarum* (1649), a collection of elegies for the Royalist Henry Hastings featuring very early poems by John Dryden and Andrew Marvell; and died poor, in the Charterhouse Hospital in 1652. Several of his plays were revived or adapted at the Restoration, setting a benchmark for well-constructed, 'serious' city comedy with place-realism elements; two of them, *The northern lass* and *A joviall crew,* enjoyed stage careers that can be measured in centuries.

Caroline drama as a whole, and the work in particular of its leading exponents, Brome, Ford, Shirley, and Massinger, was long seen as a rather decadent form, lacking the literary geniuses of the previous generation, and befitting a society soon to be swept away in the Civil War. Increasingly, though, Caroline drama is being seen as worthy of study in its own right. In the case of Brome, this realization has taken the form both of a new appreciation of the political engagement and complexity of his works, a trend begun by Martin Butler's seminal book *Theatre and crisis 1632–1642* (1984); and of the recognition of his plays' performance potential, seen, for instance, in the successful and entertaining revival of *The Antipodes* at Shakespeare's Globe Theatre in London (2002). A new online complete edition of Brome (Cave 2010) aims to provide a firmer textual basis for the efforts of readers, scholars, and particularly actors interested in Brome's plays.

SEE ALSO: Davenant, William; Ford, John; Heywood, Thomas; Jonson, Ben; Massinger, Philip; Shirley, James; Suckling, John

REFERENCES AND SUGGESTED READINGS

Berry, Herbert (1984) The Globe bewitched and *El hombre fiel. Medieval and Renaissance Drama in England* 1, 211–230.

Butler, Martin (1984) *Theatre and crisis 1632–1642.* Cambridge University Press, Cambridge.

Cave, Richard (2010) Richard Brome Online. www. hrionline.ac.uk/brome/

Clark, Ira (1992) *Professional playwrights: Massinger, Ford, Shirley, and Brome.* University Press of Kentucky, Lexington.

Haaker, Ann (1968) The plague, the theater, and the poet. *Renaissance Drama* 1, 283–306.

Kaufmann, R. J. (1961) *Richard Brome: Caroline playwright.* Columbia University Press, New York.

Miles, Theodore (1942) Place-realism in a group of Caroline plays. *Review of English Studies* 18, 428–440.

Sanders, Julie (1999) *Caroline drama: the plays of Massinger, Ford, Shirley and Brome.* Northcote House, London.

Shaw, Catherine M. (1980) *Richard Brome.* Twayne, Boston.

Steggle, Matthew (2004) *Richard Brome: place and politics on the Caroline stage.* Manchester University Press, Manchester.

Brooke, Christopher

MICHELLE O'CALLAGHAN

Christopher Brooke (c.1570–1628), lawyer, member of parliament, shareholder in the Virginia Company, and poet, was born to Robert Brooke, a wealthy citizen of York and twice lord mayor of that city, and Jane Maltby, the daughter of a York draper. It is not known whether he attended university before he entered Lincoln's Inn on 15 March 1587. Brooke's literary affiliations tell us much about the multifaceted nature of early modern literary culture. Brooke was a public poet who committed his major works to print, while also taking part in London scribal communities and tavern clubs. He first appeared in print alongside his fellow wits – his close friend John Donne, Ben Jonson, and the lawyers John Hoskyns and Richard Martin – in the mock 'Panegyric verses' which jestingly celebrated the publication of Thomas Coryate's account of his European travels, *Coryats crudities* (1611). Coryate, in turn, greeted Brooke among the 'Sireniacal Gentlemen, that meet the first Fridaie of every Moneth' at the Mermaid tavern on Bread Street in his letters sent from his Indian travels. And Brooke is also listed among the diners who gathered in mock honour of Coryate in a burlesque Latin poem, often given the title 'Convivium philosophicum' (c.1611), set at the Mitre tavern.

Brooke has long been known through his friendship with his more famous friend Donne. The two shared rooms at Lincoln's Inn in the 1590s, and Brooke was imprisoned for his role in Donne's secret marriage to Ann More. Both the poems Donne dedicates to Brooke, the mid- to late-1590s verse epistles 'Thy friend, whom thy deserts' and 'The storm', meditate on the strength of the ties binding the two men. The friendships Brooke formed at the Inns of Court, with Donne, Hoskyns, and Martin, continued throughout his life. Hoskyns, Martin, and Brooke all had a hand in the composition of a very popular political burlesque, 'The censure of a parliament fart', which circulated widely in manuscript miscellanies throughout the seventeenth century.

The poetry Brooke published from 1613 was an extension of his public office as a lawyer-MP and drew on the genres of advice poetry to discourse on the times. Like his earlier ventures with Donne, Hoskyns, and Martin, it once again testifies to the communal contexts of literary creativity in this period. The poetry he published in 1613 and 1614 is consciously collaborative and continues to draw on his social bases at the Inns of Court, although this time with a set of younger men – William Browne of the Inner Temple, and George Wither from Brooke's own inn, the Lincoln's Inn. Together with Browne, Brooke published a memorial volume, *Two elegies* (1613), to lament the death of Prince Henry.

The years from 1613 to 1616 were highly fraught politically, and this is when Brooke was most active in publishing poetry. While sitting in the 1614 'Addled' Parliament, he composed two poems for the press. He responded to Browne's dedication of the fifth eclogue of *The shepheards pipe* (1614) to him with his own eclogue, dedicated to Browne, and appended to the volume another eclogue penned by Wither, then in the Marshalsea for causing offence to a powerful courtier with his satire, *Abuses stript, and whipt* (1613). Brooke's eclogue is an elegant study in Protestant pastoral, defining its scope both as a vehicle for revelation and for political allegory. The subject of his pastoral conversation with 'Willy'-Browne is the readiness of 'Cuddy'-Brooke to write in the 'higher strain' of public political poetry, neatly advertising the publication of his *The ghost of Richard the Third* (1614). 'Cuddy'-Brooke appeared among Wither's prison visitors the following year in the second and third eclogues of *The shepherd's hunting* (1615), once again in dialogue with 'Roget'-Wither and 'Willy'-Browne.

The ghost of Richard the Third has received well-deserved attention as an example of Jacobean political poetry. The figure of Richard III had long been a vehicle for dramatizing a body politic deformed by corruption. As its title indicates, *The ghost of Richard the Third* adopts a *Mirrour for magistrates* format, and echoes passages from Richard Niccols's recently revised 1610 edition of the *Mirrour* (first published in 1559). In Brooke's hands, Richard's ghost is a vehicle for political satire, a necessary corrective that will 'startle' the sleeping nation into action. Through Richard's account of how he took advantage of a monarchical state weakened by factional divisions and corruption, Brooke expressed concerns about royal government, particularly abuses of the prerogative, which he was also voicing in parliament. Brooke returned to the theme of political corruption in the verse he contributed to the collection of elegies that prefaced the 1616 edition of *Sir Thomas Overburie his wife*, newly revised to capitalize on the trials of the earl and countess of Somerset and their accomplices for Overbury's murder.

A 'patriot' political viewpoint, which is militaristic, anti-Spanish, defends 'ancient' liberties, and complains of court corruption, infuses Brooke's public poetry. His *Poem on the late massacre in Virginia* (1622) portrays the massacre as part of a wider assault on Protestantism by the ungodly both in the Americas and in Europe. So too his 'Funeral poem in memory of Sir Arthur Chichester' (d.1624) laments the passing of Elizabethan militarism. Brooke tried but failed to get this elegy into print. Instead, he wittily prepared the poem for the censor in his prefatory epistle addressed to the licenser for the press. Brooke died in February 1628. His will records his possession of a portrait of Martin, by then also dead, and his affection for Donne, his 'deere ancient and worthie freind' (Bald 1970).

SEE ALSO: Browne, William; Coryate, Thomas; Donne, John; Hoskyns, John; Jonson, Ben; Niccols, Richard; Wither, George

REFERENCES AND SUGGESTED READINGS

Bald, R. C. (1970) *John Donne: a life.* Clarendon Press, Oxford.

Doelman, Joel (1999) Born with teeth: Christopher Brooke's *The ghost of Richard the Third* (1614). *Seventeenth Century* 14, 115–129.

Kay, Dennis (1990) *Melodious tears: the funeral elegy from Spenser to Milton.* Clarendon Press, Oxford.

Norbrook, David (2002) *Poetry and politics in the English Renaissance*, rev. edn. Oxford University Press, Oxford.

O'Callaghan, Michelle (1998) 'Talking politics': tyranny, parliament, and Christopher Brooke's *The ghost of Richard the Third. Historical Journal* 41, 97–120.

O'Callaghan, Michelle (2000) *The 'shepheards nation': Jacobean Spenserians and early Stuart political culture.* Clarendon Press, Oxford.

O'Callaghan, Michelle (2007) *The English wits: literature and sociability in early modern England.* Cambridge University Press, Cambridge.

Browne, Thomas

KATHRYN MURPHY

Sir Thomas Browne (1605–82), physician and polymath, wrote on a wide variety of topics in seventeenth-century natural philosophy, natural history, antiquarianism, philology, and religion. His works are particularly notable for a combination of natural investigations with religious reflection, while his sonorous style has been much admired and imitated.

Browne was born in London in 1605, on either 19 October or 19 November, the son of a prosperous mercer of the same name who died in 1613. In the following year his mother Anne married Sir Thomas Dutton, a courtier and soldier who squandered much of Browne's father's legacy. Dutton was scoutmaster-general in Ireland, and in 1629 took Browne on a tour of the castles and forts he commanded. Browne had an excellent education: he was sent in 1616 to Winchester College, where he received a thorough grounding in humanist letters. In 1623 he matriculated at Broadgates Hall, Oxford, which in 1624 was incorporated as Pembroke College. Browne delivered the undergraduate address at the ceremony marking the incorporation; this short Latin oration, with witty puns on the change of name, was published in 1668. His first publication also dates to 1624: a 20-line Latin poem, published in *Camdeni insignia*, an Oxford volume commemorating the death of the antiquarian William Camden. Browne's tutor was Thomas Lushington, a controversial theologian whose interests in Plato and Neoplatonism were transmitted to Browne.

Browne was admitted BA in January 1627 and proceeded MA in 1629. He then travelled to Continental Europe to study medicine at the universities of Montpellier, Padua, and finally Leiden, where he graduated doctor of medicine in December 1633, with a dissertation on smallpox. These universities were at the forefront of medical education, avant garde in promoting recent advances, such as William Harvey's discovery of the circulation of the blood, and innovative in their teaching of anatomy and natural history. Browne's travels exposed him to a variety of cultures, customs, and religious rites, and to the effects of the Thirty Years War. These experiences had an obvious influence on his writings. The first part of his *Religio medici* (*A physician's religion*,

1642) emphasizes his willingness to tolerate different rites and sects of Christianity; the second, which boasts that he understands six languages, takes pride in his openness to other cultures, their customs, and their cuisines.

Browne returned to England in 1634 to serve a medical apprenticeship. Alternative traditions place him in Oxfordshire or in Halifax, Yorkshire. The latter is more plausible, since it explains references in later correspondence with Henry Power, a natural philosopher and physician brought up in Halifax, to various inhabitants of the town as mutual acquaintances. It was during this period that Browne wrote *Religio medici*, his most famous work. Internal evidence suggests it was composed around 1635, though it is evident from surviving manuscripts, none in Browne's hand, that it was revised at a later date. The earliest version was probably intended to be read by only a small circle of acquaintances. Browne was incorporated DM at Oxford in 1637. At the prompting of friends from his student days, and of Thomas Lushington, who had left Oxford in 1632 for Norfolk, he moved to Norwich to practice. The later manuscript versions of *Religio medici*, more rhetorically elaborate and less intimate, are thought to date from Browne's early years in Norwich. By 1640, it was circulating beyond his immediate acquaintance, and had reached the intelligencer Samuel Hartlib.

In 1642 *Religio medici* was published anonymously by the bookseller Andrew Crooke, to Browne's alarm. Hearing that the courtier and natural philosopher Sir Kenelm Digby intended to publish criticisms, Browne, with Crooke, prepared an authorized edition, published in 1643 under the less memorable title *A true and full coppy of that which was most imperfectly and surreptitiously printed before vnder the name of Religio medici*, which still bore the engraved frontispiece designed for the first edition by William Marshall. Browne supplied a prefatory note 'To the Reader', in which he distanced himself from the 1642 publication, insisting that the text was corrupt, and that he had not courted public attention. He also made several alterations and additions to the text, some of which aimed to make the text less provocative.

Religio medici is divided into two parts, corresponding to the two active aspects of religion: faith and charity. In a loosely associative structure, Browne confesses his opinions and beliefs, and emphasizes his disinclination to conflict and his sympathies with the faith, customs, and opinions of other people and nations. As the title suggests, a constant theme is the paradoxical relationship between faith and reason. Physicians were proverbially assumed to be atheists, since their profession inclined them to materialism and the investigation of nature, rather than God. *Religio medici* begins with a defiant credo refuting that assumption, but faith and reason are in fruitful tension throughout. Browne declares his pleasure in confounding his reason with the mysteries of faith, while at the same time drawing attention to the paradoxes which emerge from approaching the Bible from a rational perspective. An important thread in *Religio medici* insists on the value of interpreting nature as a means both of worshipping God through wonder at the intricacy of his Creation, and of learning more about God through natural theology. Browne privileges the natural philosophical vocabulary of Plato and Paracelsus over traditional Aristotelianism, in part because it affords greater opportunities for metaphors that unite faith and reason. His advocacy of 'deliberate research' into nature as an exercise of piety anticipates Restoration justifications for the activities of the Royal Society and for natural history. The style of *Religio medici* is remarkable, at once intimate and confiding, and rhetorically ornate. Particularly striking is Browne's use of rhythm, which achieves biblical intensity through cadenced cola, and syntactic and verbal parallelisms and contrasts.

Browne's alarm at the publication was a justified recognition of *Religio medici*'s potential for controversy. Though written in the 1630s, it was published in the year in which Charles I went to war with Parliament, in an atmosphere of political and religious suspicion and antagonism, when the presses of London were busy with controversial pamphlets. Though many indications suggest that Browne was conservative and sympathetic to royalism, he preferred to keep his political statements indirect or private. In 1642, however, *Religio medici*'s reasoned ecumenism and conciliatory tone amounted to a political stance. Browne showed sympathy with several controversial positions in matters of faith, among them toleration of Catholics, and a youthful inclination, only half-heartedly repudiated, towards several heresies. His tendency both to abandon reason in favour of faith, and to pose difficulties for faith through the exercise of reason, particularly in the interpretation of Scripture, were also provocative. In addition to Kenelm Digby's *Observations upon Religio medici* (1643), Browne also drew criticism from the prolific translator and critic Alexander Ross, in *Medicus medicatus, or the physicians religion cured* (1645). Continental debates accusing Browne of atheism or defending him from it continued into the eighteenth century.

In addition to criticism, however, *Religio medici* also met with many positive responses. The seventeenth century saw 13 editions in English, seven in Latin, three in Dutch, and one in French, and there is evidence of readers as far afield as Polish Prussia and Transylvania. Many letters survive from enthused readers: Browne's broad sympathies meant that he was coopted by Quakers, Anglicans, and Catholics. The suggestive title was much imitated, including works by both Edward, Lord Herbert of Cherbury, and John Dryden entitled *Religio laici* (*A layman's faith*). His style remained influential long after the controversies over his religion had lost their vigour: among his imitators and admirers are Samuel Taylor Coleridge, Thomas De Quincey, Charles Lamb, Virginia Woolf, and Jorge Luis Borges.

Perhaps in an attempt to secure a more solid scholarly reputation, Browne's next publication was the weighty *Pseudodoxia epidemica* (1646), often referred to as the 'Vulgar Errors'. *Pseudodoxia* is a scholarly work, addressed to the learned, which in seven books sets out to expose or refute errors in a variety of fields, beginning with 'Minerall and Vegetable bodies', progressing through animals and men, to pictures, geography, and Scripture. The first book treats the general causes of error, starting with the Fall, and including credulity, mistakes in reasoning, the behaviour of crowds, and Satan. Browne's criticism of 'obstinate adherence unto Antiquity' and 'Authority' aligns him with the contemporary tendency to insist that sense and reason be elevated over the testimony of the ancients in the investigation of nature. This view is frequently associated with followers of Francis Bacon, and the composition of *Pseudodoxia* is sometimes attributed to Bacon's desideratum in his *Advancement of learning* (1605), for a 'Kalendar of popular Errors'. The 'vulgar errors' tradition was however already well established, and Browne, though he owned works by Bacon and sometimes cites him, shows few signs of the pious respect of Bacon's epigones in the Hartlib circle, or among the founders of the Royal Society.

Pseudodoxia epidemica is a massive display of erudition and wide reading. It proved popular, and made Browne's name as a learned authority. Published in six English editions in his lifetime, it was also translated into Latin, Dutch, German, and Danish. *Pseudodoxia* exhibits an interest in the exotic and fantastic. Despite its avowed aim to extirpate errors, the subjects of some chapters are evidently included for their curiosity regardless of veracity, and for the opportunity they offer to demonstrate Browne's learning and associative habits of mind. Chapters ostensibly concerned with the refutation of a single fact often mutate into essays on more general topics. Browne does not refute the belief 'That Hares are both male and female', for example, and digresses instead into questions of gender, generation, and the nature of seeds. Though his taste for the bizarre has led to an association with cabinets of curiosities and works on wonders and monsters, *Pseudodoxia* also demonstrates Browne's engagement with recent scholarship and

developments in natural philosophy. Many chapters use evidence drawn from his own experiments. Browne's mention of 'Renatus des Cartes' and citation of his *Principia philosophiae* (1644) constitutes one of the earliest references to René Descartes in English, and Browne also expresses enthusiasm for William Harvey.

Pseudodoxia is also notable for the inventiveness of its language. Though less elevated than *Religio medici*, the style is remarkable for its coinages and polysyllabic Latinity. The *Oxford English Dictionary* credits *Pseudodoxia* with almost 500 first citations; though many of these are specialist and obscure (e.g., 'albuginous', 'retromingent', 'solidungulous'), several remain in common usage (e.g., 'bisect', 'causation', 'electricity', 'exhaustion', 'invigorate').

Browne's next publication, besides a revised edition of *Pseudodoxia* in 1650, was a volume published in May 1658, whose full title reads: *Hydriotaphia, urne-buriall, or a discourse of the sepulchrall urnes lately found in Norfolk. Together with the garden of Cyrus, or the quincunciall, lozenge, or net-work plantations of the ancients, artificially, naturally, mystically considered.* The two treatises emerged from a context of gentlemanly friendship, and were addressed to friends in Norfolk. *Urne-buriall* was dedicated to Thomas Le Gros of Crostwick, and *The garden of Cyrus* to Nicholas Bacon of Gillingham, a collateral relative of Francis Bacon who kept an elaborate garden. The essays are oblique and elliptic, because of their gestation within the context of close friendships in which arcane references are more easily understood, because they are composed according to numerological and structural patterns which are not made explicit, and because of Browne's allusiveness and the scope of the fields of knowledge he surveys, including history, comparative religion, ancient philosophy, religious controversy, botany, arboriculture, optics, and generation.

Urne-buriall was prompted by the discovery of five funeral urns in a field near Walsingham in Norfolk. The first three chapters speculate on the origin of the urns, displaying Browne's antiquarian knowledge of various practices in disposing of the bodies of the dead. His conclusions are, however, awry: he believed the urns to be Roman, though they have subsequently been identified as Saxon. The anthropological and archaeological considerations are used as the prompt for meditations in the final two chapters on the vanity of memory and human knowledge, the inevitability of earthly oblivion, and the consolations of Christian belief in resurrection. These passages are among Browne's most stylistically wrought, and have been much excerpted and anthologized.

The garden of Cyrus, in comparison with the sententiousness and gravity of *Urne-buriall*, has often seemed baffling or eccentric. The ostensible topic is the layout of ancient gardens, which were planted in rows of diagonal lines, forming a net- or lattice-like pattern when viewed from above. Browne begins with an erudite account of various mythological and ancient gardens, but is soon discussing the quincunx (a pattern of four dots forming a quadrilateral, with a fifth at the point where the diagonals would meet) in whatever phenomenon he finds it: the growth of plants, the design of pyramids, ancient beds, nutcrackers, forceps, galloping horses, the function of human vision. He incorporates digressions on generation and the shapes of plants, and abandons the quincunx for circles and the number five. Such disparate materials are finally united, however, when Browne makes the quincuncial cross, contained within a circle, an emblem of God's creative power in nature. *The garden of Cyrus*'s cumulative examples of pattern in nature and art resolve into a mystical consideration of the world as the book of God, recalling similar concerns in *Religio medici*.

It is evident from close structural and thematic parallels that *Urne-buriall* and *The garden of Cyrus* were designed as companion pieces. While *Urne-buriall* considers the failure of memory, scepticism about the scope of human knowledge, burial, and death, *The garden of Cyrus* resorts to the certainties of

geometry and mathematics, and is centrally concerned with generation, seeds, and new life. Patterns of imagery reflect this: *The garden of Cyrus* counters the darkness and oblivion of *Urne-buriall* with light and vision. Structurally, each modulates into Browne's high style, and moves from its ostensible theme into mystical considerations, at the same point at the close of the fourth chapter.

The volume of 1658 was the last original work which Browne published during his lifetime. He lived, however, until 1682, and continued to write. Revised editions of *Pseudodoxia epidemica* continued to appear until the sixth in 1672. He welcomed the Restoration, and enjoyed an international reputation, which fostered correspondence with several important Continental scholars. In 1664 he was an expert witness at a witch trial in Suffolk, testifying that he believed that the accused women were witches; they were hanged. Later in the same year he was elected to an honorary fellowship of the College of Physicians, and in 1671 he was knighted by Charles II.

Works left in manuscript continued to appear after his death on 19 October 1682. Thomas Tenison, a future archbishop of Canterbury and a relative of Browne's wife Dorothy, published 13 essays, written originally as letters, on topics including natural history, scriptural criticism, music, philology, and etymology, under the title *Certain miscellany tracts* (1683). These included 'Musæum Clausum', a whimsical description of items to be included in Browne's ideal museum and library. *The works of Sir Thomas Browne* appeared in 1686, containing all the major writings published to that date. In 1690 *A letter to a friend*, a consolatory piece probably composed in several stages, combining a medical report on the death of a patient with a series of moral sententiae, was published. The bookseller Edmund Curll published *Posthumous works* in 1712, which added to the Browne canon 'Repertorium, or the antiquities of the cathedral church of Norwich', an account of the architectural features and tombstones of the cathedral; 'An account of some urnes . . . found at Brampton in Norfolk', a pedestrian description in comparison to the meditative expansiveness of *Urne-buriall*; letters between Browne and the antiquarian William Dugdale; and some short manuscript pieces. Shortly before Tenison's death in 1715, a manuscript entitled *Christian morals* was recovered from among his papers, and published in 1716. *Christian morals* is a collection of moral precepts and instructions, some of which also appear in *A letter to a friend*, written in Browne's high style. It was edited in 1756 by Samuel Johnson, whose edition also included an appreciative 'Life of Sir Thomas Browne'.

Browne corresponded with some of the leading intellectual figures in England in the period, including John Evelyn (who recorded a 1671 visit to Browne in his diary), Elias Ashmole, Henry Oldenburg, and John Aubrey, as well as writing regularly with scholarly advice or information to his son Edward. He also left a large number of notebooks and commonplace books, containing drafts, notes on reading, and records of experiments.

SEE ALSO: Aubrey, John; Bacon, Francis; Bible, the; Dryden, John; Evelyn, John; Hartlib, Samuel; Harvey, William; Herbert, Edward, Lord Herbert of Cherbury

REFERENCES AND SUGGESTED READINGS

Barbour, Reid & Preston, Claire (eds) (2008) *Sir Thomas Browne: the world proposed.* Oxford University Press, Oxford.

Huntley, Frank (1962) *Sir Thomas Browne: a biographical and critical study.* University of Michigan Press, Ann Arbor.

Killeen, Kevin (2009) *Biblical scholarship, science and politics in early modern England: Thomas Browne and the thorny place of knowledge.* Ashgate, Aldershot.

Murphy, Kathryn (2008) A man of excellent parts: the manuscript readers of Thomas Browne's *Religio medici. TLS* 5492(4 July), 14–15.

Murphy, Kathryn & Todd, Richard (eds) (2008) *A man very well studyed: new contexts for Thomas Browne.* Brill, Leiden.

Patrides, C. A. (ed.) (1982) *Approaches to Sir Thomas Browne: the Ann Arbor tercentenary lectures.* University of Missouri Press, Columbia.

Post, Jonathan (1987) *Sir Thomas Browne.* Twayne, Boston.

Preston, Claire (2005) *Thomas Browne and the writing of early modern science.* Cambridge University Press, Cambridge.

Browne, William

STEPHEN GUY-BRAY

William Browne (1590/91–?1645) is considered to be the most important of the Spenserian poets of the first half of the seventeenth century. His major works are *Britannia's pastorals*, a Christmas masque for the Inner Temple, and a book of eclogues called *The shepheards pipe*; he also wrote some shorter lyric poems as well as a number of elegies.

Very little is known for certain about Browne's life, partly because he appears to have retired from public life quite early and partly because of the commonness of his name, which has made it difficult to say that a record of a William Browne (under any spelling) is a reference to the poet. He was born in Tavistock in Devonshire. After leaving Oxford without taking a degree he was for some time a member of the Inner Temple, although he appears not to have taken a degree there either. His first publications (an elegy for Henry, prince of Wales and the first book of *Britannia's pastorals*) were in 1613; in 1614 he published *The shepheards pipe*, in 1615 the masque for the Inner Temple, and in 1616 the second book of *Britannia's pastorals*.

After this promising beginning Browne published very little. In his early career, he was connected with a number of well-known poets, in particular George Wither and the poets associated with the Inner Temple (O'Callaghan 1998). Much of his poetry from this time can be seen to some extent as coterie poetry. In the 1620s and 1630s he appears to have withdrawn from London life and to have been connected with the Herbert and Sidney families, for whom he wrote several elegies, including a famous one for the countess of Pembroke ('Underneath this sable hearse'). He had died by the end of 1645. The manuscript of the third book of *Britannia's pastorals* was discovered only in the middle of the nineteenth century in the library of Salisbury Cathedral (Brown & Piva 1978).

Edmund Spenser was Browne's poetic model throughout his career (Grundy 1969), most obviously in *Britannia's pastorals*, although he was also influenced by Italian pastoral drama (specifically by Torquato Tasso's *Aminta*). In *Britannia's pastorals*, Browne mixes the pastoral and romance genres, as Spenser did in *The Faerie Queene*, and, like Spenser, Browne attempts to write an epic that will also be thoroughly English (Swann 2000; Wright 2003). Browne did not have Spenser's narrative gifts, however, and the narrative is not a success – it is, in fact, frequently almost impossible to follow. Nevertheless, *Britannia's pastorals* contains a great deal of excellent poetry. Browne was good at evoking pathos (his shepherds and shepherdesses often find themselves in peril), but his greatest quality was probably his talent for natural description. The passages in which he describes what is recognizably his native Devonshire are especially fine.

The first book of *Britannia's pastorals* is noticeably lighter in spirit than the second, which is chiefly due to the fact that the largely latent political concerns of the first book become more prominent. Book II appears to comment unfavourably on the difference between Elizabeth and James as rulers. The incomplete third book abandons the narrative and English setting altogether and appears as an anthology of very loosely connected pastoral songs and lyrics (a number of which are pattern poems), although if Browne had finished the book he might well have added more narrative material.

The year after the appearance of the first book of *Britannia's pastorals*, Browne published *The shepheards pipe*, a collection of topical eclogues, although the precise nature of their topicality is not always clear. These eclogues are connected both to Wither (who, along with other members of the Inner Temple, contributed poems to *The shepheards pipe* and who published a connected book, *The shepherd's hunting*, in 1615) and to Spenser, with the difference, which may be significant, that while Spenser began his career with a book of eclogues before beginning his epic, Browne reversed this progression. In any case, after the publication in 1616 of the second book of *Britannia's pastorals* Browne, as far as we know, never again wrote a poem of any considerable length or ambition.

In his own lifetime Browne was considered an important English poet, but his fame did not last. Still, it has often been argued that not only Milton but also such later poets as Keats, Tennyson, and Elizabeth Barrett Browning were influenced by his work and, in particular, by his treatment of nature (Grundy 1955; 1969). Apart from the elegy for the Countess of Pembroke and a short poem beginning 'May! be thou never graced', both of which are frequently anthologized, his poetry is now difficult to find and very little of it is in print even in excerpted form. A scholarly edition of his complete works is needed and would help his works to gain the critical attention they deserve.

SEE ALSO: Herbert, Mary (Sidney), countess of Pembroke; Spenser, Edmund; Wither, George

REFERENCES AND SUGGESTED READINGS

Brown, Cedric C. & Piva, Margherita (1978) William Browne, Marino, France, and the third book of *Britannia's pastorals*. *Review of English Studies* 29 (116), 385–404.

Grundy, Joan (1955) Keats and William Browne. *Review of English Studies* 6(21), 44–52.

Grundy, Joan (1969) *The Spenserian poets: a study in Elizabethan and Jacobean poetry*. Edward Arnold, London.

Guy-Bray, Stephen (2002) *Homoerotic space: the poetics of loss in Renaissance literature*. University of Toronto Press, Toronto.

Holmer, Joan Ozark (1976) Internal evidence for dating William Browne's *Britannia's pastorals*, book III. *Papers of the Bibliographic Society of America* 70, 347–364.

O'Callaghan, Michelle (1998) Literary commonwealths: a 1614 print community, the *shepheards pipe*, and the *shepherds hunting*. *Seventeenth Century* 13(2), 103–123.

Swann, Marjorie (2000) The politics of fairylore in early modern English literature. *Renaissance Quarterly* 53, 449–473.

Wright, Gillian (1999) Giving them but their own: Circe, Ulysses, and William Browne of Tavistock. *Medieval and Renaissance Drama in England* 12, 190–217.

Wright, Gillian (2003) Whose pastorals? William Browne of Tavistock and the singing of Britannia. In: Schwyzer, Philip & Mealor, Simon (eds) *Archipelagic identities: literature and identity in the Atlantic archipelago, 1550–1800*. Ashgate, Aldershot, pp. 43–52.

Bryan, Francis

JASON POWELL

A frequent ambassador for and confidant to Henry VIII, the 'Vicar of Hell' Sir Francis Bryan (d.1550) is better known today for his nickname than his verse: his only known extant poem, 'The proverbs of Salomon', does little to uphold the reputation granted him by Elizabethans such as Francis Meres, Michael Drayton, and the printer Thomas Thynne (Powell 2009). However, his relationship with Thomas Wyatt, who dedicated his third satire and an epigram to Bryan, and his prose style in letters and in his translation of Antonio de Guevara's *Dispraise of the life of a courtier* (1548) earn him a place in the literary history of the mid-Tudor court.

The character of a restless 'Bryan', trotting constantly between foreign realms in the king's service, refusing to indulge in vice, and holding an honest name above all else, was the focus for Wyatt's third satire. There, the poet's speaking voice imitates Horace's blind seer Tiresias (from *Sermo* 2.5) by urging a dissolute and sedentary life as a solution to the financial problems 'Bryan' faced. Wyatt's Bryan refuses, and replies with a defence of royal service and

his own honesty. This portrayal fits the historical character, but only ironically, as critics consistently note (Starkey 1982). The real Bryan more often followed 'Wyatt's' advice, whether as pander for Henry VIII, as suitor to ageing widows, or as someone who seemed to store his money in a sieve. Nevertheless, Wyatt's tone changed in 'Sighs are my food', the epigram he addressed to Bryan from prison, in which he invokes a passage from Ecclesiasticus 27 in order to request that Bryan keep Wyatt's secrets from the king and the Privy Council (Brigden 1996). Bryan was indeed a diplomat, the king's trusted voice at crucial moments in arguing for the king's divorce from Katherine of Aragon, or in reporting on a momentous meeting between the French king and the emperor in 1538. His diplomatic letters are memorable for their overt disavowal of customary rhetorical formulae in favour of directness and plain language.

Bryan made his name at court as a jouster and a hunting companion of the king, and he leveraged this friendship into a lifetime of service, albeit with the periodic loss of royal favour, first as one of the 'minions' expelled from the privy chamber in 1519 (Walker 1989), and again when Henry lost confidence in him as a diplomat in 1538. Bryan, a religious conservative, managed not only to survive but to flourish in the more radical Protestantism of the Edwardian regime. He died while commanding English forces in Ireland, where he had married Joan Butler, the widowed countess of Ormond, and daughter of James fitz Maurice Fitzgerald, tenth earl of Desmond, in 1548.

Despite his lack of a university education and the claim that he would never employ an adherent of the 'new learning' (Brigden 2004), Bryan's literary activities betray a healthy respect for humanism. In 1532 his uncle John Bourchier, second Lord Berners, translated Antonio de Guevara's *Golden boke of Marcus Aurelius* from a French version at his request. Over a decade later, Bryan himself translated and had published another of Guevara's works as *A dispraise of the life of a courtier*. This interest may have owed something to the model of Wyatt, whose 1527 translation from Plutarch's *De tranquilitate animi* (*Tho. wyatis translatyon of Plutarckes boke / of the quyete of mynde*) was the first known classical moral essay printed in English. The *Dispraise*, despite its contemporary subject, borrows much from the Stoic thought and classical oratory that attracted Wyatt to Plutarch's essay. Yet Bryan's translation is arguably more successful, and his prose achieves the tautness Wyatt's early style never completely attained.

Bryan's 'Proverbs' is similarly dependent on the model of contemporary writers both for its fashionable form of ottava rima and its content, which was derived, in some places almost verbatim, from Thomas Elyot's *Banket of sapience* (?1534) (Kinsman 1979). Wyatt's apparently mocking adoption of proverbs from Bryan's poem in his satire is perhaps an indication of the limited esteem in which he held the poem. However, when they are combined with his activities as a translator and with the portrayal of him in Wyatt's satire, Bryan's 'Proverbs' suggest the importance of literary activities in the fashioning of his political identity.

The real puzzle of Bryan's writings, and an important subject for future work, relates to his possible authorship of poems in the 1557 volume *Songes and sonettes*, better known as *Tottel's miscellany*. Michael Drayton and others saw him as responsible for many of the unattributed poems there. However, some critics have questioned this claim, even while noting other possible poems of his in manuscript (Powell 2009).

SEE ALSO: Drayton, Michael; Elyot, Thomas; Meres, Francis; Wyatt, Thomas

REFERENCES AND SUGGESTED READINGS

Brigden, Susan (1996) 'The shadow that you know': Sir Thomas Wyatt and Sir Francis Bryan at court and in embassy. *Historical Journal* 39, 1–31.

Brigden, Susan (2004) Bryan, Sir Francis. In: *Oxford dictionary of national biography*. Oxford University Press, Oxford.

Burrow, Colin (1993) Horace at home and abroad: Wyatt and sixteenth-century Horatianism. In: Martindale, Charles & Hopkins, David (eds) *Horace made new: Horatian influences on British writing from the Renaissance to the twentieth century*. Cambridge University Press, Cambridge, pp. 27–49.

Heale, Elizabeth (1997) 'An owl in a sack troubles no man': proverbs, plainness, and Wyatt. *Renaissance Studies* 11, 420–433.

Kinsman, R. S. (1979) 'The proverbs of Salmon do playnly declare': a sententious poem on wisdom and governance, ascribed to Sir Francis Bryan. *Huntington Library Quarterly* 42, 279–312.

Powell, Jason (2009) Sir Thomas Wyatt and Sir Francis Bryan: plainness and dissimulation. In: Shrank, Cathy & Pincombe, Mike (eds) *The Oxford handbook of Tudor literature*. Oxford University Press, Oxford, pp. 187–202.

Rollins, H. E. (ed.) (1928–29) *Tottel's miscellany*. 2 vols. Harvard University Press, Cambridge, MA.

Starkey, David (1982) The court: Castiglione's ideal and Tudor reality, being a discussion of Sir Thomas Wyatt's 'Satire addressed to Sir Francis Bryan'. *Journal of the Warburg and Courtauld Institutes* 45, 232–238.

Walker, Greg (1989) The 'expulsion of the minions' of 1519 reconsidered. *Historical Journal* 32, 1–16.

Bryskett, Lodowick

THOMAS HERRON

Lodowick Bryskett (c.1546–c.1612), administrator and colonial settler in Ireland, is best remembered as a minor poet and translator who had the good luck to befriend two literary titans, Sir Philip Sidney and Edmund Spenser. Like James Boswell, however, he is more than just a Boswell.

Bryskett's life and family are well recorded. His father, Antonio Bruschetto, was a merchant and his parents, both Italian, settled in London before his birth. He went to school at Tonbridge in Kent and matriculated at Trinity College, Cambridge, in 1557. He left without a degree and entered the employment of Sir Henry Sidney, the three-time lord deputy of Ireland, president of Wales and father of Sir

Philip. Bryskett first travelled to Ireland with Sir Henry in 1565 and also travelled to Italy on business for him sometime before November 1569 (Bryskett's principal poetic source, the Italian courtier Bernardo Tasso, did not die until September 1569, so he could conceivably have met him there). Bryskett accompanied Sir Philip (who called him 'my Lewis') on his Continental tour (1572–74) and earned the respect of French reformer Hubert Languet and others. In Paris, Philip and his Lewis were witness to the St Bartholomew's Day Massacre (August 1572). Bryskett accompanied Sir Henry Sidney back to Ireland in 1575 and spent most of his life thereafter as a mid- to upper-level administrator in Dublin and Enniscorthy, County Wexford, where he was a landowner and sheriff (he also acquired lands in County Cork and elsewhere). His life therefore paralleled that of his acquaintance and fellow pastoral poet Edmund Spenser, who followed Lord Deputy Arthur Grey, fourteenth Baron Grey of Wilton, to Ireland as his secretary in 1580, was in the Dublin administration (1580–?1588), took over attainted lands in County Kildare (1582–?1584) and County Cork (?1588–99), and served as Bryskett's deputy clerk to the Council of Munster from around 1584 to 1589. Bryskett fled the Irish Nine Years War to London, around 1599. He served on a mission to Flanders (1601–3), where he was captured and ransomed. He was active again in Ireland in 1609, seeking to recover lands in the law courts.

Bryskett's Italian background, Irish experience, and famous companions all figure significantly in his three known works of literature. He accurately translated but also heavily adapted Giambattista Giraldi Cinthio's *Tre dialoghi della vita civile*, being the second part of *De gli hecatommithi* (1565), and published it as *A discourse of ciuill life* (1606). Additional influences include Alessandro Piccolomini's *Della institutione morale* (1560) and Stefano Guazzo's *La civil conversatione* (1574). The prose treatise is a humanist dialogue on matters moral, ethical, and philosophical, set in a cottage outside Dublin, around 1582. Bryskett

may therefore have finished the work any time after 1582 and may have translated parts of it earlier. It is dedicated to and strongly supports the administration of the highly controversial militant Protestant lord deputy of Ireland Grey of Wilton (1580–82), also patron of poets George Gascoigne and Spenser. The dialogue features Spenser as one of its interlocutors, fresh at work on *The Faerie Queene* (1590). In their company are various local luminaries, including New English administrators and military men and the lawyer and poet George Dormer, author of the ballad *The decay of Rosse*. The work's discussion of the tripartite nature of the soul; issues of providence, predestination, and free will; and advocacy of the virtuous ethical life compares favourably with (and may be a source for) episodes like the House of Temperance in *The Faerie Queene*, book II. The work has been instrumental for critics and historians as a window into the intellectual origins of *The Faerie Queene* and (for more recent critics) into the ideology of the predominantly Protestant, newly arrived colonists in Ireland, the so-called 'New English'. It is also evidence of Italian Renaissance influence in early modern Ireland and in the Dublin Pale specifically.

Bryskett's two extant poems, 'The mourning muse of Thestylis' and 'A pastoral aeglogue upon the death of Sir Philip Sidney, knight', also involve Sidney, Spenser, Ireland, and Italian sources. Both poems are published in Spenser's volume *Colin Clouts come home againe* (1595), alongside the title poem and another group lamenting Sidney, including 'The doleful lay of Clorinda', perhaps by Spenser; Spenser's 'Astrophel'; an elegy (reprinted from the miscellany *The phoenix nest*) by Sir Walter Ralegh, also a major planter in Ireland, and a few others (Bryskett's 'Mourning muse' was entered in the Stationers' Register by the printer John Wolfe on 22 August 1587, but that version is not extant). Both of Bryskett's poems rely for form and content on two poems by Bernardo Tasso: 'The mourning muse' paraphrases 'Selva nella morte del Signor Aluigi da Gonzaga', and 'A pastorall aeglogue' paraphrases Tasso's first eclogue, 'Alcippo'. Virgil is another literary precedent for the poems, as is Spenser. Spenser's alter-ego Colin Clout appears as an interlocutor in the poems, to the extent that it appears uncertain as to who wrote what part of what poem. The various shepherd-poet voices in Bryskett's poems are interwoven and blended together to a confusing and surely deliberate degree.

These poems are also graceful and affecting: Bryskett apparently felt Sidney's death in 1586 deeply. In 'A pastorall aeglogue', he recalls their Continental journey together

> Through pleasant woods, and many an vnknowne way,
> Along the bankes of many siluer streames,
> Thou with him yodest; and with him didst scale
> The craggie rocks of th' Alpes and *Appenine* . . .

But now, 'Behold the fountains now left desolate, / And withred grasse with cypress boughs be spred.' Bryskett also appropriates Sidney for his own political purposes in Ireland. Both poems open in pastoral Irish landscapes near gurgling rivers (one the Liffey near Dublin, the other the 'Orowne', most likely the Urrin in Enniscorthy). In both, Sidney's death binds the English shepherd community together in mourning, inspired by the memory of his piety and heroism.

Despite his publishing so little, Bryskett's poetic influence stretched not only to County Cork but far into the future: Spenser's *Colin Clouts come home againe* and Bryskett's two elegies are among the main sources for John Milton's *Lycidas* (1638), a pastoral elegy in tribute to the Anglican churchman Edward King, a scion of the New English King family of Boyle, County Roscommon, 'drown'd . . . on the Irish seas' en route from Chester to county Dublin (where the King family also owned a home). Milton's 'For Lycidas is dead' echoes Bryskett's '*Phillisides* is dead' ('A pastorall aeglogue') and demonstrates that Bryskett kept Sidney's poetic spirit very much alive for a future generation of Protestant poets.

SEE ALSO: Gascoigne, George; Milton, John; Ralegh, Walter; Sidney, Philip; Spenser, Edmund

REFERENCES AND SUGGESTED READINGS

Jones, Deborah (1933) Lodowick Bryskett and his family. In: Sisson, Charles J. (ed.) *Thomas Lodge and other Elizabethans*. Harvard University Press, Cambridge, MA, pp. 243–361.

Maley, Willy (1997) *Salvaging Spenser: colonialism, culture and identity*. Macmillan Press, Basingstoke.

McCabe, Richard A. (2004) Bryskett, Lodowick. In: *Oxford dictionary of national biography*. Oxford University Press, Oxford.

Plomer, Henry R. & Cross, Tom Peete (1927) *The life and correspondence of Lodowick Bryskett*. University of Chicago Press, Chicago.

Wright, Thomas E. (1990) Bryskett, Lodowick. In: Hamilton, A. C. (ed.) *The Spenser encyclopedia*. University of Toronto Press, Toronto, p. 119.

Buchanan, George

DERMOT CAVANAGH

George Buchanan (1506–82) was one of the most distinguished and influential humanists of the sixteenth century. He is best known today to historians of the period's political ideas as a notably radical theorist of constitutional thought who emphasized the importance of popular sovereignty, limited kingship, and the right to resist tyranny. Yet in his own time Buchanan was renowned as perhaps Europe's pre-eminent neo-Latin poet; he was also a dramatist of remarkable inventiveness and it is this literary side of his work that is still underexplored today.

Buchanan was born in Stirlingshire and may well have spoken Gaelic. He moved between Scotland and France during the early part of his life, studying at St Andrews and Paris, and acting as a tutor to members of the Scottish nobility. He began to translate contemporary and classical works but also to engage in independent composition, notably, in 1538, a lengthy and exceptionally vituperative poetic satire on the Franciscans ('Franciscanus'). In 1539 Buchanan became a teacher at the Collège de Guyenne in Bordeaux where one of his pupils was the young Michel de Montaigne. In the early 1540s, Buchanan began to compose drama for performance by the boys of the Collège, completing translations into Latin of Euripides' *Medea* and *Alcestis* as well as two remarkable plays of his own, also in Latin: one based on an episode from the Old Testament, *Jephthes*, and one from the New, *Baptistes*, a play on the last days of John the Baptist. Both of these works were strikingly original attempts to create a Christian humanist form of tragic drama. They also engaged with Buchanan's emerging interest in political ideas, especially the topics of tyranny and martyrdom, the nature and limits of obedience, and the scope of sovereignty. Both plays were widely admired and translated, *Baptistes* into English in notable circumstances when it was published by order of the House of Commons at the outset of the Civil War in January 1642 and given a vigorous new title: 'Tyrannicall-government anatomized, or a discourse concerning evil-councellors'.

Baptistes also advances an explicit plea for religious toleration but Buchanan was not fortunate in this respect. In 1547 he moved to Portugal to teach at a college in Coimbra and by 1550 the inquisitor-general was moved to investigate allegations of heresy against the staff. Buchanan was imprisoned for two years by the Inquisition before abjuring his errors and returning to Paris and Northern Italy, where he remained for the next five years. However, this traumatic experience did facilitate what was to become his best-known and most popular work: his acclaimed Latin version of the Psalms. This work established Buchanan as a leading neo-Latin poet, and it held the attention of a humanist readership for decades after his death, appearing in a multitude of editions. Buchanan's range as a poet was formidable, however, extending beyond purely religious themes to embrace a variety of genres and topics. His poetry responded to topical events, meditated on the nature and purpose of

political and spiritual life and, perhaps most strikingly, mounted an excoriating attack on the imperialist endeavour afflicting the 'New World'. Buchanan's poetry denounced Iberian colonialism especially. In his 'To the Brazilian colonists' ('In colonias brasilienses'), the Portuguese exploitation of Brazil was exposed in horrific detail as fostering clericalism, advancing a debased commercial greed and reducing the native population to slavery and desolation. The same impulse surfaced even in his ambitious and unfinished poem on the old Ptolemaic cosmology, *De sphaera*, which included digressions on commercial and imperial avarice.

Around 1560, Buchanan returned to Scotland, gaining the favour of Mary, Queen of Scots and, especially, the patronage of James Stewart, earl of Moray (later assassinated in 1570). He became principal of St Leonard's College in St Andrews in 1566. It is with the sensational events surrounding the murder of Mary's second husband, Henry, Lord Darnley, and the queen's forced abdication and imprisonment in 1567 that Buchanan is most well known. Buchanan sided with the queen's opponents and a vehement exposure of the queen's behaviour has been attributed to his authorship: *Ane detectioun of the duings of Marie Quene of Scottes* (1571). Buchanan took an increasingly prominent role in public life in the wake of her fall from power, acting as moderator of the general assembly of the Kirk (the Church of Scotland), attending meetings of the Privy Council, acting on various government commissions, and, most famously, becoming tutor to Mary's son, the future James VI.

These public commitments also led Buchanan's writing in new directions, most notably shaping the two works which have reinforced his reputation as one of the period's most challenging political thinkers: the contentious and widely influential treatise of 1579, *De jure regni apud Scotos dialogus* (*A dialogue on the law of kingship amongst the Scots*) and his great historical study of his native country, *Rerum Scoticarum historia*, published posthumously in 1582. The former work elaborated Buchanan's political theory, emphasizing that kingship was elective and accountable to the law. Monarchs were appointed by the people to fulfil well-defined functions and if they failed to do so they could be deposed or, in the extreme case of tyrants who flouted the law, assassinated by any citizen. Buchanan's history illustrated and vindicated similar doctrines through extensive examples drawn from the Scottish past. These works proved to be of great and lasting interest. Perhaps the most immediate and hostile response they provoked came from James VI whose vehement defence of absolutism, *The trew lawe of free monarchies* (1598), is, in part, a critical response to his old tutor. A more sympathetic audience for these works was found amongst the Sidney circle, and later John Milton was one of many engaged readers of *De jure regni* during the Civil War period; this work continued to be influential during the American Revolution. The absorption of much of Buchanan's history into the account of Scotland included in Raphael Holinshed's *Chronicles* meant that this work too enjoyed wide dissemination and also influenced Shakespeare's *Macbeth* (Norbrook 1987).

SEE ALSO: Holinshed, Raphael; James VI and I; Milton, John; Shakespeare, William

REFERENCES AND SUGGESTED READINGS

Bushnell, Rebecca W. (1994) George Buchanan, James VI and neo-classicism. In: Mason, Roger A. (ed.) *Scots and Britons: Scottish political thought and the union of 1603*. Cambridge University Press, Cambridge, pp. 91–111.

Norbrook, David (1987) *Macbeth* and the politics of historiography. In: Sharpe, Kevin & Zwicker, Steven (eds) *Politics of discourse: the literature and history of seventeenth-century England*. University of California Press, Berkeley, pp. 78–116.

Phillips, James E. (1948) George Buchanan and the Sidney circle. *Huntington Library Quarterly* 12, 23–55.

Williamson, Arthur H. (1996) George Buchanan, civic virtue and commerce: European imperialism and its sixteenth-century critics. *Scottish Historical Review* 75, 20–39.

Bullein, William

ERIN SULLIVAN

William Bullein (c.1515–76) began his professional life as a Protestant preacher, but he is best known for the witty and religiously charged medical treatises he wrote in the second half of his life. He came from a prosperous family, possibly related to that of Anne Boleyn, and it is likely that he studied at either Oxford or Cambridge, though no records exist of his enrolment. In 1550 he took up a position in a Suffolk rectory, where he was related to one of the town's prominent families, and he remained there until late 1554, when Queen Mary's rise to power prompted his resignation. Dismayed by Mary's commitment to Catholicism, Bullein soon left for the Continent, studying medicine while he was there. He returned to England by the late 1550s, practising medicine in Northumberland and Durham and moving to London in 1560. During this time Bullein's personal life was marked by scandal. Having married the widow of his late friend and patron, Sir Thomas Hilton, he soon found himself accused of murder and debt by Sir Thomas's brother William. He was found innocent of murder but spent time in a London debtors' prison, where he wrote his second book. Although Bullein never joined the College of Physicians, he seems to have cultivated a successful London practice, leasing a substantial house in Grub Street during his time in the city (Mitchell 1959).

Bullein's first two books were vernacular medical manuals intended for a non-specialist audience. *The gouernement of healthe* (1558), strongly influenced by Thomas Elyot's popular *The castel of helth* (1539), focuses on the importance of temperance, particularly regarding eating and drinking. Framed as a dialogue between a gluttonous patient and his physician, the treatise offers medical advice characteristic of the time, discussing the healthful properties of different foods, exercises, and environments, factors known in contemporary medicine as the 'non-naturals' (Siraisi 1990; Wear 2000).

The work draws on the teachings of ancient and medieval medical authorities such as Hippocrates, Galen, and Avicenna, while also including more modern references to Conrad Gesner and Leonard Fuchs. Bullein's next book, *The bulwarke of defence* (1562), addresses more specialized medical topics, such as the creation of medical compounds, their appropriate use, and guidelines for surgical procedures. Again written in dialogue form, the *Bulwarke* offers medical advice largely rooted in traditional humoral theory, though it also contains some early references to Paracelsus and his new brand of chemical medicine (Healy 2001). Bullein also includes considerable political commentary, frequently linking physical illness to wider social problems in England, such as the unjust treatment of the poor and the irresponsibility of the ruling elite. In a discussion of the healthfulness of milk, for instance, Bullein quickly launches into a critique of ingratitude, specifically singling out William Hilton, the man responsible for his imprisonment at the time (Maslen 2008).

Bullein's final two books focus on specific diseases but also expand his engagement with moral, social, and political issues. In 1562 he published *A regiment against pleurisi*, a short treatise that begins by offering a history of infectious disease and its relationship to divine judgement, followed by medical advice concerning pleurisy and its recent outbreak. Two years later Bullein published the work for which he is most remembered, *A dialogue against the fever pestilence*. Written in response to the 1563 plague, which killed roughly 20 per cent of London's population (Slack 1990), the *Dialogue* promises readers advice on how to avoid catching the disease as well as what might be done once a person falls ill. While it delivers on both of these points, it does so within a complex, multi-voiced dialogue that incorporates aspects of the morality play, medical regimen, recipe book, emblem catalogue, elegy, and, in later editions, the utopia (Healy 2001). C. S. Lewis criticized the work for trying to do too much at once, but other scholars have praised its unusual and overflowing style, aligning it with

Menippean satire, the encyclopedia or anatomy, as well as Chaucer's *The Canterbury tales* (Lewis 1954; McCutcheon 1989; Healy 2001; Grigsby 2004). Bullein's creative use of the dialogue structure later influenced pamphleteer Thomas Nashe: he claims that *Have with you to Saffron-Walden* (1596) was written 'in the nature of a Dialogue, much like Bullen'.

In addition to its unique literary form, the *Dialogue*'s concern for the poor and matters of social justice has interested recent scholars. Though many characters appear in the *Dialogue*, the central story focuses on Civis, a London citizen, and his attempt to survive the plague. In doing so he encounters many greedy individuals, including the atheistic physician Medicus, all intent on preserving their own livelihoods above the health of the commonwealth. Even Civis and his humble servant, Roger, are exposed in the end as selfish and impious, having profited from unscrupulous property dealings. The only character free from moral censure is Theologus, who appears at the end of the work to remind Civis and the reader about the corruption that comes with the pursuit of wealth, making man 'high minded, and forgetfull of hym self'. Avaricious behaviour, the *Dialogue* suggests, damages both individual and society, leading to distress among the poor, widespread spiritual impoverishment, and eventually major disease epidemics such as plague (Healy 2001; 2003).

Though scholars have debated the exact character of Bullein's Protestantism, they agree that he was fiercely reformist, both in his religious and his social views. After his death in 1576 he was buried alongside his brother Richard in St Giles Cripplegate, and in 1587 the martyrologist John Foxe was also entombed there. A monument celebrating the three reformers' lives highlighted Bullein's commitment to social welfare: 'he always had medicines, which he gave to both the rich and the poor' (Strype 1834). Such 'medicines' came in the shape of both medical prescriptions and religious advice, since Bullein believed that each had a part to play in the preservation of personal and public health.

SEE ALSO: Elyot, Thomas; Foxe, John; Nashe, Thomas

REFERENCES AND SUGGESTED READINGS

Grigsby, Bryon Lee (2004) *Pestilence in medieval and early modern English literature.* Routledge, New York.

Healy, Margaret (2001) *Fictions of disease in early modern England: bodies, plagues and politics.* Palgrave Macmillan, Basingstoke.

Healy, Margaret (2003) Defoe's *Journal* and the English plague writing tradition. *Literature and Medicine* 22(1), 25–44.

Lewis, C. S. (1954) *English literature in the sixteenth century, excluding drama.* Clarendon Press, Oxford.

Maslen, R. W. (2008) The healing dialogues of Dr Bullein. *Yearbook of English Studies* 38(1–2) 119–135.

McCutcheon, Elizabeth (1989) William Bullein's *Dialogue against the fever pestilence:* a sixteenth-century anatomy. In: Murphy, Clare et al. (eds) *Miscellanea moreana: essays for Germain Marc'hadour.* Medieval & Renaissance Texts & Studies, Binghamton.

Mitchell, William S. (1959) William Bullein, Elizabethan physician and author. *Medical History* 3 (3), 188–200.

Siraisi, Nancy (1990) *Medieval and early Renaissance medicine.* University of Chicago Press, Chicago.

Slack, Paul (1990) *The impact of plague in Tudor and Stuart England.* Oxford University Press, Oxford.

Strype, John (1834) *Annals of the Reformation and establishment of religion.* Clarendon Press, Oxford.

Wear, Andrew (2000) *Knowledge and practice in English medicine, 1550–1680.* Cambridge University Press, Cambridge.

Bunyan, John

MICHAEL DAVIES

One of the most important writers of religious literature of the later seventeenth century, John Bunyan (1628–88) is famously the author of *The pilgrim's progress*: a book long considered second only to the Bible in terms of worldwide circulation, having been translated into most languages since first publication in 1678. Bunyan's 58 published works, including several volumes of poetry, remain an outstanding collection of late seventeenth-century writings, his prose being notably rich in the use of metaphor and similitude characteristic of nonconformist scriptural style. These writings also tell us a great deal about the experiences and convictions of nonconformists who suffered persecution following the Restoration of Charles II in 1660. As a result, Bunyan holds a prominent place in the literature and the history of England from the late 1650s to the close of the 1680s, while his imaginative allegories, especially *The pilgrim's progress*, would influence generations of writers, particularly in England and America, from the end of the seventeenth century onwards.

Bunyan was born in the village of Elstow near Bedford, being baptized there on 30 November 1628. He was given an elementary schooling which, though basic, nevertheless enabled him to read and write well. As a preacher and author, Bunyan would make a virtue of his relative lack of education, claiming that the truth of his words derived not from book learning but from his own convictions and experiences, as informed by the word of God. The idea has endured that Bunyan's library consisted of no more than a Bible, a concordance, and a copy of John Foxe's *Actes and monuments*, or 'Book of martyrs' (1563). However, the rhetorical sophistication of his prose, his consummate ability to tackle opponents in debate, and his command of metaphor, imagery, and narrative, not to mention his acuity in matters doctrinal and ecclesiological, suggest that Bunyan had read more widely and more carefully than his disavowals of learning suggest. He had certainly enjoyed ballads and 'chapbook' romances as a young man, and, through marriage to his first wife, had come across devotional works such as Arthur Dent's *The plaine mans path-way to heaven* (1601) and Lewis Bayly's *The practise of pietie* (3rd edn 1613). During his religious conversion, he encountered the terrifying story of Francis

Spira's despair, as well as Luther's *Commentary on Galatians*, the theology of which confirmed Bunyan's own doctrinal thinking about justification by faith rather than by works. Bunyan must also have read the Elizabethan Calvinist divine, William Perkins, as his *Mapp shewing the order and causes of salvation and damnation* (?1663) resembles a similar 'Chart' published in Perkins's popular work, *A golden chaine* (1590).

When he was around 16, Bunyan joined the Parliamentarian forces in the English Civil War, being enlisted in the New Model Army at Newport Pagnell, from November 1644 until July 1647. Whether he saw any fighting is uncertain, but his time in the army certainly allows for speculation about his early political sympathies and possible connections to radicalism. Following his military service, Bunyan married twice: his first wife, whose name is unknown, died in 1658, leaving him with four children. A year later he married again, and had two more children with Elizabeth, his second wife. To earn a living, Bunyan followed his father's profession as a brazier or tinker. Perhaps the most significant event in his life was his religious conversion, which seems to have occurred in the early 1650s, not long after an independent congregation in Bedford had been established by John Gifford, the church's first pastor, around 1650.

From the account given in his spiritual autobiography *Grace abounding to the chief of sinners* (1666), Bunyan's conversion was long, drawn-out, and spiritually turbulent, involving months if not years of wrestling with spiritual uncertainty, convinced at times that he was damned. Such convictions were relieved periodically by flashes of assurance over salvation, and eventually by a more sustained faith gained through strenuous reading of the Bible alongside meetings with Gifford and other members of the Bedford congregation. Bunyan eventually joined Gifford's church, an Independent or Congregationalist gathering with Baptist and possibly Fifth Monarchist affiliations, around 1655 and soon became one of its most active members. By 1656–57, he had established

himself locally as a notable preacher and had debated hotly with Quakers.

Bunyan would take his opposition to Quakers into print, addressing them in his first published work, an anti-Quaker treatise: *Some gospel-truths opened* (1656). This initial foray into printed controversy was soon answered by the Quaker Edward Burrough in *The true faith of the gospel of peace contended for* (1656). Bunyan replied to Burrough's animadversions directly in *A vindication of the book called, some gospel-truths opened* (1657). These heated and sometimes acrimonious exchanges centred upon what Bunyan saw as 'the errors of the *Quakers*', and in particular the Quaker doctrines of the inner light and the inward resurrection of Christ in all believers. By contrast, Bunyan states the case for his more orthodox doctrine of salvation by grace against what, he argued, was no more than a Quaker version of salvation by works. Although Burrough responded to Bunyan's *Vindication* with *Truth (the strongest of all)* (1657), Bunyan did not reply again, and would soon face further attack from George Fox, the founder of the Society of Friends (or Quakers), in *The great mistery of the great whore unfolded* (1659).

Bunyan published next *A few sighs from hell* (1658), probably based on one of his sermons: it urges the repentance of the ungodly through a carefully developed exposition of the parable of Lazarus and Dives (Luke 16.19–31). In 1659, however, Bunyan saw into print his most important and substantial work to date: *The doctrine of the law and grace unfolded*. This work is an exemplary summary of Bunyan's 'covenant' theology, wherein the covenant of grace (or that of the gospel), as fulfilled by Christ, takes precedence over the covenant of works (or that of the Law) which had been broken by Adam in the Fall, subsequently making salvation by human fulfilment of the Law (represented most clearly by the Ten Commandments given to Moses) impossible. Faith in grace freely granted by God through Christ, whose righteousness is imputed to the faithful, thus becomes the theological centre of Bunyan's religious thinking, standing at the heart of practically everything he would write subsequently.

Had Bunyan produced nothing after 1660, the legacy of his published works up to that point – just four in total – would have been relatively small. Yet these early writings establish some of his most important characteristics, from an ability to argue around and through complex doctrinal positions, using a detailed knowledge of the Bible and its typology, to a facility with language and a style rhetorically vigorous and figuratively striking. While the anti-Quaker tracts establish Bunyan as a heavyweight controversialist, A few sighs from hell offers both a frightening vision of the fate of the damned and a powerful appraisal of social injustice, addressing the material and spiritual differences between the rich and the poor. Perhaps more than anything, though, these early writings offer the opportunity to see how unwavering Bunyan's doctrinal thinking about salvation was from the start: an aspect which – like his colloquial yet startlingly effective prose style – would characterize all of his subsequent works.

Following the return of Charles II in 1660 and the re-establishment of the Church of England in 1662, Bunyan's circumstances changed considerably. He experienced the persecutory spirit of the Restoration at first hand, being imprisoned in 1660 for refusing to stop preaching. Although the terms of his imprisonment evidently permitted him freedom to write and even to perform church duties occasionally, nevertheless he remained a prisoner of conscience for 12 years. It was against this background that Bunyan's greatest literary works appeared. While he published I will pray with the spirit (1662), an outright rejection of the Book of Common Prayer, along with works pastoral, eschatological, and millenarian in nature – Christian behaviour (1663), The holy city (1665), and The resurrection of the dead (1665) – perhaps the most important of Bunyan's writings around this time was his spiritual autobiography, Grace abounding to the chief of sinners. Scholars have rightly regarded this work as a classic Puritan conversion narrative: it details with great precision, feeling, and immediacy the spiritual turbulence experienced by the converting sinner journeying towards faith in salvation by grace. So extraordinary are the experiences Bunyan describes in this account that critics have often taken Grace abounding as evidence of his psychological instability as a young man. One of the most famous moments comes when Bunyan, believing that his enjoyment of bell-ringing is sinful, becomes convinced that the bell-tower beneath which he stands will fall upon him and so flees in terror. Yet rather than necessarily being signs of depression or neurosis, such experiences serve largely to underscore the doctrinal scheme outlined by Grace abounding as it describes the convert's progress from extreme, legalistic convictions of sin and guilt to the freedom from guilt over sin afforded by faith in grace. Equally, reading Grace abounding as little more than the product of an obsessive mode of Puritan introspection can lead to its communal contexts being overlooked. As the prefatory epistle makes clear, along with its concluding account of Bunyan's imprisonment, this conversion account has been written to comfort and support a people lost in the 'Wilderness' and now caught, as Bunyan was himself, 'between the Teeth of the Lions'.

Matters of church and community would continue to be prominent in his writings, presumably as a result of his election as pastor of the Bedford congregation on 21 December 1671 and his release from prison the following year. In 1672 Bunyan published A confession of my faith, and a reason of my practice, a work that consolidated his doctrinal beliefs and, as newly appointed pastor, clarified his congregational principles, including his view that baptism should not be a requirement of church membership. From both the Confession and the debates on baptism that followed – Bunyan publishing further defences of the principle of open communion membership against Baptist opponents in 1673 and 1674 – it becomes clear that strict denominational labels do not sit easily upon him. Though he is often described as a Baptist, it would be more accurate to refer to him as a Congregationalist or an open-communion Baptist who accepted church members without the necessity of water-baptism. Although the early 1670s saw the publication of further works in controversy, such as *A defence of the doctrine of iustification* (1672) which answered the moral theology of a Bedfordshire Church of England clergyman, Edward Fowler, Bunyan would publish numerous other doctrinal works throughout the 1670s, from *The barren fig-tree* (1673) to *Saved by grace* (1676) and *Come, and welcome, to Jesus Christ* (1678): texts elaborating his convictions on salvation by grace, as well as the active role the willing believer can play in coming to faith.

The doctrinally positive tone of these latter works certainly informs Bunyan's most famous book, with its similar message of perseverance in faith when running the race towards salvation: *The pilgrim's progress*. This religious allegory may have been conceived and written in the late 1660s and early 1670s, when persecution was fierce and when Bunyan may also have composed *The heavenly foot-man* (published first in 1698), a work that is key to his idea for an allegorical story about a man running towards heaven. *The pilgrim's progress*, however, is a major departure from anything he had produced up to this point. Rather than a straightforwardly doctrinal or sermon-like exposition, this was a sustained literary allegory, presented in the form of a 'dream-vision'. As such, it is a work of fiction: it tells of Christian's flight from the City of Destruction in order to make his way to the Celestial City. His journey leads him to encounter terrifying monsters, such as Apollyon and Giant Despair, as well as some welcoming and instructive rest-stops at the Interpreter's House, House Beautiful, and the Delectable Mountains, before he crosses the river of Death and enters the Celestial City. He also meets false or faithless pilgrims such as Talkative and Ignorance, the latter of whom reaches the Celestial City only to be cast into Hell from its very gates. Christian's pilgrimage passes, at one point, through Vanity Fair, where he and Faithful are imprisoned and the latter is put to death after the spectacular fashion of Foxe's Protestant martyrs: a searing commentary upon both the Restoration social order and ongoing persecution.

Given Bunyan's inventive adaptation of literary forms and fictive modes in *The pilgrim's progress*, including allegorical dream-vision, romance, and folk-tale, the prefatory verse 'Apology' to *The pilgrim's progress* remains a remarkable defence of his decision to use 'feigning' devices – fiction, allegory, and metaphor – as legitimate vehicles for conveying gospel 'Truth'. As such, his 'Apology' takes its place alongside Sir Philip Sidney and Edmund Spenser's defences of poetry, allegory, and romance as suitable media for their own modes of Protestantism. Bunyan's defence of allegory and metaphor in the 'Apology' also positions *The pilgrim's progress* at the centre of Restoration debates about nonconformist scriptural language and 'plain style'. It is, however, his use of similitude and dream-vision in *The pilgrim's progress*, as well as his adaptation of romance motifs, that has made it such a rich and enduring work of literature. Always popular, *The pilgrim's progress* has been subject to some radical re-evaluation in recent years across a broad range of theoretical and critical positions, from contextual and historicist to reader-response and post-structuralist approaches, Bunyan's most famous allegory sharing as much with postmodernist fiction as it does with medieval allegory or chapbook romance. The success of *The pilgrim's progress* was immediate as well as lasting: it went through 11 editions during Bunyan's lifetime and subsequently became a classic work of the English literary imagination, enjoying a rich history in terms of reception and influence. Hailed as a great work of imaginative genius by Romantics such as Samuel Taylor Coleridge and Robert Southey, *The pilgrim's progress* widely informed Victorian fiction: from Charles Dickens's *Oliver Twist* (1837–38), Charlotte Brontë's *Jane Eyre* (1847), and George Eliot's *The mill on the Floss* (1860) to

Louisa May Alcott's *Little women* (1868–69) and Mark Twain's *The adventures of Huckleberry Finn* (1884) on the other side of the Atlantic. *The pilgrim's progress* would be read by British soldiers in the trenches of the First World War and its story of trial, adventure, and perseverance would echo throughout twentieth-century popular culture, from *The Wizard of Oz* (both L. Frank Baum's children's book of 1900 and the Oscar-winning film of 1939) to Cormac McCarthy's terrifying vision of the future in his novel, *The road* (2006). Few early modern works have had such a global reach, *The pilgrim's progress* having as complex a role to play in the history of colonialism and empire as it would have in the birth of the novel (Hofmeyr 2004).

In 1680 Bunyan published *The life and death of Mr Badman*, a narrative delivered not as a 'dream' this time but as a dialogue between two fictive speakers, Wiseman and Attentive, in which Mr Badman's life and crimes are recounted via numerous digressions concerning God's providential punishments of the ungodly. This book, avoiding the romance and dream-vision elements that characterize *The pilgrim's progress*, deliberately targets ungodly social behaviour within a more realistic and this-worldly, as opposed to allegorical, setting. By contrast, Bunyan's *The holy war* (1682) returns to allegory in the high style of epic, chronicling the ongoing wars of Mansoul, a town which the forces of Shaddai and Diabolus fight to control. This allegory is, perhaps, the most sophisticated and elaborate of all of his narrative works, yet in focusing on spiritual warfaring rather than wayfaring it has never enjoyed as much popularity as *The pilgrim's progress*. In 1684, however, Bunyan returned to the format of his original allegory by publishing *The pilgrim's progress, part two*, partly to counter spurious continuations of *Part one* which had begun to appear in the early 1680s. *Part two* tells of the decision of Christian's wife, Christiana, to follow in her husband's footsteps by embarking upon her own pilgrimage to the Celestial City with her children and a neighbour called Mercy.

They undertake their journey successfully under the guidance of one Great-Heart and in the company, by the end, of a large community of fellow travellers.

Bunyan was prolific throughout the 1680s, publishing a further 13 doctrinal tracts and treatises before his death in 1688, and completing numerous others that were published posthumously by Charles Doe in 1692. Around 1683 Bunyan engaged in a controversy over whether women should be permitted to hold their own prayer meetings within the Bedford church, an issue which may have informed his decision to publish his distinctly more feminized sequel to *The pilgrim's progress* the following year. The early 1680s also saw a return to the more severe persecution of nonconformists, in response to which Bunyan wrote, among many other works, *Seasonable counsel* (1684), advocating patience and an acceptance of hardship in the face of renewed suffering. After travelling to London to give what would be his last sermon, Bunyan became ill and subsequently died on 31 August 1688.

SEE ALSO: Bayly, Lewis; Fox, George; Foxe, John; Sidney, Philip; Spenser, Edmund

REFERENCES AND SUGGESTED READINGS

Camden, Vera J. (ed.) (2008) *Trauma and transformation: the political progress of John Bunyan*. Stanford University Press, Stanford.

Davies, Michael (2002) *Graceful reading: theology and narrative in the works of John Bunyan*. Oxford University Press, Oxford.

Dunan-Page, Anne (ed.) (2010) *The Cambridge companion to Bunyan*. Cambridge University Press, Cambridge.

Greaves, Richard (2002) *Glimpses of glory: John Bunyan and English dissent*. Stanford University Press, Stanford.

Hill, Christopher (1988) *A turbulent, seditious, and factious people: John Bunyan and his church 1628–1688*. Oxford University Press, Oxford.

Hofmeyr, Isabel (2004). *The portable Bunyan: a transnational history of 'The pilgrim's progress'*. Princeton University Press, Princeton.

Keeble, N. H. (1987) *The literary culture of noncon-formity in later seventeenth century England.* Leicester University Press, Leicester.

Keeble, N. H. (ed.) (1988) *John Bunyan: conventicle and Parnassus.* Clarendon Press, Oxford.

Laurence, Anne, Owens, W. R., & Sim, Stuart (eds) (1990) *John Bunyan and his England, 1628–1688.* Hambledon Press, London.

Luxon, Thomas H. (1995) *Literal figures: Puritan allegory and the Reformation crisis in representa-tion.* University of Chicago Press, Chicago.

Newey, Vincent (ed.) (1980) *The pilgrim's progress: critical and historical views.* Liverpool University Press, Liverpool.

Owens, W. R. & Sim, Stuart (eds) (2007) *Reception, appropriation, recollection: Bunyan's 'Pilgrim's progress'.* Peter Lang, Bern.

Burton, Robert

ADAM H. KITZES

Robert Burton (1577–1640) is the author of *The anatomy of melancholy,* one of the finest books ever written on the subject. Few sources tell us about Burton's life, and we have only an outline of his career. He was born in 1577 at Lindley, in Leicestershire, second son to Ralph Burton and Dorothy Faunt. Most of his life was spent at Christ Church, Oxford. Burton was appointed vicar of St Thomas, Oxford (1616), rector of Walesby (1624) and Seagrave, Leicestershire (?1633). Early publications include two university plays, the now lost *Alba* (1605) and *Philosophaster* (1606, revised 1615), in which Duke Desiderius (Erasmus?) establishes a university in the Andalusian town of Osuna. The university is quickly besieged by Jesuit pseudo-philosophers of all disciplines. After receiving numerous complaints from the local popula-tion, the duke threatens to shut down the university altogether; he relents following the intervention of two wandering scholars, Polu-mathes and Philobiblios ('Much-Learned' and 'Lover of Books'). By the end of the play, the duke punishes the false professors, and takes several steps to restore the connections between political power and university learning.

Burton is best known for the *Anatomy,* which he spent his life writing. It was first published in 1621, with subsequent editions appearing in 1624, 1628, 1632, and 1638. A sixth edition appeared posthumously in 1651, advertised as 'this last Impression' of Burton's thinking. As one biographer remarks, 'The changes in and, especially, the additions to the successive editions of the *Anatomy* are such that putting out a new edition was … very nearly the equivalent of putting out a new book' (Nochimson 1974). He died in 1640, and his monument at Christ Church Cathedral announces that melancholy gave him life and death. The rumours that Burton took his own life on his birthday are improbable.

Burton characterized the *Anatomy* as a diversion, which he wrote to ward off his own melancholy – and to avoid discussing contro-versial religious topics. In fact the book is a comprehensive study on the disease, covering its nature, causes, prognosis, and cure. Despite the labyrinthine appearance of its tables of contents, the book is carefully structured. It is divided into three volumes, each of which is divided into sections, members, and subsec-tions. Though Burton is given to digressions, they are as clearly demarcated and carefully arranged as the official subjects from which they depart.

Burton was alert to controversies concerning anatomy and medicine; as he notes, 'Scarce two great scholars in an age, but with bitter invec-tives they fall foul one on the other, and their adherents.' He would address these by placing passages alongside each other. While he did offer his own position on occasion, he 'typically let his quotations speak for themselves and chose not to voice his own opinion or to resolve controversy' (Gowland 2006). When con-fronted with spatial limitations, he offered extensive reading lists, which typically end with the abbreviation 'etc.'. They leave one with the impression that the topics addressed are always more complex than one could possibly do justice to in a mere thousand pages.

This approach to melancholy from so many sides comes at a cost. Basic questions about the human body and disease plague Burton at every turn. There is no limit to the physical causes or symptoms of melancholy, which springs from the body as well as the mind. (Burton views the body and mind as distinct but mutually influential: one part can affect the other. He does not sever body and mind, and he makes no mention of the dualism of René Descartes.) He cannot always differentiate a symptom from a cause. Modern readers sense that the term 'melancholy' was a misnomer for a number of similar but distinct conditions which Burton lumped together in a hotchpotch, and which were not understood in themselves.

The *Anatomy* is not only a survey of melancholy, but also a springboard for any number of topics that interest Burton. Bridget Gellert Lyons (1971) notes, 'The philosophical concerns of the literature of the preceding twenty-five years are fully reflected in the *Anatomy*, which expresses a general scepticism extending to all forms of knowledge, ancient and new, Stoic and scholastic, as well as scientific.' Burton's interest in cartography and travel literature is particularly strong, and he makes frequent reference to them in order to question what we know about the shape of the world and the customs of non-European civilizations. He was also deeply interested in the social customs of his own country. His observations range from the recreational habits of the elite classes, to the grittier processes of getting and spending. While political economy had not emerged as a discipline, Burton was surprisingly attuned to the growth of international economies, along with their attendant problems, including an emerging slave trade and a growing consumerist culture in England. The pursuit of wealth, envy, and excessive luxury were as powerful causes of melancholy as any physiological disorder.

As a disease both physical and mental in its scope, as well as a cause and symptom of public disorders, melancholy eludes Burton's attempts to be comprehensive. He makes heavy use of the word 'infinite' in his descriptions of causes and symptoms, and he suggests that

melancholy is larger in scope than human language itself. It is not helpful that Burton's writing style often poses a problem for understanding. While his prose is not difficult, it is indirect. He does not always write as though he were concerned with coming to the point. These obstacles notwithstanding, Burton does express genuine concern for the 'hell in men's hearts' that melancholy brings about; and while physicians may have been undecided about the nature of the disease, he was generally mindful of the arduous process of discovery, trial, and controversy that will, hopefully, lead to genuine knowledge.

For all his dependence on authorities, Burton did make several original contributions to his subject. No writer had treated melancholy so clearly as both a cause and a symptom of faulty social and political institutions. Accordingly, his book is a medical and spiritual guidebook, as well as a study of social reform. This was especially important at a time when physicians were beginning to turn away from a humours-based physiology. His most original contribution was his section on religious melancholy. It was perhaps this section, with its treatment of ceremonies and superstitions, false prophets and enthusiasts, that contributed to the book's early popularity. Indeed, the *Anatomy* was reprinted during the 1650s, in the wake of Parliament's Blasphemy Act, which prohibited false prophets from proclaiming to be (or to be equal to) God, along with several other expressions of religious misconduct. While this was a coincidence, it was one of those coincidences that helped sustain the text's topicality.

The *Anatomy*'s extraordinary style distinguishes it from earlier formal treatises on melancholy. In many ways, what Burton wrote about was secondary to how he wrote about it. This is most notable in his witty and satirical 'Preface to the reader', written under the guise of Democritus Jr. This fictional persona, named after the famous laughing philosopher of classical Greece, informs us that the world is mad, and we are all participants in its madness. There is something reminiscent of Erasmus's

Praise of Folly (1509; first printed 1511), which was undoubtedly a model. The preface also makes us aware of our experience as readers, as we attempt to follow along the narrator's own struggle to introduce his subject. Rather than simply hand over information ready-made, Democritus Jr flatters and cajoles us with interesting leads and sharp rebukes. It is as if we are meant to experience at first hand the difficult pathways and false avenues that accompany the search for knowledge. Readers are rightly fascinated with this preface as a high point in seventeenth-century satirical prose. The book has often been reprinted under the pseudonym, even though Burton drops the persona once the preface ends.

In his preface, Burton describes his book as a cento – a patchwork text composed almost entirely from quotations. There is hardly an idea, no matter how commonplace, for which Burton fails to attach a ready supply of reference material. The range and liberality of Burton's reading material is remarkable. Several authors stand out, however. Burton is clearly drawn to Erasmus and Philip Melanchthon, both of whom he quotes regularly. Virtually every page of volume 1 mentions Girolamo Cardano. Other major figures include Juan Luis Vives, Tommaso Campanella, and Girolamo Savonarola. He has read Paolo Giovio, whose life of Pope Leo X offers a ready supply of anecdote, typically on the decadent behaviour of corrupt authority figures. For all his conventional attacks on Jesuit priests and their abuses, his favourite reading materials include several Jesuit travel narratives to Asia and the Americas. Matteo Ricci's name is more prominent than any other travel writer's, including Richard Hakluyt. Among classical authorities, Augustine is a clear favourite, followed closely by the Stoic philosophers Seneca and Cicero. On medicine, Aristotle and Galen are cornerstones, and Paracelsus figures strongly. However, Burton has consulted scores of minor medical treatises as well, and he refers to some of their intriguing discoveries, propositions, and controversies about the body and mind. While he usually names his authors, he does not give the titles of their works or their publication details.

Burton's knowledge of poetry was impressive. In addition to the classical literature he appears to have mastered, he is well versed in English poetry. Lines of verse fill the pages of volume 3, on love melancholy and jealousy. Geoffrey Chaucer, 'our English Homer', is by far his favourite resource. He borrows from 'The knight's tale', 'The wife of Bath's tale', 'The clerk's tale', *The parliament of fowls*, and *Troilus and Criseyde*. John Harington the younger's translation of Ariosto's *Orlando furioso* is a treasure trove on the pangs of love. Other favourites include Edmund Spenser and Ben Jonson ('Our arch-poet'), as well as George Buchanan, Samuel Daniel, and Michael Drayton. Christopher Marlowe and William Shakespeare appear as well, with the emphasis on their erotic poems, *Hero and Leander* (first printed 1598), and *Venus and Adonis* (1593). Robert Tofte also figures large, thanks mainly to his *The fruits of jealousie* (1615). More important than the famous names, however, are the countless English translations of classical authors, some of which are attributed to friends and family, but most of which are left anonymous. They are a testament to a large community of writers interested in the craft of poetic translation, with no thought of the accolades that come with being a famous poet.

John Ford's 1629 play, *The louer's melancholy*, borrows heavily from Burton, an early sign of the *Anatomy*'s popularity. While favourable references to Burton appear throughout the seventeenth and eighteenth centuries, the true lionizing began during the 1800s. Advertisements for modern editions would stockpile famous quotations from celebrity readers, which established the *Anatomy* as classic reading. Samuel Johnson is reputed (through James Boswell) to have risen from bed two hours early, just to read it. John Keats allegedly called it his favourite book. Not all readers shared these sentiments. One editor complains of its obscurity: 'No attempt has been made by previous editors to verify Burton's numberless quotations. His range of reading was so wide, and his references are frequently so vague and inexact, that it would be a task of the greatest difficulty to follow him through all his devious wanderings' (Shileto 1896). Still others dismissed the *Anatomy* as a sourcebook for the intellectually lazy, giving people the illusion of deep reading. Even Lawrence Sterne could not escape this taint, as he was accused of plagiarizing Burton in his *Tristram Shandy*.

The nineteenth century also saw the translation of Burton's numerous Latin passages. As the editors of the 1821 publication explain, 'To open its valuable mysteries to those who have not had the advantage of a classical education, translations of the countless quotations from ancient writers which occur in the work, are now for the first time given, and obsolete orthography is in all instances modernized.' This effort sheds light on the book's ambiguous status as a hallmark of erudition and a gateway to learning for the general population. Without such labour, it is hard to imagine the 1932 Everyman's edition, whose introduction openly acknowledges the book's darker reputation as 'the most useful book to a man who wishes to acquire a reputation of being well read, with the least trouble'. Director Elia Kazan touches on the point in his 1945 film adaptation of Betty Smith's novel *A tree grows in Brooklyn* (1943). It just happens to be Burton that protagonist Francis Nolan checks out from the library before the librarian begins to wonder what she is up to. Nolan explains it is her desire to read everything in the library – in alphabetical order!

Students and scholars looking for an introduction to the *Anatomy* would best begin with Lawrence Babb's *Sanity in Bedlam* (1959). William Mueller (1961) praises *Sanity in Bedlam* as 'the most useful, careful, and informed piece of writing yet to be done on Burton'. Mueller's *Anatomy of Robert Burton's England* (1952) is itself a useful introduction to Burton's engagement with the political, social, and religious issues that dominated his period. He characterizes Burton as a conservative reformer, who

typically proposed a 'middle way' through controversial matters. A significantly updated survey of the *Anatomy* and its contexts became available in 2006, when Angus Gowland published his *Worlds of Renaissance melancholy*. Gowland's book covers a number of subjects, including Burton's engagement with medical knowledge, his commitment to humanist learning, and his frustrations with the limited roles to which scholarship had been consigned in public life. Gowland's book is perhaps the most well-informed study of Burton ever published.

Many good studies take up Burton's style and method. Several literary studies have examined the tone of Democritus Jr, raising questions about what Stanley Fish (1972) characterized as the experience of reading the *Anatomy*. There are several interesting studies of his methodology, particularly his interest in anatomies and encyclopedias (Vicari 1989; Sawday 1997; Wong 1998; Williams 2001). As they suggest, Burton's fondness for an elaborate organization leads not to comprehensive knowledge, but only to an increasingly complex system. Paradoxically, the more Burton organizes, the more unmanageable his subject grows. It is tempting to regard the *Anatomy* as a testament to the impossibility of knowing anything through language, even to celebrate it as a precursor to postmodernist claims about how systems of knowledge undo themselves in the very process of their production. Such claims need to be tempered with recognition of Burton's concern to improve the health and well-being of his readers.

Studies of Burton's engagement with political and religious topics face several daunting obstacles. While he routinely argues that the abuses of public figures produce widespread melancholy, and while he associates melancholy with tyranny, he makes no bones about his allegiance to the king and the Church of England. Similarly, while he claims that public abuses are widespread, he deals almost entirely in abstractions. Many recent studies begin with the question of what Burton's deliberate avoidance of controversial topics implies about his own views. David Renaker (1979) and John Stachniewski (1991) have devoted attention to Burton's engagement with Archbishop Laud and his more controversial church policies. Closer to home was Laud's role as chancellor at Oxford, where his impositions on the university were a regular source of friction. Kathryn Murphy (2009) has shown that the university play *Philosophaster* was not merely a satire on false learning, but an elaborate and scathing attack on Jesuit deceptions, written in the wake of the Gunpowder Plot – and revised in the wake of public controversy over King James's Oath of Allegiance.

There is still much to learn about Burton. Only recently have critics acknowledged his familial connection with the prominent recusant scholar Arthur Faunt. It is a telling reminder that whatever personal views Burton harboured, his social connections were complex, including people who would have regarded each other as opponents. Early in the *Anatomy*, he observes, 'We can keep our professed enemies from our cities by gates, walls, and towers, defend ourselves from thieves and robbers by watchfulness and weapons; but this malice of men, and their pernicious endeavours, no caution can divert, no vigilancy foresee, we have so many secret plots and devices to mischief one another.' The city metaphor is meant to characterize the insidious nature of disease, but it also characterizes the precarious nature of early modern life, in which professed adversaries often found themselves forced to coexist in remarkably close quarters. It was a condition that seventeenth-century England knew all too well. Perhaps it was Burton's awareness of it which helped him conceptualize melancholy as a physical ailment and as a condition afflicting the body politic as a whole.

SEE ALSO: Buchanan, George; Daniel, Samuel; Drayton, Michael; Ford, John; Jonson, Ben; Marlowe, Christopher; Shakespeare, William; Spenser, Edmund; Tofte, Robert

REFERENCES AND SUGGESTED READINGS

Babb, Lawrence (1959) *Sanity in Bedlam: a study of Robert Burton's 'The anatomy of melancholy'*. University of Michigan Press, East Lansing.

Colie, Rosalie L. (1966) *Paradoxia epidemica: the Renaissance tradition of paradox*. Princeton University Press, Princeton.

Fish, Stanley (1972) *Self-consuming artifacts*. University of California Press, Berkeley.

Fox, Ruth A. (1976) *The tangled chain: the structure of disorder in 'The anatomy of melancholy'*. University of California Press, Berkeley.

Gowland, Angus (2006) *The worlds of Renaissance melancholy: Robert Burton in context*. Cambridge University Press, Cambridge.

Jackson, Holbrook (ed.) (2001) *'The anatomy of melancholy,' by Robert Burton*. New York Review of Books, New York.

Kitzes, Adam H. (2006) *The politics of melancholy from Spenser to Milton*. Routledge, New York.

Lyons, Bridget Gellert (1971) *Voices of melancholy: studies in literary treatments of melancholy in Renaissance England*. Routledge & Kegan Paul, London.

Mueller, William R. (1952) *The anatomy of Robert Burton's England*. University of California Press, Berkeley.

Mueller, William R. (1961) Review of Lawrence Babb's *Sanity in Bedlam*. *Modern Language Notes* 76, 155–157.

Murphy, Kathryn (2009) Jesuits and philosophasters: Robert Burton's response to the Gunpowder Plot. *Journal of the Northern Renaissance* 1, 109–128.

Nochimson, Richard L. (1974) Studies in the life of Robert Burton. *Yearbook of English Studies* 4, 85–111.

Renaker, David (1979) Robert Burton's palinodes. *Studies in Philology* 76, 162–181.

Sawday, Jonathan (1997) Shapeless elegance: Robert Burton's anatomy of knowledge. In: Rhodes, Neil (ed.) *English Renaissance prose: history, language, politics*. Medieval & Renaissance Texts & Studies, Tempe, pp. 173–202.

Shileto, A. R. (ed.) (1896) *Burton, Robert. 'The anatomy of melancholy.'* George Bell & Sons, London.

Stachniewski, John (1991) *The persecutory imagination: English Puritanism and the literature of religious despair*. Oxford University Press, New York.

Vicari, Patricia E. (1989) *The view from Minerva's tower: learning and imagination in 'The anatomy of melancholy'*. University of Toronto Press, Toronto.

Williams, R. Grant (2001) Disfiguring the body of knowledge: anatomical discourse and Robert Burton's *The anatomy of melancholy. ELH* 68, 593–613.

Wong, Samuel (1998) Encyclopedism in *The anatomy of melancholy. Renaissance and Reformation / Renaissance et Reformé* 22, 5–22.

C

Camden, William

BERNHARD KLEIN

William Camden (1551–1623) was an English antiquary, chorographer, and perhaps Britain's first modern historian. Admired by his Continental peers as the 'British Strabo', he is best known for two major works – *Britannia* (1586), a historical-geographical survey of the British Isles; and *Annals of the reign of Queen Elizabeth* (1615), a meticulously researched political history – both of which significantly advanced the conceptual possibilities for the writing of history.

Camden did not think of himself as an innovator but he broke new ground in several ways, for example, through the sustained attention to pioneering methodologies in the *Britannia* – such as etymology (the study of words), numismatics (the study of coins), and epigraphy (the study of inscriptions) – or through the unprecedented use of primary sources in the *Annals*. The esteem in which Camden's scholarship was held in his own time can be gleaned from the epitaph on his monument in Westminster Abbey's Poets' Corner, where he is immortalized as the 'indefatigable, judicious, and impartial Researcher into the British antiquities'. As both historian and educator – Camden was a schoolmaster for more than two decades – he had a lasting impact on a whole generation of writers. The roll-call of poets and scholars who paid tribute to Camden during his lifetime includes, amongst others, the names of Ben Jonson, Edmund Campion, John Selden, and Michael Drayton, as well as Edmund Spenser, who praised Camden in 'The ruines of time' (published in 1591) as 'the nourice of antiquitie / And lanterne unto late succeeding age'.

Camden was born in London on 2 May 1551, the son of the painter-stainer Sampson Camden and his wife, Elizabeth Curwen. From the age of seven he attended Christ's Hospital, established only a few years earlier in the recently dissolved priory of Greyfriars as a school for orphaned and poor children (Camden's background was humble though he was no orphan). In 1563, after surviving a plague infection, he transferred to St Paul's School, a reform institution founded in 1512 by John Colet on humanist principles imported from the Continent. In 1566 Camden went to Oxford (first to Magdalen College, then to Broadgate Hall, Christ Church), where he came into contact with Philip Sidney and other scholars who shared his antiquarian interests, such as George and Richard Carew. Camden's time in Oxford appears to have been fraught with difficulties, social setbacks, and a lack of recognition. He left the university in 1571 having been denied the BA degree he was seeking, though he petitioned successfully for the same degree only three years later. In 1588, after the publication and favourable reception of the *Britannia*, an MA degree was approved conditionally but never conferred; when the same degree was offered again in 1613, with Camden already in his sixties, he refused on the grounds that the honour came too late.

The Encyclopedia of English Renaissance Literature, First Edition. Edited by Garrett A. Sullivan, Jr and Alan Stewart.
© 2012 Blackwell Publishing Ltd. Published 2012 by Blackwell Publishing Ltd.

After leaving Oxford in 1571 Camden briefly disappears from the historical record until his appointment as second master of Westminster School in 1575. How and where he spent the intervening years is not known. One possibility may be that he was travelling through the kingdom, gathering materials for his chorographical writings, but there is no concrete evidence to bear out this assumption. Westminster School gave Camden a livelihood and an intellectual home for the next 22 years. Here he played a significant role in educating the contemporary social elite, boasting later in life that three current bishops and many 'persons now employed in eminent place abroad, and many of especial note at home of all degrees; do acknowledge themselves to have been my Scholars'. His students included, amongst others, Jonson, who wrote in his *Epigrammes* (printed in Johnson's 1616 workes) that he owed Camden 'all that I am in arts, all that I know', and Robert Cotton, the future antiquary, who became a lifelong friend and colleague. In 1593 Camden was made headmaster, which doubled his salary to £20.

While at Westminster Camden published the *Britannia* and wrote or edited several other works not published until after his departure from the school in 1597, including *Reges, reginae, nobiles, et alii in Ecclesia Collegiata B. Petri Westmonasterii*, a guidebook to the tombs in Westminster Abbey (known formally as the Collegiate Church of St Peter at Westminster), published in London in 1600 (and again in expanded versions in 1603 and 1606), and *Anglica, Normannica, Hibernica, Cambrica, a veteribus scripta*, an edition of historical texts related to Britain, published in Frankfurt in 1603. Taking William Lily's successful Latin grammar as a model, Camden also wrote and published a Greek school grammar in 1595, which remained a standard textbook in Britain for over a century. In 1605 Camden published *Remaines of a greater worke, concerning Britain*, a collection of material left over from the *Britannia* which he dismissed in the dedicatory epistle as 'the rude rubble and out-cast rubbish . . . of a greater and more serious worke'. In fact, the *Remaines* is a rich source of antiquarian research on a variety of topics, many of them philological in nature, others related to specific cultural artefacts and practices.

With increased public recognition as the author of the *Britannia* came new opportunities for the schoolmaster in the 1590s. On the recommendation of Fulke Greville, Camden was appointed in 1597 to the office of Clarenceux king of arms, with responsibility for all English provinces south of the river Trent. This was a position of considerable influence, one of the three highest offices in the College of Arms, which provided Camden with financial security until his death in 1623. The three kings of arms had authority in all matters related to the granting of arms, titles, and degrees in the realm, they participated in court proceedings, verified genealogies, decided on claims to inheritance and property, and were consulted on public processions as well as marriages and funerals within the nobility.

The role, which required in-depth knowledge of Britain's dynastic history, was ideal for the nation's foremost antiquarian scholar, yet his appointment from outside the college hierarchy was unusual. While it reflected Camden's growing reputation in Elizabethan public life, it may have been this favour bestowed on a novice to the world of arms and royal patronage that provoked the vitriolic response of Ralph Brooke, another senior herald in the College of Arms (but institutionally below Camden in rank, despite a much longer association with the college), who openly attacked Camden in an angry little book written in English, entitled *A discoverie of certaine errours published in print in the much commended Britannia, 1594*. A thin-skinned Camden defended himself (in Latin) against the accusation of factual errors, while conceding some ground to Brooke, in the preface to the fifth edition of the *Britannia* (1600), but this did not stop Brooke from compiling a second, much extended 'discouerie of errours' which Camden was probably aware of but which did not reach print until 1723.

Camden always kept his distance from politics and proudly confirmed to James Ussher in 1618 that he had 'never made suit to any man', yet as Clarenceux king of arms he was brought into much closer contact with the affairs of state. Some time in the 1590s William Cecil, Lord Burghley, 'willed [him] to compile a *Historie* of Q. *Elizabeths* Raigne', giving him access to his own and the queen's archives. Work on the *Annals* started during Elizabeth's lifetime, but was temporarily abandoned after Burghley's death in 1598. Uncertain about his suitability to historical study, and preferring to see himself as a chorographer, Camden eventually bowed to royal pressure (this time coming from James, who wanted to replace George Buchanan's damning account of the life of his mother Mary Queen of Scots) and returned to the project in 1608, publishing the first three books of his chronicle (covering the years up to 1589) in Latin in 1615. An English translation appeared in 1625. A fourth book, also written in Latin, taking the history up to 1603, was published posthumously in Leiden in 1625 and in London in 1627, with an English translation following in 1629.

In his final years, marked by failing health, Camden put considerable efforts into establishing a professorship in history at Oxford, the first of its kind in England, despite his earlier troubled relationship with the university. The first incumbent of the new chair, Degory Wheare, took up his post in 1622, receiving the unusually high salary of £140. The Camden chair in ancient history exists to this day, attached since 1877 to Brasenose College. Aged 72, Camden died unmarried in his house at Chislehurst on 9 November 1623, and was buried in Westminster Abbey. His monument stands next to Isaac Casaubon's and Geoffrey Chaucer's, an appropriate resting place for a man whose magnum opus proved equally inspiring to scholars and poets.

That work, whose full title is *Britannia sive florentissimorum regnorum, Angliae, Scotiae, Hiberniae, et insularum adiacentium ex intima antiquitate chorographica descriptio*, was a product of the huge contemporary interest in antiquarianism, the study of the physical traces of the past and the systematic recording and analysis of all kinds of archaeological remains, such as inscriptions, tombstones, monuments, and coins. As an intellectual movement, British antiquarianism achieved nothing less than a transformation of the nation's sense of its own collective self, seeing the past no longer as the unfolding of divine providence but as a succession of interconnected civilizational layers. Antiquarian scholars in Tudor and Stuart Britain looked back to the pioneering work of the royal librarian under Henry VIII, John Leland, who had assembled, on a nationwide itinerary lasting several years, a vast collection of notes intended to form the basis of a multi-volume chorographical description of Britain. Leland's notes never made it into print but were available to Camden in manuscript when he began work on the *Britannia*.

His purpose in writing the book, as he explained in the preface to the 1610 English translation, was to 'restore antiquity to Britaine, and Britain to his antiquity'. As the formula makes clear, the emphasis was heavily on Roman Britain; Camden's implicit aim was to present the contemporary nation as the rightful heir to Roman civilization. The idea for this approach apparently originated with Abraham Ortelius, the Flemish cartographer and 'worthy Restorer of Ancient Geographie', who had visited England in 1577 and met with Camden personally. Camden remained in contact with Continental scholars throughout his life, corresponding with luminaries such as Casaubon, Jacques-Auguste de Thou, Jan de Groot, Gerard Mercator, and of course Ortelius. European models had a formative influence on his own scholarship; the *Britannia* especially had notable precursors in Europe, such as Flavio Biondo's *Italia illustrata* of 1474 or Conrad Celtis's unfinished *Germania illustrata*.

When the first (Latin) edition of the *Britannia* was published in 1586, it was enthusiastically received. Further editions quickly followed in 1587, 1590, 1594, and 1600, with the book growing in size each time before reaching its final form in the substantially revised Latin edition of 1607, translated into English three years later by Philemon Holland in collaboration with Camden. That edition is principally a county-by-county description of England and Wales, followed by separate sections on Scotland and Ireland, and preceded by a general historical introduction. In the entries on the English and Welsh counties the focus is on local names and boundaries, on landscape features such as rivers, lakes, and mountains, on any 'places of antiquity' within the shire, and on the genealogies of the leading families of the gentry. In order to compile this data Camden travelled extensively around Britain, benefiting from the school vacations and the support of his headmaster at Westminster, though he also relied heavily on notes and printed works, and on information supplied by correspondents around the country. A second translation, by Edmund Gibson, which included lengthy additions carefully separated from Camden's original text, appeared in 1695 and is more faithful to the 1607 Latin version than Holland's translation of 1610, despite Camden's assistance with the latter.

Though the *Britannia* is, to modern readers, unmistakably a work of history, contemporaries would have recognized it as something quite different: an exemplary study of national chorography. The distinction is an important one. Chorography focused on place, whereas history focused on time, and as a genre it provided scholars such as Camden with the ideal conceptual form of regional description for promoting the contemporary project of the 'discovery of Britain'. As a concept, chorography was not original to the period but derived from classical and medieval writers. Ptolemy had defined the term – with its root in the Greek word *khōros*, 'place' – as applying to the description of particular regions rather than whole continents or the entire earth, which properly belonged to the disciplines of geography and cosmography. In its application by contemporary British scholars, chorography quickly developed a deeply patriotic agenda. Leland had already declared himself to be

'totallye enflamed wyth a loue, to se throughlye all those partes of thys your opulent and ample realme', a sentiment repeated in similar form by subsequent writers for whom the object of chorographical description – the land or counties of Britain – began to glow with affective pathos.

The *Britannia* shares this patriotic impulse with a range of other works emerging from the context of antiquarian and chorographical study, notably the maps and atlases of Britain produced by cartographers such as Christopher Saxton, John Norden, or John Speed, the county chorographies of writers such as William Lambarde, Richard Carew, or George Owen, or new forms of geographically inspired poetry, whose most prominent example is Michael Drayton's *Poly-olbion* (1612). When Camden included county maps based on the work of Saxton and Norden in the *Britannia* from the 1607 edition onwards, the conceptual proximity between the land-based focus of antiquarian study and related forms of geographical practice became clearly apparent.

There is some indication that antiquarianism began to be viewed with suspicion by the crown in the first decade of the seventeenth century. Camden and Cotton, together with James Ley and Henry Spelman, had founded the Society of Antiquaries in 1586, which counted upwards of 20 members in the 1590s. When it ceased to meet after 1607, the antiquarian Richard Carew offered as an explanation for the Society's dissolution the imminent danger to its members, whom he saw at risk of being 'prosecuted as a Cabal against the Government'. The reason for the royal dislike of antiquarian study may have been that some of the topics discussed at Society meetings – such as the ancient laws of the realm – had become too political in nature. But it is equally likely that the crown increasingly perceived the shape and history of the land itself, as promoted by chorographical works and visualized in county maps and national atlases, as a rival focus of political allegiance. While chorography never openly challenged the principle of royal sovereignty over the kingdom, it did strengthen the sense of local and national identity, possibly at the expense of forms of self-hood rooted in dynastic loyalty.

When Camden began to work in earnest on his last major project, the *Annals of the reign of Queen Elizabeth* (full Latin title: *Annales rerum Anglicarum, et Hibernicarum, regnante Elizabetha*), he was acutely conscious of switching to a different register: no longer writing as a chorographer, he now had to follow the protocols of the historian. He was initially overwhelmed, 'couered with dust and sweat', by the sheer mass of the source material he found in the archives, and offered this together with Burghley's death as the reason for the decade-long abandonment of the work. The more likely cause seems to have been his initial aversion to history as a literary form. Camden eventually approached the archive much like his collection of antiquities: by reproducing the evidence unaltered and constructing the narrative strictly around the sources he had available, without recourse to conjecture, invented speeches, personal opinion, or providential readings, the *Annals* is essentially a version of documentary history.

Camden's sources came in the form of the full archive of state papers: letters, notes, statutes, charters, diaries, official records, etc, to which he and his collaborator Cotton had privileged access. By organizing this material in the form of annals, Camden followed the example set by the Roman historian Tacitus, who had advocated year-by-year entries as the appropriate representational structure for 'great and illustrious Actions'. The form tied Camden down to a strict chronology and made it necessary to introduce a layer of reference which allowed him to identify earlier causes and later effects, and to locate single events within larger patterns of causality. His 'method', as he explained in the preface, was the example of truth and impartiality championed by the Greek historian Polybius, which for Camden meant principally the neutral and disinterested reporting of facts and events. Of course, like any other historical work, the *Annals* is not without an interpretative

authorial perspective, yet the almost exclusive reliance on recent primary sources, many of them involving historical agents still alive when Camden was writing, was a novel methodology in English historiography.

The approach enabled Camden to resist the imposition of a retrospective explanatory pattern on his sources; he chose instead to read them forward in time, sometimes anticipating outcomes but never presenting these as inevitable. The *Annals* stands as a unique achievement of early modern British historiography, ahead of its time both in the implicit recognition of the force of chance and accident in the course of history, and in the organic picture Camden paints of the Elizabethan age and the interlocking pressures of economy, society, religion, constitution, and government. The book has shaped the view of Elizabeth's reign down to the twenty-first century, making Camden one of the most influential of British historians – just as Spenser had, in a sense, predicted in 'The ruines of time': 'Cambden, though time all moniments obscure, / Yet thy just labours shall endure.'

SEE ALSO: Buchanan, George; Drayton, Michael; Greville, Fulke; Holland, Philemon; Jonson, Ben; Leland, John; Norden, John; Saxton, Christopher; Selden, John; Sidney, Philip; Speed, John; Spenser, Edmund

REFERENCES AND SUGGESTED READINGS

Baker, Herschel (1969) *The race of time: three lectures on Renaissance historiography*. University of Toronto Press, Toronto.

Fussner, F. Smith (1962) *The historical revolution: English historical writing and thought, 1580–1640*. Columbia University Press, New York.

Helgerson, Richard (1994) The land speaks. In: *Forms of nationhood: the Elizabethan writing of England*. University of Chicago Press, Chicago, pp. 105–147.

Herendeen, Wyman H. (2007) *William Camden: a life in context*. Boydell & Brewer, Woodbridge.

Levy, F. J. (1964) The making of Camden's *Britannia*. *Bibliothèque d'humanisme et Renaissance* 26, 76–97.

McRae, Andrew (1996) *God speed the plough: the representation of agrarian England, 1500–1660*. Cambridge University Press, Cambridge.

Mendyk, Stanley G. (1989) *'Speculum Britanniae': regional study, antiquarianism, and science in Britain up to 1700*. University of Toronto Press, Toronto.

Powicke, Maurice (1948) William Camden. *English Studies* 1, 67–84.

Sharpe, Kevin (1979) *Sir Robert Cotton 1586–1631: history and politics in early modern England*. Oxford University Press, Oxford.

Trevor-Roper, Hugh (1971) *Queen Elizabeth's first historian: William Camden and the beginnings of English 'civil history'*. Jonathan Cape, London.

Woolf, D. R. (1990) *The idea of history in early Stuart England*. University of Toronto Press, Toronto.

Campion, Thomas

LAUREN SHOHET

Thomas Campion (1567–1620) is unusual for his lasting contributions to both letters and music. He is known as a poet of both English and Latin verse, a composer of songs and airs, a scriptor of masques and entertainments, and a theorist of both music and verse. Interested in edgy new developments in English literature of the 1580s, when poets like Philip Sidney and prose writers like John Lyly sought to develop new literary aesthetics, Campion not only wrote poetry tapping into this innovative vein, but perhaps even more significantly showed ways to use newer styles of lyrics in English song.

Campion was born in Holborn, London, to John and Lucy Campion; his mother was the daughter of a serjeant-at-arms of the royal court. His father died when Campion was nine, followed in the next few years by his mother's second husband and his mother herself. Campion was raised thereafter by his late mother's third husband, Augustine Steward, and shared university rooms with his stepbrother. Campion was educated at Peterhouse, Cambridge, though he left without taking a degree, and at Gray's Inn, then studied medicine at the University of Caen,

receiving the degree of MD in 1605. He became well known for his English poems and short dramatic pieces from the early seventeenth century, including the major court masque King James presented for the marriage of his favourite courtier James Hay to Lady Honora Denny in 1607; poems on the 1612 death of Prince Henry; and *The lords' masque* (1613), a court masque for the marriage of Princess Elizabeth and the elector palatine.

Campion also published several books of airs between 1601 and 1617. He was unusual in composing both lyrics and music for songs; additionally, other composers, including John Dowland, used his verse for their own musical settings. Campion's airs were widely printed, performed, and admired during his lifetime; when his court masques were published, dance music from the masques, rearranged and given words, was appended for amateurs to sing at home. Campion's songs offer English explorations of ideals underwriting the Italian *seconda pratica* of composers like Claudio Monteverdi: of ways for music most effectively to serve the words it sets, eliciting an affective response by drawing out the most natural and moving elements of speech. Analogously, Campion's songs constitute musical explorations of ideals underwriting the poetic practice of sonneteers like Philip Sidney and Edmund Spenser: of ways for repetition and variation to draw out nuances of affective and poetic engagement.

Campion's poetic aesthetic is likewise of a piece with broader humanist impulses, his poetry drawing upon classical models less to imitate the past than to serve as a resource for articulating distinctive contemporary experience. His verse links universal and particular, parts and whole, individual poems or songs and the volumes that comprise them. These poems provoke a direct affective response as well as sophisticated reflection. The sonnet 'Fire that must flame', for instance, draws upon both the Petrarchan and religious resonances of 'fire', using parallel phrases, alliteration, and multiple senses of key terms like 'heaven', 'grace', and 'prayer' to create elegant formal patterns as it draws its reader into the enticing but dangerous capabilities of flame:

> Fire that must flame is with apt fuell fed,
> Flowers that wil thrive in sunny soyle are bred;
> How can a hart feele heate that no hope findes?
> Or can hee love on whom no comfort shines?
> ... Prayers move the heav'ns, but finde no grace with you;
> Yet in your lookes a heavenly forme I view:
> Then will I pray againe, hoping to finde,
> As well as in your lookes, heav'n in your minde.

Campion's masques and entertainments show how supple these dramatic forms can be, accommodating multiple agendas in performance and crafting further receptive audiences when they are printed. The *Lord Hay's masque* of 1607 presents an elaborately staged scenario: Night bemoans the impending wedding of a chaste nymph of the moon goddess Cynthia, stolen away (according to Cynthia) by the wedding god Hymen; the dawn-god Hesperus contests Cynthia's version of marriage as a violent disruption of peaceful feminine community; and the knights of Apollo celebrate together with such sylvan figures as Zephyrus and Flora. Performed before the well-lettered King James I – conventionally complimented as an Apollo figure – and marking a court wedding, the masque's action comprises at once mythological tale, the social ritual of the Hay–Denny wedding, and the structure of the Jacobean court. The masque also engages a more specifically political agenda: the king promoted this marriage between his Scottish favourite and the English Honora Denny at the same time he was negotiating union between his natal realm of Scotland and his newly inherited kingdom of England. Danced by six Scottish and six English 'knights of Apollo', the masque thus enacts the national concord James sought. At the same time, however, the masque's presentation of alternative views (Night's frank acknowledgement that brides may find their arranged marriages unappealing, for instance) make the event more nuanced than mere propaganda. The masque's effects extend beyond the courtly audience, and also

beyond naked panegyric, when the masque is published (indeed, in multiple editions), particularly because the print version recounts such performance glitches as scenery failures at key moments of the masque.

Campion's treatise on poetics (*Observations in the art of English poesie*, 1602) proposes a singular system of prosody, based on classical models that count syllables rather than the accentual system generally used in English. While his proposals did not change common practice, his reflections on the poetic peculiarities of English – 'heavier' than classical and romance languages – are compelling. Campion's final published work, entitled *Thomae Campiani epigrammatum libri II. Vmbra. Elegiarum liber vnus* (1619), revised earlier Latin poetry and included new texts, among them epigrams on medical subjects. Testaments of contemporaries suggest that in late life he was well regarded in London circles as a sympathetic friend and physician, with a continuing passion for the arts. A few years before his death, he was peripherally involved in the sensational poisoning of Sir Thomas Overbury, having served patrons in the powerful Howard family as the collector of a bribe intended to silence Tower of London guards. Campion was interrogated, but his involvement was found to have been unknowing. He died in London on 1 March 1620, possibly of plague.

SEE ALSO: Dowland, John; James VI and I; Lyly, John; Sidney, Philip; Spenser, Edmund

REFERENCES AND SUGGESTED READINGS

Davis, Walter (ed.) (1969) *Works of Thomas Campion.* Faber & Faber, London.

Curran, Kevin (2007) Erotic policy: King James, Thomas Campion, and the rhetoric of Anglo-Scottish marriage. *Journal of Early Modern Cultural Studies* 7(1), 55–77.

Davis, Walter R. (1987) *Thomas Campion.* Twayne, Boston.

Ferrell, Lori Anne (2002) The sacred, the profane, and the Union: politics of sermon and masque at the court wedding of Lord and Lady Hay. In: Lake,

Peter, Cogswell, Thomas, & Cust, Richard (eds) *Politics, religion, and popularity in early modern England.* Cambridge University Press, Cambridge, pp. 45–64.

Friedman, Lawrence S. (1988) Words into power: Renaissance expression and Thomas Campion. *English Studies* 69, 130–145.

Lindley, David (1986) *Thomas Campion.* Brill, Leiden.

Carew, Thomas

MELISSA E. SANCHEZ

Thomas Carew (pronounced 'Carey') (1594/95–1640) was a seventeenth-century poet and courtier. The earl of Clarendon's comment that Carew's life was 'spent with less Severity or Exactness than it ought to have been' has powerfully shaped the poet's reputation, but much of Carew's literary work belies his reputation as a carefree, urbane wit. Carew is closely associated with a group of lyricists known as the 'Cavalier' poets, which included John Suckling, Robert Herrick, and Richard Lovelace. Cavalier poetry focused on exploring and defining what it meant to live the good life. On the one hand, the good life was defined by pleasure, wit, and elegance; on the other, it demanded constancy, integrity, and candour.

Carew was probably born in Kent. His mother was the daughter of the lord mayor of London. His father was a civil lawyer, master in chancery, and justice of the peace for Surrey and Hampshire. After receiving his BA from Oxford, Carew began to read law at the Middle Temple, but it quickly became clear that he was not cut out to be a lawyer. In 1613 Carew left his studies to become the secretary of Sir Dudley Carleton, whom he accompanied on an embassy to Italy, where he became familiar with Italian poetry and philosophy. Carew also joined Carleton on an embassy to the Netherlands in 1616, but he was quickly dismissed for writing a satire on Carleton and his wife. The next record we have of Carew has him employed as secretary to Sir Edward Herbert (later Lord Herbert of Cherbury), whose embassy to Paris he joined in 1619. In Paris, Carew became acquainted with French poetic tradition, particularly the work of Ronsard, and probably met the Italian poet Giambattista Marino. In 1630 Carew was appointed a gentleman of Charles I's privy chamber and sewer-in-ordinary, which put him in charge of all royal dining arrangements. Carew also participated in Charles I's campaign to put down the Scottish rebellion in spring 1639. He died a year later, in March 1640. No authorized publication of Carew's work was printed until after his death, but his verse circulated widely in manuscript during his lifetime.

Carew's 'To Ben Jonson' and 'An elegy upon the death of the dean of Pauls, Dr. John Donne' have received more scholarly attention than any other of his works. The verse letter to Jonson is written in response to Jonson's own 'Ode to himself', which attacked popular taste after the humiliating failure of *The new inne.* In 'To Ben Jonson', Carew draws on Jonson's own condemnation of the pursuit of worldly recognition to urge the older poet to ignore contemporary opinion and focus instead on lasting intellectual achievement. In the elegy on Donne, Carew celebrates Donne's poetic achievement by imitating his language, style, and metaphysical conceits.

Carew is also well known for his libertine lyrics and his court masque, *Coelum Britanicum* (1634). His most famous lyric, 'A rapture', describes a sexual fantasy in explicit terms that shocked many contemporaries. *Coelum Britanicum* celebrates Charles I's attempt to reform court morals. Its plot hinges on the conceit that Jove has decided to dismantle the current constellations, which depict the divine misbehaviour immortalized by Ovid's *Metamorphoses*, and to replace them with the name 'CarloMaria' (a combination of Charles and his queen, Henrietta Maria). However, *Coelum Britanicum* is not entirely laudatory. It also includes the satirical character Momus, who critiques the hypocrisy, secrecy, and military weakness of Charles's government. *Coelum Britanicum* is especially notable for its structure. Most Caroline masques began with a short anti-masque depicting grotesque and evil characters; the masque proper banished these threats with an extensive celebration of the monarch's power and wisdom. *Coelum Britanicum*, by contrast, begins with seven anti-masques, which take up a total of 832 lines, while the four songs of the masque proper take only 247 lines. This structure places greater stress on domestic unrest and foreign threats than on the virtue of Charles's rule.

In his lesser-known poetry Carew explores the problem of individual virtue. One such poem is 'In answer of an elegiacal letter', his reply to fellow poet Aurelian Townshend, who urged him to write an elegy on the death of Gustavus Adolphus, king of Sweden and leader of the Protestant forces in the Thirty Years War. Here, Carew ironically insists that his 'lyric feet' are inadequate to the task of celebrating a martial hero. He then goes on to compare the idle pleasures of the Caroline court with the heroic struggles of war. This poem has been understood as both encapsulating and satirizing a courtly attitude of leisurely indifference. Carew also wrote 'To Saxham' and 'To my friend G.N. from Wrest', two country house poems in the mode established by Aemelia Lanyer and Ben Jonson. Both of these poems celebrate the values of modesty, truthfulness, and integrity. The former is notable for its austere winter setting, which contrasts with the lush springtime depicted in previous country house poems.

SEE ALSO: Donne, John; Herrick, Robert; Jonson, Ben; Lanyer, Aemelia; Lovelace, Richard; Suckling, John

REFERENCES AND SUGGESTED READINGS

Adamson, J. S. A. (1993) Chivalry and political culture in Caroline England. In: Sharpe, Kevin & Lake, Peter (eds) *Culture and politics in early Stuart England.* Stanford University Press, Stanford, pp. 161–197.

Butler, Martin (2009) *The Stuart court masque and political culture.* Cambridge University Press, Cambridge.

Fitzmaurice, James (1985) Carew's funerary poetry and the paradox of sincerity. *Studies in English Literature, 1500–1900* 25, 127–144.

Johnson, Paula (1976) Carew's 'A rapture': the dynamics of fantasy. *Studies in English Literature, 1500–1900* 16, 145–155.

Long, Ada & MacLean, Hugh (1978) 'Deare Ben,' 'Great Donne', and 'My Celia': the wit of Carew's poetry. *Studies in English Literature, 1500–1900* 18, 75–94.

Miner, Earl Roy (1971) *The Cavalier mode from Jonson to Cotton.* Princeton University Press, Princeton.

Nixon, Scott (1999) Carew's response to Jonson and Donne. *Studies in English Literature, 1500–1900* 39, 89–109.

Sharpe, Kevin (1987) *Criticism and compliment: the politics of literature in the England of Charles I.* Cambridge University Press, Cambridge.

Cartwright, William

DEANNE WILLIAMS

William Cartwright (1611–43) was a poet, playwright, and clergyman. Widely celebrated as a poet, dramatist, and orator, Cartwright is best known for his play *The royall slave* (1636), designed by Inigo Jones and set to music by Henry Lawes, and for *The lady-errant* (1635), which included female actors. One of the followers of Ben Jonson known as the 'Sons of Ben', Cartwright lived in Oxford for most of his life, taking holy orders in 1638, and was admired for his preaching. His poetic and dramatic expressions of royalist ideology emphasize ideals of honour and self-sacrifice. The dramatic roles performed by women in *The lady-errant* illustrate the increasing significance of women in Caroline theatre.

Born in Northway, Gloucestershire, Cartwright was a king's scholar at Westminster School and matriculated as a gentleman scholar at Christ Church, Oxford, in 1632. He made his name as a poet by contributing to various Oxford-produced collections of poetry that celebrated the Stuart monarchy, such as *Britanniae natalis* (1630), a collection of Latin poems written to celebrate the birth of Prince Charles, and Musarum Oxoniensum *pro rege soteria* (1633), which celebrated the king's survival of smallpox. He also contributed commendatory poems to Francis Kynaston's *Amorum troili et creseidae* (1635), a translation of Chaucer's *Troilus and Criseyde* into Latin, and to *Jonsonus virbius* (1638), commemorating Ben Jonson. Most of his poems remained unpublished during his lifetime, and were collected in his posthumous *Comedies, tragi-comedies, with other poems* (1651), printed by Humphrey Moseley. These included love poems such as 'To Chloe who wish'd herself young enough for me' and 'No platonique love', as well as poems of praise or commemoration such as 'In the memory of the most worthy Benjamin Jonson', as well as translations of Horace and Martial.

Cartwright's first play, *The ordinary* (1635) is the only one set in London, and its concerns are squarely within the genre of city comedy: Meanwell takes revenge upon Simon Credulous, who has cheated his father, by marrying him to the maidservant of Jane, his rich fiancée. The play is an overt imitation of Jonson, who praised it: 'My son Cartwright writes all like a man.' Many of its lines are quotations from Chaucer, and its lyrics were copied in various miscellanies.

Performed at Oxford for Prince Rupert and the elector palatine, *The lady-errant* asserts 'That each Sex keeps to its part . . . Being the female's habit is / Her owne, and the Male's his'. In this play, one of the first to give women speaking parts, women are, in fact, the majority. Set in Cyprus, *The lady-errant* concerns a faction of women who attempt to take over the reins of government while the men are away at war with Crete. In the meantime, the princess of Cyprus, Leucasia, falls in love with Charistus, the deserting prince of Crete. With the help of Machessa, a martial maid, the queen of Cyprus ultimately suppresses the rebellion, while Leucasia and Charistus are betrothed. The play illustrates Cavalier associations of women with eros and theatricality while ultimately subordinating them to royal authority and political governance.

Another one of Cartwright's 'Platonic plays', *The royall slave* (1636) was perhaps his greatest success. Performed at Christ Church, Oxford, before the king and queen, it dramatizes the story of Cratander, a handsome and able Greek slave who is captured by the Persians. Following a Persian custom, this war prisoner is made the king of Persia for three days before being sacrificed to the Sun God. Cratander's philosophical talk wins admirers in Queen Atossa and her ladies, who appeal to King Arsamnes to spare his life. Cratander insists on going through with the sacrifice, but a solar eclipse is taken as proof from the gods that he should live. Cratander is then made king of his native Ephesus. *The royall slave* was so admired that the queen wanted to see it performed by her own players at Hampton Court, with the original sets and costumes. The play's elaborate music and spectacle reflect Caroline tastes, while the sustained reflection that it offers upon the nature of monarchy and the hero's innate nobility and superiority would have spoken to immediate royalist concerns and interests. The key role played by the queen, and its demonstration of her entirely Platonic love for Cratander, was flattering to Henrietta Maria, an active participant in and patron of the theatre.

There is no evidence that *The siedge, or love's convert*, probably composed around 1638, was ever acted. Based on a story from Plutarch's *Life of Cimon*, the play concerns King Misander's desire for the virgin Leucasia, but, after stabbing her, he is converted into an ideal mate by her sheer beauty. Leucasia drinks a love potion, believing it to be poison, and falls for the king as well. It reflects not only royalist idealizations of kingship and sacrifice but also a Cavalier fascination with the Platonic implications of female beauty.

According to his printer, Humphrey Moseley, Cartwright wrote no more plays after taking orders in 1638. His only surviving sermon is *An off-spring of mercy, issuing out of the womb of cruelty* (1652), written following the Royalist victory at the battle of Edgehill. He died of a 'camp disease' that spread among soldiers billeted at Oxford. King Charles wept when he learned of his death and went into mourning.

SEE ALSO: Jones, Inigo; Jonson, Ben

REFERENCES AND SUGGESTED READINGS

Bentley, G. E. (1956) *The Jacobean and Caroline stage,* vol. 3 Clarendon Press, Oxford, pp. 126–142.

Evans, Blakemore G. (ed.) (1951) *The plays and poems of William Cartwright.* University of Wisconsin Press, Madison.

Farnsworth, Jane (2002) Defending the king in Cartwright's *The lady-errant* (1636–37). *Studies in English Literature, 1500–1900* 42, 381–398.

Goffin, R. Cullis (1918) *The life and poems of William Cartwright.* Cambridge University Press, Cambridge.

Gordon, Scott Paul (2002) The cultural politics of William Cartwright's The royal slave. In: Bruster, Douglas & Moisan, Thomas (eds) *In the company of Shakespeare: essays on English Renaissance literature in honor of G. Blakemore Evans.* Fairleigh Dickinson University Press, Madison, pp. 251–269.

Cary, Elizabeth

BERNADETTE ANDREA

Elizabeth Cary, Lady Falkland (1585–1639), is considered the first English woman to publish an original, rather than a translated, 'closet' drama and possibly the first English woman to write an extended history in prose and poetry. She also published a controversial translation of Catholic polemic later in her life. She wrote many other works, most of which remained in manuscript and many of which are considered lost. The quasi-hagiographical manuscript, *The Lady Falkland, her life* (composed between 1643 and 1650), is significant as the first extended biography to focus on an English-woman (Weller & Ferguson 1994; Wolfe 2001). Her daughter Lucy (b.1619) probably composed it with the assistance of her siblings, Mary (b.1622) and Patrick (b.1624), all of whom converted to Catholicism (although Patrick later recanted).

She was born Elizabeth Tanfield around 1585 at Burford Priory, Oxfordshire, to Sir Laurence (or Lawrence) (c.1551–1625) and Lady Elizabeth Tanfield (née Symondes) (c.1565–1629). Her father, a relatively impoverished younger brother who became a lawyer and judge, was knighted by King James I in 1604, rising to the position of chief baron of the exchequer (1607); her mother, from a gentry family in Norfolk, was niece of Queen Elizabeth I's official 'champion', Sir Henry Lee (1533–1611), a fact she did not let her lower-ranked husband forget. The Tanfields were despised for their rapaciousness, which encompassed accepting bribes to compromise judicial decisions and dispossessing their tenants by enclosing common lands.

Elizabeth, who was their only child, suffered from a strict upbringing. As the biography by her daughter records, she learned to read early, 'and loved it much'. She taught herself French, Spanish, Italian, Latin, and Hebrew. She even learned 'Transylvanian' (this could be Hungarian, as Transylvania was part of the Eastern Hungarian Kingdom at this time, or Romanian); in any case, she soon forgot this language through disuse. Among her early works were translations from Latin to English of Seneca and Louis de Blois (a sixteenth-century Flemish mystic of the Benedictine order). However, her efforts at self-education were constantly thwarted, with her mother going so far as to confine her to her room without candles to stem her voracious reading. Her father, by contrast, is represented as supporting her learning, even providing her with tomes such as John Calvin's *Institutes of the Christian religion* (definitive edition in Latin 1559 and in French 1560) when she was only 12. Other reading recorded in her biography includes Richard Hooker's *Of the lawes of ecclesiasticall politie* (first four books published in 1593; fifth book published in 1597), which argued for the *via media* of the established Church of England, but left Elizabeth in doubt of her Protestant faith; and the patristic fathers, especially St Augustine, who are represented in the biography as 'of the religion of the Church of Rome', to which she ultimately turned. The biography concludes with an extensive list of her reading, which covered poetry, history, philosophy, and theology in multiple languages.

Her writing, in addition to her early translations, included 'the life of Tamberlaine in verse', which she considered her best literary effort. She also translated Abraham Ortelius's *Le miroir du monde* (1579), from the first modern atlas, in her 'younge and tender years', as she specifies in her dedication to Sir Henry Lee. This work is extant in manuscript. Her first play, mentioned in the dedication to her second play but no longer extant, focused on the city of Syracuse in Sicily, which had been subject to Greek, Roman, and Islamic rule. Her second play, *The tragedie of Mariam, the faire queene of Jewry*, was composed as early as 1603 and published, apparently without her permission, in 1613. Based on the Catholic Thomas Lodge's 1602 translation of the first-century Jewish historian Flavius Josephus's *The antiquitie of the Jewes* and *The warres of the Jewes*, it focuses on the marital strife between Herod I (also, the Great) and his wife, Mariam (also, Mariamne), with significant political ramifications. The play's title character is notable for her outspokenness (beginning with her opening line, 'How oft have I with public voice run on') and for her refusal to hide her displeasure from her husband, who arranged to have her murdered should he be executed in Rome, among other crimes against her family. Although the play confirms Mariam is chaste, Herod (at the urging of his sister Salome) condemns her to death as an adulteress because she refuses to dissimulate her emotions, rejects his demands to comply with the codes of courtly love, and abjures his bed. She has been seen as 'a type of Christ' (Beilin 1980), a proto-feminist, and a racial bigot, among other interpretations (Schoenberg & Trudeau 2008; Raber 2009). However, the final scene, where the Nuntio memorializes her deliberate silence –

> She made no answer, but she look'd the while,
> As if thereof she scarce did notice take,
> Yet smil'd, a dutiful, though scornful, smile

– remains productively open-ended.

A play probably meant to be read rather than performed, it derives from the experiments in Senecan tragedy characteristic of the circle of writers around the countess of Pembroke, Mary Sidney Herbert, which included Michael Drayton and John Davies, both of whom had direct connections with Elizabeth from her earliest days. However, Elizabeth, who attended masques and plays during a 'golden age' for both, rendered her drama eminently performable, as recent productions have proven (Hodgson-Wright 2000). The play is now deemed canonical, at least in so far as studies of early modern women's writing are concerned.

This early literary output ensured Elizabeth's reputation as a learned woman, with Davies, in the dedicatory letter to *The muses sacrifice* (1612), lauding her as one 'of whom Minerva [the Roman goddess of wisdom and the arts] stands in feare, / lest she, from her, should get Arts Regencie'. Drayton (*Englands heroicall epistles*, 1597), John Bodenham (*Englands helicon, or the muses harmony*, 1614), Richard Bellinge (*Sixth books to the countesse of Pembrokes Arcadia*, 1624), William Sheares (*The workes of Mr. John Marston*, 1633), and others also published dedications to her. She continued to write in various genres, even though she published only one more work during her lifetime, *The reply of the most illustrious cardinall of Perron, to the answeare of the most excellent king of Great Britaine* (1630), which translation she dedicated to the French Catholic queen of Charles I, Henrietta Maria. In her epistle 'To the reader', she boldly identifies herself as 'a *Catholique*, and a Woman', and deems her translation was 'well done'. Perron in his original tract, published at Paris in 1620 as the culmination of a debate with James I that began in 1612, 'attempted to allay English Protestant suspicions about Roman Catholics as traitors' (Lewalski 1993). By necessity, this translation was published at Douai in the Spanish Netherlands (now France), a refuge for English Catholics escaping persecution. *The history of the life, reign, and death of Edward II king of England, and lord of Ireland. With the rise and fall of his great favourites, Gaveston and the Spencers* (composed c.1627; published in two versions in 1680), over which controversy about her authorship continues, was published posthumously. Like *The tragedie of Mariam*, it develops the character of a queen resisting patriarchal tyranny, in this case Isabel. Other critics argue for its relatively sympathetic portrait of Edward (Skura 1996).

In 1602 Elizabeth was disposed in an arranged marriage to a man she barely knew: Sir Henry Cary (c.1575–1633), son of Sir Edward of Berkhamstead, Hertfordshire, and Lady Katherine (née Knyvett, previously married to Henry, second Baron Paget). The financial resources Henry received through this marriage enabled him to buy his way steadily into the peerage as first Viscount Falkland, a position inherited by the Tanfield heir, the eldest son of the marriage, Lucius (b.1610). Elizabeth remained in her parental home during the first year of marriage while her husband joined English forces assisting Maurice of Nassau against the Spanish in the Netherlands. In 1603, while her husband was still abroad, Elizabeth moved into the Cary household, where her mother-in-law, who 'took away all her books', treated her harshly. Henry was captured by Spanish troops in 1605, and remained a prisoner before returning to England in 1606. Ben Jonson celebrated his valour in the epigram 'To Sir Henry Cary'. The marriage was consummated upon Henry's return, with their first child, Katherine, born in 1609 and 'married into Scotland' prior to the family moving to Ireland. Ten more children followed, with the last, Henry, born in Ireland in 1625. Elizabeth experienced bouts of depression, or 'deep melancholy', starting with her second pregnancy, possibly alternating with manic episodes. Yet, she nursed all her children, except the eldest son, Lucius, who as heir of the Tanfield estates was raised by his maternal grandparents. He accompanied his parents

to Dublin after the death of his grandparents, where he was educated at the Protestant stronghold of Trinity College; he died fighting for the Royalist forces in 1643. Ben Jonson praised him as the ideal 'Cavalier' in his famous Pindaric ode, 'To the immortall memorie, and friendship of that noble paire, Sir Lucius Cary and Sir H. Morison'.

After his return from the Netherlands, Henry pursued a meteoric career as a courtier over the next decade, with appointments as gentleman of the bedchamber, master of the jewel house, knight of the bath, comptroller of the household, and privy councillor. He was ultimately granted the title of first Viscount Falkland in the county of Fife in the peerage of Scotland in 1620, even though he was an Englishman. A staunch Protestant, he became lord deputy of Ireland in 1622, where he took up residence in Dublin with his growing family. During her residence in Ireland Elizabeth 'learnt to read Irish in an Irish Bible' and established a vocational school for 'beggar children' (Wolfe 2001), which has been described as 'a chain of child-labour sweatshops' (Rankin 2007).

As the biography by her daughter records, Elizabeth displayed an early interest in Catholicism, which was a proscribed religion for all but a few exempted members of the household of Queen Henrietta Maria. She nonetheless conformed outwardly to her husband's Protestant faith, reluctantly attending Church of England services. In 1625 she returned to England with four of her children, but without her husband. As Susan Cerasano and Marion Wynne-Davies (1996) propose, 'the harshness of his rule in Ireland and his persecution of the Irish Catholics appear to have precipitated the complete breakdown of their marriage'. The subsequent death of her daughter Katherine in childbirth, which she attended, provoked a vision of the Virgin Mary, described in the biography as 'our Blessed Lady', which further confirmed Elizabeth in her faith. Shortly after this episode, her Catholicism became public knowledge when her erstwhile friend, Susan Villiers Feilding, countess of Denbigh, sister to

George Villiers, first duke of Buckingham, informed Charles I. (Elizabeth may have written a funeral elegy for Buckingham, who was assassinated in 1628.) Her publicized conversion was greeted with general hostility, with her husband insisting upon a full separation and the king seeking her recantation. Having been previously persuaded by her husband to mortgage her jointure to finance his ventures, she lost the security of her marriage settlement and was disinherited by her father. She was consequently left without any means of support, with her mother also refusing to assist her. She issued a series of appeals, both formal and informal, to have her maintenance restored, resulting in a Privy Council decree in 1627 ordering her husband to provide for her and to pay her accumulated debts. He refused to comply with this order. In the midst of this high-stakes marital dispute, he was recalled from Ireland to England in 1629. Shortly after his return, Elizabeth published her polemical translation of *The reply of the most illustrious cardinall of Perron*, most copies of which were burnt upon their arrival in England. In 1631 Henrietta Maria mediated a partial reconciliation, and in 1633 Elizabeth succoured her husband through his gruesome end from an improperly set broken leg which, becoming gangrenous, was improperly amputated; he bled to death.

After her husband's death, Elizabeth devoted her energies to ensuring the Catholic faith of her younger children, who were under the guardianship of their Protestant elder brother, Lucius. She abducted her two sons, Patrick and Henry (Dom Placid), from Lucius's household, and they were sent to Catholic Europe, though both eventually returned to England and to Protestantism. Lord Chief Justice John Bramston interrogated her on 16 May 1636 regarding this affair, after which she was called before the Star Chamber on 25 May and threatened with imprisonment in the Tower of London. She nevertheless admitted no wrongdoing, and apparently was not incarcerated. Despite the intervention of archbishop of Canterbury William Laud, four of her daughters

became nuns at Cambrai, then in the Spanish Netherlands, with Lucy (Dame Magdalena), Mary (Dame Maria), and Elizabeth (Dame Elizabetha) received into the Benedictine convent in 1638 and Anne (Dame Clementia) in 1639. Elizabeth was never able to convince her eldest son, Lucius, to convert, even though she responded to his *Discourse of infallibility* (1645), which challenged the Catholic dogma of 'this supposed necessity of an infallible guide' in interpreting Scripture, with a polemic she 'thought the best thing she ever writ'. She died in October 1639, at the age of 53 or 54 years, in impoverished circumstances; she seems to have been given a Catholic burial in Henrietta Maria's chapel at Somerset House.

As Karen Raber (2009) summarizes, 'Cary's literary efforts were largely forgotten in the centuries following her death. She was not, however, completely unknown.' Lauded in her lifetime for her learning, and remembered thereafter as the mother of Lucius Cary, in the nineteenth century English Catholics recovered *The Lady Falkland, her life* in the context of their own struggles within England and within the English Catholic community, publishing the biography in two redactions (Richard Simpson, 1857; Georgianna Fullerton, 1883). Literary historians from the beginning of the twentieth century included sketches of her life in their biographical compendiums (Donald Stauffer, 1930; Kenneth Murdock, 1939); yet, her significant *oeuvre* of extant writings remained marginalized. While influential literary critics through the first half of the twentieth century, such as A. C. Dunstan (1908, 1914; the latter reissued with a new introduction by Stratznicky and Rowland (1992)), Maurice Valency (1940), and Alexander Witherspoon (1968), acknowledged her authorship of *The tragedie of Mariam*, they generally 'deprecate[d] the play, viewing it as inferior to its male-authored predecessors' (Gutierrez 1991). In response, feminist critics in the 1970s and 1980s, who sought to recover women's writing from such opprobrium, began to take her seriously as a literary writer, often through the lens of biographical criticism. With the publication of Barry Weller and Margaret Ferguson's *The tragedy of Mariam, the fair queen of Jewry, with the Lady Falkland, her life, by one of her daughters* in 1994, which was followed by other accessible editions (Cerasano & Wynne-Davies 1996; Purkiss 1998; Hodgson-Wright 2000), both works began to be more widely read and taught. Cary criticism accordingly expanded to include analyses of topics such as the construction of subjectivity, the negotiation of sexuality, and the 'reproduction of motherhood'; race, empire, and religion; authorship, rhetoric, and theatricality; and comparisons with writers such as William Shakespeare, John Fletcher, Thomas Middleton, and John Milton (Schoenberg & Trudeau 2008; Raber 2009). Facsimile editions have made her other two published works more accessible to scholars (Ferguson 1996; Dolan 2000), who are now pursuing archival work in manuscript collections, such as Heather Wolfe's ground-breaking efforts in Benedictine holdings (2007). One hopes that some of her 'lost' works will emerge from these investigations.

SEE ALSO: Davies, John; Drayton, Michael; Herbert, Mary (Sidney), countess of Pembroke; Jonson, Ben; Lodge, Thomas

REFERENCES AND SUGGESTED READINGS

Beilin, Elaine (1980) Elizabeth Cary and *The tragedie of Mariam*. Papers on Language and Literature 16, 45–64.

Cerasano, S. P. & Wynne-Davies, Marion (1996) *Renaissance drama by women: texts and documents*. Routledge, London.

Dolan, Frances E. (1999) *Whores of Babylon: Catholicism, gender, and seventeenth-century print culture*. Cornell University Press, Ithaca.

Dolan, Frances E. (ed.) (2000) *Recusant translators: Elizabeth Cary, Alexia Grey*. Ashgate, Aldershot.

Ferguson, Margaret (ed.) (1996) *Works by and attributed to Elizabeth Cary*. Ashgate, Aldershot.

Gutierrez, Nancy A. (1991) Valuing *Mariam*: genre study and feminist analysis. *Texas Studies in Women's Literature* 10, 233–251.

Hodgson-Wright, Stephanie (ed.) (2000) *The tragedy of Mariam, by Elizabeth Cary*. Broadview, Peterborough, ON.

Lewalski, Barbara Kiefer (1993) Resisting tyrants: Elizabeth Cary's tragedy and history. In: *Writing women in Jacobean England*. Harvard University Press, Cambridge, MA, pp. 179–211.

Purkiss, Diane (ed.) (1998) *Three tragedies by Renaissance women*. Penguin, London.

Raber, Karen (ed.) (2009) *Ashgate critical essays on women writers in England, 1500–1700*, vol. 6: *Elizabeth Cary*. Ashgate, Aldershot.

Rankin, Deana (2007) 'A more worthy patronesse': Elizabeth Cary and Ireland. In: Wolfe, Heather (ed.) *The literary career and legacy of Elizabeth Cary, 1613–1680*. Palgrave Macmillan, New York, pp. 203–221.

Schoenberg, Thomas J. & Trudeau, Lawrence J. (ed.) (2008) *Literature criticism from 1400 to 1800*, vol. 141. Thomson Gale, Farmington Hills.

Skura, Meredith (1996) Elizabeth Cary and Edward II: what do women want to write? *Renaissance Drama* 27, 79–104.

Straznicky, Marta & Rowland, Richard (eds) (1992) *The tragedie of Mariam, faire queene of Jewry*. Oxford University Press, for Malone Society, Oxford.

Weller, Barry & Ferguson, Margaret W. (eds) (1994) *Elizabeth Cary, the Lady Falkland: The tragedy of Mariam, the fair queen of Jewry, with the Lady Falkland, her life, by one of her daughters*. University of California Press, Berkeley.

Wolfe, Heather (ed.) (2001) *Elizabeth Cary, Lady Falkland: life and letters*. RTM Publications, Cambridge.

Wolfe, Heather (ed.) (2007) *The literary career and legacy of Elizabeth Cary, 1613–1680*. Palgrave Macmillan, New York.

Cary, Lucius, Lord Falkland

EDWARD PALEIT

Lucius Cary, second Viscount Falkland (1609/ 10–1643), is now chiefly known for the circle of religious and political thinkers who met on his estate of Great Tew, northwest of Oxford, during the 1630s. He was also a minor poet and religious writer and, from late 1641 till his death in battle, a leading constitutional royalist.

Cary was born in 1608, the eldest son of Sir Henry Cary (ennobled as Viscount Falkland in 1620) and his wife Elizabeth, author of *The tragedie of Mariam* (1613). In 1622, after a year at Cambridge, Cary went to Ireland when his father became lord deputy. In 1629 he inherited the Oxfordshire estates of Great Tew and Burford from his maternal grandparents and returned to England. His best friend Sir Henry Morison died the same year, prompting Cary to write a long elegy and two later anniversary poems addressed to Ben Jonson, who celebrated Cary's friendship with Morison in a famous ode (Murdock 1938; Weber 1940). Cary married Morison's sister, Lettice, in 1630, and inherited his father's title in 1633.

He spent the 1630s mainly in rural retirement. He contributed elegies to the first edition of John Donne's poems (1633) and to Jonson's memorial collection, *Jonsonus virbius* (1638), whose title he may have suggested, and also wrote dedicatory poems for George Sandys's religious translations. Nonetheless, his interests were increasingly theological: Sir John Suckling, in 'The sessions of the poets' (1637), represents him as 'so gone in divinity / That he had almost forgot his poetry'. By then Cary's manor at Great Tew had became a haven for theologians from Oxford and further afield such as Gilbert Sheldon or Henry Hammond, as well as other intellectual figures. The tenor of religious discussion there was sceptical and rationalist: though often labelled Socinian by hostile Catholic and Calvinist observers, it contributed significantly to the development of Anglicanism during the Interregnum and Restoration. Its chief expression was William Chillingworth's *The religion of Protestants* (1638), which was written at Great Tew. Falkland's own writings echo Chillingworth's, and mostly date from the mid-1630s: they include *A discourse of infallibility* (1645), a *Reply* to a response to it (1651), and some letters challenging the arguments of recent Catholic converts. All refute Rome's claim to be the only true church. Possibly this stance was encouraged by personal experience: with his mother's suspected connivance, his two younger brothers had in 1636 escaped from Great Tew to a Catholic education on the Continent. Politics and law were also discussed at Great Tew, contributing significantly to the development of natural rights theory: Thomas Hobbes, John Vaughan the lawyer, and (possibly) John Selden were guests. Edward Hyde's fervent friendship with Falkland, celebrated in his autobiography and *History of the rebellion* (1702), dates from the Great Tew period.

In 1637 William Lenthall secured Falkland's admission to Lincoln's Inn. Two years later he rode north to fight in the 'Bishops' War', a decision commemorated anxiously in poems by Edmund Waller and the young Abraham Cowley. In 1640 he was elected member of parliament for Newport, in the Isle of Wight, for both Short and Long Parliaments. Like many others, Falkland initially condemned the excesses of the Personal Rule of Charles I. In a much-circulated speech he savaged the judges over ship money, and in another attacked the Laudian bishops. He seems to have agreed with Thomas Wentworth, first earl of Strafford's attainder and maybe also Archbishop Laud's. These attitudes, however, combined with a conservative respect for constitutional and ecclesiastical tradition, which led Falkland to defend episcopacy against abolitionist 'root-and-branch' demands. His similar defence of the royal prerogative brought him Charles's gratitude, and by late 1641 he was identified with a pro-Royalist grouping in the Commons.

In January 1642 he agreed, reluctantly, to become senior secretary of state, and soon formed, with Hyde and Sir John Culpeper, a triumvirate of moderate advisers to the king. In June 1642 Falkland and Culpeper drew up the king's *The answer to the nineteen propositions*. *The answer* used classical republican language to declare that England was a precarious 'balance' of three 'estates', king, lords, and commons – significantly omitting the clergy. This formulation, rapidly appropriated by polemicists on both sides, was to become the orthodox theory of the English constitution for nearly a century (Weston 1960; Mendle 1985; Pocock 2003).

The Civil War destroyed Falkland's irenical hopes, plunging him into depression. He fought in several engagements before charging, perhaps suicidally, into a hail of musket bullets at the battle of Newbury on 19 September 1643. The climax to Abraham Cowley's abandoned epic *The Civil War*, composed in the mid-1640s, vividly registers shock and dismay at his death. Falkland was increasingly mythologized as the archetypal English gentry hero: virtuous, loyal, an opponent of ideological extremes. Pope called him 'the Just'. The legend was also something to strike against – the villain in William Godwin's skewering of English squirearchy, *Caleb Williams* (1792), is called Falkland.

SEE ALSO: Cary, Elizabeth; Chillingworth, William; Cowley, Abraham; Hobbes, Thomas; Hyde, Edward, earl of Clarendon; Jonson, Ben; Sandys, George; Selden, John; Suckling, John; Waller, Edmund

REFERENCES AND SUGGESTED READINGS

Hayward, J. C. (1987) New directions in studies of the Falkland circle. *Seventeenth Century* 2, 19–48.

Mendle, Michael (1985) *Dangerous positions: mixed government, the estates of the realm, and the making of the Answer to the XIX propositions.* Tuscaloosa, University of Alabama Press.

Murdock, Kenneth (1938) An elegy on Sir Henry Morrison, by Lucius Cary, Viscount Falkland. *Harvard Studies and Notes in English Philology and Literature* 20, 29–42.

Pocock, J. G. A. (2003) *The Machiavellian moment: Florentine political thought and the Atlantic republican tradition*, 2nd edn. Princeton University Press, Princeton.

Smith, David (1994) *Constitutional royalism and the search for settlement, c.1640–1649.* Cambridge University Press, Cambridge.

Trevor-Roper, Hugh (1987) *Catholics, Anglicans and Puritans: seventeenth-century essays.* Secker & Warburg, London.

Tuck, Richard (1979) *Natural rights theories: their origin and development.* Cambridge University Press, Cambridge.

Weber, Kurt (1940) *Lucius Cary, second Viscount Falkland.* Columbia University Press, New York.

Weston, Corinne (1960) English constitutional doctrines from the fifteenth century to the seventeenth. II: The theory of mixed monarchy under Charles I and after. *English Historical Review* 75, 426–443.

Cary, Mary

JASON E. COHEN

Mary Cary (b.1620/21, active 1645–53) was a radical millenarian author who espoused the beliefs of the Fifth Monarchy movement. Cary is known exclusively through her printed works, particularly her mature tracts, *The resurrection of the witnesses; and Englands fall from (the mystical Babylon) Rome* (1648), and *The little horns doom & downfall, or a scripture-prophesie of King James and King Charles, and of this present Parliament unfolded*, published with *A new and more exact mappe, or description of new Jerusalem's glory* (1651). Her 1647 publication, *A word in season to the kingdom of England*, advocates the political liberty of lay preachers and was sold, as were her later works, in the shop of Giles Calvert, the radical sectarian bookseller. Cary's works after 1650 bear a change of name to Mary Rande, although no further details of her life have been uncovered to date. Cary's extant production ceases after her 1653 appeal to the Barebones Parliament titled *Twelve humble proposals to the supreme governours of the three nations*, which recommended taxation to alleviate poverty, decried tithing, proposed university funding reforms, and discussed simplified laws and court procedures.

Mary Cary's strong female voice accompanies Anna Trapnel's and Elizabeth Avery's in revealing women's influence on Fifth Monarchist ideology. Cary's preface 'To the Reader' in *The little horns doom* humbly suggests that she neither fully controls her work nor requires outward validation, 'for I am a very weake, and unworthy instrument', she admits; nevertheless, she dedicates her 1651 text to three prominent anti-Royalist women: Elizabeth Cromwell,

Bridget Ireton, and Lady Margaret Rolle. Cary's acknowledgement of her passive role is accompanied by a Pauline disavowal of inward strength and a reliance on divine guidance: '[I] have not done this worke by any strength of my owne ... I could doe no more herein ... then a pensill, or pen can do, when no hand guides it.' Yet her pen and pencil carry her powerfully gendered voice: 'And if there be very few men that are thus furnished with this gift of the Spirit; how few are the women!' she exclaims. *The little horns doom* and *More exact mappe* outline Cary's vision of the fall of the papal Beast, the reign of the saints with Christ on earth, and a utopian New Jerusalem, which brings the rule of God to man and woman alike.

As a movement, Fifth Monarchism came into ascendancy following the events of 1645 and became increasingly vocal after 1649. The movement is defined by the belief that the fall of King Charles I had dual significance. First, it represented the biblical fall of the Fourth Monarchy prophesied in Daniel 7 and repeated in Revelation 12; secondly, it announced the reign of the saints. Its central figures included Christopher Feake, William Aspinwall, John Spittlehouse, and John Rogers. Like her male counterparts, Cary was distressed by the ineffectual Rump Parliament; Cary's texts, unlike the works of her contemporary Anna Trapnel, shaped Fifth Monarchist beliefs by offering trenchant critiques of the English state along with a programme for reforming her nation's human and spiritual conditions.

The little horns doom and *More exacte mappe* signal Cary's mature concerns with the 'present proceedings of God in the world' and her aim to persuade believers to desist living 'in waies contradictory to, (or crossing of) his present designes'. Cary's hermeneutics connect religious conviction to political avenues for the amelioration of the human condition through the elevation and rule of the oppressed saints. As in her extended reading of Revelation 11 in *The resurrection of the witnesses*, Cary's claims for Christ's return in *The little horns doom* hinge on a mathematical reading of scriptural dates from the book of Revelation marshalled to prove that the 1,260 years of saints' suffering have ended. Along with her assertions that the Beast no longer holds power over saints and provision of details of the Jews' deliverance to Christ in 1656, Cary's speculative calculations drive her belief that recent events are harbingers of salvation.

A new and more exacte mappe lays out the remarkable utopia that Christ's return announces. Cary's utopia envisions the natural prosperity and social equity that will reward the devout, but it also uniquely attends to political and economic issues, including marriage rights, the treatment of women and children, the supply and distribution of food and raw materials, and specific remedies for recent English crises. Cary's 1651 text concludes with extended verse passages that harshly criticize the Rump and conservative subjects who oppose the 'great designes' that God had brought to the world since 1645. Cary's verse rings out from a moment when extreme and millennial visions carried the weight of political possibility, and her concluding lyrics sound a warning to a state that failed to embody the hopes with which she infused her revolutionary message.

SEE ALSO: Avery, Elizabeth; Trapnel, Anna

REFERENCES AND SUGGESTED READINGS

Baston, Jane (1998) Mary Cary and Fifth Monarchism. *Prose Studies* 21(3), 1–18.

Capp, Bernard S. (1972) *The Fifth Monarchy men: a study in seventeenth-century English millenarianism.* Faber & Faber, London.

Capp, Bernard S. (2004) Cary, Mary. In: *Oxford dictionary of national biography.* Oxford University Press, Oxford.

Gillespie, Katharine (2004) *Domesticity and dissent in the seventeenth century: English women writers and the public sphere.* Cambridge University Press, Cambridge, pp. 25–61.

Loewenstein, David (2006) Scriptural exegesis, female prophecy, and radical politics in Mary Cary. *Studies in English Literature, 1500–1900* 46 (1), 133–153.

Malson-Huddle, Elizabeth R. (2009) Mary Cary's millennial utopia. In: Utopian literature and religion in early modern England. PhD dissertation, University of Wisconsin–Madison.

Cavendish, George

MIKE PINCOMBE

George Cavendish (1497–c.1562) was a literary late starter. He was already in his mid-fifties when he took up his pen to write his first work, the so-called *Metrical visions*, a longish dream-vision which, though apparently taking place over a single day and night, actually occupied the poet over the two years between June 1552 (or earlier) and the summer of 1554. Almost as soon as he had finished this project, Cavendish started work on another, *The life of Wolsey*, which took him from November 1554 to 24 June 1558. And then, just as suddenly as his literary career had begun, it stopped. Thus, over a roughly six-year period during the turbulent decade of the 1550s, Cavendish had written two of the classics of mid-Tudor literature.

Cavendish was born in 1497 into a well-established gentry family in Suffolk. His father, Thomas, held office at the exchequer, and it was no doubt by means of his position at the centre of the machinery of state that his eldest son George was preferred to the service of the great cardinal Thomas Wolsey around 1522. George Cavendish acted as Wolsey's gentleman usher, which required him to attend personally on his master at all times, and also involved special duties with regard to the lavish entertainments of which the somewhat megalomaniac cardinal was especially fond; Cavendish describes some of these in great detail in his *Life*. As it happens, Cavendish's own name is completely absent from the historical record for these years, and we know nothing of his activities other than what he tells us himself – not very much – in his biography of his master. When Wolsey died in disgrace in 1530, Henry VIII invited the still relatively young gentleman usher to serve him

instead; but Cavendish had come into his inheritance in 1524 and was already married with children, so he declined the offer – wisely, perhaps – and retired to his estates in Suffolk, where, most probably, he wrote the *Visions* and the *Life*.

Cavendish's account of life at the top is essentially tragic (Pincombe 2009). The *Metrical visions* is the record of a vision or dream in which the poet is visited by the phantom of his old master, who laments his woeful destiny, and then by a series of men and women – including Anne Boleyn and Henry Howard, the poet earl of Surrey – who dallied with fortune at the English court and came to grief. The whole poem is framed to suggest a likeness with one of the most prestigious books of the later Middle Ages in England: John Lydgate's *The fall of princes*, an adaptation of the Italian writer Giovanni Boccaccio's *De casibus virorum illustrium* (*On the falls of illustrious men*). But whereas in Lydgate's *Fall*, the dream-narrator 'Bochas' (Boccaccio) tells the stories of the ancient deceased in the third person, Cavendish introduced the innovation of having the fallen courtiers of his own day tell their own stories – with a very appreciable increase in the pathos of their tragedies.

The life of Wolsey is also based on the *de casibus* tragic pattern (Sylvester 1960). It tells the story of Wolsey's rise from humble circumstances to the highest position in the realm next to the king: he was not only the lord chancellor but also a cardinal and a papal legate. But, says Cavendish, Fortune and Venus conspired against him by making Henry fall in love with Anne Boleyn, a devotee of the new ideas in religion, who managed not only to have her perceived adversary Wolsey eliminated, but also to bring ruin to England by trapping her royal husband in the snares of the Reformation. Cavendish remained true to the old Roman Catholic faith throughout his life, refusing to profit from Henry's plundering of church lands, and nursing a hatred of Boleyn (and also, one suspects, a strong dislike of the king) which is evident in both the *Fall* and the *Visions*.

Cavendish's *Life of Wolsey* is an essentially medieval story, though its modern editor has noted Cavendish's 'Renaissance eye for details of splendid clothing and for scenes of pomp and luxury' (Sylvester 1959); and a more recent critic has argued on much the same grounds that this qualifies Cavendish as a paradigmatically 'Renaissance' author (Crewe 1990). But Cavendish had the professional eye of a master of ceremonies for entertainments and pageantry; and he also came from a family of mercers, so his interest in the fine fabrics they dealt in is also unsurprising. On the whole, Cavendish's poetry and prose is invigoratingly retrospective and it breathes the rich air of the late Middle Ages.

Cavendish's place in the history of Tudor literature is secure, though it is hard to decide whether either of his two works had much influence in his own time or in the decades after his death, for both remained in manuscript. But it is quite possible that William Baldwin and his colleagues had at least an idea of the format of the *Metrical visions* when they sat down in 1554 to compose the first version of *A mirrour for magistrates*, for they, too, let the fallen speak in their own voices – a considerable legacy to the history of English Renaissance poetry in itself.

SEE ALSO: Baldwin, William; Howard, Henry, earl of Surrey

REFERENCES AND SUGGESTED READINGS

Crewe, Jonathan (1990) *Trials of authorship: anterior forms and poetic reconstruction from Wyatt to Shakespeare.* University of California Press, Berkeley.

Edwards, A. S. G. (ed.) (1980) Cavendish, George. *Metrical visions.* University of South Carolina Press, Columbia.

Edwards, A. S. G. (2004) Cavendish, George. In: *Oxford dictionary of national biography.* Oxford University Press, Oxford.

Pincombe, Mike (2009) A place in the shade: George Cavendish and *de casibus* tragedy. In: Pincombe, Mike & Shrank, Cathy (eds) *The Oxford handbook to Tudor literature, 1485–1603.* Oxford University Press, Oxford, pp. 372–388.

Sylvester, Richard S. (ed.) (1959) Cavendish, George. *The life and death of cardinal Wolsey.* Early English Text Society, London.

Sylvester, Richard S. (1960) Cavendish's *Life of Wolsey*: the artistry of a Tudor biographer. *Studies in Philology* 57, 44–71.

Cavendish, Jane

RUTH CONNOLLY

The occasional poetry of Jane Cavendish (1621–69) presents a writer whose verse reiterates the importance of familial and communal ties, particularly her personal relationship with her father, William Cavendish, first duke of Newcastle. Her play *The concealed fancyes*, co-written with her sister, Elizabeth Brackley, offers a satiric retort to the hyperbole of courtship rituals. It examines the dynamics of power between women and men and refracts these concerns through a treatment of the Civil War that emphasizes its capacity to divide families and deprive them of male figureheads. Her work makes a significant contribution to the literary tradition of royalism, early modern women's writing, and the history of collaborative authorship.

Almost all Cavendish's extant writing dates from the 1640s, although she composed both literary and religious work throughout her life. Her family highly valued its members' writings. Both her father and stepmother, Margaret Lucas Cavendish, wrote and printed a range of works and Newcastle explicitly encouraged literary ambition in all his children. The search for her father's approbation underpins all of Cavendish's writing; his absences, caused by military campaigning and later exile following the Royalist defeat prompt several poems that pay homage to him (Ezell 1988; Clarke 1999) and her deference to his critical verdict is made clear in the dedications she composed to accompany the masque and play she co-wrote with Brackley.

Cavendish's writings are preserved in two folio presentation manuscripts (Bodleian Library, MS Rawl. Poet. 16, and Beinecke Library, Osborn MS b. 233), although Greer et al. (1988) print one additional poem from a Cavendish family manuscript held at the Huntington Library. Both volumes are scribal copies, made by Newcastle's secretary, John Rolleston (Coolahan 2005) and are not, as has been supposed, in Cavendish's own hand. Both volumes share an untitled pastoral masque co-written by Brackley and Cavendish and 81 poems by Cavendish, but the Bodleian volume supplies an additional eight poems and the only copy of *The concealed fancyes*, the work for which she and Brackley are best known.

Both folios are copied after 1643, the date of Cavendish's poem on her father's military victory at Adwalton Moor, 'On the 30th of June to God', and before Cavendish's marriage to Charles Cheyne in 1654, since she is referred to throughout by her family name. The Yale manuscript has a unique copy of a dedicatory letter from Cavendish to her father and in it Cavendish speaks of 'my works', referring both to the poems and to the masque that follows them, in which each scene is annotated with the initials of either Cavendish or Brackley, making it possible to distinguish each woman's contribution. The Yale manuscript may have been intended to be more representative of Jane's work since it also contains a unique copy of an anonymous commendatory poem addressed to Cavendish which refers to her 'book of verses' and regrets that her muse remains 'in garrison', a direct reference to the siege laid by Parliamentary forces to the family home of Welbeck Abbey in 1644 and an implicit one to the deliberately limited circulation of her work.

Cavendish identifies herself as a 'wit', a term which in the period encompassed both intellectual ingenuity and creativity and represented one of the highest terms of approbation for a poet, although in the same line she asks her addressee, William Cavendish, to 'whisper't low'. Most of her poetry is occasional, composed with reference to a particular person, usually a friend or family member, or a specific event. Her work participates in a poetic culture of polite compliment and more robust complaint, invoking a literary sociability in which poetry functions as a medium of dialogue and debate as well as a means of expressing bonds of affection. Cavendish redeploys the tropes of love and religious lyrics to commend her family and lament their absence, and conflates the desire of the lover for the beloved and of the devout for God with her own hope of seeing her absent father and siblings. Her poetry also criticizes men's contradictory expectations of women's behaviour, and masculine hypocrisy is explicitly satirized in *The concealed fancyes*, as the sisters Luceny and Tatteny debate how to ensure that their husbands will treat them as well after marriage as they have during courtship. The impact of the Civil War is visible in both the play and the poems, but it is foregrounded in the masque as she and Brackley use the pastoral backdrop to dramatize the war's effects on rural smallholders and its ability to break the bonds of family and marriage. A modern edition of the play is available and a number of Cavendish's poems have been anthologized, but there is currently no edition of the poetry or the masque.

SEE ALSO: Brackley, Elizabeth; Cavendish, Margaret; Cavendish, William; Rich, Mary

REFERENCES AND SUGGESTED READINGS

Bennett, Alexandra, G. (2005) 'Now let my language speak': the authorship, rewriting and audience(s) of Jane Cavendish and Elizabeth Brackley. *Early Modern Literary Studies* 11(2). http://purl.oclc.org/emls/11-2/benncav2.htm

Bennett, Alexandra G. (2008) Filling in the picture: contexts and contacts of Jane Cavendish. *Literature Compass* 5(2), 342–352.

Clarke, Elizabeth (1999) The garrisoned muse: women's use of the religious lyric in the Civil War period. In: Summers, Claude J. & Pebworth, Ted-Larry (eds) *The English Civil Wars in the literary imagination*. University of Missouri Press, Columbia, pp. 130–143.

Coolahan, Marie-Louise (2005) Presentation volume of Jane Cavendish's poetry: Yale University, Beinecke Library Osborn b. 233. In: Millman, Jill Seal & Wright, Gillian (eds) *Early modern women's manuscript poetry*. Manchester University Press, Manchester, pp. 87–96.

Ezell, Margaret (1988) 'To be your daughter in your pen': the social functions of literature in the writings of Lady Elizabeth Brackley and Lady Jane Cavendish. *Huntington Library Quarterly* 51, 281–296.

Greer, Germaine et al. (eds) (1988) *Still kissing the rod: an anthology of seventeenth-century women's verse*. Virago, London.

Wynne-Davies, Marion (2000) 'My fine delitive tomb': liberating 'sisterly' voices during the Civil War. In: D'Monté, Rebecca & Pohl, Nicole (eds) *Female communities, 1600–1800: literary visions and cultural realities*. Macmillan Press, Basingstoke, pp. 111–128.

Cavendish, Margaret

JULIE CRAWFORD

Margaret Cavendish, duchess of Newcastle (1623–73), was the author of a singularly large volume of work. She wrote in multiple genres, including poetry, plays, stories, letters, orations, biography, and autobiography, essays, and natural and political philosophy. Her work was published in 12 large folio volumes (not including subsequent editions), with a great deal of paratextual material that both apologized for and aggressively promoted the books it prefaced, punctuated, and concluded. She was, in a fulsome sense of the term, an author, and deeply invested in both the stature of that identity and the myriad uses of printed books.

Born into the Essex gentry in 1623, Margaret Lucas was two when her father died and thereafter her mother ran the large family estate. During the English Civil Wars, the Lucas estate was plundered and (eventually) sequestered. In 1643 Margaret joined Queen Henrietta Maria's court in exile as a maid of honour, first in Oxford, and then in Paris, where she met and married her fellow exile William Cavendish, marquess of Newcastle, a widower, playwright,

and former Royalist general 30 years her senior. After their marriage they lived in heavily indebted and culturally rich exile in Paris, Holland, and Antwerp. William and his brother Sir Charles Cavendish were patrons of Thomas Hobbes and René Descartes, among others, and from 1648 to 1660, William and Margaret lived in the Antwerp house that had belonged to Peter Paul Rubens. During Margaret's exile, her mother, eldest brother, and favourite sister all died, and in 1648 her youngest brother, the Royalist lieutenant Sir Charles Lucas, was executed by the Parliamentarian regime. In 1651 she visited England to petition Parliament (without success) for income from her husband's sequestered estates, and there she began her publishing career. *Poems and fancies*, a collection of poems on natural philosophy that was also perhaps the first atomic theory of nature to be published in England, appeared in 1653 while she was still in England, and *Philosophical fancies* appeared shortly thereafter. Cavendish published three more books from exile: a third volume of natural philosophy, *Philosophicall and physical opinions* (1655), and the mixed-genre volumes *The worlds olio* (1655) and *Natures pictures* (1656).

After the Restoration in 1660, the Cavendishes returned to England and set about seeking restitution and political position from Charles II, restoring the Cavendish properties and reputation (William had been the head of the Royalist forces defeated at Marston Moor in 1644), patronizing philosophers and playwrights, and writing. Between 1660 and her death, Margaret Cavendish published several revised editions of earlier volumes and seven new books, including two more books of natural philosophy, the utopian *Description of a new world, called the Blazing World* (1666), two volumes of plays, a book of orations, a volume of letters, and the book for which she is most famous, *The life of the thrice noble, high and puissant prince, William Cavendishe* (1667). She died in 1673 and was buried in Westminster Abbey.

Cavendish's books, especially those she wrote during the Interregnum, were texts written for a coterie which sought to affirm the values of exiled Royalists in the face of Parliamentarian ascendancy and rule. For example, the frontispiece included in many copies of *Natures pictures* features the Cavendish family (Margaret had no children of her own, but William had grown children from his previous marriage), in reality divided by exile, sitting together around a table, next to the fireplace of one of William's sequestered properties. The inscription for the 1656 edition highlights the family's Royalist company-keeping during the 'cavalier winter' of Royalist exile (Miner 1971). In the inscription in the second edition, published after the Restoration, Cavendish further affirms her place in the Newcastle family, fortune, and culture; the family is gathered, she writes, 'To hear me tell them Tales, as I think fit'. Even when she is not the reader herself, Cavendish frequently presumes that her work will be read aloud for an audience. In an epistle in *The worlds olio*, she asks 'those that read any of this Book, that every Chapter may be read clearly, without long stops and staies', and she admonishes readers of her first volume of plays to read the scenes 'as if they were spoke or Acted'.

Yet in printing so many of her books, Cavendish took a different path from the more familiar modes of aristocratic female authorship exemplified by the poet Katherine Philips with her Society of Friendship and by the community-oriented writings co-authored by her stepdaughters, Jane Cavendish and Elizabeth Brackley. The publishers who produced the majority of Cavendish's works, John Martin and James Allestrye, were known for publishing cutting-edge scientific and intellectual work. Cavendish circulated her writings in carefully curated presentation volumes to a wide range of interlocutors, including the major colleges of Oxford and Cambridge and the University of Leiden, and an international roster of intellectual luminaries, including the English philosophers Henry More, Joseph Glanville, and Walter Charleton, the influential French 'trumpeter of letters' Samuel Sorbière, and the Dutch diplomat and poet Constantijn Huygens. She also took great care of her books after they were printed, amending them, often consistently across an entire print run, with manuscript corrections, printed slips identifying her husband's authorship of songs and scenes, frontispiece portraits, and manually corrected titles.

Cavendish writes frequently about the nature of her authorship, telling readers about her youthful output ('the Sixteen Books I Writ in my Childhood') and her attitude towards revision ('there is more Pleasure and Delight in making than in mending'). Most remarkable is her use of paratextual materials, particularly epistles to readers, which are overwhelmingly committed to presenting Cavendish and her books as subjects of great interest if not controversy. In an epistle in *The worlds olio*, she writes: 'Some say as I heare, that my book of Poemes, and my book of Philosophical Fancies, was not my own', a charge that she indignantly denies; and in a preface to *CCXI Sociable letters* (1664) she alludes to the various 'aspersions' cast upon her books, including her recent *Orations* (1662): 'some do Censure me for speaking too Freely, and Patronizing Vice too much'. Cavendish paints a picture of an embattled, and widely read, author. While her epistles may have been intended to 'defend my Book from spightfull Invaders', as she puts it in *Poems and fancies*, they also helped to create and promote her celebrity.

Cavendish's large and heavily mediated *oeuvre* was matched by her equally large and heavily mediated personality: indeed, the claim that she was known as 'Mad Madge of Newcastle' has become something of an emblem for her life and work – a recent biography of Cavendish is titled *Mad Madge* (Whitaker 2002). Reportedly a big talker and extravagant dresser, Cavendish certainly had some notoriety in her own time, and specific, almost obsessively cited, comments about her have been taken as descriptive. For example, after reading Cavendish's *Poems and fancies*, the Royalist letter-writer Dorothy Osborne claimed that there were 'many soberer People in Bedlam', and upon meeting with Cavendish, the correspondent Mary Evelyn said she 'was surprised to find so much extravagancy and vanity in any person not confined within four walls'. Yet these comments should be considered in context. Despite their shared Royalism, Osborne had very different political views from Cavendish, and in many ways her (soon to be) husband was competing with William Cavendish for political favour. Mary Evelyn and her husband John were part of the rising class that saw itself in competition with the aristocratic privilege the Cavendishes were so actively and anxiously promoting. The 1667 visit to London in which, according to Mary Evelyn, Cavendish went on at length 'magnifying her own generous actions, stately buildings, noble fortune, her lord's prodigious losses in the war, his power, valour, wit, learning, and industry', did indeed make Cavendish seem 'amazingly vain and ambitious' to Evelyn, yet such self-promotion was how Cavendish made her political views and desires known to the alien culture of post-Restoration London, in a context of increasingly socially dominant bourgeois women. Both Osborne and Evelyn, moreover, were writers themselves and engaged in the more typical, and politically circumspect, kinds of manuscript circulation that characterized women's literary activities in the period. (Mary Evelyn compares Cavendish, unfavourably, to Katherine Philips.) Both women may thus have considered Cavendish's mode of literary self-promotion inappropriate for a wide range of reasons, and comments that have been read as testament to Cavendish's madness, or as anti-feminist, may well have been the products of political and ideological difference and competition. Notwithstanding, Osborne and Evelyn's comments testify to Cavendish's success in keeping herself, her books, and her beliefs, in the public eye.

Much of Cavendish's notoriety, in other words, seems to have been carefully scripted. The final entry in Cavendish's 1668 volume of plays, *A piece of a play*, is something of a fictionalized record of this script. *A piece* focuses on the gossip that centres on one Lady Phoenix who is, like so many of the female characters in Cavendish's plays, a partial cipher

for Cavendish herself, and whose visit to London is clearly modelled on Cavendish's own. The appropriately named gallant Monsieur Ass reports that while he has not seen Lady Phoenix himself, he is 'credibly informed, that she is as proud as Lucifer, she despises her Superiors, and scorns her Inferiors'. In contrast, Lady Phoenix's loyal, and appropriately named, servant Dormouse offers this defence: 'She may chance to seem proud to an Ass, and vain to a Buzzard, but otherwise, she is as one of her quality ought to be.' Like Lady Phoenix, Cavendish's persona, equal parts show and political retrenchment, is best understood as a performance of appropriate aristocratic privilege. Its seeming contrast to her equally compelling representations of herself as bashful, or as a retired country housewife, need not indicate Cavendish's personal confusion about her identity; rather, it illustrates the different kinds of self-presentation that she deployed at different times and for a range of purposes in a long and creative career. By the time the diarist Samuel Pepys followed her around London in 1667 so that he 'might better understand her', Cavendish had become a figure of considerable renown. As Charles North wrote from London in the same year, 'The Dutchess Newcastle is all the pageant now discoursed on', and, according to Pepys, there was 'as much expectation of her coming to Court as if it were the Queen of Sweden'. 'The whole story of the lady', he writes with a kind of admiration, 'is a romance'.

The volume and variety of Cavendish's work is such that it is almost impossible to discern a consistent picture of who she was and what she believed. There is a tantalizing moment in one of her *Sociable letters* when she suggests that 'Writers should never speak of themselves, but in Praefatory Epistles, or in a History of their own Lives, wherein they may freely declare their own Acts and Opinions'. Yet Cavendish's epistles are more artful than 'free', and her history of her own life, *A true relation of my birth and breeding* – the story purportedly without 'Feignings' that concludes *Natures pictures* (1656) – is as generically and politically determined as anything else she wrote.

Committed to defending her family and promoting an image of herself as a worthy wife and loyal Royalist, Cavendish here describes herself as 'bashful' and tells how, after her humiliating rebuttal at parliament's door, she 'whispered' to her brother-in-law to 'conduct [her] out of this ungentlemanly place'.

Readers have been equally confused about Cavendish's views on women. There is no doubt that gender was a key concern for Cavendish; she writes about it frequently, and with great aphoristic flair. Her range of 'opinions' is dizzying, ranging from strict biological determinism – in an epistle in *Poems and fancies* she argues that female brains 'work usually in a Fantasticall motion' and 'go not so much by Rules and Methods as by Choice' – to trenchant indictments of the social inequality of the sexes. In a dedicatory letter in *Philosophical and physical opinions*, she hopes that her work will serve as 'good encouragement of our sex; lest in time we should grow irrational as idiots, by the dejectedness of our spirits, through the careless neglects and despisement of the masculine sex'. Often she recurs to images and examples of 'Heroick Women' and encourages other women in ways modern feminist critics have seen as collectivist (see, for example, the epistle 'To all Writing Ladies' in *Poems and fancies*). But much more frequently, she refers to her own singular ambition for fame: 'though I cannot be Henry the Fifth, or Charles the Second', she famously writes in an epistle to *The Blazing World*, 'yet I will endeavor to be Margaret the First'.

A range of factors influenced Cavendish's 'Opinions' on gender. The *querelle des femmes*, the ancient yet resilient literary debate in which authors attacked and defended women – and enacted a reliable strategy for selling books – clearly informs her paratextual practice. The deployment of feminist and misogynistic arguments was also a display of, and thus advertisement for, an author's rhetorical and oratorical skills. That her *Orations of* (pointedly) *diverse kinds* (1662) includes powerful examples of both sorts of argument is a reminder to consider genre and voice when attempting to determine her 'real'

opinions. Orations were, as she makes clear in her title, formal speeches 'accommodated' to specific occasions. To identify one view, no matter how powerfully presented, as Cavendish's own fails both to take account of the nature of the genre and to recognize the strategically political nature of a text that presents powerful opinions and refuses to tie them tidily, or actionably, to the author herself.

Cavendish's oft-cited desire for glory – another biography is entitled *Margaret the first* – was also concerned with more than personal, gender, or literary superiority. The desire for fame that she expresses so frequently was a trope of Interregnum Royalist culture: a statement of belief in a providentially happy ending, such as the apotheosis of one's own glory, was also a statement of belief in the restoration of the monarchy. As Hero Chalmers (2004) puts it, Royalists' 'undampened urge for fame could testify to their basic right to an "extraordinary" social status'. For Cavendish, as her Lady Phoenix mode attests, this statement of belief carried over into the Restoration context in which she and her husband still had to petition for a return to 'extraordinary' social status. Her pursuit of fame was thus intimately tied to her consciousness of social rank and political position, as well as to her sense of herself as a woman and author.

Over the course of her publishing career, Cavendish's natural philosophy changed from a firm belief in atomism, the idea that the natural world was made up of individual atoms, to vitalism, the belief in a natural world organized and cohered by a kind of vital spirit. Sylvia Bowerbank (1984) suggests that the philosophy of atomism eventually sat uncomfortably with Cavendish's sense of a natural political order; if each atom were 'absolute', Cavendish wrote in a prefatory epistle to *Philosophical opinions*, there could never be 'good government' in the universe. Her belief in nature's vital connectiveness, in which, according to Lisa Sarasohn (2010), she saw nature 'as a sort of glorified housewife who performed the work of continuous creation in a cosmos where the male deity was almost as remote as the God of Spinoza', was more in keeping with her other views.

While Cavendish frequently denies any substantive education, reading, or engagement with philosophers, her work on natural science testifies to her knowledge of and engagement with both ancient and contemporary philosophy. As Emma Rees (2003) has argued, the atomism expressed in *Poems and fancies* is derived from Epicurus, and her use of poetry to express her views aligns with Lucretius' notion that poetry can produce intellectual pleasure, the highest good. The atomism outlined in *Poems and fancies*, moreover, is also similar to that of Walter Charleton, who, as his letters included in a volume dedicated to Cavendish after her death testify, took Cavendish's own writing very seriously. Cavendish's later work, such as *Observations upon experimental philosophy* (1666), also expresses familiarity with contemporary philosophy. In addition to offering direct critiques of Baconian empiricism and Robert Hooke's influential *Micrographia* (1665), she differs explicitly from Hobbes's materialism in her belief that change in motion is caused not by external forces but rather by 'vital agreement or sympathetic influence of parts, as within a single organism' (O'Neill 2001). While Cavendish's explicit denials of scholarly influence were in keeping with her self-presentation as singular and self-authored, they also express her distance from and criticism of dominant philosophical practice, particularly empiricism. Despite being the first woman invited to visit the Royal Society in 1667 – a visit that was itself somewhat controversial – Cavendish believed as much in speculation and reflection as she did in experiment.

It is thus not surprising that Cavendish's elaborately speculative work of utopian fiction, *The Blazing World*, was originally published as part of *Observations*. The central character is a romance heroine who fortuitously becomes empress of a newly found polar kingdom resplendent with marvels. The Empress rules beautifully, fortifying the military, defending her country against its enemies, and organizing the intellectuals (such as the bear- and lice-men) into a learned society of which she is head, and, ultimately, critic. *The Blazing World*'s vision of a magical mode of female rule is certainly aristocratic nostalgia for a mythical monarchical past (Trubowitz 1992), but it is also a sharp-toothed comment on the nature of power, both scholarly and political, and an often very funny feminist fantasy.

In a wonderful narrative trick, the Empress's chief counsellor and 'scribe' is one Duchess of Newcastle, who offers the Empress sage advice. At a key moment, the Empress tells a wistfully ambitious Duchess that rather than desiring 'to be Empress of a material world, and be troubled with the cares that attend Government', she should create 'a world within [her]self' that she may enjoy 'without control or opposition'. One critic sees this imaginative and internalized resolution of the Duchess's worldly ambitions as reflecting Cavendish's own 'political quietism' and turn away from attempts to reform the external world (Battigelli 1998). Another sees it as a reflection of the monarchical ideal of the independent woman who has complete dominion over herself and her work (Trubowitz 1992; see also Gallagher 1988). Cavendish's self-inscription in *The Blazing World* serves both topical and (cheekily) impertinent ends. When the disembodied spirits of the Empress and the Duchess visit the Duke of Newcastle, the Empress expresses her desire that 'some of the gold that is in the Blazing World' might be used to repair his ruined estates.

Cavendish's dramas, like other plays written during the Interregnum, were designed for coteries of like-minded readers rather than for the public stage, and offer a Royalist critique of Parliamentarianism in keeping with the literary and political posture of retreat, nostalgia, and retrenchment that characterized the 'Cavalier winter' (Wiseman 1998; Crawford 2003; Straznicky 2004). They often invoke the idealized platonic love, pastoralism, and performing women of Queen Henrietta Maria's pre-Civil War court culture. Indeed the single-sex female community in *The convent of pleasure* (1668) references practises all three. They also frequently offer fantastic resolutions to dire political situations. The 'Kingdom of Faction' is vanquished in one play (*Bell in campo*), and a 'Masculine Synod' is stymied in another (*The convent of pleasure*). Above all, the plays celebrate and seek to entrench Royalist and aristocratic values. As Cavendish writes in the preface to the 1662 volume, 'a Poet is the best Tutor, and a Theatre is the best School that is for [noble] Youth to be educated by or in'.

Yet Cavendish's plays, particularly those published in 1668, are also significantly critical of the Restoration government (Wiseman 1998; Chalmers 2004; Crawford 2005). In *The sociable companions* (1668), the war has ended, 'Soldiers are out of Credit', and the 'poor Cavaliers' cannot get 'Offices and Employments'. Cavendish's plays thus also serve as forms of petition. Among the injustices meriting redress are the fates of the families of loyal Cavaliers who were, like Lady Poor Virtue's father, Lord Morality – and William Cavendish – killed or impoverished 'in the defence of his King and Country' (*The Lady Contemplation*, 1662).

Women often play starring roles in these fantasies of triumphalism and redress. Cavendish's characters are informed by images of the 'Heroick woman' and 'femme forte', and by the widely circulated stories of actual Royalist women who defended their estates and cause during the Civil Wars, including Henrietta Maria herself. The female Generalissimo in *Bell in campo*, head of the band of 'Heroickesses' which defeats the Kingdom of Faction, is often seen as a figure for the queen, who in a contemporary letter is referred to as 'her she-majesty Generalissima' (Chalmers 2004). Military heroines appear frequently: in *Loves adventure* (1662), the heroine Lady Orphant disguises herself as a man and becomes a great military leader, winning both acclaim for her honor and the hand of Lord Singularity. Lord Singularity is, perhaps unsurprisingly, a cipher for William Cavendish, and one of William's own songs is used to celebrate the wedding.

Cavendish's plays also affirmed her partnership with her husband. As she writes in a preface to the 1668 volume, she created the stories herself, but her husband contributed scenes and verses. '[O]ur Wits', she concludes, 'join in Matrimony.' Some have seen this claim as reflecting Cavendish's need to authorize her authorship via recourse to her husband or his status. Yet the insistent 'corrections' Cavendish made to her 1668 volume in the form of cancel slips identifying sections 'Written by My Lord Newcastle', seem instead to flag, and thus highlight, their collaboration.

Cavendish's biography of her husband is in some ways another form of this collaboration. *The life* defends William's military actions and reputation, criticizes his treatment by the post-Restoration court, and recommends him for office. It points out that 'The Lieutenancy of a County' – the only substantive office Charles II offered William – 'is barely a Title of Honour, without Profit', and includes 'a Computation of My Lord's Losses, which he hath suffered by those unfortunate Warres', an accounting that includes everything from the money he spent entertaining the king to the revenues he failed to collect while in exile. In a characteristic move, Cavendish timed the publication of *The life* to coincide with their 1667 visit to London, during which the Cavendishes intended to meet with the king and address their situation.

Cavendish understood that *The life* was competing with other histories of the period, and characterizes it as both truth-telling and non-partisan. In the epistle to her husband she promises not to 'mention any thing or passage to the prejudice or disgrace of any family or particular person', and promises in the preface not to write 'in a mystical and allegorical Style' of the treacheries of her husband's enemies, or of the 'ingratitude of some of his seeming Friends'. In the volume itself she manually inked out two sections that betrayed these promises: one that claimed that William's troops stayed on duty during the wars in spite of Charles I's failure to pay them, and one that accused two of the king's top military men of 'invigilancy and carelessness'.

Yet as James Fitzmaurice (1991) has shown, rather than eliminating the embarrassing passages, Cavendish's 'erasures' actually call attention to them; the deletions were often so light one could still make out the words underneath.

Cavendish was not just defending and promoting her husband in her biography; her investment in his reputation and property was also an investment in her own. By 1667 she was taking over the management of the Newcastle estates – she would become known as quite the rack-renter – but her own property rights were somewhat perilous (Grant 1957). Because of the destruction of the Lucas estate, her dowry, upon which women's marital property rights depended, had never been paid, and William's children were jealous of the property rights she had secured. The detailed accounting that characterizes *The life* illustrates Cavendish's skills as a scrupulous estate manager and record-keeper, and her paratexts and 'corrections' illustrate her even more valuable skills as an adept, and politic, corrector of the historical record. Officially a defence of her husband, *The life* also seeks to cement Cavendish's own role as a great property-holder and thus as a person with political rights herself.

Happily, Cavendish's political views are starting to get the attention they deserve. A volume of her writings appeared in the prestigious Cambridge Texts in the History of Political Thought series (James 2003), and readers have begun to examine the nature of her Royalism (Smith 1997; Norbrook 2000; 2004; Suzuki 2003). Cavendish was also often critical of the monarchy, particularly its more absolutist forms. More specifically, she frequently highlights the value of mixed monarchy, in which counsel, rightfully held and conferred by the nobility, is the cornerstone of political order. If *The life* advertises Cavendish's skills as a politically astute and entitled member of the nobility, moreover, her *Orations* and *Letters* present them in more generically resonant and appropriate form.

Cavendish clearly understood her *Orations* as political. In one of the epistles she points out that orations are used 'to Perswade the Auditors to be of the Orators Opinion or Belief', and that hers are 'General Orations', 'viz. such as may be spoken in any Kingdome or Government, for I suppose, that in All, at least in Most Kingdomes and Governments there are Souldiers, Magistrates, Privy-Counsellours, Lawyers, Preachers, and University Scholars' – those entrusted, in other words, with the task of providing counsel. While the orations often have predictable targets of abuse, such as the rise of the commons – 'O Powerfull Voice of a Headless Monster!' – others are critical of precisely those things that plagued the Stuart monarchies: corruption, monopolies, selling of titles and offices, and 'great taxes'. Still others take the form of direct advice 'to Soveraignes' in which succeeding speakers promote opposing monarchical styles, advising the value of 'clemency' in one, for example, and of 'Absolute Power' in its successor. Yet in her 'Orations on the Form of Government', Cavendish provides a middle way. After an oration in defence of aristocracy, and one in defence of monarchy, she offers 'An other Oration Different from the two Former' which supports neither an 'Absolute Aristocraty, nor a Monarchical Government, but a Government that shall be Mixt of the two … for as the Nobles are as the Head, to Guide, Direct, Rule, and Govern the Common People, which are as the Body; so a King, or a Chief Governour, is as the Brain to that Head.' '[A] King or Chief Ruler, Joyn'd to a Grand Counsel', the speech concludes, 'is the Best Government of all.' Cavendish's orations display her considerable intellectual and rhetorical gifts, perhaps most notably in the way they can simultaneously promote a specific political view and provide a fail-safe context of deniability.

Despite their 'sociable' moniker, Cavendish's *Sociable letters* are similarly political. In his prefatory epistle to the volume William Cavendish praises the letters as having 'The Style of States-men', identifying them with the history-writing and political-advisory functions of early modern letters. Cavendish's letters – written to another woman – valorize idealized friendship between women, and the volume presents itself as contributing to a kind of social reform and political advice-giving: the style of statesmen, that is, who happen to be women. In another prefatory epistle, Cavendish claims that she writes 'under the Cover of Letters to Express the Humours of Mankind, and the Actions of Man's Life', temporarily revealing the shadowed, and thus politically pertinent, nature of her work. The women's epistolary 'Tye in Friendship' is itself a model of political integrity, less for its recounting of the 'reports we hear of publick affairs, and of particular Persons', than for its deployment of the standard Renaissance valuation of friendship as the ideal form of political integrity and constancy.

The topics of the letters range widely from beauty to ciphered tales of political careers and marriages ('Lady M.N.' recurs frequently). The letters also make frequent allusions to barely ciphered political matters and texts. In one, she responds to her interlocutor's desire for her 'Opinion of the Lord Bs. Works' by praising them – presumably Francis Bacon's *Essays* – as fit for giving 'State-Counsel and Advice'. She also frequently presents herself as a perspicacious reader of controversial texts, praising Sir W.D.'s 'Heroic Poem' (Sir William Davenant's anti-commonwealth poem *Gondibert*), criticizing a biased history of Charles I, and referencing both Plutarch and Livy. Finally, as in the *Orations*, while Cavendish consistently praises monarchy, she just as often points out that the nobles are the 'the Pillars of … Royal Government', and insists on the necessity of good counsel. Indeed the letter-writer herself is an ideal counsellor: constant in both mind and friendship, well read, and capable of great rhetorical and ideological subtlety. Like the *Orations*, Cavendish's *Sociable letters* are both advertisement for and exemplification of Margaret Cavendish's counsel.

SEE ALSO: Bacon, Francis; Brackley, Elizabeth; Cavendish, Jane; Cavendish, William; Evelyn, John; Hobbes, Thomas; More, Henry; Philips, Katherine

REFERENCES AND SUGGESTED READINGS

Battigelli, Anna (1998) *Margaret Cavendish and the exiles of the mind*. University Press of Kentucky, Lexington.

Bowerbank, Sylvia (1984) The spider's delight: Margaret Cavendish and the 'female' imagination. *English Literary Renaissance* 14, 392–408.

Chalmers, Hero (2004) *Royalist women writers, 1650–1689*. Oxford University Press, Oxford.

Crawford, Julie (2003) Convents and pleasures: Margaret Cavendish and the drama of property. *Renaissance Drama* 32, 177–223.

Crawford, Julie (2005) 'Pleaders, attorneys, petitioners and the like': Margaret Cavendish and the dramatic petition. In: Brown, Pamela Allen & Parolin, Peter (eds) *Women players in England, 1500–1660: beyond the all-male stage*. Ashgate, Aldershot, pp. 241–260.

Fitzmaurice, James (1991) Margaret Cavendish on her own writing: evidence from revision and handmade correction. *Papers of the Bibliographical Society of America* 85, 297–307.

Gallagher, Catherine (1988) Embracing the absolute: the politics of the female subject in seventeenth-century England. *Genre* 1, 24–39.

Grant, Douglas (1957) *Margaret the first: a biography of Margaret Cavendish, duchess of Newcastle, 1623–1673*. Hart-Davis, London.

James, Susan (ed.) (2003) *Margaret Cavendish: political writings*, by Margaret Cavendish. Cambridge University Press, Cambridge.

Mendelson, Sara H. (ed.) (2009) *Margaret Cavendish*. Ashgate, Aldershot.

Miner, Earl (1971) *Cavalier mode from Jonson to Cotton*. Princeton University Press, Princeton.

Norbrook, David (2000) Margaret Cavendish and Lucy Hutchinson: identity, ideology and politics. *In-between* 9, 179–203.

Norbrook, David (2004) Women, the republic of letters, and the public sphere in the mid-seventeenth century. *Criticism* 46, 223–240.

O'Neill, Eileen (ed.) (2001) *Observations upon experimental philosophy*. Cambridge, Cambridge University Press.

Rees, Emma L. E. (2003) *Margaret Cavendish: gender, genre, exile*. Manchester University Press, Manchester.

Sarasohn, Lisa T. (2010) *The natural philosophy of Margaret Cavendish: reason and fancy during the scientific revolution*. Johns Hopkins University Press, Baltimore.

Smith, Hilda L. (1997) 'A general war amongst the men . . . but none amongst the women': political differences between Margaret and William Cavendish. In: Nenner, Howard (ed.) *Politics and the political imagination in later Stuart Britain: essays presented to Lois Green Schwoerer*. University of Rochester Press, Rochester, pp. 143–160.

Straznicky, Marta (2004) *Privacy, playreading, and women's closet drama, 1550–1700*. Cambridge University Press, Cambridge.

Suzuki, Mihoko (2003) *Subordinate subjects: gender, the political nation, and literary form in England, 1588–1688*. Ashgate, Aldershot.

Trubowitz, Rachel (1992) The reenchantment of Utopia and the female monarchical self: Margaret Cavendish's *Blazing world*. *Tulsa Studies in Women's Literature* 11, 229–246.

Whitaker, Katie (2002) *Mad Madge: the extraordinary life of Margaret Cavendish, duchess of Newcastle, the first woman to live by her pen*. Basic Books, New York.

Wiseman, Susan J. (1998) *Drama and politics in the English Civil War*. Cambridge University Press, Cambridge.

Cavendish, William

MARIE-LOUISE COOLAHAN

William Cavendish, first duke of Newcastle upon Tyne (1593–1676), writer and patron, served as a Royalist commander during the First Civil War. His intellectual and political sympathies associated him with Cavalier culture and his circle embraced the major playwrights and thinkers of the day. His poetry is typical of aristocratic manuscript culture; he composed both closet drama and plays for the London stage. His unequivocal support for the female writers of his family has stood him in good stead with feminist scholars.

Cavendish was born into a family of architectural enthusiasts. His grandmother, Elizabeth Talbot, countess of Shrewsbury (commonly known as Bess of Hardwick), masterminded the construction of Hardwick Hall in Derbyshire; his father, Charles Cavendish, began a medieval castle at Bolsover. William, who was educated for some years at Cambridge and then studied the equestrian art of *manège* with Prince Henry, proceeded with Bolsover Castle after his father's death in 1617. He managed the renovation of the family seat at Welbeck Abbey, Nottinghamshire, to include a riding house and great stable, and began work on Newcastle House, Clerkenwell, in 1630. His first wife was Elizabeth (née Bassett), widow of Henry Howard. The couple had five children who survived into adulthood.

William was an avid poet. His verses on a range of subjects – love, household life, religion, and occasional poems to friends – are preserved in the Portland Papers held at the University of Nottingham. He also composed masques and plays; Lynn Hulse (1996) has published a selection of dramatic fragments from his manuscripts. His comedy, *Witts triumvirate, or the philosopher*, was written for the king and queen in 1635, although there is no evidence of its performance. The 'Newcastle manuscript', an important compilation of masques and poetry by Ben Jonson and John Donne amongst others, was generated for Cavendish and exhibits his literary tastes (Kelliher 1993).

Cavendish's closest relationship in his role as a literary patron was with Ben Jonson. As Jonson's career waned, Cavendish remained loyal, commissioning from the playwright two masques that were performed for King Charles at Welbeck in 1633 and the following year at Bolsover. His lavish expenditure on these occasions was aimed at securing a court office, with which he was rewarded in 1638 when he was appointed governor to Prince Charles, a post he held until 1641. Two of his dramatic comedies, *The varietie* (written in collaboration with James Shirley) and *The country captaine*, were performed by the King's Men at Blackfriars Theatre between 1639 and 1642.

Cavendish became commander of Royalist forces in the north during the First Civil War, leading their victory at Adwalton Moor in June 1643. But he suffered ignominious defeat at Marston Moor in July the following year, after which he left for the Continent. He headed initially for the Netherlands, and arrived at Queen Henrietta Maria's court in

Paris by April 1645. There he met and married his second wife Margaret Lucas, maid-of-honour to the queen. (His first wife, Elizabeth, had died in April 1643.) The love poems he wrote during this courtship are available in a modern edition (Grant 1956). His poems praising her as an author are included in the prefatory material to many of her published works: *Poems and fancies* (1653), *Philosophical and physical opinions* (1655), *The worlds olio* (1655), *Natures pictures* (1656), *Orations of divers sorts* (1662), *Plays* (1662), *Philosophical letters* (1664), *Sociable letters* (1664), *Observations upon experimental philosophy to which is added the description of a new blazing world* (1666).

The couple moved to Antwerp in 1648, where they resided in the former home of the artist Peter Paul Rubens. Cavendish converted the studio into a riding house, where visitors from across Europe flocked to see this famous equestrian. Here, Cavendish wrote his horseriding manual *La méthode nouvelle et invention extraordinaire de dresser les chevaux* (Antwerp, 1658), later published in English in 1667. In 1658 he collaborated with Nicholas Lanier on a royal entertainment, staged at his Antwerp home. Cavendish and his younger brother Charles, a mathematician, had long been interested in the new philosophy. In exile, his intellectual circle included Thomas Hobbes, Pierre Gassendi, René Descartes, and Marin Mersenne.

The Cavendishes returned to London in summer 1660, when William composed a royal entertainment for King Charles II (Hulse 1995). About this time, he also wrote a letter of advice to the king (Slaughter 1984). Despite being created first duke of Newcastle in 1665, Cavendish found that his services were not required at the restored royal court, and retired from public life. He continued to write poetry and plays. *The country captaine* was revived four times on the London stage between 1661 and 1668, and *The varietie* in 1669. The Duke of York's company, founded by William Davenant (who had served in Cavendish's army), staged two further plays: *The humorous lovers* in 1667 and *The triumphant widow* in 1674. Thomas Shadwell (who dedicated four of his plays to Cavendish) supervised the posthumous publication of both plays in 1677. John Dryden's *Sir Martin Marr-All*, performed in 1667, was based on Cavendish's translation of Molière's *L'Etourdi*.

Following his wife's death in 1673, Cavendish threw himself into a new architectural project, Nottingham Castle, which was unfinished at the time of his death in 1676, though instructions for its completion were left to his heirs. The couple were buried in Westminster Abbey.

Currently, Margaret Cavendish's literary legacy far outshadows that of Cavendish himself, and his daughters' writings have garnered increasing attention. His drama has benefited from a number of modern editions. Barbara Ravelhofer's recent study (2006) of *The varietie* locates the play in relation to Caroline masque culture. Modern scholarship has focused on his intellectual circle and patronage (Raylor 1994). His colourful life was first detailed by his second wife (Firth 1886). His most recent biographer argues for the significance of his architectural legacy (Worsley 2007).

SEE ALSO: Brackley, Elizabeth; Cavendish, Jane; Cavendish, Margaret; Davenant, William; Donne, John; Dryden, John; Hobbes, Thomas; Jonson, Ben; Shirley, James

REFERENCES AND SUGGESTED READINGS

Firth, C. H. (ed.) (1886) *The life of William Cavendish duke of Newcastle, to which is added the true relation of my birth, breeding, and life,* by Margaret Cavendish. London

Grant, Douglas (ed.) (1956) *The Phanseys of William Cavendish, marquis of Newcastle, addressed to Margaret Lucas, and her letters in reply.* Nonesuch Press, London.

Hulse, Lynn (1995) 'The king's entertainment' by the duke of Newcastle. *Viator* 26, 355–405.

Hulse, Lynn (ed.) (1996) *Dramatic works by William Cavendish.* Malone Society, Oxford.

Kelliher, Hilton (1993) Donne, Jonson, Richard Andrews and the Newcastle manuscript. *English Manuscript Studies 1100–1700* 4, 134–173.

Ravelhofer, Barbara (2006) Non-verbal meaning in Caroline private theatre: William Cavendish's and James Shirley's *The varietie* (c.1641). *Seventeenth Century* 21, 195–214.

Raylor, Timothy (ed.) (1994) The Cavendish circle. *Seventeenth Century* (special issue) 9(2).

Slaughter, Thomas P. (ed.) (1984) *Ideology and politics on the eve of the Restoration: Newcastle's advice to Charles II*. American Philosophical Society, Philadelphia.

Trease, Geoffrey (1979) *Portrait of a cavalier: William Cavendish, first duke of Newcastle*. Macmillan, London.

Worsley, Lucy (2007) *Cavalier: A tale of chivalry, passion and great houses*. Faber & Faber, London.

Caxton, William

MEAGHAN BROWN

William Caxton (1415/24–1492), the first Englishman to print books, was an accomplished merchant, diplomat, and translator, and is now best known for bringing the printing press to England in 1475 or 1476. His activities in importing, translating, and printing books significantly shaped the book trade and the literary public in England.

Much information regarding Caxton's life is derived from the prologues and epilogues of his printed works. His birthplace is taken from the introduction to his first published book (*The recuyell of the historyes of Troye*) where he uses it to defend the quality of his translation, declaring that he 'was born & lerned myn englissh in kente in the weeld where I doubte not is spoken as brode and rude englissh as is in ony place of englond'. The date range for his birth, between 1415 and 1424, is determined from the Mercers' Company warden's book entry for the payment of his apprenticeship fees on 24 June 1438, sometime after Caxton turned 14. His apprenticeship to the important and wealthy merchant Robert Large, who became lord mayor of London just a year after Caxton's fee was recorded, has led scholars to speculate that Caxton's family was wealthy. Caxton spent over 20 years abroad in the Low Countries and served as the governor of the English merchant population at Bruges. He lived and traded in several major cities, including Bruges, Utrecht, Ghent, and Cologne, where he learned the art of printing in the early 1470s. He was the first to publish a book in English, *The recuyell of the historyes of Troye*, which he printed in Bruges in late 1473 or early 1474. Caxton returned to England by 1476, perhaps as early as 1475, bringing with him a printing press and a thorough knowledge of fashionable and profitable publication practices. He settled in the city of Westminster, where he continued to print until within a year of his death in 1492.

Caxton was a mercer, an occupation that positioned him to be well connected and cosmopolitan. The mercers were an influential guild of merchants who dealt in the luxury goods trade, specializing in silk, linen, and fustian (a combination of linen and cotton). They also traded in small goods such as dress fittings, purses, and books. The Mercers' Company was the principal group in charge of the Merchant Adventurers' Company, a loose conglomerate of merchants who often served as agents of their government abroad, and were involved in negotiations between England, France, and the Low Countries. Caxton, apprenticed to an important member of the Mercers' Company, would have learned not only how to handle money and conduct trade negotiations, but also how to speak Dutch and French and conduct himself among people of several nationalities and stations in life.

By the mid-1450s Caxton had gained a reputation as a merchant and amassed significant capital. He moved to Bruges, a cosmopolitan trading city in the duchy of Burgundy, no later than 1453 and possibly earlier; a document from Bruges dated January 1450 cites him as surety for another merchant, John Granton, for the sum of £150. This substantial amount indicates that Caxton was already in a position of responsibility within the English merchant community in Bruges, and had probably been trading there for some time. For the next 20 years, Caxton led the life of the merchant adventurer abroad. While he probably made visits to England, he relied primarily upon factors, or mercantile agents, to manage his business there.

Caxton's trading ventures in the Low Countries were highly successful, and by April of 1465 he was elected governor of the merchant adventurers in Bruges, a position that entailed arbitrating disputes between English merchants abroad, disciplining them, and advocating for them with local officials. He was probably involved in trade negotiations on behalf of the English crown when a new treaty between England and the duchy of Burgundy was arbitrated in 1467. This treaty was confirmed with the marriage of Charles, duke of Burgundy, to Margaret, the sister of Edward IV of England in 1468. Caxton's last recorded act as governor occurs in 1470, around the time of his first recorded foray into translation, which would become *The recuyell of the historyes of Troye.*

Caxton actually published two editions of the *Recuyell,* an English translation (Bruges, ?1473–74) and the original French (Bruges, ?1474–75). Raoul Le Fèvre composed his version of the Troy story, *Le recueil des histoires de Troyes,* based on Guido delle Colonne's *Historia Troiana,* in 1464 and circulated it in manuscript in the ducal court and beyond (Blake 1985). Burgundy was well known for the production of fine manuscripts, which formed a significant export product for the region. As a mercer, Caxton's intimate interactions with local scriveners, merchants, and the court provided access to the most fashionable manuscript books. Caxton began his translation of this trendy work after it had established its popularity with the upper crust of Bruges society, making it something of a safe bet for later sale in England. This became a frequent pattern in Caxton's publications: translating and printing works that were successful in France and Burgundy for English readers.

Le Fèvre, a secretary in the Burgundian court, had dedicated the work to Duke Philip, Duke Charles's father. Caxton dedicated his English edition to Margaret, Charles's wife. The importance and critical function of Margaret of Burgundy, Caxton's purported patron for his first English book, has generated a great deal of scholarly debate. In his introduction, Caxton declares that he has translated the work 'at the comaundement of the right hye myghty and vertuouse Pryncesse hys redoubtyd lady. Margarete by the grace of god. Duchesse of Bourgoyne of Lotryk of Braband.' Claiming that he had given up the translation in despair of his poor French and uncouth English, Caxton asserts that Margaret ordered him to finish the translation after approving its high quality. Because manuscript copies of many of the works he later translated were found in the library of the ducal court, some scholars have taken this 'command' of Margaret's to indicate that she provided him with monetary support and exemplars for his new venture. Flemish manuscript books were the type of items Caxton already dealt in as a mercer, however, and he probably had access to these texts without her official patronage. In addition, dedicating the book to Margaret, sister of the sitting king of England, may have been an adept marketing tool rather than a sign that Caxton expected the sort of remuneration associated with formal patronage (Rutter 1987). Claiming the duchess's approval linked the work with the erudite, fashionable qualities of the Burgundian court, an aesthetic claim rather than a claim on her finances.

Begun in Bruges in 1469/70, the translation of the *Recuyell* was finished in Cologne in 1471, just up the Rhine. Printing had arrived in the area by 1464; Caxton may have had dealings with Cologne in his role as governor and would have known of the output of Cologne's presses. Caxton's move to Cologne was recorded in the register of aliens, and he was given permission to reside in the city from 17 July 1471 until December 1472. He was clearly still acting as a mercer in this period, which provided him with the funds to acquire practical printing experience. Caxton entered into a business partnership with the printer Johannes Schilling and the printer and typecutter Johannes Veldener (Hellinga 2002). Caxton's financing made possible the printing of Bartholomaeus Anglicus's colossal encyclopedia, *De proprietatibus rerum* (1471/72). The folio edition was much larger than Veldener's previous publications and would have required a significant outlay of capital for the paper stocks alone (the work ran to 248 folio leaves, compared to his two earlier works of 58 and 22 leaves). Caxton probably collaborated with Veldener as well on the *Gesta Romanorum* (?1473) (Blake 1991). He would have learned from Schilling and Veldener the techniques and requirements of running a printing shop, and in Cologne he acquired a press, type, and men skilled in manipulating both. In 1472 Caxton returned to Bruges, accompanied by Veldener and possibly the printers Wynkyn de Worde and Colard Mansion. There he set up a shop and printed the first book in English, the *Recuyell*, in late 1473 or early 1474. The books were then exported to England for sale, using the same outlet channels as Burgundian manuscripts before them. The *Recuyell* would have a lasting presence: this first printed Troy book was reprinted 11 times before the eighteenth century.

As he was the first publisher to focus on the English market, Caxton's selections had a broad and lasting impact on English literature. He returned to England with a press and workmen sometime after 4 September 1475, and set up his shop at the sign of the Red Pale in the Almonry of Westminster Abbey (Hellinga 1982). His earliest printing probably consisted of jobbing work – the small, ephemeral printing jobs that were paid up front – and a number of undated quarto pamphlets. One of these pamphlets, a short poetic compilation of mostly Chaucerian texts, known either by its first line, *Thou fiers god of armes, mars the rede*, or the standardized title of one of its component poems, *Anelida and Arcite* (?1477), contains the famous 'compleint of Chaucer unto his empty purse', an apt

inclusion for a short work which probably provided a quick return on the investment in paper and labour. Caxton's first major undertaking, although undated, was a folio edition of Chaucer's *The Canterbury tales* (?1476) (Needham 2007). Through the end of the 1470s, Caxton would print a series of works by Chaucer and Lydgate, ranging from individual poems in small pamphlet formats to Chaucer's translation of Boethius's *De consolatione philosophiae*.

Caxton's shop was never devoted to only one author or genre, however. Evidence from the watermarks in his paper stock indicates that the publication of the last quires of *The Canterbury tales* and the short quarto edition of Lydgate's *Temple of glas* (?1477) are contemporary with his edition of the Latin *Horae ad usum Sarum*, a perennial bestseller in the manuscript market, and the *Sarum ordinale*, a book that contained the Mass and divine office of the Sarum Use (Needham 2007). The large *Canterbury tales* would have been a significant investment of time and capital – after all, the paper had to be bought and printed before any money could be recouped – and a variety of shorter works produced at the same time would have helped to maintain the flow of money necessary for daily expenses.

From this early phase of production survives the earliest English book advertisement. Even works as well known as the Sarum Use, required for every church, cannot be sold if no one knows where to buy them. To remedy this problem, Caxton created a broadsheet advertisement which reads:

> If it plese ony man spirituel or temporel to bye ony pyes of two and thre comemoracions of salisburi vse enpryntid after the forme of this present lettre whiche ben wel and truly correct / late hym come to westmonester in to the almonesrye at the reed pale and he shal haue them good chepe. / Supplico stet cedula.

Meant to be posted around town – the Latin line which ends the piece asks that it 'please be left posted' – the advertisement served to inform customers where they might find his shop and promoted one of its chief selling points. For a buying public used to examining the quality of a manuscript hand before purchasing a book, the advertisement provided possible purchasers with a sample of the font used in Caxton's work, 'the forme of the present lettre'. Perhaps more importantly, it emphasized that his works were 'good chepe'.

By the 1480s, Caxton had competition in the form of printers operating in England, in addition to merchants who continued to import books from the Continent. Printers established themselves in Oxford, St Albans, and London; with the possible exception of the St Albans Schoolmaster Printer (about whom we know nothing except that Wynkyn de Worde referred to him as 'sometyme scole master of Saynt Albans'), these printers were all foreign-born and relied on English financial backers (Kuskin 2008). Caxton's ability to be both printer and financier allowed him flexibility with his printing programme. His new competition, like their Continental counterparts, focused primarily on Latin works and when they did move into English vernacular writings, their product often followed Caxton's lead either in subject matter or as reprints of his actual texts.

Thus Caxton's output from the 1480s would come to define the English canon for generations. He published major editions of Chaucerian poetry, including a new illustrated *Canterbury tales* (1483), the *Book of fame* (1483), and *Troilus and Criseyde* (1483). He also published major works in translation, including classics such as his own translation of *Aesop's fables* (1484), John Tiptoft, earl of Worcester's translation of Cicero's *De amicitia* and *De nobilitate*, which Caxton printed with Stephen Scrope's translation of *De senectute* (1481), and religious works like the monumental *Legenda aurea*, which Caxton translated as the *Golden legend* (1487). He printed Thomas Malory's romance *Le morte d'Arthur* (1485) with the claim that readers of his edition of Ranulf Higden's *Polychronicon* (1482), a major chronicle which included the Arthurian legend

as history, had requested he produce a work on Arthur. He was the first to print the story of the *Aeneid*, although his *Eneydos* (1490) was a romance derived not from the Latin but from Guillaume le Roy's French *Le livre des Eneydes* (1483).

Caxton also published works which are less known today, but which resonated through the literate culture of the English Renaissance in the form of multiple republications, allusions, and references. He published a number of schoolbooks and books of manners, including Lydgate's English *Stans puer ad mensam* (?1476), one of the early quarto pamphlets. In 1480 he printed the first dictionary, a dual-column French–English word list. Translations from French brought a number of popular works to English readers: Anthony Woodville's *The dictes, or sayengis of the philosophhres* (1477, 1489), a set of famous biographies originally composed in Arabic; Christine de Pizan's *Morale proverbes* (1478), a collection of moral truisms; and Alain Chartier's *Curial* (1483), a famous critique of court life. Caxton also published at least two works in the popular genre of the *ars moriendi*, *The arte [and] crafte to knowe well to dye* (1490), probably translated from French, and *The craft for to deye for the helthe of mannes sowle* (1491), probably translated from Latin (Blake 1985).

While not all of Caxton's publications have survived, translation into English was involved in a majority of the approximately 80 known works. Of these, the majority are from French, although there are a substantial number of Latin works and at least one from Dutch, *Reynart the foxe* (1481). There is no evidence that Caxton attempted any translations prior to beginning work on the *Recuyell*. Rather, as scholars such as N. F. Blake (1991) and A. E. B. Coldiron (2008) have argued, Caxton's venture into translation and his acquisition of the printing press were two parts of a premeditated programme that provided both the means of production and the seed material for a lucrative new business venture. The proven market potential of translations of works popular in the Burgundian manuscript-book market, together with a thoughtful selection of English poets and practical works, provided financial grounding for Caxton's programme of printing in English for English buyers.

The accounts of St Margaret's Church, Westminster, record the burial of William Caxton sometime in March 1492. Caxton's last printed work was probably the *Fifteen Oes* (1491). However, his assistant Wynkyn de Worde took over the rent of his shop in Westminster Abbey in 1491/92 and began printing immediately with Caxton's device, founts, and woodcuts. Consequently, there is a series of works printed in 1491 that could be attributed to either printer. As late as 1494 de Worde continued to use Caxton's name as a selling point, noting that a work was 'sette in printe in William Caxtons hows'.

Caxton was a canny and cosmopolitan businessman. He experimented with the market for printing in Latin and French while on the Continent, but made his mark publishing English works and English translations for English readers, first importing from the Continent and subsequently translating and bringing the production to England itself. He was perfectly capable of publishing in other languages; indeed, at least 15 editions of Latin works survive, as well as four editions of French works from his time in Bruges. Current research into his dealings with translators, patrons, and other printers is shedding new light on Caxton's working methods, but it is generally agreed that his choices shaped the English literary canon well into the Tudor period and beyond.

SEE ALSO: anonymity

REFERENCES AND SUGGESTED READINGS

Blake, N. F. (1985) *William Caxton: a bibliographical guide.* Garland, New York.

Blake, N. F. (1991) *William Caxton and English literary culture.* Hambledon Press, London.

Blake, N. F. (2004a) Caxton, William. In: *Oxford dictionary of national biography.* Oxford University Press, Oxford.

Blake, N. F. (2004b) Worde, Wynkyn de. In: *Oxford dictionary of national biography.* Oxford University Press, Oxford.

Coldiron, A. E. B. (2008) William Caxton. In: Ellis, R. (ed.) *The Oxford history of literary translation in English,* vol. 1: *To 1550* Oxford University Press, Oxford, pp. 160–169.

Hellinga, Lotte (1982) *Caxton in focus: the beginning of printing in England.* British Library, London.

Hellinga, Lotte (2002) Printing. In: Hellinga, Lotte & Trapp, J. B. (eds) *The Cambridge history of the book in Britain: 1400–1557.* Cambridge University Press, Cambridge, pp. 65–108.

Kuskin, William (2008) *Symbolic Caxton: literary culture and print capitalism.* University of Notre Dame Press, Notre Dame.

Needham, Paul (2007) The paper of English incunabula. In: *Catalogue of books printed in the XVth century now in the British Library.* British Museum Catalogue part XI. Hes & de Graaf, 't Goy-Houten, pp. 311–334.

Raven, James (2007) *The business of books.* Yale University Press, New Haven.

Rutter, Russell (1987) William Caxton and literary patronage. *Studies in Philology* 84, 440–470.

Sutton, Anne F. (1994) Caxton was a mercer: his social milieu and friends. In: Rogers, Nicholas (ed.) *England in the fifteenth century: Proceedings of the 1992 Harlaxton Symposium.* Paul Watkins, Stamford, pp. 118–148.

Chaloner, Thomas

TIMOTHY D. CROWLEY

Sir Thomas Chaloner, the elder (1521–65), worked within a milieu of Englishmen who adapted to shifting structures for political and religious authority in the mid-sixteenth century. He studied at Cambridge and by 1538 worked for Henry VIII's secretary Thomas Cromwell. In 1540, he accompanied Henry Knyvet at the imperial diet in Regensberg. From there, Chaloner joined the entourage of Holy Roman Emperor Charles V for a military venture in 1541 to Algeria, where he experienced shipwreck and, apparently, saved himself by hanging onto a rescue cable with his teeth after he could swim no longer (Blazer 1978). In 1545 he undertook brief diplomatic service in Spain and then became a clerk for the Privy Council. In the first year of Edward VI's reign, Chaloner helped lead England's victory over Scottish forces at the battle of Pinkie on 10 September 1547 and was knighted for that service by Edward Seymour, duke of Somerset and lord protector of England (Miller 1965; Blazer 1978). Another veteran of that battle, William Cecil, who also remained in England under the Marian regime, became a lifelong friend. When Chaloner died on 14 October 1565, he entrusted Cecil with the execution of his will and with the education of his stepson (Miller 1965; Blazer 1978). In 1557/58, Chaloner fought for Mary and Philip in their war with France, and from 1558 until 1565, he served Queen Elizabeth first as special ambassador in Germany and Flanders, then as resident ambassador in Spain.

Chaloner's literary activity complemented his service to these four Tudor monarchs, and his works often comment on political history and policy. Towards the end of Henry VIII's reign, he praised that monarch's character and policies with an epic poem in Latin, *In laudem Henrici octaui*. This panegyric ascribes to Henry the virtue of balanced military force and diplomacy amidst shifting conflicts and allegiances with French king François I and Charles V; it characterizes his government of England as stern but just; and it defends both his heavy taxation and his religious reform as prudent for the defence of the realm and for the liberation of the English people from a corrupted monastic institution. The latter section of the poem refers to the printing press as an agent for religious reformation. In the early 1550s, Chaloner seems to have associated himself with George Ferrers, a fellow veteran from the battle of Pinkie who also had worked for Cromwell in 1538, and other literary acquaintances such as Thomas Wilson, Barnabe Googe, Thomas Sackville, Thomas Phaer, and William Baldwin, who called upon Chaloner, Ferrers, and Phaer as contributors

to *A mirrour for magistrates* in 1554 (Miller 1965; Blazer 1978; Lucas 2009). The ghostly voice of Richard II that Chaloner contributed to Baldwin's *Mirrour*, not printed until after Mary Tudor's death, warns about the delicate nature of monarchical authority contingent upon the consent of willing subjects (Lucas 2009). Upon Elizabeth's accession, Chaloner revised *In laudem Henrici octaui* and presented a printed copy to the queen as a New Year's gift. The poem concludes with praise for all three children who ruled in Henry's wake, followed by entreaty that Elizabeth marry as a means to secure continuity for the Tudor dynasty. In the early 1560s, while serving Elizabeth as ambassador in Spain, Chaloner composed a second epic poem in Latin hexameters on the topic of Tudor English history, *De republica Anglicorum instauranda*, edited by William Malim and printed with *In laudem Henrici octaui* in 1579. That collection and certain state papers preserve shorter Latin poems written by Chaloner, including a lamentation of Lady Jane Grey's death in 1554.

As a translator, Chaloner produced the first English rendition of Erasmus's *Moriae encomium*, first printed as *The praise of folie* in 1549. That project followed prior translations: *Of the office of seruauntes* (1543) and *An homilie of Saint Iohñ Chrysostome* (1544). Chaloner rendered certain poems from Boethius's *The consolation of philosophy* into English verse, perhaps associating the speaker's 'banishment' mentioned in the first poem of book I with his own distance from England while living in Spain. From Ovid's *Heroides*, he translated the epistle 'Helen to Paris', preserved in a manuscript copy at the British Library (Additional MS 36529). Chaloner's diplomatic correspondence reveals that, by June 1563, his 'doings in our English rhyme' also included certain verses 'out of Ariosto'. Presumably, given his investment in heroic poetry, he translated portions of *Orlando furioso*.

Chaloner's Latin poetry was well received among educated circles in England and in Spain (Miller 1965). George Puttenham,

Francis Meres, and John Aubrey praised him among sixteenth-century English poets.

SEE ALSO: Baldwin, William; Ferrers, George; Googe, Barnabe; Meres, Francis; Puttenham, George; Sackville, Thomas, earl of Dorset; Wilson, Thomas

REFERENCES AND SUGGESTED READINGS

Blazer, Phyllis Gene (1978) The life of Sir Thomas Chaloner. PhD dissertation, State University of New York at Buffalo.

Lucas, Scott C. (2009) 'A mirror for magistrates' and the politics of the English Reformation. University of Massachusetts Press, Amherst.

Miller, Clarence H. (1965) Introduction. In: Miller, Clarence H. (ed.) The praise of Folie, by Desiderius Erasmus; trans. Thomas Chaloner. Early English Text Society, London, pp. xiii–li.

Chapman, George

ANDREW FLECK

George Chapman (1559/60–1634) may almost literally have been born with a silver spoon in his mouth, but the defining humour of his life must have been anxious and uncertain poverty. A prolific playwright, an innovative poet, an autodidactic translator, and a mercenary soldier, Chapman pieced together a tenuous existence on the edge of destitution. Despite his many brushes with misfortune, Chapman did find a few loyal patrons whose support allowed him to complete the work for which he is probably best known, the first English translation of Homer.

Chapman, whose maternal grandfather served Henry VIII, was the second son of a Hertfordshire yeoman of declining fortunes. As a young man, Chapman spent some time at Oxford without taking a degree. He briefly entered the service of Sir Ralph Sadler, who rose to prominence in the reign of Henry VIII and was reputedly the wealthiest commoner in the land when he died in 1587. Bereft of that avenue of advancement and in debt to an unscrupulous moneylender, Chapman joined the English forces fighting the Habsburg armies in the Low Countries. He returned to England a few years later and, scorning the 'prophane multitude', began to write learned, metaphysical poetry while searching for patronage. As a younger son, he did not inherit his family's property; in fact, his father left him only a silver spoon and a small monetary bequest. Perhaps the need for immediate cash drove him to the theatre. By the mid-1590s, in addition to generating speculative dedications of his first partial translations of Homer, Chapman was writing comedies for Philip Henslowe, owner of the Rose playhouse, and later for the children's companies. He continued to live hand to mouth, being imprisoned for his debts in 1600. He also ran afoul of the law for some of his provocative dramatic productions and seems to have left the theatre by around 1611. He had been given a minor position in the household of Prince Henry in 1604 and trusted that this patron would secure his future. When the young prince, who had patronized many aspiring poets, died suddenly in 1612, Chapman found himself in renewed financial straits. He again went to debtors' prison after receiving inadequate compensation for his contribution to the Memorable masque (1613), celebrating the marriage of Henry's sister Elizabeth to the elector palatine. His next patron, the king's young favourite Robert Carr, earl of Somerset, did not provide the safe haven he sought, for a scandal about the earl and his murderous wife came to light almost immediately and made some of Chapman's verse – in its praise of the lovers' temperate chastity – seem quite tactless. Chapman seems to have quarrelled with Ben Jonson, and when the irascible Jonson and Inigo Jones themselves quarrelled over the essence of courtly masques, he sided with Jones, but his ongoing financial difficulties strained even that relationship. Retreating from the expensive metropolis to the neighbourhood of his birth, Chapman continued his translations of Homer, though he would be forced to return to London occasionally to defend himself against suits for his debts. He died in London in 1634.

Modern readers usually encounter Chapman in one of three arenas. His dramatic works are among the most innovative in the age of Shakespeare. Even during his own lifetime, Chapman was recognized as one of the great English playwrights, mildly caricatured for his self-promotion in Thomas Dekker and John Webster's *North-ward hoe* (1605) Chapman's early writing for the stage began with one of the period's most popular comedies, *The blinde begger of Alexandria*, written for the Admiral's Men in 1596. It focuses on the comic deceptions and love plots of Irus, a low-born fortune-teller whose chameleon abilities made him many different things to different people. Henslowe's diary records an extraordinary number of performances in just its first run at the Rose and the comedy was revived again in 1601; the printed text presents a defective version. Chapman followed this success with *An humerous dayes myrth* (1597), an innovative play that began a vogue for 'humours' comedies – Ben Jonson would further popularize the form and Shakespeare would parody it in the Eastcheap figures of the Henriad – at the end of the century. Henslowe records additional payments to Chapman for another Admiral's Men play, *All fools but the fool, or the world runs a' wheels* (1599), which may have been revised in 1601 and printed in 1605 as *All fools*. Following Chapman's brief incarceration for debt, he redirected his talents towards the coterie theatres of the City of London, writing primarily for the boys' companies. In addition to *All fools*, Chapman wrote several popular comedies for the Blackfriars Theatre, including *May-day* (1601/2), *Sir Gyles Goosecappe* (1602), *The gentleman usher* (1602/3), *The widdowes teares* (1604/5), and *Monsieur D'Olive* (1605).

In addition to his financial difficulties, Chapman's unwise choices of material for his dramas also caused him to run afoul of the law. One lost comedy, *The old joiner of Aldgate* (1603), capitalized on a local scandal involving deceptive marriage negotiations in the neighbourhood near St Paul's (where it was performed) and caused trouble for Chapman and the players when the humiliated parties brought a lawsuit against them. In one of the most celebrated instances of Chapman's reckless contributions to satiric comic drama, he joined with Jonson and John Marston in writing a city comedy called *Eastward hoe* (1605). The play, a comic intrigue of adulterous plots, satirized the merchant citizens and other stereotypical figures of the City of London as well as the foolish schemes of ambitious gentlemen and city wives – the central plot involves the impoverished Sir Petronel Flash's duping of the vain and pretentious daughter of a wealthy London goldsmith – but dallied with controversial material in its satirical excess. Performed while King James and his court were away from London, the play commented on the king's own scheme to acquire new revenues by selling titles and mocked the influx of stereotypically impoverished Scots after 1603. For their transgressions, Chapman and Jonson were imprisoned; Chapman wrote to the king to pin the blame for the most stinging lines on Marston, who had escaped the arm of the law. His claim that their 'chief offences are but two clauses, and both of them not our own', must have succeeded in saving Chapman and Jonson from the physical disfigurement with which they were threatened. Eventually they were released, but when the play was printed, its most upsetting lines, which referred satirically to the 'industrious Scots', were censored and rewritten.

As with his city comedies, Chapman's tragedies also caused legal difficulties for him. The playwright took much of his inspiration for tragedy from recent French history, aided in part by texts written by his kinsman Edward Grimeston. In the most controversial of his tragedies, a two-part play called *The conspiracie and tragedie of Charles duke of Byron* (1608), Chapman represented the rise and fall of an influential French nobleman, Charles, duc de Biron. Biron, who was appointed marshal general of France, had been a key military figure in the rise of Henri IV during the French civil wars, but became involved in a variety of treasonous intrigues against his monarch. In the *Conspiracie*, the king recognizes Byron's importance and succeeds in curbing his plots, but in the *Tragedy*, Byron can no longer be redeemed. Convicted of his crimes, a defiant Byron ascends the scaffold and makes a half-hearted submission, cautioning others to 'Fall on your knees' in repentance 'ere ye fall' permanently from greatness. At the same time he remarks that 'danger haunts desert when he is greatest' and urges his unvanquished soul to 'Bear the eternal victory of Death!' In this tragedy, Chapman again crossed a line with the authorities, not least because Biron had received an audience in 1600 with Queen Elizabeth as Henri IV's ambassador. His arrogant plotting had attracted popular comparisons with the Queen's own erratic earl marshal, Robert Devereux, second earl of Essex, whose abortive uprising in 1601 had led to his execution. Chapman's scene of Elizabeth and Biron's meeting may have been too sensitive for the authorities. Moreover, Chapman's play dramatized a living, foreign monarch, which violated a prohibition against staging living kings. And finally, taking advantage of the authorities' temporary absence from London for Lent, Chapman added a scene in a March 1608 performance of the *Tragedie* in which Henri IV's wife and his mistress, Madame de Verneuil, confronted each other, trading insults and fisticuffs. This last scene was too much for the French ambassador, who had already complained about the initial, mildly censored production of the plays. An irate King James appeased the ambassador by incarcerating three of the actors. A diligent effort was made to arrest Chapman, but the playwright found refuge with one of the king's favourites, Ludovic Stuart, second duke of Lennox. Chapman petitioned to have the plays printed, despite the uproar he had caused, and the censored tragedies appeared later that year.

Despite his notoriety with authorities – he may also have been a collaborator with Jonson on the controversial tragedy *Sejanus* (1603) – Chapman's tragedies have suffered critical neglect. At the heart of these plays, Chapman demonstrates a commitment to Stoic philosophical ideals, particularly to his exhibition of the 'Senecal Man'. He wrote other tragedies based in French history, such as *Chabot, admirall of France* (1611/12) – set in the time of Francois I, a play printed posthumously (1639) probably with revisions by James Shirley – and the very popular *Bussy D'Ambois* (1603/4) – set in the time of Henri III – and a sequel based on a fictional brother of Bussy, *The revenge of Bussy D'Ambois* (1610/11). For his other great tragedy, Chapman drew on classical Roman history, dramatizing the consolidation of Julius Caesar's power in *Caesar and Pompey* (1604). Here Chapman most clearly articulates the heroic ideals of his tragic figures who confront mutable fortune with Stoic equanimity. Dramatizing Caesar's ambition and his contest with Pompey for dominion in Rome, the tragedy highlights the virtue of the Stoic Cato the Younger, who allies with Pompey to try to prevent Caesar's rise. Although Caesar defeats his rivals at Pharsalus, Cato refuses to acknowledge Caesar's victory, choosing suicide as a way to 'conquer conquering Caesar', and declaring with his last breath: 'Just men are only free, the rest are slaves.' This articulation of Stoic ideals and resistance to tyranny runs throughout Chapman's tragic works.

Modern readers may also know Chapman through his innovative, often metaphysical poetry. His own peers recognized his preeminence as a poet. In 1598 Francis Meres listed Chapman among those poets who 'mightily enriched' the English language and produced poetry 'gorgeously invested in rare ornaments and resplendent habiliments'. And when Robert Allot compiled his printed commonplace book, *Englands Parnassus* (1600), he included more than 80 passages from Chapman to illustrate the collection's topics. While Chapman was one of the most recognized poets of the age, he cultivated an air of exclusivity, disdaining the understanding and applause of the vulgar, common readers. As he announced at the beginning of his poetic career: 'I rest as resolute as Seneca, satisfying myself if but a few, if one, or if none like it.' Such sentiments have garnered for Chapman a reputation for obscurity beginning with Algernon Swinburne.

Chapman made this comment about writing for his own satisfaction in a preface to his first poetic work, *The shaddow of night* (1594). The piece comprises two companion poems, a hymn to night – the perfect, primal state of being preceding the act of Creation – and a hymn to Cynthia – the chaste goddess associated with the moon and the hunt. Chapman dedicated *The shaddow of night*, like his next poem *Ovids banquet of sence* (1595), to Matthew Roydon, an Elizabethan mathematician patronized by Henry Percy, ninth earl of Northumberland. One old romantic notion, exemplified in M. C. Bradbrook and Frances Yates, associated Chapman with Northumberland, Sir Walter Ralegh, and Thomas Harriot in a putatively secretive group of radical thinkers called the School of Night. In this scenario, Chapman, assisted by his 'compeers by night', might have been Shakespeare's rival poet mentioned in Sonnet 86.

Throughout his early poems, Chapman laments the decadent sensuality of the age, articulating a metaphysical ideal that complements the neo-Stoic resolve of his heroic drama. In *Ovids banquet of sence*, for instance, Chapman imagines Ovid wooing Corinna and indulging each of his five senses, only to learn that enjoying true virtue requires a refined rejection of sensuality, that 'sense is given us to excite the mind'. The poem concludes with a 'Coronet', a collection of 10 interlinked sonnets, in which the poet rejects anyone who 'prefer[s] the painted Cabinet' of the physical senses 'Before the wealthy jewel it doth store'. Similar sentiments appear in his other poetry, including his additions to Christopher Marlowe's apparently incomplete epyllion *Hero and Leander* (c. 1593), in which Chapman incorporates a more strongly moral message into the concluding sections of the poem. The completion of *Hero and Leander*, undertaken in 1598 during one of Chapman's periods of intense financial distress, demonstrates a remarkable concern with financial prodigality and lack, concluding as it does with

Leander's mangled corpse washing ashore among 'filthy usuring Rocks that would have blood, / Though they could get of him no other good'. Chapman's high moral sentiments in verse could not lift him from his own material existence, forcing him to eke out a living in any way he could.

Chapman would continue to write original verse through the first two decades of the next century. For his potentially most responsive patron, Prince Henry, Chapman wrote *Euthymiae raptus* (1609), or *Tears of peace*, on the occasion of the temporary peace agreed in the Low Countries. When Prince Henry died suddenly in 1612, Chapman wrote an epicede (or funeral song) in the prince's honour before searching for a new patron. Already indebted to the Howards for assistance during his legal troubles of the previous decade, Chapman now turned his attention on the king's favourite, Robert Carr, earl of Somerset, who married Frances Howard upon her scandalous divorce from Robert Devereux, third earl of Essex. Chapman's *Andromeda liberata* (1614) celebrated the marriage. Although he was not alone in currying favour with the royal favourite on the occasion – John Donne, for instance, wrote an eclogue and epithalamion on the marriage – Chapman's poem would seem to have been in especially poor taste, given the unsavoury cloud surrounding Howard's separation from Essex (potentially the 'rock' from which Andromeda was freed). Chapman quickly followed the poem with a defensive explanation of its allegory. The matter became an even greater scandal when Frances Howard poisoned Carr's former mentor, Sir Thomas Overbury, to quiet his objections. Chapman remained steadfast in his loyalty to Carr, however, dedicating his last poetry to the disgraced Somerset.

In *Euthymiae raptus*, Chapman records a poetic vision 'Of a most grave and goodly person . . . / With eyes turned upwards and was outward blind' – that is, of Homer, who tells Chapman that he 'didst inherit / My true sense . . . in my spirit; / And I, invisible, went prompting thee'. Homer speaks of the 'Rapture' that has come over Chapman, through the epic poet's inspiration, and driven him to produce his poetry. Chapman prefaces many of his poems with prose meditations on his poetic method and through these it becomes clear that he thought of himself as pursuing a Neoplatonic inspiration in his poetry. At the outset of *Ovids banquet*, for instance, he advocates poetic 'Enargia' – the Platonic concept of brilliant depiction of ideals glossed by him as 'clearness of representation' – which the poet can achieve only through 'high, and hearty invention expressed in most significant and unaffected praise'. As with the moral purpose in Chapman's poetry, the poet must refine his inspiration to reach a transcendent Truth, something beyond 'mere nature'. Chapman remarks that 'rich Minerals are digged out of the bowels of the earth, not found in the superficies and dust of it'. The poetic maker must strive to refine himself and his poetry if it is to have value.

Chapman also speaks of this poetic 'rapture' or divine fury in the preface to his translation of Homer's *Odyssey*, and Homeric translation is the third arena in which modern readers may have encountered the Renaissance poet. Throughout his life, Chapman returned to this task. It was this project of translation, the iambic heptameter Englishing of the Greek epics, that inspired Keats to write his sonnet 'On first looking into Chapman's Homer'. Chapman spent almost two decades translating the *Iliad*. In 1598 he published the first portions of his project, *Seaven bookes of the Iliades of Homere, prince of poets*, as well as *Achilles shield*, a partial translation of the eighteenth book of the *Iliad* in which the gods prepare a new shield for Achilles. He dedicated both to the second earl of Essex, then in his prime.

As a result of Essex's disgrace, Chapman did not initially publicize subsequent translations of Homer, but as servant to Prince Henry, he undertook to finish this work. Perhaps responding to Henry's encouragement to complete the project, Chapman concludes 1609's *Euthymiae raptus*, in which

Homer appears as a character, by assuring Prince Henry that the project of finishing the translation proceeded apace. Homer had suddenly inspired Chapman to write the 'Tears of Peace', and this had 'delay[ed] your great Command, / To end his Iliades' but now the end of the translation was in sight. Chapman had a great incentive to finish his translation, since the prince had promised him an annual pension and a three hundred pound gift when it was done. Later in 1609, Chapman published the first half of his translation of the *Iliad* with a dedication to Prince Henry commending the stoic ideal of 'govern[ing] inward'. Chapman also took up another favoured theme in his verse, that the best poetry 'to virtue moves' and is thus worthy of royal patronage. Unfortunately, Prince Henry died before Chapman could reap the rewards of completing his translation of the *Iliad* and King James did not fulfil his son's promises.

Chapman quickly completed his translation of the *Odyssey* in 1614 and 1615, then worked on translating other minor works of Homer's by 1624. Chapman's method of translation deserves some comment. In his final edition of Homer, Chapman implied that he had taught himself the languages necessary to complete the translation. However, his method seems to have been to work from the edition of Jean de Sponde, who printed the Greek text with a facing-page Latin translation. Chapman anxiously defended his method in the prefatory matter of his work, as well as his practice of interpolating amplifications into the text. In other words, Chapman may not have been faithful to Homer's words, but he strove to be faithful to the epic poet's spirit. And so he felt justified in his addendum to this final work of translation of declaring that 'The Work that I was born to do, is done'.

SEE ALSO: Dekker, Thomas; Donne, John; Jonson, Ben; Marston, John; Meres, Francis; Ralegh, Walter; Shakespeare, William; Shirley, James; Webster, John

REFERENCES AND SUGGESTED READINGS

Braden, Gordon (1987) George Chapman. In: Bowers, Fredson (ed.) *Elizabethan dramatists*. Gale, Detroit, pp. 3–29.

Braunmuller, A. R. (1992) *Natural fictions: George Chapman's major tragedies*. University of Delaware Press, Newark.

Burnett, Mark Thornton (2004) Chapman, George. In: *Oxford dictionary of national biography*. Oxford University Press, Oxford.

Snare, Gerald (1989) *The mystification of George Chapman*. Duke University Press, Durham, NC.

Snare, Gerald (1992) George Chapman. In: Hester, M. Thomas (ed.) *Seventeenth-century British non-dramatic poets*, 1st series. Gale, Detroit, pp. 45–58.

Spivack, Charlotte (1967) *George Chapman*. Twayne, New York.

Tricomi, Albert H. (1982) The dates of the plays of George Chapman. *English Literary Renaissance* 12(2), 242–266.

Cheke, John

JOHN F. McDIARMID

John Cheke (1514–57) was the central figure in a group of Protestant humanists, including Thomas Smith, William Cecil, Roger Ascham, and Thomas Wilson, who proceeded from study at Cambridge to high positions at court and in the church under Edward VI and, in some cases, again under Elizabeth I. Cheke and his circle shaped royal policy, religious reform, and literary culture in England in the middle of the sixteenth century.

Cheke was born in Cambridge on 16 June 1514, the son of a bedell in the university. He entered St John's College in 1526, became a fellow in 1529, and received his MA in 1533. University chancellor John Fisher was promoting humanistic studies in the 1520s, particularly at St John's. Protestant ideas were also coming into Cambridge and into Cheke's own family: some of his earliest surviving letters, addressed to his mother, show they shared Protestant beliefs.

Cheke made his reputation at St John's in the 1530s as an outstanding teacher of Greek.

In *The scholemaster* (first published 1570), Cheke's student Ascham recalls and celebrates Cheke's teaching techniques and his classical erudition. Cheke joined with Thomas Smith of Queens' College in pursuing a project Erasmus had brought to the fore: the reconstruction of the classical pronunciation of Greek from evidence in ancient texts. In 1540 Cheke was made regius professor of Greek. In 1542, however, his pronunciation was banned by Stephen Gardiner, now Cambridge's chancellor and Henry VIII's leading councillor. Over the ensuing months Cheke and Gardiner exchanged letters (two of Cheke's are book-length) debating pronunciations and concepts of language (these were published in Basle in 1555 as *De pronuntiatione graecae linguae*). The conservative Gardiner aimed to bring Cheke to heel because of Cheke's support for change not only in language but also in religion.

Despite this check, in 1544 Cheke was appointed a tutor of Edward, prince of Wales. This was to be his main occupation for the next eight years, including most of Edward's reign as King Edward VI. The manuscripts of Edward's school work are an important record of Renaissance education, documenting his progress through Latin and Greek grammar and composition and writers on rhetoric and moral and political philosophy, especially Cicero and Aristotle.

In the last years of Henry VIII Cheke presented the king with a series of Latin translations of Greek texts. One was of Plutarch's essay on superstition, to which Cheke added a long preface distinguishing superstition from true religion (now University College, Oxford, MS 171). This was probably in aid of the attempt by archbishop of Canterbury Thomas Cranmer in 1545/46 to persuade Henry to abolish 'superstitious' ceremonies in English worship. After Edward's accession in 1547 Cheke gave important aid to Cranmer in constructing a reformed English church. Cheke's incomplete English Gospel translation was probably a contribution to Cranmer's 1549 project for a new English Bible. Cheke helped foreign reformers whom Cranmer had welcomed to England, and in

1551 he helped produce *De obitu ... Buceri*, a printed collection of Latin prose and Latin and Greek verse on the death of the reformer Martin Bucer in Cambridge, which showcased mid-Tudor Protestant humanist culture.

Cheke's best-known book, *The hurt of sedicion*, published by John Day in 1549, is a polemic against the rebels of that year. After a short section on the Devon and Cornwall rebels who rose against the imposition of the first Book of Common Prayer, the bulk of the work is directed against the economically motivated rebels of East Anglia. Cheke violently denounces all the rebels for their disobedience and for the suffering their actions have caused. On the other hand, *The hurt* also shows that Cheke, like Smith, supported the comprehensive reform programme of the protector Edward Seymour, duke of Somerset. Cheke blames the western rebels for opposing religious reform, and the East Anglians for trying to bring about socio-economic change by violent means, and thus disrupting the orderly agrarian reform the protector had (in fact) undertaken.

Cheke weathered the power shift from Somerset to John Dudley, duke of Northumberland, and was knighted in October 1551. At the end of Edward's reign he participated in the council of Lady Jane Grey, and when Mary I made good her claim to the throne he was imprisoned. He was allowed to go abroad in 1554, and spent the next two years mostly in Padua and Strasbourg. In May 1556 Cheke was seized while travelling in the Low Countries, brought to the Tower of London, and there induced to recant his Protestantism. He died in September 1557.

Cheke's proficiency as a classicist was the foundation of his success. Admiration of the perfect eloquence already achieved in Greek and Latin did not preclude, for Cheke and his circle, belief that their native language could rise to similar heights. Cheke worked to improve English by promoting (with Smith) a rationalized spelling and (with Ascham) the use of quantitative metres in English verse. In both Latin and English Cheke used a style he apparently thought of as Ciceronian, characterized by long sentences including syntactically parallel segments, often of similar length or construction or involving parallelisms in sound. The style is one of the precursors of euphuism.

Humanists like Cheke did not pursue rhetorical excellence for its own sake; it was a tool to be used, along with classical moral and political learning, in a life of effective engagement in the affairs of the commonwealth. Cheke led the way for his colleagues from Cambridge to court; Smith and Cecil, especially, achieved leading posts under Edward and Elizabeth. Republican political values learned from Cicero informed their thought and activity; Edward's reign and the early decades of Elizabeth's were the high points of sixteenth-century English 'monarchical republicanism'. Ultimately, the rhetorical and the political were included by Cheke, and by colleagues like Ascham and Wilson, within the religious. Eloquence was granted by God, and service to the commonwealth was a mode of the sanctified life made possible by grace. A Protestantism heavily inflected by Renaissance humanism is the distinctive intellectual mode of Cheke and his circle.

SEE ALSO: Ascham, Roger; Gardiner, Stephen; Smith, Thomas; Wilson, Thomas

REFERENCES AND SUGGESTED READINGS

Alford, Stephen (2002) *Kingship and politics in the reign of Edward VI*. Cambridge University Press, Cambridge.

Goodwin, James (ed.) (1843) *The Gospel according to St Matthew and the first chapter of the Gospel according to St Mark*, trans. John Cheke. J. & J. J. Deighton, Cambridge.

Hudson, Winthrop S. (1980) *The Cambridge connection and the Elizabethan settlement of 1559*. Duke University Press, Durham, NC.

McDiarmid, John (1996) Classical epitaphs for heroes of faith: mid-Tudor neo-Latin memorial volumes and their Protestant context. *International Journal of the Classical Tradition* 3, 23–47.

McDiarmid, John (1997) Sir John Cheke's preface to *De superstitione*. *Journal of Ecclesiastical History* 48, 100–120.

Needham, Paul S. (1971) Sir John Cheke at Cambridge and court. PhD dissertation, Harvard University.

Chettle, Henry

GRANT WILLIAMS

Henry Chettle (d.1603/7) was a printer and playwright who most probably penned two famous epithets for Shakespeare long attributed to Robert Greene: 'upstart crow' and 'absolute Johannes Factotum' (Jowett 1993). That the case for reattribution of such important documentary evidence has been made a number of times and has left little impact on scholarship underscores the ease with which Chettle has been consigned to the margins of literary history. Chettle was among the most prolific of Elizabethan playwrights, but only one of his 13 plays ever saw print. His underrepresentation as a solo dramatist makes it difficult for scholars to ascertain his role as a collaborator in the six plays that survive from the 36 to which he contributed. The indifference of scholarship to the likelihood that Chettle first described the most famous writer in the English language demonstrates how easy it has been for Chettle's voice to be drowned out by those of other Elizabethans who have a stronger archival presence.

The epithets 'upstart crow' and 'absolute Johannes Factotum' are, at the very least, representative of Chettle, who struggled throughout his life to make ends meet. The son of a London dyer, Chettle was from 1577 to 1584 apprenticed to the printer Thomas East, and then went into partnership briefly with two other printers, William Hoskins and John Danter. After the partnership dissolved, Chettle worked for Danter on several projects until 1598. The epithet 'Jack of all trades', a literal rendering of 'Johannes Factotum', aptly describes his labours in Danter's printing house. Chettle wrote epistles for books going through press, such as Anthony Munday's translation of the romance *The second booke of Primaleon of Greece* (1596) and Thomas Nashe's *Have with you to Saffron-Walden* (1596). In the latter, he signs himself 'your old compositor', indicating a long association as Nashe's typesetter. Chettle was also involved in more substantive correcting and patching up of books in press, such as the pirated copy of Shakespeare's *Romeo and Juliet* (1597).

Chettle was an author, besides being a compositor, corrector, and epistle-writer. His pamphlet, *Kind-harts dreame* (1593), shows the extent to which writers could emerge out of the social space of the printing house. On the face of it, the pamphlet rails against current abuses through the voices of five apparitions who appear to the sleeping Kind-hart, an itinerant tooth-drawer. But the story is much more than a sensationalistic satire after the manner of Nashe's *Pierce Pennilesse* (1592); it clearly performs the work of the printing house even as it turns a profit for the bookseller. For Danter and others, Chettle acted as a kind of intermediary between printer and authors, his ability to gain piecemeal employment depending upon his credibility in the larger social network of literary production. *Kind-harts dreame* provides an urgent response to the allegation that Chettle forged *Greenes groats-worth of witte* (1592), an allegation that jeopardized his reputation amongst his authorial connections. Its opening epistle explains why Greene's manuscript was suspiciously in Chettle's handwriting, while apologizing to Shakespeare, whom 'Greene' attacked along with Marlowe, and vindicating Nashe from any accusations of having forged the tract. *Kind-harts dreame* rhetorically salvages the ethos of Chettle as a respectable and well-connected factotum in the printing community. In the pamphlet proper, Chettle assumes the authorial persona of Kind-hart, a benevolent go-between, who knows his place and yet takes to print in order to champion the bills presented by his deceased friends. The persona's situation of representing ghostly voices in print reflects the wish-fulfilment of Chettle, who likewise desired to continue mediating strong authorial voices.

The second epithet, 'upstart crow', is also representative of Chettle, who suddenly rose to importance on the theatre scene from quite humble origins as an apprentice. After 1597 Chettle turned his attention to playwriting, mostly collaborating with writers who worked for Philip Henslowe, the owner of London's Rose Theatre. Henslowe's famous diary identifies Chettle as the most prolific of the group and indicates that Chettle, who was always cash-strapped and was even imprisoned for debt, received more loans from him than did any other playwright, implying that Henslowe might have had a closer friendship with him than he had with the others. Out of his 36 collaborative efforts, only the following were ever printed: two Robin Hood plays, *The downfall of Robert, earle of Huntingdon* (1601) and *The death of Robert, earle of Huntingdon* (1601); *The pleasant comodie of patient Grissill* (1603); *The blind-beggar of Bednal-green* (1659); and *The famous history of Sir Thomas Wyat* (1607). Outside his collaborative work and some poetry, Chettle's primary individual efforts are *Piers Plainnes seauen yeres prentiship* (1595) and *The tragedy of Hoffman* (1631), both of which depict bleak societies in which Machiavellian scheming and deceit tear apart courtly communities.

Because Chettle left behind such a small body of identifiable work, we will probably never know how much of an upstart crow he really was. With the exception of the sustained labours of Harold Jenkins (1934) and John Jowett (1993; 1994), Chettle scholarship has naturally been minimal and sporadic. His significance for literary history lies less with textual innovation than with his involvement in the literary production of Elizabethan print culture. His career path from printer's apprentice and factotum to noteworthy writer brings to the fore the picaresque struggle to make a living through print.

SEE ALSO: Greene, Robert; Marston, John; Munday, Anthony; Nashe, Thomas; Shakespeare, William

REFERENCES AND SUGGESTED READINGS

Carson, Neil (1988) *A companion to Henslowe's diary.* Cambridge University Press, Cambridge.

Jenkins, Harold (1934) *The life and work of Henry Chettle.* Sidgwick & Jackson, London.

Jowett, John (1993) Johannes factotum: Henry Chettle and *Greene's groatsworth of wit. Papers of the Bibliographical Society of America* 87, 453–486.

Jowett, John (1994) Notes on Henry Chettle. *Review of English Studies* 45, 384–388.

Chidley, Katherine

ELIZABETH MALSON-HUDDLE

Katherine Chidley (d. c.1653), Leveller activist and religious polemicist, advocated toleration for the Independent churches. No records survive of her life before 1616 when she gave birth to her first child, Samuel; she and her husband, Daniel Chidley, a tailor, had seven more children and participated in the Shrewsbury conventicle in Shropshire. After childbirth, she refused to be churched, a practice she later denounced in her first tract; in 1629 both she and her husband were brought to the consistory court for being absent from church. The Chidley family relocated to London by the end of the 1620s and became involved with Leveller activism and separatist congregations.

In 1641 Chidley published *The justification of the Independant churches of Christ*, a comprehensive treatise presenting scriptural justification for Independent congregations in explicit response to anti-tolerationist Thomas Edwards's *Reasons against the independant government of particular congregations* (1641). Quoting 2 Corinthians 6.14–18, Chidley contends that separatist congregations obeyed God by leaving the Church of England to establish their own gatherings: 'God hath commanded all his people to separate themselves from all Idolatry and false worshipping and false worshippers (and therefore it is no Schisme) except you will make God the Author of Schisme.' Refuting Edwards's assertion that allowing separate congregations 'overthrowes the Communion of Saints', she argues that the churches in Acts were in 'sweet communication' but independent; additionally, she asserts there was no scriptural support for one church or synod to rule over all churches. In defiance of Edwards's objections that 'the government of the Independent Congregations is not of divine institution', she draws on Ephesians 4, 2 Timothy 2, and Titus, and asserts scriptural precedent for congregations electing their own priests, 'but I verily doe beleeve, that as Titus, so Timothy heard of Paul that Elders must be ordained by Election in every city'. Her thorough exegesis creates a scriptural and theological basis for Independency.

Chidley boldly entered the fray of exegetical debate dominated by educated men with her argumentative style. In 1645 she directly challenged Edwards's *Antapologia* (1644) with *A new-yeares-gift, or, a brief exhortation to Mr Thomas Edwards*. Marcus Nevitt (2006) observes that in contrast to other sectarian women writers such as Anna Trapnel, Mary Cary, and Elizabeth Poole, who styled their works as prophecies inspired by God, Chidley wrote animadversions, a polemical genre famously used by John Milton which methodically quotes and refutes a previous text. Like Milton, who also attacked the prelacy's reliance on tithes in *Animadversions upon the remonstrants defence against Smectymnuus* (1641), Chidley accuses Edwards in *A new-yeares-gift* of opposing Independent congregations to secure the maintenance of priests. With Milton and other sectarian contemporaries, she argues that episcopal government was a Catholic institution, but goes further by asserting that the very practice of ordaining priests is 'popish'. In her pleas for toleration of Independent churches, Chidley denounces the greed of priests who demanded fees the poor could ill afford.

Knowing that many educated male polemicists scorned women's writing, in *A new-yeares-gift* Chidley used her gender and wit against Edwards by observing that his arguments were so facile that a woman could easily refute them: 'I considering the many questions that you asked, and the weakenesse of your reasons and arguments, and the untruths of some of them, and how contradictory they were to one another, thought it very easie to undermine and overthrow them.' Although she deprecates her own writing and calls herself 'one of the meanest' of the separatists, she articulates her readings of Scripture with great confidence. Her analysis of the relationship between the church and its ministers appropriates the traditional analogy of the church as the bride of Christ to undermine the power of priests: 'Yea, the power of the Keyes is as absolutely the Churches, which is Christs wife, as the power of the Keyes of the Family are the Mistrises, to whom the Husband giveth full power; and I thinke no reasonable man will affirme (if her Husband give her sole power in his absence) that she is subordinate to any of her servants.' When she compares the keys of the church to a wife's possession of the keys to her household, she inverts the ecclesiastical power dynamic. If the church is Christ's wife, then she must assume authority in his absence, but the servants (i.e., the priests) remain subordinate. Chidley contends that the people comprise the church, and thus the people have more power than its servants, the ministers.

Through the late 1640s and early 1650s, Chidley continued to participate in separatist politics and served as a leader of Leveller women in London; meanwhile, she ran the family haberdashery business after her husband's death in 1649 and provided stockings for the Parliamentary army in Ireland. She often collaborated with her son Samuel, a prolific polemicist, and with him helped establish a separatist church at Bury in Suffolk in 1647. Edwards complains in the third part of *Gangreana* (1646) that 'Katherine Chidly and her sons Books (for the mother and the son made them together, one inditing, and the other writing) are highly magnified'. Scholars believe Chidley helped Leveller women compose petitions and organize large-scale protests outside of parliament in 1649 and 1653 demanding the release of Leveller leaders, including John Lilburne (Crawford 1993; Gentles 2004). As an activist and a writer, Chidley opposed episcopal and presbyterian systems of church government and advanced theological justification for Independent churches. No account of her remains after 1653.

SEE ALSO: Cary, Mary; Edwards, Thomas; Lilburne, John; Milton, John; Poole, Elizabeth; Trapnel, Anna

REFERENCES AND SUGGESTED READINGS

Crawford, Patricia M. (1993) *Women and religion in England 1500–1720*. Routledge, New York.

Gentles, Ian J. (2004) Chidley, Katherine. In: *Oxford dictionary of national biography*. Oxford University Press, Oxford.

Hinds, Hilary (2007) The paratextual profusion of radical sectarian women's writing of the 1640s. *Prose Studies* 29(2), 153–177.

Nevitt, Marcus (2006) *Women and the pamphlet culture of revolutionary England, 1640–1660*. Ashgate, Aldershot.

Mack, Phyllis (1992) *Visionary women: ecstatic prophecy in seventeenth-century England*. University of California Press, Berkeley.

Chillingworth, William

EDWARD PALEIT

William Chillingworth (1602–44) was a theologian and Anglican churchman. His chief work, *The religion of Protestants a safe way to salvation* (1638), took shape at Great Tew, the country house of his friend Lucius Cary, Lord Falkland. Its distinctively moderate, sceptical rationalism was influential within later Anglican thought and contributed to the development of secular theories of certainty later in the century. Chillingworth also wrote 10 smaller works which, like his magnum opus, touch on

certainty in faith and the Church of Rome's claims to infallibility; nine of his sermons and a few letters were published in the eighteenth century.

Chillingworth was born in Oxford in 1602, the son of a future mayor of Oxford of the same name. His godfather was William Laud, later archbishop of Canterbury. He was admitted to Trinity College, Oxford, in 1618, graduating BA in 1620 and MA in 1624; in 1628 he was awarded a fellowship. At Oxford he became notorious as a skilful disputant. In 1628 he converted to Catholicism and went to an overseas seminary (probably Douai), but returned within the year dissatisfied by Rome's claims to infallibility. Despite pressure from Laud and friends like Gilbert Sheldon, he evaded official conversion to the Church of England, finding difficulty with some of the Thirty-Nine Articles as late as 1635. In 1633 Elizabeth Cary, Lady Falkland, still believed him to be Catholic and appointed him to convert her daughters. When she found out he wasn't and expelled him, her son Viscount Falkland immediately made him tutor to his two younger brothers. At Great Tew, Chillingworth profited from a substantial library and the company of thinkers such as Sheldon, John Hales, and Falkland himself. *The religion of Protestants* presents itself partly as defending the Church of England, suggesting Chillingworth's belated conversion. In 1638 he was granted two church appointments; subsequent writings, such as *The apostolicall institution of episcopacy* (1644), which characteristically argues that despite a lack of certain proof there are insufficient grounds to deny the apostolic origin of bishops, indirectly support the cause of church and crown. During 1643 he served in the Royalist army, devising engines for the siege of Gloucester. Captured in December 1643, and in terrible health, he was harried by the Presbyterian Francis Cheynell, who later published virulent attacks on his reputation. He died on 30 January 1644.

The religion of Protestants was written in answer to the Jesuit Edward Knott's *Mercy and truth* (1634), itself a response to the Anglican

Christopher Potter's *Want of charitie justly charged* (1633), which had in turn answered Knott's *Charity mistaken* (1630). Chillingworth's tract is arranged as a defence of Potter and a point-by-point refutation of Knott, whose treatise is printed alongside. Laud commanded that church censors approve the work before publication; the delay probably allowed Knott to acquire copies of the proofs, which he used to attack Chillingworth in *Directions to be observed by N.N.* (1636), to which Chillingworth also replies.

The religion of Protestants is in style resolutely logical and moderate, eschewing the *ad hominem* savagery of much religious polemic. It famously contends that as human interpretation and transmission are fallible, there can be no absolute certainty that any Christian doctrine is true; faith consists of rationally assessing the evidence to arrive at a *degree* of certainty concerning a doctrine. The Bible, the only 'true religion of Protestants', is the word of God and therefore infallible – in principle. However, as one cannot be certain of *interpreting* it correctly, a critical assessment of probability remains necessary. Direct divine revelation is possible, but as no absolute assurance can be given of its divinity, particularly to third parties, in practice it too has only probable status. For Chillingworth God is 'charitable', offering salvation to those who rationally seek the truth even if they have mistaken beliefs: the Calvinist theory of predestination is denied. No belief is absolutely necessary for salvation; hence, heaven cannot be denied to pre-Christians, or non-Christians. Ideally the Church, as a repository of tradition – to which Chillingworth gives a high but not absolute value – assists in enquiring after truth, yet unlike the Roman church it must allow doctrinal differences to be openly disputed rather than pretend, impossibly, to infallible authority over interpretation, still less pronounce new doctrines or assume an intercessory role in salvation. Chillingworth, an ardent opponent of fanaticism, hopes that a tolerant church so constituted – perhaps the Church of England – could reunite Christendom, reversing the bloody consequences of Reformation schism.

The religion of Protestants builds on the humanist scepticism and ecumenism of Erasmus and post-Erasmians like Sebastian Castellio, as well as Hugo Grotius's *On the truth of the Christian religion* (1624), while finding echoes in the theology of Hales, Falkland, Henry Hammond, Sheldon, and others of the Great Tew circle. It was reprinted in 1664, 1674, and 1684; several eighteenth-century editions of Chillingworth's *Works* testify to continued interest in his ideas amongst Anglicans. Catholics, predictably, and Calvinists who thought he privileged reason over Scripture were immediately and vocally hostile, calling him a heretic and 'Socinian'. As an ex-Catholic convert defending regal authority and denying predestination, Chillingworth appears superficially to endorse Puritan stereotypes of Arminian Laudianism, with which Nicholas Tyacke (1987) associates him. Co-thinkers like Sheldon and Morley were influential in the post-Restoration church. However, Chillingworth's anti-sacerdotalism distinguishes him from the Laudian church, and his tolerationism from the later versions of Anglicanism which persecuted dissenters. Likewise, despite stressing toleration and the individual's sufficiency to pursue salvation, Chillingworth's scepticism towards revelation and emphasis on rational interpretation distinguish him from the radical, prophetic strain of Independency in the later 1640s and 1650s. Henry Van Leeuwen (1963) argues that his notion of doctrinal probability was taken forward by John Tillotson, contributing later in the century to the formulation of 'scientific' theories of certainty. Chillingworth's commitment to logical consistency disturbed some of his friends; Thomas Hobbes thought it dealt 'back-blows' to his own side. But John Locke thought *The religion of Protestants* a supreme example of argumentative rigour, and Chillingworth can be considered one of the finest ever products of a training in Renaissance dialectic.

SEE ALSO: Cary, Elizabeth; Cary, Lucius, Lord Falkland; Hales, John; Hobbes, Thomas; Hyde, Edward, earl of Clarendon

REFERENCES AND SUGGESTED READINGS

Mortimer, Sarah (2010) *Reason and religion in the English Revolution: the challenge of Socinianism.* Cambridge University Press, Cambridge.

Orr, Robert (1967) *Reason and authority: the thought of William Chillingworth.* Oxford University Press, Oxford.

Trevor-Roper, Hugh (1987) *Catholics, Anglicans and Puritans: seventeenth-century essays.* Secker & Warburg, London.

Tyacke, Nicholas (1987) *Anti-Calvinists: the rise of English Arminianism, c.1590–1640.* Oxford University Press, Oxford.

Van Leeuwen, Henry (1963) *The problem of certainty in English thought, 1630–1690.* Martinus Nijhoff, The Hague.

Churchyard, Thomas

LIZ OAKLEY-BROWN

The name of the Shrewsbury-born soldier and prolific writer Thomas Churchyard (?1523—1604) is relatively unknown in the twenty-first century. Yet from the satire *Davy Dycars dreame* (c.1552) to *Sorrowfull verses made on [the] death of our most soveraigne lady Queen Elizabeth* (1604), his generically diverse range of texts – including a military biography, royal progresses, chorographies, tragedies, translations, epitaphs, and liminary verses – weave their way through Tudor literary culture. Churchyard is invoked in Gabriel Harvey's so-called 'Letter book' (1573–80) and *Pierces supererogation* (1593), and William Webbe's *A discourse of English poetrie* (1586). Edmund Spenser figures the author as 'old Palemon' in *Colin Clouts come home againe* (1595), while in *Palladis tamia* (1598) Francis Meres includes Churchyard in his catalogue of writers 'most passionate among us to bewaile the complexities of love'. The second part of the anonymous university play, *The returne from Pernassus* (c.1601), features a brief discussion of Churchyard and one of his most renowned works, 'Shore's wife'. Initially published in the 1563 edition of William Baldwin's *A mirrour for magistrates*, the tragic verse focusing on Edward IV's mistress was joined in the 1587 edition by Churchyard's complaint of Thomas Wolsey (Richards 2009).

As his first appearances in print demonstrate, Churchyard's writings are often interested in social inequalities. *A myrrour for man where in he shall see the myserable state of thys worlde* (c.1552), a poem indebted to medieval estates satires, considers how 'Lordes were ones liberal, but nowe they waxe harde'. Similarly, the 28-line broadside ballad *Davy Dycars dreame*, its titular character appropriated from William Langland's *Piers Plowman* (c.1360–87), caused controversy for anticipating a time 'When truth doth tread the stretes and lyers lurke in den, / And Rex doth raigne and rule the ro[o]s t, and weedes out wicked men'. Fifteen poems were produced in response to Churchyard's perceived criticism of the Edwardian government (Lucas 2001), and all but one of these texts were eventually compiled and published as *The contention betwyxte Churchyeard and Camell* (1560). It is likely that *Davy Dycars dreame* is the poem that Churchyard alludes to in *The fortunate farewel to the most forward and noble earle of Essex* (1599). Here, the author states that he was 'troubled before the Lords of the Counsell, for writing some of [his] first verses' (Lucas 2001). In 1566, three satires articulating Churchyard's disregard for courtly behaviour also initiated published ripostes (Lucas 2001; Lyne 2006).

Little is known about Churchyard's background, though he is believed to have been a page to Henry Howard, earl of Surrey (Pincombe & Shrank 2009). However, many of the soldier-author's texts appear autobiographical, most notably his relation of Protestant martial exploits in *A generall rehearsal of warres*, part of the miscellany entitled *Churchyardes choise* (1579). Churchyard's other anthologies – *The firste parte of*

Churchyardes chippes contayning twelue seuerall labours (1575), *A light bondell of liuly discourses called Churchyardes charge* (1580), *A pleasaunte laborinth called Churchyardes chance* (1580), *Churchyards challenge* (1593), *A musicall consort of heauenly harmonie [...] called Churchyards charitie* (1595), and *A pleasant discourse of court and wars ... written by Thomas Churchyard, and called his Cherrishing* (1596) – regularly contain material which seem related to the author's personal circumstances. The speaker of 'A tragecall discourse of the unhappie mans life', for instance, announces that he was 'boern ... about the world to roem / To see the warres' (*Churchyardes chippes*). Publications such as *The thre first bookes of Ovids De tristibus, translated into Englishe* (1572), *A prayse, and reporte of Maister Martyne Forboishers voyage to Meta Incognita* (1578), 'Hir Highnesse returne from Norwich' (1578), and *The worthines of Wales* (1587) exhibit Churchyard's wider interest in early modern itinerancy.

On occasion, pamphlets such as *A warning for the wise ... written of the late earthquake chanced in London and other places, the. 6. of April 1580* (1580) and *... a description & commendation of a paper mill, now and of late set vp (neere the towne of Darthford) by an high Germayn called M. Spilman ...* (1588) produce timely responses to current events. Eschewing familial and marital networks in favour of literary and, as his dedications to powerful Elizabethan figures attest, political coteries, Churchyard's publications frequently proffer an authorial voice which strives for public recognition. Accordingly, Churchyard's prefatorial address to John Wolley in his collection of epitaphic verses, *A revyving of the deade* (1591), announces that 'the world shall see what wrong I have suffred to endure a deniall (by busie tunges) of mine owne workes'.

SEE ALSO: Baldwin, William; Harvey, Gabriel; Meres, Francis; Spenser, Edmund; Webbe, William

REFERENCES AND SUGGESTED READINGS

Adnitt, William Henry (1880) *Thomas Churchyard: a memoir.* Transactions of the Shropshire Archaeological and Natural History Society, Shrewsbury.

Bergeron, David M. (2007) The 'I' of the beholder: Thomas Churchyard and the 1578 Norwich pageant. In: Archer, Jayne, Goldring, Elizabeth, & Knight, Sarah (eds) *The progresses, pageants, and entertainments of Queen Elizabeth I.* Oxford University Press, Oxford, pp. 142–159.

Heale, Elizabeth (2002) *Authorship and autobiography in Renaissance verse: chronicles of the self.* Palgrave Macmillan, Basingstoke.

Lee, John (2000) The English Renaissance essay: Churchyard, Cornwallis, Florio's Montaigne and Bacon. In: Hattaway, Michael (ed.) *A companion to English Renaissance literature and culture.* Oxford University Press, Oxford, pp. 600–608.

Lucas, Scott (2001) Doggon Davie and Davy Dicar: Edmund Spenser, Thomas Churchyard, and the poetics of public protest. *Spenser Studies* 16, 151–165.

Lyne, Raphael (2006) Churchyard, Thomas. In: *Oxford dictionary of national biography*, Oxford University Press, Oxford.

Oakley-Brown, Liz (2008) Taxonomies of travel and martial identity in Thomas Churchyard's *A generall rehearsall of warres* and 'A pirates tragedie'. *Studies in Travel Writing* 12(1), 67–84.

Pincombe, Mike & Shrank, Cathy (2009) Prologue: The travails of Tudor literature. In: Pincombe, Mike & Shrank, Cathy (eds) *The Oxford handbook to Tudor literature, 1585–1603.* Oxford University Press, Oxford, pp. 1–19.

Richards, Jennifer (2009) Transforming *A mirror for magistrates.* In: Healy, Margaret & Healy, Thomas (eds) *Renaissance transformations: the making of English writing 1500–1650.* Edinburgh University Press, Edinburgh, pp. 48–63.

Chute, Anthony

ALAN STEWART

Anthony Chute (or Chewt) (*fl.* 1593–95) is perhaps now best known as the author of *Tabacco* (1595), an early English treatment of the popular New World import. But during his lifetime his notoriety was as a minor player in the pamphlet quarrel waged by Cambridge academic Gabriel Harvey and popular writer Thomas Nashe, in which Chute supported Harvey. Unfortunately, this means that most of what we think we know about Chute derives from the testimonies of Harvey and Nashe, in *Pierces supererogation* (1593) and *Have with you to Saffron-Walden* (1596) respectively, two less than reliable sources for biography.

Chute writes of himself briefly in an elaborate petition of May 1594 to William Cecil, Lord Burghley, applying to be a pursuivant at arms. Chute describes himself as 'a poor Gentleman and a Scollar without frends', who has a working knowledge of Latin, French, and Italian, and all parts 'belonging to blazon', suggesting an expertise in heraldry. By contrast, Nashe claims that Chute was once 'but a low Clarke, and carried an Atturnies bookes after him', merely a lawyer's servant. As 'a youth' he 'could not vnderstand a word of Latine'. He sailed with the English expedition of 1589 led by Sir Francis Drake that hoped to place the pretender Don Antonio back on the Portuguese throne, but only as 'a Captaines Boye that scornd writing and reading, and helpt him to set downe his accounts, and score vp dead payes'. And, according to Nashe, by 1596 Chute was 'dead and rotten'.

The origins of Chute's association with Gabriel Harvey are unknown, but Chute's first publication in the summer of 1593 was significantly with Harvey's publisher, John Wolfe. In *Beawtie dishonoured written under the title of Shores wife*, a poem of 1,182 lines in 197 six-line stanzas, the ghost of Jane Shore, the mistress of Edward IV, bemoans her fate. The male voicing of Shore was hardly a novelty, since Thomas Churchyard had done the same in the 1563 *Mirrour for magistrates* – and indeed had very recently (in spring 1593) printed a slightly longer version in his *Churchyards challenge*. But although Chute evidently knew Churchyard's work, his poem is more than twice as long, and less concerned with the historical characters than with 'the general moral and psychological situation' (Moore 1964). In his dedication to Sir

Edward Wingfield, Chute implies that he is a novice author, and that this poem is 'the first invention of my beginning muse', a move comparable to William Shakespeare dedicating his 'first fruits' of *Venus and Adonis* to Henry Wriothesley, earl of Southampton, in the same year.

Chute identified with the poem enough to sign himself 'Sh: Wy: for, Shores Wife' in one of his contributions to Harvey's *Pierces supererogation, or a new prayse of the old asse* (1593), a continuation of his assault on Nashe, published shortly after. Chute was the joint dedicatee of the volume, along with Barnabe Barnes and John Thorius, supposedly in reward for providing the concluding appendix materials – a sonnet, two undated letters in one of which he dubs Nashe 'a patheticall asse', and a poem, 'The asses figg', the tone of which can be gauged by its opening lines:

So long the Rhennish furie of thy braine,
Incent with hot fume of a Stilliard Clime,
Lowd-lying Nash, in liquid termes did raine,
Full of absurdities, and of slaundrous ryme.

Chute had clearly learned the lingua franca of the Harvey–Nashe dispute. A third 1593 Wolfe pamphlet, *Remonstrances, to the duke de Mayne lieu-tenant generall of the estate and crowne of Fraunce*, was 'Trulie translated out of the French coppie, printed at Paris, by Ant: Ch:', which suggests that Chute had French (although it has been noted that Chute's translations of French sources for *Tabacco* indicate a flawed grasp of the language).

No doubt in retaliation for the attack on him, Nashe portrays Chute as a man of appetites, 'who lou'd lycoras and drunke posset curd, the best that euer put cuppe to mouth', as well as tobacco ('I haue seene him *non plus* in giuing the charge, at the creating of a new Knight of *Tobacco*'). According to Nashe, 'within a yere and a halfe' of contributing to *Pierces supererogation*, probably in the late summer of 1593, Chute 'died of the dropsie, as diuers Printers that were at his burial certefide mee'. This would place Chute's death in early 1595; the last evidence of him alive is the May 1594 petition to Burghley.

One of Chute's indulgences resulted in a posthumous publication, and a literary first. In Nashe's words, Chute 'hath kneaded and daub'd vp a Commedie, called The transformation of the King of *Trinidadoes* two Daughters, Madame *Panachaea* and the Nymphe *Tobacco*', a derogatory allusion to his best-known work, entitled *Tabacco. The distinct and seuerall opinions of the late and best phisitions that haue written of the diuers natures and qualities thereof. Gathered by A.C.*, which was published posthumously in 1595. *Tabacco* falls into two parts. In the second, Chute attends to the tobacco plant, and the possibilities of its green leaf, citing works by Continental writers such as by Nicolas Monardes, Jean Liébault, Gilles Everaerts (Aegedius Everaruts), Jacques Gohory and Leo Sauvius (in fact the same man), and Leonardo Fioravanti, though he does not mention recent English-language treatments of the topic by William Harrison (1587) and Thomas Harriot (1588). The first part of the tract, however, in which he explores the practical and medicinal uses to which dried tobacco may be put, is original to Chute.

Nashe charges that 'to approue his Heraldrie' Chute 'scutchend out the honourable Armes of the smoakie Societie', and indeed the book's woodcuts include a coat of arms with a crowned man and a pipe (presumably a punning allusion to the book's dedicatee 'Maister Humphrey King, The Souereigne of Tabacco'), and an illustration of a man smoking a pipe, reputedly the first European depiction of a smoker. Chute may be the first person to write of 'drinking' tobacco, soon to become a commonplace (Wilson 1961). His pamphlet can certainly claim to be 'the first English work on tobacco' (Kane 1931), paving the way for the plethora of attacks on and defences of tobacco in the 1600s, most famously James I's *A counterblaste to tobacco* (1604).

Another claim by Nashe, that Chute wrote the poems *Procris* and *Cephalus,* seems to be mistaken: although these were licensed to Wolfe in 1595, and published by him two years later, in a dedicatory epistle they are claimed to be by Thomas Edwards.

SEE ALSO: Edwards, Thomas; Harriot, Thomas; Harrison, William; Harvey, Gabriel; James VI and I; Nashe, Thomas; Shakespeare, William

REFERENCES AND SUGGESTED READINGS

Kane, Robert J. (1931) Anthony Chute, Thomas Nashe, and the first English work on tobacco. *Review of English Studies* 7, 151–159.

Lee, Sidney (2004) Chute [Chewt], Anthony, rev. Matthew Steggle. In: *Oxford dictionary of national biography*. Oxford University Press, Oxford.

Moore, William H. (1964) An allusion in 1593 to *The taming of the shrew? Shakespeare Quarterly* 15, 55–60.

Wilson, F. P. (1961) Introduction. In: Wilson, F. P. (ed.) *Tabacco*, by Anthony Chute. Blackwell, Oxford, pp. vii–xxxix.

Clarkson, Lawrence

ARIEL HESSAYON

A manual labourer and autodidact turned preacher, polemicist, and sectary, Lawrence (or Laurence) Clarkson (c.1615–67) was the author of nine different printed works issued at London between 1646 and 1660. Born by his account at Preston, Lancashire, he may have been apprenticed and was later described as a tailor. Though his parents conformed to the Church of England's teachings, Clarkson claimed to have dissented by refusing to receive communion kneeling at a railed altar. Instead he took it sitting, administered by sympathetic preachers in the countryside. His youth, moreover, was marked by puritanical devotions: long walks to hear godly ministers, keeping the Sabbath, fasting, private prayer, and memorizing the Authorized (or King James) Version of the Bible. He took the Protestation Oath at Preston in January 1642, but with the outbreak of Civil War went to London. Much of our knowledge of his life comes from his well-known spiritual autobiography *The lost sheep found* (1660), a colourful, self-serving and indeed problematic text that should not be taken at face value. Evoking the wanderings of the children of Israel during their journey from Egypt to the promised land of Canaan and written after he had become a Muggletonian, it uses the seven churches of Revelation 2–3 as a type, recounting Clarkson's progress through seven forms of church fellowship: Episcopalian, Presbyterian, Independent, Baptist, Seeker, Ranter, and Muggletonian.

Hunting out the ablest preachers active in London – including Edmund Calamy, Thomas Case, and Thomas Brooks – and diligently reading both their works and those of Thomas Hooker, a minister who had fled to New England, Clarkson discovered his own 'small gift of preaching' while serving as a soldier under the command of Captain Paul Hobson. Following his adult baptism in the moat around the Tower of London on 6 November 1644, he began evangelizing and baptizing in Suffolk and Norfolk. This resulted in allegations of sexual misconduct during his trial at Bury St Edmunds and imprisonment. On his release he issued a recantation – no longer extant – entitled *The pilgrimage of saints* (January 1646) and allegedly turned Seeker, denying the Scriptures to be the word of God and consequently their authority as a guide to Christian conduct. Clarkson became more notorious still as 'Captain of the Rant' and disrupted the Digger plantation on the Little Heath in Cobham, Surrey. Gerrard Winstanley had either heard him preach or read Clarkson's *A single eye all light, no darkness* (c. June 1650), an 'impious and blasphemous' book subsidized by an army officer and one of three 'Ranter' writings publicly burned by order of the House of Commons in 1650. Clarkson was apprehended near Whitechapel, detained in custody and examined by a Parliamentary committee for suppressing licentious and impious practices. He confessed and was sentenced to one month's labour in New Bridewell followed by banishment, though the latter part of this decree was not executed.

Following his release Clarkson took up astrology, medicine, and magic, combining his newly acquired skills in healing and recovering stolen goods with preaching in Cambridgeshire, Essex, and Norfolk. All the same he may have remained impoverished, for a Lawrence Claxton received poor relief at London in February 1658. About this time he became acquainted with John Reeve, who had declared himself one of the 'two witnesses' of Revelation 11, and with Reeve's writings. After Reeve's death, and claiming to be the only true bishop and faithful messenger of Jesus Christ, he wrote five treatises in quick succession under the name Claxton. One was an attack on the Quakers that provoked an intemperate response in the form of John Harwood's *The lying prophet* (1659). He also quarrelled with Reeve's cousin and fellow witness of the Spirit Lodowick Muggleton who, fearing Claxton's attempt to usurp control of the Muggletonians, excommunicated him on 25 December 1660. Muggleton eventually forgave a humbled Claxton, allowing him back into the fold on condition that he desist from writing. According to Muggleton, after the Great Fire of London Claxton became involved in an ill-advised financial scheme that led to his incarceration for debt at Ludgate prison, where he died about a year later.

Clarkson's earliest surviving work, *Truth released from prison, to its former libertie* (March 1646) may have derived from a sermon on 1 Kings 18.17. Through its condemnation of the ancient Israelite King Ahab together with his wicked priests and courtiers, Clarkson implicitly charged Charles I, the Laudian clergy, and the king's counsellors with hindering the progress of England's Reformation and denying liberty of conscience to God's saints. Furthermore, drawing on Pauline notions of divine election and the belief in his calling, Clarkson, like several contemporary pamphleteers, justified unlearned lay preaching by drawing parallels with the lowly occupations of Christ and his disciples. Recognizing Clarkson's polemical talents, one of his hearers paid him £12 for the publication of his next book, *A generall charge, or impeachment of high-treason* (October 1647). Framed as a legal document, it purported to be an indictment of the enslaved 'Communality of England' on 14 charges of relinquishing their birthright – popular sovereignty – into the hands of parliament.

The title of *A single eye all light, no darkness* was a conflation of Luke 11.34 and 1 John 1.5. Here Clarkson maintained that 'sin hath its conception only in the imagination'. Indeed, 'so long as the act was in God' it was 'as holy as God'. Consequently there was no iniquity to behold with 'purer' eyes, only that the 'Devil is God, Hell is Heaven, Sin Holiness, Damnation Salvation'. These oxymorons recall the dictum of Giles Randall, the English editor of Nicholas of Cusa, that knowledge of God consisted of opposites and contradictions. Significantly, Randall owned and sold copies of Clarkson's first book. Though Randall may have discussed Cusa's writings with Clarkson, there is no clear indication in *A single eye* that Clarkson had read them. Nor does it appear that he was familiar with the German mystic Jacob Boehme's teachings. A more likely source for Clarkson's doctrines was the posthumously published sermons of Tobias Crisp, a minister who was considered an antinomian.

Claxton's Muggletonian texts – *Look about you, for the devil that you fear is in you* (1659), *A wonder of wonders* (c.1659 but no longer extant), *The Quakers downfal* (1659), *A paradisical dialogue betwixt faith and reason* (1660), and *The lost sheep found* – were largely concerned with elaborating aspects of the sect's principal doctrines. Surviving manuscript copies of two of these treatises suggest they were highly regarded until, angered by Claxton's spiritual pride, Muggleton ordered his daughter to burn some of Claxton's books before his face. Although Claxton's published writings fell into neglect outside Muggletonian circles, copies were recorded in the library of John Denis, a late eighteenth-century London bookseller. Sir Walter Scott also owned *The lost sheep found*, comparing it with John Bunyan's *Pilgrim's progress* (1678).

SEE ALSO: Bunyan, John; Coppe, Abiezer; Winstanley, Gerrard

REFERENCES AND SUGGESTED READINGS

Davis, J. C. (1986) *Fear, myth and history: the Ranters and the historians.* Cambridge University Press, Cambridge.

Hill, Christopher, Reay, Barry, & Lamont, William (1983) *The world of the Muggletonians.* Temple Smith, London.

Lamont, William (2006), *The Muggletonian history, 1652–1979.* Ashgate, Aldershot.

Smith, Nigel (1989) *Perfection proclaimed: language and literature in English radical religion, 1640–1660.* Oxford University Press, Oxford.

Cleveland, John

JEROME DE GROOT

John Cleveland (1613–58) was one of the foremost of the Royalist poets and polemicists who took the propaganda battle to the Parliamentarians in the 1640s (along with others like the journalist Sir John Berkenhead) by writing politically motivated but widely popular verse and pamphlets, which circulated extensively in manuscript as well as in print. He established a particular form of savage political satire that adapted the bodily, sexualized nature of vulgar, popular writing at the time. Cleveland's 'Epitaph on the earl of Strafford' is one of the major political poems of the Civil Wars, transcribed and copied out by scholars, aristocrats, and politicians in their commonplace books. It occasioned multiple responses and rewritings. The simplicity of the verse and the politically scabrous message are typical of Cleveland:

> [Strafford] who was hurried hence
> 'Twixt treason and convenience ...
> The prop and ruin of the state;
> The people's violent love and hate.

Cleveland catches the ambiguity and the complexity of the political situation as well as invoking the schizophrenic affections of the mob who watched the execution of Thomas Wentworth, first earl of Strafford, in 1641.

Cleveland was born in Loughborough in 1613, the eldest son of a clergyman, and entered Christ's College, Cambridge, in 1627, where he was a contemporary of John Milton. Cleveland became a Fellow of St John's College, Cambridge in 1634. He left Cambridge when it was taken over by Parliamentarian forces to join the Royalist headquarters in Oxford in 1643. Many of his best-known political poems were written at Cambridge, including the Strafford epitaph, 'A dialogue between two zealots', 'Smectymnuus', and 'To P. Rupert', although he contributed little to printed university anthologies other than an elegy for Edward King which appears in the same volume as Milton's 'Lycidas' (*Juxta Edouardo King*, 1638). His 1644 poem 'The rebel Scot', composed at Oxford, is probably his most famous and influential piece of work. Written after the Scottish invasion of England to decry their mercenary greed, Cleveland winds himself up into a fit of fury, representing himself as a prophet of stability. The Scots upset the order of the world which the king has undertaken to guarantee; their rebelliousness reveals their venality and inhumanity: 'Nature her selfe doth Scotch-men beasts confesse.' He presents himself as the poet of righteous indignation ('I am all on fire / Not all the buckets in a country quire / Shall quench my rage') and anger, and warns in a particularly strong image that 'A poet should be feared / When angry, like a comet's flaming beard'. His keen sense of the importance of poetry in the political sphere, and his effective deployment of satirical verse, can tell us much about the ways in which politics and culture were enmeshed during the Civil Wars. In 'The rebel Scot', Cleveland's rich, scabrous, and scatological imagination is given free rein and the poem consists of a long list of insults:

> Sure, England hath the hemorrhoids, and these
> On the north postern of the patient seize
> Like leeches; thus they physically thirst
> After our blood, but in the cure shall burst!

The poem not only influenced Royalist verse but the anti-Presbyterian, anti-Scots sonnets of Milton in 1646/47, and is the inspiration for Andrew Marvell's long Restoration poem 'The loyal Scot' (McDowell 2008).

The character of a London diurnall was written and published in 1644 and is a good example of Cleveland's aggressive polemic style. A piece of prose with some poems added, it demonstrates Cleveland's engagement with the print and news market-place of the 1640s, and his technique of destructive and contemptuous satire: a London diurnal (i.e., a London-based, parliamentary newsbook) 'begins usually with an Ordinance, which is a Law still-borne; dropt, before quickned by the Royall assent'. This vicious and unpleasant image is characteristic of Cleveland's Juvenalian satire, excessive and transgressive; at the same time it is (horrifically) articulate. He helped to create the image of the Puritan enemy as irreligious, hypocritical, illegal and dirty; he contributed more than most to a vicious print culture.

Throughout the war Cleveland produced this kind of verse and journalism, attacking those who would defy the king. His *Character of a moderate intelligencer* from 1645 again attacks London newsbooks and also includes several more poems attacking parliamentary committees, 'Presbyters', and Independents, concluding by scorning all of the social innovations of the city: 'I doe abhorre a woman should weare breeches / A Priest that fights, a man at Armes that Preaches.' This characteristic simplicity, social inversion, and disgusted tone expressing just how repellent such ungodly things are give Cleveland's political writings their power and directness. Cleveland was best at writing up-to-the-minute, politically detailed poetry, although he also undertook pastoral verse on a lover ('Delia') in the manner of fellow Royalist poets Robert Herrick and Richard Lovelace. Cleveland was also capable of more complex meditations on the political situation, especially as the Royalist cause stuttered towards defeat in the First Civil War: 'The king's disguise' (1645) has recently received extended critical treatment revealing this (Loxley 1997). Often his political poetry is anthologized in manuscripts alongside his more lyric, if strange, poems like 'Fuscura', which is about a bee.

Little is known of Cleveland after the end of the wars, although he did spend some time in prison in 1655. After three months in prison he wrote a petition directly to Cromwell and was released. He died in 1658. His style of writing was exceptionally suited to the hurly-burly of conflict, where slapdash but effective verse – all about punch rather than subtlety – was in demand. That said, his aggressive, politically committed poetry continued to be very popular – his *Poems* of 1651 were repeatedly reprinted throughout the 1650s and 1660s. His burlesque style would become very popular as a mode and his example was important to Samuel Butler, Jonathan Swift, and others.

SEE ALSO: Berkenhead, John; Herrick, Robert; Lovelace, Richard; Marvell, Andrew; Milton, John

REFERENCES AND SUGGESTED READINGS

de Groot, Jerome (2004) *Royalist identities.* Palgrave Macmillan, Basingstoke.

Loxley, James (1997) *Royalism and poetry in the English Civil Wars: the drawn sword.* Macmillan Press, Basingstoke.

McDowell, Nicholas (2008) *Poetry and allegiance in the English Civil Wars: Marvell and the cause of wit.* Oxford University Press, Oxford.

Clifford, Anne

JAMES DAYBELL

The life of noblewoman and diarist Lady Anne Clifford, countess of Pembroke, Dorset, and Montgomery (1590–1676), was dominated by an inheritance dispute over the Clifford titles and estates, a fractious experience that inflected the various extant writings connected to her with a strong sense of family, lineage, and posterity. The only surviving child of George Clifford, third earl of Cumberland (1558–1605) and his wife, Lady Margaret (1560–1616) – herself the youngest daughter of Francis Russell, second earl of Bedford – Anne Clifford was born at Skipton Castle on 30 January 1590, and apparently conceived on 1 May 1589 'in the Lord Wharton's house in Channell Row in Westminster'. During the course of her long life she married only twice: first, on 25 February 1609, Richard Sackville, Lord Buckhurst, third earl of Dorset (1589–1624), with whom she quarrelled bitterly; and second, on 3 June 1630, Philip Herbert, earl of Montgomery and fourth earl of Pembroke (1584–1650), Charles I's lord chamberlain, a match that brought great wealth, power, and court influence, but was no more happy than her first. She gave birth to two surviving daughters by her first marriage, Margaret (1614–76) and Isabella (1622–61), and had three sons by her first husband and two by her second, all of whom died in infancy. After Pembroke's death she enjoyed a period of more than two decades of widowhood as a redoubtable matriarch, holding the hereditary office of sheriff of Westmorland, a position she used to assert her ancestral rights. Anne Clifford died on 22 March 1676 at Brougham Castle, and was buried in a tomb of her own fashioning at the church of St Lawrence, Appleby on 14 April, laid to rest as one of the wealthiest noblewomen in later Stuart England, having bequeathed over £80,000 in heritable estates, with a rental income of £8,000 per annum.

As was customary for early modern girls of her elevated social status, Anne Clifford's upbringing and education were conducted within the household, overseen by her mother and other Russell relatives, all of whom were highly educated. Her childhood governess was Anne Taylor and she was tutored until 1602 by the poet Samuel Daniel. Of her own education Lady Anne summarized that she 'was not admitted to learn any language, because her father would not permit it; but for all other knowledge fit for her sex none was bred up to greater perfection than she'. This meant that unlike certain exceptional sixteenth-century girls she did not acquire Latin, yet account books indicate that she studied French, learned the lute from the composer Jack Jenkins, and had a dancing master, Stephen. Her formal learning was clearly bookish, as testified by the numerous volumes depicted neatly arranged in the left-hand panel of the Appleby Triptych, a biographical painting comprising a centre panel (the 'Great Picture') showing Anne, her parents, brothers, and relatives, and two wings encapsulating her life: the left, as a 15-year-old girl, and the right, as a matron in old age. Among the texts that she evidently studied during childhood were works of religion, philosophy, and science (the Bible, Augustine's *City of God*, Boethius's *Consolation of philosophy* and Agrippa's *Vanity of sciences*), works of history and geography (William Camden's *Britannia* (1585), and Abraham Ortelius's *Theatrum orbis terrarum*) as well as literature, especially romance and fiction (Ovid's *Metamorphoses*, Baldassare Castiglione's *Courtier*, Michel de Montaigne's *Essays*, Philip Sidney's *Arcadia* (1590), and the works of Chaucer and Spenser). Widely read and well educated, she was praised by the likes of John Donne and Bishop Edward Rainbow for her wide-ranging discourse, wit, and learned conversation. Reading clearly played an important role throughout her life. She inherited her mother's library, which formed the basis of an ongoing collection (some of which is depicted in the right-hand wing of the Appleby Triptych), and her household official George Sedgewick noted that she had 'a library stored with very choice books, which she read over not cursorily, but with judgement and observation'. Her diary regularly mentions her being read to aloud by servants, and a marginally annotated copy of *A mirrour for magistrates* once owned by Lady Anne appears to have been read collectively by her household in a series of daily readings over a three-month period between 21 March and 20 May 1670. Furthermore, Rainbow described the fascinating way in which her bedchamber was transformed into a kind of commonplace book for the purpose of

discourse with her servants: 'she would', he remarked, 'frequently bring out of the rich Store-house of her Memory, things new and old, Sentences, or Sayings of remark, which she had read or learned out of Authors', causing these to be written out on papers, which were then pinned up on her walls, hangings and furniture, thus dressing the room 'with the flowers of a Library'.

Unlike her mother, Clifford was never a major literary patron, but had obvious intellectual and literary interests, growing up in a rich cultural milieu; the countess of Cumberland associated with distinguished Elizabethan writers, including Edmund Spenser, Henry Constable, Samuel Daniel, and Fulke Greville. As a member of Anna of Denmark's entourage the young Anne danced in three court masques between 1609 and 1610: Ben Jonson's *Masque of beautie* (14 January 1609) and *Masque of queenes* (2 February 1610) and in Samuel Daniel's *Tethys festival* (5 June 1610) celebrating Henry's creation as prince of Wales. As the heir of Margaret Clifford, Lady Anne was lauded in her youth by her mother's clients who sought to persuade her to assume the maternal mantle as a patron of serious literary and theological works. The invitation of Daniel's dedicatory sonnet of 1607 to his former pupil ('I know you love the Muses, and you will / Be a most faithfull Guardian and a just') was echoed in Aemilia Lanyer's dedicatory poem 'To the Lady Anne, countesse of Dorcet' in *Salve Deus rex Judaeorum* (1611), which emphasized her maternal legacy of virtue and above all her bounty. While she never had the inclination to follow in her mother's footsteps, Lady Anne did, however, honour the writers associated with her family, paying tribute to her old tutor Samuel Daniel by incorporating a portrait of him into the Appleby Triptych (describing him as 'a man of Upright and excellent Spirit, as appeared by his Works') and building a tomb for him in Beckington church, Somerset, which bore the inscription 'that excellent Poett and Historian'; and in 1620 she erected a monument in Westminster Abbey for her mother's client Edmund

Spenser, proclaiming him 'The Prince of Poets in His Tyme'.

The roots of Anne Clifford's great dispute over inheritance lay in her father's decision in 1605 to bequeath his estates (for financial reasons) to his brother, Francis, fourth earl of Cumberland. Anne, his sole heir, received instead £15,000 as a portion. As her guardian, Countess Margaret initiated on her daughter's behalf what was to be a long and immensely complicated legal battle to attain the hereditary Clifford baronial titles and estates, claims which were at first refused by the earl marshal's court in 1606. After meticulous archival researches demolished the Earl Francis's case for all the estates, the countess won a victory in 1607 in the Court of Wards, which decreed that the Skipton (though not the Craven) properties were rightfully Anne's. In practice, though, her uncle kept possession. In 1612, Anne's first husband, Dorset, took over his wife's lawsuits through which he sought to extract maximum financial gain, thus further complicating proceedings. Anne refused to relinquish her claim to all her estates despite untoward pressure from her husband, rejecting in February 1617 King James's award to settle the dispute. The latter gave all estates to Earl Francis and his male heirs, and awarded £17,000 in compensation to Dorset and Anne.

Anne's struggles over her inheritance are a continuing feature of her *Diary* for the years 1616–17 and 1619, in which she figures herself as alienated from her male kin, but aided by God's providence in a protracted effort to claim her rightful title to her lands. An entry for January 1617 illustrates the enormous pressure brought to bear on her: 'The King asked us all if we would submit to his Judgement in this Case. My Uncle Cumberland, my Coz. Clifford & my Lord answered they would, but I would never agree to it without Westmoreland, at which the King grew in a great Chaffe against me.' On Dorset's death in 1624, Anne received a large jointure of lands in Essex and Sussex amounting to an income of £2,000 per annum, giving her the wealth and independence to settle her daughters' futures and turn her attentions back

towards the claim for her estates. She married the earl of Pembroke in a bid for support in her campaign against Earl Francis's heir, her cousin Henry Clifford, who was without male heirs. Under these circumstances and knowing the implications of the king's award on Henry Clifford's death, Anne made an agreement with her second husband in December 1634, guaranteeing her possession of the Westmorland lordships. Anne and Pembroke quarrelled soon after (over estates and his infidelities) and she was banished from London, living for eight years in his Wiltshire properties and then at Baynard's Castle in London during the Civil War. On the death of Henry Clifford in 1643, hostilities prevented her occupying the estates, but she nevertheless appointed officers in Westmorland and Craven. After Pembroke's death in 1650 she had the freedom to try to overturn the king's award, which led to costly and bitterly determined litigation through which she sought to eject tenants in Westmorland and to oust Henry Clifford's heir, Richard Boyle, earl of Burlington (1612–98) from the Craven lands. The rapacity with which she enforced her rights has perhaps dented her posthumous reputation.

One of the few known early modern female diarists, Anne Clifford appears to have engaged in diary-writing throughout her life, although most of the original manuscripts are not extant. What survives is a series of life writings, diary-like and otherwise, that are generally collectively known as Clifford's *Diary*. A major part of these writings is the 'Knole Diary', which survives as a late eighteenth-century transcript that includes fragmentary entries for 1603, 1616–17, and 1619, and is one of the earliest secular examples of the form, recording a mixture of personal and family affairs with public events. While mainly matter-of-fact and descriptive the *Diary* nonetheless offers some analytical commentary on emotions, motives, and judgements, and marginal entries of notable occurrences (such as 'Prince Charles created Prince of Wales') situate the personal narrative within a broader framework of public events. The years 1623 to 1649 are covered summarily by Anne in her autobiographical account of her own life, but no diary remains for this period. Annual summations of occurrences for the years 1650 to 1675 (sometimes collectively referred to as the 'Kendal Diary', though strictly not diary-like in either form or practice) were recorded in the third volume of her 'Great Books', or Books of Record, which contained vast quantities of genealogical information relating to Clifford ancestry. Unlike her earlier journal there is scant reference to national or international events here, the entries instead offering a digest of her life in Westmorland. The only original diary-like form to have survived is Anne's 'Day-Book', which covered the last 11 weeks of her life in 1676. It was dictated regularly at various times of the day to a series of amanuenses, which is attested to by the different scribal hands observable throughout. In old age, with time on her hands, she was able to record the minutiae of daily occurrences at Brougham Castle with an assiduity simply not possible during earlier stages of her life when she would have lacked such privacy and leisure.

Although Clifford's diary-writing was secular in outlook, unconstrained by the straitjacket of religious accounting that marked the daily writing habits of a woman like Lady Margaret Hoby, she was certainly pious, deeply versed in biblical and other religious texts. A supporter of the established church, she had certain Puritan leanings, though she eschewed the staunch outlook of Margaret Clifford and her tutor Daniel. Her households were pious establishments: Sedgewick writes 'The psalms of David appointed for the day she constantly read, and had three or four chapters read to her by some of her women daily', and she and her family received the sacrament at least four times a year. Her resident clergy were often in attendance upon her; she received regular visits from clergymen to preach in her private chapel; and she was active charitably, contributing financially to the upkeep of the fabric of churches and endowing almshouses.

In addition to her *Diary*, household accounts, a funeral sermon, and a substantial correspondence survives, including a letter of filial obedience penned to her father on the eve of her ninth birthday, written on paper with a decorative border; and a large number of intimate, respectful, often conspiratorial letters to her mother. She commissioned, oversaw, and contributed to a series of genealogical manuscripts which were bequeathed to her Thanet successors along with a large collection of transcripts of numerous evidences. Chief among these manuscripts were three foliosized copies of her great books of record, each comprising three volumes and produced from texts drawn up by St Loe Kniveton, whose work was rewritten and expanded with contributions from the antiquary Roger Dodsworth. These great books were commissioned to document Anne's claim to her title, and reproduced genealogies of her Vipont and Clifford forebears as well as vital documents collected from various royal courts, appended with scholarly apparatus. The books themselves formed an invaluable legal repository for Lady Anne and her legal team during her protracted inheritance disputes. These collections were added to with summaries of the lives of her predecessors and an autobiographical memorial of her life. Further commissions included two histories of her forebears, compiled by the judge and antiquary Sir Matthew Hale, as well as genealogies, a book of heraldry, several copies of Richard Robinson's description of the Earl George's voyages (one of which was illustrated), and a volume of her mother's letters. These manuscript collections, all overseen by Lady Anne, surpass mere antiquarianism in their innate practicality as a legal resource and their testimony of her lineage and titular claim. Collectively they attest to her as a family historian of some note.

Concerns with family, lineage, and posterity likewise marked Anne Clifford's extensive activities as a builder, restorer, erector of monuments, and patron of the visual arts. From the 1650s onwards she threw her energies into conserving her ancestral estates, repairing the castles of Appleby, Brougham, Brough, Pendragon, Skipton, and Barden Tower; restoring and renovating churches and chapels; and endowing and building almshouses. Through heraldic coats of arms emblazoned on funerary monuments (including those of her father and mother, and indeed her own in Appleby church), on almshouses, and throughout her castles, and on the plaques that adorned restored buildings, Lady Anne stressed the legitimacy of the rights inherited from her father and expressed a powerful sense of ancestral pride. Similar self-publicity was achieved in the commissioning of two triptych portraits (one each for her daughters Margaret and Isabella) painted by Jan van Belcamp (and possibly Peter Lely), which encapsulated the life of Anne Clifford as a young girl and elderly matriarch in opposing wing panels, and memorialized her family in the centre panel or 'Great Picture'. Moreover, through her actions as baroness and sheriffess once she entered upon her ancestral lands, Lady Clifford tenaciously defended her aristocratic privileges against her tenants, fiercely concerned to protect her rights and justify her position and posterity.

SEE ALSO: Daniel, Samuel; Donne, John; Hoby, Margaret; Jonson, Ben; Lanyer, Aemilia; Spenser, Edmund

REFERENCES AND SUGGESTED READINGS

Chan, Mary & Wright, Nancy E. (2004) Marriage, identity, and the pursuit of property in seventeenth-century England: the cases of Anne Clifford and Elizabeth Wiseman. In: Wright, Nancy E., Ferguson, Margaret W., & Buck, A. R. (eds) Women, property and the letters of the law in early modern England. University of Toronto Press, Toronto, pp. 162–182.

Chew, Elizabeth V. (2003) 'Repaired by me to my exceeeding great cost and charges': Anne Clifford and the uses of architecture. In: Hills, Helen (ed.) Architecture and the politics of gender in early modern Europe. Ashgate, Aldershot, pp. 99–114.

Clifford, D. J. H. (ed.) (1990) The diaries of Lady Anne Clifford. Sutton, Stroud.

Friedman, Alice T. (1995) Constructing an identity in prose, plaster and paint: Lady Anne Clifford as writer and patron of the arts. In: Gent, Lucy (ed.) Albion's classicism: the visual arts in Britain, 1550–1660. Yale University Press, New Haven, pp. 358–376.

Holmes, Martin (1975) Proud northern lady: Lady Anne Clifford 1590–1676. Phillimore, Chichester.

Klein, Lisa M. (2001) Lady Anne Clifford as mother and matriarch: domestic and dynastic issues in her life and writings. Journal of Family History 26(1), 18–38.

Kunin, Aaron B. (2004) From the desk of Anne Clifford. ELH 71(3), 587–608.

Lewalski, Barbara K. (1993) Claiming patrimony and constructing a self: Anne Clifford and her Diary. In: Writing women in Jacobean England. Harvard University Press, Cambridge, MA, pp. 125–151.

Matchinske, Megan (2007) Serial identity: history, gender, and form in the diary writing of Lady Anne Clifford. In: Dowd, Michelle M. & Eckerle, Julie A. (eds) Genre and women's life writing in early modern England. Ashgate, Aldershot, pp. 65–80.

O'Connor, Mary E. (2000) Representations of intimacy in the life-writing of Anne Clifford and Anne Dormer. In: Coleman, Patrick, Kowalik, Jill Anne, & Lewis, Jayne Elizabeth (eds) Representations of the self from the Renaissance to Romanticism. Cambridge University Press, Cambridge, pp. 79–96.

Orgel, Stephen (2005) Marginal maternity: reading Lady Anne Clifford's A mirror for magistrates. In: Brooks, Douglas A. (ed.) Printing and parenting in early modern England, Ashgate, Aldershot, pp. 267–290.

Spence, Richard T. (1997) Lady Anne Clifford: countess of Pembroke, Dorset and Montgomery (1590–1676). Sutton, Stroud.

Suzuki, Mihoko (2001) Anne Clifford and the gendering of history. Clio 30(2), 195–229.

Williamson, G. C. (1922) Lady Anne Clifford, countess of Dorset, Pembroke & Montgomery, 1590–1676: her life, letters and work. SR Publishers, Wakefield.

Wiseman, Susan (2003) Knowing her place: Anne Clifford and the politics of retreat. In: Berry, Philippa & Tudeau-Clayton, Margaret (eds) Textures of Renaissance knowledge. Manchester University Press, Manchester, pp. 199–221.

Clinton, Elizabeth

GARRETT A. SULLIVAN, JR

Elizabeth Clinton, countess of Lincoln (?1574–?1630), is the author of one known work, a tract in defence of breastfeeding entitled *The countess of Lincolns nurserie* (1622). Daughter of Sir Henry Knevitt of Charlton, Wiltshire, Elizabeth married Thomas Clinton (otherwise Fiennes), Lord Clinton sometime after 21 September 1584. By her own account, Clinton had 18 children, of whom as many as half died during infancy. Clinton attributed at least 'one or two' of these deaths to her use of wet nurses instead of breastfeeding the infants herself. Although few details of her life survive, it is known that her son Theophilus, who succeeded his father as earl of Lincoln in 1616, brought a suit in chancery against his mother over the guardianship of his three younger brothers. One of Clinton's daughters, Arabella, emigrated to the Massachusetts Bay Colony in 1620, but died shortly after arriving. Clinton probably died in 1630.

The countess of Lincolns nurserie should be considered in the context of seventeenth-century notions about maternal breastfeeding. For noblewomen, the employment of wet nurses was the norm, even as (and perhaps also because) the majority of early modern women breastfed their children. Breast milk was understood to have medicinal as well as nutritive properties, and was believed to be, like semen, purified blood. However, many thought the beneficial effects of breast milk to be fully realized only through the mother–infant bond. French physician Jacques Guillimeau wrote in *The nursing of children* (1612) that 'every mother should nurse her owne child: because her milke which is nothing else, but the bloud whitened ... will bee alwaies more naturall, and familiar unto him, than that of a stranger' (Salmon 1994). Guillimeau's reference to 'a stranger' captures cultural anxieties about the potentially contaminating influence of the wet nurse – anxieties brought home for Clinton by the deaths of her infant children and expressed powerfully in the

Nurserie: 'I haue found by grieuous experience, such dissembling in nurses, pretending sufficiency of milke, when indeed they had too much scarcitie; pretending willingnesse, towardnesse, wakefulness, when indeed they haue beene most willfull, most froward, and most slothfull, as I feare the death of one or two of my little Babes came by the defalt of their nurses.'

Clinton's argument in the *Nurserie* can be summed up in her assertion that 'the duty of nursing [is] due by mothers to their owne children'. She develops this claim, first, by providing evidence of that duty drawn primarily from the Bible (e.g., Abraham's wife Sarah 'gaue her sonne *Isaac* suck'); and, second, by addressing objections to the practice of breastfeeding. Clinton believes the maternal duty to breastfeed to be divinely inaugurated, and thus also to be one to which mothers are 'bound ... in conscience'. Moreover, she understands breastfeeding as the extension of childbearing itself, and thus it is part of the divine edict to be fruitful and multiply. Breast milk is produced by 'the direct prouidence of God', which prompts Clinton to ask of the mother who refuses to breastfeed, does she 'not despise Gods prouidence?'

In addressing the arguments against breastfeeding, Clinton criticizes what she takes to be the values of her fellow noblewomen: 'it is objected, that it is troublesome; that it is noisome to ones clothes; that it makes one look old, &c. All such reasons are vncomely, and vnchristian to be objected.' In adhering to such objections, these noblewomen 'argue *vnmotherly affection, idlenesse, desire to haue liberty to gadd from home, pride, foolish finenesse, lust, wantonnesse,* & the like euills'. Additionally, Clinton stresses the bad example that noblewomen's abdication of this maternal responsibility could represent for women of lower rank. What really animates her text, though, is regret at her own failure to perform what she terms her 'bounden duty', for reasons both personal and cultural: 'I knowe & acknowledge that I should have done it, and hauing not done it, it was not for want of will in my selfe, but partly I was ouerruled by anothers authority, and partly deceiued by somes ill counsell, & partly I had not so well considered of my duty in this motherly office, as since I did.' Read in light of this comment, the Nurserie can be seen as simultaneously an alternative to ill counsel; a textual rebuttal of the unspecified authority that once overruled her; and the expression of Clinton's contrite sense of both her Christian and her maternal duties.

Clinton's text features a dedicatory epistle to her daughter-in-law, Lady Bridget, countess of Lincoln, whom she commends for 'go[ing] on with that loving act of a loving mother; in giving the sweete milke of your owne breasts, to your own childe'. As such, the Nurserie contributes to the genre of the mother's advice book, other major examples of which include Dorothy Leigh's The mothers blessing (1616) and Elizabeth Jocelin's The mothers legacie, to her unborne childe (1624).

SEE ALSO: Jocelin, Elizabeth; Leigh, Dorothy

REFERENCES AND SUGGESTED READINGS

Ezell, Margaret J. M. (1987) The patriarch's wife: literary evidence and the history of the family. University of North Carolina Press, Chapel Hill.

Mahl, Mary R. & Koon, Helene (1977) The female spectator: women writers before 1800. Indiana University Press, Bloomington.

North, Marcy (2009) Women, the material book and early printing. In: Knoppers, Laura Lunger (ed.) The Cambridge companion to early modern women's writing. Cambridge University Press, Cambridge, pp. 68–82.

Salmon, Marylynn (1994) The cultural significance of breastfeeding and infant care in early modern England and America. Journal of Social History 28(2), 247–269.

Travitksy, Betty S. (2004) Clinton, Elizabeth. In: Oxford dictionary of national biography. Oxford University Press, Oxford.

Wayne, Valerie (1996) Advice for women from mothers and patriarchs. In: Wilcox, Helen (ed.) Women and literature in Britain, 1500–1700. Cambridge University Press, Cambridge, pp. 56–79.

Colet, John

DANIEL T. LOCHMAN

Renowned exegete and preacher as well as dean of St Paul's and founder of a restructured St Paul's School, John Colet (1467–1519) adapted Italian philosophy and humanist interests in the will and rhetoric to native English traditions of theology and education. He challenged the Tudor church and society by promoting an ideal Christianity rooted in the assumption that a reformed church should transform the lapsed individual and community and progressively realize a more perfect, more spiritual humanity that reciprocates God's love and action in the world.

These views emerge in Colet's comments on Paul's epistles and the opening verses of Genesis and in digressive commentary to a paraphrase of the Hierarchies of Dionysius the Areopagite. In treatises on the sacraments and the mystical body, and a sermon delivered to a convocation of clergy, Colet more directly critiques the decay he finds in the church since its inception, and he calls for a reformed, spiritualized faith within each individual and in the ecclesiastical republica. Writings printed during Colet's life or soon thereafter include a sermon delivered at the 1512 convocation of clergy in the London diocese, contributions to a Latin grammar completed by William Lily and Desiderius Erasmus for the refounded St Paul's School, and an admonition for the moral and religious well-being of the faithful. Other extant writings remained in manuscript until the close of the nineteenth century, and their chronology is still debated. Some are fragmentary and most have additions and corrections, some in the author's hand. Although the reputation of Colet has often been based largely on his relations with a network of prominent humanists, clerics, and political figures in England and Italy, Colet's writings have received attention since their publication by the Victorian scholar J. H. Lupton (1869, 1873, 1876). Today, they provide evidence of the emergence in early Tudor England of humanist rhetorical education, adaptations of Italian Neoplatonism, and the formation of 'Erasmian' approaches to the spiritual interpretation of Scripture.

An idealist said to prefer the contemplative life, Colet nevertheless maintained lifelong connections to the commerce and intellectual life of early modern London. Around 1450, his father, Sir Henry (d.1505), relocated from Buckinghamshire to London, there beginning a successful career in the Mercers' Company, eventually being named its master. After marrying Dame Christian Knyvet (d.1523), Henry twice served as lord mayor of London (1486–87, 1495–96); acquired properties in Buckinghamshire, the London area, and Sussex; and amassed wealth, some used to guarantee London's cooperation in the Magnus Intercursus, a trade agreement with the Netherlands, on behalf of King Henry VII. At his father's death, therefore, John inherited a large estate, a reservoir of royal favour still evident after Henry VIII's accession in 1509, and a sympathy for mercantile interests set against suspicion of corruption in some ecclesiastical institutions.

During the 1480s, John pursued a BA and MA at Cambridge, completing the latter in 1488. Embarking for the Continent around 1492, he resided for a time in Rome during 1493 and, in 1495, studied alongside the legist François DeLoynes in Orleans. Sears Jayne (1963) published Colet's correspondence with Marsilio Ficino and marginalia discovered on a copy – probably acquired while abroad – of Ficino's *Epistolae* (1495). Through his studies on the Continent and at Cambridge and, later at Oxford, Colet became acquainted with the works of church fathers such as Origen, Lactantius, Chrysostom, and Augustine, as Erasmus testified in a 1521 letter to Jodocus Jonas praising the lately deceased Colet (Godin 1982). Colet's writings refer also to non-Christian writers such as Plato, Cicero, Virgil, and Plotinus, as well as near-contemporaries such as Ficino, Niccolò Perotti, and Pico della Mirandola.

Back in England by 1496, Colet pursued religious studies, receiving bachelor's (1497) and doctoral degrees (1504) in divinity from Oxford. He was ordained deacon (1497) and then priest (1498). Erasmus's letter to Jonas reported the praise and large audiences Colet received for his 1498 lectures on Paul's epistles at Oxford, and he was probably then developing the interest in the *Hierarchies* of Dionysius evident in many of his writings. By the time Colet met Erasmus in 1499, he had a promising future as a learned preacher and influential ecclesiast. Elected dean of St Paul's in 1505, Colet advocated both small and large reforms, imitating the boldness of St Paul in disciplining Christian communities. Jonathan Arnold (2007) shows that he sought – unsuccessfully – to enforce statutes regulating the behaviour and benefits of minor clergy at the cathedral, in addition to challenging London's ecclesiasts and institutions, particularly the bishop of London, Richard Fitzjames. Colet's willingness to speak boldly, evident also in rhetorically elevated digressions in his writings, extended even to Henry VIII, whose preparations for warfare in France (1513) were reportedly criticized twice in sermons delivered at St Paul's, culminating in a tense private interview with the king and Colet's subsequent public affirmation of the possibility of a 'just' war. Yet Colet apparently gained Henry's respect. By 1517 the new chancellor, Thomas Wolsey, appointed Colet to the king's Privy Council.

Colet's most fully developed views appear in his religious writings. John B. Gleason (1989) observed that nineteenth-century writers promoted a view of Colet as England's prototypical Protestant and asserted that they attributed overmuch to the novelty of Colet's exegetical practice as compared to Erasmus's in the *Novum instrumentum omne* (1516), the first freshly edited Latin New Testament from Greek since Jerome's Vulgate. Inexpert in Greek but conversant with exegesis from Origen on, Colet eschewed the systematic topics of Peter Lombard's *Sentences* and the scholastic questions of Thomas Aquinas's *Summae.* Colet's commentaries are not strictly paraphrastic, grammatical, allegorical, or void of scholastic terminology, yet their mix of interpretive approaches is *sui generis*, particularly in their emphasis on a spiritual sense praised in language very similar to Erasmus's in the *Enchiridion militis christiani* (1503). Though unsystematic, Colet's exegesis unfolds in recursive digressions that emphasize central themes such as faith, love, justification, spiritual reformation, and an ideal of Christian society. The flexibility of this approach produced original, resonant readings. The *Lectures* on Romans and 1 Corinthians, for instance, emphasized through rhetorical amplification Colet's focus on the will as the means to spiritual perfection, in contrast to Ficino's scheme of salvation, which stressed contemplative intellection.

The emphasis upon will rather than intellect parallels Colet's humanist interest in the affective power of scriptural rhetoric and poetics. Colet sometimes interrupts exposition to praise God's mercy and justice or to amplify topics of thematic interest. He brings to exposition historical and rhetorical contexts thought to have shaped Paul's modulation of gentle and harsh rhetoric, in contrast to Jerome's practice of segregating such matters in prefaces. Colet often pauses to admire Paul's attention to rhetorical circumstances such as audience, place, and purpose, and he praises and imitates Paul's poetic figures, such as the mystical body, as well as the literary craftsmanship of Moses and Paul when they accommodate transcendent spiritual truths to the imagination. He weaves into his writing poetic motifs that expand biblical figures such as the 'sun' of righteousness, the shining city on the hill, and the floodwaters of sin that, together with periodic summaries, strengthen the coherence of his exposition and produce a cumulative sense of profundity.

SEE ALSO: Bible, the

REFERENCES AND SUGGESTED READINGS

Arnold, Jonathan (2007) *Dean John Colet of St Paul's: humanism and reform in early Tudor England.* I. B. Tauris, London.

Gleason, John B. (1989) *John Colet.* University of California Press, Berkeley.

Godin, André (1982) *Erasme: vies de Jean Vitrier et de John Colet.* Moreana, Angers.

Jayne, Sears (1963) *John Colet and Marsilio Ficino.* Oxford University Press, Oxford.

Lupton, J. H. (ed.) (1869) *Super opera Dionysii,* by John Colet. Bell, London.

Lupton, J. H. (ed.) (1873) *Enarratio in epistolam S. Pauli ad Romanos (Lectures on Paul's epistle to the Romans),* by John Colet. Bell, London.

Lupton, J. H. (ed.) (1876) *Opuscula quaedam theologica,* by John Colet. Bell, London.

Lupton, J. H. (1887) *The life of Dr John Colet, dean of St Paul's.* Bell, London.

O'Kelly, B. & Jarrott, C. A. L. (eds) (1985) *Commentary on first Corinthians,* by John Colet. Medieval & Renaissance Texts & Studies, Binghamton.

Collins, An

BROOKE A. CARLSON

Nothing is known about An Collins beyond her sole work, *Divine songs and meditacions composed by An Collins*, which was published in London by R. Bishop in 1653. Collins is a common surname in early modern England, and the name An was thought to be a variant on Anne, Ann, or Anna, or an article serving in lieu of a name. Critics today agree that the afore-mentioned An is a woman who was childless and in middle age when the book was sent to the printer. From her childhood on, Collins was ill. Her chronic sickness plays a large part in her turning to God in hopes of overcoming her mental and physical suffering. This same sickness kept her from performing conventional forms of female labour, which led to her writing theological meditation in poetic form.

The small octavo volume of *Divine songs* at the Huntington Library is the only version of the verses available. Since she is largely unmentioned in the works of other seventeenth-century writers, the autobiographical information we have comes from her own prose, in 'To the reader' and the metrical 'Preface' and 'Discourse'. Most of what we know is that she lived a life of pain, and that her pain led her to writing.

We can read Collins's gender in the text itself. On the first page of the 'Discourse' she writes, 'You that indeared are to pietie .../ Dain to survay her works that worthlesse seem.' Collins offers four reasons for her work, beginning with the praise of God. Secondly, she asserts that one must employ one's given talents and be held to account for them. Thirdly, she hopes that by reading her poetry a reader might be moved to read the scriptures, which she cites throughout the book. And finally, Collins hopes the text will offer the reader 'the image of her mind' so that 'They may conjecture how she was inclin'd'.

Collins begins with an epistle 'To the reader', followed by a five-page 'Preface,' and then 'Discourse'. A series of 13 songs are included, most of which explore the ways by which Collins communicates with and worships God. Physical suffering led Collins to look for solace outside of the body, in religious practice. Titles range from the first song's 'A song expressing their happiness who have communion with Christ', to the penultimate 'A song composed in time of the Civill Warr, when the wicked did much insult over the godly'. Collins's political stance is inconsistent, leading to her being read at times as a Royalist, and at times as a Puritan.

In 'A song exciting to spiritual alacrity', Collins turns to pain as the touchstone for spiritual growth:

> The sense of Love-Eternall, doth,
>   with Love, Obedience still produce,
> Which active is, and passive both,
>   So suffrings are of special use.

Connecting the physical pain of the body to spiritual worship, Collins follows a tradition of medieval and early modern women writers, such as Julian of Norwich (1342–1416),

Margery Kempe (1373–1440), and Saint Teresa of Avila (1515–82). 'Another song' makes the case for a female poetics based upon, but not always consistent with, gender:

> Yet as a garden is my mind enclosed fast
> Being to safety so confined from storm and blast
> Apt to produce a fruit most rare
> That is not common with every woman
> That fruitfull are.

The trope of a garden as the female mind, while not new, is intriguing and suggestive. As part of the reclamation process of feminist criticism, Collins's garden and birthing images can be studied next to the work of other seventeenth-century women writers to assess precisely how her own work draws on familiar preoccupations.

'Meditacions' make up the last section of her text; it is divided into five meditations with 'The preamble' followed by the meditations themselves, and concludes with 'verses on the twelfth Chapter of *Ecclesiastes*'.

Collins is controversial in that she was a woman writing when there were few women writers, and in that her religious and political views tend to be self-contradictory. In the end, Collins herself makes categorization difficult. For example, in the 'Discourse', she writes of God: 'He is incomprehensible I find ...' And then, 'Next unto God, my selfe I sought to know ...' Collins moves from an 'incomprehensible' God to what she 'sought' to do, which is know herself. Knowing herself, in the humanist manner, leads to knowing God. While the text is thus a meditation on spiritual being and self, it reveals the conflicted and contradictory state of being human. The question for Collins is how to love and be in the world. The answer Collins offers is one of meditative practice and spiritual activity. 'As doth the Hart the water brook desire / So humble Souls a Savior doth require.'

Divine songs and meditacions is important because it is one of the earliest volumes of collected poetry by a woman in the seventeenth century. In addition to its aesthetic appeal, evident in her potent imagery, the work sheds light on religion, politics, and women's experience in the seventeenth century.

REFERENCES AND SUGGESTED READINGS

Gottlieb, Sidney (2004) Collins, An. In: *Oxford dictionary of national biography.* Oxford University Press, Oxford.

Hobby, Elaine (1988) *Virtue of necessity: English women's writing, 1649–88.* University of Michigan Press, Ann Arbor.

commonplace books

ADAM G. HOOKS

An indispensable tool for Renaissance readers and writers, the commonplace book was a collection of quotations culled from various authoritative sources and organized under a series of topical headings. The practice of commonplacing served as an aid to memory by building and preserving a storehouse of acquired knowledge and, more importantly, an organizational rubric that allowed that knowledge to be retrieved and reused by the compiler. This practice encouraged an opportunistic form of reading in which texts were mined for lines or passages that possessed some practical, intellectual, or stylistic value. Once the appropriate extracts had been gathered and arranged, they could then be redeployed to support a persuasive argument or to embellish a literary work. Widely available printed commonplace books supplied convenient and efficient access to pre-selected and approved texts, offering an essential guide for readers attempting to manage the ever increasing quantity of printed material, while manuscript commonplace books kept by individuals reflected their idiosyncratic interests and intentions. A pervasive practice positioned at the intersection of script and print, composition and interpretation, commonplacing was fundamental to the ways in which people made sense of, interacted with, and actively created their textual world.

In classical rhetorical theory, as articulated by Cicero, commonplaces (derived from the Latin *loci communes*) were ideas or propositions that could be applied universally, rather than to a specific case, and as such could be used to enhance or extrapolate from an argument. As a central component of rhetoric, and thus of the grammar school curriculum, commonplacing became a staple of humanist pedagogy in the sixteenth century. Erasmus provided detailed instructions for compiling one's own commonplace book in his essential educational treatise *De copia* (1512), while providing plentiful examples in his collections of similes and proverbs, most prominently in the *Parabolae* (1514) and in the numerous and expanding editions of the *Adagia* (first published in 1500). Students were taught to excerpt passages only from works invested with the necessary degree of authority, which were almost exclusively classical texts in Latin, the language of instruction. The popular printed collections of adages, aphorisms, maxims, proverbs, and *sententiae* – wise, witty, and weighty sayings – served as sourcebooks and as models for identifying appropriately authoritative quotations. Just as important as the choice of quotations was the organizational pattern of a commonplace book, which effectively established the scope of the body of knowledge to be surveyed, and the interests that governed it. While usually arranged alphabetically, commonplace books were often assembled according to distinctly ethical or theological principles: Erasmus suggested topical divisions based on various virtues and vices; John Foxe's *Locorum communium* (1557), a largely blank book with printed subject headings designed to be filled in by the reader, manifested Foxe's religious commitments; and the writer and scholar of divinity Francis Meres ordered his *Palladis Tamia* (1598) on a topical trajectory that began with 'Of God' and ended with 'Hell'. Learning and practising the proper manner of commonplacing would serve students well throughout their lifetimes, equipping scholars in all disciplines, from theology to law to science and medicine, with the techniques and resources necessary for serious study. In *The advancement of learning* (1605), Francis Bacon emphasized the importance of compiling a commonplace book, but criticized ready-made printed versions with conventional topical divisions that simply followed an alphabetical order. Bacon preferred his own more systematic and practical method, based on direct observation rather than textual quotation, as exemplified in the *Novum organum* (1620), a work of natural philosophy that in many ways resembles a commonplace book (Blair 2003).

Commonplacing was not strictly a scholarly pursuit, for it was also central to the composition and presentation of literary works. The ubiquitous botanical vocabulary used to characterize the realm of poetry as a garden populated by choice flowers standing in the midst of rank weeds stemmed in part from the language of commonplacing. Printed commonplace books were often generally referred to as *flores poetarum*, 'the flowers of the poets', after the immensely popular *Illustrium poetarum flores* of Octavianus Mirandula, a collection of quotations from Latin poets first published in 1538, and regularly reprinted throughout the sixteenth and seventeenth centuries. The most frequently cited source for this terminology was Seneca's oft-repeated injunction on imitation, found in the *Epistulae morales*. Seneca directed readers to emulate bees, which made honey by extracting nectar from the most suitable flowers, depositing it in separate compartments of the honeycomb, and finally converting it into the sweet substance for which they are known. Likewise, readers should gather select phrases from the most excellent passages of poetry – the 'flowers' – and collect them in a commonplace book, where they can subsequently be accessed and, through a combination of diligence and talent, transformed into new poetic creations. The most admired poets were those who had mastered the art of digesting and incorporating textual material in order to compose poetry with a distinctly sweet style. Francis Meres praised Shakespeare in just these terms, citing his 'sugred' sonnets and

granting him the epithets 'mellifluous' (from the Latin for honey, *mel*) and 'hony-tongued'. This is now one of the most familiar characterizations of Shakespeare, but it emerged from a novel and radical enterprise. Meres was one of a group of scholars and stationers associated with John Bodenham, a London grocer who sponsored a series of printed commonplace books around the turn of the seventeenth century which, for the first time, used contemporary English texts as sources, rather than the traditional Latin classics. A practice that normally relied on classical *auctores* and was limited to an educated Latin readership thus became accessible in the vernacular, helping to raise the status of the developing field of English poetry, and indeed of the English language itself. *Bel-vedere* (1600), subtitled *The garden of the Muses*, began with a list of the writers from which the short, otherwise unattributed passages were drawn, while *Englands Parnassus* (1600) consisted of somewhat lengthier, attributed excerpts. By conspicuously publicizing vernacular authors, the Bodenham books identified Shakespeare and his contemporaries as suitably attractive and authoritative sources for commonplacing.

The practice of commonplacing vernacular texts quite literally made its mark on the texts themselves through the proliferation of printed commonplace markers, a typographical feature which pointed out the *sententiae* to readers (Hunter 1951). Usually taking the form of inverted commas, commonplace markers look just like modern quotation marks, but instead of indicating passages that are quoted, they indicate passages that are particularly quotable. This mark of punctuation identified a book as appropriately authoritative, while aiding in the detection and extraction of specific, preselected passages. The presence of commonplace markers encouraged readers to copy down these passages into their own manuscript commonplace books, or to forage through the text on their own to find similarly suitable passages which could likewise be copied, or simply marked with a handwritten marginal symbol. The Bodenham books both relied on and fostered the use of commonplace markers in vernacular texts. Shakespeare's narrative poem *Lucrece* (1594) included several passages marked in this way, and these passages reappear in both *Bel-vedere* and *Englands Parnassus* (Stallybrass & Chartier 2007). While poetry continued to be marked for commonplacing, the Bodenham books had an immediate effect on another class of books: printed plays, which quickly became the most desirable sources for this practice. Both early quartos of *Hamlet* (1603; 1604/5) include commonplace markers, mostly around the deliberately sententious lines of Polonius (Lesser & Stallybrass 2008). The plays of John Marston and Ben Jonson were the most thoroughly marked, though, since both authors were exceptionally aware of and committed to the practice of commonplacing. In both his poetry and plays, Marston often satirized those who failed to recognize the appropriate sources for their own commonplace books, including the work of other playwrights, such as Shakespeare's popular love story *Romeo and Juliet*. Jonson exploited the potential of print to display his formidable learning, filling the margins of his *Sejanus* (1605) with citations of classical sources, as well as commonplace markers. Jonson's penchant for highlighting *sententiae* of a political nature was in turn exploited by readers such as Sir William Drake, a political aspirant who copied extensively from *Sejanus* in his own series of manuscript commonplace books (Sharpe 2000). Commonplace markers were only the most visible sign that the practice of commonplacing encompassed the entire cycle of the production and reception of Renaissance texts. A play such as Jonson's *Sejanus*, undoubtedly a result of Jonson's own commonplacing, was presented and read as a source of *sententiae* intended to be used and reused by readers for their own practical or literary purposes.

The methodical industry required to maintain a commonplace book often proved too much for compilers, for numerous extant exemplars are only partially finished, revealing an intention unfulfilled by execution. While they incorporated a vast array of textual material, proper commonplace books should be distinguished from miscellanies, more diverse collections of texts, literary and otherwise, which could include accounts, anecdotes, recipes, and scattered notes which are not organized according to any overarching principle. Verse miscellanies often share certain characteristics with commonplace books, such as arranging poems on similar themes or by prominent authors together, but entire poems are copied, rather than notable extracts. Commonplace books and miscellanies, both in print and in manuscript, have been attended to by scholars with increasing frequency, since they demonstrate the vital, if unfamiliar, ways in which literary works circulated. Commonplacing in particular continues to be an attractive subject for study, as it provides an early modern antecedent for navigating the fragmentary textual world we are confronted with today.

SEE ALSO: Bacon, Francis; Foxe, John; Jonson, Ben; Marston, John; marginalia; Meres, Francis; Shakespeare, William; verse miscellanies, manuscript; verse miscellanies, printed;

REFERENCES AND SUGGESTED READINGS

Beal, Peter (1993) Notions in garrison: the seventeenth-century commonplace book. In: Hill, W. Speed (ed.) *New ways of looking at old texts: papers of the Renaissance English Text Society, 1985–1991*. Medieval & Renaissance Texts & Studies / Renaissance English Text Society, Binghamton, pp. 131–147.

Blair, Ann (2003) Reading strategies for coping with information overload ca. 1550–1700. *Journal of the History of Ideas* 64, 11–28.

Crane, Mary Thomas (1993) *Framing authority: sayings, self, and society in sixteenth-century England*. Princeton University Press, Princeton.

Hunter, G. K. (1951) The marking of *sententiae* in Elizabethan printed plays, poems, and romances. *The Library* ser. 5, 6(3–4), 171–188.

Lesser, Zachary & Stallybrass, Peter (2008) The first literary *Hamlet* and the commonplacing of professional plays. *Shakespeare Quarterly* 59(4), 371–420.

Moss, Ann (1996) *Printed commonplace-books and the structuring of Renaissance thought.* Clarendon Press, Oxford.

Sharpe, Kevin (2000) *Reading revolutions: the politics of reading in early modern England.* Yale University Press, New Haven.

Stallybrass, Peter & Chartier, Roger (2007) Reading and authorship: the circulation of Shakespeare 1590–1619. In: Murphy, Andrew (ed.) *A concise companion to Shakespeare and the text.* Blackwell, Oxford, pp. 35–56.

Constable, Henry

EMILY E. STOCKARD

Henry Constable (1562–1613) not only authored one of the first Elizabethan sonnet sequences, his poems also exemplify both the characteristic sonnet types: amatory and religious. Further, the marked stages in his life, first as a diplomat in the service of Anglican Protestantism, then as a Catholic in exile, coincide respectively with these two styles of verse.

By leading a life of public service, Constable followed in the footsteps of his family. He was born in 1562 to Christina Forster and Robert Constable, who was knighted on a Scottish battlefield in 1570. Following his matriculation from St John's College, Cambridge in 1580, Constable's diplomatic missions in service of the Protestant cause took him to the courts of Scotland and France, as well as to Germany, Italy, and Poland, all under the auspices of principal secretary of state Sir Francis Walsingham, his patron and long-time friend of his father.

Back at the English court in the late 1580s, Constable entered the circle of those for whom, in the fashion of Sir Philip Sidney, interests in religion, politics, and literature coincided. His literary productions during this time took the form of single sonnets addressed to such personages as Penelope Rich, Arbella Stuart, King James VI of Scotland, and his bride, Anna of Denmark. Constable's sonnet sequence *Diana* appeared first in 1592; this publication was followed in 1594 by a very different and enlarged version. Textual evidence indicates that the sonnets were composed before 1591, the publication year of Sidney's *Astrophil and Stella*, thus strengthening Constable's importance to the history of the English sonneteering tradition. In addition to these two versions of *Diana*, both published after Constable had left the country, additional manuscripts exist, one of which (the Todd manuscript, MS Dyce 44 in the Victoria and Albert Museum) was chosen as the basis for the standard modern edition (Grundy 1960). In sonnets embellished with Petrarchan figures typical of Renaissance erotic poetry, the sequence chronicles the poet's love for Diana, praising her along with other ladies of the court, while also commemorating notable births and deaths. The sequence concludes, in response to Sidney's death, with a rejection of earthly love in favour of the consolations afforded by heaven. This poetically conventional rejection of the earthly for the heavenly may have presaged Constable's actual leave-taking both of secular poetry and of the courtier's life upon his conversion to Catholicism, which, in retrospect, seem to have occurred almost simultaneously. His suspected authorship of the anonymous *Examen pacifique de la doctrines des Huguenots* (1589), translated into English as *The Catholike moderator* (1623), may have signalled this conversion, made manifest in the late summer of 1591 when Constable left the French expedition of Robert Devereux, earl of Essex, in support of Henry IV to join the Catholics.

For the rest of his life, much of it lived in exile, Constable devoted his self-proclaimed patriotic efforts to the conversion of James VI, by which means he aimed to secure not only religious toleration for his fellow English Catholics, but ultimately religious unification for his country. During this period he wrote theological tracts, now known only by contemporary references to them, and is assumed to be the author of a work that defends James's claim to the English throne. Constable's religious poetry, composed in exile (probable date 1593), extant in manuscript form, and apparently unknown to his English contemporaries, demonstrates his affiliation with Counter-Reformation devotional art and perhaps more particularly with medieval mysticism. In *Spiritual sonnets*, 17 sonnets printed in 1815 and addressed variously to God and the saints, with particular attention to Mary Magdalene, Constable turns the Petrarchan conventions of his secular poetry into a vehicle for expressing the soul's love for and ultimate unification with the divine.

Upon James's accession to the English throne in 1603, Constable was allowed to return to his family land. But in 1604 his unswerving efforts to convert the king led to a brief imprisonment in the Tower, after intercepted letters outlined plans judged to be near-treasonous. Following other short stints in prison, Constable was either exiled or allowed to leave the country for Paris in 1610. He died in Liège, Belgium, in 1613, while attending to the conversion of a Protestant divine.

In his day, Constable's poetic reputation was high; Ben Jonson and Michael Drayton ranked his secular court poetry alongside that of Sidney, and he was often praised alongside other notable poets. His religious poetry, unremarked upon by readers of his time, has in our day been rated more highly than his secular verse – a judgement perhaps rendered in light of his undoubted devotion to the Catholic cause. While Constable's convictions proved to be out of step with the politico-religious direction of his country, the forms of both his secular and his religious verse provide a minor model of its literary fashions.

SEE ALSO: Drayton, Michael; James VI and I; Jonson, Ben; Sidney, Philip

REFERENCES AND SUGGESTED READINGS

Bossy, John (1962) A propos of Henry Constable. *Recusant History* 6, 228–237.

Cousins, A. D. (1991) *The Catholic religious poets from Southwell to Crashaw.* Sheed & Ward, London.

de Oliveira e Silva, J. (1983–84) 'Plainness and truth': the secular and spiritual sonnets of Henry Constable. *University of Hartford Studies in Literature* 15–16, 33–42.

Grundy, Joan (ed.) (1960) *The poems of Henry Constable.* Liverpool University Press, Liverpool.

Guiney, Louise Imogen (1939) Henry Constable. In: *Recusant Poets.* Sheed & Ward, New York, pp. 303–318.

John, Lisle C. (1938) *Elizabethan sonnet sequences: studies in conventional conceits.* Columbia University Press, New York.

Kuchar, Gary (2006) Henry Constable and the question of Catholic poetics: affective piety and erotic identification in the *Spirituall sonnettes. Philological Quarterly* 82, 69–90.

Rogers, David (1960) 'The Catholic moderator': a French reply to Bellarmine and its English author, Henry Constable. *Recusant History* 5, 224–235.

Wickes, George (1954) Henry Constable, poet and courtier (1562–1613). *Biographical Studies 1534–1829* 2, 272–300.

Wickes, George (1957) Henry Constable's spiritual sonnets. *Month* 18, 30–40.

Copland, Robert

RUTH AHNERT

Robert Copland (*fl.* 1505–47) was active in the printing trade for over 40 years, as translator, printer, editor, and poet. The prologues and envoys he added to his works carefully document Copland's professional life from his 'fyrst werke' of translation in 1505. The reliance on these paratexts for biographical details, however, has led to disagreement concerning Copland's birth and early career. Copland's statement prefacing *Kynge Appolyn*, that he was 'folowynge the trace of my mayster Caxton', has led some scholars to conclude that Copland was William Caxton's apprentice, meaning a birth date somewhere before 1473. But Copland's reference to 'my mayster' may simply signal his respect for this influential forebear. Similarly, Frank Charlton Francis's suggestion (1961) of a northern origin for the printer derives from a beggar's comment to Copland in *The hye way to the spyttell hous* that he is 'lyke your maystershyp / of the north'.

Copland's work provides evidence of a French influence on Tudor literature. Early in his career Copland translated popular French texts for Wynkyn de Worde's press. His first recorded translation was *A complaynt of them that be to soone maryed* (c.1505), followed by *The complaynte of them that ben to late maryed* (c.1505), *The kalender of shepeherdes* (1508), *Kynge Appolyn of Thyre* (1510), and *The knyght of the swanne* (1512). Copland's preface to *The kalender* suggests that he was the driving force behind de Worde's Francophile output during this period, claiming that he read the French original and drew it to de Worde's attention. After beginning work as a printer in 1514, Copland continued to produce translations from French works, including *The maner of dauncynge of bace daunces after the use of Fraunce* (1521); *The begynnynge and foundacyon of the ... knyghtes hospytallers* (1524); a navigational route-book entitled *The rutter of the see* (1528); *The questyonary of cyrurgyens* (1542), a compendium of four surgical tracts; and *The maner to lyve well*, printed in 36 editions of books of hours (1529–56). Copland's original verse also acted as a conduit for French popular literature. His knowledge of French farce *Aves*, for example, probably underlies the poem to Mary in *The rosarye* (1521), a religious parody containing elements of the Ave Maria and the Salve Regina (Erler 1993).

Copland's translations may have been driven by a consistent desire to transmit French literary fashions in the English language, but they contributed to a print output that is notable in its heterogeneity. The range of publishers with whom Copland collaborated might account for some of this diversity. At the beginning of his printing career he shared the printing of *The deyenge creature* (1514), and *The justices of peas* (1515) with de Worde, and 10 more of his titles are identifiable as work for or with Richard Kele, John Byddell, Richard Bankes, and Michael Fawkes. Nevertheless, Copland's decision to produce specialist technical works such as the *Questyonary* and *Rutter* is striking. Sheila Ahern (1994) argues that the publication of

such texts was motivated by a desire to contribute to the public store of knowledge, rather than by financial gain, because they held little general interest. M. C. Erler (1985), however, makes the persuasive argument that the *Questyonary* was conceived as a surgical students' textbook, and printed in response to the amalgamation of the Barbers' and Surgeons' companies in 1540, a union which produced a fresh concentration on the company's training and teaching function. One might reasonably assume, therefore, that Copland's other technical volumes, such as his *Rutter* and Andrew Boorde's *Pryncyples of astronamye* (?1547), were also aimed at assured markets.

Copland's interest in market forces was both professional and creative, providing the stimulus for several of his prologues. Most notable is the preface to Copland's poem *The seuen sorowes that women have when theyr husbandes be deade* (c.1536), which provides an imaginary debate between 'Copland' the printer and a customer called Quidam. This dialogue, Thomas Betteridge (2004) argues, stages 'the effect of market forces on the circulation of knowledge' in 1520s London, for after discovering that he does not stock the kind of book that Quidam wants (a 'geest that is ful of bourdes'), for a price he is willing to pay ('a peny'), the two speakers collaborate to produce a suitably marketable text. This text is *Seuen sorowes*, one of Copland's three longer poems. Usually placed within the lascivious widow tradition, it is a parody of religious meditation on the seven sorrows of the Virgin. Unlike its analogues, Copland's poem has been praised for its attention to poignant detail: the widow's discomfort in her tight-laced mourning clothes, the distracting importunity of the beggars at the church door, and her worries over the mounting funeral expenses (Meagher 1977). The other two poems are *Jyl of Braintfords testament* (c.1535), which has been 'labelled a very late English fabliau', its scatological jokes and fart bequests owing much to Chaucer's 'Summoner's tale'; and *The hye way to the spyttell hous* (1529–34), 'a depiction of the life of the (often criminal) poor who went to London's St Bartholomew's Hospital' (Erler 2004). As in *Seuen sorowes*, Copland embeds a representation of himself in both of these texts. The preface to *Jyl* provides a fictional account of how Copland sought the origin of the saying, 'ye shall haue a fart / Of Iyll of Brantford for your paine', in which John Hardlesay gives him an 'olde scrow all ragged and rent' containing the story. In his dialogue *Hye way*, Copland plays the foil for the hospital porter's observations in a manner reminiscent of the interplay between 'More' and Hythloday in Thomas More's *Utopia* (1516).

These three poems are the dramatic culmination of a trend for self-representation that runs throughout Copland's works. His prologues and envoys show an acute awareness of posterity. The heading he applies to these pieces of prose and verse record, without fail, his role in the making of that book ('Lenuoy and excuse of Robert Coplande the translatour and Imprynter of this boke'). He also documents other details of his work that he wishes to advertise, such as the fact he produced the text of Chaucer's *The assemble of foules* (1530) from a manuscript source (now Bodleian Library, MS Bodley 638) rather than relying on an earlier printed edition. The pride Copland took in his works, and his concern for their after-life, is expressed in his envoy to *Guystarde and Sygysmonde* (1532), where he warns subsequent printers that, though he permits 'Correcyon' to the text, they should 'let thamendynge alone'. The paper trail that Copland left behind ends in 1547. In this year Boorde described him as the 'eldist printer of Ingland' (*Pryncyples of astronamye*), and the name of his successor, William Copland, appears for the first time on a colophon.

SEE ALSO: Boorde, Andrew; Caxton, William; More, Thomas

REFERENCES AND SUGGESTED READINGS

Ahern, Sheila (1994) Robert Copland (1470?–1548). In: Richardson, David A. (ed.) *Sixteenth-century British nondramatic writers*, 2nd series. Gale, Detroit, pp. 53–57.

Betteridge, Thomas (2004) *Literature and politics in the English Reformation*. Manchester University Press, Manchester.

Erler, M. C. (1985) The first English printing of Galen: the formation of the Company of Barber-Surgeons. *Huntington Library Quarterly* 48, 159–171.

Erler, M. C. (ed.) (1993) *Poems: Robert Copland*. University of Toronto Press, Toronto.

Erler, M. C. (1999) Printers' copy: MS Bodley 638 and the *Parliament of fowls. Chaucer Review* 33, 221–229.

Erler, M. C. (2004) Copland, Robert. In: *Oxford dictionary of national biography*. Oxford University Press, Oxford.

Francis, Frank Charlton (1961) *Robert Copland*. Jackson, Glasgow.

Meagher, John C. (1977) Robert Copland's *The seven sorrows. English Literary Renaissance* 7, 17–50.

Moore, W. G. (1931). Robert Copland and his *Hye way. Review of English Studies* 7, 406–418.

Phillips, Helen (1995) Aesthetic and commercial aspects of framing devices: Bradshaw, Roos and Copland. *Poetica: An International Journal of Linguistic-Literary Studies* 43, 37–65.

Sánchez-Martí, Jordi (2008) Robert Copland and *The lyfe of Ipomydon. Notes and Queries* 55, 139–142.

Coppe, Abiezer

NICHOLAS McDOWELL

Abiezer Coppe (1619–?1672) was one of the most notorious religious radicals of the English Civil Wars. He was allegedly a ringleader of the group of antinomian radicals active between 1648 and 1650 who were known by their opponents as the 'Ranters'. The Ranters were charged with believing that committing acts commonly regarded as sinful, particularly swearing, drinking, and extramarital sex, was proof of their transcendence of sin on earth and their freedom from moral law. However, the sensational, polemical image of the Ranters does not always match the evidence we have from their surviving writings of the complexity of their beliefs. Moreover Coppe's strange and powerful literary style has made him of great interest in the last 25 years to literary critics as well as to historians of religion and of the English Civil Wars; extracts from his works regularly appear in anthologies of English literature and are believed to anticipate the prophetic writings of Christopher Smart and William Blake.

Coppe was born in Warwick in 1619 and educated at Warwick School, where he was apparently something of a star pupil: the diary of Thomas Dugard, the master of Warwick School from 1633, records the young Coppe's excellence in Latin and Greek (McDowell 1997). Coppe was admitted to All Souls College, Oxford, in 1636, transferring to Merton College as a postmaster or scholar the following year. Coppe's tutor at Merton was the Presbyterian Ralph Button, to whom he seems to have been sent by the Puritan Dugard: these educational details reveal Coppe's privileged humanist and Calvinist education, far removed from the stereotype of the ignorant, libertine tub-preacher. Nonetheless it is hard to tell how far his later image has contaminated biographical accounts. Anthony Wood's colourful, hostile depiction of Coppe's time at Merton in *Athenae Oxonienses* (1691–92) includes the anecdote that he took extra food from dinner, claiming it was for his cat, when it was actually intended for a 'wanton housewife' whom he would frequently entertain in his rooms.

Upon the outbreak of civil war Coppe returned without a degree to Warwick, where Dugard supported the beginning of his career as a lay preacher. By the mid-1640s he had become a roaming Anabaptist preacher in the Midlands and Oxfordshire. As with many of those who became prominent radicals, he served as chaplain to a provincial Parliamentary army garrison in Warwickshire in 1646. By 1647/48 he had developed an association with the itinerant lay preacher Richard Coppin and with conventicles in Oxford and Berkshire, before achieving national notoriety with his ventures into print in 1649. The

Commonwealth Parliament ordered all copies of Coppe's *A fiery flying roll* (1649) to be publicly burnt, and the pamphlet provoked his imprisonment under the Blasphemy Act of 1650, although he was actually imprisoned before the Act was on the statutes. After two published recantations, Coppe was released in 1651. Little is known of his later life, but opponents doubted the sincerity of his recantation. An anonymous broadsheet of 1657 entitled *Divine fire-works* is evidently his work, written in the style of the publications of 1648–49. After the Restoration Coppe became a doctor in Surrey, having changed his name to Higham. He died in 1672.

Coppe's prose style has rightly been described as unlike anything else in the seventeenth century, even though it can be placed in a tradition of early modern radical writing (Hill 1982; Smith 1989). The liberties he takes with orthodox syntax and punctuation, and the instability of his tone, which switches between apocalyptic threat and bathetic joking, convey the sense of living in a moment in English history when all hierarchy and convention appeared to be disintegrating, and when it seemed society might be utterly renovated in anticipation of the last days prophesied in Revelation. Scholars have been baffled by Coppe's purpose even when they have admired his prose (Corns 1992). But it has become evident that Coppe's style is structured around intricate parody of the linguistic and typological forms of orthodoxy, in particular of the orthodox humanist education which he himself had experienced (McDowell 1997; 2003). Indeed the Erasmian persona of folly is at times as important a model for Coppe as the prophetic voices of the Bible.

The first published work to appear under Coppe's name was a preface to Richard Coppin's *Divine teachings* (1649). Coppin's tract dismisses the notion that a classical rhetorical education is a necessary qualification of the preacher, maintaining instead the sufficiency of the truths vouchsafed by inner experience of the Holy Spirit. Coppe's preface prepares the way for this argument through parody of the form of the ABC or hornbook, the basic text for learning to read in early modern England. He appropriates the typographical design of ABCs to re-educate the Puritan pedagogues who believe that illiteracy should be equated with damnation. The parody of educational texts is continued in *Some sweet sips, of some spirituall wine* (1649), which features an address to Coppe's former 'cronies' in Oxford in which the language and typography of Lily's grammar (first extant edition c.1542), the official text for teaching Latin in seventeenth-century England, is subject to extended mimicry. Coppe displays his own learning while locating linguistic and educational authority within the inspired individual rather than in political and religious institutions (McDowell 2003).

A *fiery flying roll*, which was printed as one pamphlet despite having separate title pages for its two parts, begins by describing Coppe's experience of spiritual crisis and conversion in powerful abstract images of death and rebirth. The title page of the first part names the author as 'his most excellent MAJESTY, dwelling in' Coppe, and it is often impossible to distinguish his voice from that of the angry God promising the apocalyptic destruction of all forms of political, religious, and social hierarchy. Coppe expresses his sympathy for the recently suppressed Levellers. The tract includes extraordinary passages influenced by picaresque narrative, in which the perfected Coppe moves around London and interacts with the poor and the criminal. The combination of prophecy, sexuality, and social radicalism in *A fiery flying roll* that was defined as blasphemous in 1649 remains provocative today.

REFERENCES AND SUGGESTED READINGS

Corns, Thomas N. (1992) *Uncloistered virtue: English political literature, 1640–1660.* Oxford University Press, Oxford.

Davis, J. C. (1986) *Fear, myth, and history: the Ranters and the historians.* Cambridge University Press, Cambridge.

Hill, Christopher (1982) Radical prose in seventeenth-century England. *Essays in Criticism* 32, 95–118.

McDowell, Nicholas (1997) A Ranter reconsidered: Abiezer Coppe and Civil War stereotypes. *Seventeenth Century* 12, 173–205.

McDowell, Nicholas (2003) *The English radical imagination: culture, religion, and revolution, 1630–1660.* Oxford University Press, Oxford.

Smith, Nigel (1989) *Perfection proclaimed: language and literature in English radical religion, 1640–1660.* Oxford University Press, Oxford.

Corbett, Richard

MATTHEW J. SMITH

Richard Corbett (1582–1635) was a poet who also served as bishop of Oxford and of Norwich. He was born in Ewell, Surrey, and entered Broadgates Hall, Oxford, in 1598 before graduating as a BA (1602) and MA (1605) from Christ Church. Corbett's literary output at Oxford consisted mostly of satires, elegies, and verse epistles, all heavily influenced by the university setting. His reputation as a performer of his own verse seems to have begun as a student. Anthony a Wood represents Corbett's Oxford reputation in terms of his 'poems, jests, romantic fancies and exploits' and notes that such wit was 'perform'd extempore' in public. These early 'jests' include Corbett's 'Upon mistris Mallett', also entitled 'Upon an unhandsome gentlewoman, who made love unto him', a poem afterwards imitated in form and content by James Smith. In addition to Corbett's adoption of satirical encomium in the style of Erasmus, 'Mistris Mallet' also showcases an early propensity towards religious stricture, characterized by open criticism of moments in English Tudor history that swung too close to the extremes of papists and Puritans, following the shrew mistress through '*Maryes* torrid dayes' and the downfall of the Spanish Inquisition.

Having been ordained a priest in 1613 and receiving a DD from Oxford in 1617, Corbett began in his verse to aim predominately at patronage and advancement, ostensibly sincere but biting towards those parties who might oppose his dedicatees. He wrote several elegies during this time, including 'An elegy upon the death of Queene Anne' (1619) and 'An elegie upon the death of his owne father' (1619). One can see the typical double agenda of Corbett's elegies in 'An elegie upon the death of *Sir Thomas Ouerbury* knight poysoned in the tower' (1613–16) wherein he implicates Overbury's poisoners both in injustice and in writing with their poison a more permanent and laudatory elegy than Corbett's own. He thus ironically bows to the 'strong poyson' of Frances Howard, ex-wife of the third earl of Essex, who orchestrated Overbury's murder,

> which did seeme to kill,
> Working afresh in some Historians quill,
> Shall now preserue thee longer, ere thou rot,
> Than could a Poem mixt with Antidot.

Although he is too often affiliated with the 'school', lines like these show Corbett at his most Metaphysical.

Corbett never commissioned the printing of these elegies, or any of his verse, during his lifetime, although some were printed in miscellanies or as appendages to works by other authors. His verse uniquely gained its relatively high popularity by circulation in manuscript form. In fact, it is noteworthy that Corbett's reputation as a cunning yet sincere wit was based on a society of readers who mostly acquired his verse by hand-to-hand or oral circulation, which for many readers implied a sense of social proximity to the author. This socio-literary context for Corbett's literature perhaps influenced his reputation as an author fully devoted to the political and aesthetic value of wit, a satirical integrity in which Thomas Fuller saw 'no destructive nature' but one that was always prepared to be 'repaid with a jest upon him'.

One of Corbett's lengthier pieces of the late 1610s that demonstrates his ability to patronize, satirize, and politicize in the genre of verse epistle is 'To the Lord Mordant upon his return from the north' (1617–18). While he would later devote himself almost entirely to the flattery of George Villiers, duke of Buckingham, Corbett's addressee in this epistle is John Mordaunt, whom Corbett treats partly as an intermediary to the viscount Villiers, who was in competition with Robert Carr, husband to Frances Howard, the subject of Corbett's recent elegiac criticism. 'To the Lord Mordant' provides an interesting window onto both Corbett's self-perception as a maturing poet and the disappointments that accompany the progress of his career. Recalling an episode when he was manhandled by the privy chamber guards because of his '*Scholler*' dress, Corbett repines that these guards did not know

> the truth,
> That I had sung *Iohn Dory*, in my youth;
> Or that I knew the day when I could chaunt
> *Chevy*, and *Arthur*, and the *Seige of Gaunt*.

Even if they had known about his balladeering past, he reasons, the disparity between the 'new *Coats*' of fashion and the more serious attire of his middle age hampers his access to possible patronage.

Despite his pessimism over the impermanence of his ballad rhapsodies in earlier years, Corbett wrote two popular ballads, 'The distracted Puritane' and 'A proper new ballad intituled The faeryes farewell: or God-a-mercy will', probably sometime in the early 1620s. Both ballads are set to popular melodies, and both are avidly anti-Puritan in content. An interesting note after the alternative title of 'The faeryes farewell' instructs '*Learned*' singers to use one tune and '*the vnLearned*' to use another. This ballad was one of the most popular works of Corbett's in his lifetime and has received the most critical attention since. 'The faeryes farewell' draws from English folklore associating fairies with superstition and Catholicism and from the anonymous *Coleorton masque* (performed in 1618), and it uses this combination of popular form and mythology to attack the iconoclasm of Puritan reform. M. E. Bradford (1973) has described the complex force of this ballad through its utilization of a popular form to draw his audience away from the Puritan ideology that opposes such verse, the same ideology that opposes the royalism of Corbett's ulterior audience, Buckingham and Laud. 'The faeryes farewell' also culls folkloristic material from the other of Corbett's major works in the 1620s, *Iter boreale* (1620–24), a verse travel narrative based on a trip north taken by Corbett and three companions, including his father-in-law, Leonard Hutten. The longest and most widely circulating manuscript of Corbett's, *Iter boreale* (printed in 1647) took its name and form from Richard Edes's Latin domestic travel narrative (1585), and its popularity spawned a host of travel narratives by authors such as Richard James, Thomas Master, Thomas Bispham, and Jeremiah Well. Corbett's travel verse records observations of historical sites, like Bosworth Field, narrates the discoveries of local folk traditions, and cues up sharp satirical attacks on Protestant extremism found in the Midlands.

In 1628 Corbett wrote the scathing 'Against the opposing the duke in parliament, 1628' that defends Buckingham against the influence of Calvinists William Prynne, John Pym, and George Buchanan, all three of whom are mentioned explicitly in the poem. Written in the year of Buckingham's assassination, 'Against the opposing the duke' was a last fervent defence of the patron whom Corbett had earlier famously defended regarding Buckingham's part in Prince Charles's proposed Spanish marriage in 'A letter to the duke of Buckingham, being with the Prince in Spain'. Corbett's later years, after he was transferred to the see of Norwich in 1632, were less literarily productive. His verse from the 1630s includes a series of celebratory poems on the birth of Charles II and 'An epitaph on Doctor Donne, deane of Pauls'. He died in Norwich in 1635.

SEE ALSO: broadside ballads; Buchanan, George; Devereux, Robert, earl of Essex; Donne, John; Prynne, William

REFERENCES AND SUGGESTED READINGS

Bradford, M. E. (1973) The prescience of Richard Corbett: observations on 'The fairies' farewell'. *Sewanee Review* 81, 309–317.

Brooks, Cleanth (1991) A merry bishop on the death of merry England: Richard Corbett. In: *Historical evidence and the reading of seventeenth-century poetry*. University of Missouri Press, Columbia, pp. 23–40.

Fisher, Joshua (2003) 'He is turned a ballad-maker': broadside appropriations in early modern England. *Early Modern Literary Studies* 9.

McRae, Andrew (2003) Satire and sycophancy: Richard Corbett and early Stuart royalism. *Review of English Studies* 54, 336–364.

Raylor, Timothy (1995) *Cavaliers, clubs, and literary culture: Sir John Mennes, James Smith, and the Order of the Fancy*. University of Delaware Press, Newark.

Coryate, Thomas

M. G. AUNE

Thomas Coryate (?1577–1617), a traveller, writer, and aspirant in the courts of Henry, prince of Wales and James I, is best known for a lengthy first-person travel narrative, *Coryats crudities* (1611) and several shorter pieces printed posthumously. Until comparatively recently, Coryate and his works, like those of other contemporary travel writers, though well known, were regarded as novelties rather than as literature worthy of study. However, as the definition of literature has expanded and especially since scholars have become interested in travel writing and cross-cultural relations during the Renaissance, Coryate and his works have attracted greater attention.

Born in Odcombe, Somerset, Coryate attended Winchester College, and then Gloucester Hall (now Exeter College), Oxford, where he studied for about three years. Though he did not complete a degree, his education and aptitude for learning languages provided him with a thorough knowledge of classical literature, history, and rhetoric. In 1608, Coryate undertook an extensive tour of Continental Europe and kept a detailed journal. Upon returning, he had the journal and commendatory verses printed as *Coryats crudities*. Inspired by the success of this journey, Coryate began a second by sailing to Istanbul. He travelled through the Middle East and walked to India where he died of dysentery in 1617. Several of his works were published posthumously.

His father, George, an ambitious rector and Latinist who dedicated verses and translations to influential figures and created a reputation for himself as a minor poet, perhaps inspired Coryate. When the younger Coryate made his way to London, he took advantage of a family friendship with a local aristocrat, Sir Edward Phelips, and his son Sir Robert. With their help, he presented himself at Prince Henry's court where he seems to have become a sort of unofficial jester. It was probably in this way that Coryate also befriended members of London's literary circles such as Ben Jonson and John Donne.

In his European travels starting in 1608, Coryate followed an itinerary through most important metropolitan areas, but also included stops at historical sites and the homes of noted scholars. Such journeys were typical for young aristocrats and members of the gentry seeking to complete a humanist education: travel provided an opportunity to learn modern languages, and to prepare for service to the crown. But Coryate's travels were unconventional in several ways. He seems to have travelled frugally and largely alone rather than with a tutor or an entourage. His writings are uncommon as his journal contains important information but also accounts of his non-scholarly adventures and misadventures.

During his initial voyage across the English Channel, for example, not only did Coryate become seasick, but he describes the experience for his readers: 'I had varnished the exterior parts of the ship with the excremental ebullitions of my tumultuous stomach.' Typically, Coryate's descriptions are lengthy, detailed, and digressive. In Calais, he mentions the governor's wooden leg and his conversation with the deputy governor about current events. Religion is a particular interest and Coryate rarely misses an opportunity to learn more about Catholicism, Judaism, or Islam. In Calais, for example, he attends Mass and witnesses 'many ceremonies that I never saw before'. He is not an objective observer, however. At the Mass, he 'observed a great profanation of the Lord's supper . . . their mutilated Sacrament' wherein congregants are given only the bread and not the wine. This for the Protestant Coryate contravenes the 'ancient practice of the Primitive Church'.

From the coast, Coryate works his way towards Paris, taking advantage of carts and other forms of transportation. Apparently out of a desire to travel inexpensively, Coryate often walks, though not as frequently as his reputation would suggest. His writings remain diverse, noting historical landmarks as well as recent events. His curiosities and biases are those of an erudite Protestant Englishman who is well aware he travels through Catholic lands. At Lyons, Coryate is thorough in his observations. He counts the number of churches (39) and evinces scepticism about the local legend that two of the churches actually built themselves. He points out historical sites, such as the place where Pontius Pilate allegedly died. And for his English readers, he describes a memorial image of the Jesuit Edmund Campion that he noticed while touring the Jesuit College. Though his inclinations are consistently sectarian, Coryate nonetheless respects the Jesuits for their learning and their library, commenting favourably on several Greek inscriptions. The Jesuits return the respect and give Coryate a tour of the institution.

Several days later, Coryate's curiosity about religion leads him to another encounter. He happens to stay at the same inn as the former French ambassador to the Ottoman Empire. In the ambassador's train are two Ottomans, one a jester, the other 'a notable companion and a great scholar' who speaks, in addition to Latin, six or seven languages. As he did with the Jesuits, Coryate starts a conversation in Latin.

The topic, according to Coryate, begins as informational and turns to religion and finally to an argument concerning the virtues of Christianity over Islam. The Ottoman, upset by Coryate's tone, breaks off the conversation and leaves. Coryate relates the discussion without judgement, and does not seem offended by the Ottoman's behaviour. Rather it seems to conform to his notion that, although he may be a learned Muslim, the Ottoman is still a Muslim and therefore unsuited to conventional scholarly disputation.

Coryate next spends six weeks in Venice. His courtly friends in London had given him letters of introduction to the English ambassador, Sir Henry Wotton, with whom he may have stayed. Coryate admits at the beginning of the Crudities that many had written about Venice before him: indeed, Venice had been a popular destination for English travellers for over a century when Coryate arrived. He plans, however, to provide readers with more, and more current, information about the city than had any previous traveller. Coryate's accounts of Venetian history, art, and architecture are heavily indebted to these earlier writers and travellers, but he also works to confirm, correct, or dismiss information that arouses his scepticism. His comparisons typically find Venice to be superior to any place he has visited before, though England also remains exceptional. Coryate's personal touches keep the descriptions lively. In a Greek Orthodox church, he finds two impressive candles, both eight feet tall and so thick he cannot reach fully around them.

True to his word, Coryate describes aspects of Venice that few writers before had included. In St Mark's Square, he finds a portrait of King James in a place of honour among portraits of the monarchs of Europe. He attends the theatre, festivals, and concerts and provides unusually detailed descriptions of the music. While nearly every English visitor to Venice is aware of the courtesans, Coryate actually visits them, and writes about them at length, not simply describing their allure and wealth, but their daily lives and what becomes of their children.

These personal encounters are perhaps the most memorable aspects of Coryate's narrative. Coryate records the details of his visit to the Venice ghetto. At a Sabbath service, he details the elements of the ceremony, expressing surprise that the attendants do not take off their hats while inside the synagogue. He carefully describes the Jews' clothes and dispels several myths about their appearance. Via information gleaned from a rabbi who speaks Latin, Coryate generates an analysis and critique of Judaism. As he did in Lyons, Coryate eventually asks the rabbi about Christianity. Unlike the Muslim in Lyons, the rabbi is in his own territory and, rather than walk away, he chases Coryate out of the ghetto. According to Coryate, ambassador Wotton happens to be passing nearby in his gondola and provides him with a safe retreat.

As he travels north towards Switzerland, Coryate is alerted both to the presence of a Spanish garrison near Lake Como and to the fact that as an Englishman he runs the risk of capture by the Inquisition. Though he enjoyed Italy and Venice especially, Coryate is comforted to move into Protestant regions in and around Switzerland and Germany, and in Zurich visits several Protestant theologians and scholars. These relationships were important enough to Coryate that he maintained correspondences with the men and printed several of their exchanges in untranslated Latin and Greek, in the Crudities.

From Basel, Coryate follows the Rhine to the coast. His writings continue to combine dense description and history along with digressive accounts of personal interest, from several pages of inscriptions copied from the Basle Münster, to the first English version of the William Tell story, to the drinking habits of the Swiss. In Germany, the mechanics of the clock in Strasbourg's cathedral, the Great Tun of Heidelberg, the Frankfurt fair, and Cologne's cathedral attract his attention. Though he continues to meet people, Coryate does not describe his encounters in nearly the detail he did in the first half of his journey. Returning home to Odcombe, Coryate brings his shoes to the church and hangs them on the wall.

According to his calculations, over five months he visited 45 cities and covered 1,975 miles.

Coryate was unconventional in his travels as well as in the uses to which he put them. While English travellers typically kept a travel journal, few ever published them. Coryate spent his first five months back in England revising his notes for just that purpose. He expanded the historical sections, added letters he had received from the scholars he had visited, two essays on travel by the German scholar Herman Kirchner, his father's collected poetry, and Latin verses by Julius Caesar Scaliger. The lengthy manuscript then circulated among Coryate's friends in London. As his writings passed from hand to hand, the readers apparently began adding verses (perhaps solicited by Coryate) that both mocked and celebrated Coryate and his achievements. Fifty-nine such verses were included in the book, including contributions from Donne, Jonson, Sir John Harington, Inigo Jones, John Owen, and Michael Drayton. Coryate also commissioned engraver William Hole to produce eight illustrations, including an elaborate frontispiece showing moments of his journey and framing a portrait of the author. Eventually, he sought to have his travel narrative printed and asked permission to dedicate it to Prince Henry. Henry consented, but only on the condition that Coryate include the poetry added by his readers.

Coryate seems to have experienced difficulty licensing and printing his book. These problems may have been a result of lack of interest from printers; alternatively, Coryate may not have known the proper procedures for publishing a book. The finished work was printed at his own expense. William Stansby, who would four years later print Jonson's *Works*, printed it with the title *Coryats crudities*. Coryate promoted his book energetically, preparing presentation copies for Prince Henry as well as the king and queen, important aristocrats, and the founder of the Bodleian Library, Thomas Bodley.

Coryate's efforts paid off and his book was quite successful. He quickly prepared a sequel using commendatory verses that he had gathered too late for the *Crudities*, along with copies of the speeches he made presenting his book, and a variety of other material loosely related to his journey. Echoing the title of the first book, *Coryates crambe* (1611) was much smaller and less elaborate. At nearly the same time, another book became available: *The Odcombian banquet*. This work was a pirated version of the verses written for the *Crudities*, printed without Coryate's permission. Coryate, angry, managed to add a conclusion to the *Crambe* in which he excoriated the unknown pirate. The pirate's identity is still unknown, but the most likely candidate is John Taylor, the 'water poet', with whom Coryate would later feud and who would become known for his manipulation of and profit from London's print culture.

In the *Crudities*, Coryate very self-consciously characterizes himself as a humanist scholar who uses his travels through Europe as a means of demonstrating his erudition and advancing himself at court. The volume's dedicatory letter to Prince Henry clearly states Coryate's desire to inspire the young men at court to travel and gain knowledge of the world. His Protestant partiality and patriotic verve would have matched the prince's interests very well. These elements alone would be enough to create interest in Coryate and his book, but Coryate's self-deprecating humour, tolerance of ridicule from others, and investment in a costly, illustrated book make him an exceptional case in Renaissance English culture.

The success of the *Crudities* may have inspired Coryate to travel further, since in 1612 he boarded a ship for Istanbul. His goal was to travel for 10 years, as did Ulysses, visiting the Holy Land, the Ottoman and Persian Empires and India. He planned to travel thriftily, taking care to walk whenever possible. He paused in Istanbul, Aleppo, and Ajmer, India, to learn the local languages and write up his notes. The tone and content of the remaining fragments of these writings are similar to the *Crudities*. Coryate portrays himself as a learned, confident, Protestant travelling through the lands that were once part of the ancient Greek and Roman Empires but have since decayed. At the same time, he is foolish, in one instance being tricked by a fortune-teller in Istanbul and having himself dubbed an English knight of Troy among ruins of what he believed was that ancient city.

Towards the end of 1614, Coryate left Aleppo for India and walked the entire distance, which he underestimated as 2,700 miles. For much of his two-year stay in India, Coryate lived with the English ambassador Sir Thomas Roe. He learned Hindustani and Persian and practised his Arabic and Turkish. Relations between the English and the Moghuls were unstable and Coryate seems to have vexed Roe with his behaviour. At one point, Coryate dressed as a beggar and made a speech before the emperor in his native Persian. This stunt earned him a reward from the emperor and enmity from Roe. Coryate was planning his return trip when he fell victim to dysentery and died in December 1617. Unfortunately, most of his journals from this journey were lost. Fragments of his accounts of the Holy Land and the Middle East were acquired by Samuel Purchas, edited, and included in his *Hakluytus posthumus* (1625). Letters he wrote home to his mother and friends were collected in two pamphlets, *Thomas Coriate traueller for the English wits* (1616) and *Mr Thomas Coriat to his friends in England sendeth greeting* (1618). Though they were illustrated, and retained Coryate's sense of humour and predilection for self-promotion, these works were not nearly as elaborate or elegant as the *Crudities*. Though fragmentary, Coryate's writings on India provide valuable insight as to English attitudes towards and interest in India. Unlike most travellers of this period, Coryate was not a merchant, nor did he work directly for the East India Company. His observations range beyond trade and economics and touch on religion, history, flora, fauna, and geography, providing a sense of what Englishmen expected to find in India and what they did find.

The first of Coryate's India pamphlets has interest beyond his travels. Included in the pamphlet is a letter from Coryate to 'the High Seneschal of the Mermaid Club'. The Mermaid Club seems to have been a drinking society in London, which met at the Mermaid tavern and included several notable political and literary figures. It was famous at the time and is mentioned in works by Jonson, Samuel Rowlands, and Francis Beaumont. However, aside from Coryate's letter, little solid evidence exists about the club or its members.

Some have argued that Coryate was one of England's first tourists, travelling out of a desire for personal experience rather than as a merchant, diplomat, or pilgrim. Others have suggested that he was, like many other contemporary travellers, an informal spy retrieving information about foreign powers. Each of these designations probably contains an element of truth. What sets Coryate apart, however, are the wise fool character he created for himself and the way he used his writings as a means of personal advancement. These two factors have helped ensure that Coryate's popularity has lasted beyond his own lifetime. His works have regularly been reprinted, his life novelized, and his journeys recreated. Though a travel writer before the genre of travel writing formally existed, Coryate managed to create for himself a remarkable level of literary immortality.

SEE ALSO: Beaumont, Francis; Donne, John; Drayton, Michael; Harington, John, the younger; Jonson, Ben; Lithgow, William; Moryson, Fynes; Purchas, Samuel; Rowlands, Samuel; Sandys, George; Taylor, John; Wotton, Henry

REFERENCES AND SUGGESTED READINGS

Allen, Daniel (2008) *The sky above, the kingdom below: in the footsteps of Thomas Coryate.* Haus, London.

Aune, M. G. (2005) Elephants, Englishmen and India: early modern travel writing and the precolonial moment. *Early Modern Literary Studies* 11(1). http://purl.oclc.org/emls/11-1/auneelep.htm

Baker, David J. (2007) 'Idiote': politics and friendship in Thomas Coryate. In: Betteridge, Thomas (ed.) *Borders and travellers in early modern Europe.* Ashgate, Burlington, pp. 129–145.

Craik, Katharine A. (2004) Reading *Coryats crudities* (1611). *Studies in English Literature, 1500–1900* 44, 77–96.

Horowitz, Elliott (2001). A 'dangerous encounter': Thomas Coryate and the swaggering Jews of Venice. *Journal of Jewish Studies* 52, 341–353.

Moore, Tim (2002). *The grand tour: the European adventure of a continental drifter.* St Martin's Press, New York.

Moraes, Dom & Srivatsa, Sarayu (2003). *The long strider: how Thomas Coryate walked from England to India in the year 1613.* Penguin, New Delhi.

Parr, Anthony (1992) Thomas Coryate and the discovery of Europe. *Huntington Library Quarterly* 55, 578–602.

Pritchard, R. E. (2004). *Odd Tom Coryate: the English Marco Polo.* Sutton, Thrupp.

Pritchard, R. E. (2004). Shakespeare and Thomas Coryate. *Notes and Queries* 51, 295–296.

Strachan, Michael (1962) *The life and adventures of Thomas Coryate.* Oxford University Press, London.

Cotton, Charles, the younger

PHILIP MAJOR

Charles Cotton (1630–87) was a Royalist poet, translator, and bibliophile. His literary reputation is based largely on the considerable commercial success he enjoyed (and, judging by his perennial impecuniousness, needed) after the Restoration, notably with his much imitated and reprinted *Scarronides* (1664–65), a burlesque of Virgil's *Aeneid*, and his co-authorship (with his close friend and protégé Izaak Walton) of the highly acclaimed fifth edition of *The compleat angler* (1676), a touchstone of Royalist and Anglican literature of contemplative retreat. To these well-received later works may be added *The scoffer scoft* (1675), a witty burlesque of Lucian, a zestful three-volume translation of Michel de Montaigne's *Essays* (1685–86) which remained the standard text for more than two centuries, and a translation from the French of Pierre Corneille's tragedy *Horace* (1671).

Though often overlooked, Cotton's pre-1660 corpus has merit and significance, and regardless of his later accomplishments would most likely have secured for him a reputation as a writer of stature. Nearly all of Cotton's original verse was published posthumously in *Poems on several occasions* (1689), but internal evidence suggests that many of these pieces, which include elegies, epistles, epitaphs, epigrams, love poems, drinking songs, and burlesques, were written during this earlier period, after which they were circulated among friends, as was customary in seventeenth-century literary circles.

Cotton was born at Beresford Hall on the border of Derbyshire and Staffordshire. His father, Charles Cotton the elder, was a friend of Ben Jonson and other poets in Jonson's circle. The death of Henry, Lord Hastings, occasioned the publication of Cotton the younger's first significant poem, 'An elegie upon the Lord Hastings', in Richard's Brome's memorial volume, *Lachrymae musarum* (1649). Participation in a collection featuring poems by such 'divers persons of nobility and worth' as Robert Herrick, Mildmay Fane, John Dryden, and Andrew Marvell indicates the respect which the young Cotton's poetic talent was accorded. It was a talent which, unlike that of these fellow contributors, was nurtured not at Oxford or Cambridge but through private tuition. Cotton's strong Royalist sympathies and literary associations are evidenced in two further early elegies: 'On the lord Derby' commemorates James Stanley, lord of the Isle of Man and close ally of the Stuarts, who was executed for treason by Parliament in 1651 following his capture at the battle of Worcester; while 'To the memory of my worthy friend, Colonel Richard Lovelace' honours the eponymous soldier and Cavalier poet of *Lucasta* fame, who died in 1657. Lovelace had dedicated his celebrated poem 'The grasshopper' to Cotton's father, Charles.

These are poems that, in the best tradition of Royalist lyric, exemplified not least by Lovelace himself, meld the disorientation and bitterness of loss with a partisan affirmation and appropriation of the deceased's virtues. Other pieces sensitively explore ideas of melancholy and concealment, and the tension between active and passive responses to political defeat. These poems again resonate with the sense of residual, buried, and, on one level, guilt-ridden Royalism pervasively communicated by Cotton's fellow loyalist poets during the 1650s. Recommendations of private retirement and companionship abound in Cotton's verse, carrying politically pregnant notions of Royalist disinterestedness in a hostile public world, and rendering his later collaboration with Walton something of a natural extension. Consolation in drink, an important motif in the influential Cavalier literary construction of a convivial community of crown supporters that also betrays the hopelessness and anguish of political and military defeat, finds a strong voice in poems such as 'Anacreontic' and 'Ode' ('Come, let us drink away the time'). The former is one of several poems explicitly critical of Cromwell's Protectorate, none more vehemently than 'The litany', a cry for freedom 'From the tedious City Lectures / And thanksgivings for Protectors'.

As with Lovelace's verse, the political potentialities of Cotton's love poetry of the 1650s, with its recurrent themes of banishment and retreat, are rich. Yet there is also a sense in which his treatment of love, numerically the most significant of his poetic subjects, strives successfully to transcend the turmoil he sees around him. Sometimes Cotton can be knowingly derivative: 'An invitation to Phyllis' is overtly if skilfully Marlovian; yet 'The entertainment to Phyliss' is a profoundly original piece saturated in gently didactic verities of classical mythology.

Cotton's 'nature' poems are also worthy of scrutiny, not least for their acknowledged impact on key Romantic poets such as Samuel Taylor Coleridge, William Wordsworth, Charles Lamb, and John Keats. The apogee of these is The wonders of the peake (1681), a hymn to the topography of the Peak District, but his earlier verse of this kind, such as 'Morning quatrains' and 'Night quatrains', is

similarly endowed with striking metaphorical experimentation and a powerful articulation of rustic simplicity, blending love of solitariness with a passionate engagement with the landscape and the changing seasons.

It was also years before the Restoration that Cotton's linguistic skills were first put to productive use. The English translation of Hobbes's seminal De cive (1650) has been persuasively attributed to him (Malcolm 1999–2000). And prefatory evidence confirms that his Morall philosophy of the stoicks (1664), a translation of Guillaume du Vair, was written in 1656, providing a piquant prose vehicle for the staunchly Royalist sentiment of endurance suffusing his verse. Cotton was an avid book collector: his rich personal library and its wide dispersal have received deserved critical attention. Despite his literary eminence, financial problems beset Cotton, forcing him to sell the family seat of Beresford Hall, Staffordshire, in 1681. He died in London six years later, and was buried in St James's, Westminster.

SEE ALSO: Brome, Richard; Dryden, John; Herrick, Robert; Hobbes, Thomas; Jonson, Ben; Lovelace, Richard; Marvell, Andrew; Walton, Izaak

REFERENCES AND SUGGESTED READINGS

Beal, Peter (ed.) (1993) Index of English literary manuscripts. Mansell, London.

Dust, A. I. (1972) Charles Cotton: his books and autographs. Notes and Queries 217, 20–23.

Hartle, Paul (1989) 'Mr. Cotton, of merry memory': Charles Cotton (1630–1687), poet. Neophilogus 73(4), 605–619.

Malcolm, Noel (1999–2000) Charles Cotton, translator of Hobbes's De Cive. Huntington Library Quarterly 61, 259–287.

Potter, Lois (1989) Secret rites and secret writings: royalist literature, 1641–1660. Cambridge University Press, Cambridge.

Turner, E. M. (1954) The life and works of Charles Cotton (1630–1687), with a biographical account of Cotton's writings. BLitt thesis, University of Oxford.

Cowley, Abraham

HENRY POWER

Abraham Cowley (1618–67) was a poet, translator, and essayist. He was renowned in his lifetime for his lyric poetry, and for his adaptations and imitations of Pindar, Anacreon, Horace, and Virgil. His posthumously published essays also found a wide audience. He was revered in his own lifetime, and by the succeeding generation of poets, but his reputation has declined steadily since the eighteenth century. His work is playful, complex, and unusually rich in metaphor.

Cowley was born in London and attended Westminster School as a king's scholar. A precocious child, he wrote later in his essay 'Of myself' that he had read all of Edmund Spenser's work before his twelfth birthday, and 'was thus made a poet as irremediably as a Child is made an Eunuch'. He published his first collection of poems, *Poetical blossomes*, in 1633, while he was still a pupil at Westminster. An expanded edition was published in 1636. He won a scholarship to Trinity College, Cambridge, in 1637, subsequently becoming a minor fellow. While at Cambridge he wrote three plays: the Latin comedy *Naufragium ioculare* and the pastoral comedy *Loves riddle* (both 1638), and the Jonsonian comedy *The guardian*, which was performed for Charles, prince of Wales when he visited the university in 1641. Cowley was to revise *The guardian* as *The cutter of Coleman Street* after the Restoration.

In March 1643 Cowley was – like many scholars with broadly Royalist sympathies – forced to leave Cambridge, and took up residence at St John's College, Oxford. Two political poems date from the later stages of Cowley's time at Cambridge. The first, which circulated in manuscript as *The Puritans lecture* before being published in 1642 as *A satyre against separatists*, describes a meeting of tedious, hypocritical, and gluttonous Puritan ministers. The second, *The Puritan and the papist*, is purportedly an attack on religious extremism in all its forms. Its major objective, though, is to point out the hypocrisy of the Puritans, whose positions often stray close to those of Roman Catholics ('Three Kingdoms thus ye strive to make your own / And like the Pope usurp a triple Crowne'). The poem shifts in its final third to a breathless attack on the Parliamentarian cause more generally. This poem must have been substantially complete by the time Cowley left Trinity, but was probably further revised at Oxford before its publication later in 1643. While at Oxford, Cowley became acquainted with members of the Great Tew circle, centred around Lucius Cary, second Viscount Falkland. He wrote, while staying in Oxford, a historical epic poem entitled *The Civil War*. Cowley wrote more or less contemporaneously with the events he describes, versifying reports from the Royalist *Mercurius aulicus*. He abandoned the poem following the Royalists' defeat, and Falkland's death, at the first battle of Newbury in September 1643. The elegy to Falkland with which the poem closes is one of his most moving passages of verse. Cowley later claimed to have destroyed the manuscript, but the first book was published in 1679, and a further two books were discovered in the Hertfordshire County Record Office and published in 1973. Curiously, Cowley records the decision to abandon the project within the poem itself: 'The trowbled Muse fell shapelesse into aire / Instead of Inck dropt from my Pen a Teare.'

In 1644 Cowley travelled to France to join the exiled court of Queen Henrietta Maria. There he associated with the circle that surrounded Thomas Hobbes and William Davenant, and worked as a spy for the royal party. An apparently unauthorized edition of his collection *The mistresse* was published by the royalist bookseller Humphrey Moseley in 1647. The love lyrics contained in it are frequently concerned with clandestine affairs, and it has been suggested that this interest in secrecy (also manifest in his later work) stems from Cowley's involvement with espionage. Thomas Corns (1992) points to the 'libertine eroticism' of the poems, and suggests that (like Richard Lovelace's *Lucasta*, 1648) the collection 'assiduously rehearses the values and enthusiasms of the

Caroline court'. For many readers, Cowley's fertile and elastic wit, which can lead him to describe his beloved's hymen as the 'slight, outward *Curtain* to the *Nuptial Bed*!' ('Maidenhead') represents the worst excesses of metaphysical poetry. Indeed, it was in his *Life of Cowley* (1779) that Samuel Johnson initiated the idea of 'a race of writers who might be termed the metaphysical poets', producing a kind of verse in which 'the most heterogeneous ideas are yoked by violence together'. Christine Rees (1980) has made a strong case for the unity and the symmetry of the collection, but does not attempt to rescue Cowley from the charge of insincerity. This failing cannot be attributed entirely to the poems' metaphysical nature. Cowley looks back to the Petrarchan tradition and the love poetry of Edmund Spenser and Philip Sidney as much as he draws on John Donne. Several poems from *The mistresse* were subsequently set as songs by, among many others, John Blow and Henry Purcell; the scores for these settings are given in a recent collection of Cowley's works (Calhoun et al. 1993).

The contemporary poet with whom Cowley had perhaps the closest relationship was Richard Crashaw. The two men met at Cambridge, and probably renewed their acquaintance in Oxford and in France. They worked together on 'On hope', a collaborative poem in which Cowley's verses against hope are answered by Crashaw's in favour. The poem was first printed in Crashaw's *Steps to the temple* (1646), but the arrangement of verses is faulty in this version, as the poets' arguments do not properly address each other. Cowley's contribution was reprinted in *The mistress*, to which he added his own defence of hope. David Trotter (1979) has looked more broadly at the way in which the two poets influenced one another. Cowley wrote an elegy 'On the death of Mr Crashaw', in which he stresses that their friendship transcended religious difference:

> his Life, I'm sure was in the right
> And I a Catholick will be,
> So far at least, great Saint, to pray to thee.

As David Hopkins and Tom Mason (1994) observe, it is entirely characteristic of Cowley to quibble on the word 'Catholick' at so solemn a moment.

Cowley returned to England in 1654, and was briefly gaoled by the parliamentary authorities. His £1,000 bail was guaranteed by Dr Charles Scarborough, to whom he addressed a poem drawing a parallel between the nation weakened by civil war and the human body ravaged by disease. His collected *Poems* were published by Moseley in 1656. This folio volume contained a slightly revised version of *The mistresse*, alongside three new sections: *Miscellanies* (including the famous translations from poems wrongly attributed to Anacreon), the *Pindarique odes*, and the *Davideis*.

The Davideis, a sacred poem of the troubles of David was envisaged as a poem in 12 books, though Cowley completed only the first four. It anticipates Milton's *Paradise lost* (1667) in casting biblical subject matter into the form of Virgilian epic. Cowley writes in the preface that he initially planned 12 books 'after the *Pattern* of our Master *Virgil*', and even goes so far as to imitate the accidental half-lines of the *Aeneid*, which Virgil left incomplete on his death (he had also done this in *The Civil War*). Criticism on the poem has focused on the question of whether Cowley's biblical subject matter represents a retreat from political events, or whether it functions (like John Dryden's *Absalom and Achitophel*, 1681) as an allegory; might the young prince David, for example, stand for the exiled prince of Wales?

According to his friend and biographer Thomas Sprat (whose 'An account of the life and writing of Mr Abraham Cowley' was included in the posthumous 1668 *Works*), Cowley began reading Pindar in the early 1650s when he was 'in a place, where he had no other Books to direct him'. This place was probably Jersey, where he travelled on behalf of Henrietta Maria in 1651. Cowley described the Pindaric mode as 'the noblest and highest kind of writing in Verse', and regretted its disappearance, remarking also that it might 'be put into the list of Pancirollus, among the lost

Inventions of Antiquity'. He translated two of Pindar's poems for the 1656 *Works*, and offered a series of original poems taking Pindar as his model. His preface promises a free translation, recognizing that 'if a Man should undertake to translate *Pindar* Word for Word, it would be thought that one *Mad-man* had translated *another*'. Cowley's translations, metrically loose where Pindar's are highly regular, sparked an interest in the poet that extended well into the following century; when Dryden, Alexander Pope, and Thomas Gray imitate Pindar, their imitation is mediated through Cowley. Even if Cowley disregards (or, some readers have felt, misunderstands) some formal aspects of his model, there is a genuine affinity between the two poets, both of whom shift rapidly from topic to topic and from metaphor to metaphor. Thus in 'The muse', a poem which describes the power of poetry to preserve, he compares (over the course of 12 lines) the function of poetry to the halting of a river's flow, to the stiffening of a slithering snake (with echoes of Moses' miracle in Exodus), to the preservation of fruit in sugar, to the magical transformation of a sheet of melting ice to a mirror, and finally to the transformation of 'this one short Point of Time, / To fill up half the Orb of Round Eternity'. Trotter (1979) draws a connection between Cowley's interpretation of the Pindaric ode, with its particular emphasis on swift movement and arbitrary connections, and his interest in Hobbes's 'radical psychology' and the free association of ideas. One of the original poems in the collection is addressed to Hobbes, and is marked (as all of Cowley's Pindarics are) by the rapidity with which the poet moves from one metaphor to another, while hailing the addressee as representing the 'living soul' of philosophy.

Stella Revard (1993) points to the poems' potential political application, and suggests that Cowley found in Pindar's famously obscure style a means of covertly expressing his unwavering Royalist sympathies. Certainly the translation of Pindar's second Olympian ode, with its emphasis on parricide, revenge, and return, anticipates the subject matter of Cowley's ode 'Upon his majestie's restoration and return' composed in 1660. Cowley was, however, keen to stress his newly apolitical stance, and wrote a preface for the volume in which he declared himself reconciled to the defeat of the royal cause and suggested that former Royalists 'lay down our Pens, as well as our Arms'. This sentiment may have been responsible for his relative fall from favour after the Restoration – as may his inclusion in the volume of the Pindaric poem 'Brutus', which celebrates the actions of the Roman tyrannicide (though the poem can in fact be read as anti-Cromwellian). After the king's return, Cowley strove to show his loyalty, publishing not only his Restoration ode, but also *The visions and prophecies concerning England, Scotland, and Ireland* (1661), an account of Cromwell's funeral, together with an extremely negative account of his character. His post-1656 verse was collected in *Verses, written upon several occasions* (1663). The volume contains a poem, 'The complaint', in which Cowley appears to bemoan his lack of royal patronage.

Samuel Johnson acknowledged the diversity of Cowley's writing, but felt that 'his power seems to have been greatest in the familiar and the festive'. He here refers specifically to the *Anacreontiques*, 11 poems in which Cowley celebrates the simple pleasures of love and wine. He describes the poems as having been translated 'paraphrastically' (anticipating Dryden's use of the term), and they often diverge wildly from their Greek models. By contrast, Thomas Stanley had produced faithful and undazzling versions of 55 of the *Anacreontea*. The most successful, and best-known, of Cowley's *Anacreontiques* is 'The grasshopper', a poem in which the insect is hailed as a true exponent of the philosophy of Epicurus ('Voluptuous, and wise withal, / Epicurean animal!'). An interest in the transient pleasures and glories is typical of Royalist poetry of the 1640s and 1650s. Lovelace also paid homage to the grasshopper during the 'Cavalier winter' and there are faint echoes of his poem in Cowley's – though whereas Lovelace's insect is a 'verdant fool' whose inevitable fate is to become 'green ice', Cowley's can retire happily once sated. Epicureanism, in fact, informs many of his poems, and such poems should be seen in the context of his broader interest in retirement and seclusion. His posthumously published *Several discourses, by way of essays in verse and prose* (in the 1668 *Works*) contains reflections in prose on the advantages of country life and withdrawal from the political arena, incorporating verse translations from Greek and Latin (and one or two original poems) which reinforce this central theme. One of the most enjoyable of these is his rendering of Horace's second *Epode*, the celebrated poem (beginning 'beatus ille ...') in praise of rural retirement; Cowley bizarrely omits from his version the final four lines – in which the speaker is revealed to be a grasping moneylender. He also includes Horace's tale of the Town Mouse and the Country Mouse in his essay 'Of agriculture'. Other essays include 'Of liberty', 'Of solitude', and the autobiographical 'Of myself'. 'The garden', dedicated to John Evelyn, has been suggested as a possible source for Andrew Marvell's poem of the same name; it draws equally on Edenic and Epicurean language.

Cowley spent the final years of the Protectorate studying botany and medicine, and was admitted to the degree of doctor of physic in 1657. He was not a member of the Royal Society, but took an interest in its activities. His *Proposition for the advancement of experimental philosophy* was published in 1661, and he contributed a prefatory poem to Thomas Sprat's *History of the Royal-Society* (1667). His 1663 poem 'On the death of Mr William Harvey', in which he imagines the natural philosopher pursuing Nature through the fibres of a tree and into the human blood stream, is one of his most wildly inventive. His interest in plants resulted in the monumental *Plantarum libri sex* – the longest neo-Latin work by any English author. The work initially promises to be a compendium of botanical information in verse, and the first two books, which deal with the properties of

herbs (published independently as *Plantarum libri duo* in 1662) are relatively conventional – though they are enlivened by direct addresses from the plants and pseudo-Ovidian transformation tales. As the work progresses (books III and IV are concerned with flowers, V and VI with trees), Cowley becomes less concerned with botany and more politically engaged. There is also a shift in metre, from lyric forms in the first four books to Virgilian hexameters for the grander subject matter of the fifth and sixth. The final book is an exploration of the place of the oak in English history; we hear of the Civil War and regicide, Charles II's escape at Worcester, the Restoration, and the recent (1665) battle of Lowestoft. An English translation of the entire work was published in 1689. Contributors included Aphra Behn (who translated the final book) and Nahum Tate.

Cowley died of pneumonia on 28 July 1667, following a brief period of Horatian retirement in Surrey. His literary executor was Thomas Sprat, who oversaw the publication of his 1668 *Works*, his *Essays*, and his *Poemata Latina*. He was buried in Westminster Abbey, next to Chaucer and Spenser. The inscription on his monument declared him to be the English Pindar, Virgil, and Horace. John Denham wrote an epitaph for him in which he said that 'To him no Author was unknown, / Yet what he wrote was all his own'. This sounds like mere commonplace, but gets to the heart of Cowley's achievement; his poetry is always learned and allusive (sometimes off-puttingly so), but he is at his most idiosyncratic while imitating others. His reputation during his lifetime and in the decades following his death was immense, but declined steadily thereafter. The past three decades have seen a modest revival of interest, perhaps owing to the increased scholarly emphasis on classical reception.

SEE ALSO: Cary, Lucius, Lord Falkland; Crashaw, Richard; Denham, John; Donne, John; Evelyn, John; Harvey, William; Hobbes, Thomas; Lovelace, Richard; Marvell, Andrew; Milton, John

REFERENCES AND SUGGESTED READINGS

Calhoun, Thomas O. (1991) Cowley's verse satire, 1642–43, and the beginnings of party politics. *Yearbook of English Studies* 21, 197–206.

Calhoun, Thomas O., Heyworth, Laurence, & Pritchard, Allan (eds) (1993) *The collected works of Abraham Cowley*, vol. 1: *Poetical blossomes, The Puritans lecture, The Puritan and the papist, The Civil War*. Newark, University of Delaware Press.

Corns, Thomas N. (1992) *Uncloistered virtue: English political literature, 1640–1660*. Clarendon Press, Oxford.

Davis, Paul (2007) *Translation and the poet's life: the ethics of translating in English culture, 1646–1726*. Clarendon Press, Oxford.

Hopkins, David (1993) Cowley's Horatian mice. In: Martindale, Charles & Hopkins, David (eds) *Horace made new: Horatian influences on British writing from the Renaissance to the twentieth century*. Cambridge University Press, Cambridge, pp. 103–126.

Hopkins, David & Mason, Tom (eds) (1994) *Selected poems*, by Abraham Cowley. Carcanet, Manchester.

Loiseau, Jean (1931) *Abraham Cowley's reputation in England*. Didier, Paris.

Mason, Tom (1990) Abraham Cowley and the wisdom of Anacreon. *Cambridge Quarterly* 19(2), 103–137.

Nethercot, Arthur H. (1931) *Abraham Cowley: the muse's Hannibal*. Clarendon Press, Oxford.

Power, Henry (2007) 'Teares breake off my verse': the Virgilian incompleteness of Abraham Cowley's *The Civil War. Translation and Literature* 16(2), 141–159.

Rees, Christine (1980) The antecedents and reputation of Cowley's *Mistress*: a problem of interpretation. *Forum for Modern Language Studies* 16(3), 224–236.

Revard, Stella P. (1993) Cowley's 'Pindarique odes' and the politics of the Inter-regnum. *Criticism* 35(3), 391–418.

Revard, Stella P. (1997) The politics of Abraham Cowley's *Anacreontiques. Ben Jonson Journal* 4, 131–150.

Starke, Sue (2006) 'The eternal now': Virgilian echoes and Miltonic premonitions in Cowley's *Davideis. Christianity and Literature* 55, 195–219.

Trotter, David (1979) *The poetry of Abraham Cowley*. Macmillan, London.

Cox, Leonard

JACQUELINE GLOMSKI

Leonard Cox (c. 1495–c. 1549) was the first Briton to write a treatise on the education of youth and the first author of an English-language treatise on rhetoric. He was a remarkable figure for his time, travelling in the 1510s in Europe as far east as Cracow, and spending 10 years in Poland and Hungary, but he was also a typical English lay humanist and reformer, and was a precursor of such scholars as Thomas Wilson, Roger Ascham, Gabriel Harvey, and Richard Mulcaster.

Cox was born around 1495 and died in or after 1549. Although his place of origin has traditionally been given as Monmouth (Wood 1691/92), Cox himself declared it to be Thame in Oxfordshire (Ryle 2003; 2004). In his Latin writings, he referred to himself as *Britannus* or *Anglus*. Details of his early life are not known, but he must have gone to the Continent at a young age. In the first half of his career he was a wandering humanist, probably spending time in Paris and, at some later point, in Prague. He matriculated at the University of Tübingen in June 1514, where he studied with the German humanist and reformer Philipp Melanchthon, and received his BA in 1516. Having been awarded the title *poeta laureatus*, Cox matriculated at the University of Cracow in September 1518 and delivered an oration there in December. In 1520 he went south, crossing into what is now Slovakia, then part of the kingdom of Hungary. He became headmaster of the school in Levoča (Lőcse), then, at the end of 1521, of the school in Košice (Kassa). Cox returned to Cracow, where in the autumn of 1525 he was again lecturing at the university and now also tutoring the protégés of his noble patrons. By the end of his stay in Cracow, he had managed to attract the support of dignitaries of the highest rank: Justus Ludovicus Decius, royal secretary and economic adviser; Piotr Tomicki, bishop of Cracow and royal vice chancellor; and Krzysztof Szydłowiecki, the grand chancellor.

By 1529 Cox was back in England, having secured employment as the master of the grammar school at Reading. He would remain in this post until 1546, except for the year 1540, when he was resident in Caerleon in south Wales after the disgrace and execution of his patron Hugh of Faringdon, the abbot of Reading. Cox supplicated for the degree of MA at Oxford in February 1530, and in 1549 he wrote in a letter to John Hales, a court official of Edward VI and founder of the grammar school at Coventry, that he possessed a licence to preach. There exists no reliable evidence after 1549 that would contribute to his biography.

Cox wrote only three books that we know for certain, the remainder of his work consisting of editions and translations: these contain prefatory poems, dedicatory letters, and footnotes that leave a trail of information contributing to our otherwise scant knowledge of his life, and of his pedagogical and religious opinions. However, his three books are of literary and historical importance. His speech to the University of Cracow, *De laudibus celeberrimae Cracoviensis Academiae oratio* (1518), praises the accomplishments of that university, especially in the disciplines of rhetoric and poetry, and in astronomy. His treatise on the education of youth, *Libellus de erudienda iuventute* (1526), influenced by Erasmus, reveals the methods and texts used in grammar-school education in early sixteenth-century Europe. Cox is best known in the history of English literature, however, for his handbook *The arte or crafte of rhetoryke* (1532, ?1535), a large part of which is an anglicized version of Melanchthon's *Institutiones rhetoricae* (1521). (For a different print / publication date for the second edition, 1530, see Carpenter 1973 [1899].)

The educational methods and theories evinced in these writings were rooted in the early sixteenth-century humanist conventions of northern Europe; Cox was chiefly influenced by Erasmus and Melanchthon, with Erasmus, especially, inspiring his inter-

est in patristics (he edited Erasmus's version of two letters of Jerome). But Melanchthon's influence was not directly responsible for Cox's conversion to the Reformation. In fact, Stephen Ryle (2003) notes that Cox 'suppresses or tones down those passages in the *Institutiones rhetoricae* in which Melanchthon expresses antipapal sentiments or doctrinal views of a reformist nature'.

Cox's earlier career contributed to the ties that the Tudor and the Jagiellonian courts cultivated in the early sixteenth century, when their two countries were eager to preserve the unity of the Christian world and to maintain the strength of that world in face of the threat of the Turkish invasions. In his later life, Cox worked as a biblical scholar and evangelical preacher in the service of the new religious circumstances brought about by the decisions of Henry VIII. Still, he managed to ride out the religious and political storms of the age, and continued to bring his scholarly work to the service of the education of youth. His contribution to the English Renaissance was his work as a schoolmaster.

SEE ALSO: Ascham, Roger; Hales, John; Harvey, Gabriel; Wilson, Thomas

REFERENCES AND SUGGESTED READINGS

Breeze, Andrew (1988) Leonard Cox, a Welsh humanist in Poland and Hungary. *National Library of Wales Journal* 25, 399–410.

Carpenter, Frederick Ives (ed.) (1973 [1899]) *Leonard Cox: The arte or crafte of rhethoryke.* University of Chicago Press, Chicago.

Glomski, Jacqueline (2007) *Patronage and humanist literature in the age of the Jagiellons: court and career in the writings of Rudolf Agricola Junior, Valentin Eck, and Leonard Cox.* University of Toronto Press, Toronto.

Ryle, S. F. (2003) Leonard Cox. In: Malone, Edward A. (ed.) *British rhetoricians and logicians 1500–1660*, 2nd series. Gale, Detroit, pp. 58–67.

Ryle, S. F. (2004) Cox, Leonard. In: *Oxford dictionary of national biography.* Oxford University Press, Oxford.

Wood, Anthony (1691–92) *Athenae Oxonienses.* Thomas Bennet, London.

Zins, H. (1994) A British humanist and the University of Kraków at the beginning of the sixteenth century: a chapter in Anglo-Polish relations in the age of the Renaissance. *Renaissance Studies* 8, 13–39.

Cranmer, Thomas

ALLYNA E. WARD

Thomas Cranmer (1489–1556) was the first Protestant archbishop of Canterbury and the key contributor to the Anglican Book of Common Prayer. He is most remembered for his role in securing Henry VIII's divorce from Katherine of Aragon and for his contributions to the Book of Common Prayer. Additionally, he was the archbishop who crowned Anne Boleyn and heard her final confession; the godfather of Prince Edward (later Edward VI); an early proponent of Henry's marriage to his fourth wife, Anne of Cleves; a subsequent proponent of Henry's divorce from Anne of Cleves; and one of the accusers of Henry's fifth wife, Katherine Howard. These facts alone show the extent to which Cranmer was at Henry VIII's total service. He was also fully committed to reforming the English church and although he signed his name to a submission to Catholic doctrines and faith when he was imprisoned during the reign of Mary I, he would, at the very last moment, recant.

Cranmer's career was launched when, in 1530, Henry VIII sent him to Rome to obtain papal approval for his divorce from Katherine of Aragon. One of Cranmer's additional tasks at this time was to translate materials in favour of the annulment into contemporary English. Two great works were produced from this effort: the manuscript *Collectanea satis copiosa* (*Sufficiently abundant collections*), and the *Gravissimae … academiarum censurae.* The former work (now British Library, MS Cotton Cleopatra E. vi) was a collection from native and Latin chronicles providing evidence from Roman and Anglo-Saxon British history that attempted to justify that the king, and not the pope, had final authority over the realm. The latter text, first published in Latin and translated into English in 1531 as *The determinations of the moste famous and mooste excellent universities of Italy and France, that it is vnlefull* [sic] *for a man to marie his brothers wyfe; that the pope hath no power to dispence therewith,* contained eight favourable opinions concerning Henry's 'great matter' (his projected divorce) that Cranmer had researched while visiting Continental universities (these had already been published in 1530 as part of a longer treatise on the matter). In his attempt to render the Latin sources into readable English Cranmer's text contains six attempts to coin English words and phrases and five first uses of English words earlier than those recorded in the old *Oxford English dictionary* (MacCulloch 1996).

In 1532 Henry made Cranmer ambassador to Germany, replacing Sir Thomas Elyot. Later, in *Pasquil the playne* (1533), Elyot would satirize Cranmer as a flatterer for this offence (Walker 2005). In Germany Cranmer married Margaret, niece of the local pastor Andreas Osiander (Margaret's surname remains a mystery). This move was to place Cranmer firmly against at least one tradition of the Catholic Church: the celibacy of its ministers. In 1532 he was also named archbishop of Canterbury, following the death of William Warham. During this time his marriage was kept a secret, with Cranmer leaving Margaret when he returned to England in January 1533. He was consecrated in March and was the first archbishop in England to swear allegiance to the papacy while also swearing loyalty firstly to his king.

In the winter months of 1536/37, the Pilgrimage of Grace and the Lincolnshire rebellion targeted Cranmer and fellow reformer Thomas Cromwell for their role in reforming the church (especially the Ten Articles) and confiscating the country parishes' taxes under these reforms. Cranmer went into hiding during this time and when the fury was quelled he published *The institution of a Christian man* (1537), also known as 'The bishop's book', which attempted to define clearly the terms of the doctrine of justification by faith alone and predestination.

In 1538 Cromwell – then still in favour – ordered that a copy of a vernacular 'Great Bible' be placed in every church and after May 1540 Cranmer's lengthy preface was included (it was sometimes referred to as 'Cranmer's Bible'). This preface expressed the importance of the vernacular Bible and the necessity of obeying the king above the pope. It is one of Cranmer's finer pieces of prose writing and was later quoted by Henry VIII when he addressed Parliament in 1545.

When the young Edward VI became king in 1547, Cranmer was able to play a more active role in liturgical and doctrinal reform in the English church. Foremost among his achievements from this period was the 1549 Book of Common Prayer, and it is here that we find his most creative writing as he translated, imitated, and adapted various source-texts to his purposes. Cranmer's rendering of the Latin prayers into rhythmical English was one of his primary aims in the project; it established the distinctive tenor of the Book of Common Prayer and had a lasting effect on English religious poetry (Gray 2007). Cranmer published *A defence of the true and Catholike doctrine of the sacrament of the body and bloud of our saviour Christ* the following year (1550). The text, the first that he authored alone, explores the nature of the eucharist and attempts to make clear the errors of the earlier church.

When it became clear that Edward VI was terminally ill, Cranmer was to make his biggest political mistake in actively supporting Lady Jane Grey as successor to the throne. He attempted to defend his actions to Queen Mary when he was called before the royal commission in 1553 but was subsequently tried for heresy with former bishops Nicholas Ridley and Hugh Latimer in 1554. Cranmer survived his two friends by five months on account of his adherence to the principle of obedience to the ordained monarch. He listened to Catholic defenders, attended mass, and signed various submissions to Catholicism. Nevertheless, his execution was eventually ordered and he was burned at the stake in 1555. On the day of his death (21 March), he recanted his earlier submissions to papal authority and, famously, thrust his right hand into the flames before him because it was the hand that, in signing the submissions, had sinned against his true, Protestant beliefs.

In *Actes and monuments* (1563) John Foxe includes a comprehensive account of the martyrdom of Cranmer, portraying him as a Protestant hero whose dedication to the Reformation was a sign of his love for his nation but which ultimately led to his gruesome execution. In Shakespeare's play *Henry VIII* (1613) Cranmer plays a minor role but voices a prophecy at the end of the play concerning Queen Elizabeth, James Stuart, and the unification of England and Scotland.

SEE ALSO: Bible, the; Book of Common Prayer, the; Elyot, Thomas; Foxe, John; Shakespeare, William

REFERENCES AND SUGGESTED READINGS

Anderson, Judith (2001) Language and history in the Reformation: Cranmer, Gardiner, and the words of institution. *Renaissance Quarterly* 54, 20–51.

Bernard, G. W. (2005) *The king's Reformation: Henry VIII and the remaking of the English church.* Yale University Press, New Haven.

Gray, Donald (2007) Cranmer and the collects. In: *The Oxford handbook of English literature and theology.* Oxford University Press, Oxford, 561–574.

Loades, D. M. (1970) *The Oxford martyrs.* Stein & Day, New York.

MacCulloch, Diarmaid (1996) *Thomas Cranmer: a life.* Yale University Press, New Haven.

MacCulloch, Diarmaid (2004) Cranmer, Thomas. In: *Oxford dictionary of national biography.* Oxford University Press, Oxford.

Ridley, Jasper (1962) *Thomas Cranmer.* Oxford University Press, Oxford.

Walker, Greg. (2005) *Writing under tyranny: English literature and the Henrician Reformation.* Oxford University Press, Oxford.

Crashaw, Richard

SEAN H. McDOWELL

While the critical fortunes of all the metaphysical poets have fluctuated, sometimes dramatically, between the original circulation of their work and the twenty-first century, none has experienced a more varied reception than Richard Crashaw (?1612–49). Since the publication of H. J. C. Grierson's landmark edition of *Metaphysical poets* (1921), which revived Crashaw for the English-speaking world, and of L. C. Martin's *The poems, English, Latin, and Greek, of Richard Crashaw* (1927), which made available his complete poetic canon, Crashaw has been celebrated for the wit, sensuality, and spiritual vision of his hymns and odes and derided for excessive emotionalism, indulgence in grotesquery, and even mental disturbance. While a few of his secular poems (e.g., 'Music's duel' and 'Wishes. To his supposed mistress') are widely anthologized in college textbooks, he is known today primarily for his religious verse, published in the seventeenth century in three collections, the Latin *Epigrammatum sacrorum liber* (1634), *Steps to the temple* (1646; rev. edn 1648), and the posthumous *Carmen Deo nostro* (1652). Even so, the many labels and clichés attached to his work in various college textbooks continue to obscure his artistry, even for those aware of the importance of his Catholicism.

Religion always figured prominently in Crashaw's life. His father William (1572–1626) was a well-known Puritan controversialist who amassed one of the most extensive private theological libraries in England (Martin 1927). If he had lived longer, his ardent Puritanism might have shaped his son's life more dramatically (Kelliher 1990). But his death in 1626 left 14-year-old Richard first in the care of two of William's lawyer patrons and then of Charterhouse School, where, under the instruction of committed royalist Robert Brook, Crashaw rigorously studied classical rhetoric and was charged to write sacred epigrams on New Testament passages every week (Warren 1939). This practice appears to have fuelled the creativity of *Epigrammatum sacrorum liber* (Parrish 1980), though we cannot be certain whether any of the school exercises written under Brook appear in that collection.

After matriculating from Charterhouse, Crashaw became a Greek scholar at Pembroke College, Cambridge, in 1631 at a time when Arminian theology and high-church ritual enjoyed great favour. His duties included writing Latin and Greek epigrams on biblical subjects. As with Abraham Cowley, with whom Crashaw later wrote the well-known dialogue 'On hope', Crashaw's reputation as a poet must have preceded him, for in the year of his admission to Pembroke, his verses appeared under the frontispiece of the second edition of the sermons of Lancelot Andrewes, the charismatic former master of Pembroke. Throughout the early 1630s, Crashaw wrote occasional verse and elegies on the deaths of students and other college figures as well as psalm translations, divine epigrams, and presumably drafts of some of the major poems that would appear in *Steps to the temple*. Indeed, whenever the college published verse collections commemorating major events in the lives of the royal family, these tended to include Crashaw's contributions, evidence of the high regard in which his contemporaries held his poetic abilities.

From his beginnings at Cambridge, Crashaw felt a natural affinity for Laudian church practices. His High Church leanings intensified after his election to a fellowship at Peterhouse in 1635, a few months after he received his BA and after the publication of *Epigrammatum sacrorum liber*. Under the direction of John Cosin, Peterhouse was rapidly developing a reputation as a Laudian stronghold, and Crashaw fit in well, becoming first its college catechist and, by 1639, the curate and catechist of Little St Mary's, the small church next door. He appears to have supported the Laudian position that the schism of the English church from Rome did not also mean a break from the apostolic tradition, and like many Laudian supporters, he owned a copy of the translation of Francis de Sales's *L'introduction à la vie dévote* that was later banned by order of King Charles I for being too 'popish' (Kelliher 1990). Anthony Low attributes the emotional emphasis of his verse more to the devout humanism of de Sales than to Ignatian meditation, a leaning Crashaw shares with George Herbert (Low 1978; Bertonasco 1971). Moreover, Crashaw was involved in the adornment of both the college chapel and Little St Mary's, and anecdotal evidence suggests his attachment to Marian devotion took hold during these years. His dedication to the religious life led him to form close ties with the Ferrar and Collet families at the religious community of Little Gidding, where the daily recitations of the Psalms and other near-monastic offices captured his imagination. Ferrar Collet, the son of Crashaw's friend Mary Collet, became one of his pupils.

The eruption of hostilities between king and parliament in the 1640s brought an end to what Crashaw must have considered an idyllic existence of study, teaching, and prayer. He left Cambridge, however, before the Parliamentary forces took charge of that city and ejected Cosin and other like-minded fellows from their offices. Thus he was spared the pain of seeing the destruction of the pictures, statuary, and other ornaments of Little St Mary's. Crashaw's personality did not lend itself to the dogged resilience that would lead Henry Vaughan and Robert Herrick, both staunch adherents of the established church, to write a 'poetry of Anglican survivalism', in Claude J. Summers' phrase (1994). Instead, he went into exile, first to Leiden and then to Paris, where he maintained connections with the court of exiled Queen Henrietta Maria. Hearing of the progressive dismantling of the Established Church he loved so dearly, Crashaw wholly embraced its most viable alternative – Catholicism. When he converted to the faith his father so vigorously opposed is not known; but he almost certainly did so by 1646, the year of *Steps to the temple. Sacred poems, with other delights of the muses* was published in London as part of Humphrey Moseley's series of poetry collections. That Moseley decided to publish

Crashaw's verse the year after he published Milton's *Poems* attests to Crashaw's popularity among knowledgeable readers of poetry.

Crashaw's decision to convert carried a great personal cost, in that it meant a separation from the Ferrars and Collets, who would not maintain a relationship with a Catholic convert, as well as from Joseph Beaumont and other Protestant friends (though he continued to associate with Cowley while abroad). It also affected the direction of his poetic sensibility. In *Carmen Deo nostro*, his last collection, he presented not only revised and longer versions of early poems, but also new poems (e.g., 'Sancta Maria dolorum', 'Hymn to the name of Jesus', and 'The office of the Holy Cross') more expressly Catholic in orientation. Moreover, the arrangement of poems accords more explicitly with Counter-Reformation aesthetics. Whereas the 1646 edition of *Steps to the temple* begins with 'The weeper' and 'The tear' before launching into a series of English epigrams on religious themes, *Carmen Deo nostro* is much more centrally Christological, beginning with poems on Christ's life and death, then turning to a consideration of Mary and then to poems about the saints. Although Thomas Car probably saw this edition through the press (Martin 1927), the arrangement maintains Crashaw's general interest in religious ritual. Indeed, Elizabeth H. Hageman (1980) has demonstrated how the 33 poems therein chronicle the liturgical year of the Roman Catholic Church. It is conceivable that Car merely shepherded a volume already well on its way to completion.

Crashaw's fortunes after his conversion were tenuous. Though accepted into the Catholic Communion, he lacked a place until, through the intercession of Queen Henrietta Maria herself, and even then after a year of waiting, he obtained a position in the retinue of Cardinal Pallotta in 1647. Austin Warren (1939) speculates that Crashaw's piety might have spurred resentment among the cardinal's Italian attendants; to protect him, the cardinal in 1649 appointed Crashaw to a minor post at Loreto, thereby removing him from Rome. It was there, in the same city as the Santa Casa, the church built around the house where Christ reputedly was conceived in the Virgin Mary, that Crashaw died a few months after his arrival.

In the 1630s, 1640s, and 1650s, Crashaw was known for his poetic wit, and some contemporaries ranked his work in the same company as Sidney, Spenser, Shakespeare, Jonson, Donne, Herbert, and other luminaries (Dunton 1692; Belasyse 1903; Roberts 1985; McDowell 2005). Some considered his epigrams required reading for youth interested in a liberal education (Holdsworth 1961). Meanwhile, the longer poems of *Steps to the temple* and *Carmen Deo nostro*, such as 'The weeper', 'Hymn in the Holy Nativity', 'A hymn to Sainte Teresa', 'The flaming heart', 'Sancta Maria dolorum', and the hymn 'To the name of Jesus', were touted for their capacity to produce strong emotional reactions in their readers. According to the preface to the 1646 edition (written probably by Joseph Beaumont, the author of *Psyche*), these poems 'shal lift' readers 'some yards above the ground' and allow them to 'tune' their souls 'into a heavenly pitch'. The emphasis falls on instilling strong, religiously affirming passions (joy, sorrow, love, grief, ecstasy, etc.) through considerations of penitence, sacrifice, and divine mystery. Considerations of the wounds, eyes, tears, blood, and milk of religious exemplars are intended to move the souls of readers heavenward.

Crashaw's poetry, then, in contrast to that of lesser English religious lyricists of the 1590s (e.g., Henry Lok and Barnabe Barnes), engages in no didactic explication. Instead, it presents religious mysteries, raptures, and miracles to produce an emotional reaction in the reader in consonance with the subject matter at hand. Crashaw places a great premium on the senses and on the sensuousness of experience: 'sweet' and 'delicious' are among his favourite adjectives, and his lines are full of colours with symbolic meanings, particularly red and white. Unlike Herbert, with whom contemporaries sometimes compared him, Crashaw does not conceal his art but calls attention to it, filling poems with antitheses, oxymora, and bold conceits sometimes flying in the face of logic. These qualities, while effective within the context of religious devotion, garnered negative reactions in subsequent centuries, particularly among readers with different religious biases (Roberts & Roberts 1990).

Towards the end of the seventeenth century, Crashaw's piety began to overshadow his poetic wit in the minds of readers. His earliest biographers began treating his poems more as the expressions of religious enthusiasm than as the artistic designs of what Sidney would have called a 'right' poet. By 1710, when Alexander Pope wrote the first extensive critical discussion of Crashaw's work in a letter to Henry Cromwell, Crashaw's poetry was reduced to a series of witty phrases not always composed under rational control (McDowell 2005). During the eighteenth and nineteenth centuries, though references to Crashaw steadily increased (Roberts 1990), poets and critics singled out only some poems as noteworthy and often treated them as exceptions. The secular poems, particularly 'Sospetto d'Herode' and 'Musicks duell', received more favourable consideration than the religious verse, which some considered extravagant and filled with superstitions or excessive emotionalism. Biases against Crashaw's Catholicism, even in supportive readers, resulted in greater praise for the musicality of the verse than for Crashaw's thought (Roberts & Roberts 1990).

Since the publication of Grierson's 1921 volume, interest in Crashaw has been greater than ever before; yet despite an overwhelmingly favourable estimation, the poetry also has suffered the vagaries of oversimplifying labels or else occasioned negative speculations about Crashaw's mental health. 'The weeper', with its expansive comparison of Mary Magdalene's eyes to 'Portable, and compendious oceans', and the epigram, 'Luke 11. Blessed be the paps which Thou has sucked', which likens Christ's chest wound to a bloody breast that Mary must suck, are the most consistent targets. Some consider the latter especially unqualified grotesquerie (Kane 1928; Adams 1955; Jacobus 1970), while William Empson (1955) remarked that the epigram called to mind an untold number of sexual perversions. Richard Geha, Jr (1966) interpreted this and other poems dealing with wounds as evidence of mental disturbance and a tireless search for an absent mother, while more recently, Vera J. Camden (1983) considered the epigram evidence of Crashaw's fears of castration or oral repression.

Countering such negative estimations, often the products of mapping modern predilections and standards of taste onto the past, the majority of critics see a greater sophistication in Crashaw's artistry. By situating the poetry within the aesthetic, cultural, and religious contexts informing it, they thereby recover what its original readers would have seen as its richness and complexity. The most prominent of these efforts has centred on recovering the extent of Crashaw's participation in the development of European aesthetics. Many critics have noted the baroque character of his work in the 'spiritualization of sense' through a heavy reliance on witty conceits (Bertonasco 1971), in the conveyance of passionate intensity through stylistic abundance (Petersson 1974), and in the predilection both for epigrammatic expressions and emblematic images (Warren 1939). Crashaw studied closely the works of Gianbattista Marino and translated some of them, most notably 'Sospetto d'Herode', his version of the first canto of Marino's *Strage degli innocenti*, and his understanding of wit and conceits owed much to Italian literary criticism. While Italian influences undoubtedly figured prominently in Crashaw's artistic development, so, too, did Spanish influences, both religious and artistic. R. V. Young (1982) contends that Spanish poetry furnished Crashaw with poetic concepts and imagery and provided an overall pattern for the sacred parody of secular English poetry. Moreover, Crashaw's fascination with the life, mystical experiences, and spirituality of St Teresa of Avila resulted in two of his finest hymns, while his sensuality and stylistic intensification to show an affinity with the Gongorism of the Spanish Golden Age.

In the face of his many Continental intersections, however, some have seen Crashaw as 'un-English' or have implicitly positioned his work outside the native Protestant English tradition of religious lyricism. Yet this point of view, as well as the persistent labelling of Crashaw as the quintessential 'baroque' poet, obscures the degree to which Crashaw shared artistic assumptions about rhetorical effects of poetry (Parrish 1980). At the height of his popularity in the mid-seventeenth century, readers appeared to value both the liveliness and verisimilitude of his renditions of religiously charged moments (McDowell 2005). While his translations and major hymns reflect decidedly Catholic choices of subject and approach, those who imitated him were not only Catholics but Protestants as well, and his English contemporaries generally appreciated his epigrammatic wit. Even while Crashaw's exuberant style, placing a premium on the poet's substantial powers of association and his lyrical use of alliteration, accords with baroque standards of ornamentation, his rhetorical purposes – to delight and move readers towards a devotional response – are much in keeping with those of other English religious lyricists, as the preface to *Steps to the temple* suggests. His is a reader-centred art, though one with a communal focus not entirely familiar to readers steeped in the post-Romantic, post-confessional poetry of the past 100 years.

Indeed, Crashaw's avoidance of confessional utterances often distorts a modern appreciation of his work. Despite the emotionalism that, in part, caused Pope to reduce his poems to gatherings of glittering expressions, the self one encounters in even the finest of Crashaw's poems is a public self. But modern readers have found seventeenth-century religious lyricism vibrant and intriguing, in part, because of its thoroughgoing meditative focus on psychological interiority. Whether it be John Donne's tempestuous wrestling with God in the Holy Sonnets, George Herbert's quieter though profound explorations of the affective problems of the spiritual life, or Henry Vaughan's accounts of the acquisition of metaphysical insights, the religious lyric typically delves into the private inner movements of a highly subjective 'I'. This focus not only enabled the lyric to serve as a form of consolation for the writer, as is attested in some of the prefaces of published collections, but was also thought to edify the sympathetic reader as well (McDowell 1999).

Crashaw, though, largely avoids what might be construed as personal expression, one reason why some critics have considered his poetry deficient in its introspection. Instead, his is an impersonal voice carefully pitched to further the devotional aims of much of his poetry. Readerly identification is not supposed to occur in the manner of a friend confiding emotional trauma to another friend but in that of a worshipper revealing the causes of his affective transports. Noting Crashaw preferred to write in impersonal forms – the epigram, the ode, the hymn – Lorraine M. Roberts (1990) attributes Crashaw's impersonality to the influence of Jesuit poets and theorists who suggested a removal of the self from poetry on the grounds that personal expression interfered with religious devotion. Though he frequently uses personal pronouns, these serve in the creation of an 'everyman' witness who mediates between the biblical or religious events depicted and the reader. The poems draw in the reader through means similar to those in Counter-Reformation baroque painting and sculpture. In those instances when the lyric 'I' is the object of focus, the poetic speaker often voices a longing for self-dissolution (McDowell 2008), definitely not the default point of view of many modern poets.

Through the widespread use of his impersonal voice, Crashaw emphasizes the power of ritual to recreate moments of religious significance and thereby invite readers to experience the sacred through the powers of memory and imagination. Eugene R. Cunnar (1994) considers liminal or threshold images, both the gateway images in such poems as 'Letter to the countess of Denbigh' and wounds and tears in works such as 'Sancta Maria dolorum', 'The weeper', and 'The flaming heart',
fundamental to the ritualized engagements between poem and reader. By dwelling on moments of martyrdom – actual or mystical – or of repentance and grief, Crashaw focuses the reader's devotional attention on intrusions of the sacred into the profane. His interest in moments of transition – between life and death, between one affective state and another – often influences his choice of subject and / or his approach to the subject. While Milton's 'On the morning of Christ's nativity' treats Christ's birth as an epic breach in history between a pagan past and a Christian future, figured in the flight of the old gods (really devils in disguise), Crashaw's nativity hymn concentrates on the present mystery of the Incarnation, the miracle of 'Eternity shut in a span'. Seventeenth-century Puritans responded negatively to Crashaw's later poems because they disagreed with its theological emphases; but any modern criticism failing to take into adequate account the poet's attempts to move the religiously minded reader from a state of liminality to one of *communitas* (Cunnar 1994) or failing to understand the principles of Counter-Reformation aesthetics so integral to his later work especially also dismisses the poetry on suspect critical grounds.

SEE ALSO: Andrewes, Lancelot; Barnes, Barnabe; Cowley, Abraham; Donne, John; Herbert, George; Herrick, Robert; Jonson, Ben; Milton, John; Shakespeare, William; Sidney, Philip; Spenser, Edmund; Vaughan, Henry

REFERENCES AND SUGGESTED READINGS

Adams, Robert Martin (1955) Taste and bad taste in metaphysical poetry: Richard Crashaw and Dylan Thomas. *Hudson Review* 8, 61–77.

Belasyse, Henry (1903) An English traveler's first curiosity: or, the knowledge of his owne countrey (April 1657). In: Historical Manuscripts Commission, *Report of the manuscripts in various collections*, vol. 2. Mackie, London, pp. 193–204.

Bertonasco, Marc F. (1971) *Crashaw and the baroque.* University of Alabama Press, University.

Camden, Vera J. (1983) Richard Crashaw's poetry: the imagery of bleeding wounds. *American Imago* 40, 257–279.

Cunnar, Eugene R. (1994) Opening the religious lyric: Crashaw's ritual, liminal, and visual wounds. In: Roberts, John R. (ed.) *New perspectives on the seventeenth-century religious lyric.* University of Missouri Press, Columbia, pp. 237–267.

Dunton, John (1692) An essay upon all sorts of learning. In: *The Young-Students-Library, containing extracts and abridgements of the most valuable books.* John Dunton, London, pp. i–xviii.

Empson, William (1955) *Seven types of ambiguity.* Meridian, New York.

Geha, Richard, Jr (1966) Richard Crashaw (1613?–1650?): the ego's soft fall. *American Imago* 23, 158–168.

Grierson, Herbert J. C. (ed.) (1921) *Metaphysical lyrics & poems of the seventeenth century: Donne to Butler.* Clarendon Press, Oxford.

Hageman, Elizabeth H. (1980) Calendrical symbolism and the unity of Crashaw's *Carmen Deo nostro. Studies in Philology* 77, 161–179.

Holdsworth, Richard (1961) Directions for a student in the universitie (circa 1637). In: Fletcher, Harris Francis (ed.) *The intellectual development of John Milton,* vol. 2. University of Illinois Press, Urbana, pp. 623–664.

Jacobus, Lee A. (1970) Richard Crashaw as mannerist. *Bucknell Review* 18(3), 79–88.

Kane, Elisha K. (1928) Meretricious verse in other literatures. In: *Gongorism and the Golden Age: a study of exuberance and unrestraint in the arts.* University of North Carolina Press, Chapel Hill, pp. 128–168.

Kelliher, Hilton (1990) Crashaw at Cambridge. In: Roberts, John R. (ed.) *New perspectives on the art of Richard Crashaw.* University of Missouri Press, Columbia, pp. 180–214.

Low, Anthony (1978) *Love's architecture: devotional modes in seventeenth-century poetry.* New York University Press, New York.

Martin, L. C. (ed.) (1927) *The poems, English, Latin, and Greek, of Richard Crashaw.* Clarendon Press, Oxford.

McDowell, Sean (1999) Edification and the reader of Donne's *Divine poems. Discoveries* 17(1), 1–2, 10–12.

McDowell, Sean (2005) From 'lively' art to 'glitt'ring expressions': Crashaw's initial reception reconsidered. *John Donne Journal* 24, 229–262.

McDowell, Sean (2008) Stealing or being stolen: a distinction between sacred and profane modes of transgressive desire in early-modern England. In: Papazian, Mary A. (ed.) *The sacred and profane in English Renaissance literature.* University of Delaware Press, Newark, pp. 132–158.

Parrish, Paul A. (1980) *Richard Crashaw.* Twayne, Boston.

Petersson, Robert T. (1974) *The art of ecstasy: Teresa, Bernini, and Crashaw.* Atheneum, New York.

Roberts, John R. (1985) *Richard Crashaw: an annotated bibliography of criticism, 1632–1980.* University of Missouri Press, Columbia.

Roberts, Lorraine M. (1990) Crashaw's sacred voice: 'a commerce of contrary powers'. In: Roberts, John R. (ed.) *New perspectives on the art of Richard Crashaw.* University of Missouri Press, Columbia, pp. 66–79.

Roberts, Lorraine M. & Roberts, John R. (1990) Crashavian criticism: a brief interpretive history. In: Roberts, John R. (ed.) *New perspectives on the art of Richard Crashaw.* University of Missouri Press, Columbia, pp. 1–29.

Summers, Claude J. (1994) Herrick, Vaughan, and the poetry of Anglican survivalism. In: Roberts, John R. (ed.) *New perspectives on the seventeenth-century religious lyric.* University of Missouri Press, Columbia, pp. 46–74.

Warren, Austin (1939) *Richard Crashaw: a study in Baroque sensibility.* University of Michigan Press, Ann Arbor.

Young, R. V. (1982) *Richard Crashaw and the Spanish Golden Age.* Yale University Press, New Haven.

Crooke, Helkiah

REBECCA LEMON

Helkiah Crooke (1576–1648), a physician, is most famous for his *Mikrokosmographia: a description of the body of man* (1615), an encyclopedic book of anatomy. The most comprehensive English study of the human body before William Cowper's 1698 *Anatomy of humane bodies, Mikrokosmographia* created some controversy upon publication: it was written in English rather than Latin; it offered explicit depictions of human anatomy, including the sexual organs; and it wrestled with competing medical models, namely the ascendant model of clinical anatomy as opposed to the established model of Galenic theory.

Crooke was the third son of Thomas Crooke, a Puritan minister from Suffolk who served as a preacher at Gray's Inn after 1582. Crooke received limited financial support from his family. He matriculated as a scholarship student at St John's College, Cambridge, receiving his BA in 1596. After studying medicine at the University of Leiden, where he defended his theses on the human body in 1597, he returned to Cambridge to pursue further medical studies, earning an MB in 1599 and an MD in 1604. After a period of working, perhaps at home in Suffolk, Crooke attempted to establish himself in London but he seems to have had some difficulty gaining the support of his peers. After an unsuccessful attempt to join the College of Physicians in 1611, he was admitted as a candidate in 1613 only to receive the opprobrium of his fellow physicians two years later with the publication of *Mikrokosmographia*. The attempts by various authorities to suppress his book on the grounds of its explicit anatomical drawings were unsuccessful, and Crooke seemed to have received at least tacit support from King James I, the dedicatee of his text. Nevertheless, the College of Physicians continued to view Crooke with some degree of suspicion, and he was elected a fellow only in 1620. In the meantime, he assumed leadership of Bedlam Hospital in 1619, where he undertook a number of significant reforms. But under suspicion of mishandling of funds, he was dismissed in 1634; he fought, unsuccessfully, for reinstatement. Crooke withdrew from the College of Physicians the following year, after which point he appears only in the notice, in the parish records of St James's, Clerkenwell, of his burial on 18 March 1648. While Crooke seemed to have suffered financially throughout his life, and while his financial troubles may have led to his resignation from the College of Physicians, nonetheless *Mikrokosmographia* continued to be in significant demand: it was published in 1615 and twice reprinted (in 1616 and 1618) before Crooke wrote a second, revised edition (1631).

Neither edition of *Mikrokosmographia* features original observation but instead, as the title page claims, collects and translates 'out of all the best authors of anatomy, especially out of Gaspar Bauhinus, and Andreas Laurentius'. Indeed, as Winfried Schleiner (2000) has established, Crooke relies heavily on André Du Laurens's *Opera anatomica* (1595). But Crooke provides detailed illustrations, drawn from Vesalius through the work of the Swiss anatomist and botanist Casper Bauhin. Furthermore, Crooke's text offers a notable exploration of how the newly emergent field of anatomy might uphold or challenge traditional Galenic medicine. Crooke does not engage entirely with new anatomy: for example, the revised edition does not take account of Sir William Harvey's discovery of the circulation of the blood, despite the fact that he mentions Harvey personally. Nonetheless, the interplay between Galenic and anatomical models does appear in the text, both in his discussion of optics, as Hilary M. Nunn (2005) illustrates, and most obviously in his extended discussions of sexual organs.

In the section of his text titled 'Of the difference of the sexes', Crooke begins by rehearsing the 'one sex' model. According to this theory, upheld by both Aristotle and Galen, men and women are two variations on one essential body, differing only in the placement of the sexual organs. Temperature variation allegedly causes this difference: men's hotter bodies result in protruding sexual organs, while women's cooler bodies retain the organs inside. Aristotle and Galen, Cooke notes, find the female body deficient: it fails to produce enough heat for the sexual organs to descend. Aristotle calls the female, as a result of her internal anatomy, 'the first and most simple imperfection of the male', 'a creature lame, occasional and accessory, as if she were not of the main, but made by the by'. But, after citing such views, Crooke disagrees with them: 'This opinion of Galen and Aristotle we cannot approve. For we think that nature as well intended the generation of a female as of a male: and therefore it is unworthily said that she is an error or a monster in nature.' Specifically, he goes on to say, Galen's views 'savour very little of the truth of anatomy'.

Thus, even if Cooke ignores Harvey's revelations on the circulation of the blood, he nonetheless challenges established views on sexual difference. With more recent practices of dissection in early modern Europe challenging the one-sex model, Crooke takes on this controversy in his text. As he writes, the precise nature of the 'accidental difference' between men and women 'is not agreed upon yet'. But, he posits, recent developments in anatomy tend to favour a model of sexual difference rather than the earlier model upholding a single sex. Scholars continue to debate the precise nature of Crooke's views on sexual difference, however, with Thomas W. Laqueur (1990) contending that Crooke upholds the one-sex theory, while Michael Stolberg (2003), Janet Adelman (1999), and others argue that Crooke forwards a model of sexual dimorphism. Perhaps the most accurate way of describing Crooke's relationship to medical controversy is to note, as Elizabeth Harvey (2002) does, how he offers an analysis of Galenic philosophy nuanced by new anatomy. In this regard, Crooke provides an unusually accessible example of the tensions brought about by the shift from Galenism to modern medicine, and the accompanying revisions in views of gender and sexuality. Not surprisingly, then, Crooke's work appears frequently in anthologies and editions of writings on early modern gender, and he has attracted particular interest among scholars of Shakespeare's *Twelfth night* and *Antony and Cleopatra*.

SEE ALSO: Harvey, William; Shakespeare, William

REFERENCES AND SUGGESTED READINGS

Adelman, Janet (1999) Making defect perfection: Shakespeare and the one-sex model. In: Comensoli, Viviana & Russell, Anne (eds) *Enacting gender on the English Renaissance stage.* University of Illinois Press, Urbana, pp. 23–52.

Birken, William (2004) Crooke, Helkiah. In: *Oxford dictionary of national biography.* Oxford University Press, Oxford.

Harvey, Elizabeth D. (2002) Anatomies of rapture: clitoral politics / medical blazons. *Signs* 27(2), 315–346.

Harvey, Elizabeth D. (2003) Sensational bodies, consenting organs: Helkiah Crooke's incorporation of Spenser. *Spenser Studies* 18, 295–314.

Laqueur, Thomas W. (1990) *Making sex: body and gender from the Greeks to Freud.* Harvard University Press, Cambridge, MA.

Nunn, Hilary M. (2005) *Staging anatomies: dissection and spectacle in early Stuart tragedy.* Ashgate, Aldershot.

Schleiner, Winfried (2000) Early modern controversies about the one-sex model. *Renaissance Quarterly* 53(1), 180–191.

Stolberg, Michael (2003) A woman down to her bones: the anatomy of sexual difference in the sixteenth and early seventeenth centuries. *Isis* 94 (2), 274–300.

Crowley, Robert

GRETCHEN E. MINTON

Robert Crowley (c.1517/19–1588) was a Protestant printer, pamphleteer, poet, and cleric. He was part of a group of reformers known as 'gospellers' who called for further reform during the reigns of Henry VIII and Edward VI and who have often been associated with the emergence of nonconformist factions. Crowley's editions, poetry, and prose tracts all reflect the religious and political climate during Edward's and Elizabeth's reigns, while also showing a connection with medieval literary traditions.

Crowley was born in Gloucestershire around 1517–19 and educated at Magdalen College, Oxford, but after his conversion to Protestantism he gave up his fellowship and left the university. From there he served as a tutor in the household of the prominent Henrician courtier Nicholas Poyntz for a brief period, but by 1546 Crowley was residing in London. He became immediately active in the printing trade, perhaps serving as a proofreader for printers John Day and William Seres. From 1549 to 1551 a large number of books bear Crowley's imprint, ranging from his own pamphlets and poetry to editions of others' works and translations into Welsh. Although he was a publisher, he probably did not have a print-shop of his own, but was a bookseller in Ely Rents, Holborn. His works are critical of Roman Catholic beliefs such as auricular confession, transubstantiation, clerical celibacy, and the sale of indulgences, but Crowley spent much more ink in criticisms against the shortcomings of his fellow Protestants, especially in economic matters.

After Nicholas Ridley, bishop of London, ordained him deacon in 1551, Crowley's activity in printing fell off sharply. With the accession to the throne of Mary in 1553 he fled to the Continent and lived among the exiles at Frankfurt-am-Main (at which point the records show that he had a wife and a child, of whom there is no subsequent trace). Returning to England after Elizabeth's accession in 1558, he held several ecclesiastical preferments, such as archdeacon of Hereford, prebendary of St Paul's, rector of St Peter's the Poor in London, and vicar of St Giles Cripplegate. Crowley was a leader in the vestiarian controversy (the organized disobedience of 37 London ministers who refused to wear the outward apparel of the Catholic Church). He was suspended from St Giles by the archbishop of Canterbury Matthew Parker in 1566 for forcibly barring choir members from a funeral because they were wearing surplices. Crowley maintained his activity in the printing world through his membership in the Stationers' Company, to which he was admitted as a freeman in 1578. Later he became a liveryman, and also bound apprentices within the company from 1580 to 1584. During this period he continued to update older texts and to write prefaces to new ones; a large number of works were also dedicated to him. Crowley died in 1588 and was buried next to John Foxe at St Giles Cripplegate.

Like many reformers, Crowley was intent upon answering the Catholic question 'Where was your church before Luther?' by proving that the Reformation was not new, but instead the continuation of an ancient tradition. In England this interest in precedent centred upon the activities of the Lollards and other proto-reformers. Crowley published William Tyndale's *Supper of the Lorde* (1547), as well as what he thought was John Wyclif's prologue to his translation of the Bible (1550; in fact written by Wyclif's follower John Purvey); but his most important edition was of William Langland's *Piers Plowman* – a work that he identified with the proto-Protestant movement of the fourteenth century. He published three editions of this work in 1550, the latter two of which included extensive marginal notes that emphasized Langland's words against the corruption of the Roman Catholic Church. Crowley also suppressed passages that supported transubstantiation or the monastic ideal, and he made other changes such as substituting the word 'Christ' for 'Mary'. The figure of the ploughman was already an important symbol to the reformers, who followed Erasmus's call to translate the Gospels so that even simple ploughmen could understand the words. Because it was wrongly equated with Wyclif, no one had dared publish *Piers Plowman* before Edward's reign. In Crowley's reading this poem was not only part of the Lollard tradition, but also a prophecy of the Edwardian Reformation. Cognizant of how difficult it was to understand Langland's dialect, Crowley updated the language and orthography for his sixteenth-century readers and explained the alliterative verse tradition to them; by doing so he highlighted aspects of the late-medieval poetic tradition that extended beyond Chaucer. Crowley was certainly interested in the apocalyptic dimension of Langland's poem, but he avoided giving this apocalypticism a contemporary historical dimension. Ultimately Crowley's interpretation of the poem focused upon ethical action; he insisted that his readers should not view this book in order to speak of wonders of the past or yet to come, but only so that they could amend their own errors. *Piers Plowman* had a tremendous impact on Crowley's own works, inspiring everything from his metre to his satirical voice to his interest in prophetic poetry.

Although Crowley is rarely remembered as an important sixteenth-century poet, the five original poetic works he wrote illustrate both a connection with an earlier poetic tradition and the theology of Protestants during Edward's reign. John King contends that Crowley's *oeuvre* 'represents something close to a norm for Edwardian poetry' (King 1978) and that he is 'the most significant poet between Surrey and Gascoigne' (King 1982). Following in the tradition of John Skelton and William Dunbar, Crowley wrote doggerel using forms such as rhyme royal, tailed rhyme, and fourteeners. He also drew on late-medieval works, including *Piers Plowman*, Chaucer's *The Canterbury tales*, and the play *The castle of perseverance*.

Crowley's *One and thyrtye epigrammes wherein are brieflye touched so manye abuses, that maye and ought to be put away* (1550) focus on various abuses in need of eradication, organized alphabetically and covering subjects such as abbeys, alehouses, blasphemous swearers, dice-players, flatterers, inventors of strange news, merchants, nice wives (who dye their hair), obstinate papists, rent-raisers, and usurers. In the preface the book asks the reader not to blame the author, who sees himself as a voice crying in the wilderness, admonishing the people to mend their ways. This motif carries on into Crowley's *Voyce of the laste trumpet* (1549), which is influenced by the medieval form of estates satire and in fact 'conflates a medieval doctrine of estates with the nascent Protestant concept of a "vocation" or "calling"' (McRae 1996). Although the title is taken from Revelation 11, the apocalyptic framework only sets the stage for 12 'lessons' that are addressed to various estates, such as beggars, yeomen, scholars, lewd priests, merchants, gentlemen, and women. All of these are lessons about proper behaviour, such as not rebelling, helping others, accepting your calling, and being content with your lot in life. Despite the fact that Crowley was outraged when the poor were abused, ultimately he was socially conservative and supported the idea that all people should respect their place in society.

Crowley's tone became less admonishing and more threatening in *Pleasure and payne, heauen and hell* (1551), in which he warns of God's ire if oppression and greedy covetousness do not cease. Crowley emphasizes charity, insisting that if you do not do good works, then God will cast you out of heaven. As the concluding dedication to the readers explains:

> For the iuste shall haue plesure and the wicked payne.
> When euery man shal aryse oute of his graue,
> And haue the spryte knyt to the body agayne,
> In heauen or in hell they shall styll remayne.

Pleasure and payne and *Last trumpet* suggest an engagement with the apocalyptic thought made popular during this period by John Bale, whose commentary on the book of Revelation, *The image of bothe churches*, was published around 1545. Crowley seemed to believe that Edward's reign signalled the millennium, but otherwise did not have an interest in specific apocalyptic predictions relating to contemporary historical events. The significance of the last judgement, as outlined in *Pleasure and payne*, as well as in Crowley's other works, is that God will punish the wicked and reward the good.

Crowley's most original poem is *Philargyrie of greate Britayne* (1551), an allegory of nearly 1,400 lines about Henry VIII's reign written in the ballad form of 'tailed rhyme'. Philargyrie, meaning 'lover of silver', stands for avarice, ruling over a land called Nodnoll (London). He first employs Hypocrisy (the Catholic Church) to serve his insatiable hunger for wealth, but then replaces Hypocrisy with Philaute ('self-love', i.e., the Protestants), who proves to be just as vicious, raising rents and beating down the common people. In the resolution Truth tells the king what is going on, and then the king calls on God to send right men to help expel evil from the kingdom. This poem, though focused on Henry's reign, also applies to Edward's; despite the success of the Reformation under the young king, Crowley was disillusioned with the reformers who were just as greedy as the Catholics they had displaced. Throughout his works Crowley was particularly vehement about the treatment of the commoners, arguing that the money from the dissolution of the monasteries should have been distributed throughout the kingdom, and not hoarded by the wealthy few.

Crowley believed that poetry should be for pleasure and delight as well as instruction: 'he saw his poetry as providing a gracious alternative to the rod, as spurring on his godly audience by reminding it of its ideals and pointing out its imperfections' (Graham 2006). His first poetic works were verse translations of the Bible. He translated the Psalms into English verse (iambic fourteeners) for an edition that was probably intended as a Protestant service book and included a simple tune which was the first music for English psalms. He also produced a verse exposition on two chapters of the book of Joel and its parallel passages in the synoptic Gospels and Acts. In this work he examines signs such as famine, pestilence, and fallen stars, but ultimately remains, as always, vague about historical parallels. His aim is to teach his readers to be like sheep who follow in the path of Christ the shepherd; such righteous living, Crowley assures his readers, will lead to eternal bliss on the last day. In all of these versifications he was attempting to make the Scripture more accessible to his readers, and thus he was anxious to publish similar works by others: these included metrical paraphrases of Psalms and Proverbs by Lady Elizabeth Fane (wife of Sir Ralph Fane, a leading retainer of Protector Somerset); and Pore Shakerlaye's metrical verses for Ecclesiastes, *The knoledge of good and iuyle* (1551). He even sought to make the Scriptures accessible to the marginalized members of the British Isles; some of his unique projects include the first Gospel translation into Welsh as well as a book teaching how to pronounce the Welsh language (both by William Salisbury).

Crowley's prose tracts contain many of the same themes apparent in his poetry and editions of others' works. One of his earliest publications was an attack on Roman Catholic doctrine in the form of a refutation of the sermon urging recantation given by Nicholas Shaxton, bishop of Salisbury, at Anne Askew's burning in 1546. However, the bulk of Crowley's output as a pamphleteer expresses outrage at economic injustice. His *An informacion and peticion agaynst the oppressours of the poore commons* (1548) is a copy of an address he made to parliament the previous year, pleading for further reformation and attacking the 'more than Turkish tyranny' of the landlords, warning them that if they did not repent of their oppression, they would not inherit the kingdom of Christ. Again Crowley styles himself as a prophet, using the Psalms and Isaiah to cry out against the abuses of the rich. Crowley was consistent in his call for distributive wealth, and he frequently used the parable of the unjust steward (Luke 16) to support this point. He was disappointed that the dissolution of the monasteries did not result in a sharing of their wealth with the poor, so he was relentless in telling the upper classes that they had a responsibility to charity. This is a surprisingly works-based theology, perhaps even at odds with a Protestant theology of grace, but it was fundamental to Crowley's vision of the ethical responsibilities of the reformers.

Crowley also anticipated the impulse to replace Catholic saints with Protestant counterparts, which was one of the driving objectives behind the most ambitious printing enterprise of the sixteenth century, John Foxe's *Actes and monuments* (1563). In 1559 Crowley published a continuation of Thomas Lanquet and Thomas Cooper's *Epitome of cronicles* (first published in 1549) augmenting it with events from the reigns of Edward VI and Mary and telling the stories of Protestant martyrs.

Owing to his criticism of Anglican reforms and his involvement in the vestiarian controversy, Crowley has often been seen as a forerunner of Elizabethan Puritanism. *A briefe discourse against the outwarde apparell and ministring garmentes of the popishe church* (1566) was Crowley's articulation of a position that became associated with this movement: indeed, the term 'Puritan' was first used during the winter of 1567–68 in connection with this controversy. Yet despite Crowley's outspoken language against the established order, he always stopped short of preaching any sort of rebellion against the monarchy because he was an Erastian, believing in the ascendancy of the state over the church in ecclesiastical matters. He called for further reformation, but his belief in the estates reinforced the idea that each class should keep in its place; as the *One and thyrtye epigrammes* note, even beggars should be happy with their lot in life. Furthermore, Crowley seems to have softened his view by the time of Elizabeth's reign. In his election-day sermon preached to the Stationers' Company in 1574, he argued that riches themselves are not evil because they are a gift from God; this sermon even shows a more tolerant attitude towards the merchants.

While the works that Crowley saw into print can tell us a great deal about the man as well as his times, his career also highlights some interesting features of the publishing trade in the sixteenth century. His name appears in colophons only from 1548 to 1551, but his prodigious output during this period points to the burgeoning of printing during Edward's reign, specifically as part of the programme to further the Reformation (as was outlined in the Royal Injunctions of 1547). It is likely that Crowley did not have a print-shop of his own, but that he was exclusively a bookseller and publisher. Evidence suggests that Richard Grafton, the king's printer, 'secretly printed all but one of the nineteen editions that bear Crowley's imprint' (King 1980), though others have argued that perhaps it was John Day who printed these works. (Dan Knauss [n.d.] has produced the most comprehensive bibliography of Crowley's works, including conjectures about printers.) In any case, Crowley was certainly connected to the most important printers of the Edwardian period, and he also made money through this venture. Although *Pleasure and payne* is dedicated to Lady Elizabeth Fane,

there is no evidence that Crowley secured patronage from her or from anybody else. Crowley's involvement with the Stationers' Company during the Elizabethan settlement is also instructive. This powerful company emerged during this period in order to exert control over what was printed, and even though Crowley's own output was focused on the period from 1548 to 1551, he clearly continued to be active well into the Elizabethan period.

SEE ALSO: Askew, Anne; Bale, John; Dunbar, William; Foxe, John; Skelton, John

REFERENCES AND SUGGESTED READINGS

Cowper, J. M. (ed.) (1872) *The select works of Robert Crowley.* Early English Text Society, London.

Graham, Kenneth J. E. (2006) Distributive measures: theology and economics in the writings of Robert Crowley. *Criticism* 47, 137–158.

Hailey, R. Carter (2001) Geuyng light to the reader: Robert Crowley's editions of *Piers Plowman* (1550). *Publications of the Bibliographical Society of America* 95, 483–502.

Johnson, Barbara (1992) *Reading 'Piers Plowman' and 'The pilgrim's progress'.* Southern Illinois University Press, Carbondale.

King, John N. (1976) Robert Crowley's edition of *Piers Plowman:* a Tudor apocalypse. *Modern Philology* 73, 342–352.

King, John N. (1978) Robert Crowley: a Tudor gospelling poet. *Yearbook of English Studies* 8, 220–237.

King, John N. (ed.) (1980) *Philargyrie of great Britayne,* by Robert Crowley. *English Literary Renaissance* 10, 46–75.

King, John N. (1982) *English Reformation literature.* Princeton University Press, Princeton.

Knauss, Dan (n.d.) Robert Crowley: a bibliography. www.scribd.com/doc/14780261/Robert-Crowley-Bibliography

Martin, J. W. (1983) The publishing career of Robert Crowley: a sidelight on the Tudor book trade. *Publishing History* 14, 85–98.

Martin, J. W. (1989) *Religious radicals in Tudor England.* Hambledon Press, London.

McRae, Andrew (1996) *God speed the plough: the representation of agrarian England, 1500–1660.* Cambridge University Press, Cambridge.

Morgan, Basil (2004) Crowley, Robert. In: *Oxford dictionary of national biography*. Oxford University Press, Oxford.

Norbrook, David (2002) *Poetry and politics in the English Renaissance*, rev. edn. Oxford University Press, Oxford.

Cudworth, Ralph

SARAH HUTTON

Ralph Cudworth (1617–88) was one of the most important religious and philosophical thinkers of the seventeenth century. He was, with Henry More, the most significant of the Cambridge Platonists, whose tolerant, rational Christianity inspired the Latitudinarian movement. Cudworth wrote much, but published few books in his lifetime. His major work, the dauntingly erudite *The true intellectual system of the universe* (published 1678), presents a coherent anti-determinist philosophy but was never completed as planned. He published a handful of sermons, the most famous being his sermon preached before the House of Commons in 1647. His unpublished manuscripts are devoted mainly to the subject of free will. Some of these were published posthumously: *A treatise concerning eternal and immutable morality* in 1731, and *Of freewill* in 1848. Although dubbed a Platonist, he drew on a wide knowledge of ancient philosophy, especially Stoicism. This humanistic dimension of his thought belies his philosophical modernity, evidenced by his debt to René Descartes. Although critical of some aspects of Cartesianism, he used Descartes's concept of body as inert extension as a premise for dualism on the grounds that since corporeality is by definition passive, it is necessary to posit an active immaterial agent, that is mind or spirit, to explain life, thought, and motion. Cudworth's philosophy responds to what he saw as the errors of modern philosophy and theology, especially the materialist philosophy of Thomas Hobbes and predestinarian Calvinism.

Cudworth was born in Somerset in 1617. His father had been a fellow of Emmanuel College, Cambridge, and Cudworth was educated at Emmanuel and became a fellow there in 1639. In 1645 he became regius professor of Hebrew and in 1654 master of Christ's College. Politically, Cudworth supported the cause of Parliament and Commonwealth, but he managed to retain his Cambridge appointments at the Restoration, probably thanks to the influence of his powerful patrons, Edward, Lord Conway, and Sir Heneage Finch. Nevertheless he was regarded with suspicion by the Restoration political establishment, and never felt secure thereafter. This may explain why he never completed *The true intellectual system*, and delayed publication of the part that he did publish. He died in 1688, after a decade as prebendary of Gloucester Cathedral, and was buried in the chapel of Christ's College.

The 'true intellectual system' that gives Cudworth's magnum opus its title is deduced from the idea of God as a perfect being, necessarily good and just, whence are derived both epistemological certainty and the principles of morality. It follows that human beings are free to act as they choose, otherwise they would not bear moral responsibility for their actions and God would be responsible for evil. Cudworth proposed the doctrine with which he is most characteristically associated, his hypothesis of 'plastic nature' (nature conceived as the spiritual agent of God in the operations of nature), in order to square divine power with freedom of action.

The true intellectual system is a philosophy of religion (Cudworth was the first English philosopher to use the term) which sought to defend religious belief in terms which were plausible 'in an Age so Philosophical'. To that end *The true intellectual system* surveys the entire corpus of classical philosophy in order to demonstrate the naturalness of belief in God. He explains pagan polytheism as a corrupted form of monotheism and atheism as the outcome of errors in reason. Much of the work consists in an analysis of the false premises of the four atheistical philosophical systems that he identifies: Hylopathian, Atomical, Hylozoic, and 'Cosmo-Plastic' (atheism that posits a world soul, but no superior divinity). His *Eternal and immutable morality* contains his fullest statement of epistemology, arguing for innate ideas and for the reality of moral distinctions. *Of freewill* defines free will as self-determination, and formulates a moral psychology to explain how the soul directs itself towards the good – themes which are extensively elaborated in Cudworth's unpublished manuscripts (British Library, Additional MSS 4978–4982).

Cudworth's early reputation rested on this mammoth refutation of atheism, but it has not stood the test of time because it was quite quickly undermined by new developments in historical philology, which destroyed some of his semantic premises. However, the book retained its value as a compendium of classical philosophy, and was recommended as such by John Locke. Erudition aside, Cudworth had a more popular legacy through his sermons, which appealed to non-dogmatic Christians. These continued to be published into the nineteenth century. Their appeal derives from their irenic Christian message and their rich imagery. Another aspect of Cudworth's theological legacy was the appropriation of his work in disputes about the Trinity, in which he was claimed by Trinitarians and anti-Trinitarians alike, from the Trinitarian controversies of the late seventeenth century to those of nineteenth-century New England.

Cudworth's philosophical influence was enduring: his writings continued to be reprinted into the nineteenth century and were translated into Latin by Lorenz Mosheim for European consumption in 1733. His philosophical legacy may be traced in works by John Ray, Lord Shaftesbury, Le Chevalier Ramsay, Richard Price, and Thomas Reid. His readers included Locke, Isaac Newton, Gottfried Wilhelm Leibniz, and Alexander Pope, who was indebted to Cudworth for his account of 'plastic nature' in 'An Essay on Man' (1732–34).

SEE ALSO: Hobbes, Thomas; More, Henry; sermons; Sterry, Peter

REFERENCES AND SUGGESTED READINGS

Darwall, Stephen (1992) *British moralists and the internal 'ought'*. Cambridge University Press, Cambridge.

Hedley, Douglas & Hutton, Sarah (2008) *Platonism at the origins of modernity*. Springer, Dordrecht.

Passmore, John Arthur (1951) *Ralph Cudworth: an interpretation*. Cambridge University Press, Cambridge.

Popkin, Richard H. (1992) *The third force in seventeenth-century philosophy*. Brill, Leiden.

Scott, Dominic (1990) Platonic recollection and Cambridge Platonism. *Hermathena* 149, 73–97.

D

Daniel, Samuel

GREGORY KNEIDEL

Little is known about the ancestry or early life of Samuel Daniel (1562/63–1619). University records at Oxford indicate that he matriculated at Magdalen College in 1581, which would suggest that he was born around 1562; his native county is listed as Somerset. He left Oxford without taking a degree and, describing himself as a 'late student in Oxenforde', he first appears in print as the translator of *The worthy tract of Paulus Jovius* (1585), a translation of the Italian author's *Dialogo dell'imprese militari et amorose* (1555). Daniel's choice of this treatise on *impresa* – a species of emblem designed to 'manifest the special purpose of Gentlemen in warlike combats or chamber tornaments' – gestures towards two traits that frame the whole of his life's work: first, his habit of importing, vernacularizing, and even nationalizing Continental and especially Italian poetic forms (the great Italianist John Florio was a lifelong friend and mentor); and secondly, his choice of the martial and the amorous, often separately but sometimes together, as the principal subjects of his poetry. These were the basic coordinates, as he saw it, for the arc of his poetic career: his personal motto, adapted from the Roman elegist Propertius, was 'Aetas prima canat veneres, postrema tumultus' ('Let youth sing of loves, later years of conflicts').

Soon after publishing *The worthy tract*, Daniel appears to have travelled to France and Italy where, he would later claim, he met Giovanni Battista Guarini, the author of *Il pastor fido*. Upon his return to England, Daniel became a tutor within the household of Mary Sidney Herbert, countess of Pembroke, the first of numerous wealthy patrons upon whom Daniel would depend for employment throughout his life. Daniel's favour within the Sidney circle was either declared or endangered in 1591 when he found (or perhaps arranged to have?) 28 of his sonnets appended to the posthumous and pirated edition of Sir Philip Sidney's *Astrophil and Stella* (c. 1582). These 28 sonnets would become the core of *Delia*, a collection of Petrarchan-themed sonnets that Daniel would publish, with a dedication to the countess of Pembroke, independently in 1592 as a revised and expanded series of 50 sonnets with a concluding ode. *Delia* was lauded by its earliest readers primarily for its easy, 'well-languaged' style (in one sonnet, Daniel chides the 'aged accents' and 'untimely words' of Spenser's *Faerie Queene*); this dulcet style attests to the influence of sixteenth-century Continental poets such as Torquato Tasso, Joachim Du Bellay, and Philippe Desportes. In part because *Delia* lacked the narrative structure of other late Elizabethan sonnet sequences, Daniel was able to revise, expand, rearrange, and republish it several times (a second 1592 issue, for example, contained 54 sonnets). Furthermore, Daniel paired it in these early editions with *The complaynt of Rosamond* (1592), a popular poetic narrative from a rival tradition that retells the

The Encyclopedia of English Renaissance Literature, First Edition. Edited by Garrett A. Sullivan, Jr and Alan Stewart.
© 2012 Blackwell Publishing Ltd. Published 2012 by Blackwell Publishing Ltd.

tragic betrayal of Henry II's beautiful but naive and ill-fated mistress Rosamond Clifford. Written in seven-line rhyme royal, *Rosamond* was modelled on the melodramatic first-person complaints of the *Mirrour for magistrates* (1559) and its later continuations, such as Thomas Churchyard's *Tragedie of Shores wife* (1587). Daniel continued in this tragic vein by publishing the Senecan closet drama *The tragedie of Cleopatra* (1594), which might be thought of as a companion piece to *The tragedie of Antonie* (1592), a translation of the French poet Robert Garnier's *Marc-Antoine* (1578) executed by the countess of Pembroke herself. Giving voice to the third, equally aggrieved member of this classical love triangle, Daniel later in the decade published *A letter sent from Octavia to her husband Marcus Antonius into Egypt* (1599), a poem in ottava rima that was loosely modelled on Ovid's *Heroides* and on Michael Drayton's *Englands heroicall epistles* (1597). In contrast to the smooth style and intimate if plaintive mood of *Delia*, these longer discursive poems use a more melodramatic style to depict love as cruel and, at the distance of ancient Egypt and medieval England at least, politically tumultuous.

The *tumultus* mentioned in Daniel's personal motto, however, refers most properly to *The ciuil wars*, a historical epic in ottava rima that he first published in 1595 and that he would continually revise and expand until it reached its final (though still incomplete) eight-book form in 1609. Its principal subject is the fifteenth-century English War of the Roses and its key themes are those of its primary classical model, Lucan's *Pharsalia* (c.61–65): the national calamity of dynastic conflict; the social cost of great individuals pursuing, legitimately or not, their political ambitions; and the desirability of 'the unjustest peace' over 'the justest warre'. *The civil wars* has been most scrutinized as a possible source for and certain parallel to Shakespeare's virtually contemporaneous second tetralogy (*Richard II*, the two parts of *Henry IV*, and *Henry V*). The uncertain dating of Shakespeare's plays and the continued revising of Daniel's epic make it difficult to ascertain the direction of influence between the two writers. Shakespeare, for example, may have borrowed from Daniel the sentimental scene of the young Queen Isabel anticipating the arrival of the newly deposed Richard II into London, a brief irruption of *veneres* amid the epic's climate of *tumultus*. But Daniel's extensive revisions to the final 1609 edition of *The ciuil wars* reveal the influence of Shakespeare's history plays, especially in the rounder psychological portrayals of the epic's protagonists. In other instances, details and motifs not found in Daniel and Shakespeare's principal prose sources, Edward Hall's *Union of the two noble and illustre famelies of Lancastre and Yorke* (1548) and Raphael Holinshed's *Chronicles* (2nd edn, 1587), can be attributed to shared classical models. The famous speech by Shakespeare's bishop of Carlisle on the horrors of civil war (*Richard II*) may echo the opening stanzas of Daniel's epic; but both certainly recall the opening lines of Lucan. Like Shakespeare's history plays, Daniel's epic is also of interest because of its role in either forming or challenging the so-called Tudor myth, that is, the semi-official Elizabethan historical propaganda, manifested most clearly in Hall and Holinshed, about the providential rise of the Tudor dynasty. Daniel was too much of an establishment figure to debunk this myth directly; and certainly the rhetoric of his epic's dedicatory epistles endorses it. Yet, in other historical and philosophical works, Daniel espouses a less providential view of history. Despite its evident popularity, Daniel eventually gave up revising *The ciuil wars* and began the related but more historiographically sophisticated *Collection of the historie of England* (1612), a prose tract that traces the emergence of Britons from their first notice in the writings of Roman historians down to the reign of Richard III.

Beyond the poles of *veneres* and *tumultus*, of the amorous and the military, lie the writings that have earned Daniel his reputation, for good or for ill, as a poet of ideas. The best of these are *Musophilus* (1599) and *A defence of ryme* (1603). The verse colloquy *Musophilus* bears a family resemblance to classical and medieval debates about the relative merits of the active way and the contemplative way of life or, in a slightly variant form, between the soldierly *miles* and the scholarly *clericus*. Daniel seems to have been provoked to write it by the assaults on what he calls 'civil learning' that were launched alternatively in the name of fashionable Renaissance scepticism, as in *A fig for Momus* (1595) by Thomas Lodge, and of grimly pessimistic Calvinism, as in *A treatise of humane learning* (published posthumously in 1633 by Fulke Greville, who is named in Daniel's poem). Although it does defend civil humanism on fairly conventional epistemological and ethical grounds, Daniel characteristically reframes the problem in nationalist terms: against the worldly Philocosmus's charge that small, isolated England is too 'narrow [a] room; in which to seek literary or scholarly fame' ('How many thousands never heard the names/Of Sidney, or of Spenser, or their books?'), the poetry-loving title character insists that England is indeed a 'theatre large enough' for poetry, eloquence, and learning to flourish, provided that its secular and religious institutions eschew the sway of vulgar opinion and embrace the Stoical virtues of self-understanding, prudence, and self-control. Daniel's prose *Defence* responds to Thomas Campion's *Observations in the art of English poesie* (1602), in which the hyper-classicizing Campion promotes the use of Latin quantitative metres in English verse. As is to be expected in such an exchange, Daniel scores points by turning Campion's arguments against him: if rhyme and accentual metre are merely 'fetters' that impinge upon the poet's freedom, how are the rules of accentual metre, with their precise arrangement of long and short vowels, any more liberating? As he had in *Musophilus*, Daniel grounds his arguments on the premises that 'Custome' stands 'before all Law' and 'Nature' stands 'aboue all Arte'. Borrowed from the Ciceronianism controversies of the early sixteenth century, these basic axioms lead Daniel to conclude that English verse and England's medieval history are 'so little in

respect' not because of any intrinsic inferiority but because of 'the clowds that gathered about our owne judgement and that makes us thinke all other ages wrapt up in mists'. In both *Musophilus* and *A defence*, Daniel is especially concerned with depicting England, somewhat paradoxically, as a 'universal island', that is, a unique and integral nation that, despite its geographical remoteness and linguistic isolation, is and indeed always has been capable of matching the towering cultural achievements of ancient Greece and Rome and of its peer nations on the Continent. The underlying historical concern of both works is *translatio studii et imperii*, the transfer of knowledge and power from one culture, one empire to another. In concert with English antiquarians and with Continental legal historians, Daniel argues that England need not import its laws, rules, and conventions, poetic or political, wholesale from ancient Greece and Rome; England's native customs and traditions are enough to build a great nation upon.

Around the time of the death of Queen Elizabeth, Daniel repackaged many of the same neo-Stoic ethical platitudes and some of the same nationalist rhetoric into a slightly more personalized and less argumentative poetic form, the verse epistle. Six verse epistles – addressed to Thomas Egerton; Henry Wriothesley, earl of Southampton; Margaret, countess of Cumberland; Lucy, countess of Bedford; and Lady Anne Clifford – first appeared in a 1603 volume entitled *A panygyrike congratulatorie*. The titular panegyric, of course, celebrated the accession of James VI to the throne of England. Thanks to the influence of the countess of Bedford, Daniel was able to deliver his poem to the king himself on 23 April of that year. And through the influence of Bedford and of James I's queen, Anna, Daniel would receive commissions to write a handful of courtly masques and pastoral tragicomedies: *Visions of the twelve goddesses* (1604), *Queens Arcadia* (1606), *Tythes festival* (1610), and *Hymens triumph* (1615). Although it was during these years that Daniel was most favoured within courtly literary circles, in 1604 he suffered a serious brush with the authorities: the title character of his historical tragedy *Philotas* – in which the protagonist, a military officer and favourite of Alexander the Great, is charged with and executed for treason – was thought to resemble Robert Devereux, the recently executed second earl of Essex. Daniel, who had, ironically enough, recently been named licenser of Children of the Queen's Revels, was called before the Privy Council to answer for himself. The scandal, however painful, was short-lived and not only was Daniel soon receiving courtly commissions again, but *Philotas* was printed in 1605 and 1607. In any event, these courtly entertainments are perhaps best known for the annoyance they caused the age's greatest masque writer, Ben Jonson; later critics have by and large agreed with Jonson that Daniel's poetic talents lay elsewhere.

As was recognized early on, those poetic talents did not include sublimity. In an early mention of Daniel from 1591, Edmund Spenser is already imploring him to 'rouse' his 'well tuned' but 'lowly' Muse and to pursue a loftier 'course'. Other deficiencies – in wit, humour, sensuousness – have been plausibly blamed on his abiding preoccupation with English history and ethical instruction. If Philip Sidney had in his *Defence of poesie* (published 1595) placed the true poet above the fact-bound historian and the syllable-counting versifier, Daniel recognized but in some ways sought to revalue Sidney's hierarchy: for example, he imagined *The civil wars* as a project that required him to 'versifie the troth, not Poetize'. And so it was no surprise that Drayton, in many ways Daniel's nearest cohort, would label him a 'too much a historian in verse'; and Jonson groused that Daniel was 'an honest man, but no poet'. But Daniel has also been lauded for his seriousness and decency, for his plain, measured, approachable style, and, from Coleridge's much later perspective, for the near stylistic equivalence of his poetry and prose. Moreover, if the range of Daniel's wit seemed narrowly bounded, the breadth of his nationalism was never limited by naive jingoism or pedantic antiquarianism. He was an early adapter and influencial vernacularizer of foreign styles and poetic forms, not only of Ovid, Lucan, and Seneca, but Du Bellay, Desportes, and Guarini as well. Likewise, he imported philosophical ideas from Michel de Montaigne, and the cyclical view of history, which he used to shield medieval England from the derision sometimes heaped on it by high Renaissance humanists, was drawn from French historiographers.

Finally, aside from his generic innovations and historiographical initiatives, Daniel is of interest because he seems to have worked competently both as a court poet dependent on powerful patrons and as a print poet catering to the buying public. There is ample evidence from Daniel's long career that shows that he assiduously sought, often gained, and sometimes lost the patronage of his social superiors, not all of whom liked each other: prefatory dedications, encomiastic poetry, occasional verse, and surviving presentation copies of his writings, to say nothing of the traces of his employment history in court records. But there is an even larger body of evidence that shows that Daniel carefully marketed his writings to cater to an eager buying public. An inveterate reviser, he also collected, combined, and in effect repackaged his writings in unusual and influential ways. *Delia*, for example, would establish the so-called 'Delian structure' of many late Elizabethan sonnet sequences, which pairs the sonnets with a poetic complaint as, to cite just one other example, in the first 1609 printings of Shakespeare's *Sonnets*. Daniel was not the first living English poet to publish his *Works* (that was John Heywood). But in the years between the death of Edmund Spenser in 1599 and the publication of Jonson's more famous *Works* in 1616, Daniel collected and published his verse – five different collected editions published during his lifetime; yet another was published soon after his death in 1619 – in a conscious effort to promote himself among patrons and in print as England's principal poet. Ironically, it is in part because Daniel so resolutely defied the fixity of print and so successfully marketed his writings – the almost 1,000 extant early print copies of his writings include five different collected editions published during his lifetime and another published soon after his death in 1619 – that anything approaching a definitive modern edition of his complete works has, despite the heroic efforts of his editors, been so difficult to produce.

SEE ALSO: Campion, Thomas; Drayton, Michael; Florio, John; Herbert, Mary (Sidney), countess of Pembroke; Jonson, Ben; Shakespeare, William; Spenser, Edmund

REFERENCES AND SUGGESTED READINGS

Hulse, Clark (1981) *Metamorphic verse: the Elizabethan minor epic.* Princeton University Press, Princeton.

Maurer, Margaret (1977) Samuel Daniel's poetical epistles, especially those to Sir Thomas Egerton and Lucy, countess of Bedford. *Studies in Philology* 74, 418–444.

Pitcher, John (2000) Essays, works and small poems: divulging, publishing and augmenting the Elizabethan poet, Samuel Daniel. In: Murphy, Andrew (ed.) *The Renaissance text: theory, editing, texuality.* Manchester University Press, Manchester, pp. 8–29.

Rees, Joan (1964) *Samuel Daniel.* University of Liverpool Press, Liverpool.

Sagaser, Elizabeth Harris (1998) Sporting the while: carpe diem and the cruel fair in Samuel Daniel's *Delia* and *The complaint of Rosamond. Exemplaria* 10(1), 145–170.

Seronsy, Cecil (1967) *Samuel Daniel.* Twayne, New York.

Woolf, Daniel R. (1990) *The idea of history in early Stuart England.* University of Toronto Press, Toronto.

Davenant, William

MARCUS NEVITT

William Davenant (1606–68), dramatist, poet, and Restoration theatre manager, was born in Oxford, the second son of Jane and John Davenant who ran a tavern owned by New College. His origins, though relatively modest, were by no means obscure since Davenant's father, a respected vintner, was elected mayor of Oxford in 1621. Nor were they as glamorous as he occasionally encouraged his friends to believe. In a famous anecdote, recorded after the Restoration by John Aubrey, Davenant would, in his cups with Samuel Butler, intimate that he was Shakespeare's bastard or at least 'seemed contented enough to be thought his Son'. Though Shakespeare probably was a frequent visitor to the Davenants' tavern, a convenient stopping point between London and Stratford, modern biographers have convincingly dismantled this myth, suggesting that Davenant might perhaps have been his godson, but no more (Edmond 1987). Either way, Davenant spent a short period studying at Lincoln College in his home town before his parents died in 1622, at which point he made his way to London, where he refused to follow the path marked out for him in his father's will which decreed that he was to be 'put to Prentice to some good marchant of London or other tradesman'. Davenant instead put himself into the service of the aristocracy, first as a page to Frances Howard, duchess of Richmond, and then as a clerk or amanuensis to Fulke Greville, Lord Brooke. It was during his employment in these households that he probably first came into contact with the influential courtiers who would later propel him towards the centre of the nation's culture and politics: Sir Henry Jermyn and Endymion Porter.

Whilst employed by Fulke Greville, Davenant began writing plays. His first plays were all set in northern Italy; they centred upon aristocratic characters and announced their author's aspiration to consort with eminent noblemen in and around the Caroline court. *The cruell brother,* performed at Blackfriars in 1627, was dedicated to Sir Richard Weston, first earl of Portland and lord high treasurer. *The tragedy of Albovine, king of the Lombards* (1629) was, more controversially, dedicated to Robert Carr, earl of Somerset, who had been banished from court in the wake of the Overbury scandal but continued to patronize artists and poets such as George Chapman; the volume was also garlanded with commendatory poems from young Oxford graduates and members of the Inns of Court, chief amongst them Edward Hyde, future earl of Clarendon, who claimed his own contribution unworthy to grace Davenant's quarto but approved of the choice of patron. *The just Italian* (performed at Blackfriars by the Queen's Men in 1629 and printed in quarto 1630), a comedy influenced by Shakespeare's *The taming of the shrew*, concerned itself with the capacity of marriage to regulate the wilful speech and rebelliousness of its central protagonist Alteza who ends the play pledging that her 'future loyaltie / Will manifest [her husband's] mercie well bestow'd'. The play, dedicated to Edward Sackville, fourth earl of Dorset, was evidently no hit, and Thomas Carew offered the author the kind of anti-populist consolation which was to become a key feature of Davenant's own work:

Repine not Thou then, since this churlish fate
Rules not the stage alone; perhaps the State
Hath felt this rancour, where men great and good,
Haue by the Rabble beene misunderstood.
So was thy Play.

Faced with the incomprehension of the 'vulgar', Davenant began to ennoble or mystify his own social status in the printed quartos of these plays by introducing an aggrandizing apostrophe into his surname. This is most striking in *Albovine*'s dedicatory epistle to Somerset, the valedictory flourish of which, at once intimate and elite in its omission of a Christian name, works to collapse the distance between patron and an author styled 'your humblest Creature D'avenant'.

This typographical innovation obsessed some of Davenant's contemporaries who saw in the degree of social advancement conferred by this most meagre of textual marks the precariousness of his parvenu status. As Davenant's star continued to rise – he was appointed Ben Jonson's successor as England's laureate poet-dramatist in 1638 and was knighted by the king for services to the Royalist cause in 1643 – one

commentator, aware that 'avenant' was no place but merely the French adjective for 'welcoming' or 'pleasant', pointed out that to 'come from Avenant means from nowhere'. This same person made explicit links between Davenant's careful refashioning of his lineage and the physical effects of the illness he contracted in the early 1630s, which was to shape the majority of contemporary and early critical responses to his work. The loss of a significant portion of his nose to venereal disease, tidied up considerably in William Faithorne's engraving of the author for the 1673 folio of Davenant's *Works*, meant that he had 'made a Notch in's name, like that in's face'. The favourable critical reception of Davenant's work offered in *The great assises holden in Parnassus* (1645) also helped establish the connection between his physiognomy and creative output when it reminded its readers that 'his Art was high, although his Nose was low'. Davenant's own playful reflections on his afflictions indicate that his sexual habits and subsequent disfigurement were a key part of his courtly identity during the 1630s. The prologue to his extremely popular comedy *The witts* (1634) made reference to himself as 'the long-sick Poet' whilst much of his occasional verse from this period made frank reference to his disease. His poem 'Madagascar', addressed to Charles I's nephew Prince Rupert, opened with jocular references to his body's 'sick offers to depart'; another to Henrietta Maria's physician, Thomas Cademan, outlined the symptoms of venereal infection – swollen cheeks, 'revolted Teeth', foaming mouth – in excruciating detail, concluding that a poem was insufficient reward for the man who had delivered him from death's door. In a poem to his friend and patron Endymion Porter, Davenant made explicit how his illness – contracted when he had been married for at least six years – was largely attributable to Cavalier excess. Only half-repenting of his rakish ways, he asked Porter to watch him as they drank and

Take care, that Plenty swell not into vice:
Lest by a fiery surfet I be led
Once more to grow devout in a strange bed.

Such attitudes did very little to hinder his advancement. The title page of many of the plays and masques written between 1635 and 1638 indicate that he was now one of the court's pre-eminent artists and was especially favoured by Henrietta Maria as 'her Majesties Servant'. *Love and honour* (1634), *The platonick lovers* (1635), and the masque *The temple of love* (performed at Whitehall on three occasions in the 1634/35 court season) were each inspired by the fashion for Neoplatonism which took hold in the queen's circle during this period. It is difficult to ascertain the nature of Davenant's allegiances in these dramas and critics disagree about the criticism or compliment therein (Sharpe 1987; Britland 2006). Even if these works broadly uphold the benignity of the royal couple's influence, it is impossible to read them as unqualified endorsements of the cult of platonic love so favoured by Henrietta Maria and some of her leading courtiers. *The platonick lovers* looks sceptically at the transformative powers of this doctrine by presenting us with a gallery of courtly characters apparently in thrall to codes of idealized affection whilst under destabilizing attack from their libidos. In what seems a wry allusion to Davenant's own deliverance by a member of the medical profession, the only thing that can effectively temper the pleasures and perils of the body are the pharmaceutical interventions of a physician-philosopher, Buonateste, and not the cult of platonic love. The dedication of the play to Sir Henry Jermyn, Davenant's close friend who had recently been imprisoned in the Tower of London for impregnating one of Henrietta Maria's attendants and refusing to marry her, clearly indicates that the appeal of chaste affection remained distant for an author who, after his recent experiences, had every reason to endorse a flight from the pleasures of the flesh.

After *The temple of love*, Davenant and theatrical designer Inigo Jones collaborated on all the remaining masques of the Caroline reign including *Britannia triumphans* (1638) and the final masque to be performed at court before the Civil War, *Salmacida spolia*, which was staged twice in 1640. This last depicts the banishment of Discord from the realm of King Philogenes ('lover of his people'); it is a pacifist attempt to unite factions at court that urges conciliation as the best way of responding to the recent Scottish rebellion. Davenant's non-belligerent message was bold since the king was known to favour a more aggressive engagement with the Scots; its boldness also reflected the central place Davenant now occupied at the Caroline court. Appointed effective poet laureate in December 1638 ahead of Thomas May who, it was rumoured, chose the Parliamentarian cause during the Civil War as a result of this decision, Davenant published his first collection of verse, *Madagascar* (1638). The 42 occasional poems in this duodecimo volume were heralded by commendatory poems by eminent Cavalier poets such as Thomas Carew and Sir John Suckling, the latter of whom exposed the gap between the author's status at court and his parlous financial standing; debt was to plague Davenant throughout his career and Suckling praised the title poem in telling terms: 'prithee / In thy next Voyage, bring the Gold too with thee.' The majority of the poems in the volume seek to entertain and find favour with the dominant influences at the Caroline court; the volume is dedicated to Jermyn and Porter, who are also the subject of eight poems, with five more addressed to Henrietta Maria (another was a micro-epic about her dwarf Jeffrey Hudson, 'Jeffereidos'). Prince Rupert is the stated addressee of the title poem about an aborted scheme to colonize Madagascar, which imagines the 'Heroique Prince' as a valiant yet merciful conqueror of Portuguese adventurers. The indigenous population of the island falls in love with the Prince's Cavalier grooming and peacefully acquiesces to his rule whilst, back at home, the poem's narrator calls for wine and inveighs against the 'Peoples common blood' and 'rude dull Mariners, who hardly can / Distinguish Buffe, or Hides from Cordovan (since Gloves they never weare)'. There are some wonderful lyric turns in the collection; one poem to Henrietta Maria struggles to comprehend the mysteries of Stuart absolutism with affecting simplicity: 'You that are more than our discreeter fear / Dares praise, with such dull art, what make you here?' Nevertheless it is hard to imagine a single book of poetry more dedicated to the vertiginous hierarchies, glamorous personalities, and boundless pleasures of the Caroline court.

It is unsurprising, then, that when the Civil War came Davenant sided with his friends and patrons. Though new quarto editions of some of his plays and a second edition of *Madagascar* did appear during the conflict, Davenant spent his war service in support of the Royalist cause. He was involved to some degree, along with Suckling and Jermyn, in the disastrous army plot to free Thomas Wentworth, earl of Strafford, from prison and wrote a *Humble remonstrance* (1641) to avoid his own looming death sentence. In the *Remonstrance* Davenant maintains his loyalty to the queen, Jermyn, and Suckling but also manipulates a form of *parrhesia*, or free speaking, reminding Parliament that he comes from a 'Nation which hath bin ever bred with liberty of speaking: and the very Mechanicks of Spaine are glad they are Spaniards, because they have liberty; and thinke, when over-speaking becomes dangerous, that then they chiefly lose the liberty of Subjects'. Spared execution, Davenant was knighted by the king for his loyalty and spent the rest of the 1640s shuttling between England and the exiled courts in France and the Low Countries, running arms, funds, and correspondence to aid the Royalist war effort.

In Paris, Davenant began working on the text that he was to regard as his crowning achievement, his unfinished epic romance of Lombard knights, *Gondibert* (1651). His third wife ensured that this was the text placed at the head of the posthumous folio edition of his *Works* (1673). Whilst writing *Gondibert* Davenant became friends with another of the English exiles in Paris, Thomas Hobbes, showing him drafts of the poem and inviting him to write an essay on the subject of heroic poetics as a companion piece to one of his own on the same subject to be printed as a preface. In these essays we see a repudiation of inspiration as the prime source of creativity (a term tainted for these authors by its association with religious sectarianism) in favour of wit, a more refined mix of instinct and reason. In his contribution Davenant offers a vigorous defence of the office of the poet and recalls Sir Philip Sidney by suggesting that 'poesy' is a discourse far superior to history and philosophy since it gives aesthetic pleasure and offers 'collateral help' through which governments might rule 'with better order and more ease'. The publication of Davenant's poem was, however, interrupted by his capture and imprisonment by Commonwealth forces who regarded him as a dangerous Royalist renegade; he published the prefatory essays almost a year before the incomplete poem they purported to elucidate. This decision, satirized by contemporaries, was carefully calculated and represented an attempt on Davenant's behalf – as he sweated for his life in the Tower – to advertise himself as a well-connected mind for hire who might be useful to a new political order eager to urge its legitimacy (Nevitt 2009). The move was successful in so far as Davenant's life was spared and it freed him to develop *Gondibert*'s prefatory arguments in an anonymous treatise entitled *A proposition for advancement of moralitie, by a new way of entertainment of the people* (1654) which explored, with typical anti-populist hauteur, the ways in which a reformed drama might find favour with Puritans and secure obedience to the current administration:

> if the peoples senses were charm'd and entertain'd with things familiar to them, they would easily follow the voices of their shepherds; especially if there were set up some Entertainment, where their eyes might be subdu'd with Heroicall Pictures and change of Scenes, their Eares civiliz'd with Musick and wholesome discourses, but some Academie where may be presented in a Theater severall ingenious Mecanicks, as Motion and Transposition of Lights ... without any scandalous disguising of men in womens habits, as have bin us'd in Playes.

During this period Davenant was on cordial terms with individuals in and around the

Council of State, most notably John Thuloe and Bulstrode Whitelock; Royalists were aghast at Davenant's apparent change of allegiance. Lady Hester Pulter, a Hertfordshire poet who had never met him, wrote a manuscript poem about him that reworks Ariosto's *Orlando furioso* (Millman & Wright 2005; Nevitt 2009). A raucous printed response was orchestrated by John Denham who collected a group of satires about Davenant's recent behaviour mockingly entitled *Certain verses written by severall of the authors friends to be re-printed with the second edition of Gondibert* (1653).The authors of these satires round on the aggrandizing apostrophe Davenant inserted into his surname, *Gondibert*'s tediousness, and its author's meagre intellectual abilities. It was his syphilitic nose, however, which became the starkest symbol for all these writers who saw in it the most material reminder of Davenant's Cavalier past and his former political allegiances: as far as they were concerned his face would never fit with the new regime.

Davenant found favour with the new administration, however, and the entrepreneurial arguments of the *Proposition* were taken up by the Cromwellian Protectorate. He was allowed to stage an entertainment – two hours' worth of staged declamations, interspersed with music, between Diogenes the Cynic and Aristophanes on the subject of the morality of 'Publique Entertainments' – which was printed as *The first days entertainment at Rutland-House* (1656). This private entertainment had a 10-day run in a single room of a building on Aldersgate street, close to Smithfield market, which Davenant had leased since his release from prison. Its mixture of music and oratory proved so successful that Davenant was permitted to stage a series of operas, first at Rutland House and then at the Cockpit in Drury Lane, to small public audiences: *The siege of Rhodes* (1656), *The cruelty of the Spaniards in Peru* (1658), and *The history of Sr Francis Drake* (1659). Whilst the latter titles can be read as offering fulsome praise of Cromwell's engagements with the Spanish and the Dutch, *The siege of Rhodes* – the first English opera – was a much more nuanced production which Davenant revised in a racier dramatic form after the Restoration, when it became Samuel Pepys's favourite play. Focusing on the eminently noble behaviour of Solyman the Magnificent, his adoration of the chaste Sicilian Ianthe, and her husband Alphonso's disablingly jealous response to this, the opera forced its audiences to re-evaluate the nature of unthinking allegiance by censuring the Christian hero's behaviour rather than the exemplary honourable actions of the typical Renaissance stage villain, the Turk. The opera also anticipated the innovations of Restoration theatre as Davenant was the first English author-impresario to introduce movable scenery and an actress, Mrs Coleman, to the professional stage in this production.

By the time Davenant died on 7 April 1668, he had long been forgiven by Charles II for his chicanery during the 1650s. As manager of one of only two licensed theatre companies, the Duke's Company, he became a central figure in Restoration cultural life. Even though he was not the biological son of Shakespeare, he successfully adapted a number of Shakespeare's plays – *Hamlet, Macbeth, The tempest* amongst them – for the changed tastes of Restoration theatre audiences and thus played an important role in cementing Shakespeare's reputation as the most revered dramatist of the period.

SEE ALSO: Carew, Thomas; Chapman, George; Denham, John; Greville, Fulke; Hobbes, Thomas; Hyde, Edward, earl of Clarendon; Jones, Inigo; May, Thomas; Pulter, Hester; Shakespeare, William; Suckling, John

REFERENCES AND SUGGESTED READINGS

Britland, Karen (2006) *Drama at the courts of Henrietta Maria.* Cambridge University Press, Cambridge.

Butler, Martin (1984) *Theatre and crisis 1632–1642.* Cambridge University Press, Cambridge.

Clare, Janet (ed.) (2002) *Drama of the English Republic, 1649–1660.* Manchester University Press, Manchester.

Edmond, Mary (1987) *Rare Sir William Davenant.* Manchester University Press, Manchester.

Harbage, Alfred (1935) *Sir William Davenant, poet venturer, 1606–1668.* Oxford University Press, London.

Jacob, James R. & Raylor, Timothy (1991) Opera and obedience: Thomas Hobbes and *A proposition for advancement of moralitie* by Sir William Davenant. *Seventeenth Century* 6, 205–250.

Millman, Jill Seal & Wright, Gillian (eds) (2005) *Early modern women's manuscript poetry.* Manchester University Press, Manchester.

Nethercot, Arthur (1938) *Sir William D'avenant: poet laureate and playwright-manager.* University of Chicago Press, Chicago.

Nevitt, Marcus (2009) The insults of defeat: royalist responses to William Davenant's *Gondibert* (1651). *Seventeenth Century* 24, 287–304.

Sharpe, Kevin (1987) *Criticism and compliment: the politics of literature in the England of Charles I.* Cambridge University Press, Cambridge.

Zwicker, Steven N. (1993) *Lines of authority: politics and English literary culture, 1649–1689.* Cornell University Press, Ithaca.

Davies, Eleanor

REBECCA TOTARO

Lady Eleanor Davies (née Touchet; 1590–1652) was a prolific writer of civil war prophecies. She was the fifth daughter in a family of seven children born to George Touchet, who was eleventh Baron Audley (1550/51–1617) and a member of parliament from 1566 until 1614. He was also governor of Utrecht in the Netherlands and governor of Kells, County Meath, Ireland, the latter position leading in 1616 to King James I granting him the earldom of Castlehaven in Ireland. At the age of 19, Lady Eleanor married Sir John Davies (1569–1626), the famous poet and attorney-general for Ireland who in 1603 had accompanied Henry Carey, Lord Hunsdon (?1524–96) to announce to James VI of Scotland that he would be the next king of England. They had two children survive beyond infancy: Lucy, who was born in Dublin in 1613 (d.1679), and Jack, about whom little is known but who appears to have died tragically in 1617, when he was very young. The family relocated to London in 1619 when Davies was recalled from Ireland. Soon thereafter, Davies arranged for Lucy's marriage to Ferdinando Hastings (1608–55), son and heir of Henry Hastings, fifth earl of Huntingdon (1586–1643). Lucy was 11, and by the age of 13, she had moved to her husband's home. This left Lady Eleanor alone and in a difficult marriage to a man more than two decades her senior.

A radical change occurred in 1625. As Davies explains in *The Lady Eleanor, her appeal* (1646), she took in a 13-year-old Scottish boy named George Carr and, it is said, helped him to overcome his hearing and speaking impediments. The boy was reputed to have had some ability at fortune-telling. That same year, Lady Eleanor had a dream: the biblical prophet Daniel spoke to her and told her that the end times were 19½ years away and that she must warn England to prepare. Her behaviour and attire changed, much to the distress of family members. In her first prophetic pamphlet, *A warning to the dragon and all his angels* (1625), Lady Eleanor offers what is primarily an exposition of Daniel 7–12. She had intended to share this warning of end times with King James I and George Abbot, archbishop of Canterbury, but King James died that year.

Undaunted, Lady Eleanor would thereafter dedicate herself almost entirely to communicating her anti-Catholic message for England, criticizing its king and church, warning them to continue to reform or the nation would face God's heavy judgement. Her husband was displeased and burned some of her writings. When he died soon thereafter, in 1626, many wondered if there had been foul play; legal disputes over land ensued, estranging Lady Eleanor from family members. In 1627, she remarried. Her new husband Sir Archibald Douglas (d.1644) was no more supportive, however, and he too attempted to prevent her from disseminating her unlicensed, printed tracts. Lady Eleanor's response was to predict his punishment. This came, she believed, when he went mad.

The tide turned more publicly against her family when in 1631 her brother Mervin Touchet (d.1631) was charged, sentenced, and hanged for the rape and sodomy of members of his household. Lady Eleanor defended him in writing but to no avail. In 1633, she came under scrutiny herself for secretly printing some of her unlicensed prophecies while on a trip to Amsterdam and for confronting William Laud, archbishop of London (1573–1645), with the threat of the coming judgement day. She was fined, saw her books burned before her, and was imprisoned in the Gatehouse prison in Westminster. This was the first of several trials and imprisonments for various offences, including, in 1639, her imprisonment in Bedlam Hospital and then in the Tower for desecrating the altar at Lichfield Cathedral. She would continue to write throughout these years, her tracts numbering more than 70 and making her, notably, the most published female prophetess of the time.

Unfortunately for her readers, much of her work is difficult to decipher. Her prose features references to biblical passages out of context mixed with her personal history, personal names turned into anagrams, and complex, unique, and often indecipherable symbolism. One of the more straightforward of these mixtures of personal and prophetic is in the opening of *Woe to the house* (1633). The names of the women of the house of Derby, whom she counted enemies, are transformed in print: Elizabeth Stanley becomes That Jezebel Slain, and Ana Stanley becomes A Lye Satann. Many of her tracts assail Archbishop Laud and Charles I in bolder terms, referring to Laud as a beast ascending from a pit to his post, for example, in *Samsons legacie* (1643). However playful this language appears, it aroused suspicion regarding both her political position and her state of mind.

Some comfort came to Davies when in 1645, 19½ years after her prophetic dream, Archbishop Laud died; this confirmed her life's work for herself if for few others. Her most dedicated supporter by that time was her daughter Lucy. In and out of gaol, Lady Eleanor struggled financially. She saw Lucy as light personified, and Lucy seems to have desired that her mother pursue her passionate prophesying and live with some degree of comfort. She died in London in 1652 and was buried in St Martin-in-the-Fields next to her first husband.

SEE ALSO: Davies, John

REFERENCES AND SUGGESTED READINGS

Cope, Esther S. (1993) *Handmaid of the holy spirit: Dame Eleanor Davies, never soe mad a ladie.* University of Michigan, Ann Arbor.

Douglas, Amy Scott (2004) Women and parliament in seventeenth-century England: sites of cultural stress from reformation to restoration. Folger Institute. www.folger.edu/html/folger_institute/cultural_stress/parliament_women.html

Feroli, Teresa (1994a) The sexual politics of mourning in the prophecies of Eleanor Davies. *Criticism* 36, 359–382.

Feroli, Teresa (1994b) Sodomy and female authority: the Castlehaven scandal and Eleanor Davies's *The restitution of prophecy* (1651). *Women's Studies* 24(1–2) 31–49.

Pickard, Richard (1996) Anagrams etc: the interpretive dilemmas of Lady Eleanor Douglas. *Renaissance and Reformation/Renaissance et Reformé* 20 (3), 5–22.

Porter, Roy (1994) The prophetic body: Lady Eleanor Davies and the meanings of madness. *Women's Writing* 1, 51–63.

Watt, Diana (1997) *Secretaries of God: women prophets in late medieval and early modern England.* Boydell & Brewer, Woodbridge.

Watt, Diana (2004) Davies, Lady Eleanor. In: *Oxford dictionary of national biography.* Oxford University Press, Oxford.

Davies, John

PENELOPE GENG

Sir John Davies (1569–1626) wrote most of his poems between 1593 and 1599 when he was a student of law at the Middle Temple. He was considered by his contemporaries to be a satiric poet of epigrams and 'gulling' sonnets. Davies treated poetry as a medium for broadcasting his classical learning and intellectual wit. He used his poems to win favour and secure patronage. Thus, Davies's brief poetic career provides scholars with a case study for the social uses of poetry during the Elizabethan era.

Davies was born in Chisgrove, Wiltshire. He enrolled at Winchester College in 1580, then at Oxford University in 1585. In 1587 he was admitted to the Middle Temple and called to the bar in 1595. Two years later, he was disbarred and banished from the Middle Temple for attacking a fellow student, Richard Martin, with a 'bastinado', or cudgel. After his disgrace, Davies retired to Oxford where he composed *Nosce teipsum* (*Know thyself*, 1599), a lengthy poem about the state of man's soul. The poem was dedicated to Elizabeth I, as was *Hymnes of Astraea* (1599), a collection of 26 acrostics set to the queen's name 'Elisa Betha Regina'. Both poems were well received by the queen. Around this time, Sir Thomas Egerton, lord keeper of the Great Seal of England, took an interest in Davies. Egerton persuaded the officials at the Middle Temple to reinstate Davies. After the death of Elizabeth I, Davies accompanied Lord Hunsdon to Scotland where he met James I. The king reportedly asked whether Davies was the author of *Nosce teipsum*, and on discovering that he was indeed, embraced the young man. From this point forwards, Davies enjoyed a brilliant legal career. In 1603 he took office as the solicitor-general for Ireland. In 1608/9, he married Eleanor Touchet, sister to the earl of Castlehaven (who was executed in 1631). Davies returned permanently to England in 1619. In 1622 he published a revised edition of his three major poems, *Nosce teipsum*, *Astrea*, and *Orchestra*. Conspicuously, the mature lawyer chose not to publish the satiric poems he wrote as a youth. On the eve of taking office as lord chief justice, Davies died from apoplexy.

Davies's poems consistently showcase his classical training and satiric wit. His *Epigrammes*, modelled after Martial's poems, were particularly popular among urbane readers. The epigram is a short poem that ends on a witty turn. English imitations of Martial's epigrams flourished during the 1590s. Davies's epigrams, written around 1594/95, circulated in manuscript before being collected and printed with Christopher Marlowe's 'Elegies' as *Epigrammes and elegies by I.D. and C.M.* at Middleborough. Copies of this book were among those burned by censors during the Bishops' Ban of 1599. In the epigrams, Davies laughs at the figure of the 'gull' or 'he which semes, and is not wize' ('Of a gull'). Among the flock of London gulls, he describes Gallus, a young braggart who returns from a 'Sommer in Friesland', speaking 'such warlike wordes/As if I could their English understand' ('In Gallum') and Publius, the 'student at the common law' who spends more time touring London's entertainments than with the textbooks by 'Ployden, Dier and Brooke' ('In Publium'). The popularity of Davies's epigrams may be gauged by his contemporary Everard Guilpin's praise: Davies was 'our English Martiall'. Davies's gulling sonnets were written around the time of the *Epigrammes*. These poems parodied the exaggerated rhetoric of Elizabethan sonneteers, the second-rate imitators of Sir Philip Sidney's *Astrophil and Stella* (c.1582). For example, Davies's Sonnet 5 ridicules the sonneteers' overuse of *copia*: 'Mine Eye, myne eare, my will, my witt, my harte,/Did see, did heare, did like, discerne, did love,/Her face, her speche, her fashion, judgement, arte.'

Besides the satiric poems, Davies wrote the semi-serious *Orchestra, or a poeme of daucing*. Composed in 1594, and published two years later, the poem describes an episode in the *Odyssey* which 'Homer forgot' about Antinous, a 'fresh and iolly Knight' who exhorts Penelope to be his dancing partner. Antinous and Penelope engage in a debate about the merits of dancing. She considers dancing a 'new rage' and a 'misgouernment' of the body. He argues that 'Daucing is Loves proper exercise'. To prove his point, he recounts the story of Love (personified) inventing dancing to bring harmony between the sexes who would otherwise remain 'A rude disordered rout . . . Of men and women'. Penelope finally changes her mind when she sees through a magical glass the queen of England dancing. The poem parallels Edmund Spenser's use of the seven-line stanza in 'Four Hymns' as well as Spenser's poetic reworking of Neoplatonic philosophy.

Davies's 1,924-line *Nosce teipsum*, written in quatrains, is his most meditative and serious poem. The poem concerns the immortality of the soul. It opens by stating a series of questions about the limitations of man's knowledge of world and self: 'What can we know? or what can we discerne? / When *Error* chokes the windowes of the mind.' According to Davies, 'Affliction' is an excellent teacher for it makes 'us looke into our selves' and it 'Teach[es] us to *know our selves*, beyond all bookes'. The structure of the poem's argument recalls Michel de Montaigne's *An apology for Raymond Sebond*. Like Montaigne, Davies asserts that 'My selfe am *Center* of my circling thought, / Onely *my selfe* I studie, learne, and *know*.' Davies rehearses theories from contemporary metaphysical schools on the existence of the soul. A clear proposition emerges: '*She* [the Soul] *is a substance*, and a reall thing.' The soul exists independent of the body and the senses. Here, Davies borrows freely from Aristotle's *De anima*. While animal and man both possess physical senses, man's mind – encompassing various cognitive functions such as memory, reason, and judgement – transcends the physical senses. Davies concludes that the soul is God's gift bestowed upon each person and that only through faith can the soul be united with the divine.

SEE ALSO: Guilpin, Everard; Marlowe, Christopher; Sidney, Philip; Spenser, Edmund

REFERENCES AND SUGGESTED READINGS

Pawlisch, Hans S. (1985) *Sir John Davies and the conquest of Ireland: a study in legal imperialism.* Cambridge University Press, Cambridge.

Sanderson, James L. (1975) *Sir John Davies.* Twayne, Boston.

Wilkes, G. A. (1962) The poetry of Sir John Davies. *Huntington Library Quarterly* 25, 283–298.

Day, John

SARAH KNIGHT

The dramatist John Day (1573/74–?1638) was born in Cawston, a village to the north of Norwich, the son of a Norfolk farmer. Day was educated in Ely, and in October 1592 was admitted as a sizar at Gonville and Caius College, Cambridge, but in May 1593 he was expelled for stealing a book. Although he did not earn a degree and left Cambridge in disgrace, Day's post-university career mirrored that of several of his contemporaries from humble backgrounds, such as Cambridge alumni Christopher Marlowe and Thomas Nashe, and somewhat misleadingly, later works such as 1608's *The parliament of bees* were attributed to 'John Daye, Cantabridg'. Day travelled to London to earn a living as a professional writer, and like his contemporaries Robert Greene and Ben Jonson, he had an artistically varied and sometimes personally controversial career.

Five years after his expulsion from Cambridge, Day surfaces again in Philip Henslowe's diary, becoming involved with the Admiral's Men when they were still based at the Rose Theatre, then working with the company for the next five years. The diary records Day's sale of the play *The conquest of Brute* to the company in July 1598. Day's play was given to Henry Chettle, apparently Day's senior collaborator within the company, and expanded into two parts (Carson 2004). The sale of this play launched Day's regular work with the company over the next few years, and he also collaborated with Chettle on *The blind beggar of Bednal-Green* (1600). The subtitle of the printed play (1659) – 'with the merry humor of *Tom Strowd* the *Norfolk* yeoman' – suggests that Day drew from his agricultural past to create one of the play's main characters and lend his work authentic East Anglian colour. The play was successful, judging by the fact that two (now lost) sequels were written in 1601 by Day and William Haughton.

Within the company, Day appears to have worked predominantly with Chettle, Thomas Dekker, and Haughton (Foakes 2002; Carson 2004). Over the next few years, Day wrote in a variety of genres. In 1599 he collaborated with Haughton on *Cox of Collumpton* and *The tragedy of Thomas Merry*, both listed in Henslowe's diary (Foakes 2002; Carson 2004), both inspired by recent murders (Pitcher 1994; Rutter 1999), and both now lost. Simon Forman saw the former play at the Rose in March 1600 (Carson 2004), and was struck by the appearance of a bear in the play that drives two homicidal brothers to suicide (Pitcher 1994). Day himself may have been involved in a murder at around the same time: the Southwark assizes record 'John Day yeoman' stabbing Henry Porter, another playwright working for Henslowe and the author of *The pleasant historie of the two angrie women of Abington* (1599). Day confessed his guilt, but the charge was altered to manslaughter and he was apparently pardoned (Hunter 2004).

Day's play-writing continued to prosper, however, and although many of his plays are now lost, the titles alone suggest an unusual versatility of subject matter, and their performance history shows that he was capable of pleasing markedly diverse theatre-going audiences. He moved with the Admiral's Company to the Fortune Theatre in 1601, and continued to write for performances at the Rose theatre, which was taken over by Worcester's Men in 1602. Henslowe's diary records regular payments to Day for plays such as *The Spanish moor's tragedy* (a collaboration with Dekker and Haughton) and *An Italian tragedy* in the autumn and winter of 1599 (Carson 2004). Day now appears to have based his plays in exotic settings, an impression further substantiated by the titles of two other lost plays, *The conquest of the West Indies* and *The conquest of Spain by John of Gaunt* (both 1601; Parr 2004).

In the early years of James VI and I's reign, Day was writing for the Children of the Queen's Revels who acted at the Blackfriars playhouse (Gurr 1996). He wrote three satirical comedies for this company: *The ile of gulls* (1606), *Law-trickes, or who would have thought it* and *Humour out of breath* (both published in 1608). The first of these plays caused a scandal: based on Philip Sidney's *Arcadia*, the play's account of rival factions from Sidney's romance was taken to be a satire of the English and Scottish nations, several actors were imprisoned, the company could no longer use the Queen's name, and the 1606 printing appears to have been censored (Chambers 1967). Prophetically, the first line of Day's prologue evokes the 'misery that waytes upon the pen/ Of the best Writers' but he seems to have escaped serious prosecution, and was soon writing again for the public playhouses, drawing once more from contemporary events in the news. *The travels of three English brothers* (1607), written with William Rowley and George Wilkins, dramatized the international escapades of the gentlemen-adventurers Anthony, Robert, and Thomas Shirley, and was staged at the Red Bull, Clerkenwell (Parr 2004).

References to Day after 1608 are less frequent: according to the Stationers' Register, he apparently co-wrote *A booke called the madde prankes of merry Moll* in 1610, and in 1620 he and Dekker co-authored *Guy of Warwick*, and also possibly collaborated on *The bellman of Paris* and *Come see a wonder* (both 1623; Chambers 1967; Parr 2004). In 1640 John Tatham wrote an elegy on Day's death in *The fancies theater*, and it is possible that he died in late 1638.

SEE ALSO: Chettle, Henry; Dekker, Thomas; Haughton, William; Marlowe, Christopher; Nashe, Thomas; Porter, Henry; Rowley, William; Sidney, Philip

REFERENCES AND SUGGESTED READINGS

Carson, Neil (2004) *A companion to Henslowe's diary*. Cambridge University Press, Cambridge.

Chambers, E. K. (1967) *The Elizabethan stage*, vol. 3. Clarendon Press, Oxford.

Foakes, R. A. (ed.) (2002). *Henslowe's diary*. Cambridge University Press, Cambridge.

Gurr, Andrew (1996). *Playgoing in Shakespeare's London*. Cambridge University Press, Cambridge.

Hunter, G. K. (2004) Porter, Henry. In: *Oxford dictionary of national biography*. Oxford University Press, Oxford.

Parr, Anthony (2004) Day, John. In: *Oxford dictionary of national biography*. Oxford University Press, Oxford.

Pitcher, John (1994) 'Fronted with the sight of a bear': *Cox of Collumpton* and *The winter's tale*. *Notes and Queries* 41(1), 47–53.

Rutter, Carol Chillington (1999). *Documents of the Rose playhouse*. Manchester University Press, Manchester.

de Vere, Edward, earl of Oxford

DAVID KATHMAN

Edward de Vere, seventeenth earl of Oxford (1550–1604), was an Elizabethan courtier poet and playwright, best known today for the movement that claims him as the 'real' author of Shakespeare's works. On the death of his father, the sixteenth earl, in 1562 he became earl of Oxford and a royal ward under the guardianship of William Cecil, later Lord Burghley, who provided him with a good education typical of a young Elizabethan nobleman. In 1571 Oxford married Burghley's daughter Anne, but the marriage was not a happy one owing to Oxford's numerous affairs, including a notorious one with Anne Vavasour which produced an illegitimate son and led to Oxford being committed to the Tower. In his youth Oxford was a favourite of Queen Elizabeth, but he fell out of royal favour because of his reckless behaviour, and squandered most of his early promise as well as his family's fortune. In 1586 Elizabeth granted him an annuity of £1,000 to prevent him from going broke. After his first wife died in 1588, Oxford remarried in the winter of 1591/92 to Elizabeth Trentham and

spent his last years out of royal favour, petitioning for various income-producing offices, before dying in 1604 (Nelson 2003).

Oxford was known in his lifetime as a poet and a patron of letters (May 1980). The first of his poems to appear in print was 'The earle of Oxenforde to the reader' in Thomas Bedingfield's 1573 translation of *Cardanus comforte*, following Bedingfield's dedicatory letter to Oxford and Oxford's prose reply. The 1576 collection *The paradyse of daynty deuises* includes eight poems attributed to Oxford (or 'E.O.', expanded in later editions to 'E.Ox.'), alongside poems by several other noblemen. Another poem of his appeared in *Brittons bowre of delights* (1591), and a half-dozen more are preserved in various manuscripts; however, the three poems attributed to him in *Englands Parnassus* (1600) are actually by Robert Greene and Thomas Campion. Altogether, 16 poems can be confidently attributed to Oxford, along with four more of doubtful authenticity. Oxford's poems vary quite a bit in quality, with some displaying considerable lyrical skill but others marred by plodding alliteration and shaky versification. They use a variety of metrical forms, ranging from tetrameter to old-fashioned fourteeners, and often have very personal themes. Oxford's poetry was praised in print by such writers as William Webbe, George Puttenham, and Francis Meres, though this praise was undoubtedly somewhat exaggerated due to his high social position.

In addition to his poetry, Oxford displayed an interest in drama, patronizing acting companies and writing some plays of his own. In 1580 he took over the earl of Warwick's players, whose leaders, John and Lawrence Dutton, were promptly lampooned in a contemporary poem as 'chameleons' because they changed liveries, from Warwick's to Oxford's. This company was involved in a riot at the Theatre outside London on 10 April 1580, and successfully toured England through most of the 1580s. Meanwhile, Oxford also patronized a company of boy actors starting about 1580, as well as tumblers, musicians, and a bear-ward. Oxford's Boys apparently merged with the

Blackfriars boys' company a few years later and performed at court in 1584 under the leadership of Oxford's secretary John Lyly, who had dedicated his influential prose work *Euphues* to Oxford in 1578. After touring intermittently in the 1590s, Oxford's Men resurfaced in London in 1600. One of their plays, *The weakest goeth to the wall*, was printed that year, and in 1602 they merged with Worcester's Men.

George Puttenham in *The arte of English poesie* (1589) praised Oxford as a writer of comedies and interludes, and Francis Meres in *Palladis tamia* (1598) included Oxford in a list of English writers who were 'the best for comedy amongst us', though much of this list was cribbed from Puttenham. Such praise was among the factors that led J. Thomas Looney to argue in 1920 that Oxford was the 'real' author of Shakespeare's works. Since then Oxford has replaced Francis Bacon as the leading candidate among those who believe that William Shakespeare did not write the works attributed to him, despite the mediocrity of most of Oxford's surviving poetry. These 'Oxfordians' believe that William Shakespeare of Stratford did not have the education or experiences that they imagine the author must have had, and that Edward de Vere did. They are forced to claim that all the evidence for Shakespeare's authorship (including the 1623 First Folio) was the result of the same elaborate conspiracy that supposedly hid Oxford's authorship, and that the plays were written much earlier than the dates generally recognized by scholars, since Oxford died 12 years before Shakespeare. Such claims, elaborated in the most detail by Charlton Ogburn (1991), are not taken seriously by Shakespeare scholars, since they discard the methods used by literary historians and rip the plays out of their historical context. Oxfordians also tend to rely on factual distortions and double standards, greatly exaggerating Oxford's accomplishments while making Shakespeare look as bad as possible, depicting him as, say, illiterate or money-grubbing. Despite occasional bursts of popular attention, Oxfordianism has never been more than a small fringe movement within the world of Shakespeare studies, and that is unlikely to change.

SEE ALSO: Bacon, Francis; Campion, Thomas; Elizabeth I; Greene, Robert; Lyly, John; Meres, Francis; Puttenham, George; Shakespeare, William; verse miscellanies, printed; Webbe, William

REFERENCES AND SUGGESTED READINGS

Elliott, W. E. Y. & Valenza, R. J. (2004) Oxford by the numbers: what are the odds that the earl of Oxford could have written Shakespeare's plays and poems? *Tennessee Law Review* 71, 323–454.

Looney, J. Thomas (1920) '*Shakespeare*' *identified in Edward de Vere, seventeenth earl of Oxford*. Frederick A. Stokes, New York.

Matus, Irvin (1994) *Shakespeare, in fact*. Continuum, New York, pp. 219–263.

May, Steven W. (1980) The poems of Edward DeVere, seventeenth earl of Oxford, and of Robert Devereux, second earl of Essex. *Studies in Philology* (special issue) 77(5).

McCrea, Scott (2005) *The case for Shakespeare: the end of the authorship question*. Praeger, Westport, pp. 154–223.

Nelson, Alan H. (2003) *Monstrous adversary: the life of Edward de Vere, 17th earl of Oxford*. Liverpool University Press, Liverpool.

Ogburn, Charlton (1991) *The mysterious William Shakespeare*, 2nd edn. EPM Publications, McLean, VA.

Dekker, Thomas

ADAM SMYTH

The career and literary output of Thomas Dekker (c.1572–1632) to a considerable extent reflects the precarious, ad hoc, sometimes even dangerous conditions under which that emerging, late Elizabethan category of author – the professional writer – worked. Much more of what Dekker wrote has been lost than survives, but his extant printed output is still considerable, and covers multiple genres: drama, royal and mayoral entertainment, commendatory verse, prologue, epilogue, jest, and satire.

He was also prolific in that particularly Renaissance form – the prose pamphlet – and wrote about, among other things, dreams, fashion, hell, the night, criminality, sin, anti-Catholicism, and cold weather. But more than anything, Dekker was a London writer, in every sense; and if a great challenge to sixteenth- and seventeenth-century literature was to find new ways of representing London's dramatic and ongoing expansion, Dekker's abundant literary output was one important response to this task.

To construct Dekker's largely undocumented biography means relying, inevitably, on inferences drawn from his own literary works. His name perhaps suggests Dutch ancestors – in *The shomakers holiday* (1600), Rowland Lacy avoids being sent to war in France by disguising himself as a Dutch shoemaker – although Dekker was almost certainly born in London: in several texts, including *The seven deadly sinnes* (1606), Dekker figures London as his mother. Dekker's familiarity with Latin authors, and his knowledge of German, French, and classical mythology, suggests a grammar school education, but he seems not to have attended university or the Inns of Court, thereby not conforming to the traditional career arc of many Renaissance writers. There is also something of the autodidact about him: in his fitfully autobiographical *Dekker his dreame* (1620), Dekker recalls how much he had learnt from 'Private Readings', rather than tutors.

Dekker was thoroughly entangled in London literary life, and in his dramatic collaborations, he worked with, among many others, Henry Chettle, Michael Drayton, Ben Jonson, John Marston, Anthony Munday, William Shakespeare, and John Webster. His talents for theatrical writing were recognized early on: hence his involvement in 1593–94, aged about 21, in the never performed play *Sir Thomas More*, alongside Anthony Munday, William Shakespeare, Henry Chettle, and perhaps Thomas Heywood. Hence, too, Francis Meres's comment in his *Palladis tamia* (1598) that among 'our best for Tragedy' are Shakespeare, Drayton, George Chapman, Jonson, and Dekker: a

canon that would surprise most twenty-first-century readers. Later, in his preface to *The white devil* (1612), Webster singled out Shakespeare, Heywood, and Dekker for particular praise.

Between 1598 and 1602, Dekker's literary energy was largely focused on producing drama for the Admiral's Men: his name frequently appears in the company's theatrical 'diary', or account book, kept by Philip Henslowe. Dekker wrote very quickly, usually in collaboration with other dramatists, and in this four-year period was in some way involved in more than 40 plays. The great majority of these titles are now lost – co-authored plays such as *The famous wars of Henry I*, and *Godwin and his three sons* (both written in March 1598, with Chettle, Drayton, and Robert Wilson). In this period, Dekker wrote seven plays as sole author, including *The gentle craft* (1599), published as *The shomakers holiday* (1600). Based on Thomas Deloney's prose fiction of 1598, and performed before Elizabeth I at court on 1 January 1600, this city comedy remains the work for which Dekker is best known. As a result, it has come to be seen (with some justification) as paradigmatic of Dekker's literary productions, in its interest in guilds and trades, and its busy, eager, commercial London setting; in its attention to characters whose economic plight seems precarious; in its use of apparently colloquial speech and (stage) Dutch, and its attempts to generate an impression of realism; and in its awareness of class divisions and also, through Simon Eyre's spectacular rise from shoemaker to lord mayor, the possibilities of dramatic social mobility.

Despite this prolific productivity, Dekker's relationship with Henslowe was tempestuous. Payments from Henslowe were cancelled, and Dekker wrote for other companies between 1600 and 1602, composing (probably) *Blurt, master-constable* (1602) for Paul's Boys, a play previously attributed to Thomas Middleton. Dekker also revised and augmented an earlier Admiral's Men's play, *Sir John Oldcastle* (1599), to create *Sir John Oldcastle, part two* (1602) for Lord Worcester's Men. This habit of reworking existing texts was a feature of Dekker's craft.

Conflict and instability were often the conditions of Dekker's writing, as well as the subjects of his plays: *Satiro-mastix* (1602), produced in both private theatre (by Paul's Boys) and in public (by the Globe's Chamberlain's Men), was one strike in the supposed War of the Theatres – a conflict between Jonson, on one side, and Dekker and Marston, on the other, based around competing ideas of the function of drama in society, and tensions between public and private theatres as well as between theatrical companies. *Satiro-mastix* responded, in particular, to Jonson's mockery of Marston and Dekker's literary merits in *Every man out of his humour* (1599), *Cynthias revels* (1600), and *Poetaster* (1601).

Dekker possessed a capacity to switch genres quickly as the occasion demanded: on the accession of James I in 1603, he collaborated with his former adversary Ben Jonson to produce the official welcome to the new monarch, *The magnificent entertainment given to King James*, and commendatory verses for Stephen Harrison's *The arch's of triumph erected in honor of James the first* (both 1604). Dekker responded to the Gunpowder Plot of 1605 with *The double PP* (1606), a virulently anti-Catholic text in which the papist is described as, among other things, a shape-shifting beast. The pamphlet vividly conveys a sense of religious conflict as alive and ongoing, even to readers today. But Dekker's greatest catalyst for creativity was the plague. When the outbreak of 1603 led to the closure of the theatres, Dekker's literary energies migrated to other forms. *The wonderfull yeare* (1603), his pamphlet reaction to both the death of Elizabeth I and the arrival of the plague, is among the strangest and – in its flinging together of diverse registers and genres, including the skeletons of dramas which could not at that moment find a stage – aesthetically compelling instances of Dekker's work. Here, and elsewhere, he demonstrated the ability to convert adversity into literary product by, in part, making adversity and

struggle his aesthetic. Other plague pamphlets followed, including *Newes from Graves-end* (1604) and, after the 1625 outbreak, *A rod for run-awayes* (1625).

When the plague passed, and the theatres reopened, Dekker switched back to drama, working for different companies at the same time. He produced *The honest whore, part one* (1604), with Thomas Middleton, and, as single author, *The honest whore, part two* (1605), both for Prince Henry's Men: the new title of Dekker's old company, the Admiral's Men. For Paul's Boys, Dekker wrote *The roaring girle* (?1605), also with Middleton. This fictional and in some ways spectacular dramatization of the life of cross-dressing thief Mary Frith ('Moll Cutpurse') has proven popular with recent readers, due in part to its apparently transgressive themes of transvestism and female criminality. Dekker's subsequent dramatic career was only occasionally successful: *The whore of Babylon* (1607) failed to please audiences, and Dekker struggled to place *If this be not good the divel is in it* (1611) with a theatrical company. It was turned down by Prince Henry's Men and, when performed by Queen Anne's Men at the Red Bull Theatre, was not a success. In the wake of these failures, Dekker turned increasingly to pamphlet writing.

In his pamphlets, Dekker was consistently interested in the improvisations and novelties of London life, particularly under moments of strain. *The great frost: cold doings in London* (1608) describes, through a dialogue between a young city man and an older country man, the river Thames's freezing, and the ensuing follies as people walk out on the ice to sell beer and wine. This prose account of the frozen Thames might be read as an answer to the minor Renaissance genre of river poetry, represented in poems by John Leland, Edmund Spenser, and Michael Drayton: a genre that, among other things, celebrated circulation and, according to some critics, a sense of a devolved, anti-centralizing politics and national identity. Dekker's Thames, while frozen, is still dynamic: the river, and London, are the site of an always emerging capitalistic creativity, whether through the selling of fruit by costermongers-on-ice, or, more generally, through the outlandish and often troubling stories cast out by London. This profligacy of narrative creates ethical problems: the pamphlet's speakers worry about how, amid these endless London stories, to discern truth from falsity. But it also represents a commercial potential: Dekker is particularly interested – in *The great frost*, and more generally – in the relationship between the telling of such tales (or rumours, or anecdotes) and the creation of obligations of credit and debt. London emerges as the necessary, if challenging, locus for the professional writer.

Dekker's London is vividly alive in the present, but it also has a historical genealogy that keeps breaking through. Thus, in *The great frost*, amid descriptions of the current freezing, Dekker includes records of frozen rivers from England's past, from the reigns of King William II (1087–1100) and King John (1199–1216), to 'the seventh yeere of Queene Elizabeth, which began upon 21 of December, and held on so extremely'. And in *The dead tearme* (1607), a dialogue between personifications of Westminster and the City in which the sins of London are lamented, Dekker includes discussion of the 'what Names London from time to time hath bin called'.

If Dekker's London is thus both a synchronic and a diachronic construction, Dekker is nonetheless fascinated by the sins of the present, particularly those that flourished at night. *The belman of London* (1608) captures London with Dekker's characteristic immediacy, as the figure of the belman walks the dark streets, discovering and anatomizing the various kinds of London rogue: the ruffler; the angler; the prigger of prances; the palliard or clapperdugeon. As was his tendency, Dekker here returns to, and revises, his own earlier writing to produce a new text – in this case, reworking 'The discoveries of Cock Wat, the Walking Spirit of Newgate', in *Jests to make you merie* (1607). The text is also indebted to Robert Greene's cony-catching pamphlets, and, as in Greene's crime writing, the detailed knowledge Dekker conveys means that the satirical

impulse of the text is complicated: an account that is notionally censorious becomes, through its intimacy with its subject, something close to an encomium. Dekker also places great stress on what he called 'drawing to the life': a kind of realism that prioritizes, among other things, lower-class figures, particularly those associated with crime, and that creates – through different registers and half-understood discourses – seemingly authentic patterns of speech: hence the inclusion, at the end of *The belman of London*, of a 'short Discourse of canting'. In his dramatic writing, this interest in the effect of authenticity led Dekker often to rework the facts of actual crimes into plays (as in, for example, *The late murder in Whitechapel, or keep the widow waking*, 1624). *The belman of London* was sufficiently successful to prompt a sequel, *Lanthorn and candle-light, or the bellmans second nights-walke* (1608), which enjoyed considerable success, and was issued in at least nine editions.

Many of these interests return in Dekker's *The guls horne-book* (1609), his most famous non-dramatic work, and his version of Fredriech Dedekind's Latin poem *Grobianus* (1558). Once more an apparently satirical portrait of London behaviour – in this case, the fashionable, ridiculous modes of the town gallant – is complicated by the detail, intimacy, and sheer verve of the writing, as Dekker records how a gallant ought to behave as he walks up and down the aisle of St Paul's, or drinks in a tavern, or displays himself in a theatre (where the key, as Dekker puts it, is to master the art of 'spreading your body on the stage', to become conspicuous). *The guls horne-book* combines two important strands in English Renaissance literary culture – the (mock) conduct book, and the portrait of London life in which the narrator is not detached but implicated – and, partly as a result, remained popular for much of the century.

Perhaps unsurprisingly, given this focus on sin, and the precariousness of authorship, Dekker was himself no stranger to charges of criminality. In 1598, he was imprisoned in

Poultry Compter for debt: Henslowe paid for his release, along with that of Dekker's dramatic collaborator Henry Chettle, at a cost of about 40 shillings. Other imprisonments for debt followed, including, in 1612, a seven-year incarceration in the King's Bench prison for an unpaid £40 debt to the coach-maker John Webster, father of the playwright. The recusancy charges Dekker faced in 1626 and 1628 reflect almost certainly not religious heterodoxy but that he was staying away from church to elude his debtors. Dekker experienced other encounters with the law, too: in 1608 he was charged with breaching the peace against an Agnes Preston, and in 1625 he faced conspiracy and libel charges in the Star Chamber for his role in the co-authored, and now lost, *The late murder in Whitechapel, or keep the widow waking*, written with Ford, Rowley, and Webster. While publishers, booksellers, and printers might make considerable money through the book trade, the position of authors was weak. With no patron, and – unlike Shakespeare – no share in a theatrical company, and no income from acting, Dekker was solely reliant on his pen. Even the most successful work yielded scant rewards, and debt and professional writing were constant companions: as can be seen in the careers of Thomas Nashe and Robert Greene, the latter of whom died deep in debt, abandoned by friends, and living with a prostitute called Nell Ball. During his 1612–19 period of imprisonment, Dekker's first wife, Mary, died (1616). Thomas and Mary Dekker had three daughters: Dorcas (b.1594); Elizabeth (b.1598); and Anne (b.1602). Upon his death in 1632, Dekker's second wife, Elizabeth, renounced the administration of his estate, presumably in an attempt to avoid inheriting Dekker's unravelled finances.

While in prison, Dekker was able to continue his literary output, albeit in an attenuated form: the capacity of writers to work, and publish, while in prison is a striking and, to modern readers, surprising feature of Renaissance literary culture. Among other productions, Dekker revised *The great frost* (1608) into *The cold*

yeare (1614); produced commendatory verses for John Taylors *Taylors Urania, or his heavenly muse* (1615); and drew inspiration from his bleak circumstances by writing vignettes of six prison characters (including 'A prisoner', 'A creditor', and 'A common cruel jailor') for the collection of short sketches of biographical 'types', or characters, included in *Sir Thomas Overburie his wife* (1616).

After his release from prison, Dekker published *Dekker his dreame*, written in verse and careering prose, and in part a reflection of his experiences in prison, where, he says, in this enforced sleep, his hair turned white due to the 'ghastly objects' he saw. The pamphlet recounts Dekker's experiences upon dreaming of an encounter with Satan and an exploration of the afterlife. The text is also a good example of Dekker's persistent interest in writing about sound: Dekker's hell is full of 'bawling reprobate[s]', and (his neologism) 'plangiferous paines'. But Dekker's real subject, here, seems to be writing itself: his repeated stress on the difficulty of his subject (conveyed in sometimes comical marginal notes), and his sustained meta-literary unpacking of his own intentions and methods, creates a powerful sense of the arduous labour of authorship. This difficulty and struggle is also conveyed in the preface to *Jests to make you merie*, co-written with George Wilkins, in which Dekker laments 'what a miserable and endless labour does he undertake that in a few scribled sheetes hopes to wrap up the loves of all men'. The jests in this text often concern the precariousness of the worlds of writing, publishing, and bookselling. *Newes from hell* (1606), expanded into *A knights conjuring* (1607), explores similar concerns.

In this period after prison, Dekker also returned to writing drama, producing, among other plays, *The virgin martir* (1620) with Philip Massinger, and *The noble Spanish souldier* (1622) and *The wonder of a kingdome* (1623), both with John Day. As had been the case with his earlier theatrical work, Dekker's creativity relied on both collaboration and the revising of existing texts. Both mechanisms underpin his still popular play, *The witch of Edmonton* (1621; printed 1658), written with William Rowley and John Ford, and drawing heavily on a pamphlet by Henry Goodcole, *The wonderfull discouerie of Elizabeth Sawyer, a witch, late of Edmonton, her conviction and condemnation and death* (1621). Many of the plays from this late period are now lost, including *The bellman of Paris*, written with John Day (1623). The loss of so much work is certainly related to Dekker's lack of a sustained connection with a single theatrical company, and the scattered, disordered nature of his writing life; but it usefully reminds modern readers, more broadly, of the partial and fragmentary corpus of Renaissance writing that has descended to the twenty-first century. Dekker's writing serves another important reminder, too: that modern, post-Romantic assumptions about authorship (the solitary, dematerialized genius) simply do not work for most forms of Renaissance literature. The version of authorship that Dekker lived was largely collaborative; newly professionalized, and acutely self-conscious, and shifting away from an aristocratic culture based around patronage (Dekker's pamphlets mock the flattery demanded by patrons); precarious, and frequently unmoored, and never far from the possibility of imprisonment; prolific, quickly responsive to events in the world, and adept at sudden shifts between genres; and, most of all, fascinated and challenged by an expanding, dynamic London that was Dekker's most powerful context and source.

SEE ALSO: Day, John; Drayton, Michael; Ford, John; Greene, Robert; Jonson, Ben; Marston, John; Nashe, Thomas; Rowley, William; Taylor, John; Wilson, Robert

REFERENCES AND SUGGESTED READINGS

Gasper, Julia (1990) *The dragon and the dove: the plays of Thomas Dekker.* Clarendon Press, Oxford.

Manley, Lawrence (2005) *Literature and culture in early modern London.* Cambridge University Press, Cambridge.

McLuskie, Kathleen (1993) *Dekker and Heywood: professional dramatists.* St Martin's, New York.

Raymond, Joad (2006) *Pamphlets and pamphleteering in early modern Britain.* Cambridge University Press, Cambridge.

Smith, David L. et al. (eds) (2003) *The theatrical city: culture, theatre and politics in London, 1576–1649.* Cambridge University Press, Cambridge.

Twyning, John (1998) *London dispossessed: literature and social space in the early modern city.* St Martin's Press, New York.

Twyning, John (2004) Dekker, Thomas. In: *Oxford dictionary of national biography.* Oxford University Press, Oxford.

Delaval, Elizabeth

SHAINA TRAPEDO

Lady Elizabeth (Livingstone) Delaval (1649–1717) was an aristocrat, an attendant at court, and an amateur memoirist. Her unpublished meditations offer insight into the life of a noblewoman living and writing in England during the latter half of the seventeenth century. Delaval was the only child of Sir James Livingston, earl of Newburgh, and Katherine Howard. Lord Newburgh's Royalist activities forced him to flee with his wife, who died in exile. The young Delaval was left with her paternal aunt, Lady Stanhope, at Nocton, Lincolnshire. Even after her father's return and his subsequent remarriage, she was raised by her grandmother and Lady Stanhope without much involvement from her father.

Between 1662 and 1671, Delaval wrote prayers and meditations on papers she collected. At the age of 14 she notes the religious reason for her undertaking: 'It is most profitable to make our past sin's . . . the subject of our present meditation's that wee may be humble'd and God glorified.' The recording of one's transgressions was a common seventeenth-century practice. However, it appears that Delaval may have intended her writings for a wider audience. In 1670 she wrote a table of contents listing her first 12 meditations and a brief introduction that reaffirms her motivation for writing, to discipline the soul. Only in the eighteenth century did she gather her papers and copy them into a leather-bound volume, adding headers and autobiographical content between sections. Although the diary focuses on her life and relationships, the meditations deploy the second-person pronoun and consider a variety of matters from personal devotion to broader social issues like education and primogeniture.

The entries from age 14 to 15 catalogue the sinful traits of her youth, namely envy, vanity, and gossiping. Delaval establishes a spirited and slightly narcissistic tone in her opening admission that 'there is so much fier in my naturall temper that whether I ether love or hate, tis with the greater violence imagenable'. As a youth she claims 'my cheife imployment was sowing discord in the family' and repeatedly chastises herself for being a 'great sinner'. She recalls that, in addition to reading romances and visiting her grandmother, she spent her early years at Nocton directing amateur theatricals with the servants in her household as she lacked peers with whom to interact.

The meditations written during her appointment as 'First Maide of the Prevy Chamber to the queen' express Delaval's disdain for court life. While she characterizes her London cohort as 'voluntary slaves', she admits to repeatedly neglecting her devotional service in favour of the attention of gentlemen and the indulgence of material pleasures. To maintain appearances, Lady Betty, as she came to be known, incurred heavy debts, which forced her to return to Nocton.

Delaval's entries between the age of 16 and 20 demonstrate increasing awareness of her maturing rhetoric. She writes that she is able to engage in reasonable argument and speak passionately to end disputes about undesirable suitors. While many entries consider mundane aspects of life, like eating too much fruit and the pain of removing worms from her gums, Delaval's writing in her late teens becomes more socially conscious. She asks God to give her a 'greatfull heart' for 'placing me above the

meanest people since by my advantage off birth I often gaine opertunity's of advanceing thy glory'. Although she prays for her family to be spared from the plague (or 'dreadfull arrow of God'), she wonders 'how can a Christian now refraine from shedding plenty of tear's day by day, considering that the very last weeke, there were 5 thousand persons, in London ... who are now cut and ly in there graves'. Her meditations candidly explore the capacity for human compassion and repentance from a Christian perspective.

In her eighteenth year Delaval fell in love with James, Lord Annesley. During their courtship she writes that her mind is preoccupied by a 'growing passion' which distracts her from her prayers. When Lady Stanhope rejected the match, Annesley proposed an elopement, to which her father consented. Nevertheless, Delaval held out for the approval of the family's matriarch. Despite common conceptions about seventeenth-century patriarchism, Delaval's entries reveal to what extent women exercised control over marriage arrangements at the time. The relationship eventually ended when Annesley's father, the earl of Anglesey, threatened to disinherit him if he refused another match. After this episode, Delaval appears to have lost the 'fier' of her youth and describes herself in a state of 'continuall mallancoly'. She prays in her diary for God to grant her a pious man that 'may serve thee with his whole heart and that we may ever love one another faithfully'. Unfortunately it appears her request was not granted. In 1670 she accepted an offer to marry Robert Delaval and resigned herself to an unhappy marriage.

The entries after her marriage are characterized by a tone of restrained antagonism towards her husband and an abject longing for a closer relationship with God. While she resents her husband's frail health, drinking, and 'aflicted soul', she admits partial responsibility for their marital troubles due to her 'proud ill natured words, [that] to often tempted him to fall into fury'. In addition to her thoughts on matrimony, Delaval writes a great deal about her struggle with the command 'by God to honnour my parents'. Although she yearned for her father's favour as a child, his 'unkindnesse' led to her gradual detachment. Nevertheless, she still prayed to be forgiven for her sins, 'particularly my neglect of dutys to a dying father'. Though Delaval lived until 1717, the meditations end in 1672. After Sir Robert died in 1682, she married a man 14 years her junior. In 1689 she fled England after being implicated in a Jacobite plot and is believed to have died in France.

Throughout her entries Delaval repeatedly compares herself to King David, citing the Psalms and Scripture, as she records her lapses into sin. At the beginning of the manuscript her prayers carry a remorseful yet hopeful tone, asking God to 'give me grace each minute to improve and fill my heart'. Midway through the manuscript, she acknowledges the repetitiveness of her own text, noting with amazement 'how often I confess the same offences'. By the end of the manuscript, she demonstrates a more humble and world-weary spirit, admitting, 'Oh Lord, I dare not say have patience with me ... I am nothing, I have nothing worthy to offer.' While it is devoted largely to a personal struggle with sin, Delaval's narrative also reveals much about the education, marriage, and social consciousness of an Englishwoman from a prominent family in the late seventeenth century.

REFERENCES AND SUGGESTED READINGS

Greene, Douglas G. (ed.) (1978) *The meditations of Lady Elizabeth Deleval*. Northumberland Press, Gateshead.

Ezell, Margaret J. M. (1988) *The patriarch's wife: literary evidence and the history of the family*. University of North Carolina, Chapel Hill.

Greer, Germaine (ed.) (1989) *Kissing the rod: an anthology of seventeenth-century women's verse*. Farrar, Straus & Giroux, New York.

Snook, Edith (2005) *Women, reading, and the cultural politics of early modern England*. Ashgate, Aldershot.

Walker, Kim. (1996) *Women writers of the English Renaissance*. Twayne, New York.

Deloney, Thomas

ROZE HENTSCHELL

One of London's best-known balladeers in the late sixteenth century, Thomas Deloney (d. c.1600) went on to write four works of prose fiction featuring the lives of English artisans. The date and place of Deloney's birth is not known, though he probably died in London in 1600. He was a yeoman in the Weavers' Company, the London guild that regulated silk textile production. Scholars have speculated that Deloney may have been born in the mid-sixteenth century in Norwich, where Flemish and French Protestant refugees had settled; Deloney's surname appears to be of French origin, and many of the European immigrants in Norwich participated in the silk-weaving trade, which would become Deloney's profession. His first known ballad (1586) was published in Norwich, indicating a possible connection to the city. Ultimately, however, there is no hard evidence that he was born there. By 1586, Deloney is known to have been living in London. Parish records from St Giles, Cripplegate, indicate the October birth of a son to 'Thomas Delonie silkweaver'. While there is no record of grammar school attendance, Deloney's earliest publication demonstrates that he received some formal education. *A declaration made by the archbishop of Collen upon the deede of his mariage* (1583) is a translation from Latin of the archbishop of Cologne's defence of his plan to marry. Deloney's version, published as a pamphlet, includes Pope Gregory's reply and the archbishop's response. Dedicated to the bishop of London, Deloney's text indicates a strong Protestant leaning.

While Deloney's prose fiction has received the majority of critical attention, he had a successful career as a balladeer. Most of his surviving ballads were collected in two volumes, *The garland of good will* (which was entered in the Stationers' Register in 1593 and 1596, though the earliest extant edition is from 1626) and *Strange histories of kings, princes [and] dukes* (earliest extant edition from 1602).

Twenty-seven ballads, at least some of which were previously published as broadsides, comprise *The garland. Strange histories* contains 11 ballads, based largely upon on Raphael Holinshed's *Chronicles* as well as a dialogue in prose 'betweene Ladies, being Shepheards on *Salsburie* plaine'. *The garland* is a miscellany of verse on several themes, including medieval royalty, Arthurian legend, biblical stories, and contemporary political matters. While one and perhaps both of the collections of ballads appeared in Deloney's lifetime, we do not know what involvement, if any, he had in collecting and organizing the verse or seeing it into print. Several of Deloney's ballads were published only in broadside form, most marked with the initials 'T.D.'. Deloney's contemporaries refer to several other non-extant ballads. The ephemeral nature of broadside ballads, and the fact that such a large number of Deloney's ballads do survive, indicates that many more are probably lost.

Deloney's ballads cover a wide range of themes and topics and capitalize on subjects that were popular in his own day such as the so-called 'good-night ballads' (in 'The lamentation of Mr Page's wife'), in which a criminal speaks in the first person shortly before his or her execution. Deloney's ballads primarily focus on England's medieval past, particularly the exploits of royalty. In 'Of King Edward the second, being poisoned', for example, Deloney narrates an inglorious detail of English history, the supposed 1327 attempted poisoning and eventual murder of Edward II. In 'A song of the banishment of two dukes, Hereford and Norfolke', he recounts Richard II's banishment in 1398 of two advisers. Following chronicle history closely, Deloney vilifies Norfolk and emphasizes that Hereford was 'prudent' and 'wise', thus deserving of his eventual title of Henry IV. Deloney's ballads also explore England's immediate past, often in service to Protestant, nationalist sentiment. 'A most joyfull songe' tells the story of the 1586 arrest and execution of the conspirators – described as 'Englishmen with Romish harts' – against Queen Elizabeth. 'A joyful new ballad' recounts

the taking of majestic Spanish ships during the defeat of the Spanish Armada in 1588.

While Deloney had a keen interest in English history, a striking feature of his ballads is the extent to which they focus on and often laud women. Even the ballads devoted to historical subjects often centre on female protagonists. 'A mournfull dittie, on the death of Rosamond' and 'A new sonnet, conteining the lamentation of Shores wife' both focus on the mistresses of kings (Henry II and Edward IV, respectively), and Deloney tends to be sympathetic towards women who have been cast as historical villains. 'The imprisonment of Queene Elenor' is a first-person narrative of Eleanor of Aquitaine's support of the rebellion against Henry II and her subsequent imprisonment. 'A song of Queene Isabel' recounts Edward II's wife's treachery against her husband by raising an army in opposition to him. While clearly bold in their actions against their husbands, the portrayal of the women in both ballads is nevertheless sympathetic as they operate in the best interest of their nation.

Much of what we know about Deloney comes from the words of his fellow authors. Robert Greene sees rogues and low-lifes – the central figures in his *Defence of conny-catching* – as subjects more befitting of 'T.D. whose braines beaten to the yarking up of Ballads, might more *lawfully* have glaunced at the quaint conceites of conny-catching and cross-biting'. In *Pierces supererogation*, Gabriel Harvey groups Deloney with Philip Stubbes and Robert Armin as 'botchers in print'. In *Have with you to Saffron-Walden*, Thomas Nashe more generously refers to Deloney's first collection of ballads ('the balletting silk-weaver, hath rime enough for all miracles and wit to make a *Garland of good will*') as well as the penury of his primary profession of silk-weaving (he has fallen on hard times, a result of the 'silencing of his looms'). Will Kempe's *Nine daies wonder* gives us a likely death date (1600) for Deloney. Complaining of ballads written about him, Kempe seeks to find the author: 'I have made a privie search, what private Jigmonger of your jolly number, hath been the

Author of these abhominale ballets written of me: I was told it was the great ballet-maker T. D., alias Tho. Deloney ... but I was given since to understand your late generall Tho. dyed poorely, as ye all must do, and was honestly buried: which is much to bee doubted of some of you.'

During his ballad-writing years, Deloney was twice wanted for arrest by the London authorities for writing documents that criticized government policy. The same year that Deloney wrote *The book for the silkweavers*, which has not survived, he collaborated with 14 other silk-weavers on a letter, 'Complaint of the yeomen weavers against the immigrant weavers' (1595). Written to the French and Dutch churches in London, the authors register their displeasure with the Dutch and French cloth-workers, who had come to England to flee religious persecution, but who were perceived as impinging on the methods and rights of the native weavers. The lord mayor of London called for the confiscation of all copies of the letter and threw Deloney and the others in Newgate prison. In 1596, Deloney was charged with composing a ballad on the shortage of grain. While the actual ballad has not survived, evidence of its offensive subject matter is found in a letter from the lord mayor, who sought to arrest him. Critics have considered the ballad's content as licentious because it offended the queen, who in the ballad apparently speaks in a familiar manner with her working-class subjects. The mayor's alarm, though, may possibly have lain in the resemblance between Deloney's ballad and a 1595 royal proclamation that promised relief of the poor. While the proclamation is vague about how this will be achieved, Deloney's ballad calls the poor workers to take action in specific ways and thus undermines the authority of the royal document. While the printer and publisher were both gaoled for their part in the production of the ballad, officials never apprehended Deloney. Deloney would later incorporate ballads in his prose works; but it appears that after this incident, he gave up balladeering as his primary form of writing.

Deloney's literary reputation rests primarily on the four prose narratives that he wrote during the late 1590s, all of which were quite popular. As romantic fictional narratives, these texts explore the prose form for storytelling. What distinguishes Deloney from authors such as John Lyly, George Gascoigne, Robert Greene, and Philip Sidney – all of whom wrote prose romances in the Elizabethan period – is not only his own modest class background, but also the fact that his texts centre on the artisan and merchant classes. On the one hand, Deloney's novels celebrate and idealize the labour and products of England's working class. His characters are virtuous, generous, and industrious and, as a result, are rewarded for their contributions to both community and nation. On the other hand, the narratives are not always straightforward celebrations of hard work. In *Jack of Newbery*, for example, several characters who achieve success do so through happenstance and dumb luck; Jack himself gains his fortune after he is tricked into marrying the rich widow of his former master. In *Thomas of Reading*, the title character is murdered for his money despite a life of generosity. In the two-part *The gentle craft*, the shoemaker Simon Eyre becomes wealthy, and eventually London's lord mayor, not through industry, but rather as a result of a fortunate business deal. While critical interest in Deloney's novels has rightfully centred on his exploration of the under-represented artisan classes, it would be a mistake to claim that Deloney has a singular vision of what that class stands for or how it functions in the world of commercial production and exchange. Likewise, while Deloney demonstrates the possibility of upward social mobility, so does he suggest that the results of this mobility are not without their problems.

A fictionalized tale of the improbable rise to fame of an early sixteenth-century broadcloth weaver named John Winchcombe (a conflation of a father and son of the same name), Deloney's best-known and most popular prose work (and probably his first), *Jack of Newbery* (entered into the Stationers' Register in March 1597), is an account of the life of an artisan turned citizen. The title character's advance-ment from weaver-servant to the premiere master-clothier in all of Berkshire is so cele-brated that even the king, Henry VIII, recog-nizes Jack as a national treasure. The text focuses on Jack's rise, his fame, his generosity, and his involvement in representing the plight of the beleaguered broadcloth workers: his busy workshop employs hundreds of men, women, and children; his reputation as a vir-tuous man leads the queen (Katherine) to enlist his help in military efforts; he helps raise a debtor out of poverty and into a position of London alderman; and, together with a union of clothiers, he successfully petitions the king to loosen commercial restrictions and put the labourers back to work. Given the sympathetic portrayal of Jack's fame as the reward for a life of hard work, it is no wonder that readers have regarded Deloney as a benevolent proponent of the citizen classes whose writing confirms social stratifications. More recent critics have offered a corrective to this, emphasizing Deloney's activist impulses in a tumultuous decade. If *Jack of Newbery* celebrates weavers, it is at least partly to emphasize the importance of the labour of the cloth industry and, in turn, to protest the treatment of cloth workers at the hands of the government in the 1590s, a time when the cloth industry was facing a major depression. The contentious relationship between Lord Wolsey and Jack supports this. *Jack* also contains several chapters that are aligned with the jestbook tradition. In one, Will Summers, the king's clown, is publicly humiliated by being beaten with a bag of wet 'dog droppings' after he distracts the maiden spinners from their work and attempts to procure kisses from them. In another, an Ital-ian merchant attempts to woo the wife of one of Jack's weavers, resulting in a bed trick where the merchant finds himself in the dark with a hog. While the comedic episodes seemingly are not germane to Jack's story, they focus on characters that would harm the integrity of his great household, and thus are figured as ene-mies who must face the shameful consequences of their actions.

Part one of *The gentle craft* (entered into the Stationers' Register in October 1597) shifts Deloney's focus from those involved in the cloth industry to shoemakers and is divided into three separate narratives of the origins and history of that trade. The initial story involves a knight, Hugh, and his steadfast love for Winifred. After she rebuffs him, Hugh consorts with a group of 'cordwainers', who are loyal to Hugh even after he follows Winifred into death for religious convictions. The relics of the hero, 'St Hugh's bones', become the tools of the craftsmen. The second narrative, also a type of hagiography, involves the princely brothers, Crispianus and Crispine, who, in an effort to flee from the tyrant Maximus, take refuge among a group of shoemakers. When Crispine falls in love with and marries Maximus's daughter, Crispianus declares that 'a shoe-maker's son is a prince born', announcing the recurring theme of the text. The final story (most well known as the source for Thomas Dekker's *The shomakers holiday*) involves the improbable rise of Simon Eyre from a shoe-maker's apprentice to sheriff to London's lord mayor. Simon's wife plays a central role in her husband's ascent, which is achieved through savvy business dealings. As with *Jack of Newb-ery*, the members of the household also figure prominently in the narrative. The second part of *The gentle craft* is more episodic than the first. The stories are about shoemakers rather than the craft of shoemaking, thus de-empha-sizing an idealized portrait of an industry (such as that we see in part one and in *Jack*). One narrative thread concerns an eligible bachelor, the Westminster shoemaker Richard Casteler, who is pursued by several women, including Long Meg of Westminster, a historical figure from a popular jestbook of 1582. Another set of narratives revolves around a rich shoemaker, Lusty Peachy, though the stories are only tan-gentially connected to him. While shoemaking is lauded in both parts of *The gentle craft*, the texts are less concerned with national politics than are his narratives about cloth workers.

Thomas of Reading (of which the first extant copy dates from 1612), which again takes up the cloth industry, appears to have resonated with the populace (it was the source for four plays – none of which are extant – and a novel). The story takes place during the reign of Henry I (early twelfth century), and revolves around six clothiers from the western and northern counties, their wives, and households. As in *Jack*, the profession of clothier is represented as one which supports the poorer portions of the population and is admired by the king. And as in that earlier novel, the output of the industry is represented in fantastical terms (the text opens with the king forced off the road as 200 wagons of cloth make their way to London). But, unlike in *Jack*, we don't have a full – however idealized – picture of the many aspects of the cloth-making industry, as the text focuses almost entirely on rich clothiers. The tone of *Thomas of Reading* is decidedly bleaker than that of the other novels, and the ending veers towards tragedy as the title character is killed by greedy innkeepers. The text exposes the problems that accompany growing wealth. One clothier is almost killed by the rest for his dalliance with another's wife. The wives of the wealthy clothiers are vain and jealous of the wives of London merchants: 'what reason is there', one wife wonders, 'but we should be as well maintained?' Another clothier is abandoned by his servants once he falls on hard times, although he is eventually restored to wealth by his fellow clothiers. Woven through and ending the novel is a traditional romance story of the king's brother Robert, who falls in love with Margaret, a daughter of an earl, whose penury forces her to enter into service in a clothier's household. Yet even this plot ends ambivalently, with Margaret eventually deciding to enter a convent. While Deloney concludes his novel with a catalogue of the financial generosity of the 'worthy' clothiers, he also suggests he's on to more grand subjects: if his text is 'curteously accepted', Deloney will be encouraged to try 'greater matters'.

It is arguable that Deloney's desire to turn towards more lofty subjects was achieved in *Canaans calamitie* (earliest extant edition 1618), a long poem describing the destruction of Jerusalem. Modelled on Josephus's second-century narrative of the destruction of Jerusalem, Deloney's poem – like Thomas Nashe's prose narrative, *Christs teares over Jerusalem* – serves as a lamentation and warning for London for its sinful path. The text was reprinted several times in the seventeenth century.

SEE ALSO: Dekker, Thomas; Gascoigne, George; Greene, Robert; Harvey, Gabriel; Holinshed, Raphael; Lyly, John; Nashe, Thomas; Sidney, Philip; Stubbes, Philip

REFERENCES AND SUGGESTED READINGS

Hentschell, Roze (2008) *The culture of cloth in early modern England: textual constructions of a national identity.* Ashgate, Aldershot.

Lawlis, Merritt E. (1960) *Apology for the middle class: the dramatic novels of Thomas Deloney.* Indiana University Press, Bloomington.

Linton, Joan Pong (1998) *The romance of the new world: gender and the literary formations of English colonialism.* Cambridge University Press, Cambridge.

Stevenson, Laura Caroline (1985) *Praise and paradox: merchants and craftsmen in Elizabethan popular literature.* Cambridge University Press, Cambridge.

Suzuki, Mihoko (2003) *Subordinate subjects: gender, the political nation, and literary form in England, 1588–1688.* Ashgate, Aldershot.

Wright, Eugene P. (1981) *Thomas Deloney.* Twayne, Boston.

Denham, John

HENRY POWER

Sir John Denham (1614/15–1669) was a poet, translator, and courtier. He was educated at Trinity College, Oxford, though he seems to have left without taking a degree. He then studied common law at Lincoln's Inn, and was called to the bar in 1639. His earliest surviving work is a translation from Virgil's *Aeneid* (books II to VI, with gaps) undertaken in 1636. This survives in the commonplace book of Lucy Hutchinson (Denham had been a student at Lincoln's Inn alongside Hutchinson's brother, Allen Apsley, in the 1630s), and formed the basis for his later translations from Virgil. In 1641 Denham was called as a witness for the defence at the trial of Thomas Wentworth, first earl of Strafford, and wrote an elegy following Strafford's execution. The version now commonly printed was evidently revised after the Restoration, as it refers to the 1661 reversal of Strafford's attainder, but an earlier version survives.

'Coopers Hill,' the poem for which Denham is now chiefly remembered, was published in 1642 and repeatedly revised and refined over the next 16 years. A substantially altered version was published in 1655. In 1667 Moses Pengry translated it into Latin. Heavily influenced by Virgil's *Georgics*, it is a 'prospect poem' in which the speaker, from his vantage point near Egham, on the Thames, surveys the surrounding countryside, and reflects on its political, historical, and aesthetic significance. Published when the country was on the brink of civil war, it draws a contrast between England's glorious history – as represented in the landscape – and her uncertain future. Denham is supportive of Charles's position but again deplores Strafford's fate, comparing him to a noble stag, harried by hounds and put out of its misery by a 'mortal shaft' from the king. The passage of the Thames itself serves as a metaphor for kingship. Denham writes that when the people

strive to force
His channel to a new, or narrow course;
No longer then within his banks he dwells,
First to a torrent, then a Deluge swells.

Denham also uses the Thames as an aesthetic model, hoping that his verse might be (like the river's flow) 'Though deep, yet clear, though gentle, yet not dull,/Strong without rage, without ore-flowing full'. These lines were frequently imitated during the late seventeenth century, and throughout the eighteenth. Then, as now, Denham's particular achievement was held to be the development of the heroic

couplet (Sowerby 2006). 'Coopers Hill' also provided the template for a number of eighteenth-century loco-descriptive poems, notably Alexander Pope's *Windsor-forest* (1713). *The Sophy*, a verse tragedy set in the court of the shah of Persia, was probably written during the first half of 1642 (and was published with 'Coopers Hill' in August of that year). Like 'Coopers Hill,' it addresses the uneasy political situation, telling the story of the infiltration of the Persian monarchy by an evil counsellor.

Denham was also an influential theorist of translation, advocating the 'translation with latitude' later recommended by John Dryden. He does this in his 1648 poem on Richard Fanshawe's translation of Giovanni Guarini's *Il pastor fido*. Denham praises Fanshawe for pursuing a 'new and nobler way' of translation, and thereby preserving the 'flame' rather than the 'ashes' of the original. In the preface to *The destruction of Troy* (his version of book II of the *Aeneid*), he further stresses the creative aspect of translation, comparing the act of translating poetry to an alchemical process. The translator must add something in the course of the experiment, or risk the evaporation of all meaning. Denham followed his own advice. His translations, though sometimes faithful, are highly political documents. Notoriously, at the close of *The destruction of Troy* he makes Priam's death closely resemble the regicide: 'On the cold earth lies th'unregarded King,/A headless Carkass, and a nameless Thing.' Dryden slightly adapted the couplet for his own translation in 1697, and acknowledged the debt in a footnote. Denham's other significant translations include 'The passion of Dido for Aeneas' (a version of book IV of the *Aeneid* which also draws on the 1636 rendering) and 'Sarpedon's speech to Glaucus' from book XII of the *Iliad*. Both were published for the first time in his 1668 *Works*.

During the Civil War and Interregnum, Denham worked briefly as a Royalist agent, fleeing to the Continent when his role was uncovered (supposedly because the authorities recognized that a document in his keeping had been written by Abraham Cowley).

Lack of money forced him to return to England in 1653. After the Restoration, Denham was made surveyor of the king's works, and was consequently responsible for organizing the coronation of Charles II. Although his predecessor in the role had been Inigo Jones, and he was to be succeeded by Sir Christopher Wren, Denham had little practical architectural knowledge. Nonetheless, an interest in architectural matters can be detected in his work – especially in *The destruction of Troy*, in which Priam's palace is recast as a neo-Palladian villa. In 1661 Denham was returned as a member of parliament for Old Sarum. His last poem was 'On Mr Abraham Cowley, his death and burial among the ancient poets'. Cowley died in 1667, and Denham outlived him by only eight months, and was also buried in Westminster Abbey.

SEE ALSO: Cowley, Abraham; Dryden, John; Fanshawe, Richard; Hutchinson, Lucy; Jones, Inigo

REFERENCES AND SUGGESTED READINGS

Caldwell, T. (2004) John Dryden and John Denham. *Texas Studies in Language and Literature* 46(1), 49–72.

Davis, Paul (2007) *Translation and the poet's life: the ethics of translating in English culture, 1646–1726.* Clarendon Press, Oxford.

de Groot, Jerome (2008) John Denham and Lucy Hutchinson's commonplace book. *Studies in English Literature* 48(1), 147–163.

O'Hehir, Brendan (1968) *Harmony from discords: a life of Sir John Denham.* University of California Press, Berkeley.

O'Hehir, Brendan (1969) *Expans'd hieroglyphics: a critical edition of Sir John Denham's 'Cooper's Hill'.* University of California Press, Berkeley.

Sowerby, Robin (2006), *The Augustan art of poetry: Augustan translations of the classics.* Clarendon Press, Oxford.

Venuti, Lawrence (1993) The destruction of Troy: translation and royalist cultural politics in the Interregnum. *Journal of Medieval and Renaissance Studies* 23(1), 197–219.

Devereux, Robert, earl of Essex

ANDREW GORDON

Robert Devereux (1565–1601), second earl of Essex, was the most prominent courtier of the late sixteenth century, a poet in his own right as well as a leading literary patron of the period. His military exploits brought him great popular acclaim, and his spectacular fall from grace in a treasonous but ineffectual uprising sent shock waves through the country, leaving a mark upon the literary culture of the seventeenth century.

Born in 1565, Essex succeeded to the earldom at the age of 10 and rose to prominence as a protégé of his stepfather, Robert Dudley, earl of Leicester, eventually eclipsing Sir Walter Ralegh to become the last significant favourite of Elizabeth's reign. Essex's rivalry with Ralegh was played out in courtly poetry, the earl adopting a passionate but direct plain style that contrasted with the highly ornamental verses of his opponent (May 1991). Essex adapts the amorous poetics of the Elizabethan court in poems such as 'Change thy minde since she doth change', a strident critique of female falsehood which bluntly announces: 'She was false, bid her adew,/She was best but yet untrue.' In the sonnets 'To pleade my faith where faith hath noe reward' and 'The waies on earth have paths and turnings knowne', Essex figures the unjust reward for his services to the crown in the form of a lover's complaints that reproachfully exhort his mistress to 'Forget my name since you have scorned my love'. His poems invite interpretation as a commentary upon his relations with Elizabeth, identifying the subject of his poetry variously as 'She in whom my hopes did lye' ('Change') and 'her whom all the world admird' ('To plead'); even his lengthy penitential work 'The passions of a discontented mind' is identified in manuscripts as written while a prisoner in the Tower. The theme of Essex's extant poetry overlaps with a number of the highly stylized letters he composed to Elizabeth which also circulated in manuscript, and the connection between these twin forms of literary composition is illustrated by the poem 'Happy were hee', which concludes with a poetic valediction 'Your majesty's exiled servant, / Rob: Essex' (Gordon 2010). Essex's poetry was not published during his lifetime but circulated widely in manuscript and several poems were set to music. His poems have been edited by May (1980) along with verses attributed to him by contemporaries.

The traditional image of Essex as a glamorous courtier has recently been revised by historian Paul Hammer (1999) who shows that the earl assembled a skilled secretariat and network of international contacts to promote himself as a statesman and replacement for the ageing William Cecil, Lord Burghley, the leading figure within Elizabeth's Privy Council. Essex exploited occasions such as the accession day tilts of 1595 to further these claims, employing Francis Bacon's talents to devise the strategic entertainment sometimes known as *Of love and self-love*. Bacon, who would later be among the prosecutors at Essex's treason trial, was one of a number of trained minds associated with the earl in the 1590s, along with Sir Henry Wotton and Sir Henry Saville. The earl attracted bids for literary patronage from numerous authors, including Edmund Spenser and George Chapman, but his circle was particularly associated with the political history of Tacitus. When John Hayward's Tacitean history *The life and raigne of King Henrie IIII* (1599), with its account of the abdication of Richard II (a politically sensitive issue in Elizabeth's latter years), was published with a dedication to Essex, the book and the earl were investigated by the authorities. This text has been returned to by scholars exploring the parallel of Richard II and Elizabeth, particularly in connection with the performance of *Richard II* commissioned by followers of Essex at the Globe Theatre on the day before the Essex uprising in February 1601 (Barroll 1988; Lemon 2001).

The earl's public image as a martial hero was established early with valorous displays in Leicester's Netherlands campaign and furthered by his subsequent actions in Portugal and France; the 1596 Cadiz expedition was widely seen as a glorious victory for Essex, although it failed to enrich the crown. Essex's desire to translate his martial authority into broader political influence was frustrated by Sir Robert Cecil's emergence as his father's successor in the later 1590s; Essex was appointed earl marshal, a largely symbolic role. Increasingly disaffected with court life, he employed scribal publication to disseminate texts such as *An apologie of the earle of Essex against those which iealously, and maliciously, tax him to be the hinderer of the peace and quiet of his country* (1598), which urged war with Spain, and several controversial letters that criticized Elizabeth's actions. Essex was also prominently featured in contemporary libels that condemned courtly corruption, which was invariably associated with the Cecil faction, and that complained against alleged mistreatment of the earl. His 1599 appointment as lieutenant governor of Ireland to suppress the rebellion led by Hugh O'Neill, earl of Tyrone, gave rise to public expectations of success captured in the prologue to act V of Shakespeare's *Henry V*, which pictured 'the general of our gracious empress, … from Ireland coming, / Bringing rebellion broached on his sword', welcomed home by 'the peaceful city' of London. However, the challenges of ill health, poor resources, and constraints upon his authority led Essex to desert his post and return to England unannounced to claim an audience with Elizabeth. This would be the last time he met with his sovereign. He was confined thereafter to house arrest, and his conduct in Ireland was censured at a hearing at York House in June 1600. The following year, on 8 February 1601, he made a desperate bid to rally popular support in London, intending to lead his followers to Westminster to gain the ear of the monarch. The result instead was a trial for treason, and his execution in the Tower of London on 25 February.

The fall of Essex was mourned in ballads, poems, and song, and had a long afterlife within contemporary reflections on court corruption and political resistance. Letters, texts, and verses associated with him were among the most widely circulated manuscript materials of the seventeenth century. Scholars have explored resonances and allusions to Essex's fall in numerous works but particularly in drama, including Ben Jonson's *Poetaster* and *Sejanus*, Samuel Daniel's *Philotas*, Thomas Dekker's *Sir Thomas Wyat*, Shakespeare's *Troilus and Cressida*, and Thomas Heywood's *The royall king, and the loyall subject*.

SEE ALSO: Bacon, Francis; Chapman, George; Daniel, Samuel; Dekker, Thomas; Hayward, John; Heywood, Thomas; Jonson, Ben; Ralegh, Walter; Shakespeare, William; Spenser, Edmund; Wotton, Henry

REFERENCES AND SUGGESTED READINGS

Barroll, J. Leeds (1988) A new history for Shakespeare and his time. *Shakespeare Quarterly* 39, 441–464.

Fox, Alistair (1995) The complaint of poetry for the death of liberality: the decline of literary patronage in the 1590s. In: Guy, John (ed.) *The reign of Elizabeth I: court and culture in the last decade.* Cambridge University Press, Cambridge, pp. 229–257.

Gordon, Andrew (2007) 'A fortune of paper walls': the letters of Francis Bacon and the earl of Essex. *English Literary Renaissance* 37(3), 319–336.

Gordon, Andrew (2010) *Copycopia*, or the place of copied correspondence in manuscript culture: a case study. In: Daybell, James & Hinds, Peter (eds) *Material readings of early modern culture: texts and social practices, 1580–1700.* Palgrave Macmillan, Basingstoke, pp. 65–81.

Hammer, Paul E. J. (1999) *The polarisation of Elizabethan politics: the political career of Robert Devereux, 1585–1597.* Cambridge University Press, Cambridge.

Lemon, Rebecca (2001) The faulty verdict in 'The Crown v. John Hayward'. *Studies in English Literature, 1500–1900* 41(1), 109–132.

Manning, John J. (ed. and intro.) (1991) *John Hayward's The life and raigne of King Henrie IIII.* Camden Society 4th series. Royal Historical Society, London.

Marotti, Arthur F. (1995) *Manuscript, print, and the English Renaissance lyric.* Cornell University Press, Ithaca.

May, Steven M. (1980) The poems of Edward de Vere, seventeenth earl of Oxford and of Robert Devereux, second earl of Essex. *Studies in Philology* (special issue) 77(5).

May, Steven W. (1991) *The Elizabethan courtier poets: the poems and their contexts.* University of Missouri Press, Columbia.

Salmon, J. H. M. (1991) Seneca and Tacitus in Jacobean England. In: Levy Peck, Linda (ed.) *The mental world of the Jacobean court.* Cambridge University Press, Cambridge, pp. 169–188.

Digby, Kenelm

DAVID B. GOLDSTEIN

Sir Kenelm Digby (1603–65), writer, translator, natural philosopher, courtier, and bibliophile, was one of the century's most versatile and flamboyant characters. A prolific author in a variety of genres, referred to in his day as 'the Mirandola of his age' and now recognized as a father of modern embryology, he is remembered in literary circles chiefly for his posthumously published cookbook.

Digby, the eldest son of Sir Everard Digby (c.1578–1606) and Mary Digby, née Mulsho (c.1581–1653), was born just before Everard's execution for involvement in the Gunpowder Plot. Digby was educated by Jesuits and at the age of 15 entered Gloucester Hall, Oxford, under the tutelage of Thomas Allen, one of the founders of the Bodleian Library and a Catholic sympathizer. In 1630 he converted to Anglicanism, probably in order to hold office, but by 1635 he was Catholic again, and remained a prominent figure in the English Catholic noble community throughout his life. In 1619, Digby completed his education with a grand tour of the Continent, during which he claims to have fended off Marie de' Medici's amorous attentions. He spread rumours of his own death and decamped for Italy, eventually resurfacing in Spain as a participant in the marriage negotiations over Charles, prince of Wales, to the infanta. He was knighted for his role in the ultimately abortive effort in 1623.

Upon his return to England, Digby was reunited with his childhood playmate and adolescent crush, Venetia Stanley (1600–33). Venetia was a famous beauty, of high birth and low fortunes. Believing the reports of

Digby's death, she had become embroiled in various sexual liaisons. They married secretly in 1625. Venetia gave birth to three sons, only one of whom, the estranged John, survived their father. Venetia herself, having become increasingly more devout as Kenelm grew more philandering, died suddenly in 1633. Digby immediately and theatrically forswore his former carefree life, donned a black mourning cloak, and dedicated the rest of his days to intellectual, religious, and diplomatic pursuits. He never remarried, but neither did he lose his rakish volubility, to judge from anecdotes like one recounted in Ann, Lady Fanshawe's memoir.

Digby recorded his relationship with Venetia in several forms. The most elaborate is his memoir, *Loose fantasies*, which was printed only in 1827 but was published widely in manuscript. The memoir, which Digby revised substantially after Venetia's death, chronicles his youthful adventures through 1628, culminating in a privateering raid that he led against French ships at the Venetian port of Iskenderun (Scanderoon), a voyage of which he also kept a daily log. His *roman à clef* is a consummate display of self-fashioning, presenting him as a handsome courtier full of daring and *sprezzatura*. After Venetia's death, Digby commemorated her in a group of letters and memoranda, also unprinted in his lifetime yet widely circulated, entitled 'In praise of Venetia'. He commissioned Van Dyck to paint a deathbed portrait of her, and dedicated several lyric poems to her. Other writers, chief among them Ben Jonson, who enjoyed Digby's patronage, contributed poems to her memory. Digby returned the favour after Jonson's death by orchestrating the publication of one of the most important literary volumes of the age, Jonson's 1640 *Works*. His other great gift to literary history was the donation of several hundred manuscripts, both from his own collection and inherited from his old Oxford don, Allen, to the Bodleian Library in 1634. In 1643 he published *Observations on the 22. stanza in the 9th canto of the 2d. book of Spencers Faery Queen*, an insightful

Aristotelian gloss on a notoriously difficult passage (Schoenfeldt 1999).

Throughout the turmoil of mid-century politics, Digby managed to make himself useful to all sides. He was close to Queen Henrietta Maria, and became her chancellor in 1643. Though Parliament arrested him and sequestered his estate, he won it back along with a pension, and helped Cromwell negotiate with France in 1654–55. Meanwhile, he produced an astonishing range of publications, many of which were frequently reprinted during his life. In 1638, three years after his reconversion to Catholicism, he published *Conference with a lady about a choice of religion*, an exchange of correspondence regarding the potential conversion of Lady Purbeck; it was reprinted along with his translation of the *Treatise of adhering to God* of Albertus Magnus in 1654. On a similar theme is a disquisition he published in French about the nature of true religion. While under house arrest, he produced (supposedly in 24 hours) a commentary on Sir Thomas Browne's *Religio medici* (1643) that was subsequently often included in printings of the original. The year 1651 saw the publication of another exchange of letters on religion, this time between Kenelm and his cousin Lord George Digby, dating from the same period.

It was in philosophy and science that Digby produced the works for which he was best known during his lifetime. He was a close associate of Hobbes, Descartes, and above all Thomas White. Digby (as well as White) attempted to integrate several strands of thought often considered incompatible – mechanism, atomism, and Aristotelianism. He claimed to have been given a 'sympathetic powder' that cured wounds when applied to the weapon that had caused them, for which he offered an atomist explanation, though the real one probably had more to do with cleaning the wound. His *Discourse concerning the vegetation of plants* was the first to introduce the notion of embryonic development. His magnum opus, the twin treatises *Of bodies* and *Of mans soul*, set out to synthesize the new philosophy with

Aristotelian thought. The treatise on the soul tries majestically to argue for the immortality of the soul from natural principles, with almost no recourse to religious faith. Five English and two Latin editions were published of the treatises, the last in 1669, four years after Digby's death. In fact, five of his works were published in 1669, demonstrating the esteem in which his ideas were held, though he died burdened with debts. Yet he proved to be on the wrong side of the development of the new science, which was soon to move decisively away from Aristotle. Digby may have sensed this, since although he was a founding member of the Royal Society, he gradually stopped attending its meetings.

Digby's cookbook, *The closet of the eminently learned Sir Kenelme Digbie Knight opened*, was one of those 1669 volumes. Its recipes were gathered and printed posthumously by George Hartman, his former steward. Hartman had published another collection under Digby's name, *Choice and experimented receipts in physick and chirurgery* (1668), which is primarily medical. He went on to bring out two more, both in his own name but drawn from Digby's papers: *A choice collection of rare chymical secrets and experiments in philosophy* (1682), focusing on chemistry and alchemy; and *The true preserver and restorer of health* (1684), a revision and expansion of all three (Stevenson & Davidson 1997). Digby had been collecting recipes since at least the early 1620s, and the *Closet* exhibits an international range, including the first Chinese recipe in English (for tea-infused eggs). It is also the first cookbook to recommend bacon and eggs for breakfast. The recipes are often attributed to their originators, which provides a window onto the network of social – usually elite Catholic – relationships within which Digby operated. Furthermore, the rhetoric of his recipes differs from most cookbooks of the period in its level of detail and in its hunger for experimentation, a hunger that surely suffused all aspects of Digby's life.

SEE ALSO: Browne, Thomas; Fanshawe, Ann; Hobbes, Thomas; Jonson, Ben; recipe books

REFERENCES AND SUGGESTED READINGS

Bright, H. A. (ed.) (1877) *Poems from Sir Kenelm Digby's papers*. Roxburghe Club, London.

Cope, Jackson (1999) Sir Kenelm Digby's rewritings of his life. In: Hirst, Derek & Strier, Richard (eds) *Writing and political engagement in seventeenth-century England*. Cambridge University Press, Cambridge, pp. 52–68, 200–202.

Foster, Michael (2004) Digby, Sir Kenelm. In: *Oxford dictionary of national biography*. Oxford University Press, Oxford.

Petersson, R. T. (1956) *Sir Kenelm Digby, ornament of England*. Jonathan Cape, London.

Pyle, Andrew (2000) *Dictionary of seventeenth-century British philosophers*. Thoemmes, Bristol.

Schoenfeldt, Michael (1999) *Bodies and selves in early modern England: physiology and inwardness in Spenser, Shakespeare, Herbert, and Milton*. Cambridge University Press, Cambridge.

Stevenson, Jane & Davidson, Peter (eds) (1997) *The closet of Sir Kenelm Digby opened*. Prospect Books, Blackawton.

Donne, John

RAMIE TARGOFF

John Donne (1572–1631) was one of the most original poets of the early seventeenth century, and his verse has engaged readers and students for hundreds of years. Donne was born in London, son of ironmonger John Donne and Elizabeth Heywood, whose father was the playwright John Heywood. On his mother's side, Donne was related to the families of John Rastell and Sir Thomas More, and like them, Donne was raised as a Roman Catholic. He matriculated from Hart Hall, Oxford, in October 1584, but left without taking a degree. His subsequent whereabouts are unknown until May 1592, when he was admitted to Lincoln's Inn. In 1596 and 1597 he served on the Cadiz and Azores missions led by Robert Devereux, earl of Essex, and on his return to England, he was appointed secretary to lord keeper Sir Thomas Egerton, and sat in the 1601 Parliament. By this time, Donne was presumably a practising Protestant. It is believed that many of his satires and erotic elegies can be dated to the 1590s, when they circulated in manuscript to a coterie audience. None of these was published in print, however, until the posthumous 1633 collection, *Poems*. In December 1601 Donne married Lady Egerton's niece Ann More in a secret ceremony, which led to a short imprisonment in the Fleet, and dismissal from his post. The Donnes left London, moving to Pyford and then to Mitcham in Surrey, where Donne worked as a lawyer, applying for state appointments in vain. Ann Donne gave birth to 12 children, before dying in childbirth in August 1617.

The Mitcham years saw Donne reading heavily in both law and casuistry and also writing: his Holy Sonnets, and the prose works *Biathanatos* (1607–8), the anti-Catholic *Pseudo-martyr* (1610) and *Ignatius his conclave* (?1610), date from this period. The only poems published during his lifetime, the two *Anniversaries* – 'An anatomy of the world' (1611) and 'Of the progress of the soul' (1612) – were written as elegies for Elizabeth, daughter of his patron Sir Robert Drury. After travelling with the Drury family on the Continent in 1611/12, Donne moved into their London household until 1621. He became associated with James's favourite, Robert Carr (later earl of Somerset), and sat as member of parliament for Taunton in the 1614 Parliament.

Increasingly drawn to the ministry, Donne was ordained into the Church of England in 1615, becoming a royal chaplain later that year and a reader of divinity at Lincoln's Inn in 1616; he received the degree of doctor of divinity at Cambridge University in 1618. In 1619/20 Donne served as chaplain on an embassy to Germany by James Hay, Viscount Doncaster. He became dean of St Paul's in November 1621, a position he held until his death; his sermons were immensely popular, with several of them being printed (160 survive). Donne died on 31 March 1631, and was buried in St Paul's Cathedral, acclaimed as a poet and preacher by many luminaries, most famously by Thomas Carew.

Donne thus began life as a Roman Catholic, and died as a prominent minister in the Protestant Church of England. He began his writing career as a poet of courtly love lyrics and satires, and ended by composing almost exclusively devotional texts (meditations, hymns, sermons). Within literary history, Donne is best known for having invented a school of poetry known as 'metaphysical'. The term, the meaning of which has been a source of continued controversy, was coined by his contemporary William Drummond, and later reiterated by John Dryden. In the eighteenth century Samuel Johnson criticized Donne's so-called metaphysics as merely a poetic effect. What Johnson identified as a practice of '*discordia concors*', by which 'the most heterogeneous ideas are yoked by violence together', had, in his eyes, no serious philosophical purpose – it was driven merely by the desire 'to say what [he] hoped had never been said before'.

A serious grappling with Donne's metaphysics came only in the early twentieth century, when Herbert J. C. Grierson (1921) published a new edition of Donne and his contemporaries. Grierson was committed to reading Donne as a poet who should be counted as 'metaphysical not only in virtue of his scholasticism, but by his deep reflective interest in the experiences of which his poetry is the expression, the new psychological curiosity with which he writes of love and religion'. Grierson's case for Donne's metaphysical seriousness was at once exploited and undermined, however, by T. S. Eliot's *Times Literary Supplement* review of Grierson's volume, and his much lengthier exposition of Donne in the Clark Lectures at Cambridge five years later. Although Eliot praised Donne for having a 'unified sensibility' of feeling and thought that no subsequent poets possessed, he did not identify this sensibility as particularly metaphysical. Indeed, he announced that the 'invention and use of the term metaphysical' to describe Donne's poetry sprang 'from what . . . is hardly better than an accident'. According to Eliot, both Dr Johnson and Dryden mistakenly classified the 'profundity of thought and learning' in Donne and his contemporaries as 'metaphysical'. This characterization, Eliot insists, libels the name of metaphysics more than it illuminates these authors. For Eliot, and in fact for Johnson as well, what united this immensely gifted group of poets is a shared preoccupation with certain forms of expression – wit, elaboration, hyperbole, conceit – and not a metaphysical subject (Eliot 1951; 1993).

This conception of early seventeenth-century poetry was immensely productive for many mid-twentieth-century scholars, who found in both Johnson's critique and Eliot's qualified praise a vocabulary for judging Donne's rhetorical acrobatics. Donne was simultaneously admired for his poetic gifts and reviled for his apparent lack of seriousness: a man of multiple faiths and professions, Donne could not safely be said to believe in anything in particular. The darling of the New Critics, who valued the sheer complexity of his verse shorn of any historical context, Donne became increasingly harder to assess in the latter decades of the twentieth century, when scholars developed much more complex understandings of the relationship between Renaissance authors and their culture. To the extent that Donne's works could be contextualized, they needed to be selectively chosen: critical studies on single genres in which Donne worked (love lyrics, sermons) or on individual texts (the *Anniversaries*; the *Devotions*) proliferated, but very few attempts were made to reconcile the various strands of his career. When such accounts were given, the assessments were overwhelmingly negative: this was a poet, put simply, whom we had no reason to trust.

That Donne underwent a series of profound changes over the course of his career is neither controversial nor problematic. But to assume as a consequence that there were no underlying commitments, no pervasive beliefs, no gnawing fears, no obsessive desires that connect his remarkably varied works, would be to make a grave mistake. Donne was an author deeply engaged with the world in which he lived – with its religious, scientific, cultural, political, sexual, and artistic developments – and this world raised for him a persistent set of questions. Although the answers to the questions may

vary, the questions themselves vary very little. Not all of them fall under the rubric of metaphysics, although many of them do. Taken as a whole, however, they give the overwhelming impression that Donne was a poet with a set of lifelong preoccupations, and that we can learn more from and about his works when we take him seriously.

KNOWLEDGE

In a letter to his dear friend Sir Henry Goodyer, Donne described himself as having a 'Hydroptique immoderate desire of humane learning and languages'. As any reader of his poetry or prose immediately grasps, Donne was a terrifically learned, and curious, man. Rarely content to embrace any given position without a proper investigation, he circles round and round a subject until he reaches the best conclusion he can. He describes this probing technique in Satire III, in which he rehearses the different branches of Christianity available to him, until he concludes with an astonishing relativism: 'As women do in divers countries go/In divers habits, yet are still one kinde/So doth, so is Religion.' To find Truth, whose existence in any broad sense Donne has already called into question, one cannot simply follow in the path of one's forefathers. Instead, he imagines a process of mental or spiritual labour equivalent to ascending a steep mountain:

> On a huge hill,
> Cragged, and steep, Truth stands, and hee that will
> Reach her, about must, and about must goe;
> And what the hills suddenness resists, winne so;
> Yet strive so, that before age, deaths twilight,
> Thy Soule rest, for none can work in that night.

Whether Donne ever achieved the restfulness that comes with advanced age, as he imagines in Satire III, remains very much in question: one of the most appealing features of his later works is their continued restlessness, their insatiable desire for more, rather than fewer, paths of enquiry.

Donne was an avid, even insatiable reader – he declares his hope, in an undated letter to Goodyer, that he might 'die reading' – and he was also an insatiable writer. In a letter written towards the end of his life, 'To my worthy friend F.H.', Donne confesses that he has 'not yet utterly delivered my self from this intemperance of scribling'. Although he was on the whole ambivalent about sharing his poems with the world, he was never ambivalent about the act of 'scribling', and he wrote copiously throughout his life. The publication of his works seems in general to have been of little interest or concern to him – so long as the texts were written, they assumed not only a material form, but a promise of material permanence. In a letter to Susan, countess of Montgomery, he explains his preference for the written, over the spoken, word: 'Madam, Of my ability to doe your Ladiship service, any thing spoken may be an embleme good enough; for as a word vanisheth, so doth any power in me to serve you; things that are written are fitter testimonies, because they remain and are permanent.' The idea that 'things that are written' will last forever was a fantasy that Donne only sometimes entertained. In 'A funerall elegie' written to commemorate Elizabeth Drury, daughter of his patron Robert Drury, he describes his own poem as 'carcasse verses': since Elizabeth's soul has been removed with her death, the verses themselves cannot help but be 'sickly, alas, short-liv'd, aborted'. But in his love lyric 'The canonization', he celebrates his poetry as the equivalent of enduring funerary monuments; like a 'well wrought urne becomes/the greatest ashes', his verse will survive, and commemorate, their love.

PERMANENCE

The challenge of achieving permanence haunted Donne throughout his life. As a young lover, he sought a kind of constancy in love that always seems to have evaded him. In 'Song: goe, and catche a falling starre', he lists a series of impossible tasks, culminating in finding a 'woman true, and faire':

> If thou findst one, let mee know,
> Such a pilgrimage were sweet;
> Yet doe not, I would not goe,
> Though at next doore wee might meet,
> Though shee were true, when you met her,
> And last, till you write your letter,
> Yet shee
> Will bee
> False, ere I come, to two, or three.

Or, in 'Woman's constancy', he begins: 'Now thou hast lov'd me one whole day/Tomorrow when thou leav'st, what wilt thou say?' The fickleness is not one-sided, however, and by the end of the poem the speaker questions his own faithfulness as well:

> Vaine lunatique, against these scapes I could
> Dispute and conquer, if I would
> Which I abstaine to doe
> For by to morrow, I may thinke so too.

Donne's fear of mutual inconstancy fuels even moments of mutual pleasure: 'Stand still', he instructs his beloved in 'A lecture upon the shadow', attempting to seize and then dilate, the moment at noon when the sun stands 'just above our head'. Although Donne is not a poet of *carpe diem* – he lacks the insouciant disregard for the future, and embrace of the present, which characterize that genre – he experiences the genre's fundamental premise: that on the other side of today is a horizon of eternal darkness. 'Love is a growing, or full constant light', he concludes, 'And his first minute, after noone, is night.'

Donne's fears about constancy are not limited to his erotic poems. Throughout his writings, he expresses frustration over the vicissitudes of time and his inability to capture those moments he would most like to prolong. Hence he begins his 1623 prose meditation, the *Devotions upon emergent occasions*, with a cry of despair over his seemingly instantaneous fall from health to sickness: 'Variable, and therefore miserable condition of man! This minute I was well, and am ill, this minute.' Or, in Holy Sonnet XIX, 'Oh to vex me, contraryes meet in one', he laments his own inability to sustain for any length of time a sincere state of devotion:

I durst not view heaven yesterday; and to day
In prayers, and flattering speeches I court God
Tomorrow I quake with true feare of his rod.

DEATH

The single change that preoccupied Donne
most throughout his life was the change
wrought by death, when the fundamental bond
between body and soul – as he calls it in 'The
extasie', 'that subtle knot that makes us man' –
will be rent asunder. Donne's poetry and prose
are filled with dreadful anticipations of this
moment, which produce in turn some of his
most dramatic, imaginative writing. His sympathy first and foremost is directed to the body,
which moves from life to death with terrifying
suddenness at the moment of the soul's departure. Here is his account of this passage in the
Devotions:

> But for the *body*, how poore a wretched thing is
> *that*? wee cannot expresse it *so fast*, as it growes
> *worse* and *worse*. That *body* which scarce *three*
> *minutes* since was such a *house*, as that that *soule*,
> which made but one step from thence to *Heaven*,
> was scarse thorowly content, to leave that for
> *Heaven*: that *body* hath lost the *name* of a *dwelling*
> *house*, because none dwels in it, and is making
> haste to lose the name of a *body*, and dissolve to
> *putrefaction*.

Donne's sympathy lies not only with the body,
however, but also with the soul, which leaves its
former home with real reluctance – it was, he
tells us, 'scarse thorowly content, to leave that
for *Heaven*'. The idea that the soul is not
unequivocally joyful at the prospect of leaving
the body is one of the great themes of Donne's
writings, as we see most spectacularly in his
long commemorative poem, *The second anniversarie*. In this poem, misleadingly titled 'The
progresse of the soule', he represents his soul as
clinging to its earthly flesh even as it glimpses
images of the heavenly bliss that awaits it.
Despite endless efforts to rouse his soul to
depart this mortal world, he finds it clinging
firmly to the body. 'Up, up, my drowsie Soule',

he futilely beseeches, 'where thy new eare/Shall
in the Angels songs no discord heare'. The soul,
however, will not budge.

Donne explains the difficulty the soul feels in
leaving the flesh as an entirely natural phenomenon. In an Easter day sermon composed more
than a decade after *The second anniversarie*, he
gives this justification for the attachment
between the two parts of the self: 'Naturally
the soule and body are united, [and] when they
are separated by Death, it is contrary to nature,
which nature still affects this union; and consequently the soule is the lesse perfect, for this
separation.' That the soul could be 'lesse perfect' due to its division from the body is not
something many Protestants, let alone Protestant divines, would have supported, and yet
Donne sounds this note again and again in
his sermons. 'Never therefore dispute against
thine own happinesse,' he warns, 'never say,
God asks . . . the soule, and hath no respect to
the body . . . All that the soule does, it does in,
and with, and by the body.'

Unlike the marriage between husband and
wife, which is limited to the mortal world,
Donne regards the marriage between soul and
body as ultimately eternal, interrupted only by
the interval between death and resurrection
when the two parts of the self are forced to
endure a temporary separation. As he preaches
in a funeral sermon for his friend, Sir William
Cockayne,

> As farre as man is immortall, man is a married
> man still, still in possession of a soule, and a body
> too . . . For, though they be separated *a Thoro &*
> *Mensa*, from Bed and Board, they are not
> divorced . . . Though the soule be *in lecto florido*,
> in that bed which is always green, in an everlast-
> ing spring, in *Abrahams bosome*; And the body
> but in that green-bed, whose covering is but a
> yard and a half of Turfe, and a Rugge of grasse,
> and the sheet but a winding sheet, yet they are not
> divorced; they shall returne to one another
> againe, in an inseparable re-union in the
> Resurrection.

This 'inseparable re-union' is the state of permanence Donne longs for: a permanence that

will free him forever from the trauma of separation that he fears most of all.

Donne's anxieties about the separation of body from soul take many different forms, but perhaps the most persistent involves his dwelling upon the condition of the corpse in the ground. From his early love poems through his late sermons, Donne was preoccupied with the rotting of human flesh, and he envied those who would be alive on the Last Day and hence be spared the interval between death and rebirth: as he describes it in Holy Sonnet VII, 'you whose eyes/Shall behold God, and never tast deaths woe'. The metaphor from 'The relique' that Eliot singled out as the epitome of Donne's poetic powers – 'a bracelet of bright hair about the bone' – is in fact a grim synecdoche for the physical remains of himself and his lover, intertwined not in one another's arms, but in the union of a solitary lock of hair, and a bone whose flesh has melted away.

Donne's macabre humour is more pronounced in 'The relique' than in his devotional works – addressing the imagined grave-digger ready to place another corpse on top of his, he asks with indignation: 'Will he not let us alone/And thinke that there a loving couple lies?' But Donne's obsession with maintaining the integrity of our bodily remains pervades his writings. Even in his final sermon, 'Deaths duell', which he preached as a dying man, he dwells on the horror of mixing one's remains with those of fellow corpses:

> When those bodies that have beene the *children* of *royall parents*, and the *parents* of *royall children*, must say with *Iob*, to corruption thou art my father, and *to the Worme thou art my mother and my sister*. *Miserable riddle*, when the *same worme* must bee *my mother*, and *my sister*, and *my selfe*. *Miserable incest*, when I must bee *maried* to my *mother* and my *sister*, and bee both *father* and *mother* to my *owne mother* and *sister*.

Behind all of this dark imagining is his profound concern that his body will not be perfectly restored at the Resurrection, that pieces of him might go astray. Donne wants above all to be once again himself, to be entirely and completely the same man. As he affirms in another sermon, however far his body may be scattered through the corners of the world – 'this Eastern, and Western, and Northern, and Southern body' – it shall be brought together again, 'and be identically, numerically, individually the same man. The same integrity of body, and soul, and the same integrity in the Organs of my body, and in the faculties of my soul too; I shall be all there, my body, and my soul, and all my body, and all my soul.' This is Donne's greatest hope of self-fulfilment, and he expends enormous amounts of imaginative and psychic energy convincing himself of its ultimate certainty.

PERFORMANCE

To say that Donne looked forwards with great longing to the resurrection of his body is not also to say that he lived a strictly other-worldly life. One of the most striking features about Donne's poetry and prose alike is their engagement with the world, their palpable effort to represent or dramatize the multiple experiences that he had. This is something that Eliot observed in his discussion of Donne's 'unified sensibility': 'Tennyson and Browning are poets, and they think; but they do not feel their thought as immediately as the odour of a rose. A thought to Donne was an experience; it modified his sensibility.' After Donne, Eliot argued, poets suffered from a 'dissociation of sensibility', an inability to fuse feeling and thought into a single experience. Another way to describe what Eliot identifies in Donne, or a more tangible manifestation of what he means, is to register how relentlessly *present* Donne's language is – present in its tense, present in its address, present in its accommodation of changes that occur over the course of the poems themselves.

Although Donne never wrote plays, he is an extremely dramatic writer, and his style is nothing if not performative. A poem like 'The flea' is in effect a theatrical scene in which one of the actors is silent: each stanza reflects a response to the mistress's unrepresented actions, as the speaker shifts his position this way and that to accommodate the new position that he finds himself in. In 'Elegie XIX: going to bed', we witness Donne undressing his mistress, garment by garment with great rhetorical exuberance; the opening couplet of this poem, 'Come, Madam, come, all rest my powers defie/ Until I labour, I in labour lie', situates us as voyeurs at the very moment of seduction. The challenge of persuading his mistress to come to his bed – the very same challenge that drives 'The flea' – is one that he clearly relishes: this is the 'labour' of his poetry, and he seems to embrace the process as much as the end itself.

Donne's language is performative not only for being theatrical, but also for adhering to what the twentieth-century philosopher J. L. Austin (1962) means by the term: a language of 'speech-act' in which words are themselves forms of action. Although Donne's poems do not always technically adhere to Austin's definition of the speech-act, his language is forceful and active in exactly the way that Austin describes. It does not describe the acts of seducing, persuading, complaining, lamenting: it performs these acts for us. 'For God's sake hold your tongue and let me love,' he scolds in 'The canonization'; 'So, so, break off this last lamenting kisse,' he exclaims in 'The expiration'; 'Let me powre forth/My teares before thy face, whil'st I stay here,' he petitions in 'A valediction: of weeping'; 'At the round earths imagin'd corners, blow/Your trumpets, Angells', he instructs, in Holy Sonnet VII; 'Batter my heart, three person'd God,' he commands in Holy Sonnet XIV. These are the lines that open each of these poems, and in each case they demand some kind of immediate response.

SELF-SCRUTINY

Donne's demands for action are not only directed at others: he also uses his poems as vehicles to provoke changes or resolutions in himself. In this sense, the poems resemble the soliloquies of Hamlet or Iago, in which Shakespeare shows his character reaching an often startlingly different conclusion from where the speech began. The most obvious examples of Donne's representation of mental change over the course of a single poem comes in the Holy Sonnets, which repeatedly begin from a position of ignorance or arrogance (or both), only to reach a state of repentance. That Donne manages to effect this change in the space of 14 lines is both a testament to his skills of rhetorical compression, and a reflection of his understanding of the way that sonnets themselves work.

In the traditional Petrarchan sonnet, the ninth line is known as the *volta*, or turn, and here the poet can move from whatever he or she has established in the opening octave to a different position in the final sestet. The *volta* creates, then, an inherent drama in the sonnet, which Donne puts to great effect in his devotional poems. Hence in Holy Sonnet XI, 'Spit in my face you Jewes, and pierce my side', he begins by imagining himself as a substitute for Christ's sacrifice. By line 9, he has learned that what seemed like an act of self-sacrifice was in fact an act of hubris, and he backs down: 'Oh let me then, his strange love still admire.' Or in Holy Sonnet IX, he opens with bravado and outrage:

> If poisonous mineralls, and if that tree
> Whose fruit threw death on else immortall us,
> If lecherous goats, if serpents envious
> Cannot be damn'd; Alas, why should I bee?

This defiant challenge to God's justice is then forcefully retracted, again, at line 9: 'But who am I, that dare dispute with thee/O God?'

A longer, subtler version of the poem as occasion for (and not simply description of) devotional reformation comes in 'Goodfriday, 1613. Riding westward'. This poem opens with an intellectualized excuse for riding in the wrong direction – away from Christ – on this holy day, an excuse informed by cosmology rather than piety. 'Let mans Soule be a Sphere,' the speaker begins, as if putting a hypothetical case in an academic exercise, 'and then, in this / The intelligence that moves, devotion is.' The *volta* in the poem, at line 15, concedes the first bit of emotional truth: the speaker is not merely being 'carryed towards the West' by the influence of celestial forces. He is actively avoiding the East: 'Yet dare I' almost be glad', he admits, 'I do not see / That spectacle of too much weight for mee.' Over the course of the subsequent lines, the speaker conveys through a series of rhetorical questions exactly why he cannot bear to confront the 'spectacle' of Christ's sacrifice: 'Could I behold those hands'; 'Could I behold that endless height'; 'If on these things I durst not looke, durst I / Upon his miserable mother cast mine eye?'

This second set of excuses for why his back has been turned on Good Friday provokes in turn the poem's second *volta*: the speaker recognizes that what is missing from his outward gaze is already inscribed within his soul. 'Though these things, as I ride, be from mine eye,' he declares, 'They' are present yet unto my memory / For that looks towards them.' Having acknowledged his possession of Christ's sacrifice as part of his own God-given memory, the speaker is now ready to confront Christ directly, and he registers this readiness by shifting from the third to the second person. No longer referring to Christ from a safe distance, he addresses him as 'thou': 'and thou look'st towards mee / O Saviour, as thou hang'st upon the tree.' The poem ends with a personal petition to Christ, a petition of intimacy and intensity that was entirely unavailable to the speaker when he began some 40 lines earlier. The poem has served, then, as a preparation to prayer.

SELF-REVISION

If we think of Donne's poems as vehicles for self-reflection or change, the relationship between the devotional lyrics and many of the *Songs and sonnets* becomes much easier to grasp. In a poem like 'A valediction: of my name in the window',

he begins with the idea that he might leave his name engraved in a pane of glass as a substitute for his physical presence in his mistress's chamber during his period of absence. Over the course of the poem, he shifts his understanding of what purpose the engraved name should serve – having begun as an embodiment of his 'firmnesse' in love, it becomes, in turn, a 'deaths head' to teach mortality; 'my ruinous Anatomie', awaiting the return of his 'Muscle, Sinew, and Veine'; and an enraged lover defending himself against her other suitors. None of these uses of the name fully satisfies the speaker, however, and the speaker concludes by rejecting his conceit altogether:

> But glasse, and lines must bee,
> No meanes our firme substantiall love to keepe;
> Neere death inflicts this lethargie,
> And this I murmure in my sleepe.

The poem enacts, in other words, the failure of the poet's idea.

A similar, but more successful version of metaphorical trial and error occurs in 'A valediction: forbidding mourning', where we witness the poet thinking through what the single best image would be to describe the relationship between himself and his beloved. The challenge of this poem is the same as 'A valediction: of my name in the window' – namely, how to sustain the bond between lovers when they cannot physically be together. But here, rather than leave behind a token of himself (the doomed engraving in the window), Donne leaves behind the gift of metaphor. Imagine us as two souls 'which are one', he tells his beloved, souls that cannot be torn asunder, but instead are further extended, 'like gold to ayery thinnesse beate'. This gorgeous metaphor of gold beaten out so thin as to be barely substantial, like a gauzy veil in a Fra Angelico canvas, does not entirely satisfy him, however, and he moves in the next stanza to replace it. Having decided, perhaps, that an image of oneness may not be the most apt or most comforting, he begins anew with an image for their twoness:

If they be two, they are two so
As stiffe twin compasses are two,
Thy soule the fixt foot, makes no show
To move, but doth, if the'other doe.

This is the perfect metaphor, Donne seems to decide, for the simultaneous oneness and twoness of the lovers. Like the legs of the compass, the lovers are parts of a single being and remain connected to each other physically whether near or far. They are also, however, distinct beings whose identities can be articulated independently.

Donne conveys his own satisfaction with this image by not replacing it. The poem ends with an extended explication of how the metaphor works, as if supplying a close reading of his own:

And though it in the center sit,
Yet when the other far doth rome,
It leanes, and hearkens after it,
And growes erect, as that comes home.
Such wilt thou be to mee, who must
Like th'other foot, obliquely runne;
Thy firmnes makes my circle just,
And makes me end, where I begunne.

What Donne wants to achieve in this poem of valediction – in all of his poems of valediction – is the reassurance of coming back together again. The metaphor of beaten gold did not give him this, but the metaphor of the compass does. It lets him 'end, where I begunne'; it brings him where he wants to be: home.

VIVACITY

To affirm that Donne is a metaphysical poet helps us focus on his lifelong engagement with philosophy and theology and science; it allows us, as well, to connect individual works that would otherwise be separated by chronology or genre. To affirm that Donne is a metaphysical poet does not, however, capture the tremendous vivacity of his writings, the impression they give of immersing us in his presence. Donne is, to be sure, a metaphysical poet, but

he is also a physical poet, a sensual poet, a poet who is concerned with the world around him. His writing possesses above all an urgency, an insistence that its voice be heard. At his most affirmative, Donne teaches us to savour the pleasures of being alive. As he declares in 'The anniversarie': 'Let us love nobly, and live.'

SEE ALSO: Carew, Thomas; Devereux, Robert, earl of Essex; Drummond, William; Dryden, John; Shakespeare, William

REFERENCES AND SUGGESTED READINGS

Austin, J. L. (1962) *How to do things with words.* Harvard University Press, Cambridge, MA.

Carey, John (1981) *John Donne: life, mind, and art.* Faber & Faber, London.

Eliot, T. S. (1951) *Selected essays.* Faber & Faber, London.

Eliot, T. S. (1993) *The varieties of metaphysical poetry*, ed. Ronald Schuchard. Harcourt Brace, New York.

Grierson, Herbert J. C. (ed.) (1912) *The poems of John Donne.* 2 vols. Clarendon Press, Oxford.

Grierson, Herbert J. C. (ed.) (1921) *Metaphysical lyrics and poems of the seventeenth century: Donne to Butler.* Clarendon Press, Oxford.

Marotti, Arthur F. (1986) *John Donne, coterie poet.* University of Wisconsin Press, Madison.

Potter, George R. & Simpson, Evelyn M. (eds) (1953–62) *The sermons of John Donne.* 10 vols. University of California Press, Berkeley.

Raspa, Anthony (ed.) (1975) *Devotions upon emergent occasions*, by John Donne. McGill-Queen's University Press, Montreal.

Targoff, Ramie (2008) *John Donne, body and soul.* University of Chicago Press: Chicago.

Douglas, Gawin

ELIZABETH ELLIOTT

In the *Eneados* (1513), Gawin Douglas (c.1476–1522) produced the first complete verse translation of a classical poem in any British vernacular. Printed in London in 1553, Douglas's scholarly rendering of Virgil influenced the translation of Henry Howard, earl of Surrey, and bears witness to Douglas's talent as a poet in his own right. A member of one of the most powerful aristocratic families of his day, Douglas was born around 1476. As the younger son of Archibald Douglas, fifth earl of Angus, his ambitions were directed towards an ecclesiastical career; graduating from the University of St Andrews in 1494, Douglas later became bishop of Dunkeld (1516). In the wake of the Scottish defeat at Flodden in 1513, he became increasingly involved in the factional politics of his time, and he died in London as an exile, in 1522.

Only two extant poems can be securely attributed to Douglas, but contemporary evidence indicates that his literary output was larger. The allegorical poem *King Hart* is no longer regarded as being his, although the case for 'Conscience', a satirical poem on ecclesiastical corruption ascribed to him in the sixteenth century, is more credible. Douglas's earliest extant work, *The palice of honour* (c.1501), is an allegorical dream-vision reflecting literary influences encompassing Geoffrey Chaucer, John Gower, and John Lydgate, and perhaps also William Dunbar's *Goldyn targe*, although the relationship between these two Scottish poems remains the subject of critical debate. Surviving in editions printed at London and Edinburgh during the sixteenth century, *The palice* focuses on the nature of honour and the means by which it might be obtained, and it displays a particular concern with poetry. In common with Dunbar and David Lindsay, Douglas invokes the canonical English poets alongside those of his own nation, complementing the tribute paid in his later work to Chaucer as the supreme facilitator of vernacular writing in a British context. In *The palice*, he adapts the language of Lowland Scotland to accommodate his own rhetorical ambition, developing an aureate style suited to the classical subject matter of his allegory, and to the courtly audience anticipated in the poem's dedication to James IV. Yet, for all its sophistication, much of the poem's impact derives from its juxtaposition of the grand and the familiar, in the mixture of Latinate and common speech, and in the intrusion of elements

from contemporary life into the landscape of classical mythology. This coalescence is reflected in the narrator's disruption of Venus' court in procession with a bitter song, and his subsequent trial, an episode that recalls the civic pageantry of the Scottish burghs, and draws on criminal law to comic effect.

In the *Eneados*, Douglas's concern with the textual accuracy of his translation presents an early instance of the influence of Italian humanist principles, yet his work is also informed by earlier models of translation that prioritize the exposition of meaning, routinely treating the apparatus of glosses as an integral part of the source. Douglas incorporates material from the commentary tradition in a manner consistent with this praxis, and his text is especially indebted to Jodocus Badius Ascensius's edition of Virgil, published in 1501. His inclusion of the thirteenth book composed by the humanist Maffeo Vegio follows contemporary editorial practice. Douglas was not writing primarily for clerics, however, and although the *Eneados* is dedicated to his kinsman Henry, Lord Sinclair, he anticipates a British readership for his poem beyond a more particular audience of cultivated Scots.

To his translation in heroic couplets, Douglas appends a prologue for each book of Virgil's poem, and several epilogues. Sometimes treated as poems in their own right, by both critics and early readers, these additions exhibit metrical versatility, and several are remarkable for the degree of attention they afford to description of the natural world. Providing a space for Douglas to censure the paganism of classical Rome, the prologues are also the site of critical reflection on the *Eneados* itself. Douglas locates his work in relation to that of William Caxton and of Chaucer, highlighting their distortions of Virgil's text to emphasize the importance of his own enterprise. His translation is conceived as a service to Scotland, and he is among the first to use the term 'Scots' to distinguish his tongue from 'sudron', or English, at a time when 'Scots' was associated with Gaelic, rather than the 'Inglis' language of the Lowlands. Douglas's work parallels that of Virgil, as an act of literary production that translates the authority associated with classical antiquity into a new contemporary and national setting. In justifying his need to borrow from Latin, French, and English in order to amend the deficiency of Scots, Douglas points to the presence of Greek words in Latin, highlighting a precedent that authorizes and underlines his own role in forging a prestigious Scottish vernacular.

Regarded by David Lindsay as the greatest of Scots writers, Douglas was during his own lifetime the dedicatee of books by John Mair and Alexander Myln. His work was popular in England and Scotland, and, in addition to the 1553 print, the *Eneados* survives in five manuscript copies. The influence of Douglas's poetry has been traced in Thomas Sackville's 'Induction' to the 1563 edition of the *Mirrour for magistrates*, and in the work of writers including John Bellenden and John Rolland.

SEE ALSO: Caxton, William; Dunbar, William; Howard, Henry, earl of Surrey; Lindsay, David; Mair, John; Sackville, Thomas, earl of Dorset

REFERENCES AND SUGGESTED READINGS

Bawcutt, Priscilla (1976) *Gavin Douglas: a critical study.* Edinburgh University Press, Edinburgh.

Bawcutt, Priscilla (ed.) (2003) *The shorter poems of Gavin Douglas*, 2nd edn. Scottish Text Society, Edinburgh.

Coldwell, D. F. C. (ed.) (1957–64). *Virgil's Aeneid translated into Scottish verse by Gavin Douglas*. 4 vols. Scottish Text Society, Edinburgh.

Gray, Douglas (2006) Gavin Douglas. In Bawcutt, Priscilla & Hadley Williams, Janet (eds) *A companion to medieval Scottish poetry*. D. S. Brewer, Cambridge, pp. 149–164.

Parkinson, David (ed.) (1992) *The palis of honoure*, by Gawin Douglas. Medieval Institute Publications, Kalamazoo.

Dowland, John

PENELOPE GENG

John Dowland (?1563–1626) was a highly successful English composer of lute ayres.

The commercial success of his printed song-books encouraged other musicians, including Philip Rosseter, Thomas Campion, Robert Jones, and John Attey, to follow suit by using print to build their reputations, attract patronage, and mould the musical taste of the English population.

Little is known of Dowland's birth, childhood, or early career. From 1580 to 1584, he lived in Paris while in the employment of Sir Henry Cobham, the English ambassador to France. In 1588, he returned to England and received a bachelor of music degree from Oxford; sometime before 1597, he received one from Cambridge. From 1588 to 1592, Dowland's music was performed at several royal occasions. After 1592, he travelled to Europe, stopping at the courts of Henry Julio, duke of Brunswick and Moritz, landgrave of Hesse, at Kassel. While travelling in Florence, he was approached by a Catholic faction plotting to assassinate Elizabeth I. To disassociate himself from the conspiracy, Dowland fled to Nuremberg and composed a letter to Sir Robert Cecil, dated 10 November 1595, in which he emphasized his loyalty to his queen and country. In 1597, he returned to London on the intelligence that he might be promoted to court musician. However, the untimely death of his then patron Henry Noel left him empty-handed. Dowland returned to the Continent. Between 1598 and 1606, he held the well-paid position of court musician at the court of Christian IV of Denmark. In 1612 he attracted the patronage of Theophilus Walden, Lord Howard; later that year, he achieved his goal of being appointed musician for the Jacobean court, a position he held until his death.

In 1597 Dowland published 21 of his songs as *The first booke of songes or ayres of foure partes with tableture for the lute*. The English ayre denotes songs intended to be sung in solo voice or in parts. Although related to the Italian madrigal, the ayre is strophic in form and less contrapuntal than the madrigal. In the dedicatory epistle to Sir George Carey, his patron, Dowland draws attention to the vulnerable position of the professional musician. Only his patron can 'vouchfast to uphold my poore fortunes'. Dowland writes humbly of his hope that Carey might extend his 'gracious protection' to the present publication. In the letter to the reader, he stresses 'how hard an enterprise it is ... to commit our private labours to the publike view'. His dedicatory epistles to Lucy Russell, countess of Bedford, in *The second booke* (1600) and John Souch in *The third booke* (1603) contain similar yearnings for patronage, friendship, and protection. His letter to Sir Robert Cecil (1595) reinforces the anxiety he expresses in his publications. In it he alleges that he has been passed over for promotion because of the court's perception of his Catholic affiliation (Gibson 2007). Even after he had become an established figure in the music scene, Dowland spoke anxiously about the public's reception of his works. In the epistle to the reader to *The third booke*, Dowland states his 'hope' that his work 'shall not be wrackt on land by curious and biting censures'.

Dowland's books are large folios in a tablebook format so that 'all the partes together, or either of them severally may be song to the Lute, Orpherian or Viol de gambo'. The verso contains the song, the various verses, and the lute accompaniment written in tablature. It can thus be sung as a solo song. The facing recto contains parts for three additional voices (tenor, bass, and alto), making for a four-part song. These parts are placed on the page in such a way that they can be read by singers sitting to the right and opposite the principal singer or the soloist. Dowland's *First booke* was a major commercial success: it was reprinted in 1600, 1603, 1606, and 1613. In 1600, Dowland published *The second booke of songs or ayres*. The manuscript was sent to the printer from Denmark where Dowland was employed as 'Lutenist to the King of Denmark'. This was followed by *The third and last booke of songs or aires* (1603), *Lachrimae, or seaven teares, figured in seaven passionate pavans* (1604), and *A pilgrimes solace* (1612).

Besides ayres, Dowland also composed various kinds of dance music including pavans, galliards, and jigs. Towards the end of his life, he turned to writing religious music. In the epistle to the reader in *Lachrimae*, he highlights his ability to bring out 'new songs with olde, grave with light that every eare may receive his severall content' and attributes the eclecticism to his 'earnest desire to satisfie all'. In the early seventeenth century, Dowland's popularity with common audiences appeared to be on the wane. In *A pilgrimes solace*, he speaks of the 'strange entertainment' he has received by 'Cantors' and the 'young men, professors of the Lute' who say 'what I do is after the old manner'. In a sonnet in *Minerva Britanna* (1612), Henry Peacham portrays his friend as 'Philomel, [who] in silence sits alone', abandoned by the 'Ingrateful times, and worthless age of ours'.

In *Lachrimae*, Dowland includes a piece called 'Semper Dowland semper dolens' ('Ever Dowland, ever doleful'), thereby drawing a self-conscious comparison between himself and the melancholic complainants of his works. Dowland's songs depict an emotional landscape marked by solitude, abandonment, darkness, and despair. In 'Sorrow sorrow stay' (*The second booke*), the phrase 'but down, down, down, down, I fall' is set to a descending musical line, the sound mirroring perfectly the sense of the words. It is debatable whether the melancholic themes in the ayres reflect Dowland's mindset. Evidence against a biographical reading is strong. First, Dowland reminds the reader in *Lachrimae* that tears are not 'shed always in sorrowe, but sometime in joy and gladnesse'. Secondly, it is unknown whether Dowland composed the lyrics to the ayres. Finally, Dowland's ayres echo a popular and established genre, that of the lover's complaint, which is reproduced in poetry and art, in Sir Philip Sidney's *Astrophil and Stella* (c.1582) and in Nicholas Hilliard's 'A youth leaning against a tree among roses' (c.1588), respectively. The success of Dowland's *Bookes* serves as a reminder of the popularity of the complaint genre in Renaissance England.

SEE ALSO: Peacham, Henry; Russell, Lucy, countess of Bedford; Sidney, Philip

REFERENCES AND SUGGESTED READINGS

Boyd, Morrison C. (1962) *Elizabethan music and musical criticism*. University of Pennsylvania Press, Philadelphia.

Caldwell, John (1991) *The Oxford history of English music*, vol. 1. Oxford University Press, Oxford.

Gibson, Kirsten (2007) How hard an enterprise it is: authorial self-fashioning in John Dowland's printed books. *Early Music History* 26, 43–89.

Pattison, Bruce (1948) *Music and poetry of the English Renaissance*. Methuen, London.

Poulton, Diana (1982) *John Dowland*. University of California Press, Berkeley.

Spring, Matthew (2001) *The lute in Britain: a history of the instrument and its music*. Oxford Univesity Press, Oxford.

Toft, Robert (1984) Musicke a sister to poetrie: rhetorical artifice in the passionate airs of John Dowland. *Early Music* 12(2), 191–199.

Wells, Robin Headlam (1985) John Dowland and Elizabethan melancholy. *Early Music* 13(4), 514–528.

Dowriche, Anne

NICOLE A. JACOBS

Anne Dowriche (born before 1560, died in or after 1613) was a reformist poet most notable in literary, religious, historical, and feminist traditions for writing *The French historie* (1589), a verse translation of and elaboration upon Jean de Serres's *Commentariorum de statu religionis et reipublicae in regno Galliae* (*Commentary on the condition of religion and state in the kingdom of France*) (1572–75). Raised and educated at Mount Edgcumbe in Cornwall, the family home her father built, she was the daughter of Sir Richard Edgcumbe and Elizabeth Tregian. The exact dates of her birth and death are unknown, but she is mentioned in her father's will of July 1560 and is known to have been alive in 1613. Her family had been active in national and local politics since the reign of Henry VIII, and her writing provides evidence of her own political and religious agenda.

On 29 November 1580 she married Hugh Dowriche of Sandford, Devon, who was then rector of Lapford and later rector of Honiton. Her husband was educated at Hart Hall, Oxford, concluding his studies in 1581 and receiving his licence to preach in 1583. The Dowriches shared their commitment to promoting the Puritan cause in England. Anne contributed two poems to Hugh's *The jaylors conversion* (1596) in which she proclaims that the elect must overcome the temptation of sin and accept God's will. They had at least three sons, Elkana, Walter, and Hugh, and three daughters, Mary, Anne, and Elizabeth.

The French historie offers a vivid account of three significant events in the French Wars: the persecution of the Huguenots who gathered for a prayer meeting on the rue St Jacques in Paris in 1557, the martyrdom of French counsellor Annas Burgeus (Anne du Bourg) in 1559, and the murder of Admiral Gaspard de Coligny, which marked the beginning of the St Bartholomew's Day Massacre in 1572. Dowriche's poem relies upon additional sources and intertexts in Thomas Tymme's *The three partes of commentaries containing the whole and perfect discourse of the ciuil warres of Fraunce* (1574), François Hotman's *De furoribus Gallacis* (*On the French commotions*) (1573), and Innocent Gentillet's *Discours contre Machiavel* (*Discourse against Machiavelli*) (1576). However, Dowriche's lengthy speeches, theatrical devices, and focus on the roles of kings and counsellors in a godly kingdom distinguish her verse history. Despite the recent triumphs of Protestants in England – the execution of Mary Queen of Scots, and the defeat of the Spanish Armada had taken place in the two years prior to the publication of *The French historie* – Dowriche's poem reveals ongoing Puritan concerns over the Catholic threat in England.

Although Dowriche claims to have had 'slender skill' in prosody, she uses poulter's measure, a form consisting of alternating iambic hexameter and pentameter, in crafting a narrative in which Satan becomes a figure for the Catholic interference in French politics and religion. Her method of presenting historical material bears resemblance to John Foxe's *Actes and monuments* (1563), as she admits to 'amplifying the circumstance' for poetic and rhetorical effect. Like the Geneva Bible, her verse is interspersed with marginal commentary and biblical references. The poem includes pathetic detail, such as images of mothers with recently severed arms reaching for their children who are being brutally murdered, and fathers urging their children to maintain forbearance as Christ tests their faith in the face of death.

More significantly, *The French historie* reveals that Dowriche was conversant in Continental and English resistance theory as well as in the biblical examples that underwrite much of its authority. Several speeches by Huguenot leaders challenge the jurisdiction of the king and his counsel over matters of personal faith. For instance, Annas Burgeus justifies Huguenot rebellion against tyranny, asking, 'then judge again, and tell me if you can: / Which is best; to serve the Lord, or follow sinfull man?' That this work is dedicated to Dowriche's brother Pearse Edgecumbe, a long-standing member of parliament, and that she asks him to 'find here manie things for comfort worthie the considering and for policie the observing', suggests that the poem aspires to influence popular political thought in England. The consistent scholarly attention paid to *The French historie* over the past decade shows how Anne Dowriche's treatment of sixteenth-century French Huguenot resistance helped to inform seventeenth-century Puritan rebellion in England.

SEE ALSO: Bible, the; Foxe, John

REFERENCES AND SUGGESTED READINGS

Aughterson, Kate (2004) Dowriche, Anne. In: *Oxford dictionary of national biography*. Oxford University Press, Oxford.

Beilin, Elaine V. (1996) Anne Dowriche. In: Richardson, David A. (ed.) *Sixteenth-century British non-dramatic writers*, 4th series. Gale, Detroit, pp. 79–84.

Beilin, Elaine V. (2000) 'Some freely spake their minde': resistance in Anne Dowriche's *French historie*. In: Burke, Mary E., Donawerth, Jane, Dove, Linda L., & Nelson, Karen (eds) *Women, writing, and the reproduction of culture in Tudor and Stuart Britain*. Syracuse University Press, Syracuse, NY, pp. 119–140.

Chedgzoy, Kate (2004) This pleasant and sceptered isle: insular fantasies of national identity in Anne Dowriche's *The French historie* and William Shakespeare's *Richard II*. In: Schwyzer, Philip & Mealor, Simon (eds) *Archipelagic identities: literature and identity in the Atlantic archipelago, 1550–1800*. Ashgate, Burlington, pp. 25–52.

Martin, Randall (1999) Anne Dowriche's *The French history*, Christopher Marlowe, and Machiavellian agency. *Studies in English Literature, 1500–1900* 39, 69–87.

Matchinske, Megan (2004) Moral, method, and history in Anne Dowriche's *The French historie*. *English Literary Renaissance* 34(2), 176–200.

Sondergard, Sidney L. (2002) *Sharpening her pen: strategies of rhetorical violence by early modern English women writers*. Susquehanna University Press, Selinsgrove.

Suzuki, Mihoko (2009) Warning Elizabeth with Catherine de' Medici's example: Anne Dowriche's *French history* and the politics of counsel. In: Cruz, Anne J. & Suzuki, Mihoko (eds) *The rule of women in early modern Europe*. University of Illinois Press, Chicago, pp. 174–193.

Trease, G. E. (1974–77) Dowrich and the Dowrich family of Sandford. *Devon and Cornwall Notes and Queries* 33, 208–211.

Woods, Susanne, Travitsky, Betty S., & Cullen, Patrick (eds) (2001) *The poets, I: Isabella Whitney, Anne Dowriche, Elizabeth Melville (Colville), Aemilia Lanyer, Rachel Speght, Diana Primrose, Anne, Mary and Penelope Grey*. Ashgate, Burlington.

Drant, Thomas

FRED SCHURINK

Thomas Drant (c.1540–78) was born in Hagworthingham, Lincolnshire, the son of a farmer. He matriculated at St John's College, Cambridge in 1558 and received his BA in 1561, MA in 1564, and BD in 1569, having been appointed a fellow of the college in 1561. During the 1560s, Drant acted as domestic chaplain for Edmund Grindal, bishop of London, and towards the end of the decade he left Cambridge for a successful career as a Church of England clergyman, holding the position of archdeacon of Lewes, Sussex, from 1570 to his death in 1578. His main significance for literary history is as the first English translator of Horace's *Satires*, *Epistles*, and *Art of poetry* (1566–67), but he also contributed to debates over quantitative verse in English in the 1570s and wrote a number of other works in English and neo-Latin.

Drant's translation of Horace's *Satires* was published alongside an English version of the Old Testament book of Lamentations and occasional poems in English and Latin as *A medicinable morall* (1566). He explicitly connects the two verse translations in the volume, claiming that whereas the prophet Jeremiah (to whom Lamentations is attributed) weeps at sin, Horace laughs at it. This notion reflects Drant's understanding of the genre of satire as a scathing attack on the iniquity of humankind and of Horace's poems as straightforward condemnations of vice rather than the multivocal meditations on a variety of subjects suggested by the original title of the work, *Sermones* (Burrow 1993; Mukherjee 2000).

While he sees a close relationship in purpose between Horace's *Satires* and the book of Lamentations, Drant's approach to the translation of the two works diverges sharply. His translation from the Bible, the word of God, shows a great concern with fidelity to the text. Horace's *Satires*, in contrast, are subject to substantial changes to fit the moral and religious norms of Elizabethan England. Drant makes major additions to, and omissions from, four *Satires*. He expands 1.1 to underscore the moral; replaces Horace's frank account of sexual mores in 1.2 with criticism of extravagant dress; replaces 1.5 (describing a journey to Brindisi, which evidently did not fit Drant's conception of the genre) with an anti-Catholic satire, which appears to be directed against the hotter sort of Protestants too; and condemns gluttony and drunkenness instead of the ostentation and extravagance of the wealthy at social functions

in 2.8 (Medine 1972; Mukherjee 2000). Moreover, Drant frequently substitutes Elizabethan words and concepts for Horace's original Roman ones. His vigorous colloquialism found favour with C. S. Lewis (1954) – otherwise no friend of 'drab age verse' – who praised Drant's translation for its homely and lively expression. More frequently, however, critics have condemned his occasionally ponderous alliterative fourteener couplets and stern moral tone for lacking the urbanity and wit of Horace's verse (Lathrop 1933; Mukherjee 2000).

Drant's versions of Horace's *Satires* were reprinted with new translations of the Roman author's *Art of poetry* and *Epistles* as *Horace his arte of poetrie, pistles, and satyrs* in the following year (1567). In keeping with the more recognizably literary character of this publication, Drant's renderings of Horace's other poems are noticeably more faithful to the original than the earlier translations, although he again freely modernizes the Roman poet's expression. In the prefatory material, Drant emphasizes the didactic intent of Horace's verse and defends his pursuit of the humanities as a contribution to, rather than a diversion from, the study of divinity.

His attempts to reconcile religion and humanism, and the tensions between them, are equally evident in his other works. Drant's first publication, *Impii cuiusdam epigrammatis apomaxis* (*Refutation of a certain impious epigram*) (1565), was a work of religious controversy in a humanist form: a Latin verse parody of Richard Shacklock's Latin epitaph of the Catholic bishop of Chester, Cuthbert Scott, followed by English translations of the poems. Drant's sermons, including one delivered at court warning Elizabeth against the dangers of Catholicism in the wake of the Northern Rebellion (published in 1570 and 1572 and reissued together in 1584), echo the subjects of his poetry and deal with the question of the relation between the study of classical literature and divinity (Medine 1972; Mears 2005).

In a Latin poem ('De Iliade Homeri . . .') that has been dated to 1568/69, Drant wrote that he had renounced profane literature for sacred writing at the behest of his patron Grindal (Medine 1972), and his remaining works of poetry are all on religious subjects. *Epigrams and sentences spirituall in vers* (1568), dedicated to Grindal, is an English translation of the poetry of Gregory of Nazianzus, the fourth-century bishop of Constantinople. Four years later, Drant issued a Latin verse paraphrase of Ecclesiastes (*In ... Ecclesiasten paraphrasis poetica*, 1572). His last publication, once more dedicated to Grindal, consists of a long Latin poem on the duties of a bishop, *Praesul*, followed by a collection of miscellaneous verse in Latin addressed to many of the key figures in Elizabethan England, *Sylva* (1576) (Binns 1990). In addition, Drant contributed several liminary poems to publications by other authors and wrote a number of poems in manuscript that are apparently now lost, including a translation of the first five books of Homer's *Iliad*.

Drant's experiments with Latin verse, as well as his association with St John's College, Cambridge, the centre of the quantitative movement in Tudor England, may have led him to consider the possibility of writing quantitative verse in English. He discussed his ideas with Philip Sidney, and Edmund Spenser refers to a set of rules for writing English poetry in classical metres by Drant (now lost) in a letter to Gabriel Harvey of 1580 and chided Harvey for breaking Drant's rules a year earlier. While the experiment with quantitative verse was eventually abandoned by Spenser and other English authors, it left its mark on the development of poetry in the period, and represent another facet of Drant's impact on the literary culture of Elizabethan England.

SEE ALSO: Harvey, Gabriel; Sidney, Philip; Spenser, Edmund

REFERENCES AND SUGGESTED READINGS

Binns, J. W. (1990) *Intellectual culture in Elizabethan and Jacobean England: the Latin writings of the age.* Francis Cairns, Leeds.

Burrow, Colin (1993) Horace at home and abroad: Wyatt and sixteenth-century Horatianism. In: Martindale, Charles & Hopkins, David (eds) *Horace made new: Horatian influences on British writing from the Renaissance to the twentieth century.* Cambridge University Press, Cambridge, pp. 27–49.

Lathrop, Henry Burrowes (1933) *Translations from the classics into English from Caxton to Chapman 1477–1620.* University of Wisconsin Press, Madison.

Lewis, C. S. (1954) *English literature in the sixteenth century, excluding drama.* Clarendon Press, Oxford.

McConchie, R. W. (2004) Drant, Thomas. In: *Oxford dictionary of national biography.* Oxford University Press, Oxford.

Mears, Natalie (2005) *Queenship and political discourse in the Elizabethan realms.* Cambridge University Press, Cambridge.

Medine, Peter E. (ed.) (1972) *Horace his arte of poetrie, pistles, and satyrs Englished (1567) by Thomas Drant.* Scholars' Facsimiles & Reprints, Delmar.

Mukherjee, Neel (2000) Thomas Drant's rewriting of Horace. *Studies in English Literature, 1500–1900* 40, 1–20.

Shrank, Cathy, Pincombe, Mike, Bryson, Alan, & Schurink, Fred (2009) *The origins of early modern literature: recovering mid-Tudor writing for a modern readership.* www.hrionline.ac.uk/origins

Wheeler, Angela J. (1992) *English verse satire from Donne to Dryden: imitation of classical models.* Winter, Heidelberg.

Drayton, Michael

PHILIP SCHWYZER

Though the poet and dramatist Michael Drayton (1563–1631) lived into the reign of Charles I and produced his most significant work under King James, he remains inextricably associated with the values and preoccupations of the Elizabethan era. Even in his lifetime, both his contemporaries and Drayton himself were inclined to regard him as a throwback to an earlier and more high-minded era. Yet his sober morality can be understood, at least in part, as a mannered poetic pose, and this quintessential Elizabethan was a keen observer and satirist of early Stuart politics and social values.

Drayton was born within a year and a few miles of William Shakespeare, in the village of Hartshill, Warwickshire, in 1563. Like Shakespeare, Drayton made his way to London in his mid-twenties to seek a literary career as both poet and playwright. Yet unlike his close contemporary, who seems to have observed a sharp division between the literary and dramatic world of the capital and the domestic sphere of Stratford-upon-Avon, Drayton remained deeply attached to the region of his birth, finding both his poetic inspiration and his most significant patrons there. Indeed, he would seem rather more deserving than Shakespeare of the title of 'bard of Avon': Drayton modelled his ideal of the laureate poet in large part on the semi-mythic figure of the Welsh bard, and in his greatest poem, *Poly-olbion* (1612), he celebrates the river Avon, tracing its course through Warwickshire and allowing it to sing in praise of the regional hero Guy of Warwick.

The son of either a tanner (Newdigate 1961) or a butcher (according to John Aubrey), the young Drayton appears to have found employment as a servant in the household of Thomas Goodyer, younger brother of Sir Henry Goodyer. A reference in a late work to his having spent his youth as a 'proper goodly page' almost certainly exaggerates his status at this time within the Goodyer household. Yet Drayton maintained a lifelong connection with this important Warwickshire family, and would eventually identify Sir Henry's daughter, Anne Goodyer, as his Petrarchan mistress 'Idea'. Although some biographers have woven tales of his unrequited love for Anne, he was also on good terms with her husband, Sir Henry Rainsford, to whom he dedicated a moving and accomplished elegy on his death in 1622.

In the 1590s Drayton produced a remarkable and varied series of works in many of the key late-Elizabethan poetic genres. His first printed work was *The harmonie of the church* (1591), a series of paraphrases of biblical passages in sundry poetic styles and metres. In the epistle to the reader Drayton takes pains to emphasize that he is not merely seeking to display his virtuosity or wit, demonstrating an anxiety about the purpose of poetry that would resurface throughout his career. His next work was *Idea: the shepheards garland* (1593), a collection of pastoral eclogues in the style of Edmund Spenser's *Shepheardes calender*, with Drayton's pastoral persona going by the name of Rowland. No less than Spenser, Drayton was clearly drawn to pastoral as marking, in classical tradition, the first step in a poetic career. From the outset, it would seem, he harboured laureate ambitions. Nor did his sense of poetic destiny abandon him in later years; the frontispiece to the 1619 edition of his *Works* shows him crowned with a wreath of laurel.

In 1594 Drayton produced the first version of his sonnet sequence *Ideas mirrour: amours in quatorzains*. There is no indication that these sonnets were dedicated to Anne Goodyer or any other real individual at this stage, though the last sonnet features what seems to be an anagrammatized reference to Mary Sidney Herbert, countess of Pembroke. Drayton repeatedly reworked and drastically altered both the tone and the content of the *Idea* sequence throughout his career, instilling many of the poems with a playful self-consciousness. In an introductory sonnet first printed in 1605 he insists that his lyrics are not the fruit of passion, but only of his constantly shifting mood and interests: 'My active Muse is of the worlds right straine,/That cannot long one fashion entertaine.' Later, in 1619, he revised these lines to refer not to the world's but to 'the English strain'. Ironically, the interest in defining Englishness demonstrated here and elsewhere in his sonnets (one poem meditates on the bounds of the English language, whilst another enumerates English rivers in a manner prefiguring *Poly-olbion*) is one aspect of Drayton's poetic character that remained consistent throughout his career.

Another group of poems first produced in the mid-1590s and reworked several times in ensuing decades were a set of complaints or 'tragedies' in the popular mode of the *Mirrour for magistrates* (1559). Among the tragic figures from the medieval English past resurrected by Drayton's pen were *Peirs* [Piers] *Gaveston*

(1593), *Matilda* (1594), and *Robert duke of Normandy* (1596). The complaint of Gaveston has attracted critical attention for its depiction of Gaveston's homosexual relationship with Edward II. Drayton, who apparently never married, has been seen as sympathetic in his depiction of love between men, though he subsequently whittled away much of the poem's erotic content, perhaps to avoid being seen to reflect scandal on the Jacobean court (Hammond 2002). Like his sonnets, Drayton's exercises in the complaint genre convey a deep awareness of and preoccupation with his literary predecessors and competitors. Thus, his Matilda enumerates the many female victims of jealousy who have previously been the subject of verse complaints, including Thomas Churchyard's Jane Shore, Thomas Lodge's Elstred, Samuel Daniel's Rosamund, and Shakespeare's Lucrece.

If Drayton began his poetic career with the ambition of excelling, or at least making a name for himself, in every established genre, the exercise of writing the complaints seems to have awakened in him a deep fascination with the English past which would come to underlie all of his most important subsequent productions. It was not long before he made his first stab at a national epic. *Mortimeriados* (1596) recounts the civil wars that beset the reign of Edward II, conflicts which had been the subject of Christopher Marlowe's *Edward II* earlier in the decade and indeed of Drayton's tragedy of Gaveston. This poem was heavily revised in 1603 as *The barrons wars*; here the seven-line stanza of *Mortimeriados* gives way to one of eight lines, which Drayton considered more appropriate to his sombre subject.

Drayton's crowning success in the 1590s was *Englands heroicall epistles* (1597), a collection of versified letters exchanged between famous pairs of men and women from English history. Individually dedicated to a range of patrons, the exchanges include letters between Rosamund and Henry II, King John and Matilda, Owen Tudor and Catherine of France, and Lady Jane Grey and Guildford Dudley. Unlike most of Drayton's prior productions, these were not modelled on the successful works of his contemporaries, but on the classical example of Ovid's *Heroides*. His most popular work during his own lifetime, *Englands heroicall epistles* was reissued in 1598, 1599, 1600, and 1602, and thereafter in sundry editions of Drayton's *Poems*. The inclusion of 'Notes from the chronicle history' after each epistle marks the first appearance of the quasi-scholarly apparatus which would become increasingly prominent in later poems, most notably in John Selden's 'Illustrations' for *Poly-olbion*.

Drayton was also remarkably active as a collaborative playwright in the later 1590s. Philip Henslowe's diary associates him with more than 20 plays written for the Admiral's Men, usually sharing authorship with Thomas Dekker, Henry Chettle, and/or Anthony Munday. As in the verse he produced in this period, Drayton was strongly though not exclusively drawn to subjects from English history. He had a hand in lost plays on Richard Cordelion, Owen Tudor, and Cardinal Wolsey, as well as *The first part of Sir John Oldcastle* (1600), the only one of these collaborative works to be printed and to survive. Drayton's career as a playwright seems to have been comparatively brief; as the vogue for history plays came to an end around the dawn of the new century, Drayton turned away from the stage. In 1607–9 he was a leading investor in the short-lived playing company the Children of the King's Revels, but he does not appear to have had a hand in any of the plays known to have been in their repertoire. In later years he never troubled himself to revise, preserve, or print any of his dramatic works, marking a great contrast with his attitude to his poetry.

Like so many of his literary contemporaries, Drayton made a conspicuous effort to welcome and attract the attention of James I upon his accession to the throne, producing *To the majestie of King James: a gratulatorie poem* (1603) and a subsequent paean celebrating the king's entry into London. *Moyses in a map of his miracles* (1604) has also been seen as an attempt to appeal to the new ruler's interest in divinity. Drayton was chided for his prematurity in welcoming James by Henry Chettle in *Englands mourning garment* (1603), who advised him that "twas a fault to have thy Verses seene / Praising the King, ere they had mournd the Queen'. There is no evidence that James himself was offended by this faux pas, but he certainly made no effort to acknowledge or to reward Drayton for his pains. Drayton in turn soon abandoned hope of royal patronage, and would increasingly set himself against the cultural and political mores of the Stuart court, defiantly upholding the poetic and personal values associated with the reign of the late queen. If he did not mourn Elizabeth's passing in 1603, he more than made up for this omission in subsequent years and decades.

Drayton's longest and most important poem, *Poly-olbion*, belongs to the Jacobean era, though it had its inception in the reign of Elizabeth. As early as 1598, Francis Meres had reported that 'Michael Drayton is now penning in English verse a Poem called *Polyolbion* Geographical and Hydrographicall of all the forests, woods, mountains, fountaines, rivers, lakes, flouds, bathes, and springs that be in England'. This is a fairly accurate summation of Drayton's aims, but for the fact that *Poly-olbion*, the first instalment of which finally emerged in 1612, is as much an historical work as a geographical and hydrographical one. The poem's project is indeed not dissimilar to John Leland's quest earlier in the sixteenth century to encapsulate the history and topography of the nation in a single work. Drayton found the structuring principle that eluded Leland in the figure of the 'Muse'; the poem's central character, she glides serenely over the English and Welsh landscape, recording the songs and conversations of the nymphs and spirits of rivers, hills, and woods. The first edition of *Poly-olbion* is divided into 18 songs, in the course of which the Muse, entering Britain via the Channel Isles and the south-western peninsula, traverses southern England and some parts of the Midlands, as well as Wales.

Drayton's chief sources for the topographical information and associated traditions in *Poly-olbion* include William Camden's *Britannia*, Christopher Saxton's *Atlas*, Raphael Holinshed's *Chronicles* (including William Harrison's 'Description of England'), and Humphrey Llwyd's *Breviary of Britayne*. Among the charming features of the work as originally printed are the maps, based on Saxton's county maps, in which the landscape is populated by sundry nymphs and deities. The frontispiece of the first edition has also attracted critical attention; it features a female personification of Britain, reminiscent of Elizabeth, flanked by smaller figures of the male conquerors Brutus the Trojan, Julius Caesar, Hengist the Saxon, and William the Conqueror. The comparative smallness and marginality of the royal figures suggests a perspective in which the identity of the land itself is of more significance than its transitory rulers.

As Richard Helgerson (1992) has argued, the poem emerges from and crystallizes the tendency in Elizabethan chorography and antiquarianism to privilege the history of the land over that of the monarchy, and the regional and particular over the national and homogeneous. Drayton was undeniably attracted to a vision of Britain incorporating the nations of England, Scotland, and Wales in an ancient and unified identity – in this, at least, he was in harmony with James I, though comparatively few Jacobean subjects shared in this enthusiasm. Yet the idiosyncrasies of the regions and nations that composed Britain, and indeed the tensions between them, were at least as important to Drayton as the commonalities. In particular, he found himself profoundly drawn to the history and literary culture of Wales. The front matter to *Poly-olbion* includes a special dedication 'to my friends the Cambro-Britons', in which Drayton affirms his commitment to Llwyd's vision of Wales as extending as far as the Severn. The borders and rights of Wales become a matter of controversy in several of the early songs, including Song 4, where Wales and England vie over ownership of the island of Lundy, only to be informed (in Song 5) that the unification of Britain has obviated the question.

Recent readings of *Poly-olbion* have explored its treatment of the natural world and of the human impact on the landscape from an eco-critical perspective. Although it would be anachronistic to term Drayton an early modern environmentalist, his concern with the problem of deforestation, in particular, resonates with the ecological thinking of later eras. Laments over the wanton felling of ancient woods recur throughout the poem, notably in Songs 3 and 17. There is thus an unresolved tension in *Poly-olbion* between a vision of the land as standing apart from and above mere human history, and a vision of the land as appallingly vulnerable to the abuses of her short-sighted inhabitants.

Whereas in *Englands heroicall epistles* the poet had supplied his own annotations, Drayton employed his friend the legal scholar John Selden to supply the 'Illustrations' to the first part of *Poly-olbion*. This choice assuredly adds greatly to the volume's fascination, for Selden's attitude to the hoary traditions associated with British antiquity is diametrically opposed to Drayton's. The 'Illustrations' repeatedly undercut Drayton's appeals to mythic ancestry by attributing them to medieval superstition and mendacity. Yet the overall effect is surprisingly harmonious, making *Poly-olbion* a poly-vocal work wherein the poet and annotator find common ground in their deep engagement with the puzzling and contradictory traces of the British past.

Drayton issued a second part of *Poly-olbion* in 1622, though without further notes from Selden. The new instalment contained 12 more songs, covering the Midlands and north of England as far as Cumberland and the Scottish Borders. Drayton had apparently finished the work by 1619 if not earlier but, as he wrote to the Scottish poet William Drummond, he had been unable to come to agreement with the booksellers, terming them 'a company of base knaves, whom I both scorn and kick at'. Drayton hoped that Drummond might put him in touch with his publisher in Edinburgh, perhaps on the assumption that a Scottish stationer would be more welcoming of a poem with a British theme. It is not clear, however, whether Drayton still (or, indeed, ever) intended to write a further set of songs covering Scotland. The conclusion of the second part, announcing the completion of the poet's 'strange Herculean toyle', suggests otherwise.

Drayton's last years, following the apparent abandonment of the *Poly-olbion* project, saw the production of some of his most powerful and troubling verse, whilst demonstrating that his commitment to variety was undiminished. Whereas *The battaile of Agincourt* (1627) pursued the epic and nationalistic themes of *The barrons wars*, *Nimphidia, the court of fayrie* (published in the same volume) saw an escape into domains of pure fancy. Fairies and nymphs also populate the world of his last work, *The muses Elizium* (1630). Here Drayton figures himself as a Satyre, banished from Felicia (England) owing to deforestation and the contempt in which the modern generation holds the Muses (problems which, typically, the poet sees as closely linked – both springing from a failure to respect custom and the principle of sustainability). Drayton died in December 1631, having outlived almost all the major literary figures of his generation. In spite of his self-proclaimed estrangement from Caroline society, he received a notable funeral, attended by the gentlemen of the Inns of Court, and was buried in Westminster Abbey.

SEE ALSO: Chettle, Henry; Daniel, Samuel; Drummond, William; Harrison, William; Herbert, Mary (Sidney), countess of Pembroke; Llwyd, Humphrey; Lodge, Thomas; Meres, Francis; Saxton, Christopher; Selden, John; Shakespeare, William; Spenser, Edmund

REFERENCES AND SUGGESTED READINGS

Brink, Jean R. (1990) *Michael Drayton revisited.* Twayne, Boston.

Curran, John E., Jr (1998) The history never written: bards, druids, and the problem of antiquarianism in *Poly-olbion. Renaissance Quarterly* 51, 498–526.

Galbraith, David Ian (2000) *Architectonics of imitation in Spenser, Daniel, and Drayton.* University of Toronto Press, Toronto.

Hadfield, Andrew (2000) Spenser, Drayton, and the question of Britain. *Review of English Studies* 51, 582–599.

Hammond, Paul (2002) *Figuring sex between men from Shakespeare to Rochester*. Oxford University Press, Oxford.

Hardin, Richard (1973) *Michael Drayton and the passing of Elizabethan England*. University Press of Kansas, Lawrence.

Helgerson, Richard (1983) *Self-crowned laureates*. University of California Press, Berkeley.

Helgerson, Richard (1992) *Forms of nationhood: the Elizabethan writing of England*. University of Chicago Press, Chicago.

McEachern, Claire (1996) *The poetics of English nationhood, 1590–1612*. Cambridge University Press, Cambridge.

Newdigate, Bernard (1961) *Michael Drayton and his circle*. Blackwell, Oxford.

Prescott, Anne Lake (1991) Marginal discourse: Drayton's muse and Selden's 'Story'. *Studies in Philology* 88, 307–328.

Warley, Christopher (2005) *Sonnet sequences and social distinction in Renaissance England*. Cambridge University Press, Cambridge.

Drummond, William

MICHAEL R. G. SPILLER

William Drummond of Hawthornden (1585–1649), always given the title of his estate to distinguish him from other William Drummonds of his day, has a claim to be reckoned the greatest Scots lyric poet between William Dunbar at the beginning of the sixteenth century and Robert Burns at the end of the eighteenth. Like many of his contemporaries in the court and society of James VI and I, he was both well read in French and Italian literature, and a tolerable classicist; he did not strive to be original in lyric composition, but observed and used the stylistic features of late Petrarchist and early Mannerist rhetoric. But where others imitated, Drummond absorbed, from Horace, Francesco Petrarch, Pietro Bembo, Torquato Tasso, Giovanni Guarini, and Giambattista Marino, as well as from Philip Sidney, Samuel Daniel, and, it is suggested, Shakespeare, whose

sonnets he appears to have known. From these writers and others, he took the themes, the phrases, and the mannerisms that suited his own habitual preoccupations with mutability and eternity, and set them to more splendid, and sometimes subtler, melodies in verse than most of his contemporaries could manage. He can be pedantic and vain of his learning; he has not the fierce disruptive wit of John Donne, or the modest terse profundity of George Herbert, but though he never knew John Milton, whose politics he would have abhorred, when Drummond's melodious plangency works well, it is the younger Milton of whom he most often reminds us.

He was born in 1585 at Hawthornden Castle near Edinburgh, the eldest son of Sir John Drummond (1553–1610), who was a gentleman usher to James VI. He was well educated, graduating MA in 1605 from the College of Edinburgh, later to become Edinburgh University; he then went to Paris and Bourges to study law. After returning home in 1608 with nearly 400 books, not to any great extent of a legal nature, he visited London in 1610, allegedly meeting some of the poets of the city, including a number of Scots who had followed James VI south. He returned on the death of his father in August of that year, inheriting the Hawthornden house and estate. This enabled him to live the life of a quiet country laird, which with few absences he did for the rest of his life. He had the means and leisure to read extensively, his interests extending to Spanish literature, and seems to have rejected law for poetry, with a conscious embracing of the Horatian ideal of virtue achieved through knowing, as he said,

What sweet delight a quiet life affords,
And what is it to be of bondage free,
Farre from the madding worldlings hoarse discords.

If he remained without honours or court notice, he had the friendship of the leading poets of his day, including Ben Jonson, who visited him at Hawthornden in 1618. He was honoured by the city of Edinburgh, being made a burgess at a council banquet in 1626. Drummond had three illegitimate children by an unknown woman in the years 1625–28, of whom two survived to adulthood. In 1632 he married Elizabeth Logan (d.1679), by whom he had eight children, of whom three survived him: Elizabeth, Robert, and his heir William (d.1713). He died on 4 December 1649, from complications of the pyelonephritis that had plagued him for more than two decades.

His literary career divides into the poetic, before 1635, and the historical and political thereafter. His principal poetic works are his *Poems* of 1616, consisting mainly of sonnets, madrigals, and epigrams, and *Flowres of Sion* (1623, 2nd edn 1630) consisting almost entirely of religious and philosophical lyrics, together with his prose essay 'A cypresse grove', a meditation on death, foreshadowing Sir Thomas Browne's *Hydriotaphia* (1658). His monarchical loyalty led him to write and publish *Forth feasting: a panegyrick to the kings most excellent majestie* to celebrate James VI and I's visit to Scotland in 1617. Drummond also wrote pageants for Charles I's entry into Edinburgh in 1633, printed as *The entertainment of the high and mighty monarch Charles, king of Great Britaine, France and Ireland* (1633).

He wrote *A history of Scotland from the year 1423 until the year 1542*, which occupied him for about 10 years from 1633, and was posthumously published in 1655. Drummond was a monarchist, but was hostile to any compulsion of belief, whether from kings or from presbyteries, and he wrote a number of moderationist tracts, mostly privately circulated, from *Irene: a remonstrance for concord, amity and love amongst his majesty's subjects* (1638), recommending passive obedience to the king, through to *Skiamachia* (1643), a strongly anticlerical pamphlet. Through all the Scottish troubles he lived quietly and unpersecuted, but he did receive a letter thanking him for his loyalty from the marquis of Montrose, leader of the Royalist army, after the battle of Philiphaugh (1646).

Drummond has been well served by editors ever since Edward Phillips, Milton's nephew, published *Poems, by that most famous wit, William Drummond of Hawthornden*, in 1656. With the cooperation of Drummond's son William, John Sage and Thomas Ruddiman published the poems and much of Drummond's prose writings as *The works of William Drummond of Hawthornden* (1711). Following the bequest in 1782 of Drummond's surviving manuscripts (now in the National Library of Scotland) to the Scottish Society of Antiquaries, there were four editions of his poems in the nineteenth century, and from the Milton scholar David Masson in 1873 came the eminently readable *Drummond of Hawthornden: the story of his life and writings*. In 1913 L. E. Kastner published the two-volume edition which all students of Drummond now use, *The poetical works of William Drummond of Hawthornden, with 'A cypresse grove'*. A parallel piece of meticulous scholarship was based on Drummond's own gift in 1626 of a substantial part of his Hawthornden library to what was to become the University of Edinburgh: R. H. MacDonald's *The library of Drummond of Hawthornden* (1971). MacDonald followed this with a generous selection of Drummond's work, *William Drummond of Hawthornden: poems and prose* (1976), which has an admirable short critical introduction. Curiously, given the devotion of Drummond to European literature, there has been little interest from scholars beyond Scotland: French Rowe Fogle's very romantic *Critical study of William Drummond of Hawthornden* (1952) and Eloisa Paganelli's modest but erudite *La poesia di Drummond of Hawthornden* (1972) stand almost alone. The best account of the European side of Drummond is R. D. S. Jack's section on his borrowings in *The Italian influence on Scottish literature* (1972). A serviceable account of Drummond's life and the available source material is by M. R. G. Spiller in the *Oxford dictionary of national biography* (2004), and there is a critical assessment by the same author in the first volume of *The history of Scottish literature*, edited by R. D. S. Jack, *Origins to 1660* (Spiller 1987).

Kastner's thoroughness bequeathed a critical problem to the twentieth century: in the annotations to the poems in his edition, he traced wherever he could the source material in European literature that Drummond had used, revealing the extent of Drummond's imitations. Experienced Renaissance scholars, aware of the lingering presence of the Romantic ideal of passionate sincerity in lyric verse, have shown themselves conscious of the need to explain how Drummond's poems should be read (MacDonald 1971; Jack 1972; Spiller 1987). There is certainly a challenge to our conventional notions of lyric verse in the discovery that such a splendid and vibrant sonnet as 'Now while the night her sable vaile doth spread', ending with the moving couplet, "I wake, muse, weepe, and who my heart hath slaine/See still before me to augment my paine', is adapted from a sonnet by Drummond's uncle, William Fowler, who adapted his from a sonnet by Petrarch, who was himself indebted to a poem by Statius. The realization that Drummond so often echoed the voices of others, while it would not in the least have perturbed his contemporaries, may have something to do with his relative underrepresentation in modern anthologies.

SEE ALSO: James VI and I; Jonson, Ben

REFERENCES AND SUGGESTED READINGS

Fogle, French Rowe (1952) *Critical study of William Drummond of Hawthornden*. King's Crown Press, New York.

Jack, R. D. S. (1972) *The Italian influence on Scottish literature*. Edinburgh University Press, Edinburgh.

Jack, R. D. S. (ed.) (1987) *The history of Scottish literature*, vol. 1: *Origins to 1660*. Aberdeen University Press, Aberdeen.

Kastner, L. E. (ed.) (1913) *The poetical works of William Drummond of Hawthornden, with 'A cypresse grove'*. Manchester University Press, Manchester.

MacDonald, R. H. (1971) *The library of Drummond of Hawthornden*. Edinburgh University Press, Edinburgh.

MacDonald, R. H. (ed.) (1976) *William Drummond of Hawthornden: poems and prose*. Edinburgh University Press, Edinburgh.

Masson, David (1873) *Drummond of Hawthornden: the story of his life and writings*. Advocates' Library, Edinburgh.

Paganelli, Eloisa (1972) *La poesia di Drummond of Hawthornden*. Adriatica, Bari.

Phillips, Edward (ed.) (1656) *Poems, by that most famous wit, William Drummond of Hawthornden*. William Rands, London.

Ruddiman, Thomas & Sage, John (eds) (1711) *The works of William Drummond of Hawthornden*. Maitland Club.

Spiller, M. R. G. (1987) Poetry after the Union. In: Jack, R. D. S. (ed.) *The History of Scottish Literature*, vol. 1: *Origins to 1660*. Aberdeen University Press, Aberdeen, pp. 141–162.

Spiller, M. R. G. (2004) Drummond, William. In: *Oxford dictionary of national biography*. Oxford University Press, Oxford.

Dryden, John

HENRY POWER

John Dryden (1631–1700) was a poet and translator whose most significant achievements were his translations from Greek and Latin poetry. He was a convert to Roman Catholicism, and a prominent supporter of the Stuart dynasty.

Dryden was brought up in Northamptonshire. From 1644, he attended Westminster School as a king's scholar, where he was taught by Richard Busby (who was also responsible for the early education of Robert Hooke, John Locke, and Christopher Wren). While still at Westminster he contributed an elegy to *Lachrymae musarum* (1650), a volume of elegies mourning the death of Henry, Lord Hastings; Dryden's contribution displays a broad range of classical reference and looks back to the metaphysical poets. In 1650 he moved to Trinity College, Cambridge, and took his degree in 1654. Thereafter, he seems to have entered the service of the Protectorate, probably securing a post through his cousin, Sir Gilbert Pickering, who was lord chamberlain in Cromwell's administration. When Cromwell died in 1658, Dryden walked in the procession (the official record tells us) alongside Andrew Marvell and John Milton, as one of the secretaries for the Latin and French tongues.

Dryden's first major poem was an elegy on Oliver Cromwell. His 'Heroique stanzas' (printed 1659), 'Consecrated to the Glorious Memory' of the lord protector, were intended for publication alongside poems by Andrew Marvell and Thomas Sprat. In the event, this projected volume did not appear, and William Wilson published Dryden's poem alongside Sprat's, with Edmund Waller's elegy replacing Marvell's, as *Three poems upon the death of his late highnesse Oliver lord protector of England, Scotland, and Ireland* (1659). Dryden's poem is highly complimentary towards Cromwell, stressing his desire for peace, and comparing him to a physician who has acted to end England's 'consumption', war: 'He fought to end our fighting, and essayed / To stanch the blood by breathing of the vein.' The 'breathing of the vein' was widely interpreted by later critics as referring to the regicide. When the poem was mischievously reprinted in 1681 (presumably by those who wished to highlight Dryden's radically altered political stance), the words were italicized, and a dagger placed in the margin.

On the Restoration of the monarchy, Dryden changed tack, producing *Astraea redux* (1660), a poem which celebrates the return of a golden age, in language and imagery recalling Virgil's fourth 'messianic' eclogue. Charles is hailed both as 'Prince of Peace' and as a second Augustus, and the institution of monarchy is praised. Dryden's support for the idea of kingship was unwavering after 1660, although some have suggested an ongoing sympathy with the republican cause (Haley 1997). Nevertheless, much of his work is informed by the experience of the Civil War and the fault-lines it left in English culture. His 1667 poem *Annus mirabilis, the year of wonders, 1666* looks at the events of that year – above all, the naval battles against the Dutch and the Great Fire of London – and praises Charles's clemency and

steadfastness in the face of cataclysm. Dryden also predicts the emergence of a stronger nation and capital from this disaster ('Methinks already from this chymic flame / I see a city of more precious mould'), and the poem closes with a triumphalist assertion of England's glorious future as a major trading power. The poem as a whole is remarkable for its lively use of metaphor (particularly striking is the anthropomorphizing account of the fire's progress through London), as well as for its constant classicizing. Like 'Heroique stanzas', it is written in quatrains of the sort used by William Davenant in *Gondibert* (1651). Doubtless because of his newly established loyalty, Dryden was appointed poet laureate in succession to Davenant in 1668. He was appointed historiographer royal two years later.

Dryden was a prolific dramatist, and for 20 years after the Restoration the theatre was his major source of income (he was a shareholder in the King's Company and from 1668 was contracted to provide them with three plays a year). He was also an intelligent theorist of drama. His essay *Of dramatick poesie* (1668) is dialogic in form, consisting of a discussion between four imaginary characters (based on his associates, and with Dryden himself represented as 'Neander'). These characters debate the merits and shortcomings of English, French, and classical drama, and of blank and rhymed verse. Dryden composed several highly successful comedies in the years following the Restoration, most notably *Marriage a-la-mode* (1671, printed 1673). He achieved his greatest theatrical success in the field of heroic drama – that is, plays in rhymed verse, addressing weighty subjects. The most notable examples are *Tyrranick love* (1669, printed 1670), *The conquest of Granada* (1670, printed 1672), and *Aureng-Zebe* (1675, printed 1676). He also adapted several plays by Shakespeare, whom he praised effusively in *Of dramatick poesie*. *The tempest* (1667, printed 1668) was written with Davenant. *All for love* (1677, printed 1678) was his reworking of *Antony and Cleopatra*, and his first venture into blank verse. *Troilus and Cressida* (1679) to some extent normalizes

Shakespeare's difficult plot. Perhaps his strangest dramatic work is *The state of innocence and fall of man*, his operatic adaptation of *Paradise lost*, for which he had to seek Milton's personal approval. The play was never staged, but was published in 1677 (three years after its composition) and frequently reprinted. Much of Dryden's drama articulates the same strongly pro-Stuart position as his public verse.

Troilus and Cressida was published by the bookseller Jacob Tonson, and this initiated a productive arrangement that would last for the rest of Dryden's life. In 1680 he published a version of Ovid's *Heroides*, by several hands, to which he himself contributed three translations. Tonson and Dryden also collaborated, over the next two decades, on four volumes of miscellanies, published in 1684, 1685, 1693, and 1694. Two further volumes were published in 1704 and 1709, after Dryden's death. These miscellanies were instrumental in stimulating and satisfying a public appetite for translations from the classics, and they contain many of Dryden's finest translations. *Sylvae* (1685) contains excerpts from *De rerum natura* (including his powerfully sympathetic rendering of Lucretius' mortalist argument 'Against the fear of death'), alongside selections from Virgil and Horace. Dryden was also an influential theorist of translation, articulating in its clearest form the famous tripartite division between metaphrase ('turning an author word by word, and line by line, from one language into another'), paraphrase ('translation with latitude'), and imitation ('where the translator [if now he has not lost that name] assumes the liberty not only to vary from the words and sense, but to forsake them as he sees occasion') (Preface to *Ovid's epistles*). His own clear preference was for paraphrase.

From the 1670s, Dryden established a reputation as a satirist. In 1676 Thomas Shadwell attacked him in the dedication to the printed version of his play *The virtuoso*. This was only the latest in a series of attacks, and Dryden responded with a satire on Shadwell, which (though it may only have been intended as a throwaway piece) has become one of his best-known poems. *Mac Flecknoe* (1676) constructs a conspicuously unimpressive literary ancestry for Shadwell (who regarded himself as a successor to Ben Jonson), making him the heir to the dunce poet Richard Flecknoe. The language of the poem draws on Milton and Virgil, and also makes precise allusions to the work of Flecknoe and Shadwell. It has been enormously influential; most significantly, the central premise of Alexander Pope's *Dunciad* (1728) is taken from the poem. *Mac Flecknoe* is one of the earliest 'mock heroic' poems in English, applying lofty epic diction to base subject matter. It circulated initially in manuscript. An unauthorized edition was published in 1682, and it was included in Tonson's *Miscellaneous poems* of 1684.

Dryden produced a satire of a different sort during the Exclusion Crisis. In the late 1670s the Whig opposition, under the leadership of Anthony Ashley Cooper, first earl of Shaftesbury, sought to exclude the Roman Catholic James, duke of York (Charles II's brother) from the line of succession, and to replace him with Charles's illegitimate son, James Scott, duke of Monmouth. Shaftesbury was charged with treason in the summer of 1681, and Dryden's poem, *Absalom and Achitophel*, which was published in November of that year, may have been intended to influence the outcome of his trial. It seems more likely that it was an attempt to sway public opinion more broadly. Many later critics have accepted Tonson's claim that the poem was written at the king's request. It is a biblical allegory (based on the story of Absalom's rebellion in the second book of Samuel), in which Charles II appears as the benevolent but over-sexed David (who 'after heaven's own heart, / His vigorous warmth did variously impart / To wives and slaves'), Shaftesbury as the sly Achitophel, and Monmouth as the well-loved but impressionable Absalom. The poem ends with a glance back to *Astraea redux*, and the promise of a second Restoration. A second part to *Absalom and Achitophel* appeared in 1682, largely written by Nahum Tate, but with Dryden contributing some passages (notably a renewed attack on Shadwell).

In the same year, he published *The medall*, a satire on Shaftesbury and his supporters, who had struck a medal to support his acquittal.

Dryden's approach to satire – his interest in its connection to lofty literary forms such as epic and didactic, as well as his belief that its ultimate aim 'is the amendment of vices by correction' (Preface to *Absalom and Achitophel*) – was informed by his deep knowledge of the Roman satirists. In 1692 Tonson published *The satires of Juvenal and Persius*, and Dryden himself contributed translations of five of Juvenal's 16 satires (1, 3, 6, 10, and 13), and was personally responsible for recruiting the other contributors. He also translated all six of Persius' poems, and wrote the 'Discourse concerning the original and progress of satire' with which the volume opens. Dryden's translations frequently update the contexts and settings of his models, and he does much to bring them into line with contemporary taste – or at least with his own. Persius' famously impenetrable style, which Dryden attributes partly to the Roman poet's 'close way of thinking', is made more readily accessible; Dryden's Persius offers a clear-headed, sane exposition of his Stoic philosophy. The moral, rather than the scurrilous, aspect of Juvenal's satire is stressed. Dryden does not, however, expunge the obscene passages in either satirist – perhaps indicating his faith in the concept of the satiric persona. (He had toned down the more explicit passages of Lucretius when translating from *De rerum natura*.) The 'Discourse' itself is a well-informed guide to the origins of satire, and the etymology of the term. Its structure is digressive, and Dryden reveals in passing his own frustrated ambitions to write a historical epic.

During the 1680s, Dryden also published two poems which explore his attitude to religious belief. In *Religio laici, or a laymans faith* (1682), he assesses the shortcomings of various religious positions, including Roman Catholicism, Deism, and nonconformist Protestantism, before eventually declaring in favour of the Anglican Church. By the time he wrote *The hind and the panther* (1687) his religious affiliations had changed, along with those of the

nation. In February 1685 the Roman Catholic James II acceded to the throne. At some point in the same year, Dryden converted to Roman Catholicism (John Evelyn records his having attended Mass in January 1686). In *The hind and the panther* he seeks to justify that conversion. It is an extended beast fable in three parts, in which the various forms of Christianity are represented as different animals. The Church of England is a panther, while the Roman Catholic Church is 'A milk-white Hind, immortal and unchanged', and the other denominations become apes, bears, boars, foxes, and wolves. The first part describes these various denominations, the second concentrates on doctrinal issues, and the third on the situation under James II. The poem ends with an embedded fable of the Buzzard and the Pigeons, told by the Hind, in which she stresses the dangers of trying to replace James with, for example, William of Orange.

Following the Williamite revolution of 1688, Dryden was deprived of the roles of poet laureate and historiographer royal. On this occasion there was no change of tack; he was steadfast in his Catholicism and (even if only implicitly) in his support for the Stuart house. It is hard not to see a trace of Dryden himself in the disconsolate figure of Umbricius who trudges away from Rome in his version of Juvenal's third satire: 'conducted on my way by none: / Like a dead member from the body rent; / Maimed and unuseful to the government'. Certainly, Dryden's situation in the last 12 years of his life should dispel any lingering suspicions that he was prepared to blow with the prevailing wind.

Dryden returned to the theatre after 1688, driven by financial necessity to write several new plays: the tragedy *Don Sebastian* (1689, printed 1690), the comedy *Amphitryon* (1690), which draws on versions of both Plautus and Moliere, and *Cleomenes: the Spartan heroe* (1692). His final play was *Love triumphant* (1694). He wrote the libretto for Henry Purcell's opera *King Arthur* (1691). He also, in this period, continued to write original poems. The best known of these is 'Alexander's feast' (1697), a poem on the power of music, often praised in the eighteenth century for its energy. Most of Dryden's time, though, was spent on translation – which also became his major source of income. The *Satires of Juvenal and Persius* appeared in 1692, and 1693 saw the appearance of *Examen poeticum* – the third Tonson miscellany – to which Dryden contributed several translations from Ovid's *Metamorphoses* (the whole of book I, and selections from books IX and XIII). He is highly critical of Ovid in his preface, noting his frequent 'boyisms' and violations of decorum – but his exuberant mode of translation suggests that he may have valued these qualities more than he acknowledges.

In 1694 Dryden signed a contract with Tonson to translate the complete *Works of Virgil*. He devoted the next three years to this task, and the resulting work, published by subscription in 1697, became the standard English Virgil for the next century. Dryden's Virgil is not typical of his practice as a translator. Previously, he had translated only fragments of authors that reflected his own interests and enthusiasms. At the same time, it is the culmination both of his own poetic career and of a half-century of poetic activity: a translation of the most revered Roman poet into fluent and balanced heroic couplets. In his preface, Dryden acknowledges his debt to (among others) Abraham Cowley, John Denham, Milton, Edmund Spenser, and Edmund Waller. The *Works of Virgil* is a highly political document: an imperialist text translated by a disenfranchised poet. There is an emphasis, in the *Aeneid*, on Aeneas' mission to restore an outcast dynasty. He is the man, we learn in the proem, who 'His banish'd gods restor'd to rites divine, / And settled sure succession in his line'. The lines can hardly fail to evoke the exiled Roman Catholic Stuarts. Dryden's postscript stresses the difference between his circumstances and those of Virgil: 'What *Virgil* wrote in the vigour of his Age, in Plenty and at Ease, I have undertaken to Translate in my Declining Years: struggling with Wants, oppress'd with Sickness, curb'd in my Genius,

lyable to be misconstrued in all I write.' Although Dryden refused to dedicate the *Works of Virgil* to William III, as Tonson asked, Tonson (an ardent Whig) still managed to pay the king a compliment, surreptitiously adapting the illustrations for the *Aeneid* so that the hero shared William's hooked nose.

Dryden's last major work was *Fables ancient and modern* (1700), an anthology consisting largely of translations from Homer, Ovid, Geoffrey Chaucer, and Boccaccio. His translation of the first book of the *Iliad* is lively and idiosyncratic, mixing moments of comedy with high drama. He announces in the preface that he finds Homer 'more suitable to my temper' than Virgil, contrasting Homer's fire and impetuosity with Virgil's care and propriety. He also announces his intention to translate the *Iliad* in its entirety. His translations of Chaucer are free, coming closer to Dryden's own category of Imitation than his more usual Paraphrase; he frequently omits material, and introduces ideas and images of his own. He writes in his preface to the *Fables* that he holds Chaucer 'in the same veneration as the Grecians held Homer, or the Romans Virgil'. He died two months after the publication of the *Fables*, and was buried in Chaucer's grave in Westminster Abbey.

Dryden's reputation was high during the eighteenth century. Samuel Johnson stressed the advances he made in metre (especially the refinement of the heroic couplet) and the variety of his work. He praised him for demonstrating 'the true bounds of a translator's liberty', adding that 'What was said of Rome, adorned by Augustus, may be applied by an easy metaphor to English Poetry adorned by Dryden, ... he found it brick, and he left it marble.' From the late eighteenth century, Dryden's reputation went into steep decline – partly, no doubt, because of a mistaken view of his work as straightforwardly 'Augustan'. The past few decades have seen a revival of interest in his work, particularly among scholars interested in the theory and practice of translation, and in the reception of classical literature.

SEE ALSO: Cowley, Abraham; Davenant, William; Denham, John; Evelyn, John; Marvell, Andrew; Milton, John; Shakespeare, William; Spenser, Edmund; Waller, Edmund

REFERENCES AND SUGGESTED READINGS

D'Addario, Christopher (2004) Dryden and the historiography of exile: Milton and Virgil in Dryden's late period. *Huntington Library Quarterly* 67(4), 553–572.

Davis, Paul (2007) *Translation and the poet's life: the ethics of translating in English culture, 1646–1726.* Clarendon Press, Oxford.

Haley, D. B. (1997) *Dryden and the problem of freedom.* Yale University Press, New Haven.

Hammond, Paul (2000) *John Dryden and the traces of classical Rome.* Clarendon Press, Oxford.

Hammond, Paul & Hopkins, David (eds) (2000) *John Dryden: tercentenary essays.* Clarendon Press, Oxford.

Harth, Philip (1993) *Pen for a party: Dryden's Tory propaganda in its contexts.* Princeton University Press, Princeton.

Hopkins, David (1986) *John Dryden.* Cambridge University Press, Cambridge.

Sowerby, R. (2006) *The Augustan art of poetry: Augustan translations of the classics.* Clarendon Press, Oxford.

Winn, James A. (1987) *John Dryden and his world.* Yale University Press, New Haven.

Zwicker, Steven N. (1993) *Dryden's political poetry: the arts of disguise.* Princeton University Press, Princeton.

Zwicker, Steven N. (1996) The paradoxes of tender conscience. *ELH* 63(4), 851–869.

Zwicker, Steven N. (ed.) (2004) *The Cambridge companion to John Dryden.* Cambridge University Press, Cambridge.

Dunbar, William

ELIZABETH ELLIOTT

A key figure in the canon of early Scottish literature, William Dunbar (c.1460–1513/30) is remarkable for his rhetorical virtuosity, and for the rich generic diversity of his poetic corpus. Dunbar locates himself within a vernacular literary tradition stemming from Chaucer, and his work had a significant impact on the poetry of sixteenth-century Scotland. Identified as a graduate of St Andrews University, Dunbar was probably born around 1460; by 1504, he had become a priest. Between 1500 and 1513, he was a salaried member of King James IV's household, and his poetic career is bound up with the culture of the Scottish court. Accounts from the period following the death of James IV at the battle of Flodden in September 1513 are incomplete, but Dunbar's absence from the records after May of that year suggests that he was dead long before his talent was memorialized by his poetic successor David Lindsay, in 1530.

Dunbar's poetry reflects a keen sense of authorial self-consciousness. Protesting against the misappropriation of his name and maltreatment of his verses in 'Schir, I complane off iniuris', he elsewhere defines himself as a 'makar', a term that emphasizes the craftsmanship of poetry. Some indication of his early reputation is provided by the six poems represented amongst the few surviving 'Chepman and Myllar prints' (c.1508), early products of Scotland's first press, set up by Walter Chepman and Andrew Myllar. Dunbar's poetic self-construction is informed by a distinctive conception of national tradition, articulated in poems such as 'I that in heill wes and gladnes'. In this powerful meditation on death, he depicts himself as part of a line of Scottish poets, whose predecessors are Chaucer, John Gower, and John Lydgate. Dunbar's sense of a poetic heritage that is at once indebted to and separate from English writing corresponds to the contemporary designation of the language of Lowland Scotland as 'Inglis'. For Dunbar, the trio of English poets had facilitated vernacular writing: in *The goldyn targe*, he praises them as superlative illuminators of the language of Britain, an 'ile' previously 'bare and desolate / Off rethorike or lusty fresch endyte'. The traditional label applied to Dunbar, 'Scottish Chaucerian', aptly reflects this, though its application is controversial because it suggests passive imitation.

Dunbar's work also exposes the tensions arising from intercultural contact within Scotland. Many of the poetic insults he trades with Walter Kennedy in *The flyting of Dunbar and Kennedy* (1508) express antagonism towards the Gaelic culture associated with the Highlands, and to Gaelic poetry. He presents a cruelly satirical response to ethnic difference in 'Lang heff I maed of ladyes quhytt', a parodic blazon of a black woman that evokes the Tournaments of the Black Lady held at James's court in 1507 and 1508. Yet Dunbar's sardonic wit was also directed against other targets, including himself, and he voices trenchant criticisms of contemporary abuses of power and the neglect of social responsibilities in works that reflect the role of the poet as moral adviser.

Dunbar's involvement in court life finds expression in pieces that survive in manuscript addressing public occasions: he celebrates the marriage of James IV and Margaret Tudor (1503) in a dream-vision. Titled 'The thrissill and the rois' by Dunbar's eighteenth-century editor, Allan Ramsay, the poem makes innovative use of the thistle, recently adopted as a Stewart emblem, to represent the king. James also appears in the more traditional heraldic guises of lion and eagle, while his bride takes the form of a Tudor rose. Epithalamium is combined with advice to princes, as the poem's celebration of order encompasses instruction in morality and good governance. Other occasional poems with a public function include an elegy composed in honour of the diplomat Bernard Stewart, who visited Scotland in 1508, and a eulogy lamenting his death the same year. Yet Dunbar also composed lyric poems inspired by more everyday events: a dance in the queen's chamber, a migraine, a difference of opinion with another courtier. His petitionary verses in particular have been singled out as reflecting the individualism fostered by the competitive nature of the courtier's life, and their introspective quality cultivates the impression of a personal voice.

In Dunbar's corpus, poems of religious devotion and courtly allegories of love, such as the aureate *Goldyn targe* (printed c.1508), rub shoulders with bawdy poems appealing to a more popular audience. Dunbar's longest poem, *The tretis of the tua mariit wemen and the wedo* (printed c.1507?) synthesizes refined and lewd elements, drawing on the *chanson d'aventure* to frame a narrative informed by the medieval tradition of anti-feminist writing. Observed by the hidden narrator, three beautiful, and apparently courtly, women talk about their experience of marriage in the most ribald terms. In a parodic version of religious teaching, the wives learn from the widow how best to fool the eyes of the world and do as they please.

Although popular in the sixteenth century, Dunbar's poetry was subsequently neglected until the publication of the poet Allan Ramsay's anthology *The evergreen* in 1724. Ramsay's edition appropriated Dunbar's poetry in the service of a vernacular revival, positioning the poet's 'Inglis' as the historic representative of a distinctive Scots voice that stood in contrast to the anglicized literature of the eighteenth century. For Hugh MacDiarmid in the early twentieth century, Dunbar's linguistic virtuosity functioned as inspiration for a similar revival, in the movement termed the 'Scottish Renaissance'.

SEE ALSO: Lindsay, David

REFERENCES AND SUGGESTED READINGS

Bawcutt, Priscilla (1992) *Dunbar the makar*. Clarendon Press, Oxford.
Bawcutt, Priscilla (ed.) (1998) *The poems of William Dunbar*. 2 vols. Association for Scottish Literary Studies, Glasgow.
Burrow, John (2006) William Dunbar. In: Bawcutt, Priscilla & Hadley Williams, Janet (eds) *A companion to medieval Scottish poetry*. D. S. Brewer, Cambridge, pp. 133–148.
Mapstone, Sally (ed.) (2001) *William Dunbar, 'the nobill poyet': essays in honour of Priscilla Bawcutt*. Tuckwell, East Linton.
Mapstone, Sally (ed.) (2008) *The chepman and myllar prints*. Digitized facsimiles with introduction,

headnotes and transcription [DVD]. Scottish Text Society / National Library of Scotland, Edinburgh.

Dury, John

AYESHA MUKHERJEE

The son of an exiled Church of Scotland minister, John Dury (or Durie) (1596–1680) was a reformer and preacher whose itinerant career was spent advocating educational reform and religious tolerance. Born in Edinburgh, he grew up in the Netherlands where he enrolled at Leiden University in 1611. After attending the French Huguenot academy in Sedan in 1615 and working as a tutor from 1621 to 1623, he became a preacher for the Walloon Reformed church in Cologne. However, Dury resigned in 1626 following a crisis of faith. He next became secretary to James Spens, English ambassador to Sweden. It was as minister to Scottish and English settlers connected with the English Company of Merchant Adventurers in Elbing, Poland, that Dury met his first patron, Thomas Roe, and established connections with Samuel Hartlib and Johannes Amos Comenius, whose vision of reform he shared. In theological terms, Dury's work laid consistent emphasis on practical or ethical (rather than scholastic or doctrinal) approaches to Christianity. He advocated tolerance based on the establishment of universally accepted 'fundamental' doctrines.

While Dury maintained and expanded his wider European network, he also tried to convince English divines to support his irenic ideals. In the early 1630s, he started to concentrate on negotiations for the union of Lutheran and Calvinist churches in Germany and attempted to gain the support of leaders from other parts of Europe. In England, his proposals were encouraged by Calvinist figures such as Joseph Hall and John Davenant, but his efforts to convince William Laud were unsuccessful. Dury continued his conferences with leaders of church and state in England, Scotland, Holland, Denmark, and Germany throughout the 1630s. During this time, he lived mainly on donations from Roe and Hartlib. The 1640s constituted a particularly active phase in his life when he moved to England and worked closely with Hartlib and Comenius. As Dury's 1641 pamphlets *A summary discourse concerning the work of peace ecclesiasticall* and *A memoriall concerning peace ecclesiasticall* demonstrate, before the outbreak of the Civil Wars, he was engaged in peacemaking efforts, trying to persuade Laud, Charles I, and the Puritans to settle their differences and to support pan-continental Protestantism. Dury was appointed tutor to Charles I's younger children (James, Elizabeth, and Henry) from 1647 to 1649; after Charles's death, however, he supported the Commonwealth and the Protectorate, urging all Englishmen to take the Oath of Allegiance to the Commonwealth in *Considerations concerning the present engagement* (1649) on the grounds that the very existence of the new republican state demonstrated it to be the will of divine providence. In 1650 he translated John Milton's *Eikonoklastes* (1649) into French. He provided rhetorical support to the new government, pleading for religious settlement and exhorting Cromwell to take the lead in this matter. In 1659 Cromwell sent Dury to the Continent to further on his behalf the institution of worldwide Protestant cooperation, a mission aborted by Cromwell's death.

A fascinating aspect of Dury's corpus is the opportunity it affords for reconstructing his travels, negotiations, and networks. There are more than 80 printed works which range from brief pamphlets to long volumes. His activities are referred to in the writings of many of his contemporaries. These offer evidence of his constant travel throughout Protestant Europe and hold a wealth of information regarding the relationships between churches and the diplomatic negotiations between states. As Dury's own medium of negotiation was primarily through personal conferences and communications with key individuals or groups, he meticulously recorded these interactions. As his biographers have pointed out, this gives a full picture of his network which included rulers and statesmen, leading churchmen, and literary figures and philosophers. This variety in his network of correspondents, each with their own field of concerns, is reflected in Dury's varied irenic strategies and rhetorical ploys for persuasion.

Structurally, Dury felt that Christian unity could be achieved by the establishment of a series of councils designed to adjust local and national differences, culminating in a universal conference on faith, order, and duty. He thought Covenant theology a useful way of forming this consensus. This belief was allied to his dislike of Protestant scholasticism and debates over confessional differences. Instead, Dury was interested to establish a theological discipline of 'practical divinity' (deriving in part from German pietism and practical mysticism) which laid emphasis on Christianity as a way of life rather than 'an attitude of intellectual assent' (Batten 1944). Dury's ideas of educational reform were thus closely linked to his irenic projects. Following Comenius, he believed in educational reform as a tool for achieving Christian unity. He was prolific on this topic and his strategies for reforming education included the establishment of a college of Jewish studies to encourage the conversion of Jews and Protestant unity in Europe. Powerful expositions of his educational ideas are found in *The reformed school* (1649) and *The reformed librarie-keeper* (1650). Allied with this was the lobbying for state-sponsored Baconian reform of learning which he pursued alongside Hartlib, and which finds expression in works such as Considerations tending to the happy accomplishment of *Englands reformation* (1647) and *A seasonable discourse* (1649).

Dury rapidly lost favour after the Restoration. Until his death in 1680 he continued negotiations abroad without official support, and was able to arouse interest among the churches of Holland, Switzerland, and Germany. His later writings, such as *Brevis disquisitio de articulis veri Christianismi* (1672), are characterized by a more pietist, introspective tone, and they enlarged the scope of his irenicism to argue for the unity of Protestants and Roman Catholics. Critical accounts of Dury have cast him in different, often opposite, ways – as a genuine advocate of

Christian unity (Batten 1944) and Jewish 'redemption' (Wilensky 1960), as narrow-minded and intolerant (Roth 1934), or as something of an opportunist who tried to balance his doctrine of unity and to stay afloat in a rapidly altering religious and political climate (Milton 1994; Young 1998).

SEE ALSO: Bacon, Francis; Hall, Joseph; Hartlib, Samuel; Milton, John

REFERENCES AND SUGGESTED READINGS

Batten, J. M. (1944) *John Dury, advocate of Christian reunion.* University of Chicago Press, Chicago.

Hartlib Papers Project (2002) *The Hartlib papers,* 2nd edn. CD-ROM. University of Sheffield, Sheffield.

Mandelbrote, Scott (1997) John Dury and the practice of irenicism. In: Aston, Nigel (ed.) *Religious change in Europe 1650–1914.* Clarendon Press, Oxford, pp. 41–58.

Milton, Anthony (1994) 'The unchanged peacemaker'? John Dury and the politics of irenicism in England, 1628–1643. In: Greengrass, Mark, Leslie, Michael, & Raylor, Timothy (eds) *Samuel Hartlib and universal reformation: studies in intellectual communication.* Cambridge University Press, Cambridge, pp. 95–117.

Rae, T. H. (1998) *John Dury and the royal road to piety.* Peter Lang, Frankfurt.

Roth, Cecil (1934) *A life of Menasseh ben Israel.* Jewish Publication Society of America, Philadelphia.

Webster, Charles (1970) *Samuel Hartlib and the advancement of learning.* Cambridge University Press, Cambridge.

Wilensky, M. L. (1960) Thomas Barlow's and John Dury's attitude towards the readmission of the Jews to England [part 2]. *Jewish Quarterly Review* 50(1), 256–268.

Young, John T. (1998) *Faith, alchemy and natural philosophy: Johann Moriaen, reformed intelligencer, and the Hartlib Circle.* Ashgate, Aldershot.

Dyer, Edward

ELIZABETH HODGSON

Edward Dyer (1543–1607) was among the first of the Elizabethan courtly poets, with an influence in courtly literary circles, especially on Philip Sidney and the Sidney coterie, far beyond his modest manuscript *oeuvre*. His amorous laments circulated and were imitated in private collections and then anthologies during Elizabeth's reign. Dyer's development of a more fictionalized and yet immediate poetic persona helped reinvent the new Elizabethan Petrarchan and elegiac modes so characteristic of Sidney, Walter Ralegh, Edmund Spenser, William Shakespeare, and others.

Edward Dyer was born in 1543 in Somerset; his father, Thomas Dyer, had become landed gentry courtesy of minor service to the court of Henry VIII. Dyer may have studied at Oxford, though he does not appear to have taken a degree. He first appeared as a visible member of Elizabeth I's court in the 1560s. Through his client relationships with, first, Robert Dudley, earl of Leicester, and then later both Robert Devereux, second earl of Essex, and William Cecil, Lord Burleigh, as well as in his own right, Dyer established a presence in court which lasted until the end of Elizabeth's reign. He was granted stewardship of the queen's royal Oxfordshire manor of Woodstock, was awarded monopolies for tanning and for locating concealed crown lands, functioned as Elizabeth's envoy to the Low Countries and Bohemia in the 1580s, and was knighted in 1596. He never married, and died at Winchester House, his estate on London's South Bank, bankrupt, in 1606.

Current scholars attribute 12 poems with certainty to Dyer; there are a handful more which may be his. Ralph Sargent's *Life and lyrics of Edward Dyer* (1968) and Steven May's *The Elizabethan courtier poets* (1991) offer the most scholarly editions of Dyer's small *oeuvre*. The earliest work, 'The songe in the oke', was part of an entertainment for Elizabeth I during her stay at Woodstock in 1575, published 10 years later in *The Queanes majesties entertainment at Woodstock*. A number of poems by and attributed to Dyer were included in miscellanies like *The phoenix nest* (1593), *Englands Helicon* (1600), and *A poetical rapsody* (1602); one is quoted in Sidney's 1598 *Arcadia*.

George Puttenham in his *Arte of English poesie* (1589) refers to several lines from poems he attributes to Dyer.

The most literarily influential of Dyer's poems is 'Bewayling his exile he singeth thus' (the first line of which is 'He that his mirthe hathe lost'), which was referred to by John Harington in his translation of Ludovico Ariosto's *Orlando furioso* (1591), sanctified in Robert Southwell's 'Dyer's phancy turned to a sinner's complaint', imitated in sonnet 83 of Fulke Greville's *Caelica* (first printed in 1633), translated into Scots by James Murray, and imitated again by James VI in his (at the time unpublished) poem 'If mourning might amend'. His shorter lyric 'The lowest trees have tops' was found in over 20 manuscripts and in three print collections, and is considered 'one of the most enduringly popular of all Elizabethan lyrics' (May 1991). One of the poems most frequently anthologized today under Dyer's name, 'My mind to me a kingdom is', has been with considerable evidence also attributed to Edward de Vere, earl of Oxford (May 1975).

In addition to many extant letters about court and literary matters which have not yet been published, Dyer's main contribution in his lifetime was to begin the revival of amorous English verse at court. English court poetry almost vanished in the religious tensions of both Edward VI's and Mary I's reigns. Even in the first decade of Elizabeth's reign court literature was largely Latin verse or prose works in the humanist or Protestant traditions. Dyer and Oxford began in the early 1570s to revive what rapidly became a torrent of secular amorous verse along Petrarchan lines, most significantly in the sonnet craze of the later Elizabethan era fuelled by Sidney's *Astrophil and Stella* (c. 1582).

Dyer was a close and influential older friend to Philip Sidney and indeed to the larger Sidney family, and a prominent member of the literary coteries which included Edmund Spenser, Fulke Greville, and Gabriel Harvey, exchanging poems and poetic theories, letters and commendatory dedications. Dyer's obvious interest in a wide variety of English verse forms (iambic pentameter, but also poulter's measure, heptameter couplets, ballad metre, octameter couplets, and trochaic hexameter) clearly both influenced and was influenced by the technical experiments engaged in by Sidney, Harvey, Greville, and Spenser as they sought to develop distinctively English poetic sophistication and range, but Dyer seems to have been resistant to their attempts to recreate classical quantitative metre in English verse.

The return of a fictional poetic 'I' to English poetry began with Dyer. Thomas Wyatt had perfected an earlier version of this voice, 'They flee from me that sometime did me seek' being a particularly fine example. Dyer's poems reinvent such insistent self-reflections: lines like 'there is no griefe that may with mine compare', and 'I sowed the soile of peace, my blisse was in the spring' not only are examples of the heavy alliteration and strong metre so characteristic of mid-sixteenth-century verse but also reveal the self-revelatory voice that Dyer's poems helped to revive in courtly circles. In particular, the early poetic forms of the Elizabethan devotional cult are evidenced in his suitor's lamentations: 'It was a Heaven to me to view thy face Devine/Wherin besides Dame Venus' stayne great Majesty did shine.'

Dyer's fluid and flexible identity as a courtier-lover-poet was a persona that Sidney, Ralegh, and others adopted enthusiastically in the second half of Elizabeth's reign. More generally, poetic comments on and investments in the life of the English court were clearly a common language for many of Dyer's younger friends, like Spenser and Harvey, and such a venue for literature continued in the courtly and anti-courtly pastorals of not just Spenser but also Ben Jonson, Shakespeare, and others in the next generation.

Though clearly a minor poet with a very modest literary output, Edward Dyer helped to initiate the poetic forms we associate with the Elizabethan era. Through his friendships and coteries he was clearly an influence on the literary and courtly figures of his day, though (or perhaps because) so few of his works reached the wider public.

SEE ALSO: Greville, Fulke; Harvey, Gabriel; Puttenham, George; Ralegh, Walter; Sidney, Philip; Spenser, Edmund

REFERENCES AND SUGGESTED READINGS

Berry, Edward (1998) *The making of Sir Philip Sidney.* University of Toronto Press, Toronto.

Garrett, Martin (ed.) (1996) *Sidney: the critical heritage.* Routledge, London.

May, Steven (1975) The authorship of 'My mind to me a kingdom is'. *Review of English Studies* 26, 385–394.

May, Steven (1991) *The Elizabethan courtier poets: the poems and their contexts.* University of Missouri Press, Columbia.

Sargent, Ralph M. (1968) *The life and lyrics of Sir Edward Dyer.* Clarendon Press, Oxford.

E

Edwards, Richard

JENNIFER RICHARDS

The Somerset-born Richard Edwards (1524–66) matriculated from Corpus Christi College, Oxford, in 1540. Four years later, he graduated BA and was elected a probationer fellow at Corpus Christi. From 1546 he was a lecturer in logic at Christ Church. Edwards's career extended beyond the precincts of the university when he became a gentleman of the Chapel Royal in 1553 and was subsequently appointed master of the children of the chapel in 1561. He was now placed at the heart of university and court life. (He was also admitted as honorary fellow to Lincoln's Inn two years before his death in 1566.) Edwards probably devised many court masques and tournaments and was involved in the preparations for the queen's progress to Oxford University in 1566 (King 2001). But it is as a poet and playwright that he is best known. He is the compiler of *The paradyse of daynty devises* (1576), a miscellaneous collection of poems by different hands, to which he contributed 10 poems. *Paradyse*, Ros King (2001) claims, was 'perhaps the most successful of all the Elizabethan printed anthologies'; it was reprinted with new poems in 1577, 1578, 1580, 1585, 1590, 1596, 1600, and 1606.

Friendship is one of the key themes of this anthology. It is not just that many of the poems celebrate faithful friends; the anthology is also an expression of friendship, as poets answer each other, offering a different perspective on the same sayings. Among the poems contributed by Edwards is 'Faire woordes makes fooles fain'. Edwards's youthful narrator is advised by his father before he leaves for the court to think on 'this proverb olde'. Initially, he cannot see its value, but the experience at court of 'hollow hartes' changes his mind, leaving him to muse that 'Faire speache alway doeth well, where deedes insue faire woordes'. Exactly the same topic is taken up and developed by other poets in this anthology, including one who signs his poems 'R.D.' But this poet argues instead that it is only deeds, not words, that count.

Friendship is also the subject of Edwards's two university plays: *Palamon and Arcyte* and *Damon and Pithias*. The former play is now lost, though its content and performance history have been recreated from contemporary eye-witness testimonies, including that of one of the actors, Miles Windsor (King 2001). Performed at Christ Church during Elizabeth I's visit to Oxford in 1566, this play reworked Geoffrey Chaucer's 'The knight's tale', a story of two men battling for the same woman's love (the story also provides the plot for William Shakespeare and John Fletcher's *The two noble kinsmen*). In so doing, King (2001) suggests, it tackled a key contemporary political concern: the negotiations and machinations of Elizabeth's courtiers and counsellors over the question of who the new queen might marry.

The Encyclopedia of English Renaissance Literature, First Edition. Edited by Garrett A. Sullivan, Jr and Alan Stewart.
© 2012 Blackwell Publishing Ltd. Published 2012 by Blackwell Publishing Ltd.

In contrast, *Damon and Pithias*, first performed at Whitehall during the Christmas season in 1564–65 (and printed in 1571), is not obviously addressing any particular situation, despite its final fulsome praise of Elizabeth. But this play does link friendship and counsel in interesting ways. The tyrant it portrays, Dionysius of Syracuse, is reformed by the spectacle of the virtuous friendship of the two eponymous friends. Edwards describes the play in his prologue as a 'tragicomedy', and he may well be offering an answer to another play of counsel, Thomas Norton and Thomas's Sackville's tragic history, *Gorboduc* (1561/62) (Richards 2012). After all, both plays dramatize the failures of counsel: a character called Eubulus (literally, good counsel) is ignored in each. But in *Damon and Pithias* a tragic denouement is averted. True friendship, not court sycophancy, wins the day.

The 'fountainhead' for this confidence in the transformative effects of virtuous example is probably Thomas Elyot's political and educational work *The boke named the governour* (1531). In a chapter on friendship Elyot suggests repeatedly through a series of ideal examples, including that of Damon and Pythias, that it is the 'embodiment of abstract virtues in fictional characters that transforms readers' (Cartwright 1999). Edwards is probably referencing Elyot. Just like *The boke named the governour*, this play is full of classical *sententiae* drawn from Cicero's *De amicitia* (*On friendship*). Yet, at the same time, we would do well to take this ideal with a pinch of salt; indeed, it is undercut at several points (King 2001; MacFaul 2007; Richards 2012). It is not only that the reiteration of the ideal becomes ridiculous, or that Damon, the elder friend of the two, is often both naive and pompous, but rather that the character who most frequently cites Cicero in a reproving way is the amoral courtier Aristippus. Finally, we might note that it is the 'slave' Stephano who invariably gives the most sensible advice, not least because he refuses to accept platitudes:

Oft-times I have heard, before I came hither,
That no man can serve two masters together –
A sentence most true as most men do take it …
And yet by their leave that first have it spoken,
How that may prove false, even now I will open.

Such questioning may offer a different way of linking friendship and counsel: it is not just virtuous example but also considered reflection that makes a difference.

Edwards was revered by his literary contemporaries, among them Barnabe Googe, who commended his skill as a writer in a eulogy 'Of Edwardes of the chappell' in his *Eglogs* (1563). In our own time there has been little interest in him, and indeed, he has been 'dismissed as one of the old-fashioned academic poets from whose dreadful scansion and conventional platitudes Shakespeare mysteriously sprang' (King 2001). But there is nothing platitudinous about Edwards's recycling of familiar sayings, and recent work, including King's fine modern edition of *Damon and Pithias*, means that he is finally beginning to attract the attention he deserves.

SEE ALSO: Googe, Barnabe; Elyot, Thomas; Fletcher, John; Norton, Thomas; Sackville, Thomas, earl of Dorset; Shakespeare, William

REFERENCES AND SUGGESTED READINGS

Cartwright, Kent (1999) *Theatre and humanism: English drama in the sixteenth century.* Cambridge University Press, Cambridge.

Cavanagh, Dermot (2003) *Language and politics in the sixteenth-century history play.* Palgrave Macmillan, Basingstoke.

Kewes, Paulina (2011) *Drama, history, and politics in Elizabethan England.* Oxford University Press, Oxford.

King, Ros (ed.) (2001) *The works of Richard Edwards: politics, poetry and performance in sixteenth-century England.* Manchester University Press, Manchester.

MacFaul, Tom (2007) *Male friendship in Shakespeare and his contemporaries.* Cambridge University Press, Cambridge.

Richards, Jennifer (2012) Male friendship and counsel in Richard Edwards' *Damon and Pythias*. In: Betteridge, Tom & Walker, Greg (eds) *The Oxford handbook to Tudor drama.* Oxford University Press, Oxford.

Edwards, Thomas

ANN HUGHES

Thomas Edwards (c.1599–1648), Presbyterian preacher and polemicist, is best known as the author of *Gangraena*, a ramshackle and intemperate 'heresiography', attacking the growth of gathered churches, separatist religious sects, and heterodox opinions in England in the 1640s. *Gangraena, or a catalogue and discovery of many of the errors, heresies blasphemies and pernicious practices of the sectaries of this time*, published in three parts in February, May, and December 1646 and amounting to more than 800 pages, was one of the most notorious and significant publications produced during a conflict in which print was central to mobilization and debate.

Edwards was a Cambridge-educated Puritan, a London lecturer in the 1630s, and was subject to harassment by the Laudian establishment, and indeed throughout the 1640s he remained a lecturer rather than a parochial minister, specializing in dynamic and provocative denunciations of religious toleration in the high-profile pulpit at Christ Church, Newgate, in London. *Gangraena* was Edwards's response to the growth of radical religious congregations and to arguments for religious liberty published by William Walwyn, Roger Williams, and others. Edwards argued that any deviation from a compulsory national church opened the floodgates to horrendous blasphemy, social dislocation, and anarchy and he made no distinctions between apparently respectable Independents or Congregationalists (many of whom he was acquainted with) and radical sectaries. Indeed it was the laxity of Independents who for Edwards had unleashed the horrors that he describes in luxuriating, alarmist detail: the women preachers, soldiers baptizing horses, the books denying the divinity of Christ. He believed that the precious opportunity to establish a reformed national church, so hopeful when the Long Parliament met in 1640, was being sabotaged by this eruption of sectarianism, blasphemy, and heresy.

Gangraena is a complex, lively, and interactive text, based on the cooperation of readers as much as the paranoid energy of its author. Edwards printed letters describing sectarian misdeeds from orthodox correspondents, as well as material transmitted orally by eyewitnesses whose respectability and veracity was carefully established through the piling on of circumstantial detail. The provocations of men like the Baptist Samuel Oates, made notorious in part 1, were amplified in the later volumes as anxious, active readers sent further reports.

Other sections consisted of selective quoting from a host of 'dangerous' books. One of John Milton's divorce tracts, for example, was the source for error 154 in *Gangraena* part 1, 'That 'tis lawful for a man to put away his wife upon indisposition, unfitness or contrariety of mind'. This was then followed by an uncorroborated error 155, ''Tis lawful for one man to have two wives at once', and Milton was made more guilty by association with a woman preacher – known to us only through her appearance in *Gangraena*, one Mrs Attaway who had looked into 'Master Milton's doctrine of divorce' and resolved upon reading it to leave her 'unsanctified husband' and run away with another married man. Above all, Edwards loved lists, beginning part 1 with a list of 176 errors, and adding increasingly complicated lists of errors, conclusions, and proposals for action in subsequent volumes. It was as if by numbering the excesses around him he could control them, but his frequent additions and revisions succeeded only in revealing that he felt overwhelmed. Edwards also provided many vivid pen portraits of the travels, writings, and preaching of 'audacious men and their daring books', Hugh Peter, John Goodwin, William Walwyn, and Laurence Clarkson among them. In part 3 he offered angry discussion of the democratic political claims of John Lilburne and Richard Overton who were to become leaders of the Levellers the following year, but as memorable was his accusation that Lilburne was 'a player at cards, one who will sit long with company at wine and tippling, and hath done all he hath for money'.

Edwards's *Gangraena* (book and author were always closely associated) was much cited by fellow Presbyterians in 1646–48, and subject to attack in a score of pamphlets by John Goodwin, Marchamont Nedham, John Saltmarsh, and William Walwyn. Milton got some revenge when 'shallow Edwards' featured in his sonnet against the 'New forcers of conscience under the Long Parliament' (1646). *Gangraena* had a dramatic if fleeting impact on religious and political conflict in the 1640s, intensifying the polarization of Parliamentarians, particularly in London, between Presbyterians and Independents in 1646–47. The bitter conflicts involving city, parliament, and army, as well as their increasingly unhappy Scottish allies, culminated in violent Presbyterian protests in London in July 1647 and the occupation of the city by the New Model Army in response. Edwards fled in panic from the Independent army in the summer of 1647, taking shelter with the English Presbyterian church in Amsterdam where he died some six months later. His works were still read and cited through the seventeenth century although his intemperate intolerance became increasingly embarrassing to Presbyterians as their hopes of controlling a reformed English church evaporated.

From the nineteenth century at least, *Gangraena* has been used as a source of information on the heterodox movements Edwards denounced, notably by the great Milton scholar David Masson and the leading historian of mid-seventeenth-century English radicalism, Christopher Hill. More recently the difficulties of using such polemical material as reliable evidence have been highlighted and *Gangraena* is now more commonly studied within discussions of the importance of printed debate and propaganda in the English Revolution in the 1640s, and of the interplay between printed, manuscript, and oral means of communication in early modern culture.

SEE ALSO: Clarkson, Laurence; Lilburne, John; Milton, John; Nedham, Marchamont; Overton, Richard; Walwyn, William

REFERENCES AND SUGGESTED READINGS

Davis, J. C. (1984) *Fear, myth and history: the Ranters and the historians.* Cambridge University Press, Cambridge.

Hill, Christopher (1972) *The world turned upside down.* Maurice Temple Smith, London.

Hughes, Ann (2004) *Gangraena and the struggle for the English Revolution.* Oxford University Press, Oxford.

Lake, Peter, & Como, David (2000) 'Orthodoxy' and its discontents: dispute settlement and the production of 'consensus' in the London (Puritan) underground. *Journal of British Studies* 39, 34–70.

Raymond, Joad (2003) *Pamphlets and pamphleteering in early modern Britain.* Cambridge University Press, Cambridge.

Elizabeth I

HELEN HACKETT

As well as ruling England from 1558 to 1603, Elizabeth I (1533–1603) was a prolific and skilful writer, composing poems, speeches, translations, letters, and prayers. She also presided over one of the most remarkable periods of English literature, and was herself the subject of much of that literature.

Elizabeth was born in 1533, the daughter of Henry VIII and his second queen, Anne Boleyn. She received the advanced humanist education befitting a Renaissance princess, with a curriculum including several languages, classical literature, Bible study, and Protestant theology. At the age of 11 she translated from French *Le miroir de l'âme pécheresse* (*The glass of the sinful soul*) by Marguerite de Navarre as a New Year's gift for her last stepmother, Queen Katherine Parr. The following New Year, 1546, she presented her father with a translation of Queen Katherine's own *Prayers and meditations* into Latin, French, and Italian (Mueller & Scodel 2009a). These works were presented in beautifully handmade copies which demonstrated Princess Elizabeth's skills not only as a linguist, but also as a needlewoman (she embroidered the covers) and as a practitioner of elegant and remarkably neat italic handwriting.

During the reign of her half-brother Edward VI (1547–53), Elizabeth faced danger as Thomas Seymour, lord admiral and brother of the lord protector, plotted to marry her and make an attempt on the throne. Elizabeth's letters of self-exoneration written during this crisis (Marcus et al. 2000) demonstrate both her precocious rhetorical skills and her remarkable self-belief, qualities that became even more essential after the accession of her Catholic elder half-sister Mary in 1553. Over the next five years Elizabeth was regarded with increasing hostility by her sister, and was for a time imprisoned in the Tower of London on suspicion of treason.

From her own accession in 1558 to her death in 1603, Elizabeth used her public utterances to cultivate popular belief in the mutual love between herself and her subjects. A printed account of her procession through the streets of London to her coronation in January 1559 records her gestures and words as much as the pageants performed for her along the route; the author, Richard Mulcaster, describes the city on that day as 'a stage wherein was showed the wonderful spectacle of a noble-hearted princess toward her most loving people'. Elizabeth would continue to deploy the rhetoric of mutual love right up until her renowned 'Golden Speech' to Parliament in 1601. She would also return at various times to the image of herself as a theatrical performer, as in an oration to a parliamentary delegation in 1586: 'we princes, I tell you, are set on stages in the sight and view of all the world duly observed.'

Elizabeth's public speeches seem to have been delivered sometimes from prepared scripts, but most often extempore or from memory (Marcus et al. 2000). Many of the surviving records of them were made by auditors from notes or from their own memories, and were in some cases corrected later by the queen or by others; some speeches exist in several different versions. Elizabeth's actual spoken words, then, are elusive, but the written versions of the speeches often had wide circulation, and have their own life as literature and as contributions to the construction of the queen's public image. As early as her first speech to Parliament in February 1559 she began to fashion herself as the Virgin Queen: 'in the end this shall be for me sufficient: that a marble stone shall declare that a queen, having reigned such a time, lived and died a virgin.' As her reign proceeded, and especially after the failure of her last marriage negotiation (with the French king's brother, François, duc d'Anjou) in 1582, she increasingly presented herself as the spouse and mother of the nation. In one characteristic speech Elizabeth interspersed stern statements of authority – 'I am your anointed queen. I will never be by violence constrained to do anything' – with assertions of her solidarity with her ordinary subjects, gained through her early tribulations – 'if I were turned out of the realm in my petticoat, I were able to live in any place of Christendom.'

Gender was a constant issue to be negotiated, in a period when many believed that it was unnatural for a woman to be a monarch, that women did not and should not possess the 'masculine' qualities necessary to a strong ruler, and that it was unnatural too for a woman to remain unmarried. Elizabeth's consequent careful efforts to represent herself as balancing masculine and feminine qualities in one person have attracted particular attention from later ages, especially since the growth of feminism in the twentieth century. Although, again, we cannot be sure of the exact words she spoke at the time, her most quoted utterance has become her speech to the troops at Tilbury during the Armada crisis of 1588: 'I know I have the body but of a weak and feeble woman, but I have the heart and stomach of a king and of a king of England too.'

Some Elizabethan literary critics praised their queen as the best poet of the age. We may suspect some sycophancy, but her surviving poems do indeed show literary skill. 'The doubt of future foes' was apparently written soon after the flight to England of Mary Queen of Scots,

Elizabeth's cousin and a dangerous Catholic claimant to her throne, in 1568. Elizabeth memorably dubs Mary 'the daughter of debate', and creates a vivid sense of political and personal insecurity: 'falsehood now doth flow / And subjects' faith doth ebb.' Indeed, Elizabeth's poems often gesture towards private anxieties and sufferings behind the public role of monarch: 'A hapless kind of life is this I wear'; 'I grieve and dare not show my discontent.' There is a playful wit as well, however, as in an exchange of poems with her favourite Sir Walter Ralegh. In reply to Ralegh's self-pitying and rather lofty lament that Fortune has taken Elizabeth's favour from him, she retorts: 'Ah, silly Pug, wert thou so sore afraid? / Mourn not, my Wat, nor be thou so dismayed.'

Elizabeth's letters, too, habitually assert her authority and put the recipient in his place, whether conveying advice and reprimands to fellow rulers such as James VI of Scotland and Henry IV of France, or chastising wayward favourites like Robert Dudley, earl of Leicester, and later Robert Devereux, earl of Essex. Her correspondence shows her liking for figurative language: she tells James VI, for instance, that 'laws resemble cobwebs whence great bees get out by breaking and small flies stick fast for weakness'. Again the letters often reveal her sense of humour, and sometimes a more intimate and informal side of her personality, as when she writes to Leicester, 'Rob, I am afraid you will suppose by my wandering writings that a midsummer moon hath taken large possession of my brains this month.'

The prayers composed by Elizabeth similarly range from those clearly designed for public consumption, to those apparently for more personal use, which may give us some indication of her private thoughts and feelings. They reveal that Elizabeth's conception of herself as mother of her people went beyond her public oratory; she frequently drew upon an Old Testament text which was popular with Protestant theologians and which described godly rulers as nursing fathers and mothers of the church (Isaiah 49.23). She also habitually referred to herself as the handmaid of God,

in a striking echo of the words of the Virgin Mary in response to the Annunciation (Luke 1.38). It is clear from Elizabeth's prayers that she profoundly believed herself to be the agent of God in promoting the Protestant faith, but that nevertheless she was no feminist: she repeatedly emphasized her status as the weaker vessel, chosen by God as his instrument precisely because of her feminine deficiency, in order to demonstrate all the more vividly the miraculousness of his power.

Elizabeth's activity as a translator was truly prodigious. The remarkable translations of her childhood may well have been undertaken as acts of duty, but her continued output after her accession suggests a desire to maintain and develop her linguistic proficiency, a pleasure in literature, and a real personal enjoyment of the process of translation. In the middle years of her reign she translated Seneca's *Epistulae morales* 107 (*Moral epistles*, c.1567), Cicero's *Epistulae ad familiares* (*Familiar letters*, c.1579), and a choral ode from *Hercules Oetaeus* (*Heracles on Oeta*, attrib. Seneca, c.1589) (Mueller & Scodel 2009a). But it was towards the end of her life, as she passed into her sixties, that she became most prolific, working on Cicero's *Pro M. Marcello* (*For Marcus Marcellus*, c.1592), Boethius's *De consolatione philosophiae* (*Consolation of philosophy*, 1593), Plutarch's *De curiositate* (*Of curiosity*, 1598), and Horace's *De arte poetica* (*Art of poetry*, 1598) (Mueller & Scodel 2009b). This range, volume, and level of translation would be impressive for any individual, but is especially so when we consider that Elizabeth was ruling England at the same time.

The Boethius is especially extraordinary: it runs to nearly 300 pages in a modern edition, but according to Thomas Windebank, Elizabeth's clerk, to whom she dictated parts of the text, it took her only between 24 and 30 working hours, spread over less than a month. Not surprisingly it bears marks of haste, including grammatical errors, compressions, and rough-hewn syntax, and where Elizabeth writes in her own hand it is very much less formal and tidy than that lapidary script of her youth. These characteristics are shared with others of her later translations, but the Boethius also has a distinctive and compelling muscular energy, especially in the lyric passages. The work dates originally from the sixth century; Boethius was imprisoned on charges of treason, and describes his dialogues with the allegorical figure of Lady Philosophy as she leads him out of despair to acceptance of divine providence. It had been translated by a previous English monarch, King Alfred. After Elizabeth's death, the historian William Camden explained that Elizabeth had turned to Boethius for consolation following her dismay at the conversion of Henry IV of France to Catholicism. Be this as it may, this work's theme and mood of stoicism in the face of worldly mutability are certainly consistent with many other parts of Elizabeth's literary output.

Elizabeth understood that the arts were a vital medium for the creation of her image and the dissemination of her power. Her portraits showcased her sumptuous costumes and jewels, and included symbols of her virginity such as a phoenix, a sieve, or an ermine (Strong 1987). She recognized that although painters and poets depended on her for favour and patronage, she also depended upon them to celebrate and mythologize her. When Paul Melissus, an eminent German poet, wrote a Latin epigram in her praise, she replied with grace and wit: 'vatum es princeps; ego vati subdita, dum me / Materiam celsi carminis ipse legis' ('you are prince of poets, I, a subject / To a poet when you choose me as the theme / Of your high song'; Mueller & Marcus 2003 Marcus et al. 2000). Edmund Spenser made her the subject of his epic romance *The Faerie Queene* (1590, 1596), in which England was depicted allegorically as Faeryland, and aspects of Elizabeth were diversely personified as Gloriana, Belphoebe, Britomart, Una, Mercilla, and more. Similarly to Elizabeth's own rhetoric in performances like the Tilbury speech, Spenser dealt with the anomaly of an unmarried woman ruler by blending masculine and feminine qualities in personae like Belphoebe, a virgin huntress, and

Britomart, a warrior-woman. However, as well as attempting to fuse Elizabeth's opposing aspects as ruler and as woman, he also split them in two: he explained that Gloriana represented Elizabeth as 'a most royall Queene or Empresse', while Belphoebe represented her as 'a most vertuous and beautifull Lady'. This and similar dualities in representations of Elizabeth by other authors are often seen as reflecting the legal and political idea of the 'Queen's two bodies', whereby Elizabeth possessed a body politic (the timeless, superhuman essence of monarchy) and a body natural (her temporal, human, personal identity).

Numerous entertainments were written for Elizabeth. Some were staged on her progresses, such as *The lady of May* by Sir Philip Sidney (1578/79); others were for court performance, including George Peele's *The arraygnment of Paris* (c.1581). Often such dramas reached across the boundary between stage and audience to include their royal spectator: Sidney's play required a judgement from the queen to determine its ending, while in Peele's work the three goddesses Pallas, Juno, and Venus resolved their quarrel over a golden apple by resigning the trophy to Elizabeth. Other court dramas included John Lyly's *Endimion* (c.1585), Ben Jonson's *Cynthias revels* (1600), and Thomas Dekker's *Old Fortunatus* (1599), which begins with two old men travelling to the temple of Eliza, and commenting self-consciously on the literary refraction of Elizabeth into multiple personae: 'Some call her Pandora; some Gloriana, some Cynthia: some Belphoebe, some Astraea: all by several names to express several loves.'

Many courtiers composed literary works about their queen, often using the fashionable convention of Petrarchan love poetry. This represented the poet as a servant adoring a chaste and unattainable mistress; it was thereby a convenient way of allegorizing and managing the anomaly of a court in which ambitious men were subject to a powerful woman. Sir Walter Ralegh was one of the leading courtier poets, and helped to promote the representation of Elizabeth as the moon goddess, Diana or

Cynthia. This persona could be used to praise Elizabeth as virginal, radiant, and endlessly self-renewing; indeed, as she aged, increasingly extravagant claims were made for her eternal youth, and even her immortality. The idea was that by triumphing over the flesh as a perpetual virgin, she had also conquered the temporal decay of the flesh. But the moon image was double-sided, and could also be a means of implying supposed feminine fickleness and instability, and even sinister and occult associations, as in Ralegh's disillusioned manuscript poem 'The ocean to Cynthia', possibly written while he was in disgrace in the Tower in 1592.

As the supreme governor of the English church and the figurehead of the English nation, Elizabeth was an immensely symbolic figure. As well as being at the centre of court poetry, she was the subject of numerous popular ballads throughout her reign. At her accession in 1558, a writer named William Birch wrote 'A song between the Queen's majesty and England', in which the nation woos its new bride: 'Come over the bourn, Bessy, / Sweet Bessy, come over to me.' At her death in 1603, comparisons with the Virgin Mary, which had been avoided or carefully negotiated over the course of the reign because of Protestant suspicion of Mariolatry, finally burst out in elegies: 'In heaven's chorus so at once are seen / A virgin mother and a maiden queen.' Through the reign of her successor James I, Elizabeth was increasingly depicted as a kind of Protestant saint, as dissatisfaction with her successor grew (Watkins 2002).

SEE ALSO: Birch, William; Dekker, Thomas; Devereux, Robert, earl of Essex; James VI and I; Jonson, Ben; Lyly, John; Parr, Katherine; Peele, George; Ralegh, Walter; Sidney, Philip; Spenser, Edmund

REFERENCES AND SUGGESTED READINGS

Berry, Philippa (1989) *Of chastity and power: Elizabethan literature and the unmarried queen*. Routledge, London.

Doran, Susan & Freeman, Thomas S. (eds) (2003) *The myth of Elizabeth*. Palgrave Macmillan, Basingstoke.

Farrell, Kirby & Swaim, Kathleen M. (eds) (2003) *The mysteries of Elizabeth I: selections from 'English Literary Renaissance'*. University of Massachusetts Press, Amherst.

Frye, Susan (1993) *Elizabeth I: the competition for representation*. Oxford University Press, Oxford.

Hackett, Helen (1995) *Virgin mother, maiden queen: Elizabeth I and the cult of the Virgin Mary*. Macmillan Press, Basingstoke.

Marcus, Leah S., Mueller, Janel, & Rose, Mary Beth (eds) (2000). *Elizabeth I: Collected works*. University of Chicago Press, Chicago.

May, Steven W. (ed.) (2004) *Elizabeth I: selected works*. Washington Square Press, New York.

Montrose, Louis (2006) *The subject of Elizabeth: authority, gender, and representation*. University of Chicago Press, Chicago.

Mueller, Janel & Marcus, Leah S. (eds) (2003) *Elizabeth I: autograph compositions and foreign language originals*. University of Chicago Press, Chicago.

Mueller, Janel & Scodel, Joshua (eds) (2009a) *Elizabeth I: translations, 1544–1589*. University of Chicago Press, Chicago.

Mueller, Janel & Scodel, Joshua (eds) (2009b) *Elizabeth I: translations, 1592–1598*. University of Chicago Press, Chicago.

Strong, Roy (1977) *The cult of Elizabeth: Elizabethan portraiture and pageantry*. Thames & Hudson, London.

Strong, Roy (1987) *Gloriana: the portraits of Queen Elizabeth I*. Thames & Hudson, London.

Watkins, John (2002) *Representing Elizabeth in Stuart England*. Cambridge University Press, Cambridge.

Wilson, Elkin Calhoun (1966 [1939]) *England's Eliza*. Octagon, New York.

Elyot, Thomas

CATHY SHRANK

The only son of Sir Richard Elyot (one of the king's serjeant-at-arms, justice of the assize for the western circuit, and a judge in the court of common pleas), Sir Thomas Elyot (c.1490–1546) would have been trained for public service from his youth. In the preface to his 1538 Latin–English dictionary, Elyot presents himself as self-taught, educated in his father's house and 'not instructed by any other teacher from his twelfth year, but led by himself into liberal studies and both sorts of philosophy [i.e., natural and moral]' (translation: Lehmberg 2004). However, despite fashioning himself as an autodidact, Elyot attended the Inns of Court, having been admitted to his father's inn, the Middle Temple, in November 1510. He may also have studied at Oxford (Lehmberg 2004). That said, neither of these institutions would have provided him with the humanistic grounding which so obviously informs his writings.

Elyot's learning was doubtlessly shaped by other influences, which may have included the intellectual circle round Sir Thomas More (Hogrefe 1959). The scant evidence for intimacy between Elyot and More is bolstered by the biographical sketch of More published by the Catholic theologian Thomas Stapleton in *Tres Thomae* (1588), which is undoubtedly partisan and published at a critical point for the reputation of Catholics in England. However, the evidence is not inconsequential: Elyot wrote to Henry's chief minister, Thomas Cromwell, about his alleged 'amity' with More (see below); he also credits More's friend Thomas Linacre with inspiring his interest in medicine. The preface of the 1541 edition of Elyot's *Castel of helth* acknowledges the role played by the 'worshipful physician' Linacre, who – 'perceiving [him] by nature inclined to knowledge' – 'read unto [him] the works of Galen … with some of … Hippocrates'. A *terminus ad quem* for this tutelage is supplied by Linacre's death in 1524; since Elyot's birth date is uncertain, the occurrence of this interaction 'before that [he] was 20 years old' is less helpful.

Elyot was the author of at least 12 books printed by the king's printer, Thomas Berthelet, between 1531 and 1545. These works cover an impressive range of genres and subjects. His earliest, *The boke named the governour* (1531), is a treatise on governance in three books: the first describes the ideal education for 'inferior magistrates' (those statesmen below the sovereign, with responsibilities for governing and counselling); the second two outline the qualities that governors should possess or develop (affability, fortitude, magnanimity) and what vices they should abhor (ambition, obstinacy). As a treatise on education, *The governour* was followed by *The educacion or bringinge vp of children* (1530), a translation from Plutarch's *Moralia* dedicated to his sister Margery Puttenham (mother of George Puttenham, the likely author of *The arte of English poesie*). The early 1530s also saw Berthelet publish Elyot's *Doctrinall of princis* (?1533), a translation from Isocrates which advises rulers on how they should govern (advocating the virtues of counsel), and two political dialogues about the problems of counsel: *Of the knowledge which maketh a wise man* (1533) stages a series of conversations between Plato and his fellow philosopher Aristippus in which they debate whether or not Plato should have spoken out against tyranny at the court of the Dionysius of Sicily; *Pasquil the playne* (1533) presents a glimpse into a corrupt court, where flattery and complicit silence (represented by the characters Gnatho and Harpocrates) have the ear of the king, whilst the only forthright speaker (Pasquil) lacks a counsellor's requisite ability to 'temper his language' and remains exiled beyond the city walls, unable to influence policy. A third dialogue, *The defence of good women* (1540), dedicated to Henry VIII's fourth wife, Anne of Cleves, acts as a further meditation on the necessary qualities of a ruler (which should include discretion and prudence) and advocates political moderation; ostensibly a eulogistic account of the life of Queen Zenobia of Palmyra, it is recurrently read as a paean to Henry's first queen, Katherine of Aragon (Walker 1996). Elyot's continued interest in political writing and theories of governance is evidenced by *The image of governance* (1541), a life of the Roman emperor Alexander Severus. Elyot also compiled a printed commonplace book, *The bankette of sapience* (1534); a major Latin–English dictionary (1538), the first to be based on classical sources (Lehmberg 2004), which was republished, revised, and expanded as *Bibliotheca*

Eliotae in 1542; and a medical handbook, *The castle of health* (?1536), which he revised and corrected in editions of 1539 and 1541. His devotional works are a translation of *A swete and deuoute sermon of holy saynt Ciprian*, printed with his translation of *The rules of a christian lyfe made by Picus, erle of Mirandula* (1534), and *A preservative agaynste deth* (1545), an *ars moriendi*, which – fittingly – was to be his last published work: he died the following year, on 26 March 1546.

Elyot is also credited with three anonymous works (Lehmberg 1960), two printed by Berthelet and one in Cambridge by the immigrant printer-bookseller John Siberch: these texts are *Hermathena* (1522), a dialogue imitating Lucian attributed to 'Papyrius Geminus Eleates' ('Geminus' is a Latin form of Thomas; 'Papyrius' describes his role as writer); *How one maye take profite of his ennmies* (?1531), a translation of a section of Plutarch's *Moralia*; and *A dialogue between Lucian and Diogenes* (?1532), a translation of Lucian's *Cynicus*, which debates the various merits of 'the life hard and sharp' and 'the life tender and delicate'. However, none of these texts appear in Elyot's list of his works in the preface to *The image of governance*.

Despite its generic diversity, Elyot's output is nevertheless characterized by a recurrent desire to 'counsel' his compatriots by disseminating, in the vernacular, various bodies of knowledge, be they political, philosophical, moral, medical, linguistic, or spiritual: Elyot frequently describes his engagement with these different spheres as a means of providing 'counsel'. As he writes in *The governour*, 'the end of all doctrine and study is good counsel'. Elyot's sense that, as an author, he was meeting – rather than competing with – his public duty is borne out by the prefatory material to his works, which often draws attention to the way in which he felt that he was combining intellectual and political activities, either in practice (by beavering away on his texts at the same time as fulfilling certain political duties) or in spirit; for example, the dedicatory epistle to the 1539 edition of the *Castel of helth* describes how he revised the text whilst 'attending on the parliament ...

being a member of the lower house'. *A preservative agaynste death* makes analogies between Elyot's role of sheriff and as author: 'for since it pertaineth to my office, and also the laws of this realm do compel me to punish transgressors, how much more is it my duty to do the best that I can, by all study and means to withdraw men from transgressing the laws and commandments of God?'

That Elyot occasionally justifies his authorial excursions (most obviously in the proem of the 1541 edition of the *Castel of health*, where he berates those who say 'it beseemeth not a knight' to write such things and that 'he might have been much better occupied') does indicate that not everyone was of his opinion. Nonetheless, it is noticeable that Elyot was the only one of his social peers printed by Berthelet (the others being Sir Anthony Cope, Sir Anthony Fitzherbert, and Sir Richard Morison) to have his coat of arms included in the first (and usually subsequent) editions produced between 1534 and his death in 1546. Elyot's works may contain the sole examples of authorial coats of arms in Berthelet's output because he was the only armigerous writer printed by Berthelet to be sufficiently prolific to merit investing in such a woodcut, but that Elyot was so productive and that he was willing for his works to be identified with him as a gentleman is a striking indication of his belief that, through writing, he was performing the public service expected of someone of his rank and position. Elyot also tended to dedicate his works to those at the centre of power: *The governour*, *Bankette of sapience*, the 1538 *Dictionary*, and the 1542 *Bibliotheca* are dedicated to Henry VIII; the first and second editions of *Castel of helth* (?1536, 1539) to Cromwell; and *The image of governance* to 'all the nobility of this flourishing realm of England'. That he did so suggests his belief in the public import of his writings, which he describes in the 1541 *Castel of helth* as 'labours', undertaken 'for the fervent affection which [he has] ever borne toward the public weal of [his] country'. Elyot's humanism is thus marked as much by his civic intentions – working for what he perceives as the public good, neglecting, as he puts it in *Image*, 'the increase of [his] private commodity' in favour of 'the writing of books for others' necessity' – as by his persistent recourse to classical texts as an inspiration, model, or direct source.

Elyot's concern to profit his country extends to his attitude to the English language. Not only does he regularly translate works out of Greek or Latin, so that, as he argues in *Doctrinall of princis*, 'they which do not understand Greek nor Latin, should not lack the commodity and pleasure which may be taken in reading thereof', but his works of translation are also intended to test his own vernacular, to 'assay if our English tongue might receive the quick and proper sentences pronounced by the Greek'. Part of his response to classical texts is thus an endeavour to improve the vulgar tongue, then viewed by many as lacking semantic variety and elegance. Through his writing, Elyot strove to expand English vocabulary, by broadening the grammatical usages of existing words (e.g., coining 'womanliness' from 'womanly' in 1538) or by fashioning new words through foreign borrowings, a method which necessitates Elyot's characteristic use of doublings, in which he pairs neologisms with their familiar counterparts (as in 'devulgate or set forth' and 'animate or give courage', to give examples from the prefatory material to *The governour*). Elyot is consequently credited by the *Oxford English dictionary* with some 455 first recorded usages, including 'acumen', 'adherence', and 'adulterate'. As with his ventures into medical writing, however, Elyot's linguistic endeavours seem to have incurred a hostile reception in some quarters, to judge by his irritable defence of his attempts 'to augment our English tongue, whereby men should as well express more abundantly the thing that they conceived in their hearts . . ., having words apt for the purpose': 'There was no term new made by me of a Latin or French word,' he insists in *Of the knowledge which maketh a wise man*, 'but it is there declared so plainly by one mean or other to a diligent reader that no sentence is thereby made dark or hard to be underst[oo]d.'

Across Elyot's works there is this recurrent sense of the author's need to defend himself against 'the assaults of malign interpreters' (*The governour*). That impression of feeling hard-done-by is apparent from his extant letters, mostly addressed to Cromwell, with whom he established a lasting friendship in the 1520s, based on their mutual love of books, or 'similitude of studies' (Wilson 1976). 'I perceive other men advanced openly to the place of counsellors which neither in the importance of service neither in charges have served the king as I have done,' he complains to Cromwell in 1532, some months after his recall from his position of ambassador to Emperor Charles V (Wilson 1976).

Elyot's career played out against the backdrop of the Henrician Reformation, and the subsequent religious and political upheavals. In terms of his faith, Elyot seems to have occupied a conservative position: his will provides for prayers for the dead (Lehmberg 1960). However, he was prepared in a letter to Cromwell in autumn 1536 to denounce many of the rituals of the Church of Rome as 'vain superstitions, superfluous ceremonies, slanderous jugglings, counterfeit miracles, arrogant usurpations of men called "spiritual"' (Wilson 1976). Elyot's self-presentation as an enthusiastic supporter of Henry's 'due reformation of the said enormities' is possibly heightened by his attempt in this letter to distance himself from a now politically dangerous friendship with Thomas More, executed the previous year for refusing to subscribe to the Oath of Supremacy, which recognized Henry as head of the English church. However, it may also be – as Elyot explains in an earlier letter – that his desire for 'necessary reformation' caused 'no little contention' between him and those of More's persuasion (Wilson 1976). Certainly, Elyot was willing to profit personally from the dissolution of monastic property (asking Cromwell to help him acquire such lands on a number of occasions), and in 1535 he had served on a commission to visit Oxfordshire monasteries (Lehmberg 1960).

Nonetheless, the turbulent politics of the 1530s and 1540s resonate through Elyot's *oeuvre*: debates about charity and good works (flashpoints of Reformation controversy) inform the pages of his *Bankette of sapience*; the trial of a renowned heretic, John Lambert, is used to illustrate Henry's majesty in the dedicatory epistle to the 1538 *Dictionary*. Greg Walker, Elyot's most assiduous recent critic, argues persuasively for topical readings of even his seemingly apolitical works. His 1534 translation of Cyprian's *Sermon* is, for example, dedicated to his step-sister, 'the right worshipful sister dame Susan Kingston', 'not only for [their] alliance, but also much more for [her] perseverance in virtue and works of true faith'; Susan is, moreover, enjoined to share the work 'with our two sisters religious', Dorothy and Eleanor Fettiplace (Susan's sisters and Elyot's step-sisters), probably – like Susan – then resident at the Bridgettine House of Syon, a religious house subjected to particular pressure in 1534 for its connection with Anne Barton, 'the Maid of Kent', who was executed in April that year for prophesying Henry's death should he divorce Katherine of Aragon and marry Anne Boleyn (Walker 2005). Dedicating a sermon in which Cyprian encourages the faithful to stand firm during times of oppression to members of a beleaguered religious establishment at such a politically sensitive moment would seem far from being a neutral statement of personal devotion.

It is less easy to gauge Elyot's response to what many critics and historians have perceived as the increasing tyranny of Henry's reign, partly because Elyot's modes of resistant writing are habitually and wisely oblique, and partly because we need to be wary of reading accounts of extreme punishment through twenty-first-century spectacles. Tyranny and the failure or vulnerability of counsel are recurrent concerns of Elyot's works (from *The governour* through *Pasquil* and *Of the knowledge* to *The image of governance*). Nonetheless, we cannot necessarily equate ruthlessness with tyranny; Elyot himself differentiates 'mercy' from 'vain pity' in *The governour* and defines

'Severitas' in his 1538 *Dictionary* as 'gravity, constantness, properly in ministering justice'. The challenge – for modern readers, as it was for early modern witnesses / political agents – is to distinguish justifiable harshness from irrational, impassioned 'wrath', the true sign of tyranny, when the ruler loses sight of the reason and self-control that should distinguish humans from beasts.

Elyot is sometimes seen as an elitist writer because his focus in *The governour* is on the education of the aristocracy and gentry, conducted within private households. This whiff of elitism is compounded by his suspicion of the emergent term 'commonweal', which – apparently aspiring for semantic precision – he prefers to classify as 'public weal', since 'common' connotes holding 'everything in common, without discrepancy of any estate or condition'. However, the form and content of Elyot's books belie that sense of social exclusivity. Printed in the vernacular, they made available to a reading public a considerable body of scholarship, much of which had been previously restricted to those with classical languages. As such, his printed works performed on a large scale what Elyot's will did in miniature, as he bequeathed his books not to his heirs (his sister and then his nephew, Margery and George Puttenham), but to be sold, with the proceeds distributed to poor but promising scholars (Lehmberg 1960). The extent to which Elyot was motivated by a desire to disseminate knowledge to his compatriots is exemplified by the difference between his medical works and those of his mentor, Linacre: where Linacre translated Galen's works from Greek into Latin for fellow doctors and other learned men, such as philosophers (as the title page to Linacre's 1521 translation of Galen's *De temperamentis* indicates), Elyot's *Castel of helth* was designed to serve as a practical handbook, allowing 'ordinary men and women to diagnose their own complaints' (Lehmberg 2004).

Elyot's works were widely read. Eleven of the 12 works of acknowledged authorship went through more than one edition (the exception being his last publication, *A preservative agaynste death*; the conservative tenor of this 1545 *ars moriendi* would not have accorded with Edward VI's evangelical regime, which followed less than two years later). Four of Elyot's works saw at least one Elizabethan edition, printed a decade or more after his death, a further sign of their popularity: *Bibliotheca Eliotae* (1559); *Bankette of sapience* (1564, c.1575); *The governour* (1565, 1580); *The castel of helth* (?1560, ?1561, 1572, 1576, 1580, 1587, 1595). *Castel of helth* – clearly the most lastingly popular of Elyot's works – even had a final, Jacobean edition, issued in 1610 by William Jaggard, one of the less scrupulous printers of Shakespearean quartos.

SEE ALSO: More, Thomas; Morison, Richard; Puttenham, George; Wyatt, Thomas

REFERENCES AND SUGGESTED READINGS

Baker, David Weil (1999) *Divulging Utopia: radical humanism in sixteenth-century England.* University of Massachusetts Press, Amherst.

Baumann, Uwe (1998) Sir Thomas Elyot's *The image of governance*: a humanist's *Speculum principis* and a literary puzzle. In: Stein, Dieter & Sornicola, Rosanna (eds) *The virtues of language.* John Benjamins, Amsterdam, pp. 177–199.

Foley, Stephen Merriam (1994) Coming to terms: Thomas Elyot's definitions and the particularity of human letters. *ELH* 61, 211–230.

Hogrefe, Pearl (1959) *The Sir Thomas More circle.* University of Illinois Press, Urbana.

Hogrefe, Pearl (1967) *The life and times of Sir Thomas Elyot, Englishman.* Iowa University Press, Ames.

Lehmberg, Stanford E. (1960) *Sir Thomas Elyot, Tudor humanist.* University of Texas Press, Austin.

Lehmberg, Stanford E. (2004) Elyot, Sir Thomas. In: *Oxford dictionary of national biography.* Oxford University Press, Oxford.

Major, John M. (1964) *Sir Thomas Elyot and Renaissance humanism.* University of Nebraska Press, Lincoln.

Shrank, Cathy (2009) Sir Thomas Elyot and the bonds of community. In: Pincombe, Michael & Shrank, Cathy (eds) *Oxford handbook of Tudor literature.* Oxford University Press, Oxford, pp. 154–169.

Swain, David W. (2008) 'Not lernyd in physicke': Thomas Elyot, the medical humanists, and vernacular medical literature. In: Dutcher, J. M. & Prescott, A. L. (eds) *Renaissance historicisms: essays in honor of Arthur F. Kinney.* University of Delaware Press, Newark, pp. 54–68.

Walker, Greg (1996) *Persuasive fictions: faction, faith, and politics in the reign of Henry VIII.* Scolar Press, Aldershot.

Walker, Greg (1999) Dialogue, resistance and accommodation: conservative literary responses to the Henrician Reformation. In: Amos, N. S., Pettegree, A., & van Niewp, H. (eds) *Humanism and education in a Christian society.* Ashgate, Aldershot, pp. 89–111.

Walker, Greg (2005) *Writing under tyranny: English literature and the Henrician Reformation.* Oxford University Press, Oxford.

Wilson, Kenneth J. (ed.) (1976) *The letters of sir Thomas Elyot.* University of North Carolina Press, Chapel Hill.

Wilson, Kenneth J. (1985) *Incomplete fictions: the formation of English Renaissance dialogue.* Catholic University of America Press, Washington, DC.

emblem books

WILLIAM E. ENGEL

Emblems were part of virtually every literary form and aesthetic practice of the Renaissance. No domestic or public space was left unfilled by some appropriate emblematic decoration (Manning 2002). The designs for such ornamentation in many cases can be traced to specific emblem books (Bath 1994). To this end, books of emblems frequently were indexed topically by virtues, vices, and other commonplace themes. Strictly speaking, an emblem consisted of a picture, motto, and poem. The *pictura*, or image, was likened to the body of the device, and the *inscriptio*, or word, to the soul; the *subscriptio*, or verse commentary, brought out a connection between the two main components.

Much of the popularity of emblems can be traced to their epigrammatic quality. The emblem calls on the reader to tease out and consider a series of concealed meanings.

As such, emblem books express even as they are exemplary expressions of the easy commerce between verbal and visual registers of thought during the Renaissance. This same ingenious relation between word and image was a defining feature of *imprese*, those witty devices which were a standard feature of romance narratives and epic poetry such as Philip Sidney's *Arcadia* and Edmund Spenser's *Faerie Queene*. An *impresa* (Italian for 'device') combined an image and motto to signal a person's resolve, aspiration, or intention. Originally used as part of the lavish pageantry of late-medieval chivalry and later in Renaissance tournaments, special shields were carved and painted which identified each contestant. For example, in Shakespeare's *Pericles* the recently shipwrecked hero, down on his luck, enters the tilts with 'A withered branch that's only green at top; / The motto: *In hac spe vivo* [In this hope, I live].' King Simonides glosses this 'pretty moral' by explaining to the princess, 'From the dejected state wherein he is, / He hopes by you his fortunes may flourish.' His gloss models how emblems were interpreted in this period.

The riddle tradition of late antiquity also played a part in the development of emblem literature, where a gnomic description of an object or quality challenged the reader to discover its identity. Although many of these have come down to us in books, initially they were part of the impromptu entertainments at celebratory feasts where contestants tried to outdo one another in good-natured verbal combat. Indeed, from their origin in the mid-sixteenth century, emblems were attended by a kind of festive, intellectual playfulness (Manning 2002). Readers delighted in resolving for themselves the conundrum posed by an emblem, thereby coming to a new understanding of some larger moral or truth as a result of having engaged in this kind of sophisticated play of words and images. Emblem writers and their audiences appreciated the paradoxical value of 'speaking pictures' and 'mute poesy' in line with Horace's analogy *ut pictura poesis* ('as is painting, so is poetry'). Deciphering an emblem required that the reader

look beyond what the image depicted and what the words said to come to a richer and more complicated interpretation of the larger matter thus being presented. As such, emblems call for and set in play a synthetic model of reading that stresses the dynamic relationship between image and text.

Andrea Alciato, an Italian lawyer and humanist, is considered the father of the emblem not only because his *Emblematum liber* (1531) was the first book devoted exclusively to emblems but also because his influence runs through the whole tradition (Daly 1989). Although the emblem was conceived originally as a collection of Greek epigrams translated into Latin, pictures quickly became a distinguishing feature of this novel literary form. For example, the picture of a beehive in a helmet, when taken together with the motto *Ex bello pax* ('From war, peace') and an explanatory poem, amplified the meaning that weapons of war may be turned into the works of peace. The book's initial success convinced Alciato to issue a more carefully edited version with better woodcuts. More than 100 editions, including vernacular translations, were published throughout Europe during the sixteenth and seventeenth centuries.

The emblem was part of a broad-based cultural movement associated with humanist learning that resulted in a host of different practical applications, including civic, moral, and political uses. Treatises and commentaries either using or alluding to emblematic material formed an important thread in the development of the essay form pioneered by Michel de Montaigne and Francis Bacon (Raybould 2009), both of whom were admired in their own day more as statesmen than as authors. Along the same lines, the first printed emblem book by an Englishman, Geoffrey Whitney's *Choice of emblemes* (Leiden, 1586), was part of a series of cultural exchanges aimed at strengthening the pro-Protestant Anglo-Dutch alliance. The publication of this book was motivated less by the humanistic ideals of literary imitation than by current politics; it was composed at a time when the English forces under the command of Robert Dudley, earl of Leicester, were in the Low Countries opposing Spanish oppression. Individual emblems in the collection were dedicated to Whitney's Dutch hosts and to members of the English military contingent, with many of the images recalling allegorical designs on the triumphal arches built to welcome Dudley as he passed through the major cities of the United Provinces in 1585 (Manning 2002).

Both Protestants and Catholics perceived great value in emblems. Despite periodic hostility towards the use of images, emblems remained popular in Reformation England (Gilman 1983). Francis Quarles, a poet much admired by Puritans, generated moral lessons for his extraordinarily successful *Emblemes* (1635) by using designs taken mainly from a Jesuit emblem book, Herman Hugo's *Pia desideria* (1624). Emblem books with more mundane applications include later seventeenth-century versions of Philip Ayres's *Emblemata amatoria* (c.1680), intended as a gift for ladies and printed in a format suited to fit securely and secretly in one's pocket. Others were designed for school children, such as Johannes Amos Comenius's *Orbis sensualium pictus* (*The visible world in pictures*) (1657), which can be credited with making illustrations a regular feature of textbooks and primers. Some emblem books followed sequential programmes, such as Quarles's aptly titled *Hieroglyphikes of the life of man* (1638); while more esoteric volumes, especially Michael Maier's *Atalanta fugiens* (*Fleeing Atalanta or philosophical emblems of the secrets of nature*) (1617), with its 50 emblems, epigrams, prose commentaries, and musical fugues, hinted at an alchemical progression towards perfection – the moral interpretation of the series paralleling a movement from the generation of wind (Boreas' offspring) in the first emblem to the production of the fiery spirit (Mansion of Dragons) in the last, such that 'preservers of the Chemical treasures should be called Keepers of the Golden Fleece'. Despite their different aims and target audiences, all emblem books were fundamentally didactic. Like

collections of adages full of sententious wisdom, and like illustrated editions of Aesop's fables full of moral instruction, emblems served a combined educational and recreational purpose consistent with Horace's dictum that poetry should teach and delight.

Among the most enduring of the English emblem books was George Wither's *Collection of emblemes, ancient and moderne* (1635), 'disposed into lotteries' with an appended pattern for constructing a spinning dial to locate emblems pertinent to one's present situation much in the same way randomly picked verses from Virgil had served previous generations. Indicative of how emblems circulated freely and easily from one book to another, this volume was conceived by a London publisher who employed Wither to write illustrative verses for 200 circular emblems by Crispin de Passe first printed in Gabriel Rollenhagen's *Nucleus emblematum* (1611, 1613). The frontispiece was executed by William Marshall, who also contributed 79 plates to Quarles's *Emblemes*, and, among other frontispieces, engraved the allegorical 'Pourtrature of his sacred majestie' for *Eikon basilike* (1649).

Another important strand in the development of emblem literature involved festival books, which recorded the designs used in civic pageants and royal entries. Emblem books often supplied the patterns for the triumphal arches used in such processions, which, in turn, found parallel expression in the architectural designs of allegorical frontispieces and title pages. Emblems, traceable in many cases to specific books, provided images for decorating private drawing rooms, great halls, tapestries, leaded-glass windows, fireplace tiles, and all manner of furniture but especially chairs, bed-headboards and wedding chests (Bath 1994). This aspect of the tradition has led to a field of study in its own right called 'applied emblematics' (Böker & Daly 1999).

Emblems also figured prominently in the design and adornment of theatres (Yates 1969). Moreover, dumb shows and meticulously choreographed processions were elaborate versions of pages in an emblem book in both form and function. Individual emblems frequently show up in plays, whether as a passing allusion or as part of the dramatic action. For example, in John Marston's *Antonio and Mellida* (c.1599), an importunate suitor gives a device to Rosaline: 'a glow-worm, the word *splendescit tatum tenebris*', which he glosses as 'O lady the glow-worm figurates my valour, which shineth brightest in most dark, dismal and horrid achievements'. She offers a variant interpretation, however, which both mocks him and makes clear her own intentions: 'Or rather your glow-worm represents your wit, which only seems to have fire in it, though indeed 'tis but an *ignis fatuus* [will o' the wisp] and shines only in the dark dead night of fools' admiration.' The well-established tripartite structure of the traditional emblem – image, motto, and commentary – provided the dramatist with an ideal way to display his ingenuity. In John Webster's *The white divel* (1612), an emblem is thrown through the window for a duped husband. The image, we are told, is a stag weeping for the loss of its horns; the motto, *Inopem me copia fecit* is translated as 'Plenty of horns hath made him poor of horns.' Finally, the reference to cuckoldry is explained by one of the characters with respect to the play's unfolding plot (Daly 1998). This pause in the dramatic action to puzzle out an emblem was intended to imprint a key issue on the audience's memory. The mnemonic quality of emblems and emblematic quality of memory images would have been taken for granted during the period.

Another kind of book, best described as a symbol dictionary, enjoyed a resurgence of popularity coincident with the proliferation of emblem books. Natalis Comes's *Mythologiae* (1567) contends that the ancients intended their tales and genealogies of the gods to be construed allegorically. Vincenzo Cartari's *Imagini delli dei de gl'antichi* (1571), which focuses on the various aspects and attributes of the classical deities, includes outlandish images ingeniously explained in the margins. Cesare Ripa's *Iconologia* (1603) contains descriptions of over 150 illustrations of commonplace themes arranged alphabetically, thus making it an ideal source book for painters and sculptors, as for poets and orators, in search of telling details with which to embellish their compositions. Such handbooks likewise served in the construction of artificial memory systems designed to put one in mind of an orderly array of ideas whether for sermons, legal cases, or table talk. Treatises on the art of memory urged that one make use of all kinds of hieroglyphics and sententious phrases, whether those taken from mythographic texts or from emblem books (Willis 1621). Alexander Ross's *Mystagogus poeticus, or the muses interpreter* (1647) was among the more popular English mythographic handbooks written in the style of the *Ovide moralisé* tradition (where allegories from Ovid were elaborated), in part because of the occasional anti-Catholic expositions presented in the course of his interpretations of classical figures and stories.

Emblem-related research during the nineteenth century resulted in valuable studies of classical sculpture, coins and insignia, Dances of Death, books of hours, and *biblia paupera* (called Paupers' Bibles because for reasons of economy they illustrated parallel scenes from the Old and New Testaments). In the mid-twentieth century, iconographically oriented investigations carried out mainly by art historians tracked the earliest uses and later transformations of key images, such as Time's scythe and Mary's lily. A concurrent movement aimed at determining the provenance and print runs of extant emblem books paved the way, in the last 30 years, for massive cataloguing and indexing projects. Scanning technology and electronic databases have made available a wide range of texts for comparative studies of the customs and circumstances surrounding the use of particular emblems both in their original and in later, transposed settings.

SEE ALSO: Bacon, Francis; Fletcher, John; Marston, John; Quarles, Francis; Shakespeare, William; Sidney, Philip; Spenser, Edmund; Webster, John; Whitney, Geoffrey; Wither, George

REFERENCES AND SUGGESTED READINGS

Bath, Michael (1994) *Speaking pictures: English emblem books and Renaissance culture.* Longman, London.

Böker, H. & Daly, Peter M. (eds) (1999) *The emblem and architecture: studies in applied emblematics.* Brepols, Turnhout.

Daly, Peter M. (ed.) (1989) *Andrea Alciato and the emblem tradition.* AMS Press, New York.

Daly, Peter M. (1998) *Literature in the light of the emblem,* 2nd edn. University of Toronto Press, Toronto.

Daly, Peter M. (ed.) (2008) *Companion to emblem studies.* AMS Press, New York.

English Emblem Book Project (n.d.) http://emblem.libraries.psu.edu

Gilman, Ernest B. (1983) Word and image in Quarles' *Emblemes. Critical Inquiry* 6(3), 385–410.

Glasgow University Emblem Website (n.d.) www.emblems.arts.gla.ac.uk

Höltgen, Karl Josef (1986) *Aspects of the emblem: studies in the English emblem tradition and the European context.* Reichberger, Kassel.

Manning, John (2002) *The emblem.* Reaktion Books, London.

OpenEmblem Portal (n.d.) http://media.library.illinois.edu/projccts/oebp/SPT–Home.php

Raybould, Robin (2009) *Emblemata: symbolic literature of the Renaissance.* Grolier Club, New York.

Willis, John (1621) *The art of memory.* Sowersby, London.

Yates, Frances Amelia (1969) *Theatre of the world.* University of Chicago Press, Chicago.

Evelyn, John

ANGUS VINE

John Evelyn (1620–1706) was a diarist and writer whose interests ran from education to horticulture, and from bibliography to numismatics. He was also a respected advocate of the arts, publishing works on sculpture, painting, and architecture, and was one of the founding fellows of the Royal Society.

Evelyn was born on 31 October 1620 at Wotton in Surrey. From the age of five, he lived with his maternal grandfather, John Stansfield, in Lewes. In 1630 he was enrolled in the free school at Southover, where he remained until 1637, when he was admitted to the Middle Temple. The same year he was also admitted as a fellow commoner to Balliol College, Oxford, matriculating on 29 May, but he did not take a degree. For much of the 1640s he travelled on the Continent in the company of fellow Royalist exiles. In Paris he became acquainted with the ambassador there, Sir Richard Browne, and in June 1647 he married Browne's daughter Mary. Shortly afterwards he returned to England, and in 1652 he and Mary took the lease of Sayes Court, her family home in Deptford.

Evelyn's fame today comes mostly from his voluminous *Diary.* From the age of 11 he kept notes of his life, perhaps in the waste leaves of an almanac, from which the *Diary* was later composed. (It was not until 1684 that he kept a diary on a daily basis.) The first part of the *Diary,* which covers events from his birth to his visit to Rome in 1644, was written in 1660, while the second part, which covers the next period of his life to 1684, dates from 1680–84. Many of the entries reflect this belatedness: the account of his tour of Italy in the 1640s, for example, is not an eye-witness report, but was written up later with the aid of guidebooks published at the time. Subjects to attract Evelyn's curiosity include politics, major events, such as the Great Fire of London, strange fauna and flora, and operations and experiments. On 3 June 1658, for example, he described a prodigious whale beached in shallow water by Sayes Court, while on 10 October 1667 we learn that he attended the dissection of a 'poore curr, kept long alive after the *Thorax* was open, by blowing with bellows into his lungs', which he described as 'an experiment of more cruelty than pleased me'. There are two main sources for the *Diary*: the *Kalendarium* (British Library, Additional MSS 78323–78325), which covers his life from 1620 to 1697, and the *De vita propria,* written in 1697, which returns to the events of the first 24 years of his life. The remainder of the *Diary,* from 1697 to 1706, was entered on a series of loose sheets.

Evelyn never intended to publish his *Diary*, and so it was on other works, in particular his books on horticulture, that his contemporary reputation rested. In 1664 he published his best-known work: the *Sylva, or a discourse of forest-trees*. Other horticultural works include a translation of Nicolas de Bonnefons's *Le jardinier françois*, published in 1659, a translation of the sieur le Gendre's *La Manière de cultiver les arbres fruitiers*, published in 1660 as *The manner of ordering fruit-trees*, and a report on the discovery in Spain of an old seed-drill, the 'sembrador', published in the *Philosophical Transactions of the Royal Society* in June 1670. He was also the author of the encyclopedic, but unfinished, *Elysium Britannicum*, a history of gardens, on which he worked for much of his life. As well as writing about gardens, he was also the creator, at Sayes Court, of one of the best-known and mostly richly documented gardens in early modern England.

Other works by Evelyn include three Royalist tracts printed in 1659–60: *An apologie for the royal party*, *A character of England*, and *The late news or message from Bruxels unmasked*. Evelyn never strayed from the staunchly Royalist politics of his youth, although his confessional identity was more complicated than this might suggest. During the 1650s he worked on a translation of Lucretius's materalist epic *De natura rerum*, but only the first book ever appeared in print, in 1656: his correspondence reveals that his decision not to publish further books was influenced by fear of how the translation of such material might be received. His later works turn away from horticulture and politics to the arts. In 1661 his *Sculptura, or the history, and art of chalcography* appeared, a history of copperplate engraving written along lines drawn up by Francis Bacon. The same year he also published *Instructions concerning erecting of a library*, a translation of Gabriel Naudé's *Advis pour dresser une bibliothèque*. Other works on the arts include translations of Roland Fréart's *Parallèle de l'architecture antique et de la moderne* (1664) and *Idée de la perfection de la peinture* (1668), and *Numismata* (1697), a work justly praised for its exposition of why people collect coins and medals.

Evelyn died on 27 February 1706 at the house of his son in Dover Street, London. For a long time, his reputation was mixed. Despite being a founder member of the Royal Society, he has often been dismissed as a virtuoso who lacked the rigour and flair for abstraction of friends such as Robert Boyle or Sir William Petty. By the same token, his *Diary* has never attracted the attention of Samuel Pepys's, in part because Evelyn is so much more guarded than his contemporary about his private life. But since the British Library's acquisition of a large part of his library and the Evelyn family archive, there has been a resurgence of interest in him. The horticultural works, in particular, have attracted attention, with Evelyn now restored to his rightful position in garden theory and history.

SEE ALSO: Bacon, Francis; Boyle, Robert; Petty, William

REFERENCES AND SUGGESTED READINGS

Harris, Francis (2003) *Transformations of love: the friendship of John Evelyn and Margaret Godolphin*. Oxford University Press, Oxford.

Harris, Francis & Hunter, Michael (2003) *John Evelyn and his milieu*. British Library, London.

Hunt, J. D. (2001) *Greater perfection: the practice of garden theory*. Thames & Hudson, London.

Hunter, Michael (1995) *Science and the shape of orthodoxy*. Boydell Press, Woodbridge.

O'Malley, Terese & Wolschke-Bulmahn, Joachim (1998) *John Evelyn's 'Elysium Britannicum' and European gardening*. Dumbarton Oaks, Washington, DC.

F

Fage, Mary

GARRETT A. SULLIVAN, JR

Next to nothing is known about Mary Fage (*fl.* 1637), the author of *Fames roule* (1637). The volume's title page identifies Fage as 'wife of Robert Fage the younger, Gentleman'. There is reason to believe that she was the daughter of Edward Fage (d.1638), that she married her cousin, and that she hailed from Doddinghurst, Essex. For all of Fage's relative anonymity, *Fames roule* is a text that centres on some of the most famous people of her day, members of the court of Charles I. (With the exception of the queen and her daughters, women are not alluded to in the work.) Robert Fage would seem to have had court connections, although it is not clear if either he or his wife spent much time in Westminster, and Fage's poems 'give little evidence of actual familiarity with the politically powerful persons she lists' (Travitsky 1999).

Fames roule contains anagrams and acrostic verses that focus on over 400 court figures; the poems are arranged in terms of precedence, beginning with verses devoted to 'CHARLES our great monarch' and concluding with those 'To the right worshipfull Richard Weston, knight, one of the barons of the *Exchequer*'. Fage establishes a distinctive pattern over the course of her poems. She identifies a member of the court as dedicatee, and then offers first an anagram on that person's name, and second an acrostic verse that develops a theme articulated in the anagram. For instance, in the verses dedicated 'To the most illvstrious Prince, *James*, duke of *Yorke. James Stuarte*', Fage anagrammatizes Stuart's name as 'Av! I seem a star'. She then develops an acrostic that extends the emphasis on the celestial:

> I Seem a Star Au; may your grace well say,
> Amongst our glorious STARRES, who light display,
> Making all *Europe* to behold your light.

The verses dedicated to Charles I offer a noteworthy exception to the pattern, as the acrostic on his name is followed with another that passes twice through the alphabet, concluding each time with the letter 'W'. Charles is the only court figure to receive this alphabetical tribute; the length of the other anagrammatic poems is constrained by the names of the principals.

Fage undoubtedly aims at a virtuosic display designed to impress members of court and, presumably, to secure patronage (although it is unusual for a writer to curry favour with so many potential patrons in a single volume). At the same time, her poetic efforts need to be considered in light of Renaissance conceptions of language. In *The arte of English poesie* (1589), George Puttenham writes that the '*Anagrame, or posie transposed*' is 'a thing if it be done for pastime and exercise of the wit without superstition [is] commendable inough and a meete study for Ladies, neither bringing them any great gayne nor any great losse vnlesse it be of

The Encyclopedia of English Renaissance Literature, First Edition. Edited by Garrett A. Sullivan, Jr and Alan Stewart.
© 2012 Blackwell Publishing Ltd. Published 2012 by Blackwell Publishing Ltd.

idle time'. Puttenham's definition invites a condescending view of Fage's efforts as the products of female idleness, perhaps motivated by the hope of a 'great gayne' in the form of patronage. At the same time, in alluding to 'superstition' Puttenham both registers and disparages the period idea that the (re)arrangement of words could have quasi-magical or supernatural effects. This view underwrites various kinds of magical thinking, such as belief in the medical efficacy of spells or word charms (Pollard 2007). As for anagrams specifically, they were sometimes understood as having prognosticatory power (Fleming 2001). Even if a given poet did not subscribe to such views, much of the potency of anagrammatic verse depends upon the conceit that it reveals a truth about the person whose name is anagrammatized – a conceit partly underwritten by the ancient Adamic association of a word with the essence of the thing it denotes.

For example, when an anagram references the scandalous affair between Robert Carr and the married Francis Howard, countess of Essex, by transforming Howard's name to 'Car findes a whore' (Folger Shakespeare Library, MS V. a. 162), we are invited to believe that, with its letters rearranged, Howard's name betrays her corrupt nature, much as Fage's anagram reveals James Stuart's stellar one. Fage's verses certainly demonstrate the wit and assiduity that she hopes will please her dedicatees, but they also tease her readers with the notion that her verse has a quasi-magical revelatory power. As she puts it in an epistle dedicated to a number of court eminences, she 'adventured to present each of you with with a glimps of his owne glory naturally innated in your Names'.

More broadly, *Fames roule* celebrates the court in a year marked by great political turmoil, including a Scottish uprising in response to Charles's efforts to impose Anglicanism, Puritan charges of government censorship, and an unpopular ruling on the levying of the ship money tax (Travitsky 1999). In the years leading up to the Civil War, members of the court, and royalists more generally, would have perceived *Fames roule* as the welcome articulation of their 'innated' if increasingly beleaguered glory.

SEE ALSO: Puttenham, George

REFERENCES AND SUGGESTED READINGS

Fleming, Juliet (2001) *Graffiti and the writing arts in early modern England.* University of Pennsylvania Press, Philadelphia.

Pollard, Tanya (2007) Spelling the body. In: Floyd-Wilson, Mary & Sullivan, Garrett A., Jr (eds) *Environment and embodiment in early modern England.* Palgrave Macmillan, Basingstoke, pp. 171–186.

Travitsky, Betty S. (1999) Relations of power, relations to power, and power(ful) relations: Mary Fage, Robert Fage, and *Fames roule.* In: King, Sigrid (ed.) *Pilgrimage for love: essays in early modern literature in honor of Josephine A. Roberts.* Arizona Center for Medieval and Renaissance Studies, Tempe, pp. 95–112.

Travitsky, Betty S. (2004) Fage, Mary. In: *Oxford dictionary of national biography.* Oxford University Press, Oxford.

Travitsky, Betty S. & Prescott, Anne Lake (eds) (2000) *Female and male voices in early modern England: an anthology of Renaissance writing.* Columbia University Press, New York, pp. 277–282.

Walker, Kim (1996). *Women writers of the English Renaissance.* Twayne, New York.

Fairfax, Edward

DENNIS AUSTIN BRITTON

Unquestionably, the literary legacy of Edward Fairfax (?1568–?1632/35) is his *Godfrey of Bulloigne, or the recoverie of Jerusalem. Done into English heroicall verse* (1600), a translation of Torquato Tasso's *Gerusalemme liberata* (1580). In his time Fairfax was regarded as an important English poet, evidenced by the fact that Robert Alott frequently quotes lines from *Godfrey* in his miscellany, *Englands Parnassus, or the choysest flowers of our moderne poets* (published just months after *Godfrey*).

Little is known about Fairfax's life; much of what is known about him and his lost works comes from biographical sketches written by his nephew, Brian Fairfax. Edward was the illegitimate son of Sir Thomas Fairfax. He was born in Leeds sometime between 1560 and 1575, and he died in Yorkshire in 1635. From Brian Fairfax we know that Edward authored a long verse work entitled *History of Edward the black prince*, which is now lost, and a pastoral poem of 12 eclogues, of which only two of the remaining four are complete. The primary concerns of the eclogues are religious and anti-Catholic: for example, in the fourth eclogue the shepherd Eglon laments that his favourite lamb has been seduced and bound in chains by a fox (the Catholic Church), and in an unnumbered eclogue the shepherds Hermes and Lycaon enact a debate between True Church and False Church. Additionally, two short poems by Fairfax are extant: 'An epitaph upon King James' and 'Epitaph on Lady Fairfax'.

Godfrey is the first complete translation of *Gerusalemme liberata* to appear in England. Its appearance, however, develops out of an already established English admiration for Italian epic romance in general and Tasso's poem in particular. Fairfax's translation appears after Scipio Gentili's Latin translation – dedicated to Philip Sidney and published in 1584 – of a small portion of the poem, as well as after Richard Carew's 1594 dual-language edition of the first five books.

Most of the scholarship on *Godfrey* attends to differences between Fairfax's version of the poem and Carew's, and to differences between his translation and Tasso's original. Carew's is a very literal, word-for-word translation of Tasso's poem. Although Fairfax follows Tasso's poem rather closely (his stanzas correspond with Tasso's in number and content), C. P. Brand (1965) suggests that Fairfax is much more likely than Tasso to moralize. Charles G. Bell (1954) notes that Fairfax adds nearly 50 classical allusions. These additions are often fairly conventional (e.g., beautiful virgins are compared to Cynthia and brave warriors to Mars). Fairfax's fondness for such comparisons, conventional or otherwise, is nonetheless

a testament to *Godfrey*'s indebtedness to Edmund Spenser's *Faerie Queene*.

Fairfax must have had an edition of Spenser's epic nearby when he translated the *Liberata*; there are moments in *Godfrey* when it is clear that Fairfax is imitating Spenser's imitation of Tasso. An often noted example is Fairfax's imitation of Spenser's *carpe florem* lay in the Bower of Bliss – itself an imitation of the bird's song in Armida's pleasure garden in the *Liberata* – for his translation of the bird's song in Armida's garden. Additional Spenserian influences are seen, as Colin Burrow (1993) suggests, in that Fairfax's heroes often violently feel and respond to erotic impulses. In this, Fairfax's characters are more similar to Spenser's than to Tasso's, who seem to have far more emotional and erotic restraint (compare, for example, Fairfax's and Tasso's treatments of Tancred while he fights and after he kills Clorinda). Such Spenserian influence and differences between *Godfrey* and *Liberata* may ultimately be the result of the poem being '*Done into English*'. Giulia Totó (2008) argues that Fairfax attempted to produce a translation that corresponds with Elizabethan expectations for an English heroic poem.

Godfrey received royal admiration. The first edition of the poem was dedicated to Queen Elizabeth, and in the dedicatory epistle to the 1624 edition of the poem, the printer, John Bill, informs Prince Charles that King James ordered the second edition, and that Godfrey is 'an example of pietie and valour ioyned together, to redeeme one countrey to the honour of Christ'. It then becomes clear in the second edition's dedicatory poem that Prince Charles is imagined as the English Protestant Godfrey, that Charles would '*leade an armie to expel those drones, / That doe usurpe* HIERU-SALEM and ROME'.

Apart from *Godfrey*, Fairfax's most studied work is *Daemonologia*, which circulated in manuscript sometime after 1621 and was first published in 1859. In *Daemonologia*, Fairfax describes the bewitching of four young women (three are his daughters) by a group of local women. The narrative takes place at the height of English anxieties about witchcraft, and the text gives insight into the symptoms of bewitched persons (e.g., trances, visitations by invisible entities, and vomiting pins) and offers a detailed account of the processes by which a group of women were tried as witches. The cases against the women were eventually thrown out of court because of insufficient evidence, but Fairfax never doubted that his daughters had been bewitched.

SEE ALSO: Spenser, Edmund; Sidney, Philip

REFERENCES AND SUGGESTED READINGS

Bell, Charles G. (1947) A history of Fairfax criticism. *PMLA* 62, 644–656.

Bell, Charles G. (1954) Fairfax's Tasso. *Comparative Literature* 6, 26–52.

Brand, C. P. (1965) *Torquato Tasso: a study of the poet and of his contribution to English literature.* Cambridge University Press, Cambridge.

Burrow, Colin (1993) *Epic romance: Homer to Milton.* Clarendon Press, Oxford.

Dodge, R. E. Neil (1927) The text of the *Gerusalemme liberata* in the versions of Carew and Fairfax. *PMLA* 144, 681–695.

Gibson, Marion (ed.) (2003) *Witchcraft and society in England and America, 1550–1750.* Cornell University Press, Ithaca.

Nash, Ralph (1957) On the indebtedness of Fairfax's Tasso to Carew. *Italica* 34, 14–19.

Totó, Giulia (2008) Fairfax's *Godfrey* and the building of a national literary identity. *The Italianist* 28, 5–23.

Fanshawe, Ann

DAVID B. GOLDSTEIN

Ann, Lady Fanshawe (1625–80), a Royalist writer, was known during her life primarily as the wife of Sir Richard Fanshawe, the translator and diplomat. She left two unpublished works, a memoir and a cookbook, both of which are of significant historical and literary importance.

Most of what we know about Lady Fanshawe is reported in her memoir. She was born Ann Harrison, on 25 March 1625, in St Olave, London. Her father, Sir John Harrison (d.1669), from rather undistinguished gentry stock, succeeded in business, buying a coat of arms and a large estate. Her mother, Margaret Fanshawe (d.1640), was the daughter of Robert Fanshawe of Fanshawe Gate, Derbyshire. Ann reports in her memoir that her childhood was peaceful, 'with great plenty and hospitality, but no lavishness'. She describes herself as a 'hoyting girle', or wild child, though trained also (under her mother's tutelage) in all the skills appropriate to her gender and class, such as dancing, music, needlework, and French (Loftis 1979). Upon her mother's death, Ann took charge of her father's accounts, and her new responsibilities coincided with a period of great turmoil for the family. In 1642 her father, an avowed royalist, was imprisoned and his estate sequestered, forcing the Harrisons into relative impoverishment. The Civil War inaugurated a long period of struggle for the Fanshawe family, punctuated by intervals of relative calm and ease. Even at the end of her life Ann was still petitioning the court for money and back pay lost during and after the war.

Ann married Richard Fanshawe (1608–66), her second cousin, on 18 May 1644. 'We never had but one mind throughout our lives,' writes Ann of what seems to have been a happy and companionate partnership. Ann dedicated her intellectual and financial resources to supporting her husband's political endeavours. Richard played important roles in the courts of both Charles I and II, and their travels took the couple to France, Ireland, Scotland, Portugal, and Spain, where Richard was ambassador from 1664 until his death.

Lady Fanshawe composed her memoir in 1676, and addressed it to her surviving son, Richard (1665–94). She apparently never meant to publish the work, intending it rather as a memorial of the deeds of a family and father that the son never knew. The memoir is written in a laconic style that hides a wealth of nuance, complexity, and emotion. Fanshawe found herself at the heart of many of the major incidents of the war and its aftermath.

The 'hoyting girl' shows herself in a few of these instances, usually in the service of her family or husband. Memorable episodes include her escape from Cork during Cromwell's 1649 invasion of the city; her forging of a pass in order to escape England and rejoin her husband in France in 1659; and a cross-dressing episode straight out of Renaissance romance, in the face of a Turkish galleon on the high seas. Throughout her travels, Ann meticulously records both ethnographic details of her environs, and the copious gifts that she both offers and receives. The descriptions of these gifts, and of the noble society in which she circulates, help paint a complex picture of the material networks in which a woman of her class would have been engaged and enmeshed.

One of the major themes of the memoir is the drama of motherhood. Ann is nearly always pregnant, and the spectre of childhood death is never far from the memoir's pages. She records the births of 14 children and suffers several miscarriages, including one of triplets. Especially excruciating is the death of her first-born daughter, Ann (1646–54), of whom Fanshawe writes, 'We both wished to have gone into the grave with her.' Four daughters and her son Richard appear to have survived her.

Lady Fanshawe began compiling her book of receipts (Wellcome History of Medicine, London, Western M MS 7113) in 1651, while Richard was away on the king's ultimately ruinous Scottish campaign. The cookbook was dedicated to her eldest surviving daughter, Katherine (b.1652, d. after 1705), and was also probably not intended for publication. Fanshawe's book contains a variety of culinary and medicinal recipes in several hands, including those of Ann, Sir Richard, Katherine, and an amanuensis. Among the most important are what may be the first recipes in England for ice cream and jarred jam, as well as one of the earliest English drawings of a chocolate pot, probably a gift during their time in Spain. The recipes are frequently attributed to the nobles and commoners from whom they were gathered, including several recipes from Sir Kenelm Digby, who is also the subject of a humorous

story in the memoir. Although many seventeenth-century households maintained manuscript receipt books, to find a surviving cookbook and memoir by the same author is rare, and affords opportunities to see the memoir (which contains many descriptions of food gifts and meals) through the lens of the recipes, and vice versa.

SEE ALSO: Digby, Kenelm; Fanshawe, Richard; recipe books

REFERENCES AND SUGGESTED READINGS

Davidson, Peter (2004) Fanshawe, Ann, Lady. In: *Oxford dictionary of national biography.* Oxford University Press, Oxford.

Findley, Sarah & Hobby, Elaine (1981) Seventeenth century women's autobiography. In: Barker, Francis et al. (eds) *1642: literature and power in the seventeenth century.* University of Essex, Colchester, pp. 11–36.

Loftis, John (ed.) (1979) *The memoirs of Anne, Lady Halkett and Ann, Lady Fanshawe.* Clarendon Press, Oxford.

Potter, David (2008) The household receipt book of Ann, Lady Fanshawe. *Petits Propos Culinaires* 80, 19–32.

Purkiss, Diane (2006) *The English Civil War: papists, gentlewomen, soldiers, and witchfinders in the birth of modern Britain.* Basic Books, New York.

Rose, Mary Beth (1986) Gender, genre, and history: seventeenth-century English women and the art of autobiography. In: Rose, M. B. (ed.) *Women in the Middle Ages and the Renaissance: literary and historical perspectives.* Syracuse University Press, Syracuse, NY, pp. 245–278.

Fanshawe, Richard

EDWARD PALEIT

Sir Richard Fanshawe (1608–66) was a prolific, multilingual translator and poet of the mid-seventeenth century. His chief works are a translation of Battista Guarini's *Il pastor fido*, the founding text of Renaissance tragicomedy (1647; the second edition of 1648 is interesting for its arrangement of supplementary poems and translations), and a translation of the Portuguese national epic *Os lusiadas* by Luís vaz de Camões (1655). A gentleman writer, Fanshawe spent his public life serving the Stuarts as a diplomat and soldier.

Born in 1608 in Ware, Hertfordshire, the son of a royal official, Fanshawe was educated for a time in Thomas Farnaby's school in London. He spent three years at Cambridge, but left without a degree. In 1626 he entered the Inner Temple, but later abandoned the law. His diplomatic career began when in 1635 he became secretary to Sir Walter Aston, ambassador to Spain. When civil war broke out he joined the Royalist court at Oxford. He married his cousin Ann Harrison in 1644. The same year he became secretary of war to Prince Charles, and apart from a brief sojourn in London during 1648, served him continuously until defeat at Worcester in 1651. After some years of unhappy retirement, Fanshawe rejoined Charles in exile in 1658. He was made secretary of the Latin tongue in 1659, and master of requests in 1660, the same year he was knighted. Between 1660 and 1664 he served as envoy extraordinary, then ambassador, to Portugal (where he negotiated Charles's marriage to Catherine of Braganza), and afterwards as ambassador to Spain. He died in Madrid in June 1666.

Fanshawe composed and translated from the late 1620s onwards, though without publication: a rare exception is a commendatory poem for his then friend Thomas May's *Supplementum Lucani* (1640). A famous, typical early work is his 'Ode' responding to Charles I's 1630 proclamation enjoining gentry to return to their estates. This poem blends a golden age vision of rural England, modelled on Virgil and Horace, with a sense of coercive royal power and the possibility of bloodshed in Arcadia. The fusion of the dystopian and the idyllic reappears in his translation of Guarini's *Il pastor fido* (1590), composed in the early 1640s and published in 1647 after Royalist defeat, with a dedicatory poem by Sir John Denham. Arcadian drama, especially tragicomedy, had

strong associations with the pre-war Caroline court and its cults of matrimony and pastoralism. The play's dedication to Prince Charles aligns its setting – Arcadia, cursed by a goddess – with strife-riven England, and parallels Arcadia's salvation through royal marriage with Charles's own matrimonial prospects. The second edition of *Il pastor fido* (1648), published when the Fanshawes had compounded for their estates and (briefly) settled in London, adds several other translations and poems from 1630 onwards in an arrangement designed to counsel Prince Charles about the future. Challenging him to play the role of a benign, constitutional Augustus, it also conveys awareness of the failures of Caroline aesthetics and ideology. Fanshawe identifies himself mostly with a war-weary Horace, to whom he turned again after the catastrophe of Worcester: *Selected parts of Horace, prince of lyrick* (1652), a set of 56 translations, voice the typical themes of Royalist poetry in defeat – drink, friendship, *otium*, the desperate hope for a new Augustus. Most of these translations reappeared in Alexander Brome's *The poems of Horace* (1666).

Fanshawe's translation of Camões's epic, titled *The lusiad*, was composed at Tankersley Park, near Sheffield, probably during 1653/54. Its representation of Portuguese commercial and military sea power, which may reflect on the English Republic's recent maritime successes, suggests a new model for English epic and perhaps the English nation. The inclusion of a prefatory translation of Petronius Arbiter's mini-epic on the Roman civil war distinguishes Fanshawe's from republican epic (Petronius, in Fanshawe's reading, is criticizing his contemporary Lucan, famously translated by the parliamentarian Thomas May), but also challenges the anti-inspirational poetics of William Davenant's *Preface to Gondibert* (1651). The translation's relationship to *Paradise lost*, whose first edition possibly recalls its 10-book structure, has long been noted. Some argue that Milton's epic constitutes a republican retort to the translation's mercantile-imperialist, dynastic values; for David Quint (1993), specific allusions to Fanshawe enable Milton to recast colonial discovery and conquest as Satan's fatal journey to earth.

Tankersley also witnessed the translation of two Spanish court entertainments by Don Antonio de Mendoza (published posthumously, in 1670), *Querer por solo querer* and *Fiestas de Aranjuez*. In 1659 Fanshawe returned to Arcadian drama, publishing a Latin translation of John Fletcher's *The faithfull shepheadess* (c.1608–9). A collection of his later diplomatic correspondence was printed in 1701. The remainder of Fanshawe's poetic works, including Latin translations from Camões, English translations of Boethius and Martial, as well as other English and Latin poems, remained in manuscript until more recently. Lady Ann Fanshawe's autobiography, which contains much on Fanshawe though not on his writings, received a modern edition in 1979. In the past, Royalist translation has been easy to ignore; the critical work of Potter (1989), Parry (1990), and Pugh (2010) has permitted a measure of rehabilitation.

SEE ALSO: Brome, Alexander; Davenant, William; Denham, John; Fanshawe, Ann; Fletcher, John; May, Thomas; Milton, John

REFERENCES AND SUGGESTED READINGS

Davidson, Peter (ed.) (1997) *The poems and translations of Sir Richard Fanshawe*. 2 vols. Oxford University Press, Oxford.

Parry, Graham (1990) A troubled Arcadia. In: Healy, Thomas & Sawday, Jonathan (eds) *Literature and the English Civil War*. Cambridge University Press, Cambridge, pp. 38–55.

Potter, Lois (1989) *Secret rites and secret writing: royalist literature 1641–1660*. Cambridge University Press, Cambridge.

Pugh, Syrithe (2010) *Herrick, Fanshawe, and the politics of intertextuality: classical literature and seventeenth-century royalism*. Ashgate, Aldershot.

Quint, David (1993) *Epic and empire: politics and generic form from Virgil to Milton*. Princeton University Press, Princeton.

Smith, Nigel (1994) *Literature and revolution in England, 1640–1660*. Yale University Press, New Haven.

Farnaby, Thomas

EDWARD PALEIT

Thomas Farnaby (c.1575–1647), who flourished in the early seventeenth century, is a noteworthy figure in the history of English education. A highly successful private schoolmaster, he published some popular manuals on grammar, rhetoric, and composition and was one of the first Englishmen to edit and publish major classical poets. He was well known in London intellectual circles before the Civil War.

Farnaby's early life is known chiefly through what his son Francis divulged to Anthony a Wood. He was born around 1575 in London. In 1590 he matriculated at Merton College, Oxford, but abandoned study shortly afterwards to be taught by the Jesuits in Spain. Forsaking their discipline too, he fought in the Low Countries and apparently sailed with Francis Drake and John Hawkins. He ended up teaching reading and writing in Cornwall. In 1605 he was licensed to teach grammar and Latin at Martock, Somerset, under the anagrammatic pseudonym 'Bainrafe'. This was, presumably, to avoid suspicions of Catholicism, although later Farnaby was clearly a member of the Church of England, serving as a canon of St Paul's. His second wife, Anne, was a daughter of John Howson, bishop of Durham.

Farnaby's private school, based in Cripplegate in the City of London, probably opened towards the end of the first decade of the seventeenth century. It provided a conventional humanist curriculum based around Latin and Greek grammar, rhetoric, and major classical authors. The school was favoured by scions of the titled classes – in a letter, Farnaby terms his pupils *nobiles* – but also the children of wealthy citizens such as Edward King,

Milton's 'Lycidas', to whose memorial volume Farnaby contributed a Latin elegy. In 1623 a year's tuition cost around £20 per pupil. The school was sizeable at peak, although Wood's claim of 300 pupils sounds exaggerated. Amongst its under-masters were Alexander Gil the younger. In 1636 Farnaby was forced to move his school to Kent because of the plague. His was the first private school to seriously rival the humanist grammar schools in reputation, though it did not survive its founder.

Farnaby supplemented his pedagogical reputation by vigorous publication. In 1612 he brought out an edition of the Roman satirists Persius and Juvenal, in a format modelled on John Bond's recent editions of Horace (Farnaby used the same publisher, Richard Field). The volume's success – revised editions followed in 1615, 1621, and 1633 – inspired him to publish Seneca's tragedies (1613, 1624, and 1634), Martial's epigrams (1615 and 1633), and Lucan (1618). Farnaby was the first Englishman to edit and publish commentaries on these texts in England. A selection from the *Greek anthology*, a multi-authored arrangement of classical and post-classical Greek occasional poems translated into Latin and English by various authors (including himself), was published in 1629. Editions of Virgil's works (1634) and Ovid's *Metamorphoses* (1636) followed; an edition of Terence was completed after his death by Meric Casaubon and published in 1651. Contemporaries admired Farnaby's editions chiefly for the clarity and brevity of his commentaries, which were drawn from his teaching notes, and almost certainly aimed at students or secular readers rather than scholars. They were frequently reprinted at home and abroad. Farnaby's editions did not, however, represent the cutting edge of humanist textual scholarship: indeed he usually took his lections from Continental scholars like Daniel Heinsius or Hugo Grotius, occasionally making erratic use of manuscripts in English libraries.

Farnaby also published a number of pedagogical textbooks, all with the primary purpose of facilitating Latin composition. His early works, the *Figurae, tropi et schemata* (first known edition 1616), a brief description of typical rhetorical figures and how to use them, and *Phrases elegantiores* (first known edition 1625), a list of useful Latin phrases under English word-headings, were cheaply produced compositional aids, little more than pamphlets; some editions have perished without trace. In 1625 Farnaby expanded *Figurae* into his *Index rhetoricus*, a breviary of rhetorical theory and terms drawing on a universe of classical and Renaissance authorities, with a particular emphasis on style. This influential work had revised editions in 1629, 1633, 1640, and 1646 and was frequently reprinted abroad and (after Farnaby's death) at home. The 1633 edition added Farnaby's 'oratorical formulae' (previously published in John Clarke's *Formulae oratoriae* of 1630), and in 1640 the work was further swelled by the *Index poeticus* (originally published separately, in 1635), an index of references to passages in Latin and neo-Latin poetry, sorted by name and topic. Collectively, these works condensed the wealth of humanist compositional resources into easy, accessible formats, at some cost to finer distinctions. In the late 1630s Farnaby received royal encouragement to prepare an authorized grammar: the *Systema grammaticum* (1641), however, failed to establish a new standard.

Farnaby's pedagogical efforts, in print and in the schoolroom, brought him considerable reward. He was incorporated MA by Oxford University in 1616 and probably at Cambridge before then. In 1630 he bought an estate in Kippington near Sevenoaks, Kent, for £2,200, later adding lands in Sussex. The range of dedicatory poems written by and for him indicates his prominence in London intellectual life and sometimes further afield. His editions of the satirists and Seneca earned commendatory poems from Ben Jonson – an early friend, though they later fell out over a debt – and his Lucan from John Selden. His correspondence with the linguist Isaac Vossius survives and he also had contact with Dutch scholars such as Pieter Schrijver and Daniel Heinsius. In 1633 Charles I granted Farnaby a 21-year embargo on imports of foreign, pirated editions of his published works.

Farnaby's career nosedived somewhat in the 1640s: appointed in June 1643 as a parliamentary licenser for 'books of Philosophy, History, Poetry, Morality, and of Arts', the following month he was involved in a Royalist uprising in Kent, and imprisoned in Newgate and then Ely House (where he continued to teach privately). Released in 1645, he died two years later on his Kent estate.

SEE ALSO: Jonson, Ben; Milton, John; Selden, John

REFERENCES AND SUGGESTED READINGS

Nadeau, Ray (1950) Thomas Farnaby: schoolmaster and rhetorician of the English Renaissance. *Quarterly Journal of Speech* 36, 340–344.

Serjeantson, R. W. (2001) Thomas Farnaby. In: Malone, Edward A. (ed.) *British rhetoricians and logicians, 1500–1660*, 1st series. Detroit, Gale, pp. 108–116.

Fell, Margaret

ELIZABETH MALSON-HUDDLE

Margaret Fell (1614–1702), often regarded as the mother of the Quaker movement, served energetically as a leader, a writer, and a defender of early Quakers. After George Fox (1624–91), the charismatic founder of the sect, converted her and her daughters to Quakerism in 1652, Fell immediately began to use her gentry status, her connections, and her wealth to lend financial and political assistance to the Society of Friends. Her first husband, Thomas Fell (d.1658), a distinguished judge and local politician, did not convert; however, he protected Quakers from persecution and invited them to hold meetings at his home, Swarthmoor Hall, in Ulverston, Lancashire. Swarthmoor continued to provide an important refuge and organizational center for the movement throughout Fell's lifetime. It was there that Margaret died in 1702.

Fell's polemical writing and activism advocated religious tolerance for peaceable sectarians and sought release for imprisoned Quakers. Between 1655 and 1657, Fell wrote letters to Cromwell, who esteemed her, protesting Quaker persecution and asking him to fulfil his promise to protect 'liberty of conscience'. By the Restoration, Quakers, estimated to be 50,000 strong, had become the largest religious sect in England. After the uprising of Fifth Monarchists in 1661, persecution of dissenters substantially increased under Charles II. The passage of the Quaker Act in 1662, which required citizens to sign an Oath of Allegiance to the king, and the Conventicles Act in 1664, which made Quaker meetings illegal, resulted in corporal punishment and the imprisonment of many Friends. Fell and Fox were frequently arrested and sometimes spent long periods in prison. Fell repeatedly visited the king and begged him in letters and pamphlets to release imprisoned Friends and to tolerate peaceable Quakers. In *A declaration and an information*, a tract 'Delivered into the Kings hand' in 1660, she equates religious toleration with 'civil Rights and Liberties of Subjects, as freeborn English men'. As an organizer, Fell worked closely with Fox, supporting his missionary travels and often obtaining his release from prison. The two Quaker leaders married in 1669.

Fell's writings, like those of religious dissenters such as John Milton and Gerrard Winstanley, condemned the clergy, whom she called 'hirelings', protested tithes, and the persecution of nonconformists. Like radical sectarians such as the Diggers and the Fifth Monarchists, she refuted the privileges of wealth and birth and asserted that God was not a 'respecter of persons'. With other sectarians and Friends, she believed God's judgement and the millennial rule of Christ's kingdom were imminent. She employed the fiery rhetoric of millennialism to threaten the nations' leaders if they continued to persecute God's saints, the Quakers. In her letter to Colonel West in 1653, she prophesied, 'But he is coming to confound, and throw down that filthy Idol, which they call their Worship, which is odious in his sight.'

Fell's millennial expectations also inspired her to reach out to Jewish leaders and communities on the Continent to convert them to Quakerism; she wrote four pamphlets to the Jews, had them translated into Dutch and Hebrew, and distributed them in Holland. Achsah Guibbory (2000) observes that the Quakers, with other revolutionaries who supported the readmission of Jews to England in the 1650s, believed the conversion of the Jews to be necessary for messianic redemption. Like Mary Cary, the prophetic Fifth Monarchist writer and other radical polemicists of the period, Fell asserted that Old Testament prophecies of the Israelites applied to the Quakers, who had become God's new chosen people. In *A loving salutation to the seed of Abraham among the Jewes*, she writes, 'Now this is unto you all, who are out of the light, from the seed which hath obtained the promise, that ye may come to partake of the same, and be brought to the fold where there is one Shepheard.'

When she refused to sign the Oath of Allegiance to the king in 1664, Fell suffered four years in prison and temporary loss of her estate. During her imprisonment, she wrote her defence of female ministry, *Womens speaking justified*. Using her detailed knowledge of scripture, she highlights the importance of women in the Gospels, such as the vital role played by the women who found Jesus absent from his tomb: 'if their hearts had not been so united and knit unto him in love, that they could not depart as the men did, but sat watching, and waiting, and weeping about the Sepulchre untill the time of his Resurrection, and so were ready to carry his Message, as is manifested, else how should his Disciples have known, who were not there?' Her defence also provides alternative interpretations of key passages often cited by clergy to silence women, such as Paul's prohibition of women speaking in church in 1 Corinthians 14.34–35. Fell risked her property and her life to promote Quakerism and to advocate liberty of conscience; her work remains significant for scholars of early Quakerism, millennialism, early modern women

writers, and the development of religious toleration.

SEE ALSO: Cary, Mary; Fox, George; Milton, John; Winstanley, Gerrard

REFERENCES AND SUGGESTED READINGS

Braithewaite, William C. (1955) *The beginnings of Quakerism.* Cambridge University Press, Cambridge.

Garman, Mary, Applegate, Judith, Benefiel, Margaret, & Meredith, Dorothea (eds) (1996) *Hidden in plain sight: Quaker women's writings 1650–1700.* Pendle Hill, Wallingford, PA.

Guibbory, Achsah (2000) Conversation, conversion, messianic redemption: Margaret Fell, Menasseh ben Israel, and the Jews. In: Summers, Claude J. & Pebworth, Ted-Larry (eds) *Literary circles and cultural communities in Renaissance England.* University of Missouri Press, Columbia, pp. 210–234.

Kunze, Bonnelyn (1994) *Margaret Fell and the rise of Quakerism.* Stanford University Press, Stanford.

Kunze, Bonnelyn (2004) Fell, Margaret. In: *Oxford dictionary of national biography.* Oxford University Press, Oxford.

Loewenstein, David & Morrill, John (2002) Literature and religion. In: Loewenstein, David & Mueller, Janel (eds) *The Cambridge history of early modern English literature.* Cambridge University Press, Cambridge, pp. 703–706.

Mack, Phyllis (1992) *Visionary women: ecstatic prophecy in seventeenth-century England.* University of California Press, Berkeley.

Fenner, Dudley

EMMA ANNETTE WILSON

Puritan writer and preacher Dudley Fenner (1558–87) was a pioneering advocate of the English vernacular, a writer of radical theological works, and author of a textbook in English, *The artes of logike and rethorike* (1584), based on the work of French Protestant logician Petrus Ramus. Controversial in several aspects of his professional life, Fenner died in exile in the Low Countries, but his public championing of the English language in theological, pedagogical, and literary forms was innovative and merits further investigation.

Born in Kent in 1558, Fenner matriculated at Peterhouse College, Cambridge, in 1575 where he encountered the controversial theologian Thomas Cartwright, with whom he would later share an English ministry in the Netherlands. He did not graduate, but instead, as he recorded later (in *A parte of a register*, published in 1593), was forced in the mid-1570s to leave the university without a degree, probably because of his emergent Puritanism. He preached briefly in the Kent parish of Cranbrook before travelling to Antwerp and Middelburg to serve the Merchant Adventurers in a ministry shared with Walter Travers and, later, Cartwright.

In 1583 Fenner returned to England as a preacher in Cranbrook. In October 1583 archbishop of Canterbury John Whitgift issued three articles instigating increased homogeneity in religious services in England, most controversially that preachers use only the Book of Common Prayer in their sermons, a deeply unpopular edict among more radical ministers. When Whitgift campaigned to make ministers subscribe to the articles, Fenner, together with Josias Nicholls of Eastwell, led a group of 17 Kent preachers who refused to do so. Fenner was one of several co-authors of *A parte of a register*, a formal petition on this matter brought to the lower house of convocation around 1586. Although the petition itself failed in the house of convocation, it was deemed to be of sufficient public interest to be printed overseas in 1593 by Richard Schilders, printer to the states of Zealand, who also printed the majority of Fenner's posthumous publications in the 1590s. Fenner also penned his own polemic entitled *A defence of the godlie ministers* at around this time; this was published in England in 1587.

As one of the leaders of the non-subscribers, Fenner was suspended from his ministry and made to answer to 17 charges brought against him. In his response to the seventeenth and last charge, the connections between his religious convictions and his advocacy of the English vernacular are apparent: he was charged with having baptized children in his parish with outlandish, unsuitable names such as More-Fruit, Dust, From-Above, and Joy-Againe. He did not deny this, but rather set out to justify his act: he argued that names such as Samuel, Zacherye, or Tymothie (*sic*) were meaningful in their Hebraic and Hellenic languages of origin, and that the names he had allowed his parishioners to select were simply English equivalents, names with clear moral meanings which parishioners could understand in their native language. He lived by example in this, calling his four daughters More-Fruit, Faint-Not, Free-Gift, and Well-Abroad. Choosing names with vernacular moral impetus was a widespread controversial practice amongst English Puritans, and was memorably parodied on stage by Ben Jonson in *The alchemist* (1610) and *Bartholomew Fayre* (1614) in his characters Tribulation Wholesome, and Zeal-of-the-land Busy. Fenner was a high-profile defendant of this practice, and in *The order of the housholde* (1584) he specified the selection of names as a duty of a father. This text was published together with his vernacular textbook, *The artes of logike and rethorike*, and in the same year he produced an English translation of the Song of Songs, further substantiating his promotion of the vernacular in theological and educational contexts.

Fenner's impassioned defence did not enable him to win his case: he was one of only a handful of preachers whose suspensions were not lifted, and in 1585 he went in voluntary exile to the Netherlands, reuniting with the Merchant Adventurers as their preacher in Middelburg. There he published *Sacra theologia* (1585), a major work on Calvinist theology in which his Ramist affiliations are clearly visible, as every divine question considered is dichotomously divided and scrutinized in accordance with the order of Ramist analysis. Although he was to die in 1587, aged just 29, only two years after the initial publication of his *Sacra theologia*, this text remained of sufficient interest to be translated into English by Henry

Finch and published in 1599. Likewise in the 1590s an edition of his *Short and profitable treatise* concerning recreations emerged, suggesting the continued interest and relevance of Fenner's works after his death.

To date Fenner has not attracted much scholarly study. Patrick Collinson (1983; 2006) and Nicholas Tyacke (1979) have brought his theological writing to critical attention, but his *Artes of logike and rethorike* merits further enquiry in terms of its aims for vernacular education, and as a contribution to the development of logic and rhetoric in this period. First published anonymously by Richard Schilders in Middelburg, the text was popular enough to merit a second edition in 1588 which identified Fenner as its author. It also underwent a revival of interest during the Interregnum, when it appeared in *A compendium of the art of logick and rhetorick in the English tongue* (1651), served as a source for John Smith's *The mysterie of rhetorique unvail'd* (1657), and reappeared again in *The art of rhetoric, with a discourse of the laws of England* (1681), misattributed for many years to Thomas Hobbes. *The artes of logike and rethorike* was based on the work of Petrus Ramus, whose *Dialecticae libri duo* (1543) and its vernacular translation *La dialectique* (1555) aimed to reform scholastic education by presenting material concisely. Fenner's work embodies these principles of accessibility, setting forth precepts simply, and following them with examples which he draws from the Bible, thereby uniting his educational approach with his theology. Roland MacIlmaine had produced an English-language translation of *The logike of the moste excellent philosopher P. Ramus martyr* in 1574, but Fenner's was the first English translation of Ramist rhetoric.

Logic and rhetoric were the central subjects of early modern pedagogy. Published in a period when education was generally in Latin, Fenner's book represents a significant attempt to render this knowledge accessible to a far wider readership by presenting it in a language they could understand. He was one of only a handful of sixteenth-century writers to attempt this project, and the only one to do so without holding a university degree: Thomas Wilson presented a scholastic logic, *The rule of reason* (1551) and a Ciceronian rhetoric, *The arte of rhetorique* (1553), while Abraham Fraunce produced *The lawiers logike* (1588), and the *Arcadian rhetorike* (1588). Both Wilson and Fenner received the patronage and protection of Robert Dudley, earl of Leicester, but Fenner's works in discourse and theology represent a much more controversial advocacy of the English vernacular.

SEE ALSO: Cox, Leonard; Fraunce, Abraham; Jonson, Ben; Wilson, Thomas

REFERENCES AND SUGGESTED READINGS

Collinson, Patrick (1983) *Godly people: essays on English Protestantism and Puritanism.* Hambledon Press, London.

Collinson, Patrick (2006) What's in a name: Dudley Fenner and the peculiarities of Puritan nomenclature. In: Fincham, Kenneth & Lake, Peter (eds) *Religious politics in post-Reformation Britain.* Boydell Press, Woodbridge, pp. 113–127.

Crane, Mary Thomas (1993) *Framing authority: sayings, self, and society in sixteenth-century England.* Princeton University Press, Princeton.

Grafton, Antony & Jardine, Lisa (1986) *From humanism to the humanities: education and the liberal arts in fifteenth- and sixteenth-century Europe.* Duckworth, London.

Howell, W. S. (1961) *Logic and rhetoric in England, 1500–1700,* 2nd edn. Russell & Russell, New York.

Mack, Peter (2002) *Elizabethan rhetoric: theory and practice.* Cambridge University Press, Cambridge.

Tyacke, Nicholas (1979) Popular Puritan mentality in late Elizabethan England. In: Clark, Peter, Smith, Alan G. R., & Tyacke, Nicholas (eds) *The English Commonwealth 1547–1640: essays in politics and society presented to Joel Hurstfield.* Leicester University Press, Leicester, pp. 77–92.

Fenton, Geoffrey

ALISON TAUFER

The most noteworthy contribution to Elizabethan literature by Geoffrey Fenton

(1539–1608), like that of his contemporary William Painter, was the introduction of the Continental novella to England. Unlike Painter's *Palace of pleasure* (1566), however, Fenton's *Certaine tragicall discourses* (1567) does not appear to have had any significant influence on the drama of his time. Fenton's writing is marked by its moral didacticism as well as a rhetorical style that includes the heavy use of antithesis, alliteration, amplification, parallelism, and repetition. Fenton's elaborate rhetoric contributed significantly to the development of the Elizabethan prose style later termed 'euphuism', which appears in such works as George Pettie's *Petite pallace of Pettie his pleasure* (1576), John Lyly's *Euphues* (1578), and Robert Greene's *Planetomachia* (1585) and *Penelopes web* (1587).

Geoffrey Fenton was born around 1539 in Fenton, Nottinghamshire, to Henry Fenton and Cecily Beaumont Fenton. Although there is no evidence that he attended either Oxford or Cambridge, he appears to have been well educated. Fluent in French and Latin, Fenton also knew Spanish and Italian. After more than a decade of steady literary output devoted to the translation of Continental texts (1567–79), Fenton turned to politics and in 1580 was appointed the secretary of state for Ireland by William Cecil, Lord Burghley. While serving in Ireland, Fenton regularly reported to Elizabeth I on the activities of his fellow administrators. Although his reports earned Fenton Elizabeth's good will and trust, they seriously compromised his relationships with his superiors and colleagues. In 1585, Fenton married Alice Weston, daughter of Robert Weston, former lord chancellor of Ireland. They had a son, William, and daughter, Catherine. Although Fenton was made principal secretary of the Irish Council in 1587, knighted in 1589, and confirmed for life to the post of secretary of state in 1604, his career in Ireland was marked by continued conflict with the Irish Council. He died on 19 October 1608 and is buried in St Patrick's Cathedral.

Fenton's literary works are adaptations more than translations in that he often significantly altered his sources to fit his own moral and religious viewpoints. Although Fenton translated Italian and Spanish texts, it appears that his adaptations are all from French translations of the originals. Fenton's first and most significant work is *Certaine tragicall discourses*, a collection of 13 tales adapted from François Belleforest and Pierre Boaistuau's *Histoires tragiques, extraits des oeuvres Italiennes de Bandel* (1559), a French version of Matteo Bandello's *Novelle* (1554). This text is his only work of fiction; the rest of his literary output consists of religious, historical, and philosophical tracts. A translation based on a 1567 sermon by the Spanish reformer Antonio de Corro, entitled *An epistle or godlie admonition, of a learned minister of the gospel of our savior Christ, sent to the pastors of the Flemish church in Antwerp* (1569), critiques the doctrine of transubstantiation. *A discourse of the civile warres and late troubles in France* (1570) depicts the events of France's Third War of Religion and is based on the *Memoires de la trezième guerre civile et des derniers troubles de France sous Charles IX* attributed to Jean de Serres, a French Huguenot. *Actes of conference in religion, holden at Paris, betweene two papist doctours of Sorbone and two godlie ministers of the church* (1571) records a debate over the validity of the Catholic Mass as opposed to the sacrament of the Last Supper. Although the text was originally written by Simon Vigor, archbishop of Narbonne, Fenton managed to convert it into an anti-Catholic tirade. Fenton adapted *Monophylo* (1572), a dialogue concerning love and its relationship to marriage, from Etienne Pasquier's *Le monophyle* (1554). A prescription for government based on the religious authority of scripture, *A forme of Christian pollicie gathered out of French* (1574) is a translation of the work of the French canon Jean Talpin. *Golden epistles, contayning varietie of discourse, both morall, philosophicall, and divine* (1575) draws from Jean de Guterry's French translation (1556, 1559) of Antonio de Guevara's *Epistolas familiares* (1539–41), a series of didactic letters to various dignitaries and nobles.

Fenton's last and most ambitious work, second only to *Certaine tragicall discourses* in its importance, is *The historie of Guicciardin, containing the warres of Italie* (1579), based on Francesco Guicciardini's *Storia d' Italia* (1537–40), an account of the period between Lorenzo de' Medici's death in 1492 and the Treaty of Cambrai between François I and Charles V in 1529. Dedicated to Queen Elizabeth, the text was used extensively by Abraham Fleming in the 1587 edition of Holinshed's *Chronicles*. The publication of the *Historie of Guicciardin* marked the end of Fenton's literary career.

SEE ALSO: Elizabeth I; Fleming, Abraham; Greene, Robert; Holinshed, Raphael; Lyly, John; Painter, William; Pettie, George

REFERENCES AND SUGGESTED READINGS

Barry, J. (2006) Sir Geoffrey Fenton and the office of secretary of state for Ireland, 1580–1608. *Irish Historical Studies* 35, 137–159.

Fellheimer, Jeanette (1945) Geoffrey Fenton's *Histoire of Guicciardin* and Holinshed's *Chronicles* of 1587. *Modern Language Quarterly* 6, 285–298.

Salzman, Paul (1985) *English prose fiction 1558–1700: a critical history*. Clarendon Press, Oxford.

Taufer, Alison (1994) Geoffrey Fenton. In: Richardson, D. A. (ed.) *Sixteenth-century British nondramatic writers*, 2nd series. Gale, Detroit, pp. 117–121.

Ferrers, George

MIKE PINCOMBE

George Ferrers (c.1510–1579) is perhaps still best known to students of English Renaissance literature as William Baldwin's principal collaborator in the composition of *A mirrour for magistrates* (1st edn 1559). Ferrers wrote five 'tragedies' – first-person complaints spoken by phantoms of the deceased English nobility from Richard II to Richard III – for the work; he may have helped recruit some of the other poets, too. Moreover, according to Baldwin's preface, it was Ferrers who suggested that it would be a good idea to continue the sequence

of tragedies back to the invasion and colonization of Britain by the Trojan refugee Brutus; and this may be his greatest legacy to English poetry, since that is exactly what motivated later continuations of the *Mirrour* by John Higgins in 1574 and Thomas Blenerhasset in 1578 (Human 2008). In this respect, we might even claim that this larger *Mirrour* project, as opposed to the original scheme often referred to as 'Baldwin's *Mirrour*', should perhaps be called 'Ferrers's *Mirrour*' – a tribute to his wider vision and ambition for the work.

However, while all this is in itself no mean achievement, in his own time Ferrers was more familiar as the impresario who devised, managed, and acted in the spectacular Christmas revels staged for the pleasure of the young Edward VI in 1551/52 and 1552/53 (Westfall 2001). Sadly, no scripts survive for these shows, but from the descriptions which have come down to us we may form some sense of Ferrers's theatrical imagination. Since Edward was fervently Protestant, it is no surprise that these entertainments were anti-papal in content; but their often grotesquely imaginative character – they mix cats, astronomers, Turks, hydras, and bagpipes – testify to the loss of a playful mid-Tudor theatrical genius.

Born around 1510 into a well-established gentry family in Hertfordshire, George Ferrers was one of a large group of talented and ambitious young men recruited to the service of Henry VIII's chief minister Thomas Cromwell during his ascendancy in the 1530s, most of whom seemed to have survived the fall of their master in 1540 and gone on to fame and fortune in the decades that followed. Ferrers seems to have had a knack for pleasing people; he got on very well not only with Cromwell, but also with Henry VIII, with Edward Seymour, duke of Somerset, lord protector to Edward VI, and, especially, with the young king himself, as his position of master of the king's revels indicates. And despite his attacks on the pope in these shows, after Edward's death we find Ferrers loyally manning the walls when Sir Thomas Wyatt the younger marched against London in the first year of the reign of the Catholic Queen Mary. Though he was probably inclined towards Protestantism, then, his chief loyalty seems to have been to the crown.

This point is worth consideration, given that the little criticism there is of Ferrers's poetry tends to be occupied with deciphering his political and thus confessional loyalties. A strong case has recently been advanced for Ferrers as an evangelical Protestant whose poems for the *Mirrour* are meant to console his co-religionists under Mary, and to vindicate the policies of their former leader, the duke of Somerset (Lucas 2003); but topical allegory is a notoriously slippery analytical tool and more work needs to be done on his five poems before we can be assured one way or the other. On the other hand, laying aside these political readings, we may note that Ferrers, unlike Baldwin, was genuinely interested in the historical aspect of the tragedies, which in the original version run from the reign of Richard II to that of Henry VII; indeed, he may have written a chronicle history of the reign of Mary for Richard Grafton's 1569 *Chronicle*. Ferrers had a keen interest in constitutional history: his translation of *Magna carta* was published in 1534 when he was in his mid-twenties; and he burrowed away in the state archives and used the parliament rolls to flesh out his *Mirrour* poems rather than merely relying on the chronicles like other writers.

Ferrers's career as a courtier came to an end in the summer of 1555, when he overplayed his part as an informer against Princess Elizabeth, who stood accused of using witchcraft against her sister, Queen Mary (Campbell 1934). Thereafter his name disappears from the court record. This faux pas and the fall from grace that followed it rehearses at the level of farce the *de casibus* tragedy that chiefly occupied him as a poet. Indeed, Ferrers is the most likely candidate for the person who so carefully revised the 1571 and 1578 editions of the *Mirrour* after Baldwin's death in 1563.

But Ferrers may have been finally reconciled with Elizabeth 20 years later, when he was presented to her at the spectacular entertainment laid on for her at Kenilworth Castle by Robert Dudley, earl of Leicester, in 1575. Using his well-tried skills as a courtly artist one more time, Ferrers contributed verses to a device concerning the liberation of the captive Lady of the Lake; since this seems to have been a figure for the young Princess Elizabeth, he may at last have found a way to apologize.

SEE ALSO: Baldwin, William; Grafton, Richard; Higgins, John

REFERENCES AND SUGGESTED READINGS

Campbell, Lily B. (1934) Humphrey duke of Gloucester and Elianor Cobham his wife in *The mirror for magistrates. Huntington Library Bulletin* 5, 119–156.

Campbell, Lily B. (ed.) (1938) *The mirror for magistrates.* Cambridge University Press, Cambridge.

Human, Elizabeth M. A. (2008) House of mirrors: textual variation and the *Mirror for magistrates. Literature Compass* 4, 772–790.

Lucas, Scott (2003) The consolation of tragedy: *A mirror for magistrates* and the fall of the 'good duke' of Somerset. *Studies in Philology* 100, 44–70.

Westfall, Suzanne (2001) The boy who would be king: court revels of King Edward VI, 1547–1553. *Comparative Drama* 35, 271–290.

Woudhuysen, H. R. (2004) Ferrers, George. In: *Oxford dictionary of national biography.* Oxford University Press, Oxford.

Fisher, Payne

JASON PEACEY

Payne Fisher (1616–93) was one of the mid-seventeenth century's tragicomic figures, a poet who struggled to negotiate turbulent times, whose limited finances and meagre talents combined to produce an *oeuvre* more noticeable for its volume than its quality, and who used print in novel ways in order to grub for money and patronage. Born in 1616, the son of a Dorset gentleman, Fisher was educated at St Paul's School, Oxford, and Cambridge, but became a professional soldier, first on the

Continent, then in the Bishops' Wars in England, and also in Ireland. During the Civil War he fought for Charles I, at least until the battle of Marston Moor, after which he suffered imprisonment by Parliamentarians, defected to their cause, and served once again in Ireland. After 1648, Fisher devoted himself almost entirely to literature, and, having accommodated himself to the Republic, became poet laureate to both Oliver and Richard Cromwell. After the Restoration, he lived entirely by his pen, which ensured protracted periods in debtors' prison, before his death in 1693.

Fisher's life and poetry are inseparable. The bulk of his verse relates directly to the events he witnessed and to the patrons he courted, and provides invaluable biographical evidence. The earliest poems, such as 'The cryes of Ulster', date from Ireland in the early 1640s, while others were penned on campaign with the Royalist army, and reveal a fervent anti-Puritanism. These works were then collected and revised in prison in the mid-1640s, doubtless in order to secure release and patronage. For the rest of his life, Fisher's topical, heroic, panegyrical, and ceremonial poetry, often in Latin hexameters or English blank verse, was used to secure personal advancement, and his contemporary fame and historical importance rest largely upon his unusual literary tactics and career during the Commonwealth. His circle of friends included Edward Benlowes, John Hall, and Marchamont Nedham, and like some of these he secured republican patronage despite a Royalist past. This probably reflected his willingness to flatter men in power, and his potential as a propagandist. What makes him distinctive is the frequency with which he used poetry as a means of approaching political grandees, and the success with which he used printed presentation copies as a means of self-promotion. Anthony a Wood regarded Fisher as a 'true time-server', who used publication in order to 'shark money from those who delighted to see their names in print'.

Fisher's first major published work, *Hyberniae lachrymae* (1648), emerged from his experience in Ireland, but more important was his

poetic reflection upon the Parliamentarian victory at *Marston-moor* (1650). It was this work which prompted official consideration of how best to encourage Fisher as a propagandist, resulting in occasional payments of between £50 and £100 in return for 'good service'. Such payments ensured that new works came thick and fast during the early 1650s. Verses celebrating Cromwell's military victories, such as *Veni, vidi, vici* (1652) and *Irenodia gratulatoria* (1652), appeared with dedications to powerful politicians, and dedicatory verses from propagandists like Nedham, and were often published by official printers. Fisher was also commissioned to research and write an account of the battle of Dunbar, and although this was never completed, he did compose verses in honour of England's victorious navy, in *Pro navali anglorum* (1653). Fisher consciously saw his role as being that of glorifying the republican regime, and he gave himself the title 'historiographer' to Cromwell: with the establishment of the Protectorate this position was formalized. In return for financial rewards, he wrote and published countless verses, often with official support, to mark key political events and anniversaries, such as Cromwell's inaugurations as protector in 1654 and 1657, marriages within the political elite, and the deaths of courtiers and military figures. Although not salaried, Fisher's official position was evident from his participation in Cromwell's funeral procession.

The major difficulty with Fisher's work during the 1650s, however, centres upon distinguishing between official and unofficial works. Fisher was somewhat innovative in using printed poetry – often in the form of individual poems printed on single sheets – in order to flatter potential patrons and to solicit financial rewards or supplementary employment. He certainly worked for George Monck in the mid-1650s, as part of his lifeguard as commander-in-chief in Scotland, and also used his pen to flatter European powers. Verses presented to the Venetian ambassador in 1656 secured a specially minted medal, commissioned by the Doge and valued at £12, and other verses were dedicated to Cardinal Mazarin, doubtless for similar purposes. The boundary between his private works of self-promotion and his official poetry is complicated further by the tendency to compile both kinds of verse together in collected works, such as *Inauguratio Olivariana* (1654) and *Piscatoris poemata* (1656).

For his poetry and his self-promotion, Fisher was widely mocked by contemporaries. This emerges nicely from an episode in April 1658, when he delivered a speech in Oxford to mark the death of Archbishop James Ussher – subsequently printed as *Armanchanus redivivus* (1658) – only to be roundly jeered by his audience. Reporting the episode to his father, John Locke observed that 'never did any man take so much pains to be ridiculous'. Such derision, as well as his changing of sides, probably guaranteed that Fisher's fortunes after 1660 were far from secure. He continued to use presentation copies of verses in order to flatter and to secure money from public figures such as Samuel Pepys; Edward Hyde, first earl of Clarendon; George Monck; and Joseph Williamson. The most important work of his life, an attempt to catalogue tombs and monuments around London, was probably a commercial venture, albeit an unsuccessful one. Such tactics continued during Fisher's long imprisonment for debt after 1673, which saw a steady stream of poetry as well as works on heraldry and history, and works in honour of his own family.

SEE ALSO: Benlowes, Edward; Hall, John, of Durham; Nedham, Marchamont

REFERENCES AND SUGGESTED READINGS

Carpenter, Andrew (2003) *Verse in English from Tudor and Stuart Ireland*. Cork University Press, Cork.

Firth, C. H. (1900) The battle of Dunbar. *Transactions of the Royal Historical Society* 14, 19–52.

Jenkins, Harold (1952) *Edmund Benlowes (1602–1676): biography of a minor poet*. Athlone Press, London.

MacLean, Gerald (1990) *Time's witness: historical representation in English poetry, 1603–1660*. University of Wisconsin Press, Madison.

Norbrook, David (1999) *Writing the English republic*. Cambridge University Press, Cambridge.

Fitzgeffrey, Henry

ROBERT DARCY

Henry Fitzgeffrey (d.1639/40) was the author of a single volume of poetry, *Satyres and satyricall epigrams*, published in 1617 and republished with four elegies by different authors in 1618 and 1620 as *Certain elegies, done by sundrie excellent wits, with satyres and epigrames*. The original volume, divided into three 'books' of formal verse satire, epigrams, and 'humours', belongs to a body of writing that imitated the ancient Roman satires of Horace, Persius, and Juvenal, and the epigrams of Martial. It also owes an immediate debt to Elizabethan satirists such as Joseph Hall and John Marston, and epigrammatists such as John Weever, who helped adapt the classical genres into English form in the late 1590s. The second son of a knight, Fitzgeffrey had been a king's scholar at Westminster School and had matriculated as a pensioner at Trinity College, Cambridge, in 1611. At the time of his pamphlet's appearance, Fitzgeffrey was a law student at Lincoln's Inn where he was admitted to the bar in 1621. Little is known of the remainder of his adult life, except that he died in 1639/40.

Fitzgeffrey's production of satirical poetry for print demonstrates that the genre condemned by the Bishops' Ban of 1599 had not only continued to have a coterie audience at the Inns of Court – probably as a pastime carried over from university days – but also had been allowed to return to the press without facing censorship. The publication of Fitzgeffrey's only volume of poetry came in the year following the death of his elder brother, George, whose will indicates that he was heavily in debt and that much of this debt passed to Henry by way of sureties Henry had made on his brother's behalf (Eccles 1982). Such circumstances might suggest a monetary motive for the publication that followed.

As was true of Fitzgeffrey's work, satires and epigrams can be general and typological as well as topical; when topical, they offer an apparent view into the immediate social and political world of the poet. Fitzgeffrey's subjects are standard among satirists: they include the beleaguered state of poetry as every untalented wit attempts to write it, the ubiquitous flouting of moral living and good behaviour, and the comedy of social habits. It is unclear exactly how earnest the volume is about presenting itself as a serious piece of writing; Fitzgeffrey's friends from Lincoln's Inn contribute laudatory poems that appear throughout the volume, one suggesting that the poet's surname ('Fitz' means 'son of') aptly describes him as the son of the most famous literary Geoffrey – that is, Chaucer. Such overblown praise may or may not hint at an intentional irony at work throughout the publication, especially in the context of the first satire's complaint about books of bad poetry that always include

> a dozen verses . . .
> With commendations of the Author's stuff,
> And in Hyperboles his Name extol
> Yond Homer, Virgil, Ovid, Juvenal.

While Fitzgeffrey's satires and epigrams reference London life and social trends and behaviours, his 'humours' are presented as 'Notes from Black-Fryers' purporting to be specific observations of play-goers at the indoor Blackfriars Theatre. Although not unrelated to classical satire, Fitzgeffrey's 'humours' are a more distinctly English variation, relating in satirical poetry the visual experience of the London playhouse. For instance, he comments on the Blackfriar's cross-dressing female audience members:

> Now *Mars* defend vs! seest thou who comes yonder?
> Monstrous! A *Woman* of the *masculine Gender* . . .
> Out, point not man! Least wee be beaten both.
> Eye her a little, marke but where shee'l goe,
> Now (by this hand) into the Gallants Roe.

Such observations in Fitzgeffrey's work have been cited by scholars such as Natasha Korda (2004) in assessing the role of women on the early modern stage and in the audience. More specifically, Fitzgeffrey's association of theatre and the medical 'humours' derives in part from the way theatrical representation was thought to reveal human temperament. In its specific terminology, however, the theatre of 'humours', a dramatic sub-genre popular in the 1590s, also dates to the Poetomachia, or war of the theatres, of 1599–1601, during which Ben Jonson on one side, and John Marston and Thomas Dekker on the other, wrote unflattering satirical portraits of one another in several of their comedies. Because Jonson was the author of the comedies *Every man in his humor* (1598) and *Every man out of his humor* (1599), he came to be dubbed a 'humourist' for his participation in writing topically satirical theatre. Fitzgeffrey, too, undertakes such 'humorous' work, and his organization of his book into satires, epigrams, and humours follows the triad of 'satirist, epigrammatist, and humourist' targeted by *The whipping of the satyre* (1601), a work by John Weever excoriating the trend of satirical writing in the years just prior to its publication. (John Weever had himself previously been a published epigrammatist.)

Of the overt references to living people in the commendatory verses, most – like Fitzgeffrey's room-mate, Nathanial Gurlyn, and 'true friend' Thomas Fletcher – are of no historical note. One contributor of commendatory verse, John Stephens, is known to have written a play and published satires. Of special note is a mention of 'crabbed Websterio / The Playwright, Cartwright: whether? Either! Ho –', almost certainly a fleeting reference to the dramatist John Webster, whose coach-maker father is mockingly evoked as a builder of carts, and whom Fitzgeffrey could well have seen while attending performances at the Blackfriars.

SEE ALSO: Dekker, Thomas; Jonson, Ben; Marston, John; Webster, John; Weever, John

REFERENCES AND SUGGESTED READINGS

Eccles, Mark (1982) Brief lives: Tudor and Stuart authors. *Studies in Philology* 79(4), 50–51.

Davenport, Arnold (1951) *The whipper pamphlets*. Liverpool University Press, Liverpool.

Korda, Natasha (2004) The case of Moll Frith: women's work and the 'all-male stage'. *Early Modern Culture* 4. http://emc.eserver.org/1-4/korda.html

Steggle, Matthew (2004). Fitzgeffrey, Henry. In: *Oxford dictionary of national biography*. Oxford University Press, Oxford.

Fleming, Abraham

CLARE PAINTING-STUBBS

During his working life Abraham Fleming (1548/52–1607) wrote, translated, indexed, contributed poetry to, recommended, proofread, and edited 50 known texts, and as a 'learned corrector' for the printer Richard Tottell it is likely he worked anonymously on many more. Fleming was most likely born in Holborn, London, between 1548 and 1552. It is not known where he was schooled but he had a good understanding of Latin and a working knowledge of French and Greek. He attended Peterhouse, Cambridge, tutored by Dr Andrew Perne, from 1570 until 1582 and interspersed his studies with long periods spent in London working in the burgeoning book trade, initially as a writer and translator and later as an editor. From 1575 to 1589 Fleming wrote, contributed to, or produced 50 printed books, ranging from broadsides and pamphlets to folio books containing thousands of pages and covering a wide range of themes. His Calvinist beliefs were evident in his texts. In the mid-1580s, Fleming was employed briefly as a 'learned corrector' or editor by the printer Richard Tottell. Printers and booksellers from the higher ranks of the Stationers' Company such as Ralph Newberie, Thomas Middleton, and Henry Denham (a printer known for the quality of his fonts) all enjoyed long working relationships with Fleming and some of his finer printed works, such as *Diamond of devotion* (1581), were produced during these associations. Although he was never an antiquary, Fleming is best known for his work on the second edition of Raphael Holinshed's *Chronicles* (1587). It was Fleming who compiled the third volume, known as the 'Continuation', which covered the period from 1576 to 1586; he also proofread, indexed, and edited almost all of the three-million-word, three-volume text single-handed. Holinshed's *Chronicles* was one of the last printed books on which Fleming is known to have worked; evidence suggests that he was collecting material for a third edition of Holinshed but this was never produced.

In August 1588 Fleming was ordained deacon and priest at Peterborough Cathedral and joined the household of the lord high admiral of England, Charles Howard. Fleming was also curate at St Nicholas, Deptford, and it is possible that here he assisted in the burial of the playwright Christopher Marlowe. Between 1589 and 1606 Fleming delivered eight sermons at the prestigious establishment pulpit of Paul's Cross in the grounds of St Paul's Cathedral. Fleming died intestate at his brother's house in Bottesford, Leicestershire, on 19 September 1607 and was buried under the chancel of St Mary the Virgin, Bottesford, among the earls and countesses of Rutland to whom his brother Samuel Fleming had been chaplain. His legacy was his printed texts, dozens of manuscripts, and a vast contribution to the Elizabethan public sphere.

Fleming's texts fall roughly but not exclusively into two categories: those that he authored between 1575 and 1581 and those from 1581 until 1589 that he embellished or corrected for others. *Holinshed's chronicles* is often viewed as the epitome of Fleming's career. It was certainly a massive and complex undertaking, but his most important texts are his early English translations of Virgil. In 1575 Fleming produced two ground-breaking editions of the *Eclogues*, one in verse (now lost) and one in prose. What makes this achievement remarkable is that before Fleming, there were no complete Virgilian texts available in English, and Fleming's editions were cheaply produced. Almost anyone who could read would be able to access this text, previously confined to the Latin-educated. In the 1580s he also produced a number of Latin–English–French dictionaries or *Alvearies*, one of which also included Greek. At least one of Fleming's own pamphlets, *Straunge and terrible wunder* (1577), was translated into French and appeared in France as *Histoire mervelleuse* (1578). It was this fantastical pamphlet that gave rise to the legend of 'Black Shuck' in Bungay, on the Norfolk–Suffolk border.

The translating of scholarly texts into English and making them accessible and affordable to anyone was a consistent theme of Fleming's work. In 1576 he translated Aelian from Greek into English; he also 'gathered' and translated *A panoplie of epistles* containing letters of Pliny, Cicero, Isocrates, and Roger Ascham. Given that it was a large volume at over 400 pages, it is likely that less wealthy readers were able to purchase unbound sections from it more cheaply. Fleming also produced *Of Englishe dogges* (1576, an English translation of John Caius's *De cannibus Britannicus*), which proved extremely popular and is still in print today. Many of Fleming's books, such as *Blasing starrs* (1576, 1618), show evidence of second or third print runs, which suggests that they kept selling out. Some of Fleming's texts seem to have been aimed specifically at educating women and children and demonstrate his genuine love of language and word-play. His *Conduit of comfort* (1579) was used by Katherine Paston to educate her son William in the mid-seventeenth century. Similarly, *Diamond of devotion*, which echoes earlier girdle books, is laid out in six themed sections that worked on many levels, providing children with familiar ABCs and colourful metaphors whilst adults could look for hidden meanings and acrostic tags. In *Diamond* Fleming takes the reader on a moral journey along 'The Footpath of Faith' into a garden where one would encounter 'A Swarme of Bees' ('Be a louer of wizedome, she shall beautifie thy head with manifolde graces') or 'A Plant of Pleasure', where the first letter of each line spells ABRAHAM FLEMING.

Fleming was undoubtedly popular and well known among the ordinary people of London. When the much-loved philanthropist William Lambe died in 1580, it was to Fleming that his executors turned for an *Epitaph* and *Memoriall* to 'Master William Lambe'. In the past Fleming has been regarded as a poor poet, a peripheral and even a ridiculous figure, but he was clearly highly regarded, enormously productive, very popular, and a key player in establishing the public sphere, making English books available to anyone and everyone.

SEE ALSO: Ascham, Roger; Holinshed, Raphael

REFERENCES AND SUGGESTED READINGS

Clegg, Cyndia Susan (2004) Fleming, Abraham. In: *Oxford dictionary of national biography.* Oxford University Press, Oxford.

Clegg, Cyndia Susan (ed.) (2005) Introduction. In: *The peaceable and prosperous regiment of blessed Queene Elisabeth: a facsimile from Holinshed's 'Chronicles' (1587).* Huntington Library, San Marino.

Donno, Elizabeth Story (1989) Abraham Fleming: a learned corrector in 1586–87. *Studies in Bibliography* 42, 200–211.

Fletcher, John

JENNIFER FORSYTH

John Fletcher (1579–1625) was a Jacobean dramatist who wrote approximately 52 plays, both singly and in collaboration with other dramatists, between about 1606 and his death in 1625. He co-wrote at least three plays with William Shakespeare, *The two noble kinsmen* (1612–13), *Henry VIII* (1612–13), and the lost play *Cardenio* (1612), and took over as chief dramatist for the King's Men in 1613 after Shakespeare retired. In addition to his collaborations with Shakespeare, Fletcher is best known today for comedies and tragicomedies collaboratively written, first with Francis Beaumont and later with Philip Massinger.

John Fletcher was born in 1579 in Rye, Sussex, into a family of clergy, poets, and diplomats. Two years after his birth, his father, Richard Fletcher, Jr, became Queen Elizabeth I's chaplain and was later bishop of Bristol, Worcester, and then London. However, he had fallen from favour by the time of his death in 1596. Fletcher's uncle Giles Fletcher (known as 'the elder') was a diplomatic envoy and poet; Giles's sons, Phineas and Giles ('the younger'), both became rectors and poets.

John Fletcher has often been identified as the 'Mr Fletcher of London' who attended Bene't (Corpus Christi) College at Cambridge, which was his father's alma mater, between 1591 and 1598. If this is true, he may also be the Fletcher who received his BA in 1595 and his MA in 1598. He was a professional playwright from approximately 1606 until his death by plague in 1625. The two playwrights with whom he collaborated most were Beaumont and Massinger, but scholars have also identified Nathan Field, Ben Jonson, James Shirley, William Rowley, Thomas Middleton, John Webster, and John Ford as occasional collaborators, in addition to Shakespeare. He was buried in Southwark Cathedral.

Fletcher began writing plays for the Jacobean theatre both on his own and in conjunction with Francis Beaumont. The Beaumont and Fletcher collaborations lasted until 1612 or 1613 and were apparently written initially for the Children of Paul's and Children of the Queen's Revels but increasingly for the King's Men after they began performing at the Blackfriars theatre in 1608. John Aubrey later famously claimed that during the time of their collaborations, Beaumont and Fletcher 'lived together on the Bankside not far from the playhouse, both bachelors; lay together; had one wench in the house between them, which they did so admire; the same clothes and cloak, & c.; between them'. Beaumont stopped writing for the stage around 1612 or 1613, perhaps because of his marriage in 1613, and he died in 1616, most likely of a stroke. The best known of the Beaumont–Fletcher collaborations today, which number among the most famous plays in Fletcher's corpus, are the tragicomedies *Philaster* (1608–9) and *A king or no king* (1611), and the tragedy *The maids tragedy* (1610).

Around the time of Beaumont's retirement, Fletcher collaborated with Shakespeare on *The two noble kinsmen*, *King Henry VIII*, and *Cardenio* for the King's Men, performing at the Globe and Blackfriars theatres. (The last of these three may be the basis for *The double falsehood* [1727], attributed to Lewis Theobald.) Fletcher also continued writing plays alone and with other playwrights such as Nathan Field. A few years after becoming chief dramatist for the King's Men, he began working regularly with Philip Massinger, with whom he would continue to collaborate for most of the rest of his career. Fletcher's greatest successes continued to be in the field of comedy and tragicomedy, though he and Massinger wrote respected tragedies as well. Of the 11 plays credited to Fletcher and Massinger, only *Beggers bush* (1622), *Rollo, duke of Normandy* (1613–25), and *The sea-voyage* (1622) enjoyed great popularity after their lifetimes. Fletcher's name was linked tightly enough with Massinger's, however, that the poet and playwright Sir Aston Cockayne wrote:

Plays they did write together, were great friends,
And now one grave includes them in their ends:
So whom on earth nothing did part beneath
Here in their fames they lie in spite of death.

In 1647 Fletcher became only the third Renaissance playwright, along with Jonson and Shakespeare, whose collected works appeared in a folio collection. Although Fletcher collaborated with numerous playwrights throughout his career, the collection was titled *Comedies and tragedies written by Francis Beaumont and John Fletcher gentlemen*. Ironically, hardly any Beaumont–Fletcher collaborations were included; they were added for the printing of the second folio collection in 1679. In contrast, Massinger's significant contributions to the collection were only glancingly referred to.

While Fletcher was spectacularly successful for most of his active career, as the folios attest, his career got off to a rocky start. His first known solo play, a tragicomedy called *The faithfull shepheardesse* (1608–9), failed in the theatres. The genre was controversial with critics, both on the Continent and in England, where Philip Sidney complains of plays that are 'neither right tragedies nor right comedies' and refers to the result as 'mongrel tragicomedy'. After the theatrical failure of his play, *The faithfull shepheardesse* was printed, and Fletcher wrote a defence and definition of tragicomedy, which appeared in the preface. He followed the arguments made by the Italian author Giovanni Battista Guarini, explaining to the English audience that 'A tragicomedy is not so called in respect of mirth and killing, but in respect it wants deaths, which is enough to make it no tragedy, yet brings some near it, which is enough to make it no comedy; which must be a representation of familiar people, with such kind of trouble as no life be questioned; so that a god is as lawful in this as in a tragedy, and mean people as in a comedy.'

Despite this inauspicious start, one of the greatest legacies of Fletcher's work is now considered to be his contribution to the development of tragicomedy. Fletcher was one of the most popular practitioners of Jacobean tragicomedy, which blends many of the hallmarks of the kind of romantic comedy frequently found in Shakespeare's well-known mature comedies, for example, with darker strands that invoke, even if only momentarily, the passions and violence of tragedies. Common themes and tropes include a female lead who is chaste and loyal despite being accused of sexual betrayal, a jealous man who commits violence (or threatens to) against a woman, a male protagonist whose virtue is questionable, a cross-dressed woman, magical or supernatural elements, and an ending that relies upon forgiveness. These plays demonstrate the idea of mingling not only genres but also content, blending the high-born with the low-born and the serious with the slapstick. Shock and titillation also figure prominently, though the sweet and the lyrical also appear. Sometimes, as a result of presenting the comic and tragic elements at

the same time, a tragicomic play creates a mixed mode of emotional confusion where spectators are not certain whether to laugh or to cry.

Most of these qualities of tragicomedy appear in *Philaster*, which remains the best-known example of a Fletcherian tragicomedy, and one which is often compared with Shakespeare's *Cymbeline*. In *Philaster*, the chaste and loyal heroine is the princess Arathusa, who is falsely accused of sleeping with her page, Bellario. In fact, Arathusa is loyal to the point of being willing to die to protect Philaster, her love. Philaster becomes jealous, and his violence against not just one but two women is infamous: believing that Arathusa has betrayed him, Philaster offers Arathusa the choice of killing him or having him stab her; she chooses to die, and Philaster stabs her (though, as it turns out, not fatally). His virtue is further called into question by the events that follow. Driven off by a 'Country Fellow' who, appalled at seeing a man attacking a woman, in turn wounds Philaster, and afraid of being identified as the man who had injured Arathusa, Philaster then finds the sleeping Bellario. Without offering Bellario a chance to defend himself, Philaster stabs Bellario to make it look as though Bellario is the one who had been wounded by the Country Fellow and had therefore been the one guilty of attacking Arathusa. At the end of the play, Bellario reveals that he is actually Euphrasia, a lord's daughter, who had fallen in love with Philaster before the beginning of the play and who had dressed as a boy to serve him. Finally, the ending relies upon forgiveness: all of the major wrongs are forgiven, even those committed by characters who seem unrepentant at the end.

Other tragicomic traits are seen more prominently in *A king or no king*, also a collaboration with Beaumont. *A king or no king* tells the stories of the romantic lives of two royal couples and of a comically spineless captain who is repeatedly dishonoured by being beaten, kicked, and disarmed. Bessus, the cowardly captain, serves the king and interacts with him. He also provides the farcical element to coincide with an otherwise serious moment: when the king contemplates seducing his own sister and asks Bessus if he will serve as a go-between, Bessus, rather than being shocked or horrified, as the audience presumably is, merely agrees, offering to bring the king's mother for him to sleep with afterwards if he wishes. Thrills of horror also occur as the king comes close to sleeping with the woman he believes to be his sister. Despite their darker aspects, both *Philaster* and *A king or no king* have comic resolutions where mistaken identities are straightened out, misunderstandings resolved, injustices corrected, and true lovers joined.

Fletcher's popularity during his lifetime is attested by the number of his plays that found commercial success in the theatres and which were printed in quarto and folio. The 1647 folio contains 34 plays and one masque; the 1679 folio adds 16 plays which had previously appeared in quartos to make up a total of 50. More recent attribution studies have removed a few plays as not being by Fletcher and have identified a few more, including the collaborations with Shakespeare. In addition to the plays, the 1647 folio also included 37 commendatory poems by such authors as Ben Jonson, Robert Herrick, James Shirley, and Richard Brome, in which the poets compare Fletcher favourably with the best playwrights of the period, with John Denham famously referring to Jonson, Shakespeare, and Fletcher as 'the triumvirate of wit'. The word 'wit', which could refer to a range of qualities reflecting a person's understanding, skill, judgement, or ability as a writer to thrill and surprise audiences, appears 100 times in praise of Fletcher and his collaborators. One of the effects of this wit was evidently Fletcher's ability to affect his audiences emotionally, which was also frequently admired by his contemporaries; the commendatory poets also tend to emphasize the natural, unforced elegance of his language. This elevated view of Fletcher's merits survived for a century after his death. In the first couple of years after King Charles II's restoration to the throne of England allowed for the resumption of public theatrical performances, one theatrical company performed 27 Fletcher plays to three each by Shakespeare and by Jonson. Dryden said that Jonson was great 'for the study' but Fletcher was 'for the stage'.

Fletcher's popularity waned during the eighteenth century, however, as his vibrant and often bawdy plays failed to match neoclassical sensibilities and the taste for greater poetic decorum. Many Romantic poets were fans: John Keats read Beaumont and Fletcher 'with great pleasure', for instance, and requested that his epitaph be based on a line from *Philaster*, and his brother George recorded that their family kept pictures of Beaumont and Fletcher on either side of a miniature of Keats on the mantel. Nineteenth-century audiences were, in general, less interested in Renaissance drama, with the exception of some of Shakespeare's plays, and Fletcher's works continued to languish. By the early twentieth century, after T. S. Eliot (1919) wrote scathingly that 'The blossoms of Beaumont and Fletcher's imagination draw no sustenance from the soil, but are cut and slightly withered flowers stuck in the sand', and that 'the evocative quality of the verse of Beaumont and Fletcher depends upon a clever appeal to emotions and associations which they have not themselves grasped; it is hollow. It is superficial with a vacuum behind it', even those critics who wrote book-length studies of Fletcher ranked him among the minor playwrights.

More recently, scholarship has often defended Fletcher's merit. Much of this work derives from his association with Shakespeare, focusing either on their collaborations or on comparisons between similar works by the two authors. Such comparisons remain fertile sites for exploring how two different authors respond to the same subject or genre, as scholars compare struggles for marital power in Fletcher's *The womans prize, or the tamer tamed* (1618) and its Shakespeare original, *The taming of the shrew*; depictions of Cleopatra in *The false one* (1621) and *Antony and Cleopatra*; the genre of revenge tragedy in *The maids tragedy* and *Hamlet*; tragicomedy in *Philaster* and *Cymbeline*; or desert isles and utopian governments in *The sea-voyage* and *The tempest*, for example.

Other critics have turned to a more bio-graphical tradition to examine the anecdotes about Fletcher's closeness to his collaborators through the lens of gender and sexuality. Homo-eroticism and the sexuality of Fletcher, his collaborators, and their characters have also frequently been the subject of investigation. Since discussions of Fletcher's female charac-ters have always been one of the primary foci of interest in his plays, critics interested in gender and sexuality and gendered identity construction have also found Fletcher's plays a productive source of material. Feminist dis-cussions of rape (threatened or actual) and other forms of violence against women appear in studies on *Philaster, The maide in the mill* (1623), *Valentinian* (1610–12), and *The queene of Corinth* (1617), and explorations of gender, sexuality, and identity construction have shown particular interest in such plays as *Loves cure* (?1625), *The loyall subject* (1618), *Philaster*, and *The maids tragedy*.

Postcolonial critics and scholars interested in political history have also found Fletcher's works ripe for investigations into England's internal politics and increasing exploration of and trade with non-European countries. For instance, Philip J. Finkelpearl's (1990) response to Coleridge's assertion that Beaumont and Fletcher were 'servile *jure divino* royalists' frames the Fletcherian collaborations in the context of both the authors' families' political stances and England's domestic politics, and Gordon McMullan (1994) looks both inwards towards the court and social life of England and outwards towards the colonies. Even though fictional plays cannot be taken as serious repre-sentations of historical reality, they can serve as reminders of the tensions produced by imag-ining cross-cultural encounters: with Russia in *The loyall subject*; with a utopian Amazonian nation in *The sea-voyage*; with moors and Islam in *The knight of Malta* (1618); with Roman conquest and England's own former colonial status in *Bonduca* (1609–14); with (historically inaccurate) paganism in Tidore, Indonesia, in *The island princesse* (1621); and so on. These recent studies have posed significant challenges

to the assumption that Fletcher's plays are mere entertainment and suggested that they com-ment on the most significant issues of the day.

SEE ALSO: Beaumont, Francis; Brome, Richard; Denham, John; Herrick, Robert; Jonson, Ben; Massinger, Philip; Rowley, William; Shakespeare, William; Shirley, James

REFERENCES AND SUGGESTED READINGS

Avery, Emmett L. (1956) The Shakespeare ladies club. *Shakespeare Quarterly* 7, 153–158.

Child, Harold (1927) Revivals of English dramatic works 1901–1918, 1926. *Review of English Studies* 3, 169–185.

Dobson, Michael (1992) *The making of the national poet: Shakespeare, adaptation, and authorship, 1660–1769.* Clarendon Press, Oxford.

Eliot, T. S. (1919) Ben Jonson. *Times Literary Sup-plement* (13 Nov.), 638.

Finkelpearl, Philip J. (1990) *Court and country pol-itics in the plays of Beaumont and Fletcher.* Prin-ceton University Press, Princeton.

Griswold, Wendy (1986) *Renaissance revivals: city comedy and revenge tragedy in the London theater, 1576–1980.* University of Chicago Press, Chicago.

Hoy, Cyrus (1956–62) The shares of Fletcher and his collaborators in the Beaumont and Fletcher canon. *Studies in Bibliography* 8–9, 11–15.

Leech, Clifford (1962) *The John Fletcher plays.* Harvard University Press, Cambridge, MA.

Masten, Jeffrey (1992) Beaumont and/or Fletcher: collaboration and the interpretation of Renaissance drama. *ELH* 59, 337–356.

Masten, Jeffrey (1997) *Textual intercourse: collabo-ration, authorship, and sexualities in Renaissance drama.* Cambridge University Press, Cambridge.

McLeod, Randall (1981–82). Un 'editing' Shak-speare. *SubStance* 10–11, 26–55.

McMullan, Gordon (1994) *The politics of unease in the plays of John Fletcher.* University of Massachu-setts Press, Amherst.

Rulfs, Donald J. (1948) Beaumont and Fletcher on the London stage 1776–1833. *PMLA* 63, 1245–1264.

Squier, Charles L. (1986) *John Fletcher.* Twayne, Boston.

Wallis, Lawrence B. (1968) *Fletcher, Beaumont and company: entertainers to the Jacobean gentry.* Octagon Books, New York.

Wilson, John Harold (1928) *The influence of Beaumont and Fletcher on Restoration drama.* Ohio State University Press, Columbus.

Fletcher, Phineas

MATTHEW J. SMITH

Phineas Fletcher (1582–1650) is most famous for his ambitious epic *The purple island, or the isle of man*, his prolific literary output, his literary relation to Spenser, and his prominent literary family (including his father Giles Sr, his brother Giles, and his cousin, the playwright John Fletcher). He was born in Kent, and studied at Eton and King's College, Cambridge. At Cambridge, he took his BA in 1604, his MA in 1608, and was ordained in 1611, the same year that he was appointed a fellow of King's College. Fletcher experienced a dramatic change in location and lifestyle in 1615 when he left Cambridge for a chaplaincy in the house of Sir Henry Willoughby in rural Derbyshire. Fletcher then took a rectorship in Norfolk in 1621 and remained a country parish priest the rest of his life.

Because Fletcher wrote or began to write most of his literary works before his move to the country, Cambridge had an intoxicating and ubiquitous influence on his work. Beginning with his first publication, an elegy (1603) occasioned by Queen Elizabeth's death, hardly a hymn, lyric, or verse epistle of Fletcher's doesn't draw explicit inspiration from Cambridge and the River Cam, his 'Chame'. Concurrent with this obsession with Cambridge is Fletcher's use of the pastoral stage of Kent, where he spent substantial time. Fletcher references Kent and Cambridge to create a productive poetic competition between pastoral allure and adventurous student life. In 'To E.C. in Cambridge, my sonne by the university', he remarks how 'Kentish powerfull pleasures here enchain me'. In 'To my ever-honoured cousin W.R. Esquire', Fletcher announces a specific allegiance to 'The muddy Chame [which] doth me enforcéd hold'. Other verse expresses resentment for

Cambridge's silencing of Philomel and a yearning for what 'To my beloved cousin W.R. Esquire' describes as Kent's Ovidian 'loud-tunéd thrush'.

While these shorter verses were not published until 1633, in *Poeticall miscellanies* along with *The purple island, or the isle of man* and *Piscatorie eclogs*, they were mostly composed before 1615. The *Miscellanies* predominately use rhyme royal, sometimes with an alexandrine on the last line, but Fletcher experimented with alterations on this – often *abababcc* and with the additional alexandrine. *Piscatorie eclogs*, also composed before 1615, is an imitation of Spenser's *The shepheardes calender*, replete with dialogues, complaints, a singing contest, praises of the rustic life, transparently topical lamentations, and love-sick consolations. Generally, the *Eclogs* amplify the concerns of the *Miscellanies*, depicting shepherd boys fishing on the banks of the Cam as structural reminders of the biographical tension between Cambridge and Kent. Thirsil is Fletcher's own poetic persona, as is clear in the second eclogue, probably written after 1614, in which he laments his departure from Cambridge.

Most of Fletcher's major works were begun before his departure from Cambridge and carry the marks of this event, but Fletcher's sole play, *Sicelides* (1631), holds a particularly conflicted relation to it. After expecting, in March 1615, a spectacular playing before the king and his company, which included Prince Charles and John Donne, *Sicelides* instead suffered an aborted performance at a Cambridge festival due to James's sudden departure the morning of the performance day. Just as the *Piscatorie eclogs* adopt Spenserian conventions, *Sicelides* is marked by the disguises, higher and lower romantic plot levels, and *deux ex machina* of Elizabethan comedies.

Most of Fletcher's other major literary works were started before but completed after this disappointment. All of his major verse was published while under the patronage of Edward Benlowes from 1627 to 1633. These include *Venus and Anchises*, published in 1628 by Thomas Walkley as *Brittain's Ida* and originally attributed to Spenser. A possible reason for its false attribution is its sensuality, perhaps less appropriate for a country parish priest than for the pre-clerical Fletcher of 1610. The epyllion is in the vein of Shakespeare's *Venus and Adonis* but distinguished by its pastoral frame narrative where Thirsil, 'hiding neerer came', sings the mythic tale in order to 'tame' his 'raging fire'. The Ovidian character of *Venus* contrasted with the topical polemicism of *Apollyonists*, which was written a year later than and published a year prior to *Venus*; it exhibits a variety of poetic forms that indicates just how devoted Fletcher was to the vocation of *poesie*, particularly in the years before his rectorship. *The locusts, or Apollyonists* is an expanded translation of his *Locustæ vel pietas jesuitica*, a Latin narrative of the Gunpowder Plot. The 1611 manuscript of *Locustæ* was dedicated to Prince Henry and a year later to Prince Charles, but its dedicatee in print (1627) was Roger Townshed, a former patron of Giles the younger, whose poem *Christs victorie, and triumph* (1610) influenced the theological narrative of *Apollyonists*.

Although he began writing it as early as 1606, Fletcher considered *The purple island* (1633) his crowning achievement. So named for the purple dirt of the earth from which God created humans, the 12-canto epic combines pastoral, science, and spiritual warfare and allegorizes the body and soul as an island. *The purple island* weaves and digresses its way, in a fashion evocative of unmapped exploration, through descriptions of the human body, mind, and passions. Its predominant content is allegorical pastoral description like that found in *The Faerie Queene*, but, unlike Spenser's, Fletcher's landscapes are seldom marked by action, with the restrained exception of the world, the flesh, and the devil's attack on the soul. Fletcher's allegory is influenced by that of *The Faerie Queene*'s House of Alma episode, where Guyon explores the architecture of the soul and is restored to health. Still, Fletcher does not refrain from explaining the hermeneutic of his long allegory in reference to the

Fall, which left man with the task of rediscovering his body. Thus, despite its 'proclivitie / To ruin', he says, the body must be viewed at an allegorical distance, where 'we by leaving find, [that which we] by seeking lost'. Fletcher's last writings focused on religious topics: *The way to blessednes, a treatise or commentary on the first psalme* (1632), *Joy in tribulation* (1632), and the posthumously printed *A fathers testament* (1670).

Fletcher's seventeenth-century reputation suggests recognition of his prolific dedication to the poetic vocation. Francis Quarles calls him the 'Spencer of his age', and Izaak Walton offers particular praise for his eclogues. In his *Lives* (1687), however, William Winstanley hints at the incongruence between the quality of Fletcher's works and his less impressive reputation, admitting that his reader 'perhaps hath never seen the Book'. Indeed, after 1633 Fletcher's verse was not again published until 1771 in Edinburgh and, later in that century, twice more in London (1783, 1787). Modern readers have primarily appreciated Fletcher as a latter-day Spenser.

SEE ALSO: Benlowes, Edward; Fletcher, John; Quarles, Francis; Spenser, Edmund

REFERENCES AND SUGGESTED READINGS

Baldwin, R. G. (1961) Phineas Fletcher: his modern readers and his Renaissance ideas. *Philological Quarterly* 10, 462–475.

Cory, H. E. (1912) Spenser, the School of the Fletchers, and Milton. *University of California Publications in Modern Philology* 2 (supplement 5), 311–373.

Grundy, Joan (1969) *The Spenserian poets: a study in Elizabethan and Jacobean poetry*. Edward Arnold, London.

Kastor, Frank (1978) *Giles and Phineas Fletcher*. Twayne, Boston.

Langdale, A. B. (1937) *Phineas Fletcher: man of letters, science, and divinity*. Columbia University Press, New York.

Piepho, Lee (1984) The Latin and English eclogues of Phineas Fletcher: Sannazaro's *Piscatoria* among the Britons. *Studies in Philology* 81, 461–472.

Quint, David (1991) Milton, Fletcher and the Gunpowder Plot. *Journal of the Warburg and Courtauld Institutes* 54, 261–268.

Florio, John

WILLIAM E. ENGEL

John Florio (1553–1625) had a profound impact on Elizabethan language and literature because of his systematic promotion of foreign-language study, and his liberal attitude towards translation which favoured exuberance of expression over linguistic precision. He used lively dialogues to teach Italian while at the same time instructing his readers in etiquette, gentility, and the social graces. Through his ebullient translations, most notably of Jacques Cartier's *Navigations* (1580) and Michel de Montaigne's *Essayes* (1603), he introduced many words that have become part of everyday speech, such as 'conscientious', 'facilitate', 'amusing', 'regret', and 'emotion' (Yates 1934).

The son of an Italian Protestant refugee who fled the Inquisition, Florio was born in London during the reign of Edward VI. His father was in the employ of the Pembroke family and tutor to Lady Jane Grey, 'the nine-day queen', about whom he wrote a sympathetic biography. Florio's family prudently went to Antwerp when Queen Mary, a devout Catholic, came to the throne in 1553. While in exile he was sent to a grammar school renowned for its reformed Protestant theology supervised by Pier Paolo Vergerio, one of the most distinguished Italian refugees in the Grisons canton of Switzerland. Florio took advantage of the humanist curriculum at the University of Tübingen where he was registered in 1563, but seems to have left before receiving a degree (Yates 1934).

Upon returning to England he fell in with influential proponents of the Protestant cause, most notably Robert Dudley, earl of Leicester, as a consequence of both his family's previous association with the Herbert and Sidney circle and his own broad humanist learning. He married Samuel Daniel's sister (her Christian name is unknown and no record of the marriage has been discovered) who was in the household of Mary Sidney Herbert, countess of Pembroke, and came into contact with the literary coterie at the Pembroke country seat, Wilton. It was here that Florio probably transcribed Philip Sidney's *Arcadia* and assigned the chapter headings that still are used today.

Florio traded on his foreignness throughout his career, fashioning himself as 'Giovanni' when it suited his purposes, even though he had never been to Italy. This explains in part why his dialogues are set in London and include discussions of local interest such as going to a comedy at the Bull Theatre, walking to the Exchange, and catching a boat at Paul's Wharf. Florio's double-columned dialogues, with Italian on one side and English on the other, present vivid portraits of everyday life and supply readers with a cache of witty maxims that could be used in polished conversation in either language. It was written initially as an entertaining study guide for his well-connected pupils, but Florio correctly assumed there was a wider audience for his *Firste fruites* (1578).

Florio was in residence at Oxford in 1576 tutoring Emmanuel Barnes, the eldest son of Richard Barnes, bishop of Durham, who matriculated from Magdalen and was later incepted to MA in 1581. As Barnes's servitor, Florio was granted room and board and could attend lectures without paying fees. It was during this time at Magdalen that he became friends with Daniel, as well as with Richard Hakluyt who commissioned him to translate Giovanni Battista Ramusio's Italian version of Cartier's *Navigations and discoveries*. Beginning in 1583 Florio worked with the French embassy in London where he became acquainted with Giordano Bruno, the celebrated mnemonist and philosopher, then a guest of the French ambassador, Michel de Castelnau. He returned to Oxford in 1586, this time Brasenose College, where he tutored the bishop of Durham's fourth son, the poet Barnabe Barnes.

Banking on the success of his first book, Florio published his *Second frutes* (1591).

It bristles with snappy dialogues that at times recall the stage banter of an impatient master and his saucy servant – especially the recurring characters Torquato and Ruspa who respectively play these roles. There is also a digest of 6,000 proverbs and excerpts from important Italian writers which constitute what amounts to a reading list for anyone wanting to be considered – or at least to appear – well educated.

By 1594 Florio had become attached to Henry Wriothesley, earl of Southampton, to whom he dedicated his dictionary *A worlde of wordes* (1598). Shakespeare had previously dedicated his two narrative poems *Venus and Adonis* (1593) and *The rape of Lucrece* (1594) to Wriothesley. It is likely that he would have come into contact with Shakespeare during these years and, given his pronounced affinity for foreign phrases and excessive augmentation, may have been the model for the schoolmaster Holofernes in *Love's labour's lost*. With Florio, things must not be said once only; they must be said at least twice and sometimes three or four times in paired or balanced phrases.

With the accession of King James, Florio became groom of the privy chamber to Queen Anna and tutored Prince Henry. As part of his ongoing effort to stoke the renewed interest in Italian culture which he had spent his entire career advancing, Florio published a much-expanded version of his dictionary, *Queen Anna's new world of words* (1611). His influence as a purveyor of Continental tastes is most evident in his translation of Montaigne's *Essayes* (1603, 1613, 1632), which was immediately absorbed by English readers and precipitated a vogue for the new essay form. Among the first generation of writers indebted to Florio's *Essayes* were Jonson, Sir Walter Ralegh, Robert Burton, and John Webster.

Early twentieth-century research on Florio tended to focus on specific borrowings from his translation of Montaigne, especially by Francis Bacon and by Shakespeare. Many studies qualified Bacon's debt to Montaigne, while others traced his influence on later English essayists. Source hunters found distinct echoes of Florio's translation of Montaigne's essay 'On cannibals' in Shakespeare's *The tempest*, especially Gonzalo's speech on the Golden Age in act II. Recent studies on marginal annotations in extant copies of Florio's Montaigne have addressed issues of appropriation (Hamlin 2010). This can be seen as part of a general trend towards documenting the fluid movement between manuscript and print culture in the seventeenth century (Ioppolo 2006).

Florio died in 1625, ending his days in poverty because his royal pension had either lapsed or not been paid. He left a widow, Rose (née Spicer), whom he had married in 1617, and a daughter, Aurelia. His works eventually became the property of Giovanni Torriano who regarded himself as Florio's successor, publishing new editions of his language tutorials, proverbs, and dictionary expanded and adapted to the needs of a later generation.

SEE ALSO: Bacon, Francis; Daniel, Samuel; Greville, Fulke; Hakluyt, Richard; Herbert, Mary (Sidney), countess of Pembroke; Jonson, Ben; Ralegh, Walter; Shakespeare, William; Sidney, Philip; Webster, John

REFERENCES AD SUGGESTED READINGS

Anderson, Judith H. (1996) *Words that matter: linguistic perception in Renaissance England.* Stanford University Press, Stanford.

Conley, Tom (1986) Institutionalizing translation: on Florio's Montaigne. In: Weber, Samuel, Sussman, Henry, & Godzich, Wlad (eds) *Demarcating the disciplines: philosophy, literature, art.* University of Minnesota Press, Minneapolis, pp. 45–60.

Hamlin, William M. (2010) Florio's Montaigne and the tyranny of 'custome': appropriation, ideology, and early English readership of the *Essayes. Renaissance Quarterly* 63, 491–544.

Ioppolo, Grace (2006) *Dramatists and their manuscripts in the age of Shakespeare, Jonson and Middleton.* Routledge, London.

Matthiessen, F. O. (1931) *Translation: an Elizabethan art.* Harvard University Press, Cambridge, MA.

Wyatt, Michael (2005) *The Italian encounter with Tudor England: a cultural politics of translation.* Cambridge University Press, Cambridge.

Yates, Frances A. (1934) *John Florio: the life of an Italian in Shakespeare's England*. Cambridge University Press, Cambridge.

Ford, John

LISA HOPKINS

John Ford (1586–?1639/53) was the major tragic dramatist of the Caroline era. Because of its eye-catching title and sensational subject matter, *'Tis pitty shee's a whore*, first published in 1633, continues to be performed on stage, with the role of Giovanni often proving attractive to big-name actors, and was also made into a film (1972). It is, however, the quieter and less popular *The broken heart*, also published in 1633, which really gives the strongest sense of Ford's distinctive power and voice, while his *Perkin Warbeck* (1634), the final, very belated manifestation of the Renaissance vogue for history plays, offers both a hypnotic image of riddled and mysterious identity and an important intervention in the contemporary debate about the changing contours of British national identities.

Like his most characteristic drama, Ford himself is an understated and elusive figure. He was born in 1586, the second son of a Devon gentleman, Thomas Ford. He was perhaps not on good terms with his father, who left him only £10 when he died in 1610 (though the bequest might also indicate that he was already financially independent and not in need of more). His mother, Elizabeth Popham, was more probably a formative influence in his life, for she was the niece of the lord chief justice Sir John Popham, who was briefly imprisoned in Essex House during the ill-fated rebellion of Robert Devereux, earl of Essex, and presided over numerous trials, including those of Essex and of Sir Walter Ralegh. Both these events find an echo in his great-nephew's works: when Ford first started publishing in 1606, one of the two works that he brought out that year, *Fames memoriall*, was an elegy on Charles Blount, earl of Devonshire, whose widow was Essex's sister Penelope; Penelope had apparently called for Popham's head when the Essex conspirators detained him. The story of Penelope, the Stella of Sir Philip Sidney's *Astrophil and Stella* sequence, has also been seen as lying behind *The broken heart*, not least because the names of the hero and heroine of Ford's play, Orgilus and Penthea, both seem to echo Sidneian names. Ralegh, meanwhile, figures prominently in Ford's prose tract *The golden meane*, published in 1613. It may also have been the influence of Popham that secured his great-nephew admission to the Middle Temple, where Ford proceeded in 1602 after a year or so at Exeter College, Oxford. Most of the few subsequent traces of Ford associate him with the Middle Temple, though he was expelled in 1605 for failing to pay his buttery bill and not readmitted until 1608. He may or may not have been the John Ford who protested in 1617 against the wearing of caps in hall, or he may have been the John Ford who was recorded as living somewhere near Holywell Street in 1619 or before (Howarth 1965). Apart from this little or nothing is known of his life, and apart from an epigram addressed to him in 1640, there is no trace at all after the publication of his last play *The ladies triall* in 1639.

Outside the archival record a very few things can perhaps be gleaned or inferred about the dramatist and the circle in which he moved. Apart from a rather formulaic-sounding allusion to a 'cruel Lycia' in his 1606 elegy *Fames memorial* there is no evidence of any emotional attachments, but there are some signs of familial and friendship connections. Apart from her influential uncle, Elizabeth Popham also brought her son another connection, with the important south Wales Stradling family; Ford would certainly have shared intellectual interests with his contemporary Sir John Stradling, the translator of Justus Lipsius, while Sir Edward Stradling was the vice admiral and close friend of Sir Kenelm Digby, whose *Private memoirs* foreshadows the plot of *The broken heart*: Stelliana, like Penthea, initially refuses Theagenes on the grounds that she had agreed to marry Mardontius and 'she would never suffer that one man should possess her, and another such a gage of a former, though half-constrained, affection'; and Stelliana's father, like Ford's prince of Argos, is called Nearchus, while the real-life equivalent of Digby's Mardontius may well have been John Mordaunt, earl of Peterborough, who was the dedicatee of *'Tis pitty shee's a whore*. Others to whom Ford dedicated or with whom he exchanged commendatory verses included his cousin John Ford of Gray's Inn and other Inns of Court men; fellow dramatists including Barnabe Barnes, John Webster, Philip Massinger, James Shirley, and Richard Brome; and a clutch of noblemen, many of whom seem to have been opposed to the policies of Charles I.

Ford's earliest work appears to have consisted entirely of prose and poetry, or if there were any plays they have not survived. As well as *Fames memoriall*, 1606 also saw *Honor triumphant*, a series of chivalric propositions apparently designed to accompany the festivities proposed for the visit of James I's brother-in-law, Christian IV of Denmark. A 1612 elegy for the Devon-born Master William Peter, briefly and controversially assigned to Shakespeare, is now generally agreed to be Ford's, and in 1613 he published a devotional poem, *Christes bloodie sweat*, and a moralizing prose tract, *The golden meane*, followed by the rather similar *A line of life* in 1620. He also wrote an elegy on Sir Thomas Overbury in 1616 and may have added two 'characters' for the second edition of Overbury's poem 'A wife' in 1614. In 1621 he collaborated with Thomas Dekker and William Rowley on the domestic tragedy *The witch of Edmonton*, followed by two further collaborations with Dekker, *The Welsh ambassador* in 1623 and *The sun's-darling* in 1624. Ford's name is also associated with a number of lost plays, including *An ill beginning has a good end* (?1613) and *Beauty in a trance*, which was acted at court by the King's Men in 1630, as well as some further collaborative works with Dekker, *The Bristow merchant*, *The fairy knight*, and *The late murther of the son upon the mother* (on the last of which Webster also worked).

Of these early plays, *The witch of Edmonton* is perhaps both the most interesting in its own right and the most characteristically Fordian. Based, like so many domestic tragedies, on a true and recent story, the execution of Elizabeth Sawyer of Edmonton for alleged witchcraft, it brought an unusually secularizing, and indeed one might almost say sociological, perspective to bear on the events it depicts. Though it does not rule out the possibility of genuinely supernatural evil (and indeed shows us the devil in the guise of a talking dog), it also strongly stresses the material, social, and economic factors at work and clearly shows both how convenient and how misleadingly simplistic a diagnosis of witchcraft can be. In Frank Thorney and his ill-fated wife Susan it also gives us sketches of what will become the quintessential Fordian character, persisting unwaveringly in a course that will obviously lead to disaster, while in the names Warbeck and Katherine we get another hint of what is to come.

Ford's first solo-authored play appears to have been *The lovers melancholy*, which was published in 1629 with the information that it had been acted at the Blackfriars. This sensitive, lyrical play, which owes debts to both *King Lear* and Burton's *Anatomy of melancholy* and is also infused with something of the mood and atmosphere of *Twelfth night*, tells the story of Eroclea, who loved and was loved by Palador, prince of Cyprus, but was banished by his tyrannical father before the play began, leading her father Meleander to go mad from grief and Palador to sink into an apparently incurable melancholy, whose cause he will not divulge to anyone. Once the tyrannical old king dies and Eroclea returns, disguised as a boy, nothing stands in the way of a happy ending except that both Palador and Meleander have been too deeply distressed (in Palador's case, we might now say depressed) for any cheap, glib lifting of spirits on their parts to be emotionally or dramatically satisfying. Instead they must both recover slowly, with delicate, indirect assistance from those around them, until they are finally ready to resume their places in the world again.

It is, above all, a play about minds and hearts connecting, and in what would become a hallmark of Fordian dramaturgy, language proves both essential and problematic in forging those connections, working best when it is oblique and allusive rather than direct and when words are supplemented and supported by metre, rhythm, or music.

It is difficult to be sure of the order of composition of Ford's independently written plays, but it is often suggested that the two plays acted at the Blackfriars were followed by a decisive move to Christopher Beeston's Phoenix, in which case the other Blackfriars play, *The broken heart*, would have followed directly after *The lovers melancholy*. There are certainly marked similarities between the two, in that *The broken heart* too is a quiet, lyrical play in which characters suffer in ways to which language is barely equal: as Havelock Ellis (1888) observed in one of the finest pieces of Ford criticism ever written, 'It is the grief deeper than language that he strives to express . . . He is a master of the brief mysterious words, so calm in seeming, which well up from the depths of despair. He concentrates the revelation of a soul's agony into a sob or a sigh. The surface seems calm; we scarcely suspect that there is anything beneath; one gasp bubbles up from the drowning heart below, and all is silence.' Here too the plot has been set in motion by an event which is now in the past but which is still playing itself out and continuing to shape the lives of the characters: the decision by the military hero Ithocles to force his sister Penthea to marry the ageing and insanely jealous Bassanes rather than Orgilus, whom she loves and to whom their father had betrothed her. The play opens with Orgilus determined to avenge this, so he pretends to leave Sparta, where this spare, stoical story is appropriately set, but actually remains in the disguise of a poor scholar to see Penthea. She, however, spurns him on the grounds that she is no longer a virgin (although there are strong signs that Bassanes is in fact impotent). She is then reconciled with Ithocles after the latter tells her of his love for the princess Calantha. Having passed this on to Calantha, Penthea starves herself, goes mad, and dies. Orgilus kills Ithocles in revenge and then confesses what he has done to Calantha, now the queen; she orders his death and then dies of a broken heart herself. Her cousin Nearchus, prince of neighbouring Argos, takes over the kingdom in what has often been seen as a reflection on the accession of James VI and I after the death of Elizabeth. The real power of the play, though, lies not in the political allegory but in the chillingly compelling spectacle of character after character choosing to lock themselves into a wholly restrictive and ultimately fatal course of action because to do so seems to be their only way of preserving a sense of self.

The cost of maintaining a chosen identity is also at the heart of *Perkin Warbeck*, arguably Ford's finest and most distinctive achievement after *The broken heart*. This elegiac play, steeped in the sense of its own belatedness, tells the story of a young man who says, and apparently believes, that he is the younger of the two Princes in the Tower (the two young sons of Edward IV, generally believed to have been murdered by Richard III), supposedly preserved from death by some means which is never explained. Arriving in Scotland to seek help from James IV, he is at first received as genuine and given the king's cousin Lady Katherine Gordon as his wife, and James offers him support in an expedition into England. When the English fail to rally to his standard and Perkin himself proves a distinctly half-hearted warrior James withdraws his support, but Katherine does not, and her love and loyalty become the emotional focus of the play, even though it is never clear that she actually believes that Perkin is really who he says he is. Perkin himself, however, maintains his claim to royalty to the bitter end, even after he has been captured by Henry VII and promised his life if he will confess that he is an impostor; once again, it is the cost of maintaining one's identity that is at the heart of Ford's tragic vision.

There is a rather different emphasis in *'Tis pitty shee's a whore*. The hero Giovanni, who has an affair with his own sister, makes her pregnant, and eventually kills her and cuts out her heart, is, like Orgilus in *The broken heart*, a self-styled revenger in fruitless quest of a revenge plot, so in a sense generic belatedness is at work here too; but *'Tis pitty* is also genuinely contemporary in its strong interest in anatomy – Giovanni has been a student at Bologna, home of a famous anatomy theatre – and above all in its obsessive probing of what the terms *heart* and *blood* might be taken to mean in the wake of the 1628 publication of William Harvey's discovery of the circulation of the blood. Ford can also be seen as daringly modern in the boldness of his treatment of incest, and it is no surprise that *'Tis pitty* has been the play of his that has spoken most loudly in recent times, as evidenced by its adoption by Maurice Maeterlinck and Angela Carter, its use as an intertext in Tom Stoppard's play *The real thing* and the visible influence it exerts on Stephen Poliakoff's 1991 film *Close my eyes*.

Ford's other plays are less famous and less powerful than the big three, but by no means devoid of interest. The tragedy *Loves sacrifice*, which like *The broken heart* and *'Tis pitty* was published in 1633, was considered lubricious and decadent in the nineteenth and early twentieth centuries because its heroine Biancha is extravagantly praised for not technically committing adultery even though she makes it quite clear to everyone, including her husband, that she very much wants to. It makes best sense when read in terms of the cult of platonic love fostered by Henrietta Maria, and so feels more dated than Ford's other work. The two tragicomedies which Ford brought out in the late 1630s, *The fancies chast and noble* and *The ladies triall*, both offer some very delicately sketched characterization and language in the scenes with Flavia and Spinella respectively, but by this stage in Ford's writing career the aesthetic of reticence has taken such deep root that these scenes must perforce be supplemented by others, which mainly consist of woefully laboured and cumbersome comedy. Perhaps most interesting is *The queen*, which appeared anonymously during the Interregnum but which has since been accepted as Ford's. This tragedy takes a number of plot elements from Gervase Markham and Lewis Machin's *The dumbe knight*, but collapses the two largely separate plots of that play to create some evocative characters who, as so often in Ford, are determined to adhere to their chosen identities even when to do so promises nothing but death or disaster.

Ford's interest in silent suffering, so understandable in a Stoic but so perverse in a dramatist, might neatly mirror the self-destructiveness of so many of his characters, but it also meant that he was likely always to be a minority taste, so it is little wonder that there was not much interest in him for a century and a half after his plays first appeared. It was, predictably enough, the Romantics who first responded to both his aesthetic agenda and his transgressiveness, with Mary Shelley revisiting one of his works in her novel *The fortunes of Perkin Warbeck* and Caroline Lamb borrowing names from the heroines of two others for her *Glenarvon* and *Ada Reis*, as well as projecting a novel called *The witch of Edmonton*. It was also during this period that first Henry Weber and then William Gifford made Ford available outside private libraries by their editions of 1811 and 1827 respectively, and the first serious criticism subsequently began to emerge. It was *The broken heart* which found most favour in this early period; the more disturbing *'Tis pitty* was slower to emerge from the shadows until Artaud discussed it under the rubric of theatre of cruelty, while in the 1970s the Italian film director Giuseppe Patroni Griffi found in its representation of incest a powerful metaphor for his own homosexuality. Even there, though, there is a sense that *'Tis pitty* can be understood and responded to only if it is treated as being about something other than what it is, while *Perkin Warbeck* and *The broken heart*, apart from one landmark production each by the Royal Shakespeare Company, are rarely if ever staged at all. Ford, then, is a playwright who still fascinates but whose essential qualities remain elusive, a not unfitting fate for a dramatist whose favoured communicative tools were reticence and silence.

SEE ALSO: Dekker, Thomas; Harvey, William; Rowley, William; Shakespeare, William; Webster, John

REFERENCES AND SUGGESTED READINGS

Artaud, Antonin (1970) *The theatre and its double*, trans. Victor Corti. Calder & Boyars, London.

Billing, Christian (2004) Modelling the anatomy theatre and the indoor hall theatre: dissection on the stages of early modern London. *Early Modern Literary Studies* (special issue) 13. http://extra.shu.ac.uk/emls/si-13/billing/index.htm

Carter, Angela (1994) John Ford's *'Tis pity she's a whore*. In: *American ghosts and old world wonders*. Vintage, London.

Ellis, Havelock (ed.) (1888) *John Ford*. T. Fisher Unwin, London.

Foster, Verna Ann & Foster, Stephen (1988) Structure and history in *The broken heart*: Sparta, England, and the 'truth'. *English Literary Renaissance* 18, 305–328.

Hopkins, Lisa (1994) *John Ford's political theatre*. Manchester University Press, Manchester.

Howarth, R. G. (1965) John Webster, property-owner? *Notes and Queries* 12(6), 236–237.

Neill, Michael (ed.) (1988) *John Ford: critical revisions*. Cambridge University Press, Cambridge.

Fox, George

HILARY HINDS

George Fox (1624–91) was one of the founders and first leaders of the early Quaker movement (the Society of Friends), which began in the early 1650s in the midst of the religious, political, and social upheaval of the English Revolution. Quakers – and not least Fox himself – were, from the outset, prolific writers and publishers, adept at using broadsheets and pamphlets to counter opposition and to convince potential converts of their interpretation of Christianity. Quakerism's central tenet was that the inward light of Christ dwelt within everyone, and that belief and salvation consisted in turning to and living by that light. This more universalist and radically inward interpretation of Christianity contrasted with the predominant Calvinist-derived understanding of salvation or damnation as predestined by God and thus beyond the reach of human action, and was at the root of the often vitriolic opposition encountered by the movement. The literary record left by Fox and other early Quakers – from the early pamphlets of the 1650s to Fox's magisterial *Journal*, published posthumously in 1694 – is at once a powerful testimony to the courage and resolve of Friends to speak their truth to a resistant or hostile power; a vivid picture of the intensity and intricacy of the disputes between different religious affiliations, and of the volatile but exhilarating context of the turbulent 1650s; and a fascinating record of the development of the distinctive idiom of this radical religious group.

Fox, the son of a Leicestershire weaver, was, by his own account, born into a godly and upright family. Nonetheless, like so many English men and women at the time, he found himself increasingly spiritually troubled and dissatisfied with the forms of religious practice, whether mainstream or radical, available to him. He left home at 19 in a state of 'despair and temptations', travelling for several years in the Midlands and to London seeking guidance, but he obtained no comfort from the ministers he consulted. From 1646 to 1648 he received a number of 'openings' or revelations from God concerning the universality and sufficiency of the indwelling light; the irrelevance of the clergy, the established church, and the universities; and the ungodliness of oath-taking and gestures of social deference such as doffing the hat. These became the basis of Quaker belief and practice. At the same time, he was commanded by God 'to go abroad into the world . . . to turn people from the darkness to the light', initiating what was to become his lifelong itinerant proselytizing mission.

In 1651 Fox's journeying took him north into Yorkshire, where he was joined by James Nayler and Richard Farnworth among others, and then into Lancashire and Westmorland. Here, in the spring and summer of 1652, the movement swiftly gained momentum, gathering adherents from the groups of Seekers – those dissatisfied with existing modes of orthodox and radical religion – in the area that has since been dubbed 'the Quaker Galilee', extending from Sedbergh in West Yorkshire to Swarthmoor Hall, near Ulverston in Westmorland, the home of the redoubtable Margaret Fell. After she and most of her family were convinced by Fox, Fell used her organizational capacities to further the movement, and allowed her house to become an indispensible base for Fox. In the early years, as the movement spread south and then across to Ireland and the Atlantic colonies, its leadership was in the hands of Fox, Nayler, and a number of other 'Public Friends' or itinerant ministers such as William Dewsbery, Richard Farnworth, and Edward Burrough, but by the latter part of the 1650s, and particularly after Nayler's notorious conviction and public punishment for blasphemy in 1656, Fox distanced himself from Nayler and increasingly established himself as the sole leader and the movement's pre-eminent voice and presence.

Following the Restoration in 1660, and as a counter to the 1661 anti-monarchist uprising instigated by another radical religious group, the Fifth Monarchists, the movement adopted the pacifist and more quietist stance associated with the Quakers today. Fox continued his work of expanding and consolidating the movement, both at home and abroad, most notably travelling to the Atlantic colonies of Barbados, Jamaica, and mainland America from 1671 to 1673. In these post-Restoration years the Quakers experienced some fractious internal disputes regarding the more formalized system of meetings established by Fox, which was seen by some as compromising the reliance on the inward light as the sole guide to action. Fox, Fell, and many other Friends also endured prolonged periods of imprisonment for continuing to hold meetings for worship, and for their refusal to swear oaths, as well as being subject to fines and the confiscation of property. Following Fox's death in 1691, it was determined by the Second Day Morning Meeting, the Quaker licensing body, that the

collection of papers designated by Fox as his 'great Jornall' would be prepared for the press; the resulting *Journal*, transcribed and heavily edited by Thomas Ellwood, was published in 1694.

From the outset, Quakers had an instinct for the rich possibilities of the written word. The movement published its first pamphlets in 1653: 27 Quaker titles appeared that year, seven of them authored or co-authored by Fox (Peters 1995), and the rate of publication increased thereafter, as the movement moved south and established strong bases in London and Bristol. This recourse to the printed word was quickly identified as one of the means by which Friends were able to attract so many new followers, the Church of England minister Francis Higginson complaining as early as 1653 about 'these printed Libels, and . . . Manuscripts that flye as thick as Moths up and down the Country'. Indeed, for a movement predicated on the importance of silent worship, where no one spoke unless 'moved of the Lord' to do so, the frequent recourse to the passionate and strategic deployment of language is striking. Kate Peters (1995) has shown how itinerant Quaker preachers used printed books and pamphlets, sent in advance of their arrival, to prepare a community for visiting Friends, or else to follow up and consolidate a recent visit. Moreover, from relatively early in the movement's history, Quakers were careful to copy and retain their manuscript letters and papers and to archive their printed works. The result is an unusually full record of the literary activities of a seventeenth-century radical religious movement.

The form and style of Fox's writings of the 1650s are indicative of the character and agenda of the early movement as a whole. Many publications were collaborative, collecting together papers written or dictated by a number of the early leaders: *Severall papers, some of them given forth by George Fox; others by James Nayler* (1653) is an early example of this practice, as is the more substantial *Saul's errand to Damascus* (1653), which included his answer to an anti-Quaker petition of the same year, rebuttals of further criticisms levelled at him, and a transcript of Nayler's blasphemy trial at Appleby-in-Westmorland (now Cumbria). The practice of collaborative publication continued through the decade and beyond, conveying a sense of the importance of the collectivity of Quaker voices to the establishment of the agenda, priorities, and defining practices during the movement's formative years. Publication for early Friends had little to do with the singular identity of the author, and everything to do with the urgency of the need to counter opposition and to persuade readers of the primacy of the light within.

These early writings were also characteristic in their insistently and overtly dialogic mode of address. Fox's writing addresses a series of sharply demarcated constituencies of reader: those hostile to Friends, particularly the clergy, were warned and frequently berated in blistering and uncompromising terms; those potentially 'tender' to the Quaker message were exhorted to turn to the light that shone within each of them; and those Friends already convinced of this doctrine were encouraged to remain steadfast in the face of hostility and to remember the sufficiency of the indwelling Christ. Sometimes all three modes of address co-exist within a single text, resulting in an extraordinary divergence of affective register. Topics addressed were also diverse, including everything from the manifestly weighty, such as the nature of the inward light (*A testimony of the true light of the world*, 1656), to the apparently slight, such as his defence of Quakers' rejection of fine apparel (*The serious peoples reasoning and speech*, 1659). The result is a body of writing characterized not only by a diversity of focus but also by extremities of tone and style, from the ecstatic to the belligerent.

Unsurprisingly, given the movement's persistent experience of vehement opposition, persecution, judicial punishment, and imprisonment, Fox learnt early the power and possibilities of adversarial discourse. His *Journal* includes a contemporary account of his 1652 trial for blasphemy in Lancaster which, had he been found guilty, could have resulted in banishment on pain of death. Fortunately for Fox, Judge Thomas Fell (Margaret Fell's husband and sympathetic to Fox, though never a Quaker), a shrewd and experienced advocate, participated in the trial proceedings, and Fox was acquitted. The incident was a powerful indicator of the transformative power of disputation, and many of Fox's publications through the 1650s share this adversarial stance, taking the form of point-for-point rebuttal and refutation of criticism. *Saul's errand to Damascus*, for example, includes a petition submitted to the Council of State by some of the gentry, justices of the peace, and ministers of Lancaster against Fox and Nayler, complaining of their beliefs and behaviour, and urging 'the speedy suppressing of these evils'. Over the next 12 pages, Fox answers each criticism and objection made in the petition, as well as a number made elsewhere.

Many of Fox's other publications of the 1650s take the form of refusals and counter-arguments, a tendency which showed no signs of abating by the end of the decade: *The great mistery of the great whore unfolded* (1659) answered 79 extant anti-Quaker books and 35 other kinds of oppositional text (Moore 2000). Even in texts with a quite different tone and purpose, such as the anti-clerical and millenarian *The lambs officer* (1659), the courtroom remains a palpable presence: this text is built around the rhetorical repetition (some 50 times in 21 pages) of a question asked of the clergy of England, 'Are you guilty, or not guilty?' In their writings, as in their lives, Quakers forged their spiritual and social identities through this often pugnacious oppositional stance, apparent not only in the tradition of written 'Sufferings' with which they are associated, but also in the persistent publication of textual rebuttals. Quaker belief was, in its early years, established more through the vigorous refutation of erroneous characterizations than by the formation of a credo.

If the form of Fox's early prose owes much to the back and forth of disputation and controversy, its stylistic texture is constituted in part from its saturation with biblical references, imagery, and syntactic structures, and in part from the powerful immediacy of a seventeenth-century secular vernacular. Drawing on and echoing in particular the Old Testament prophets such as Isaiah, Ezekiel, and Daniel, as well as the Gospels, the epistles of St Paul, and Revelation, Fox's prose reverberates with scriptural references and images. The first page of *The lambs officer*, for instance, includes these words:

> Now Christ said, false Prophets should come, *Mat*. 7.24. & Antichrist, which should have the Sheeps cloathing, but inwardlie ravening Wolves; . . . and in the *Rev*. all that dwelt upon the earth went after them, and the Dragon made war with the Woman, and she fled into the Wilderness, the true Church, and the Man-child was caught up to God.

The Bible was the common cultural currency at this time; unanswerably authoritative as well as familiar, capacious, and flexible, it provided an idiom and imagery that is in turn ecstatic, angry, millenarian, apocalyptic, incantatory, and prophetic. Fox's reliance upon the Bible is matched by an evocative use of contemporary colloquial English: for instance, he answers the objections of 'the worlds Teachers & Professors' to Quakers' plain garb by asking 'doest not see thy self ill-favored with all these Ribbands tashling about thy hands, & flaping upon thy hat, and great bunches as big as a hand flaping at the backs of women like a Besome [broom]'. Fox variously captures and deploys the language and rhythms of the Bible and of the market-place, a combination which enables his writing to evoke both a timeless religious sonority and the pulse and energy of contemporary parlance.

However powerful Fox's publications of the 1650s might be, his literary reputation rests principally on his later *Journal*. Dictated to his stepson-in-law Thomas Lower in the mid-1670s, it was, after Fox's death in 1691, prepared for publication by Thomas Ellwood (Milton's student and friend), who substantially edited, reordered, and regularized the account. On its publication, a copy was sent to every Quaker meeting, a fact indicative of the importance accorded not only Fox himself but also his account of the genesis and development of the movement. It has remained an indispensable source for historians of Quakerism ever since, although one that has also been subject to critical scrutiny regarding the extent to which its retrospection downplays the confrontational radicalism of the early years.

The *Journal* is, like so many Quaker publications, a composite text, not in its authorship, but in its constitution. Its backbone is Fox's retrospective chronological account of his life as dictated to Lower, the early part of which details the spiritual torment of his youth in terms familiar from the many Puritan spiritual autobiographies of the time. The *Journal* offers a strong sense of the interiority of the young Fox, who is tormented by uncertainty over his spiritual state and salvific destiny. Following his 'convincement', however, the tenor of the narrative changes, becoming more of a chronicle of Fox's itinerant ministry, detailing places visited, Friends convinced, and opponents rebutted, and offering thereby a history of the establishment and evolution of the movement from its inception through to the mid-1670s. This latter (and longer) part of the narrative evinces little of the interiority of its subject, relying instead on the recounting of event and encounter to convey the transformative power of the inward light.

Embedded within this retrospective account, however, are numerous epistles and papers written at the time of the events being recounted. For example, among Fox's recollections of the events of 1652 there are interpolated, in addition to the transcript of his trial at Lancaster, letters to the people of Ulverston, 'to false Christs', to Parliament and army officers, several addressed to his *bête noire*, the Ulverston priest William Lampitt, and one addressed to 'the first stirrerr up of Strikers, stoners, persecutors, stockers, mockers and Imprisoners in the north', John Sawrey, one of the justices of the peace who had tried him at Lancaster. 'Thou was mounted up,' he tells Sawrey, 'and set thy nest on high but never got higher than the ffowles, & now art runn with the ffoxes & ffallen into the earth, that the earthlynesse and Covetousnesse hath swallowed thee up.' There are also many contemporary epistles of encouragement and instruction written to Friends; in 1656, for example, he addressed them on the power of the indwelling Christ to bring them 'out of the state that Adam is in the fall driven from god to knowe the state that he was in before hee fell', and offered advice as to how to stand steadfast in that light: 'Though you may have Tasted of the power & beene Convinced & have felt the light yett Afterwards you may feell a winter storme Tempest haile … frost & cold & a wilderness & Temptations be patient & still in the power & still in the light.' Contemporary letters such as these, whether the bitter excoriation of Sawrey, the exultant promise of prelapsarian perfection to Friends, or the vivid metaphorical characterization of the testing arduousness of persistent persecution, hardly suggest an attempt to excise an earlier polemical tone. Instead, the pre-Restoration Quaker fervour, itself of a piece with the furious and optimistic ferment of those revolutionary years, sits alongside the sparser and more perfunctory chronicle recalling the journeys and events of those earlier times. It is the counterpoint, the polyphony, of these two accounts that gives the *Journal* its special character, its complexity, and its power as a historical document, combining in one volume as it does a temporal and vocal multiplicity.

While retrospection might have tempered the account of the early years to some degree, the *Journal* also still speaks the language of the millenarian passion, fury, and optimism of the 1650s, when flux and uncertainty still seemed to promise the inauguration of a new, more just, and more godly dispensation. Its richness in no small measure derives from its dual identity as both a contemporary testament of the immediacy and urgency of Quakerism's early years, and a reflective, perhaps moderating, retrospective engagement with them.

SEE ALSO: Fell, Margaret; Milton, John

REFERENCES AND SUGGESTED READINGS

Barbour, Hugh (1964) *The Quakers in Puritan England*. Yale University Press, New Haven.

Bauman, Richard (1983) *Let your words be few: symbolism of speaking and silence among seventeenth-century Quakers*. Cambridge University Press, Cambridge.

Braithwaite, William C. (1955) *The beginnings of Quakerism*, 2nd edn. Cambridge University Press, Cambridge.

Cope, Jackson I. (1956) Seventeenth-century Quaker style. *PMLA* 71, 725–754.

Ingle, H. Larry (1994) *First among Friends: George Fox and the creation of Quakerism*. Oxford University Press, Oxford.

Loewenstein, David (1995) The war of the lamb: George Fox and the apocalyptic discourse of revolutionary Quakerism. In: Corns, Thomas N. & Loewenstein, David (eds) *The emergence of Quaker writing: dissenting literature in seventeenth-century England*. Frank Cass, London, pp. 25–41.

Moore, Rosemary (2000) *The light in their consciences: the early Quakers in Britain 1646–1666*. Pennsylvania State University Press, University Park.

Mullett, Michael (ed.) (1994) *New light on George Fox 1624–1691*. Ebor Press, York.

Ormsby-Lennon, Hugh (1991) From shibboleth to apocalypse: Quaker speechways during the Puritan revolution. In: Burke, Peter & Porter, Roy (eds) *Language, self and society: a social history of language*. Polity Press, Cambridge, pp. 72–112.

Peters, Kate (1995) Patterns of Quaker authorship, 1652–1656. In: Corns, Thomas N. & Loewenstein, David (eds) *The emergence of Quaker writing: dissenting literature in seventeenth-century England*. Frank Cass, London, pp. 6–24.

Peters, Kate (2005) *Print culture and the early Quakers*. Cambridge University Press, Cambridge.

Foxe, John

MARK RANKIN

John Foxe (1516/17–1587), martyrologist, is best known as the compiler of the *Actes and monuments of these latter and perillous dayes touching matters of the church*, a collection of narratives and documents that has been known since its publication in 1563 as *The book of martyrs*. This work has shaped the English Protestant imagination more thoroughly than any other work besides the English Bible.

Born in Boston, Lincolnshire, Foxe matriculated at Brasenose College, Oxford, in about 1534, graduating as a BA in 1537. He took his MA from Magdalen College in 1543 but by 1545 had resigned his fellowship, presumably over the requirement that he enter the priesthood as a condition of tenure. Foxe worked as a tutor in the household of Sir William Lucy in Warwickshire and then, more prominently, at Mountjoy House, the London residence of Mary Fitzroy, the dowager duchess of Richmond. There he came into contact with a number of prominent evangelicals, including the dramatist and scholar John Bale, who would exert a strong influence upon the structure and content of *The book of martyrs*. Following the death of Edward VI in 1553 and the accession of the Catholic Mary to the English throne, Foxe fled to Strasbourg and Frankfurt before eventually settling in Basle. In Strasbourg he published the first of two Latin martyrologies, the *Commentarii rerum in ecclesia gestarum* (1554), at the presses of the prominent humanistic printer Wendelin Rihel. It incorporates an account of the persecution of John Wycliffe and other late-medieval Christians whose activities Foxe and other sixteenth-century Protestants described as foreshadow-ing their own evangelical sensibility. At Frankfurt Foxe allied himself with John Knox, the future Scottish reformer, in preferring the use of an updated version of the 1552 Book of Common Prayer among the English congregation there. Foxe migrated to Basel, after a series of controversies made Knox's position untenable, and took up a position as learned corrector in the printing house of the humanist publisher Johannes Oporinus. Now reunited with Bale, who also worked for Oporinus, Foxe found himself at the centre of overlapping networks of evangelical and humanistic scholarship. Oporinus and fellow printer Nicholas Brylinger published Foxe's second Latin martyrology, the *Rerum in ecclesia gestarum ... commentarii*

(1559), which radically expanded the scope of its predecessor to include narratives of the deaths of Protestants burnt alive under Queen Mary I (Freeman 2004a).

Foxe returned to England that same year, following the accession of Elizabeth to the throne, and immediately commenced work on his vernacular martyrology. Foxe's associate in Basle, Edmund Grindal, now bishop of London, had assembled documents concerning the Marian persecutions and passed these on to Foxe, who augmented them from his own researches into local diocesan records (Wabuda 1993). The first edition of *The book of martyrs* emerged from the presses of the well-connected master printer John Day, who enjoyed the influential patronage of Sir William Cecil, later Lord Burghley, during Edward's, Mary's, and Elizabeth's reigns (Evenden 2008). Day financed the inclusion of more than 50 dramatic woodcut illustrations in this book, the bulk of which were cut specifically for this edition, probably by Dutch artisans (Evenden & Freeman 2002). *The Book of martyrs* extended its history of the 'true' Protestant church back to the year 1000 and drew upon numerous sources, some of which, including works by Bale and the Lutheran historian Matthias Flacius, Foxe had previously used, and others which represented fresh findings.

At nearly two million words, this imposing book told the history of the 'true' church's struggle against the 'false' papal church of Antichrist. Soon after its publication it met with hostile reception among exiled English Catholic readers, who vilified the work memorably. In one noteworthy instance, for example, Foxe's book becomes a 'devilish dirty dunghill' of 'foul heretical and traitorous martyrs' (Thomas Stapleton, *A counterblast to M[aster] Hornes vayne blast* 1567). The most sustained reply on this front came from Nicholas Harpsfield (alias Alan Cope), who devoted one of his *Dialogi sex* (*Six dialogues* 1566) to exposing Foxe's alleged errors. The second edition of the *Book of martyrs*, published by Day in 1570, responded to this critique either by removing or substantially justifying the inclusion of passages from the 1563 edition. It also radically expanded its history of the medieval church. This decision allowed Foxe polemically to demonstrate the purported apostolic origin of the English church and rewrite the history of 'true' religion to include a tendentious representation of early Christianity as an evangelical Protestant phenomenon. The book dramatically increased in size to more than three million words and incorporated a remarkably large fold-out illustration titled 'A table of the ten first persecutions of the Primitive Church' that comprises three folio-sized woodcuts pasted together. Indeed, the project required such an investment that Day exhausted his paper supply. Authorities required copies to be placed in parish churches and cathedral libraries. The third edition of the *Book of martyrs* appeared in 1576, printed on less expensive paper but not otherwise reduced in scope. A fourth edition, in 1583, represents the last on which Foxe and Day collaborated. These two latter editions restored selected documents that had been excised from earlier editions and supplied a small number of new woodcut illustrations. Abridgements of the *Book of martyrs* appeared as soon as 1589, but Foxe never made an attempt to abridge his lengthy work (Evenden & Freeman 2004; King 2006).

Foxe's literary achievement across the entirety of his career is not insignificant. His written output includes works of pastoral care, works of apocalyptical theology and religious controversy, and English translations of important writings of Continental reformers. Two Latin closet dramas attributed to him survive: *Titus et Gesippus*, written during his Magdalen years, and *Christus triumphans*, published by Oporinus in 1556. The latter is Foxe's first attempt to apply the book of Revelation to the history of the Protestant church. Under the shaping influence of Bale, Foxe directed his early martyrological research towards Wycliffe and the English Lollards, and he also absorbed Bale's apocalyptic outlook, which appears most memorably in *The image of both churches*

(c.1545), Bale's commentary on Revelation. Bale modified the Augustinian thesis concerning the cataclysmic struggle between two cities, one of God and one of the Devil. For Bale this conflict manifested itself in the form of eternal opposition between the 'true' Protestant and 'false' Roman Catholic churches. In particular, Bale followed the twelfth-century mystic Joachim de Fiore in equating the figure of the Whore of Babylon from Revelation 17 with the papacy and arguing that the advent of final apocalypse was imminent. In the *Book of martyrs* Foxe expanded Bale's argument by equating the 1,000-year imprisonment of Satan described in Revelation 20 with the period of relative quietude within the church transpiring between the cessation of persecution following the conversion of Emperor Constantine in 313 and the renewal of persecution against Wycliffe during the fourteenth century. Foxe's involvement as an exorcist during the 1570s and his own commentary on Revelation, which remained unfinished at his death, complemented his esoteric speculations. In addition to producing translations of works by Martin Luther and two other German reformers, Johannes Oecolampadius and Urbanus Rhegius, Foxe also composed treatises in opposition to the use of the death penalty against adulterers; in favour of the use of excommunication to maintain church discipline; and in response to the Portuguese bishop Hieronymo Osorio (who had attempted to convert Queen Elizabeth). Among his other works are two editions of a guided commonplace book designed to improve memorization and a sermon which he delivered in London following the conversion of a certain Nathaniel, a Spanish Jew, to Christianity (Freeman 2004a).

It is the *Book of martyrs* and its two Latin predecessors, though, which afford the chief evidence for Foxe's significance. The recent completion of an online variorum critical edition of the *Book of martyrs*, with support from the British Academy and the Humanities Research Institute at the University of Sheffield, has reinvigorated Foxe studies (Foxe 2004). The widespread availability of a reliable, annotated edition of the first four versions of the *Book of martyrs* has enabled scholars to dismantle a number of long-accepted theses. It is now clear, for example, that Foxe did not especially favour England, as was once thought, as a divinely ordained elect nation. His work does describe England's providential opportunity to advance the cause of the gospel. Indeed, the 1563 edition incorporates a dedication to Queen Elizabeth as a latter-day Constantine, and accounts of English martyrs under Mary remain the primary focus of the book. Nevertheless Foxe always views the 'true' church as international in scope. Persistent rumours of Foxe's supposed inaccuracies have also been put to rest (Collinson 1985). Foxe is not the author of the *Book of martyrs* in the modern sense but rather its compiler who gathered documents drawn from archival research, field interviews undertaken by informants, and eyewitness testimony. These data, of course, are not always reliable, but Foxe himself had no interest in fabricating details. Another of the major advances in Foxe scholarship has been greater awareness of his disassociation from the Church of England factional debates in which his reputation had been locked since his own lifetime. Considerable light now shines upon the ways in which 'Foxe' has afforded shifting cultural capital to neo-Catholics, Presbyterians, high-church Anglicans, and dissenters within the English Protestant tradition (Freeman 1999; 2004b; King 2001; 2006).

Foxe's work is invaluable both as a record of events and as a literary text. As a historian Foxe must be used cautiously, for both he and his informants framed details in order to advance the book's overall claim that the 'true' Protestant church constituted a persecuted minority. Documents which survive among Foxe's extant papers indicate the ways in which the martyrologist and others edited texts, both before Foxe received them and prior to their inclusion in the *Book of martyrs*. The work sometimes preserves information that is not recorded elsewhere, and, at the very least, modern readers ought to understand that its account of religious history fed into a triumphant, 'Whiggish' discourse of English Protestant victory over its enemies. Sir Francis Drake read aloud from the book during his 1577–80 circumnavigation of the globe, and records indicate that the *Book of martyrs* was one of the first books carried to New England. It is possible to read this book as a Protestant manifesto, even though it incorporates a remarkably wide variety of texts and genres. In addition to martyrology, this work includes verse of various sorts, tragedy, tragicomic adventure stories, fanciful tales of providential judgement, trial narratives, letters, and more. Figurative language and stylized set speeches abound, as Foxe employs satire, rhetorical tropes, and ironic digression in transitional passages inserted between documents. Either Foxe or Day is also presumably responsible for the inclusion of marginal glosses which afford colourful commentary upon the text proper (Collinson 1985; Wabuda 1993; Loades 1997; Freeman 1999; King 2004; 2006).

In composing the text, Foxe explicitly repudiates medieval hagiography by constructing it as an alternative to Catholic compilations such as *The golden legend*. This thirteenth-century anthology aligns martyr narratives with traditional feast days associated with Catholic saints. In one of his prefaces, Foxe denigrates this book on grounds that it promulgated fables. Indeed, the 1563 and 1583 editions of the *Book of martyrs* include a Protestant 'Kalendar' of martyrs to replace those included in accounts of saints' lives. For Foxe, it was the 'truth' of the cause for which individuals died that made them martyrs, and the *Book of martyrs* shares with early modern Catholic martyrologies the tendency to describe victims as stoical, even cheerful, at the moment of suffering. Foxe's work ascribes numerous stylized speeches to persons who are burnt alive as heretics. The purported dying words of Jesus ('Father, into thy hands I commend my spirit') and St Stephen ('Lord Jesus, receive my spirit') undergo modification as formulaic dying words spoken at the moment of martyrdom (King 2006).

Indeed, the Bible constitutes the most prominent source for the *Book of martyrs*, and biblical language and imagery infuse it to a significant extent. To cite one prominent example: Foxe obtained his narrative of the imprisonment of Princess (later Queen) Elizabeth during the reign of her half-sister, Mary I, from a number of informants. According to this account, the princess described the manner of her submission to her captors *tanquam ovis* ('like a sheep') in an explicit reference to the messianic prophecy found within Isaiah 53.7. Foxe anticipates Edmund Spenser and others in satirizing Catholic tormentors as hypocritical foxes and wolves. They prey upon martyrs, who constitute 'godly' sheep. This deliberate use of imagery derives from Christ's words in the Sermon on the Mount (Matthew 7.15) and assigns a serio-comic tone to martyr narratives that can verge on the macabre and gruesome. Dedicatory verses and ballads appear scattered throughout the book, as do a wide range of epigrams which employ various stanza forms. Puns, jokes, and other similar devices add flavour and transform this collection into much more than merely a gathering of documents (Freeman 2002; King 2004).

Research into key problems of the *Book of martyrs* has produced fruitful dividends in recent years. New knowledge has emerged concerning, but not limited to, the nature and layout of the book's striking illustrations, its treatment of sources, its Continental influences and analogues, and the ways in which it was read (Loades 1997; 1999; 2004; Highley & King 2002). The work employs a complex arrangement of large and small woodcut images that were replaced by copperplate engravings in the ninth and final of the 'old' folio editions (1684). These pictures, it has been argued, increased the market appeal of the book to include the illiterate. The 1563 edition in particular incorporated a significant amount of Latin text and employed a range of typefaces that included black letter and italic as well as roman (King 2006). The iconography of these images suggests clear Continental antecedents (Loades 1997). Indeed, Foxe drew upon notable contemporary Continental martyrologies by Jean Crespin (1554–56) and Adriaan van Haemstede (1559) in ways that are still being explored. The study of Foxe's treatment of sources has led to deeper understanding of Foxe's relationship with his erstwhile mentor, John Bale, who is known to have edited substantial segments of the *Book of martyrs* himself (Freeman 1998), and to knowledge of Foxe's connection to the humanist ecclesiastical circles which gathered around leading intellectuals in the religious establishment. Matthew Parker, archbishop of Canterbury, for instance, pioneered Anglo-Saxon studies by overseeing a research team which edited (unscrupulously, by modern standards) early medieval documents in order to demonstrate the antiquity of the English Protestant church. Parker had obtained knowledge of manuscripts in part through consultation with Bale, and his financial patronage of Day included the commissioning of a complete font of Anglo-Saxon type that may be seen in the 1570 edition of the *Book of martyrs*. Scrutiny of Foxe's extant papers has yielded evidence of manuscript networks connecting not only Foxe's intellectual milieu, but also English Protestants more broadly, and scholars have used these data to rewrite received understanding concerning the nature of literary transmission during this period (Freeman 2004b). Finally, readers of the *Book of martyrs* possess enhanced understanding of the ways in which the work fits into broader narratives of the history of the book, which transcend and intersect the story of the reception of this particular book (King 2006). Memorable martyrological woodcut illustrations invited hand-written marginal commentary, as did the more 'political' images which display what Foxe viewed as the regrettable subordination of royal to papal authority. From the sixteenth century to the twentieth, the book's many abridgements themselves afford evidence of reader response. Foxe's book lies at the heart of Protestant 'grand' narratives of national greatness, and scholars have accordingly suggested interesting findings concerning the ways in which readers from Foxe's time to the relatively recent past have accepted his polemical claims as wholly normative (Netzley 2006).

The *Book of martyrs* is a highly relevant and enduring text, and Foxe's place as a major canonical figure seems certain. Shakespeare, Spenser, and Milton all certainly read this book and internalized its perspective. The question of how this fascinating work shaped *their* works may be the most intriguing, and substantial, one of all.

SEE ALSO: Bale, John; Day, John; Elizabeth I; Knox, John; Milton, John; Shakespeare, William; Spenser, Edmund

REFERENCES AND SUGGESTED READINGS

Collinson, Patrick (1985) Truth and legend: the veracity of John Foxe's *Book of martyrs*. In: Duke, A. C. & Tamse, C. A. (eds) *Clio's mirror: historiography in Britain and the Netherlands*. De Walberg, Zutphen, pp. 31–54.

Evenden, Elizabeth (2008) *Patents, pictures and patronage: John Day and the Tudor book trade*. Ashgate, Aldershot.

Evenden, Elizabeth & Freeman, Thomas S. (2002) John Foxe, John Day and the printing of the *Book of martyrs*. In: Myers, Robin, Harris, Michael, & Mandelbrote, Giles (eds) *Lives in print: biography and the book trade from the Middle Ages to the 21st century*. Oak Knoll Press, New Castle, DE, pp. 23–49.

Evenden, Elizabeth & Freeman, Thomas S. (2004). Print, profit and propaganda: the Elizabethan Privy Council and the 1570 edition of Foxe's *Book of martyrs*. *English Historical Review* 119, 1288–1307.

Foxe, John (2004) *Acts and monuments . . .: the variorum edition*. www.johnfoxe.org

Freeman, Thomas S. (1998) John Bale's book of martyrs? The account of King John in *Acts and monuments. Reformation* 3, 175–223.

Freeman, Thomas S. (1999) Texts, lies and microfilm: reading and misreading Foxe's *Book of martyrs. Sixteenth Century Journal* 30, 23–46.

Freeman, Thomas S. (2002). 'As true a subiect being prysoner': John Foxe's notes on the imprisonment of Princess Elizabeth, 1554–5. *English Historical Review* 117, 104–116.

Freeman, Thomas S. (2004a) John Foxe: a biography. In: Foxe, John *Acts and monuments . . .: the variorum edition*. www.johnfoxe.org

Freeman, Thomas S. (2004b) Publish and perish: the scribal culture of the Marian martyrs. In: Crick, Julia & Walsham, Alexandra (eds) *The uses of script and print, 1300–1700*. Cambridge University Press, Cambridge, pp. 235–254.

Freeman, Thomas S. (2004c) Foxe, John. In: *Oxford dictionary of national biography*. Oxford University Press, Oxford.

Highley, Christopher & King, John N. (eds) (2002) *John Foxe and his world*. Ashgate, Aldershot.

King, John N. (2001) 'The light of printing': William Tyndale, John Foxe, John Day, and early modern print culture. *Renaissance Quarterly* 54, 52–85.

King, John N. (2004) Literary aspects of Foxe's *Acts and monuments*. In: Foxe, John *Acts and monuments . . .: the variorum edition*. www.johnfoxe.org

King, John N. (2006) *Foxe's 'Book of martyrs' and early modern print culture*. Cambridge University Press, Cambridge.

Loades, David (ed.) (1997) *John Foxe and the English Reformation*. Scolar Press, Aldershot.

Loades, David (1999) *John Foxe: an historical perspective*. Ashgate, Aldershot.

Loades, David (2004) *John Foxe: at home and abroad*. Ashgate, Aldershot.

Netzley, Ryan (2006) The end of reading: the practice and possibility of reading Foxe's *Actes and monuments. ELH* 73, 187–214.

Wabuda, Susana (1993) Henry Bull, Miles Coverdale, and the making of Foxe's *Book of martyrs*. In: Wood, Diana (ed.) *Martyrs and martyrologies*. Blackwell, Oxford, pp. 245–258.

Fraunce, Abraham

CHRISTOPHER MARTIN

Later derided by Ben Jonson (in one of his frequent uncharitable moods) as a 'fool', and but meagerly attended by modern scholarship, Abraham Fraunce (?1559–?1592/93) nonetheless displayed sufficient energy and talent in his day to earn the support of a no less discerning Sir Philip Sidney, and remained an active member of the circle of Mary Herbert, countess of Pembroke – one of the most powerful and influential patronage agencies of the time – throughout the brief but prolific publishing career that followed. Little enough biographical detail survives, with even his date of death a matter of dispute: while more recent literary historians trace his demise to 1592 or 1593, after which he disappears from public records, others have speculated that, like Sidney's other close companion Fulke Greville, he survived well into the next century. For all that, Fraunce perhaps offers a more representative picture of applied early modern sensibilities and intellectual curiosity than do the brilliant and groundbreaking careers of the cultural celebrities with whom he consorted.

Although Fraunce was destined to live exclusively in the shadow of his revered patron, he flourished there, offering a rich if eccentric return on Sidney's sponsorship. After gaining the young Philip's notice sometime in the mid-1570s, Fraunce under his support entered St John's College, Cambridge, where he took his BA in 1580 and his MA in 1583. Subsequent attendance at Gray's Inn culminated in his passage to the bar in 1588. After Sidney's own premature death in 1586, Fraunce was recognized as a sufficiently close member of the entourage to walk in his state funeral procession. More significantly, he thereafter retained the good favour of Sidney's siblings Mary and Robert, to whom he became (in Gavin Alexander's apt description) a 'living legacy' of sorts from Philip, and he dedicated all of his works either to the dead courtier-hero's memory or to members of the family.

Fraunce's creative and scholarly ambitions were backed by a ranging and incisive intellect. Almost all of his projects were conspicuously the fruit of earlier exchanges with Sidney, whose humanist interests and poetic enthusiasms he profoundly shared. His first surviving piece, the unpublished Latin drama *Victoria* completed sometime before 1583, is a comedy whose breathlessly overwrought plot-line betrays as much the influence of Boccaccian or Chaucerian *fabliaux* as it does Plautus or Terence. The year after Sidney's death, he turned his hand to an English rendition of

Thomas Watson's Latin pastoral *Amyntas*. It was in 1588, however, that the publication of three substantial works in rapid succession made clear the full extent of Fraunce's vast literary pluck. His *Insignium, armorum, emblematum, hieroglyphicorum, et symbolorum*, a learned treatise on courtly *imprese*, was followed by the twin handbooks *The lawiers logike* and *The Arcadian rhetorike*, both of which illustrate their topics with eclectic but shrewdly chosen exempla from classical and contemporary authors. Fraunce compiled his religious verse in *The countess of Pembrokes Emanuel* of 1591, and followed up the same year with *The countess of Pembrokes Ivychurch*, an homage of sorts to Heliodorus, Virgil, and Tasso. His final work, *The third part of the countess of Pembrokes Ivychurch* (1592), would in many respects mark his most significant undertaking in its retailing and free rethinking of Ovidian mythology.

Easy to catalogue, Fraunce's output remains difficult to characterize. Several hallmark preoccupations, often at work in combination, best distinguish his productivity: a translator's desire to adapt Latin texts creatively into the vernacular; a tenacious (converse) drive to adapt English verse to classical quantitative measures; a deep intuition of the occult meanings behind mythic narrative and visual iconography alike, along with a tireless hermeneutic impulse to explicate these; and a capacity to draw upon extraordinarily broad reading to exemplify the logical principles and rhetorical tropes he had mastered in his formal legal training. In the hexameter lines of his *Lamentations of Amintas*, we first encounter his efforts to approximate classical quantitative verse in English, something that had preoccupied Sidney in the early draft of his *Arcadia* eclogues. This formal experimentation would obtain to the end of his career, where in the *Ivychurch* it makes for some especially bizarre yet fascinating reading. That text's daring attempts to interpret the esoteric significance of the Ovidian tales it refurbishes – in the context of a communal pastoral dialogue, no less – offers an impressive glimmer of Fraunce's boundless creative reflexes.

Fraunce's innovative and enterprising temperament is on display equally in the textbook setting of his 1588 manuals, where his aim to promote the revolutionary rhetorical methodology of Peter Ramus and Omer Talon meets with his equally passionate designs to see English poets on an even footing with classical and modern Continental authors. Where *The lawiers logike* resorts extensively to Spenser's already influential *Shepheardes calender* to illustrate its precepts, *The Arcadian rhetorike* even more startlingly intersperses familiar verse passages from antiquity to the present with excerpts from Sidney's as yet unpublished works (the manuscripts to which he clearly enjoyed a privileged access), in what collects into an anthology-like survey of foreign and vernacular poetic techniques. Under Fraunce's bold direction, English seamlessly enters the canon of European letters, and in so doing fulfils aspirations voiced from Richard Tottel's preface to his watershed *Songes and sonettes* of 1557 down to Sidney's own more contemporary *Defence of poesie*.

No mere amateurish if dedicated hanger-on, Fraunce made an earnest effort to shape and broker the literary reputation of his benefactor. If his efforts failed adequately to advance the kinds of technical developments he saw as instrumental to English literature's emergence onto a wider European stage, he nonetheless stands out for his initiative to democratize his sources. A writer who remained proud of his primary role as 'an Universitie man', he took seriously his academic mission to popularize and explicate the texts he so fervidly admired. The obvious delight he took in his self-appointed task, and the quirky results he realized, provide an oblique glimpse of Elizabethan intellectual exuberance: one that affords valuable insight into the cultural ambience that nourished the remarkable literary achievements for which we best remember the era.

SEE ALSO: Greville, Fulke; Herbert, Mary (Sidney), countess of Pembroke; Jonson, Ben; Sidney, Philip; Sidney, Robert, earl of Leicester; Spenser, Edmund; Watson, Thomas

REFERENCES AND SUGGESTED READINGS

Alexander, Gavin (2006) *Writing after Sidney: the literary response to Sir Philip Sidney, 1586–1640.* Oxford University Press: Oxford.

Martin, Christopher (2006) 'Made plaine by examples': parceling Philip Sidney in Abraham Fraunce's *Arcadian rhetorike. Sidney Journal* 24, 67–82.

Petrina, Alessandra (1999) Polyglotta and the vindication of English poetry: Abraham Fraunce's *Arcadian rhetorike. Neoplilologus* 83, 317–329.

Pomeroy, Ralph S. (1987) The Ramist as fallacy hunter: Abraham Fraunce and *The lawiers logike. Renaissance Quarterly* 40, 224–246.

Woudhuysen, H. R. (1996) *Sir Philip Sidney and the circulation of manuscripts, 1558–1640.* Clarendon Press, Oxford.

Fulwell, Ulpian

ALLYNA E. WARD

Ulpian Fulwell (1545/46–1584/86) was born in Wells in Somerset. He began his studies to become a clergyman in 1563, after his father died, and was ordained on 15 September 1566. In 1570 he became the rector of Naunton in Gloucestershire. During this period he was engaged to a woman whom he later learned was already married. He subsequently married Eleanor Warde, who died in 1577, and then Marie Whorwood on 14 April 1578, with whom he had six children. In 1576 he was fined for negligence of the rectory (perhaps a sign that he was focusing on his literary career): his clerk was illiterate and many children had failed to learn the catechism. In 1579 he matriculated from St Mary's, Oxford, but there is no record of his obtaining a degree before he died. There is also no record of when or where Fulwell died; it was sometime before July 1586 when the Naunton rectory was seeking a new clergyman.

Fulwell's popular comic interlude, his only known drama, *Like will to like quoth the devill to the collier* (first performed in 1562, published in 1568) focuses on the rewards of heaven to lure men to virtue, and thus offers a strong contrast to contemporaneous poems that focus solely on the hellish results of wickedness, such as Richard Robinson's *The rewarde of wickednesse* (1574). The full title reads: *A pleasant enterlude, intituled, Like will to like quoth the Deuill to the collier wherin is declared what punishments followe those that will rather liue licentiously: then esteeme and followe good councell. And what benefits they receiue that apply them selues to vertuous liuing and good exercises.* Although he specifies that his purpose is to show how debauchery is punished, Fulwell is primarily concerned to offer an example to the godly. Hence, the interlude is described as 'pleasant', the emphasis in the title is on the rewards for good behaviour, and the only punishment for sinful living that Fulwell's interlude describes is death without everlasting life rather than death and everlasting torment in hell.

The characters are stock figures from the morality tradition; there is even a Vice, Nichol Newfangle, the godson of Lucifer. Towards the middle of the interlude Good Fame, Honour, God's Promise, and Virtuous Life appear and remind the reader that God will grant salvation to those who ask for it. In the scene following this reminder, Rafe Roister and Tom Tospot resist the advances of the Vice character, and pray to God for mercy. Newfangle is deterred by their call to God and he tells them to leave, but, before they depart, Roister and Tospot beat Vice with his own tools. Newfangle's other two victims – Cutbert Cutpurse and Pierce Pickpurse – are not so fortunate and do not reject Vice until they are on the gallows awaiting their execution. In this post-morality interlude, it is too late for the sinners. Their cries for mercy are ignored and can only serve as a warning.

In Fulwell's account God is merciful and offers salvation to those who seek it out before the moment of death. In the end Lucifer commends Newfangle for ensnaring Cutpurse and Pickpurse and they leave the stage together. In the final song Fulwell repeats the eponymous line, that 'like will is to like', reminding us that if a man is sinful then Satan must be his guiding influence, and equally, where faith is present then God must have planted grace. The text does not, as is claimed in the title, declare what punishments follow for those who are matched with Satan; it is, after all, a pleasant interlude and not a tragedy.

Ultimately, Fulwell brings virtue and grace together in a morally 'good' frame of reference that includes salvation and contrasts these with vice, Satan, evil, and consequent damnation. First, he explains that like is matched to like and then he explains how Satan corresponds to the damned. In Fulwell's pairing of Satan and sinful people he suggests that sinful behaviour is instigated by figures that come from hell, while those with God's grace are naturally virtuous. The problematic implication of this is that it makes Satan an equal adversary to God; both God and Satan are able to 'plant' a path towards either sin or virtue. The moral message in the concluding song is that the faithful, and also the virtuous, have been offered the gift of grace and therefore also salvation.

In 1575 Fulwell published *The flower of fame*, dedicated to William Cecil, Lord Burghley. This is a short treatise in praise of Henry VIII in the style of *A mirrour for magistrates*, which includes a short section on three notable queens: Anne Boleyn, Jane Seymour, and Katherine Parr. *The flower of fame* also offers a brief account of the battle of Haddington, in Scotland, during the reign of Edward VI. Finally, in 1576, Fulwell printed his most controversial work, *Ars adulandi, the art of flattery*, dedicated to Mildred Cecil, Lady Burghley. The text is based on Lucian's *The parasite* (which suggests that being parasitic is the best form of art) and Erasmus's colloquy *Pseudocheus and Philetymus*. It is a collection of eight short dialogues on flattery, which is identified as the 'eighth liberal science'. The speaker chides contemporary evils, especially flattery, in society and the church; the content caused the court of high commission to require a public recantation of some offensive parts. Fulwell published a revised second edition in 1579 and a third edition of the text appeared a little later, though it is undated.

SEE ALSO: Baldwin, William; Parr, Katherine

REFERENCES AND SUGGESTED READINGS

Bevington, David (1962) *From mankind to Marlowe: growth of structure in the popular drama of Tudor England.* Harvard University Press, Cambridge, MA.

Buchanan, R. (1984) Introduction. In: Buchanan, R. (ed.) *Ars adulandi, or the art of flattery by Ulpian Fulwel: a critical edition with a biography of the author.* University of Salzburg, Salzburg, pp. i–lxxx.

Craik, T. W. (1958) *The Tudor interlude: stage, costume and acting.* Humanities Press, New York.

Eccles, M. (1982) Brief lives: Tudor and Stuart authors. *Studies in Philology (Texts and Studies)* 79, 51–53.

Farnham, Willard (1932) The progeny of *A mirror for magistrates. Modern Philology* 29, 395–410.

Gough, Alfred B. (1917) Who was Spenser's bon font? *Modern Language Review* 12, 140–145.

Happé, Peter (ed.) (1991) *Two moral interludes.* Oxford University Press, for Malone Society, Oxford.

Kathman, David (2004) Fulwell, Ulpian. In: *Oxford dictionary of national biography.* Oxford University Press, Oxford.

Ribner, Irving (1950) Ulpian Fulwell and his family. *Notes and Queries* 195, 444–448.

Ribner, Irving (1951) Ulpian Fulwell and the court of high commission. *Notes and Queries* 196, 268–270.